# Microsoft®

# Excel 2000

## Illustrated Introductory

# Microsoft®

# Excel 2000

## Illustrated Introductory

Tara Lynn O'Keefe
Elizabeth Eisner Reding

MICROSOFT OFFICE
Microsoft®
OFFICE
USER SPECIALIST

**APPROVED COURSEWARE**

**COURSE
TECHNOLOGY**
™

**THOMSON LEARNING**

Australia • Canada • Mexico • Singapore • Spain • United Kingdom • United States

## Microsoft Excel 2000—Illustrated Introductory is published by Course Technology

| | |
|---|---|
| Senior Product Manager: | Kathryn Schooling |
| Product Managers: | Jennifer A. Duffy, Rebecca VanEsselstine |
| Associate Product Manager: | Emily Heberlein |
| Production Editors: | Elena Montillo, Jennifer Goguen |
| Developmental Editors: | Rachel Biheller Bunin, India Koopman |
| Marketing Manager: | Karen Bartlett |
| Editorial Assistant: | Stacie Parillo |
| Composition House: | GEX Publishing Services |
| QA Manuscript Reviewers: | Jeff Schwartz, John Freitas, Jon Greacen, Matt Carroll |
| Text Designer: | Joseph Lee, Joseph Lee Designs |
| Cover Designer: | Youngs Design |

**For more information contact:**

Thomson Learning
Berkshire House
168-173 High Holborn
London, WCIV 7AA

or find us on the World Wide Web at: www.thomsonlearning.co.uk

**Disclaimer**

Course Technology reserves the right to revise this publication and make changes from time to time in its content without notice.

ISBN 1-86152-828-0

Printed in Croatia by Zrinski

# Satisfy your Microsoft Office 2000 Needs with the Illustrated Series

## Office 2000 MOUS Certification Coverage

The Illustrated Series offers a growing number of Microsoft-approved titles that cover the objectives required to pass the Office 2000 MOUS exams. After studying with any of the approved Illustrated titles (see list on inside cover), you will have mastered the Core and Expert skills necessary to pass any Office 2000 MOUS exam with flying colors. In addition, **Excel 2000 MOUS Certification Objectives** at the end of the book map to where specific MOUS skills can be found in each lesson and where students can find additional practice.

## Helpful New Features

The Illustrated Series responded to customer feedback by adding a **Project Files List** at the back of the book for easy reference. We also added new conceptual lessons to units to give students the extra information they need when learning Office 2000.

## New Exciting Case and Innovative On-Line Companion

There is an exciting new case study used throughout our textbooks, a fictitious company called MediaLoft, designed to be "real-world" in nature by introducing the kinds of activities that students will encounter when working with Microsoft Office 2000. The **MediaLoft Web site**, available at www.course.com/illustrated/medialoft, is an innovative Student Online Companion which enhances and augments the printed page by bringing students onto the Web for a dynamic and continually updated learning experience. The MediaLoft site mirrors the case study used throughout the book, creating a real-world intranet site for this chain of bookstore cafés. This Companion is used to complete the WebWorks exercise in each unit of this book, and to allow students to become familiar with the business application of an intranet site.

## Course Assessment

How well do your students *really* know Microsoft Office? Course Assessment is a performance-based testing program that measures students' proficiency in Microsoft Office 2000. Course Assessment is available for Office 2000 in either a live or simulated environment. You can use Course Assessment to place students into or out of courses, monitor their performance throughout a course, and help prepare them for the MOUS certification exams.

# Preface

Welcome to *Microsoft Excel 2000—Illustrated Introductory Edition*. This highly visual book offers users a hands-on introduction to aspects of Microsoft Excel 2000 and also serves as an excellent reference for future use. If you would like additional coverage of Microsoft Excel 2000, we also offer *Microsoft Excel 2000—Illustrated Second Course*, a logical continuation of the Introductory Edition.

## ▶ Organization and Coverage

This text contains eight units that cover basic through intermediate Excel skills. In these units, students learn how to build, edit, and format worksheets and charts, work with formulas and functions, and manage workbooks.

## ▶ About this Approach

What makes the Illustrated approach so effective at teaching software skills? It's quite simple. Each skill is presented on two facing pages, with the step-by-step instructions on the left page, and large screen illustrations on the right. Students can focus on a single skill without having to turn the page. This unique design makes information extremely accessible and easy to absorb, and provides a great reference for after the course is over. This hands-on approach also makes it ideal for both self-paced or instructor-led classes.

Each lesson, or "information display," contains the following elements:

Each 2-page spread focuses on a single skill.

Clear step-by-step directions explain how to complete the specific task, with what students are to type. When students follow the numbered steps, they quickly learn how each procedure is performed and what the results will be.

Concise text that introduces the basic principles discussed in the lesson. Procedures are easier to learn when concepts fit into a framework.

---

## Unit F — Excel 2000

# Controlling Page Breaks and Page Numbering

The vertical and horizontal dashed lines in worksheets indicate page breaks. Excel automatically inserts a page break when your worksheet data doesn't fit on one page. These page breaks are dynamic, which means they adjust automatically when you insert or delete rows and columns and when you change column widths or row heights. Everything to the left of the first vertical dashed line and above the first horizontal dashed line is printed on the first page. You can override the automatic breaks by choosing the Page Break command on the Insert menu. Table F-2 describes the different types of page breaks you can use. ✎ Jim wants another report displaying no more than half the hourly workers on each page. To accomplish this, he must insert a manual page break.

### Steps

1. Click cell A16, click Insert on the menu bar, then click Page Break
   A dashed line appears between rows 15 and 16, indicating a horizontal page break. See Figure F-13. After you set page breaks, it's a good idea to preview each page.

2. Preview the worksheet, then click Zoom
   Notice that the status bar reads "Page 1 of 4" and that the data for the employees up through Charles Gallagher appears on the first page. Jim decides to place the date in the footer.

   **QuickTip**
   To insert the page number in a header or footer section yourself, click 🔲 in the Header or Footer dialog box.

3. While in the Print Preview window, click Setup, click the Header/Footer tab, click Custom Footer, click the Right section box, click the Date button 🔲

4. Click the Left section box, type your name, then click OK
   Your name, the page number, and the date, appear in the Footer preview area.

   **QuickTip**
   To remove a manual page break, select any cell directly below or to the right of the page break, click Insert on the menu bar, then click Remove Page Break.

5. In the Page Setup dialog box, click OK, and, still in Print Preview, check to make sure all the pages show your name and the page numbers, click Print, then click OK

6. Click View on the menu bar, click Custom Views, click Add, type Half N Half, then click OK
   Your new custom view has the page breaks and all current print settings.

7. Click Insert on the menu bar, then click Remove Page Break

8. Save the workbook

TABLE F-2: Page break options

| type of page break | where to position cell pointer |
|---|---|
| Both horizontal and vertical page breaks | Select the cell below and to the right of the gridline where you want the breaks to occur |
| Only a horizontal page break | Select the cell in column A that is directly below the gridline where you want the page to break |
| Only a vertical page break | Select a cell in row 1 that is to the right of the gridline where you want the page to break |

▶ EXCEL F-12  MANAGING WORKBOOKS AND PREPARING THEM FOR THE WEB

---

Hints as well as trouble-shooting advice, right where you need it — next to the step itself.

Quickly accessible summaries of key terms, toolbar buttons, or keyboard alternatives connected with the lesson material. Students can refer easily to this information when working on their own projects at a later time.

Every lesson features large-size representations of what the students' screen should look like after completing the numbered steps.

FIGURE F-13: **Worksheet with horizontal page break**

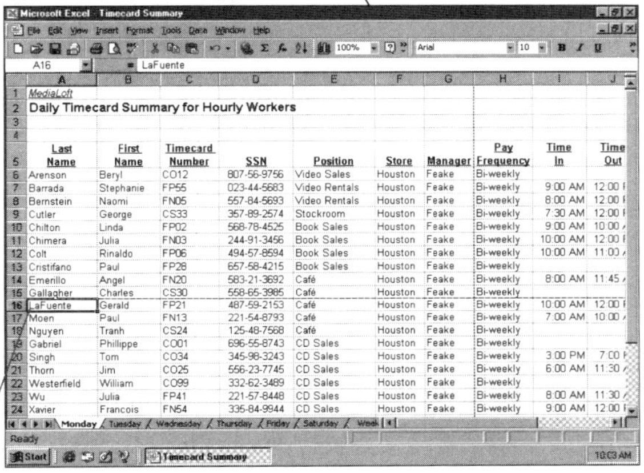


Dashed line indicates horizontal break after row 15

Excel 2000

**CLUES TO USE**

### Using Page Break Preview

By clicking View on the menu bar, then clicking Page Break Preview, or clicking Page Break Preview in the Print Preview window, you can view and change page breaks manually. (If you see a dialog box asking if you want help, just click OK to close it.) Simply drag the page break lines to the desired location. See Figure F-14. To exit Page Break Preview, click View on the menu bar then click Normal.

FIGURE F-14: **Page Break Preview window**

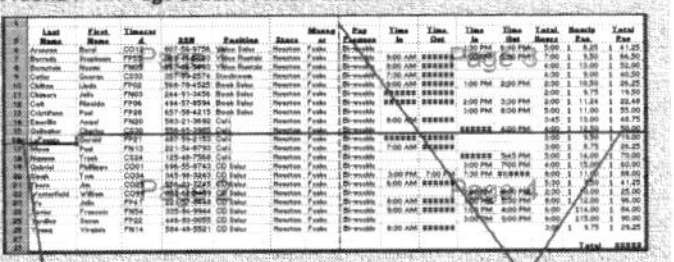

Cell pointer in cell A16

Drag page break lines to change page breaks

MANAGING WORKBOOKS AND PREPARING THEM FOR THE WEB EXCEL F-13

Clues to Use boxes provide concise information that either expands on one component of the major lesson skill or describes an independent task that is in some way related to the major lesson skill.

The page numbers are designed like a road map. Excel indicates the Excel section, F indicates the sixth unit, and 13 indicates the page within the unit.

# Other Features

The two-page lesson format featured in this book provides the new user with a powerful learning experience. Additionally, this book contains the following features:

## MOUS Certification Coverage

Each unit opener has a MOUS next to it to indicate where Microsoft Office User Specialist (MOUS) skills are covered. In addition, there is a MOUS appendix which contains a grid that maps to where specific Core Excel MOUS skills can be found in each lesson and where students can find additional practice. This textbook thoroughly prepares students to learn the skills needed to pass the Excel 2000 MOUS exam. *Microsoft Excel—Illustrated Complete, 0-7600-6064-9,* teaches students the Expert skills needed for the Excel 2000 Expert MOUS exam.

## Real-World Case

The case study used throughout the textbook, a fictitious company called MediaLoft, is designed to be "real-world" in nature and introduces the kinds of activities that students will encounter when working with Microsoft Excel 2000. With a real-world case, the process of solving problems will be more meaningful to students. Students can also enhance their skills by completing the Web Works exercises in each unit by going to the innovative Student Online Companion, available at **www.course.com/illustrated/medialoft**. The MediaLoft site mirrors the case study by acting as the company's intranet site, further allowing students to become familiar with applicable business scenarios.

## End of Unit Material

Each unit concludes with a Concepts Review that tests students' understanding of what they learned in the unit. The Concepts Review is followed by a Skills Review, which provides students with additional hands-on practice of the skills. The Skills Review is followed by Independent Challenges, which pose case problems for students to solve. At least one Independent Challenge in each unit asks students to use the World Wide Web to solve the problem as indicated by a Web Work icon. The Visual Workshops that follow the Independent Challenges help students develop critical thinking skills. Students are shown completed Web pages or screens and are asked to recreate them from scratch.

# Instructor's Resource Kit

The Instructor's Resource Kit is Course Technology's way of putting the resources and information needed to teach and learn effectively into your hands. With an integrated array of teaching and learning tools that offers you and your students a broad range of technology-based instructional options, we believe this kit represents the highest quality and most cutting edge resources available to instructors today. The resources available with this book are:

**MediaLoft Web site**  Available at **www.course.com/illustrated/medialoft**, this innovative Student Online Companion enhances and augments the printed page by bringing students onto the Web for a dynamic and continually updated learning experience. The MediaLoft site mirrors the case study used throughout the book, creating a real-world intranet site for this fictitious company, a national chain of bookstore cafés. This Companion is used to complete the WebWorks exercise in each unit of this book, and to allow students to become familiar with the business application of an intranet site.

**Instructor's Manual**  Available as an electronic file, the Instructor's Manual is quality-assurance tested and includes unit overviews, detailed lecture topics for each unit with teaching tips, an Upgrader's Guide, solutions to all lessons and end-of-unit material, and extra Independent Challenges. The Instructor's Manual is available on the Instructor's Resource Kit CD-ROM.

**Course Test Manager**  Designed by Course Technology, this Windows-based testing software helps instructors design, administer, and print tests and pre-tests. A full-featured program, Course Test Manager also has an online testing component that allows students to take tests at the computer and have their exams automatically graded.

**Project Files**  Project Files contain all of the data that students will use to complete the lessons and end-of-unit material. A Readme file includes instructions for using the files. Adopters of this text are granted the right to install the Project Files on any standalone computer or network. The Project Files are available on the Instructor's Resource Kit CD-ROM, the Review Pack, and can also be downloaded from www.thomsonlearning.co.uk.

**Solution Files**  Solution Files contain every file students are asked to create or modify in the lessons and end-of-unit material. A Help file on the Instructor's Resource Kit includes information for using the Solution Files.

**Figure Files**  Figure files contain all the figures from the book in bitmap format. Use the figure files to create transparency masters or in a PowerPoint presentation.

**WebCT**  WebCT is a tool used to create Web-based educational environments and also uses WWW browsers as the interface for the course-building environment. The site is hosted on your school campus, allowing complete control over the information. WebCT has its own internal communication system, offering internal e-mail, a Bulletin Board, and a Chat room.

Course Technology offers pre-existing supplemental information to help in your WebCT class creation, such as a suggested Syllabus, Lecture Notes, Figures in the Book / Course Presenter, Student Downloads, and Test Banks in which you can schedule an exam, create reports, and more.

# Brief Contents

# Contents

## Excel 2000

# Contents

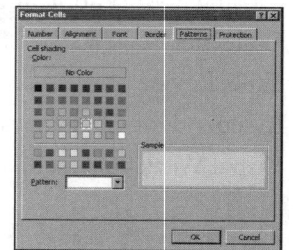

## Formatting a Worksheet

# Working with Charts

# Working with Formulas and Functions

# Contents

## Managing Workbooks and Preparing Them for the Web

## Automating Worksheet Tasks

## Using Lists

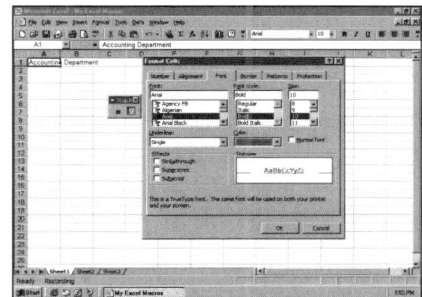

# Contents

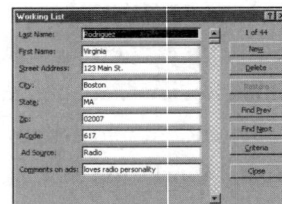

Unit
A

# Getting
## Started with Excel 2000

### Objectives

► **Define spreadsheet software**
► **Start Excel 2000**
► **View the Excel window**
MOUS ► **Open and save a workbook**
MOUS ► **Enter labels and values**
MOUS ► **Preview and print a worksheet**
MOUS ► **Get Help**
► **Close a workbook and exit Excel**

In this unit, you will learn how to start Microsoft Excel 2000 and use different elements of the Excel window. You will also learn how to open and save existing files, enter data in a worksheet, and use the extensive Help system. ✎ Jim Fernandez is the office manager at MediaLoft, a nationwide chain of bookstore cafés selling books, CDs, and videos. MediaLoft cafés also sell coffee and pastries to customers. Jim uses Excel to analyze a worksheet that summarizes budget information for the MediaLoft Café in the New York City store.

# Defining Spreadsheet Software

Microsoft Excel is an electronic spreadsheet program that runs on Windows computers. You use an **electronic spreadsheet** to perform numeric calculations rapidly and accurately. See Table A-1 for common ways spreadsheets are used in business. The electronic spreadsheet that you produce when using Excel is also referred to as a **worksheet**. ⟋ Excel helps Jim produce professional-looking documents that can be updated automatically so they always have accurate information. Figure A-1 shows a budget worksheet that Jim created using pencil and paper, while Figure A-2 shows the same worksheet Jim created using Excel.

## Details

### The advantages of using Excel include:

### Enter data quickly and accurately

With Excel, you can enter information faster and more accurately than when using the pencil-and-paper method. For example, in the MediaLoft NYC Café budget, certain expenses such as rent, cleaning supplies, and products supplied on a yearly plan (coffee, creamers, sweeteners) remain constant for the year. You can copy the expenses that don't change from quarter to quarter, and then use Excel to calculate Total Expenses and Net Income for each quarter by simply supplying the data and formulas.

### Recalculate data easily

Fixing typing errors or updating data using Excel is easy, and the results of a changed entry are recalculated automatically. For example, if you receive updated expense figures for Quarter 4, you simply enter the new numbers and Excel recalculates the worksheet.

### Perform a what-if analysis

One of the most powerful decision-making features of Excel is the ability to change data and then quickly view the recalculated results. Anytime you use a worksheet to answer the question "what if," you are performing a **what-if analysis.** For instance, if the advertising budget for a quarter is increased to $3,600, you can enter the new figure into the worksheet and immediately see the impact on the overall budget.

### Change the appearance of information

Excel provides powerful features for enhancing a spreadsheet so that information is visually appealing and easy to understand. You can use boldface type and shade text headings or numbers to add emphasis to key data in the worksheet.

### Create charts

Excel makes it easy to create charts based on information in a worksheet. With Excel, charts are automatically updated as data changes. The worksheet in Figure A-2 includes a pie chart that graphically shows the distribution of the MediaLoft NYC Café's budget expenses for the year 2000.

### Share information with other users

Because everyone at MediaLoft is now using Microsoft Office, it's easy to share worksheet data among colleagues. For example, you can complete the MediaLoft budget that your manager started creating in Excel. Simply access the files you need or want to share through the network or from a disk, and then make any changes or additions.

### Create new worksheets from existing ones quickly

It's easy to take an existing Excel worksheet and quickly modify it to create a new one. When you are ready to create next year's budget, you can open the file for this year's budget, save it with a new file name, and use the existing data as a starting point.

FIGURE A-1: Traditional paper worksheet

## MediaLoft NYC Café Budget

|  | Qtr1 | Qtr 2 | Qtr 3 | Qtr 4 | Total |
|---|---|---|---|---|---|
| Net Sales | 48,000 | 76,000 | 64,000 | 80,000 | 268,000 |
| Expenses |  |  |  |  |  |
| Salary | 13,000 | 13,000 | 13,000 | 13,000 | 52,000 |
| Rent | 3,500 | 3,500 | 3,500 | 3,500 | 14,000 |
| Advertising | 3,600 | 8,000 | 16,000 | 20,000 | 47,600 |
| Cleaners | 1,500 | 1,500 | 1,500 | 1,500 | 6,000 |
| Pastries | 2,500 | 2,500 | 2,500 | 2,500 | 10,000 |
| Milk/Cream | 1,000 | 1,000 | 1,000 | 1,000 | 4,000 |
| Coffee/Tea | 4,250 | 4,250 | 4,250 | 4,250 | 17,000 |
| Sweeteners | 300 | 300 | 300 | 300 | 1,200 |
| Total Expenses | 29,650 | 34,050 | 42,050 | 46,050 | 151,800 |
| Net Income | 18,350 | 41,950 | 21,950 | 33,950 | 116,200 |

FIGURE A-2: Excel worksheet

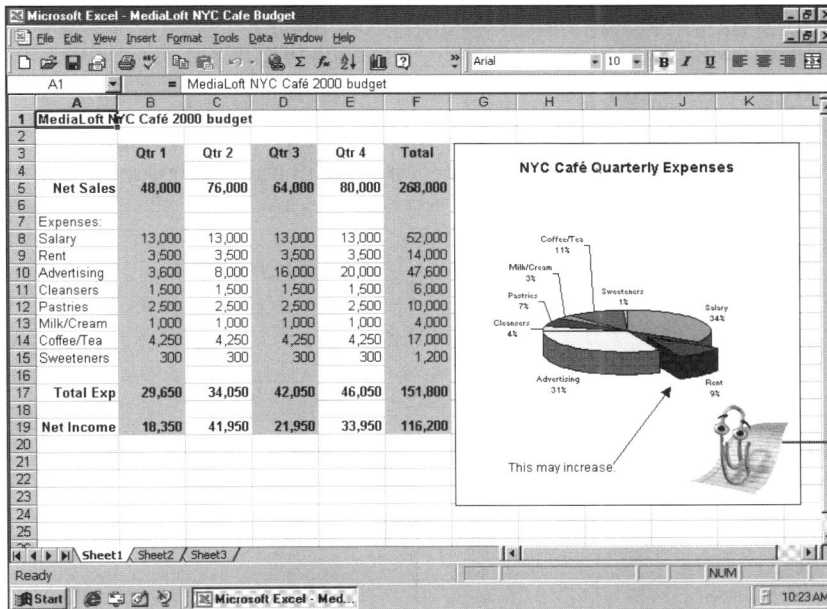

Office Assistant provides help when needed

TABLE A-1: Common business uses for spreadsheets

| spreadsheets are used to: | by: |
|---|---|
| **Maintain values** | Calculating numbers |
| **Represent values visually** | Creating charts based on worksheet figures |
| **Create consecutively numbered pages using multiple workbook sheets** | Printing reports containing workbook sheets |
| **Organize data** | Sorting data in ascending or descending order |
| **Analyze data** | Creating data summaries and short-lists using PivotTables or AutoFilters |
| **Create what-if data scenarios** | Using variable values to investigate and sample different outcomes |

# Starting Excel 2000

To start any Windows program, you use the Start button on the taskbar. A slightly different procedure might be required for computers on a network and those that use Windows-enhancing utilities. If you need assistance, ask your instructor or technical support person. ✐ Jim is ready to begin work on the budget for the MediaLoft Café in New York City. He begins by starting Excel.

## Steps

**1.** Point to the **Start button** 🔳Start on the taskbar

The Start button is on the left side of the taskbar and is used to start programs on your computer.

**2.** Click 🔳Start

Microsoft Excel is located in the Programs group, which is at the top of the Start menu, as shown in Figure A-3.

**Trouble?**

If you don't see the Microsoft Excel icon, consult your instructor or technical support person.

**3.** Point to **Programs**

All the programs on your computer, including Microsoft Excel, are listed in this area of the Start menu. See Figure A-4. Your program list might look different depending on the programs installed on your computer.

**4.** Click the **Microsoft Excel program icon** on the Programs menu

Excel opens and a blank worksheet appears. In the next lesson, you will familiarize yourself with the elements of the Excel worksheet window.

FIGURE A-3: **Start menu**

Microsoft Excel
is located in
this group

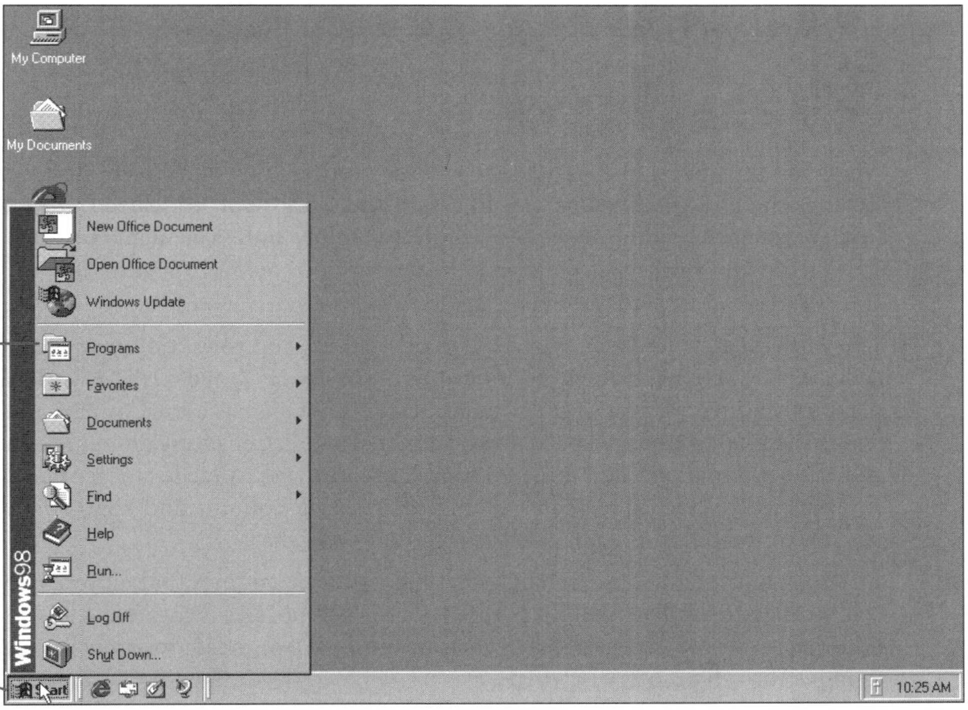

Click here to
open the Start
menu

FIGURE A-4: **Programs list**

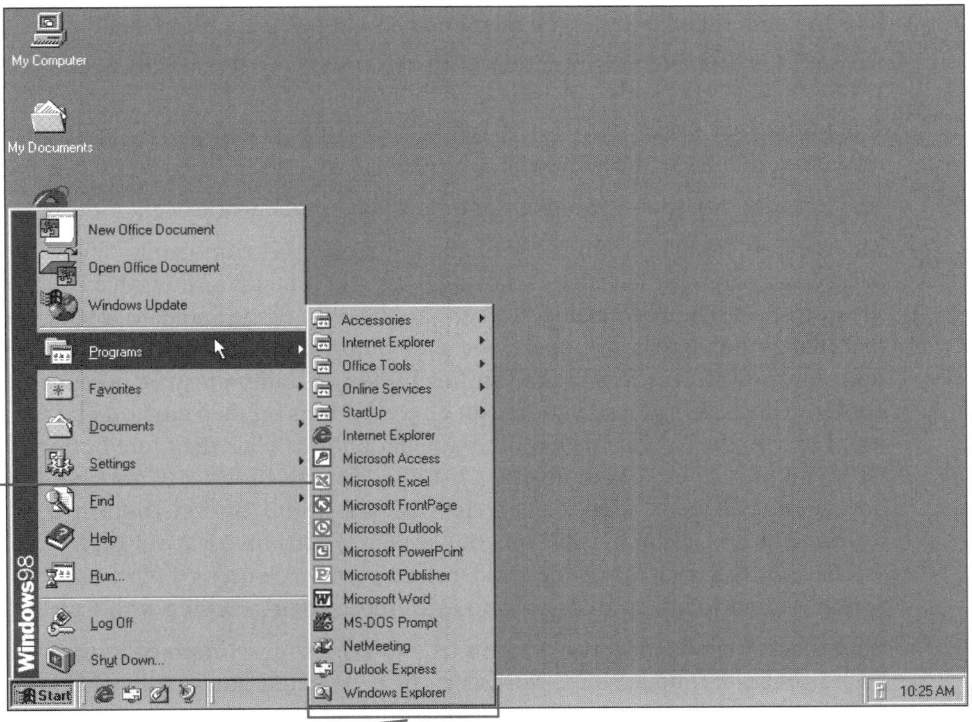

Microsoft Excel
program icon

Your list of programs
might vary

Figure A-3 Start menu items:
New Office Document
Open Office Document
Windows Update
Programs
Favorites
Documents
Settings
Find
Help
Run...
Log Off
Shut Down...
Windows98
Start
10:25 AM

Figure A-4 Programs list:
New Office Document
Open Office Document
Windows Update
Programs
Favorites
Documents
Settings
Find
Help
Run...
Log Off
Shut Down...

Accessories
Internet Explorer
Office Tools
Online Services
StartUp
Internet Explorer
Microsoft Access
Microsoft Excel
Microsoft FrontPage
Microsoft Outlook
Microsoft PowerPoint
Microsoft Publisher
Microsoft Word
MS-DOS Prompt
NetMeeting
Outlook Express
Windows Explorer

10:25 AM

My Computer
My Documents

GETTING STARTED WITH EXCEL 2000 EXCEL A-5

Excel 2000

# Viewing the Excel Window

When you start Excel, the **worksheet window** appears on your screen. The worksheet window includes the tools that enable you to create and work with worksheets. Jim needs to familiarize himself with the Excel worksheet window and its elements before he starts working with the budget worksheet. Compare the descriptions below to Figure A-5.

**Trouble?**

If your worksheet does not fill the screen as shown in Figure A-5, click the Maximize button in the worksheet window.

The **worksheet window** contains a grid of columns and rows. Columns are labeled alphabetically (A, B, C, etc.) and rows are labeled numerically (1, 2, 3, etc.). The worksheet window displays only a tiny fraction of the whole worksheet, which has a total of 256 columns and 65,536 rows. The intersection of a column and a row is a **cell**. Cells can contain text, numbers, formulas, or a combination of all three. Every cell has its own unique location or **cell address**, which is identified by the coordinates of the intersecting column and row. For example, the cell address of the cell in the upper-left corner of a worksheet is A1.

The **cell pointer** is a dark rectangle that highlights or outlines the cell you are working in. This cell is called the **active cell**. In Figure A-5, the cell pointer is located at A1, so A1 is the active cell. To activate a different cell, just click any other cell or press the arrow keys on your keyboard to move the cell pointer elsewhere.

The **title bar** displays the program name (Microsoft Excel) and the filename of the open worksheet (in this case the default filename, Book1). As shown in Figure A-5, the title bar also contains a control menu box, a Close button, and resizing buttons, which are common to all Windows programs.

The **menu bar** contains menus from which you choose Excel commands. As with all Windows programs, you can choose a menu command by clicking it with the mouse or by pressing [Alt] plus the underlined letter in the menu name. When you click a menu, a short list of commonly used commands may appear at first; you can wait or click the double arrows at the bottom of the menu to see expanded menus.

The **name box** displays the active cell address. In Figure A-5, "A1" appears in the name box, indicating that A1 is the active cell.

The **formula bar** allows you to enter or edit data in the worksheet.

The **toolbars** contain buttons for frequently used Excel commands. The **Standard toolbar** is located just below the left edge of the menu bar and contains buttons that effect operations within the worksheet. The **Formatting toolbar**—to the right of the Standard toolbar—contains buttons that change the worksheet's appearance. Each button contains a graphic representation of its function. For instance, the face of the Printing button contains a printer. To choose a button, simply click it with the left mouse button. Not all the buttons on the Standard and Formatting toolbars are visible on the screen. To view other toolbar buttons, click the More Buttons button ⬚ at the right end of each toolbar to display a list of additional buttons. Throughout the lessons in this book, you will need to remember to click the More Buttons button if a button you are instructed to click is not visible on your screen. When you use a button from the More Buttons list, Excel adds it to your visible toolbar. That's why each user's toolbars look unique. Be sure to read the Clues to Use in this lesson to learn more about working with Excel's toolbars.

**Sheet tabs** below the worksheet grid let you keep your work in collections called **workbooks**. Each workbook contains three worksheets by default and can contain a maximum of 255 sheets. **Sheet tabs** can be given meaningful names. **Sheet tab scrolling buttons** help you move from one sheet to another.

The **status bar** is located at the bottom of the Excel window. The left side of the status bar provides a brief description of the active command or task in progress. The right side of the status bar shows the status of important keys such as [Caps Lock] and [Num Lock].

FIGURE A-5: Excel worksheet window elements

Title bar
Menu bar
Standard toolbar (your toolbar may look different)
Name box
Cell pointer highlights active cell
Formula bar
Sheet tab scrolling buttons

Resizing buttons
Close button
Formatting toolbar (your toolbar may look different)
More Buttons button
Worksheet window

Sheet tabs          Status bar          Your Office Assistant may appear in a different location, or not at all

CLUES TO USE

## Personalized toolbars and menus in Excel 2000

Excel toolbars and menus modify themselves to your working style. The Standard and Formatting toolbars you see when you first start Excel include the most frequently used buttons. To locate a button not visible on a toolbar, click the **More Buttons button** on that toolbar to see the list of additional toolbar buttons. As you work, Excel promotes the buttons you use to the visible toolbars, and demotes the buttons you don't use to the More Buttons list. Similarly, Excel menus adjust to your work habits, so that the commands you use most often automatically appear on the shortened menus. Click the double arrow at the bottom of a menu to view additional menu commands. You can return toolbars and menus to their default settings by clicking Reset my usage data on the Options tab of the Customize dialog box, as shown in Figure A-6. Resetting your usage data erases changes made automatically to your menus and toolbars. It does not affect the options you customize.

FIGURE A-6: Customize dialog box

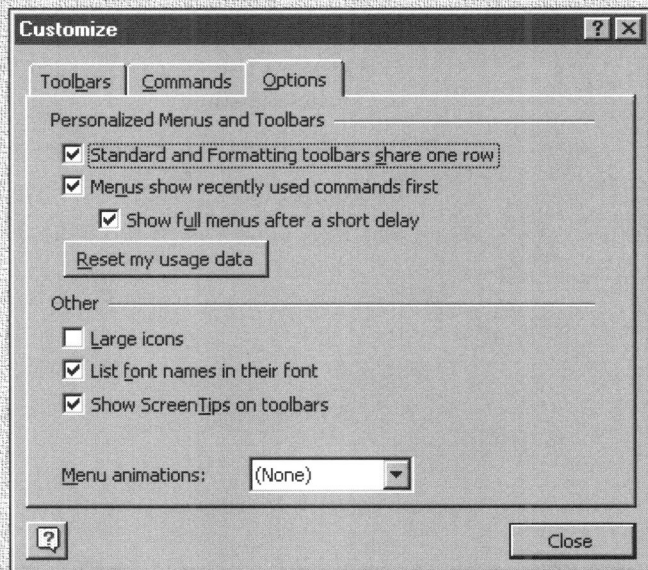

# Opening and Saving a Workbook

Sometimes it's more efficient to create a new worksheet by modifying one that already exists. This saves you from having to retype information that can be reused from previous work. Throughout this book, you will create new worksheets by opening a file from your Project Disk, using the Save As command to create a copy of the file with a new name, and then modifying the new file by following the lesson steps. Use the Save command to store changes made to an existing file. It is a good idea to save your work every 15 minutes or before printing. Saving the files with new names keeps your original Project Disk files intact, in case you have to start the lesson over again or you wish to repeat an exercise. ▰▰▰ Jim wants to complete the New York City MediaLoft Café budget that a member of the accounting staff has been working on. Jim opens the budget workbook and then uses the Save As command to create a copy with a new name.

## Steps 1234

1. **Insert your Project Disk in the appropriate disk drive**

2. **Click the Open button 🖻 on the Standard toolbar**
   The Open dialog box opens. See Figure A-7.

3. **Click the Look in list arrow, then click the drive that contains your Project Disk**
   A list of the files on your Project Disk appears in the Open dialog box.

4. **Click the file EX A-1, then click Open**
   The file EX A-1 opens.

5. **Click File on the menu bar, then click Save As**
   The Save As dialog box opens with the drive containing your Project Disk displayed in the Save in list box. You should save all your files to your Project Disk, unless instructed otherwise.

6. **In the File name text box, select the current file name (if necessary), type MediaLoft Cafe Budget, as shown in Figure A-8, then click Save**
   Both the Save As dialog box and the file EX A-1 close, and a duplicate file named MediaLoft Café Budget opens, as shown in Figure A-9. The Office Assistant may or may not appear on your screen. As you will learn, toolbars and menus change as you work with Excel. It is a good idea to return toolbars and menus to their default settings when you begin these lessons.

7. **Click Tools on the menu bar, click Customize, make sure the Options tab in the Customize dialog box is displayed, click Reset my usage data to restore the default settings, click Yes in the alert box or dialog balloon, then click Close**

Click to display a list of available drives and folders

Your folder may differ

Your files and folders display here

The selected filename will appear here

FIGURE A-8: **Save As dialog box**

Current drive or folder (yours may differ)

Your list of files might be different

Type the new filename here

FIGURE A-9: **MediaLoft Cafe Budget workbook**

Because toolbars adapt as you work, your toolbars may not match the figures

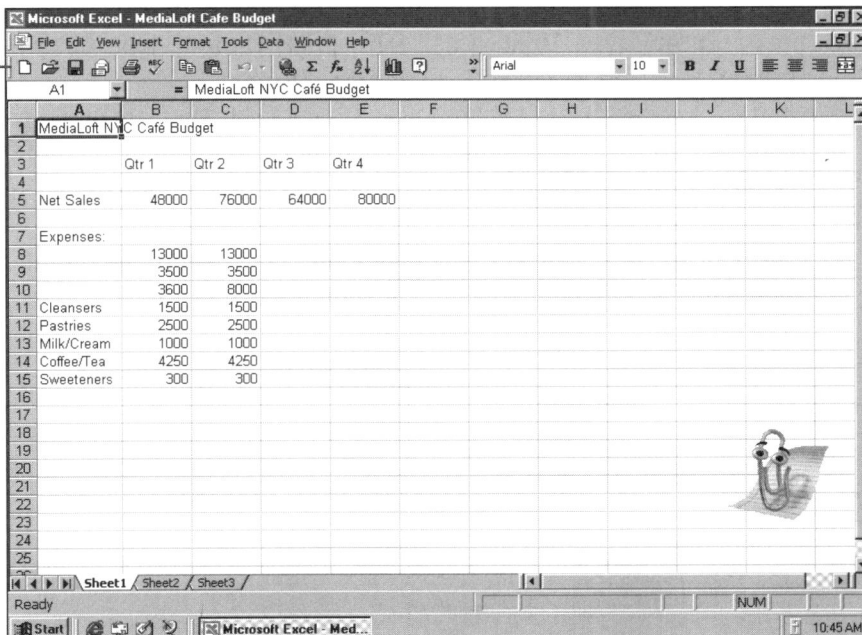

| | A | B | C | D | E |
|---|---|---|---|---|---|
| 1 | MediaLoft NYC Café Budget | | | | |
| 2 | | | | | |
| 3 | | Qtr 1 | Qtr 2 | Qtr 3 | Qtr 4 |
| 4 | | | | | |
| 5 | Net Sales | 48000 | 76000 | 64000 | 80000 |
| 6 | | | | | |
| 7 | Expenses: | | | | |
| 8 | | 13000 | 13000 | | |
| 9 | | 3500 | 3500 | | |
| 10 | | 3600 | 8000 | | |
| 11 | Cleansers | 1500 | 1500 | | |
| 12 | Pastries | 2500 | 2500 | | |
| 13 | Milk/Cream | 1000 | 1000 | | |
| 14 | Coffee/Tea | 4250 | 4250 | | |
| 15 | Sweeteners | 300 | 300 | | |

Excel 2000

# Entering Labels and Values

Labels are used to identify the data in the rows and columns of a worksheet. They also make your worksheet more readable and understandable. You should try to enter all labels in your worksheet before entering the data. Labels can contain text and numerical information not used in calculations, such as dates, times, or addresses. Labels are left-aligned by default. **Values**, which include numbers, formulas, and functions, are used in calculations. Excel recognizes an entry as a value when it is a number or begins with special symbols: +, -, =, @, #, or $. All values are right-aligned by default. When a cell contains both text and numbers it is not a valid formula; Excel recognizes the entry as a label. ◄━━━ Jim needs to enter labels identifying the rest of the expense categories, and the values for Qtr 3 and Qtr 4 into the MediaLoft Café Budget worksheet.

**Steps**

1. Click cell **A8** to make it the active cell

   Notice that the cell address A8 appears in the name box. As you work, the mouse pointer has a variety of appearances, depending on where it is and what Excel is doing. Table A-2 lists and identifies some mouse pointers. The labels in cells A1:A15 identify the expenses.

2. Type **Salary**, as shown in Figure A-10, then click the **Enter button** ☑ on the formula bar

   The label is entered in cell A8 and its contents display in the formula bar. You can also confirm a cell entry by pressing [Enter], pressing [Tab], or by pressing one of the arrow keys on the keyboard. If a label does not fit in a cell, Excel displays the remaining characters in the next cell to the right as long as it is empty. Otherwise, the label is **truncated**, or cut off.

3. Click cell **A9**, type **Rent**, press [Enter] to complete the entry and move the cell pointer to cell A10, type **Advertising** in cell A10, then press [Enter]

   The remaining expense values have to be added to the worksheet.

4. Click cell **D8,** press and hold the left mouse button, drag the ✛ pointer to cell **E8** then down to cell **E15,** then release the mouse button

   Two or more selected cells is called a **range**. The active cell is still cell D8, the cells in the range are shaded in purple. Since entries often cover multiple columns and rows, selecting a range makes working with data entry easier.

5. Type **13000**, press [Enter], type **3500** in cell D9, press [Enter], type **16000** in cell D10, press [Enter], type **1500** in cell D11, press [Enter], type **2500** in cell D12, press [Enter], type **1000** in cell D13, press [Enter], type **4250** in cell D14, press [Enter], type **300** in cell D15, then press [Enter]

   All the values in the Qtr 3 column have been added. The cell pointer is now in cell E8.

6. Using Figure A-11 as a guide, type the remaining values for cells E8 through E15

   Before confirming a cell entry you can click the Cancel button on the formula bar or press [Esc] to cancel or delete the entry.

7. Type your name in cell A17, then click the **Save button** 🖫 on the Standard toolbar

   Your name identifies the worksheet as yours when it is printed.

## Trouble?

If you notice a mistake in a cell entry after it has been confirmed, double-click the cell, use [Backspace] or [Delete] to make your corrections, then press [Enter]. You can also click Edit on the menu bar, point to Clear, then click Contents to remove a cell's contents.

## QuickTip

To enter a number that will not be used as part of a calculation, such as a telephone number, type an apostrophe (') before the number.

**TABLE A-2: Commonly used pointers**

| name | pointer | use to | |
|---|---|---|---|
| **Normal or Cross** | ✛ | Select a cell or range; indicates Ready mode | |
| **I-beam** | I | Edit contents of formula bar | |
| **Select** | ⬈ | Select objects and commands | |

FIGURE A-10: Worksheet with initial label entered

Name box ——

Cancel button —

Enter button —

Formula bar —

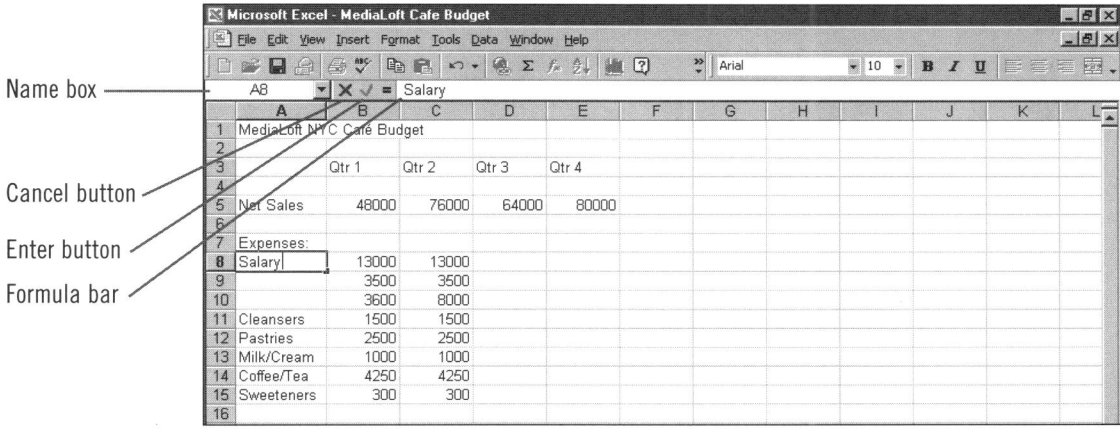

FIGURE A-11: Worksheet with new labels and values

Type these values —

Labels entered —

Values entered —

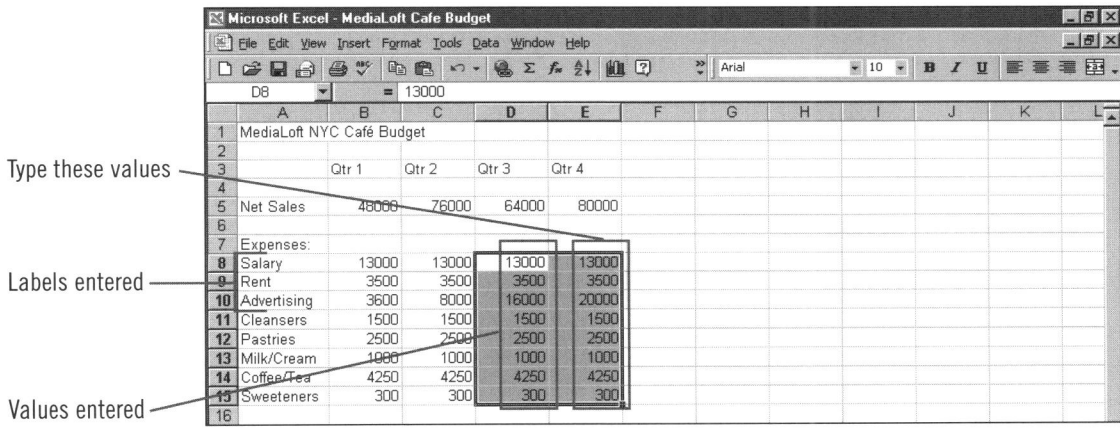

## Navigating a worksheet

With over a million cells available to you, it is important to know how to move around, or **navigate**, a worksheet. You can use the arrow keys on the keyboard ([↑], [↓], [←], [→]) to move a cell or two at a time, or [Page Up] or [Page Down] to move a screenful at a time. To move a screen to the left press [Alt] [Page Up]; to move a screen to the right press [Alt] [Page Down]. You can also simply use your mouse pointer to click the desired cell. If the desired cell is not visible in the worksheet window, use the scroll bars or the Go To command to move the location into view. To return to the first active cell in a worksheet, click cell A1, or press [Ctrl][Home].

# Previewing and Printing a Worksheet

When a worksheet is completed, you may want to print it to have a paper copy to reference, file, or give to others. You can also print a worksheet that is not complete to review your work when you are not at a computer. Before you print a worksheet, you should save any changes. That way, if anything happens to the file as it is being sent to the printer, you will have your latest work saved to your disk. Then you should preview it to make sure it will fit on a page the way you want. When you preview a worksheet, you see a copy of the worksheet exactly as it will appear on paper. Table A-3 provides additional printing tips. ✎ Jim is finished entering the labels and values into the MediaLoft Café budget. Since he already saved his changes, he previews and prints a copy of the worksheet to review on the way home.

## Steps

1. **Make sure the printer is on and contains paper**
   If a file is sent to print and the printer is off, an error message appears.

**Trouble?**

If 🔍 is not visible on your Standard toolbar, click the More Buttons button ≫ to view additional toolbar buttons.

2. **Click the Print Preview button 🔍 on the Standard toolbar**
   A miniature version of the worksheet appears on the screen, as shown in Figure A-13. If there were more than one page, you could click the Next button or the Previous button to move between pages. You can also enlarge the image by clicking the Zoom button.

3. **Click Print**
   The Print dialog box opens, as shown in Figure A-14. To print, you could also click File on the menu bar, then click Print Preview.

4. **Make sure that the Active Sheet(s) option button is selected and that 1 appears in the Number of copies text box**
   Adjusting the value in the Number of copies text box enables you to print multiple copies. You could also print the selected range, the values you just entered, by clicking the Selection option button.

5. **Click OK**
   The Printing dialog box appears briefly while the file is sent to the printer. Note that the dialog box contains a Cancel button. You can use it to cancel the print job provided you can catch it before the file is sent to the printer.

### CLUES TO USE

#### Using Zoom in Print Preview

When you are in the Print Preview window, you can enlarge the image by clicking the Zoom button. You can also position the mouse pointer over a specific part of the worksheet page, then click it to view that section of the page. Figure A-12 shows a magnified section of a document. While the image is zoomed in, use the scroll bars to view different sections of the page.

**FIGURE A-12: Enlarging the preview using Zoom**

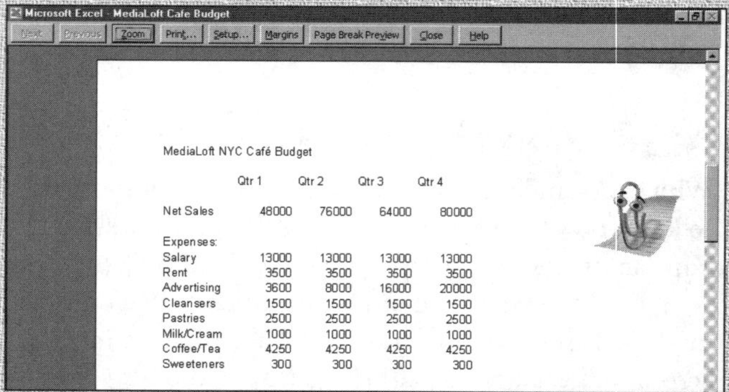

FIGURE A-13: **Print Preview screen**

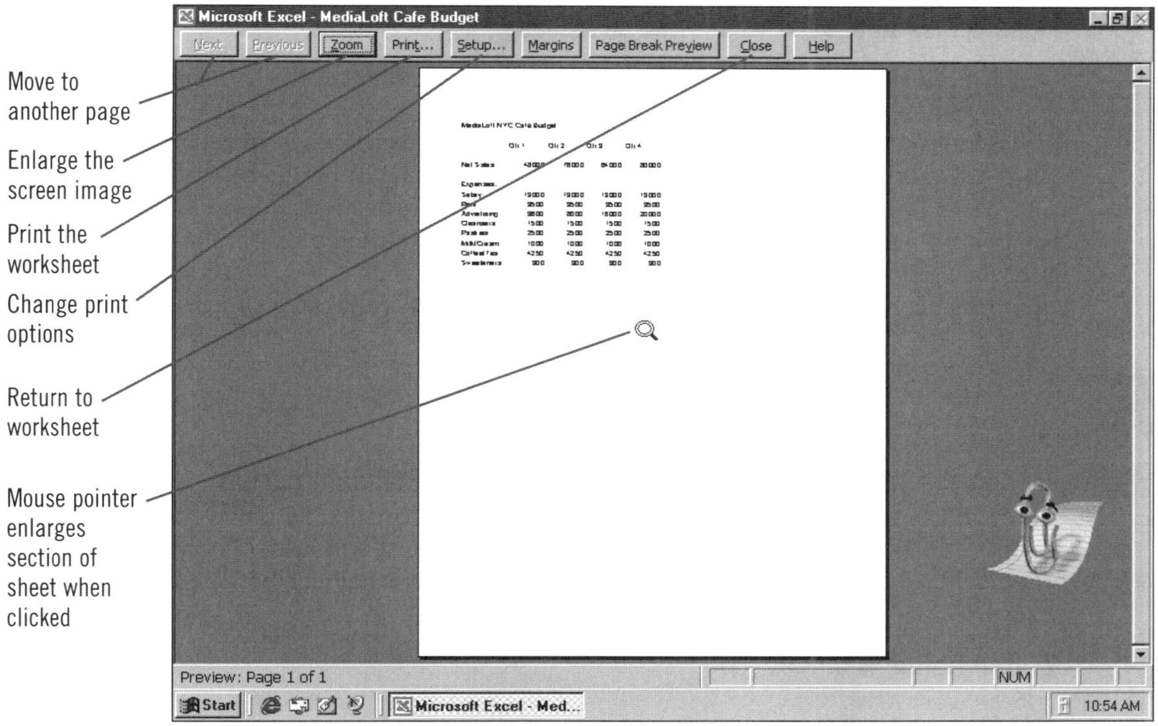

Move to
another page

Enlarge the
screen image

Print the
worksheet

Change print
options

Return to
worksheet

Mouse pointer
enlarges
section of
sheet when
clicked

FIGURE A-14: **Print dialog box**

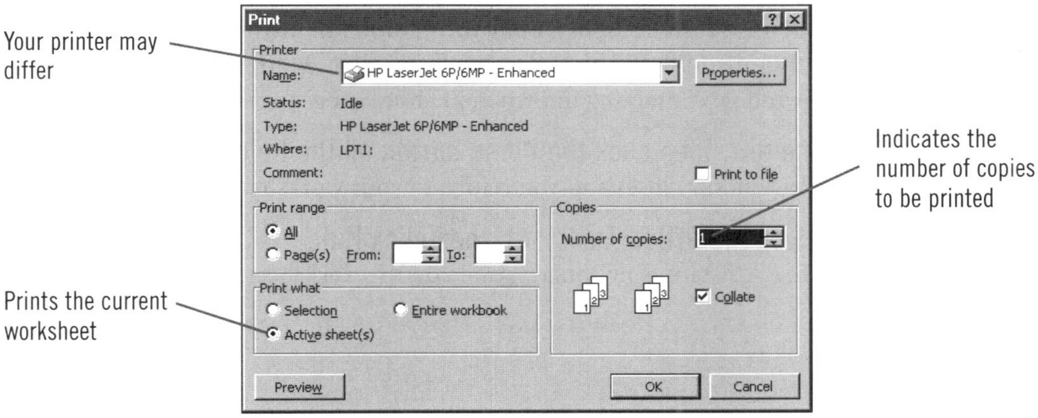

Your printer may
differ

Indicates the
number of copies
to be printed

Prints the current
worksheet

TABLE A-3: **Worksheet printing tips**

| before you print | recommendation |
|---|---|
| Save your work | Make sure your work is saved to a disk |
| Check the printer | Make sure that the printer is turned on and is online, that it has paper, and that there are no error messages or warning signals |
| Preview the worksheet | Check the formatted image for page breaks, page setup (vertical or horizontal), and overall appearance of the worksheet |
| Check the printer selection | Use the Printer setup command in the Print dialog box to verify that the correct printer is selected |
| Check the Print what options | Verify that you are printing either the active sheet, the entire workbook, or just a selected range |

# Getting Help

Excel features an extensive **Help system** that gives you immediate access to definitions, explanations, and useful tips. The animated Office Assistant provides help in two ways. You can type a keyword to search on, or access a question and answer format to research your help topic. The Office Assistant provides **ScreenTips** (indicated by a light bulb) on the current action you are performing. You can click the light bulb to access further information in the form of a dialog box that you can resize and refer to as you work. In addition, you can press [F1] at any time to get immediate help. Jim wants to find out more about ranges so he can work more efficiently with them. He knows he can find more information using the animated Office Assistant.

## Steps

**QuickTip**

If it's displayed, you can also click the Office Assistant to access Help.

1. **Click the Microsoft Excel Help button** [?] **on the Standard toolbar**
   An Office Assistant dialog box opens. You can get information by typing a word to search on in the query box, or by typing a question. If the text within the query box is already selected, any typed text will automatically replace what is highlighted. The Office Assistant provides help based on text typed in the query box.

2. **Type Define a range**
   See Figure A-16.

3. **Click Search**
   The Office Assistant searches for relevant topics from the help files in Excel and then displays the results.

**QuickTip**

Clicking the Print button in the Microsoft Excel Help window prints the information.

4. **Click See More if necessary, click Name cells in a workbook, then click Name a cell or a range of cells in the Microsoft Excel Help window**
   A Help window containing information about ranges opens. See Figure A-17.

5. **Read the text, then click the Close button on the Help window title bar**
   The Help window closes and you return to your worksheet.

6. **Right-click the Office Assistant, then click Hide**
   The Office Assistant is no longer visible on the worksheet.

### CLUES TO USE

#### Changing the Office Assistant

The default Office Assistant character is Clippit, but there are others from which you can choose. To change the appearance of the Office Assistant, right-click the Office Assistant, then click Choose Assistant. Click the Gallery tab, click the Back and Next buttons until you find an Assistant you want to use, then click OK. (You may need to insert your Microsoft Office 2000 CD to perform this task.) Each Office Assistant makes its own unique sounds and can be animated by right-clicking its window and clicking Animate! Figure A-15 shows the Office Assistant dialog box.

**FIGURE A-15: Office Assistant dialog box**

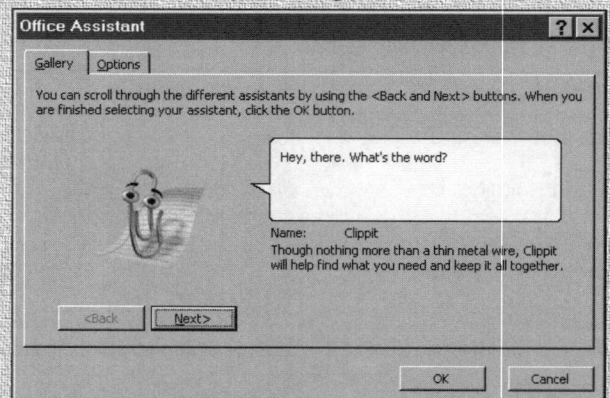

Office Assistant

Gallery | Options

You can scroll through the different assistants by using the <Back and Next> buttons. When you are finished selecting your assistant, click the OK button.

Hey, there. What's the word?

Name: Clippit
Though nothing more than a thin metal wire, Clippit will help find what you need and keep it all together.

<Back    Next>

OK    Cancel

**FIGURE A-16: Office Assistant**

The Office
Assistant on
your screen
may offer a list
of options to
choose from

What would you like to do?

Define a range

Options    Search

Type request
here

Click to close
the dialog
balloon

**FIGURE A-17: Help window**

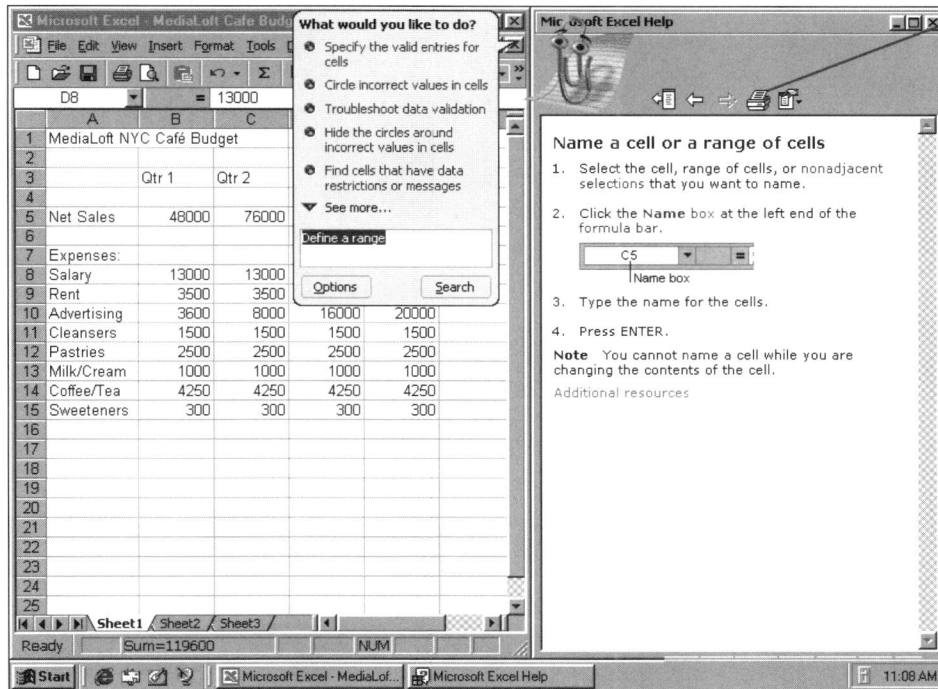

Click to print
Help topic

What would you like to do?
- Specify the valid entries for cells
- Circle incorrect values in cells
- Troubleshoot data validation
- Hide the circles around incorrect values in cells
- Find cells that have data restrictions or messages
- See more...

Define a range

Options    Search

**Name a cell or a range of cells**

1. Select the cell, range of cells, or nonadjacent selections that you want to name.

2. Click the **Name** box at the left end of the formula bar.

   C5    =

   Name box

3. Type the name for the cells.

4. Press ENTER.

**Note** You cannot name a cell while you are changing the contents of the cell.

Additional resources

Excel 2000

# Closing a Workbook and Exiting Excel

When you have finished working you need to save the file and close it. When you have completed all your work in Excel you need to exit the program. You can exit Excel by clicking Exit on the File menu. ◄═══ Since Jim has completed his work on the MediaLoft Café budget, he is finished using Excel for the day. He closes the workbook and then exits Excel.

## Steps

**QuickTip**

You could also click the workbook Close button instead of clicking the File menu.

1. **Click File on the menu bar**
   The File menu opens. See Figure A-18.

2. **Click Close**
   Excel closes the workbook and asks if you want to save your changes; if you have made any changes be sure to save them.

**Trouble?**

To exit Excel and close several files at once, click Exit on the File menu. Excel will prompt you to save changes to each open workbook before exiting.

3. **Click File on the menu bar, then click Exit**
   You could also click the program Close button to exit the program. Excel closes and you return to the desktop. Memory is now freed up for other computing tasks.

FIGURE A-18: **Closing a workbook using the File menu**

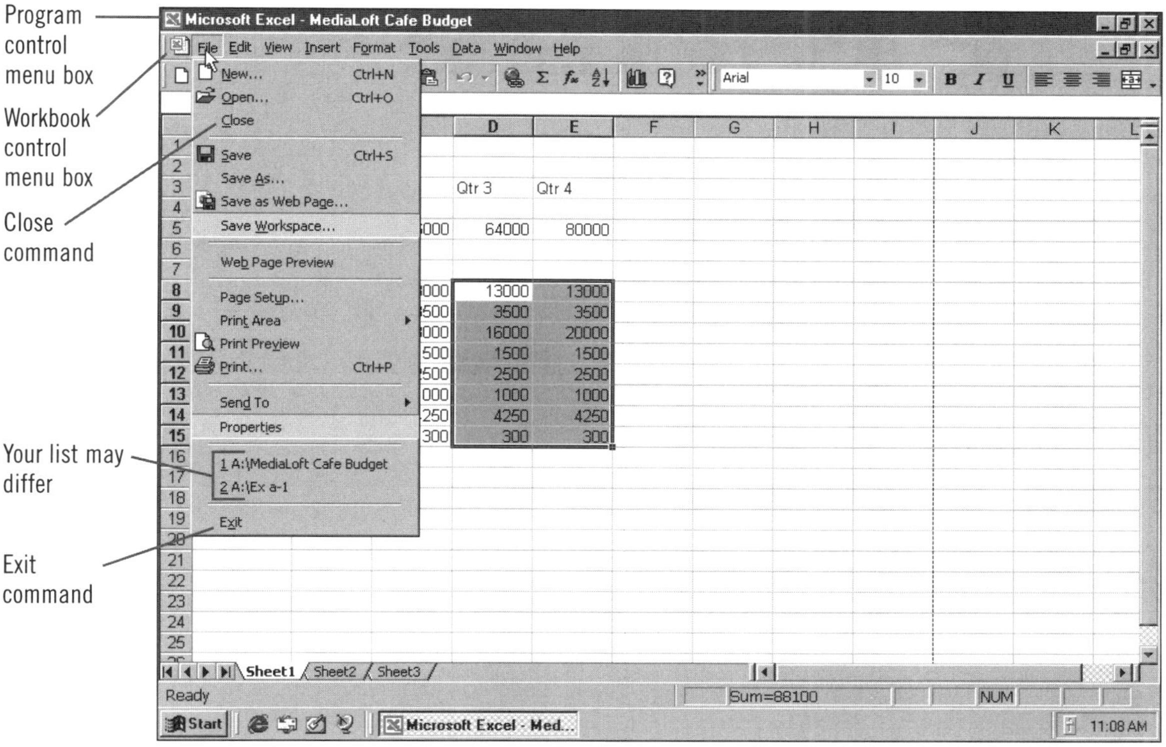

Program control menu box

Workbook control menu box

Close command

| Microsoft Excel - MediaLoft Cafe Budget | _ | 8 | X |

| File | Edit | View | Insert | Format | Tools | Data | Window | Help |

| New... | Ctrl+N |
| Open... | Ctrl+O |
| Close |
| Save | Ctrl+S |
| Save As... |
| Save as Web Page... |
| Save Workspace... |
| Web Page Preview |
| Page Setup... |
| Print Area |
| Print Preview |
| Print... | Ctrl+P |
| Send To |
| Properties |
| 1 A:\MediaLoft Cafe Budget |
| 2 A:\Ex a-1 |
| Exit |

Arial    10    **B** *I* U

|   | D | E | F | G | H | I | J | K | L |
| 1 | | | | | | | | | |
| 2 | | | | | | | | | |
| 3 | Qtr 3 | Qtr 4 | | | | | | | |
| 4 | | | | | | | | | |
| 5 | 64000 | 80000 | | | | | | | |
| 6 | | | | | | | | | |
| 7 | | | | | | | | | |
| 8 | 13000 | 13000 | | | | | | | |
| 9 | 3500 | 3500 | | | | | | | |
| 10 | 16000 | 20000 | | | | | | | |
| 11 | 1500 | 1500 | | | | | | | |
| 12 | 2500 | 2500 | | | | | | | |
| 13 | 1000 | 1000 | | | | | | | |
| 14 | 4250 | 4250 | | | | | | | |
| 15 | 300 | 300 | | | | | | | |

Your list may differ

Exit command

Sheet1 / Sheet2 / Sheet3

Ready    Sum=88100    NUM

Start    Microsoft Excel - Med...    11:08 AM

# Practice

## ► Concepts Review

Label the elements of the Excel worksheet window shown in Figure A-19.

FIGURE A-19

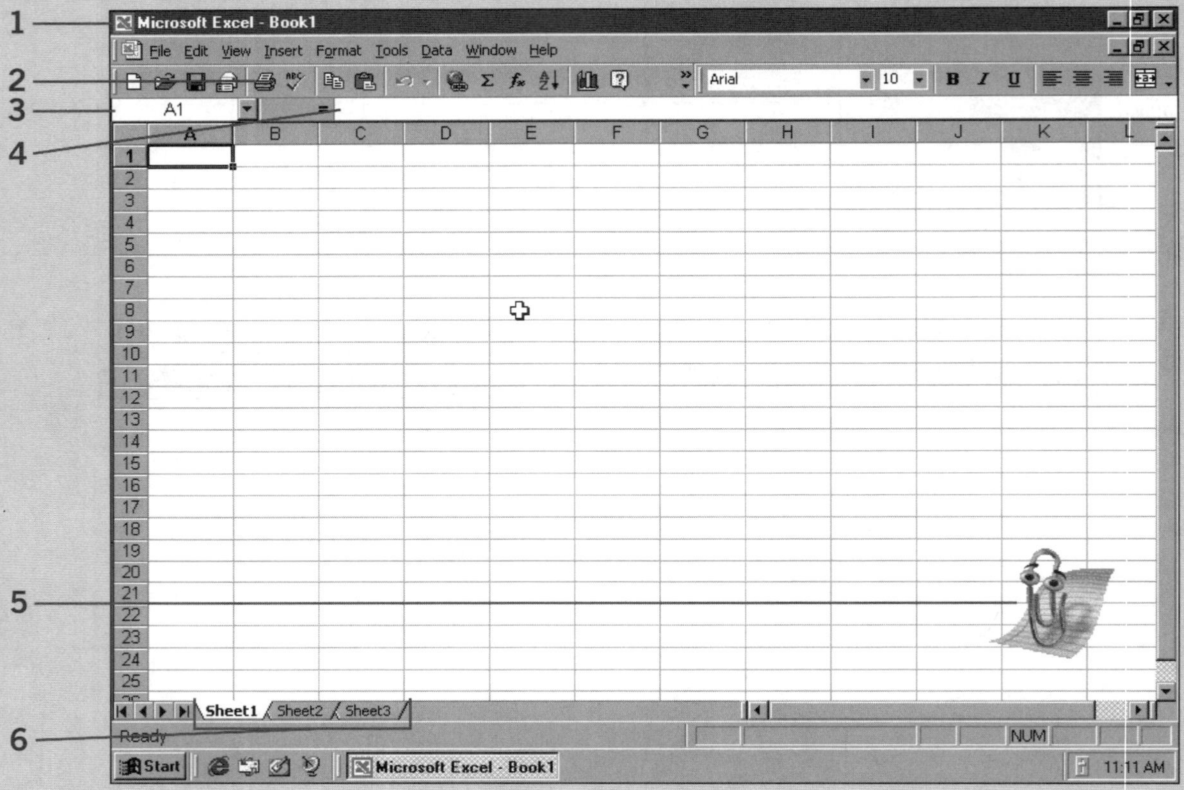

Match each term with the statement that describes it.

7. Cell pointer
8. Button
9. Worksheet window
10. Name box
11. Cell
12. Workbook

a. Area that contains a grid of columns and rows
b. The intersection of a column and row
c. Graphic symbol that depicts a task or function
d. Collection of worksheets
e. Rectangle indicating the active cell
f. Displays the active cell address

Select the best answer from the list of choices.

**13. An electronic spreadsheet can perform all of the following tasks, *except***
   **a.** Display information visually.
   **b.** Calculate data accurately.
   **c.** Plan worksheet objectives.
   **d.** Recalculate updated information.

**14. Each of the following is true about labels, *except***
   **a.** They are left-aligned by default.
   **b.** They are not used in calculations.
   **c.** They are right-aligned by default.
   **d.** They can include numerical information.

**15. Each of the following is true about values, *except***
   **a.** They can include labels.
   **b.** They are right-aligned by default.
   **c.** They are used in calculations.
   **d.** They can include formulas.

**16. What symbol is typed before a number to make the number a label?**
   **a.** "
   **b.** !
   **c.** '
   **d.** ;

**17. You can get Excel Help any of the following ways, *except***
   **a.** Clicking Help on the menu bar.
   **b.** Pressing [F1].
   **c.** Clicking ⃞.
   **d.** Minimizing the program window.

**18. Each key(s) can be used to confirm cell entries, *except***
   **a.** [Enter].
   **b.** [Tab].
   **c.** [Esc].
   **d.** [Shift][Enter].

**19. Which button is used to preview a worksheet?**
   **a.** 📋
   **b.** 🔍
   **c.** 💾
   **d.** 🖨

**20. Which feature is used to enlarge a print preview view?**
a. Magnify
b. Enlarge
c. Amplify
d. Zoom

**21. Each of the following is true about the Office Assistant, *except***
a. It provides tips based on your work habits.
b. It provides help using a question and answer format.
c. You can change the appearance of the Office Assistant.
d. It can complete certain tasks for you.

# ▶ Skills Review

**1. Start Excel 2000.**
a. Point to Programs in the Start menu.
b. Click the Microsoft Excel program icon.

**2. View the Excel window.**
a. Identify as many elements in the Excel worksheet window as you can without referring to the unit material.

**3. Open and save a workbook.**
a. Open the workbook EX A-2 from your Project Disk by clicking the Open button.
b. Save the workbook as "Totally Together Fashions" by clicking File on the menu bar, then clicking Save As.

**4. Enter labels and values.**
a. Enter the labels shown in Figure A-20, the Totally Together Fashions worksheet.
b. Enter values shown in Figure A-20.
c. Type the label "New Data" in cell A2, then clear the cell contents in A2 using the Edit menu.
d. Type your name in cell A10.
e. Save the workbook by clicking the Save button.

FIGURE A-20

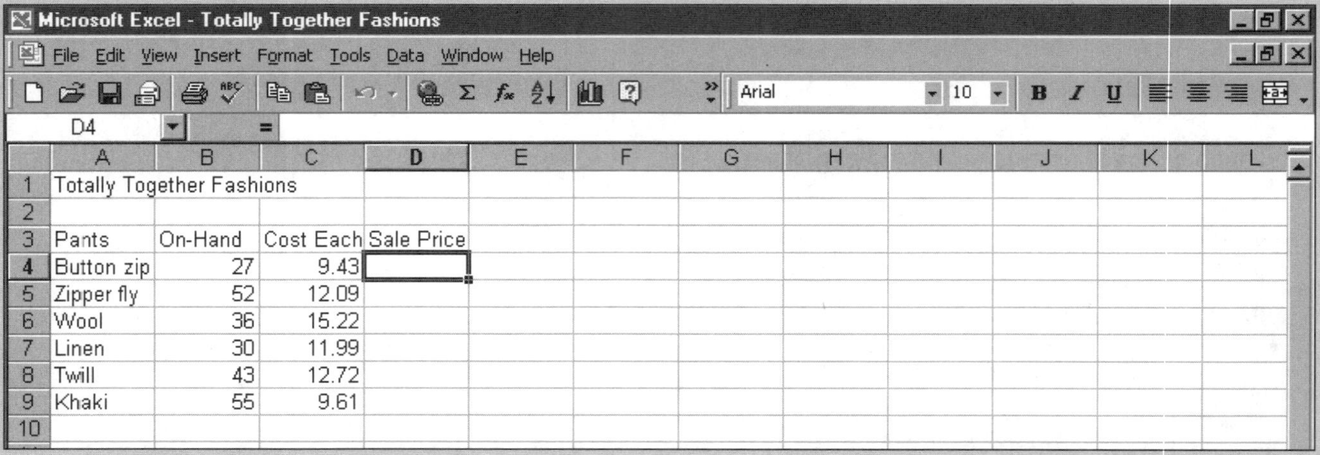

**5. Preview and print a worksheet.**
   **a.** Click the Print Preview button.
   **b.** Use the Zoom button to see more of your worksheet.
   **c.** Print one copy of the worksheet.

**6. Get Help.**
   **a.** Click the Office Assistant button if the Assistant is not displayed.
   **b.** Ask the Office Assistant for information about changing the Excel Office Assistant.
   **c.** Print information offered by the Office Assistant using the Print topic command on the Options menu.
   **d.** Close the Help window.

**7. Close a workbook and exit Excel.**
   **a.** Click File on the menu bar, then click Close.
   **b.** If asked if you want to save the worksheet, click No.
   **c.** If necessary, close any other worksheets you might have opened.
   **d.** Click File on the menu bar, then click Exit.

# ▶ Independent Challenges

**1.** The Excel Help feature provides definitions, explanations, procedures, and other helpful information. It also provides examples and demonstrations to show you how Excel features work. Topics include elements such as the active cell, status bar, buttons, and dialog boxes, as well as detailed information about Excel commands and options.

   To complete this independent challenge:

   **a.** Start Excel and open a new workbook.
   **b.** Click the Office Assistant.
   **c.** Type a question that will give you information about opening and saving a workbook. (*Hint*: You may have to ask the Office Assistant more than one question.)
   **d.** Print the information.
   **e.** Return to your workbook when you are finished.
   **f.** Exit Excel.

Excel 2000

**2.** Spreadsheet software has many uses that can affect the way work is done. Some examples of how Excel can be used are discussed in the beginning of this unit. Use your own personal or business experiences to come up with five examples of how Excel could be used in a business setting.

To complete this independent challenge:

**a.** Start Excel.

**b.** Open a new workbook.

**c.** Think of five business tasks that you could complete more efficiently by using an Excel worksheet.

**d.** Sketch a sample of each worksheet. See Figure A-21, a sample payroll worksheet, as a guide.

**e.** Open a new workbook and save it as "Sample Payroll" on your Project Disk.

**f.** Give your worksheet a title in cell A1, type your name in cell B1.

**g.** Enter the labels shown in Figure A-21.

**h.** Enter sample data for Hours Worked and Hourly Wage in the worksheet.

**i.** Save your work, then preview and print the worksheet.

**j.** Close the worksheet and exit Excel.

FIGURE A-21

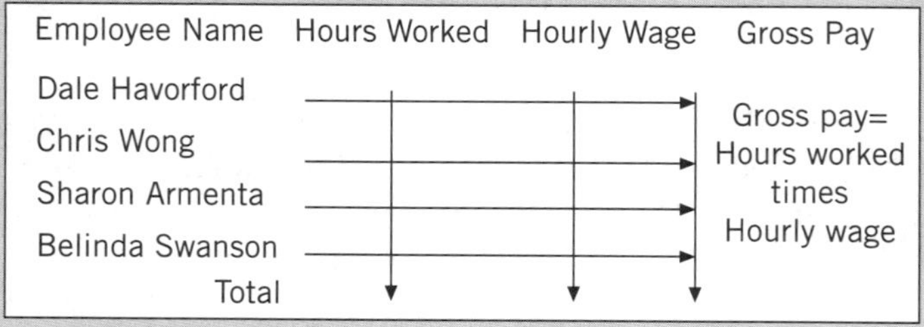

**3.** You are the office manager for Christine's Car Parts, a small auto parts supplier. Although the company is just three years old, it is expanding rapidly, and you are continually looking for ways to make your job easier. Last year you began using Excel to manage and maintain data on inventory and sales, which has greatly helped you to track information accurately and efficiently. The owner of the company has just approved your request to hire an assistant. This person will need to learn how to use Excel. Create a short training document that your new assistant can use as a reference while becoming familiar with Excel.

To complete this independent challenge:

**a.** Draw a sketch of the Excel worksheet window and label the key elements, such as toolbars, title bar, formula bar, scroll bars, etc.

**b.** For each labeled element, write a short description of its use.

**c.** List three ways to get Help in Excel. (*Hint*: Use the Office Assistant to learn all of the ways to get Help in Excel.)

**d.** Create a sketch for three of the following spreadsheet uses: accounts payable schedule, accounts receivable, payroll, list of inventory items, employee benefits data, income statement, cash flow report, or balance sheet. (*Hint*: Make up data for these sketches.)

**e.** Start Excel.

**f.** Create a new workbook and enter the values and labels for a sample spreadsheet. Make sure you have labels in column A. Enter a title for the worksheet and put your name in cell A1.

**g.** Select the range which includes the column labels.

**h.** Use the Print dialog box to print the selected range.

**i.** Preview the entire worksheet.

**j.** Save the workbook as "Christine's Car Parts" on your Project Disk, and then exit Excel.

WEB WORK

**4.** To make smart buying decisions, you can use the World Wide Web to gather the most up-to-date information available. MediaLoft employees have access to the Web through the company's intranet. An **intranet** is a group of connected networks owned by a company or organization that is used for internal purposes. Intranets use Internet software to handle the data communications, such as e-mail and Web pages, within an organization. These pages often provide company-wide information. As with all intranets, the MediaLoft intranet limits access to MediaLoft employees.

Imagine that your supervisor at MediaLoft has just given you approval for buying a new computer. Cost is not an issue, and you need to provide a list of hardware and software requirements. You use Excel to create a worksheet using data found on the World Wide Web to support your purchase decision.

To complete this independent challenge:

**a.** Start Excel, open a new workbook and save it on your Project Disk as "New Computer Data."

**b.** List the features you want your ideal computer to contain (e.g. CD-ROM drive, etc.).

**c.** Connect to the Internet, go to the MediaLoft intranet site at http://www.course.com/illustrated/MediaLoft, then click the Research Center link.

**d.** Use any of the links to computer companies provided at the Research Center to compile your data.

**e.** Compile data for the components you want. When you find a system that meets your needs, include that in your list. Be sure to identify the system's key features, such as the processor chip, hard drive capacity, RAM, and monitor size. List any extra/upgrade items you want to purchase.

**f.** When you are finished gathering data, disconnect from the Internet.

**g.** Make sure all components are listed and totaled. Include any tax and shipping costs the manufacturer charges.

**h.** Indicate on the worksheet your final purchase decision. Enter your name in one of the cells.

**i.** Save, preview, and then print your worksheet.

**j.** Close and exit Excel.

Excel 2000

# ▶ Visual Workshop

Create a worksheet similar to Figure A-22 using the skills you learned in this unit. Save the workbook as "Carrie's Camera and Darkroom" on your Project Disk. Type your name in cell A11, then preview and print the worksheet.

**FIGURE A-22**

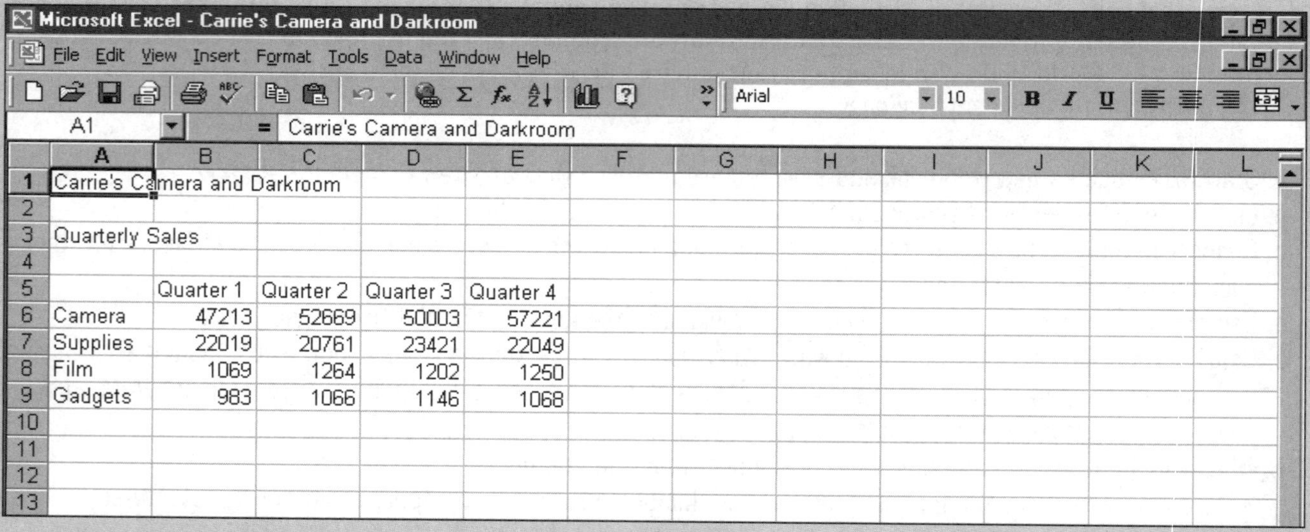

| | A | B | C | D | E | F | G | H | I | J | K | L |
|---|---|---|---|---|---|---|---|---|---|---|---|---|
| 1 | Carrie's Camera and Darkroom | | | | | | | | | | | |
| 2 | | | | | | | | | | | | |
| 3 | Quarterly Sales | | | | | | | | | | | |
| 4 | | | | | | | | | | | | |
| 5 | | Quarter 1 | Quarter 2 | Quarter 3 | Quarter 4 | | | | | | | |
| 6 | Camera | 47213 | 52669 | 50003 | 57221 | | | | | | | |
| 7 | Supplies | 22019 | 20761 | 23421 | 22049 | | | | | | | |
| 8 | Film | 1069 | 1264 | 1202 | 1250 | | | | | | | |
| 9 | Gadgets | 983 | 1066 | 1146 | 1068 | | | | | | | |
| 10 | | | | | | | | | | | | |
| 11 | | | | | | | | | | | | |
| 12 | | | | | | | | | | | | |
| 13 | | | | | | | | | | | | |

# Building
## and Editing Worksheets

### Objectives

- ▶ **Plan and design a worksheet**
- MOUS ▶ **Edit cell entries and work with ranges**
- MOUS ▶ **Enter formulas**
- MOUS ▶ **Introduce Excel functions**
- MOUS ▶ **Copy and move cell entries**
- MOUS ▶ **Understand relative and absolute cell references**
- MOUS ▶ **Copy formulas with relative cell references**
- MOUS ▶ **Copy formulas with absolute cell references**
- MOUS ▶ **Name and move a sheet**

Using your understanding of the basics of Excel, you can now plan and build your own worksheets. When you build a worksheet, you enter text, values, and formulas into worksheet cells. Once you create a worksheet, you can save it in a workbook file and then print it. ✐ Jim Fernandez has received a request from the Marketing department for a forecast of this summer's author events and an estimate of the average number of author appearances. Marketing hopes that the number of appearances will increase 20% over last year's figures. Jim needs to create a worksheet that summarizes appearances for last year and forecasts the summer appearances for this year.

# Planning and Designing a Worksheet

Before you start entering data into a worksheet, you need to know the purpose and approximate layout of the worksheet. You should also familiarize yourself with the mouse pointers you will encounter; refer to Table B-1. ◆━━ MediaLoft encourages authors to come to stores and sign their books. These author events are great for sales. Jim wants to forecast MediaLoft's 2001 summer author appearances. The goal, already identified by the Marketing department, is to increase the year 2000 signings by 20%. Using the planning guidelines below, work with Jim as he plans this worksheet.

**Details**

### In planning and designing a worksheet it is important to:

#### Determine the purpose of the worksheet and give it a meaningful title
Jim needs to forecast summer appearances for 2001. Jim titles the worksheet "Summer 2001 MediaLoft Author Events Forecast."

#### Determine your worksheet's desired results, or "output"
Jim needs to begin scheduling author events and will use these forecasts to determine staffing and budget needs if the number of author events increases by 20%. He also wants to calculate the average number of author events since the Marketing department uses this information for corporate promotions.

#### Collect all the information, or "input", that will produce the results you want
Jim gathers together the number of author events that occurred at four stores during the 2000 summer season, which runs from June through August.

#### Determine the calculations, or formulas, necessary to achieve the desired results
First, Jim needs to total the number of events at each of the selected stores during each month of the summer of 2000. Then he needs to add these totals together to determine the grand total of summer appearances. Because he needs to determine the goal for the 2001 season, the 2000 monthly totals and grand total are multiplied by 1.2 to calculate the projected 20% increase for the 2001 summer season. He'll use the Paste Function to select the Average function, which will determine the average number of appearances for the Marketing department.

#### Sketch on paper how you want the worksheet to look; identify where to place the labels and values
Jim decides to put store locations in rows and the months in columns. He enters the data in his sketch and indicates where the monthly totals and the grand total should go. Below the totals, he writes out the formula for determining a 20% increase in appearances for 2000. He also includes a label for the location of the average number of events calculations. Jim's sketch of his worksheet is shown in Figure B-1.

#### Create the worksheet
Jim enters the labels first to establish the structure of the worksheet. He then enters the values—the data about the events—into his worksheet. Finally, he enters the formulas necessary to calculate totals, averages, and forecasts. These values and formulas will be used to calculate the necessary output. The worksheet Jim creates is shown in Figure B-2.

## Summer 2001 MediaLoft Author Events Forecast

|  | June | July | August | Total | Average |
|---|---|---|---|---|---|
| Boston | 15 | 10 | 23 | | |
| New York | 14 | 10 | 12 | | |
| Seattle | 12 | 13 | 6 | | |
| San Diego | 10 | 24 | 15 | | |
| Total | June Total | July Total | August Total | Grand Total | |
| 20% rise | Total X 1.2 | | | | |

FIGURE B-2: Jim's forecasting worksheet

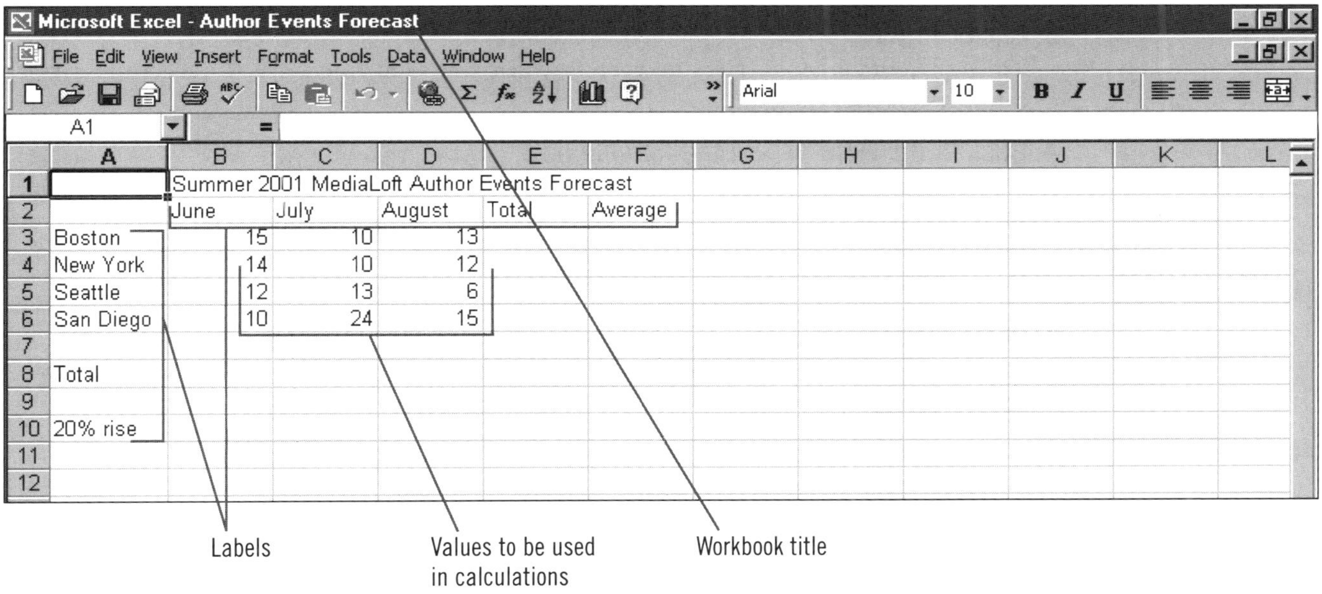

Labels

Values to be used in calculations

Workbook title

TABLE B-1: Commonly used pointers

| name | pointer | use to |
|---|---|---|
| **Normal** | ⊕ | Select a cell or range; indicates Ready mode |
| **Copy** | ⬚ | Create a duplicate of the selected cell(s) |
| **Fill handle** | ✛ | Create an alphanumeric series in a range |
| **I-beam** | I | Edit contents of formula bar |
| **Move** | ⬚ | Change the location of the selected cell(s) |

# Editing Cell Entries and Working with Ranges

You can change the contents of any cell at any time. To edit the contents of a cell, you first select the cell you want to edit. Then you have three options: you can click the formula bar, double-click the selected cell, or press [F2]. This puts Excel into Edit mode. To make sure you are in Edit mode, look at the **mode indicator** on the far left side of the status bar. ✎ After planning and creating his worksheet, Jim notices that he entered the wrong value for the August Seattle events, and that Houston should be entered instead of San Diego. He fixes the event figures, replaces the San Diego label, and corrects the value for July's Houston events.

**Steps 1 2 3 4**

1. Start Excel, click **Tools** on the menu bar, click **Customize**, click the **Options tab** in the Customize dialog box, click **Reset my usage data** to restore the default settings, click **Yes**, then click **Close**

2. Open the workbook **EX B-1** from your Project Disk, then save it as **Author Events Forecast**

3. Click cell **D5**
   This cell contains August Seattle events, which you want to change to reflect the correct numbers for the year 2000.

4. Click to **the right of 6** in the formula bar
   Excel goes into Edit mode, and the mode indicator on the status bar displays "Edit." A blinking vertical line called the **insertion point** appears in the formula bar, and if you move the mouse pointer to the formula bar, the pointer changes to $I$, which is used for editing. See Figure B-3.

5. Press **[Backspace]**, type **11**, then click the **Enter button** ☑ on the formula bar
   The value in cell D5 is changed or edited from 6 to 11. Additional modifications can also be made using the [F2] key.

6. Click cell **A6**, then press **[F2]**
   Excel is in Edit mode again, and the insertion point is in the cell.

**QuickTip**

The Redo command reverses the action of the Undo command. Click the Redo button ⤵ on the Standard toolbar if you change your mind after an undo.

7. Press **[Backspace]** nine times, type **Houston**, then press **[Enter]**
   The label changes to Houston. If you make a mistake, you can either click the Cancel button ✗ on the formula bar *before* accepting the cell entry, or click the Undo button ⤺ on the Standard toolbar if you notice the mistake *after* you have accepted the cell entry. The Undo button allows you to reverse up to 16 previous actions, one at a time.

8. Double-click cell **C6**
   Double-clicking a cell also puts Excel into Edit mode with the insertion point in the cell.

9. Press **[Delete]** twice, then type **14**
   The number of book signings for July in Houston has been corrected. See Figure B-4.

10. Click ☑ to confirm the entry, then click the **Save button** 🖫 on the Standard toolbar

**FIGURE B-3: Worksheet in Edit mode**

Your toolbars may not match the toolbars in the figures

Edit mode indicator — Insertion point in formula bar — Pointer used for editing

**FIGURE B-4: Edited worksheet**

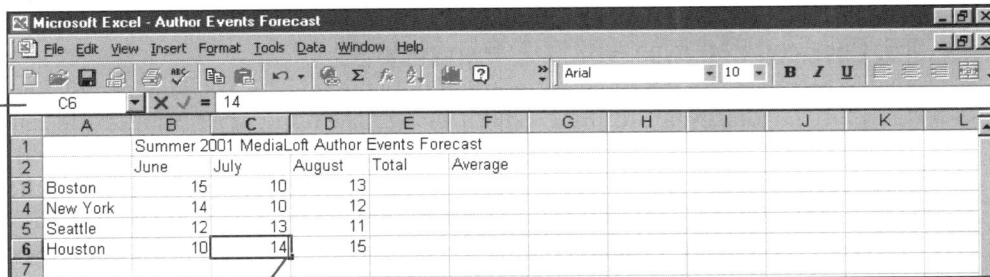

Name box

Insertion point in cell

## Using range names in a workbook

Any group of cells (two or more) is called a range. To select a range, click the first cell and drag to the last cell you want to include in the range. The range address is defined by noting the first and last cells in the range separated by a colon, for example A8:B16. Once you select a range, the easiest way to give it a name is by clicking the name box and typing in a name. Range names—meaningful English names— are usually easier to remember than cell addresses. You can use a range

name in a formula (for example, Income-Expenses) or to move around the workbook more quickly. Simply click the name box list arrow, then click the name of the range you want to go to. The cell pointer moves immediately to select that range. To clear the name from a range, click Insert on the menu bar, point to Name, then click Define. Select the range name you want to delete from the Define Name dialog box, click Delete, then click OK.

# Entering Formulas

You use **formulas** to perform numeric calculations such as adding, multiplying, and averaging. Formulas in an Excel worksheet usually start with the formula prefix—the equal sign (=) and contain cell addresses and range names. Arithmetic formulas use one or more **arithmetic operators** to perform calculations; see Table B-2. Using a cell address or range name in a formula is called **cell referencing**. If you change a value in a cell, any formula containing that cell reference will be automatically recalculated using the new value. In formulas using more than one arithmetic operator, Excel uses the order of precedence rules to determine which operation to perform first. ◢━━ Jim needs to total the values for the monthly author events for June, July, and August, and forecast what the 20% increase in appearances will be. He performs these calculations using formulas.

## Steps 1234

**1.** Click cell **B8**
This is the cell where you want to enter the calculation that totals the June events.

**2.** Type = (the equal sign)
Placing an equal sign at the beginning of an entry tells Excel that a formula is about to be entered, rather than a label or a value. "Enter" appears on the status bar. The total number of June events is equal to the sum of the values in cells B3, B4, B5, and B6.

### Trouble?

If the formula instead of the result appears in the cell after you click ☑, make sure you began the formula with = (the equal sign).

**3.** Type **b3+b4+b5+b6**, then click the **Enter button** ☑ on the formula bar
Notice that the result of 51 appears in cell B8, and the formula appears in the formula bar. Also, Excel is not case-sensitive: it doesn't matter if you type upper or lower-case characters when you enter cell addresses. See Figure B-5.

**4.** Click cell **C8**, type **=c3+c4+c5+c6**, press [Tab]; in cell **D8**, type **=d3+d4+d5+d6**, then press [**Enter**]
The total appearances for July, 47, and for August, 51, appear in cells C8 and D8 respectively.

**5.** Click cell **B10**, type **=B8*1.2**, then click ☑
To calculate the 20% increase, you multiply the total by 1.2. The formula in cell B10 multiplies the total events for June, cell B8, by 1.2. The result of 61.2 appears in cell B10 and is the projected value for an increase of 20% over the 51 June events. Now you need to calculate the 20% increase for July and August. You can use the **pointing method**, by which you specify cell references in a formula by selecting the desired cell with your mouse instead of typing its cell reference into the formula. Pointing is a preferred method because it eliminates typing errors.

### QuickTip

Press [Esc] to turn off a moving border.

**6.** Click cell **C10**, type **=**, then click cell **C8**
When you click cell C8, a moving border surrounds the cell. This **moving border**—as well as the mode indicator—indicates the cell that is copied in this operation. Moving borders can display around a single cell or a range of cells.

**7.** Type *1.2, then press [Tab]
The calculated value 56.4 appears in cell C10.

**8.** In cell **D10**, type **=**, click cell **D8**, type *1.2, then click ☑
Compare your results with Figure B-6.

**9.** Click the **Save button** 🖫 on the Standard toolbar

FIGURE B-5: Worksheet showing formula and result

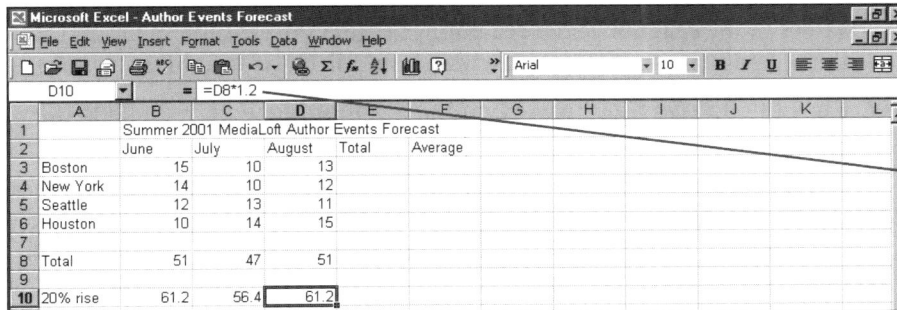

Formula in formula bar

Calculated result in cell

FIGURE B-6: Calculated results for 20% increase

Formula calculates 20% increase over value in cell D8 and displays result in cell D10

TABLE B-2: Excel arithmetic operators

| operator | purpose | example |
|---|---|---|
| + | Addition | =A5+A7 |
| – | Subtraction or negation | =A5-10 |
| * | Multiplication | =A5*A7 |
| / | Division | =A5/A7 |
| % | Percent | =35% |
| ^ (caret) | Exponent | =6^2 (same as 6*6) |

CLUES TO USE

## Order of precedence in Excel formulas

A formula can include several mathematical operations. When you work with formulas that have more than one operator, the order of precedence is very important. If a formula contains two or more operators, such as 4 + .55/4000 * 25, the computer performs the calculations in a particular sequence based on these rules: Operations inside parentheses are calculated before any other operations. Exponents are calculated next, then any multiplication and division—from left to right. Finally, addition and subtraction is calculated from left to right. In the example 4 + .55/4000 * 25, Excel performs the arithmetic operations by first dividing 4000 into .55, then multiplying the result by 25, then adding 4. You can change the order of calculations by using parentheses. For example, in the formula (4+.55)/4000 * 25, Excel would first add 4 and .55, then divide that amount by 4000, then finally multiply by 25.

**BUILDING AND EDITING WORKSHEETS** EXCEL B-7 ◄

# Introducing Excel Functions

Functions are predefined worksheet formulas that enable you to do complex calculations easily. Like formulas, functions always begin with the formula prefix = (the equal sign). You can enter functions manually, or you can use the Paste Function to select the function you need from a list. ➤ Jim uses the SUM function to calculate the grand totals in his worksheet and the AVERAGE function to calculate the average number of author events per store.

**Steps** 1 2 3 4

**1. Click cell E3**

This is the cell where you want to display the total of all author events in Boston for June, July, and August. You use **AutoSum** to create the totals. By default, AutoSum sets up the SUM function to add the values in the cells above the cell pointer. If there are one or fewer values in the cells above the cell pointer, AutoSum adds the values in the cells to the left of the cell pointer—in this case, the values in cells B3, C3, and D3.

**Trouble?**

If you don't see Σ on your toobar, click the More Buttons button » on the Standard toolbar.

**2. Click the AutoSum button** Σ **on the Standard toolbar, then click the Enter button** ✓ **on the formula bar**

The formula =SUM(B3:D3) appears in the formula bar. The result, 38, appears in cell E3. The information inside the parentheses is the **argument**, or the information to be used in calculating a result of the function. An argument can be a value, a range of cells, text, or another function.

**3. Click cell E4, click** Σ **, then click** ✓

The values for the Boston and New York events are now totaled.

**4. Click cell E5, then click** Σ

By default, AutoSum sets up a function to add the two values in the cells above the active cell, as you can see by the formula in the formula bar. You can override the current selection by manually selecting the correct range for this argument.

**5. Click cell B5, drag to cell D5 to select the range B5:D5, then click** ✓

As you drag, the argument in the SUM function changes to reflect the selected range, and a ScreenTip appears telling you the size of the range by row and column.

**6. Click cell E6, type =SUM(** , point to cell **B6**, drag to cell **D6**, press **[Enter]**, click cell **E8**, type **=SUM(** , point to cell **B8**, drag to cell **D8**, press **[Enter]**, click cell **E10**, type **=SUM(** , point to cell **B10**, drag to cell **D10**, then click ✓ to confirm the entry

See Figure B-7 to verify your results. Now the Paste Function can be used to select the function needed to calculate the average number of author events.

**Trouble?**

If the Office Assistant opens, click No, don't provide help now.

**7. Click cell F3, then click the Paste Function button** *fx* **on the Standard toolbar**

The Paste Function dialog box opens. See Table B-3 for frequently used functions. The function needed to calculate averages—named AVERAGE—is included in the Most Recently Used function category.

**QuickTip**

Modify a function's range by clicking the Collapse dialog box button, defining the range with your mouse, then clicking the Expand dialog box button to return to the Paste Function window.

**8. Click AVERAGE in the Function name list box, click OK, the AVERAGE dialog box opens; type B3:D3 in the Number 1 text box, as shown in Figure B-8, then click OK**

**9. Click cell F4, click** *fx*, verify that **AVERAGE** is selected, click **OK**, type **B4:D4**, click **OK**, click cell **F5**, click *fx*, click **AVERAGE**, click **OK**, type **B5:D5**, click **OK**, click cell **F6**, click *fx*, click **AVERAGE**, click **OK**, type **B6:D6**, then click **OK**

The result in Boston (cell F3) is 12.6667; the result in New York (cell F4) is 12; the result in Seattle (cell F5) is 12; and the result in Houston (cell F6) is 13, giving you the averages for all four stores.

FIGURE B-7: Worksheet with SUM functions entered

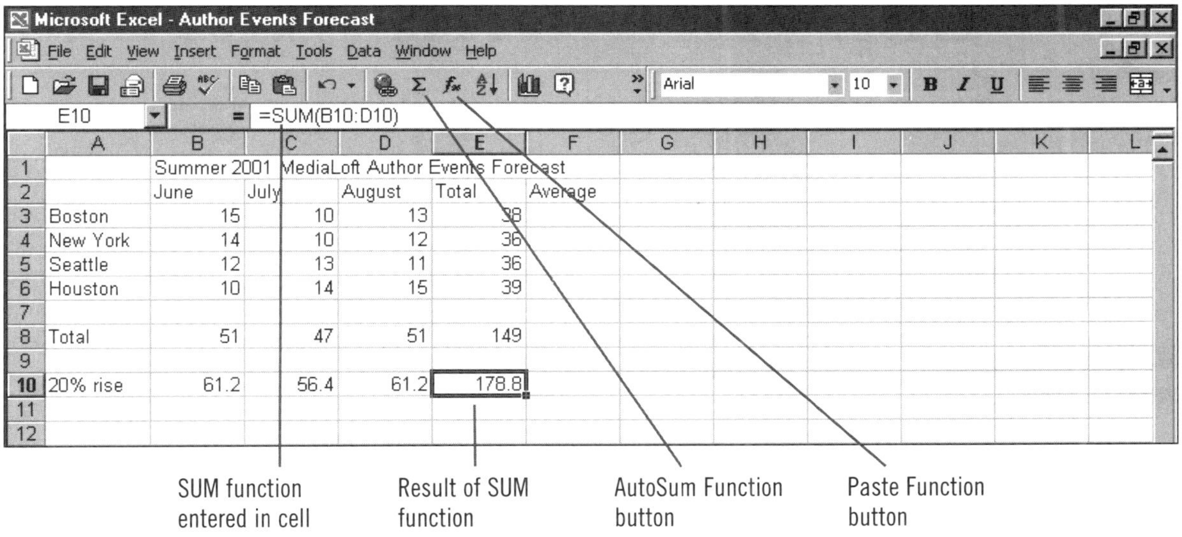

| | A | B | C | D | E | F | G | H | I | J | K | L |
|---|---|---|---|---|---|---|---|---|---|---|---|---|
| | E10 | | = | =SUM(B10:D10) | | | | | | | | |
| 1 | | Summer 2001 | MediaLoft Author Events Forecast | | | | | | | | | |
| 2 | | June | July | | August | Total | Average | | | | | |
| 3 | Boston | 15 | 10 | 13 | 38 | | | | | | | |
| 4 | New York | 14 | 10 | 12 | 36 | | | | | | | |
| 5 | Seattle | 12 | 13 | 11 | 36 | | | | | | | |
| 6 | Houston | 10 | 14 | 15 | 39 | | | | | | | |
| 7 | | | | | | | | | | | | |
| 8 | Total | 51 | 47 | 51 | 149 | | | | | | | |
| 9 | | | | | | | | | | | | |
| 10 | 20% rise | 61.2 | 56.4 | 61.2 | 178.8 | | | | | | | |
| 11 | | | | | | | | | | | | |
| 12 | | | | | | | | | | | | |

SUM function entered in cell

Result of SUM function

AutoSum Function button

Paste Function button

FIGURE B-8: Using the Paste Function to create a formula

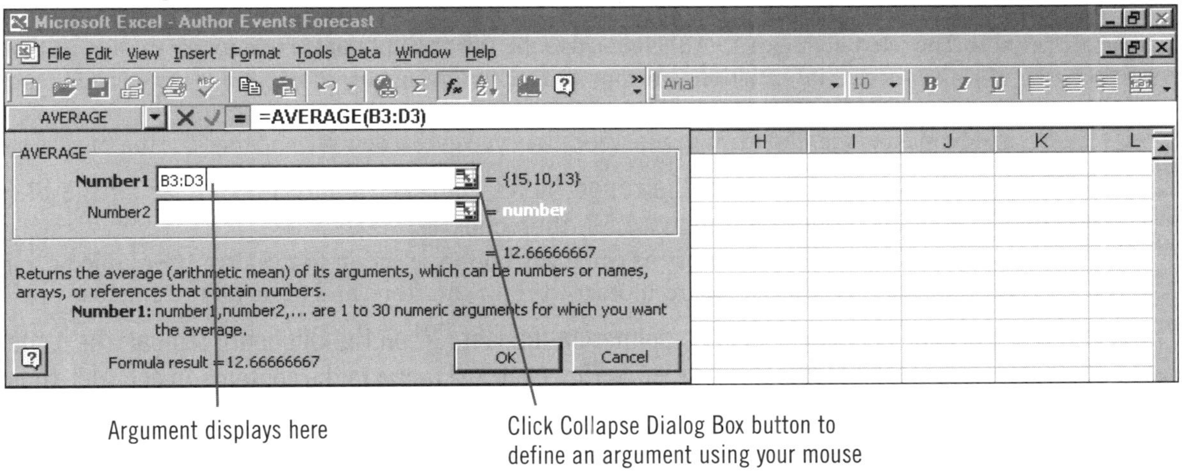

AVERAGE | = =AVERAGE(B3:D3)

AVERAGE
Number1  B3:D3  = {15,10,13}
Number2  = number

= 12.66666667
Returns the average (arithmetic mean) of its arguments, which can be numbers or names, arrays, or references that contain numbers.

Number1: number1,number2,... are 1 to 30 numeric arguments for which you want the average.

Formula result =12.66666667        OK        Cancel

Argument displays here

Click Collapse Dialog Box button to define an argument using your mouse

TABLE B-3: Frequently used functions

| function | description |
|---|---|
| SUM(*argument*) | Calculates the sum of the arguments |
| AVERAGE(*argument*) | Calculates the average of the arguments |
| MAX(*argument*) | Displays the largest value among the arguments |
| MIN(*argument*) | Displays the smallest value among the arguments |
| COUNT(*argument*) | Calculates the number of values in the arguments |

CLUES TO USE

## Using the MIN and MAX functions

Other commonly used functions include MIN and MAX. You use the MIN function to calculate the minimum or smallest value in a selected range; the MAX function calculates the maximum or largest value in a selected range. The MAX function is included in the Most Frequently Used function category in the Paste Function dialog box, while the MIN function can be found in the Statistical category. Like AVERAGE, MIN and MAX are preceded by an equal sign and the argument includes a range.

# Copying and Moving Cell Entries

Using the Cut, Copy, and Paste buttons or the Excel drag-and-drop feature, you can copy or move information from one cell or range in your worksheet to another. You can also cut, copy, and paste data from one worksheet to another to make corrections, and add information using the Office Clipboard, which can store up to 12 items. ◀━━━ Jim needs to include the 2001 forecast for spring and fall author events in his Author Events Forecast workbook. He's already entered the spring report in Sheet2 and will finish entering the labels and data for the fall report. Jim copies information from the spring report to the fall report.

**Steps 1 2 3 4**

1. **Click Sheet 2 of the Author Events Forecast workbook**
   To work more efficiently, existing labels can be copied from one range to another and from one sheet to another. You see that the store names have to be corrected in cells A6:A7.

2. **Click Sheet 1, select the range A5:A6, then click the Copy button [📋] on the Standard toolbar**
   The selected range (A5:A6) is copied to the **Office Clipboard**, a temporary storage file that holds the selected information you copy or cut. A moving border surrounds the selected range until you press [Esc] or copy additional information to the Clipboard. To copy the most recent item copied to the Clipboard to a new location, you click a new cell and then use the Paste command.

3. **Click Sheet 2, select the range A6:A7, click the Paste button [📋] on the Standard toolbar, select the range A4:A9, then click [📋]**
   The Clipboard toolbar opens when you copy a selection to the already occupied Clipboard. You can use the Clipboard toolbar to copy, cut, store, and paste up to 12 items.

4. **Click cell A13, place the pointer on the last [📋] on the Clipboard toolbar, the contents of range A4:A9 display in a ScreenTip, click [📋] to paste the contents in cell A13, then close the Clipboard toolbar**
   The item is copied into the range A13:A18. When pasting an item from the Clipboard into the worksheet, you only need to specify the top left cell of the range where you want the selection to go. The moving border remains active. Now you can use the drag-and-drop technique to copy the Total label, which does not copy the contents to the Clipboard.

5. **Click cell E3, position the pointer on any edge of the cell until the pointer changes to [⬚], then press and hold down [Ctrl]**
   The pointer changes to the copy pointer [⬚]. When you copy cells, the original data remains in the original cell. When you move cells, the original data does *not* remain in the original cell.

6. **While still pressing [Ctrl], press and hold the left mouse button, drag the cell contents to cell E12, release the mouse button, then release [Ctrl]**
   As you drag, an outline of the cell moves with the pointer, as shown in Figure B-9, and a ScreenTip appears tracking the current position of the item as you move it. When you release the mouse button, the Total label appears in cell E12. You now decide to move the worksheet title over to the left. To use drag and drop to move data to a new cell, do not press [Ctrl].

7. **Click cell C1, position the pointer on the edge of the cell until it changes to [⬚], then drag the cell contents to A1**
   Once the labels are copied, you can easily enter the fall events data into the range B13:D16.

8. **Using the information shown in Figure B-10, enter the author events data for the fall into the range B13:D16**
   Compare your worksheet to Figure B-10.

FIGURE B-9: **Using drag and drop to copy information**

Copy button

Paste button

More Buttons button

Copied cell

Outline of copied cell

Drag-and-drop pointer with ScreenTip

FIGURE B-10: **Worksheet with Fall author event data entered**

| | Fall | September | October | November | Total |
|---|---|---|---|---|---|
| 11 | | | | | |
| 12 | Fall | September | October | November | Total |
| 13 | Boston | 16 | 10 | 13 | |
| 14 | New York | 12 | 15 | 16 | |
| 15 | Seattle | 17 | 10 | 18 | |
| 16 | Houston | 14 | 11 | 12 | |
| 17 | | | | | |
| 18 | Total | | | | |

Sum of selected range displays in status bar

### Using the Office Clipboard

The Office Clipboard lets you copy and paste multiple items such as text, images, tables, or Excel ranges within or between the Microsoft Office applications. The Office Clipboard can hold up to 12 items copied or cut from any Office program. The Clipboard toolbar, shown in Figure B-11, displays the items stored on the Office Clipboard. You choose whether to delete the first item from the Clipboard when you copy the thirteenth item. The collected items remain in the Office Clipboard and are available to you until you close all open Office applications.

FIGURE B-11: **The Office Clipboard**

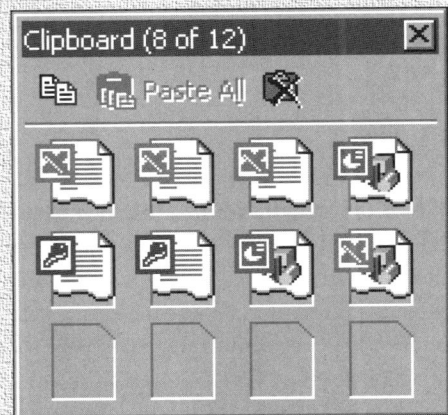

Clipboard (8 of 12)

Paste All

# Understanding Relative and Absolute Cell References

Like a label or value, an existing formula can be copied to a new location. This enables you to work efficiently by copying a working formula to multiple locations. When copied, a cell reference within a formula is automatically copied *relative* to its new location. This is called a **relative reference**. You can, however, choose to copy a cell reference with an absolute reference or a mixed reference. An **absolute reference** always cites a specific cell when the formula is copied. Jim often copies existing worksheet formulas and makes use of many types of cell references.

### Use relative references when cell relationships remain unchanged

When Excel copies a formula, all the cell references change to reflect the new location automatically. Each copied formula is identical to the original, except that the column or row is adjusted for its new location. The outlined cells in Figure B-12 contain formulas that contain relative references. For example, the formula in cell E5 is =SUM(B5:D5). When copied to cell E6, the resulting formula is =SUM(B6:D6). The original formula was copied from row 5 to row 6 within the same column, so the cell referenced in the copied formula increased by one row.

### Use an absolute cell reference when one relationship changes

In most cases, you will use relative cell references—the default. Sometimes, however, this is not what is needed. In some cases, you'll want to reference a specific cell, even when copying a formula. You create absolute references by placing a $ (dollar sign) before both the column letter and row number for a cell's address using the [F4] function key (on the keyboard). Figure B-13 displays the formulas used in Figure B-11. Notice that each formula in range B15:D18 contains both a relative and absolute reference. By using an absolute reference when referring to cell $B$12 in a formula, Excel keeps that cell reference (representing the potential increase) constant when copying that formula.

### Using a mixed reference

When copying formulas, the alternative to changing a cell reference relative to its new location and referring to a specific cell location as an absolute reference, is a mixed reference. A mixed reference contains both a relative and absolute reference. When copied, the mixed reference C$14 changes the column relative to its new location but prevents the row from changing.

In the mixed reference $C14, the column would not change but the row would be updated relative to its location. Like the absolute reference, a mixed reference can be created using the [F4] function key. With each press of the [F4] key, you cycle through all the possible combinations of relative, absolute, and mixed references ($C$14, C$14, $C14, C14).

FIGURE B-12: Location of relative references

Cells containing
relative references

FIGURE B-13: Absolute and relative reference formulas

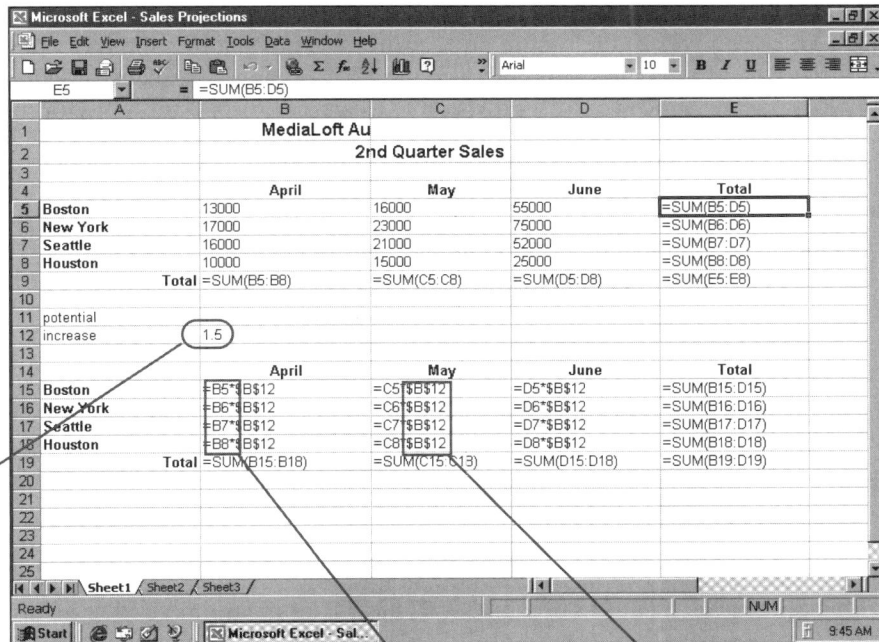

Cell referenced in
absolute formulas

Relative references

Absolute references

Excel 2000

# Copying Formulas with Relative Cell References

Copying and moving formulas allows you to reuse formulas you've already created. Copying formulas, rather than retyping them, is faster and helps to prevent typing errors. ✎ Jim wants to copy the formulas that total the appearances by region and by month from the spring to the fall. He can use Copy and Paste commands and the Fill Right method to copy this information.

**Steps** 1 2 3 4

1. Click cell **E4**, then click the **Copy button** 📋 on the Standard toolbar
   The formula for calculating the total number of spring Boston author events is copied to the Clipboard. Notice that the formula =SUM(B4:D4) displays in the formula bar.

2. Click cell **E13**, then click the **Paste button** 📋 on the Standard toolbar
   The formula from cell E4 is copied into cell E13, where the new result of 39 appears. Notice in the formula bar that the cell references have changed, so that the range B13:D13 appears in the formula. This formula contains **relative cell references** which tell Excel to copy the formula to a new cell, but to substitute new cell references so that the relationship of the cells to the formula in its new location remains unchanged. In this case, Excel adjusted the formula so cells D13, C13, and B13—the three cell references immediately to the left of E13— replaced cells D4, C4, and B4, the three cell references to the left of E4.
   Notice that the bottom right corner of the active cell contains a small square, called the **fill handle.** You can use the fill handle to copy labels, formulas, and values. You use the fill handle to copy the formula in cell E13 to cells E14, E15, and E16.

3. Position the pointer over the **fill handle** until it changes to **+** , press the **left mouse button**, then drag the fill handle to select the range **E13:E16**
   See Figure B-14.

4. Release the mouse button
   Once you release the mouse button, the fill handle copies the formula from the active cell (E13) and pastes it into each cell of the selected range. Again, because the formula uses relative cell references, cells E14 through E16 correctly display the totals for the fall author events.

5. Click cell **B9**, click **Edit** on the menu bar, then click **Copy**

6. Click cell **B18**, click **Edit** on the menu bar, then click **Paste**
   See Figure B-15. The formula for calculating the September events appears in the formula bar. You can use the Fill Right command to copy the formula from cell B18 to cells C18, D18, and E18.

7. Select the range **B18:E18**

8. Click **Edit** on the menu bar, point to **Fill**, then click **Right**
   The rest of the totals are filled in correctly. Compare your worksheet to Figure B-16.

9. Click the **Save button** 💾 on the Standard toolbar

**CLUES TO USE**

### Filling cells with sequential text or values

Often, we fill cells with sequential text: months of the year, days of the week, years, and text plus a number (Quarter 1, Quarter 2, . . . ). You can easily fill cells using sequences by dragging the fill handle. As you drag the fill handle, Excel automatically extends the existing sequence. (The contents of the last filled cell appears in the name box.) Use the Fill Series command on the Edit menu to examine all of the available fill series options.

FIGURE B-14: Selected range using the fill handle

Formula in cell E13 will be copied to E14:E16

Fill handle

Mouse pointer

FIGURE B-15: Worksheet with copied formula

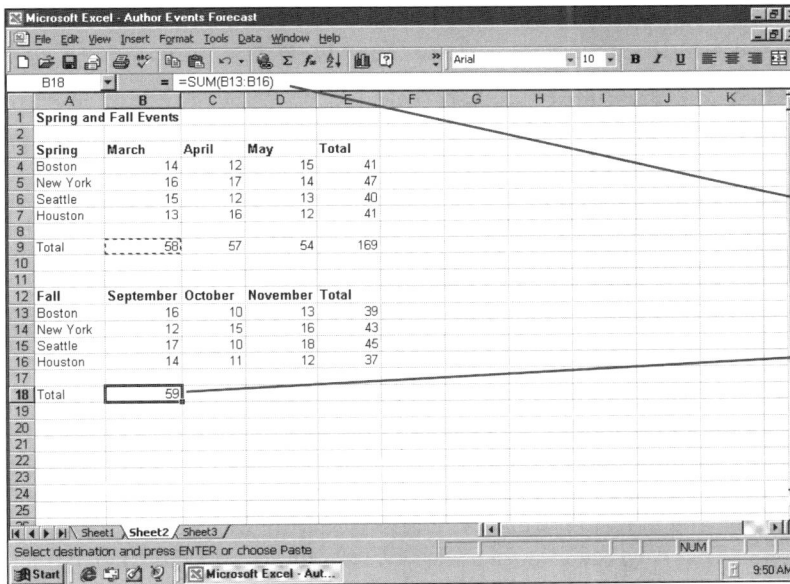

Copied formula cell references

Copied formula result

FIGURE B-16: Completed worksheet with all formulas copied

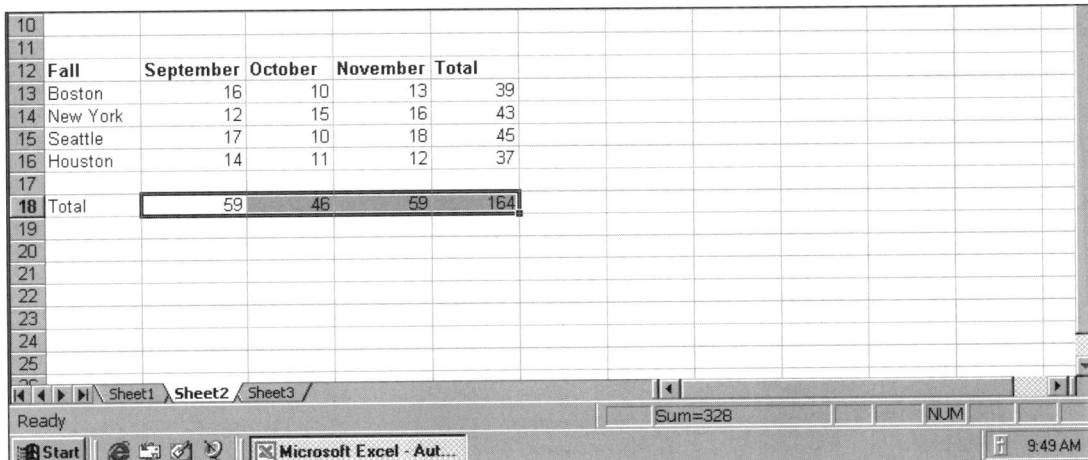

# Copying Formulas with Absolute Cell References

When copying formulas, you might want a cell reference to always refer to a particular cell address. In such an instance, you would use an **absolute cell reference**. An absolute cell reference always refers to a specific cell address when the formula is copied. You identify an absolute reference by placing a dollar sign ($) before the row letter and column number of the address (for example $A$1). The staff in the Marketing department hopes the number of author events will increase by 20% over last year's figures. Jim decides to add a column that calculates a possible increase in the number of spring events in 2001. He wants to do a what-if analysis and recalculate the spreadsheet several times, changing the percentage that the number of appearances might increase each time.

**Steps 123 4**

1. Click cell **G1**, type **Change**, then press [→]
   You can store the increase factor that will be used in the what-if analysis in cell H1.

2. Type **1.1**, then press **[Enter]**
   The value in cell H1 represents a 10% increase in author events.

3. Click cell **G3**, type **What if?**, then press **[Enter]**
   Now you create a formula that references a specific address: cell H1.

4. In cell **G4**, type **=E4*H1**, then click the **Enter button** ☑ on the formula bar
   The result of 45.1 appears in cell G4. This value represents the total spring events for Boston if there is a 10% increase. To determine the value for the remaining stores, you copy the formula in cell G4 to the range G5:G7.

**QuickTip**

Before you copy or move a formula, check to see if you need to use an absolute cell reference.

5. Drag the fill handle to select the range **G4:G7**
   The resulting values in the range G5:G7 are all zeros. When you copy the formula it adjusts so the formula in cell G5 is =E5*H2. Since there is no value in cell H2, the result is 0, an error. You need to use an absolute reference in the formula to keep the formula from adjusting. That way, cell H1 will always be referenced. You can change the relative cell reference to an absolute cell reference using [F4].

6. Click cell **G4**, press **[F2]** to change to Edit mode, then press **[F4]**
   When you press [F2], the **range finder** outlines the equation's arguments in blue and green. When you press [F4], dollar signs appear, changing the H1 cell reference to an absolute reference. See Figure B-17.

7. Click the **Enter button** ☑ on the formula bar
   The formula correctly contains an absolute cell reference and the value remains unchanged at 45.1. The fill handle can be used to copy the corrected formula in cell G4 to G5:G7.

8. Drag the fill handle to select the range **G4:G7**
   The correct values for a 10% increase display in cells G4:G7. You complete the what-if analysis by changing the value in cell H1 from 1.1 to 1.25 to indicate a 25% increase in events.

9. Click cell **H1**, type **1.25**, then click ☑
   The values in the range G4:G7 change to reflect the 25% increase. Compare your worksheet to Figure B-18. Since events only occur in whole numbers, the numbers' appearance can be changed later.

FIGURE B-17: Absolute cell reference in cell G4

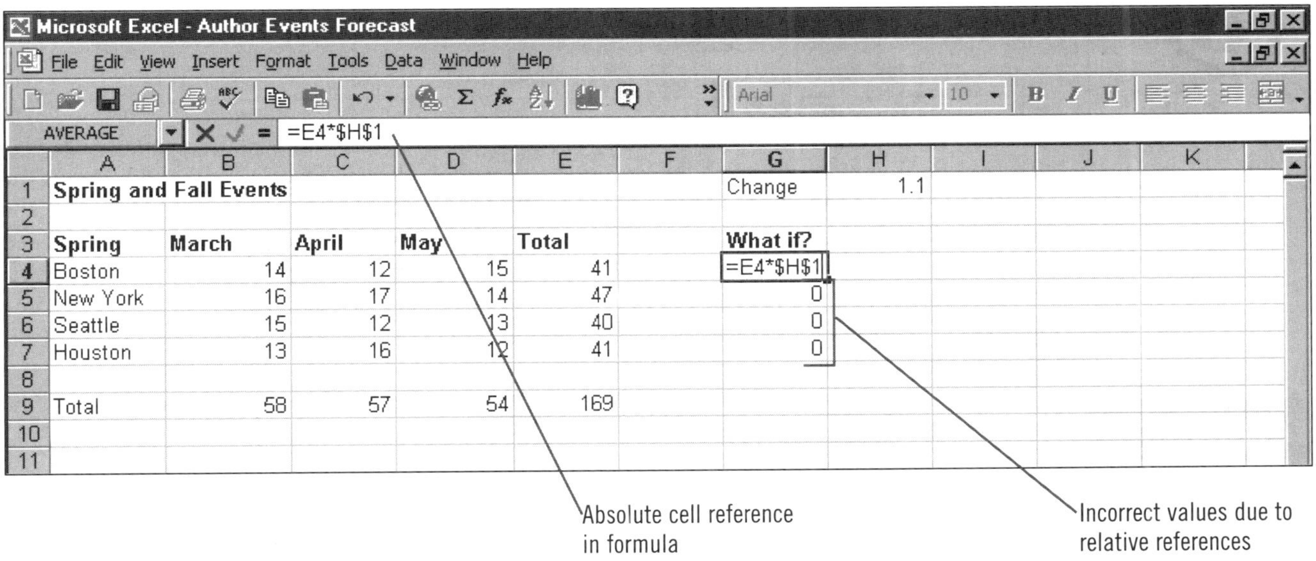

Absolute cell reference
in formula

Incorrect values due to
relative references

FIGURE B-18: Worksheet with what-if value

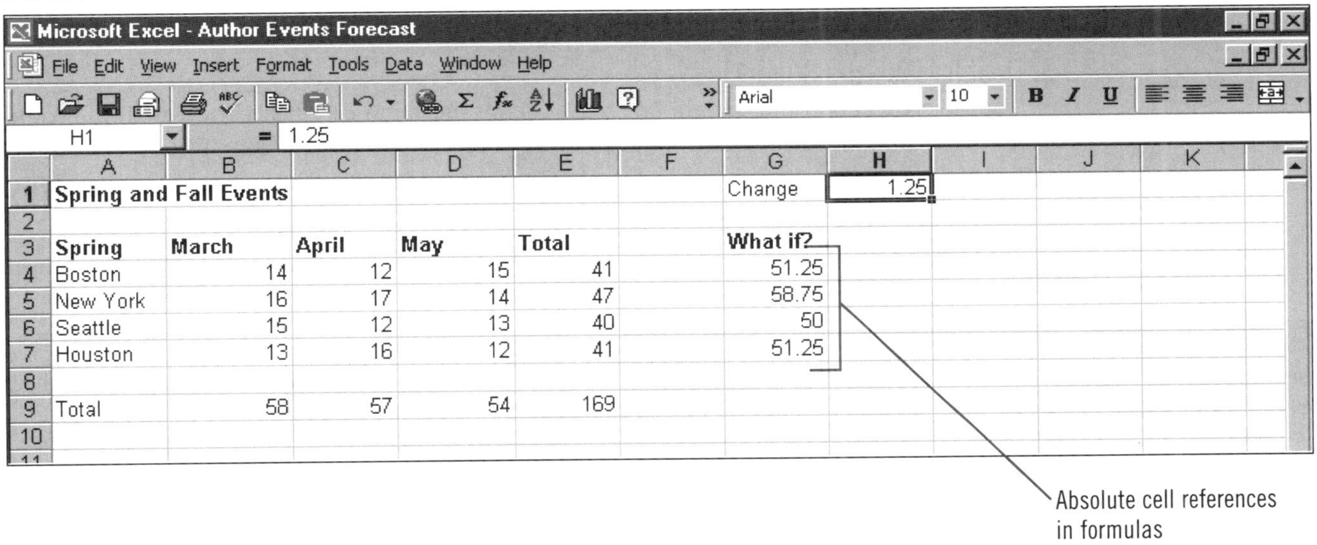

Absolute cell references
in formulas

**CLUES TO USE**

## Copying and moving using named ranges

You can give a range of cells an easy-to-remember meaningful name, such as "2001 Sales." If you move the named range, its name moves with it. Like any range, a named range can be referenced absolutely in a formula by using the $ symbol. To copy or move a named range, you can "go to" it quickly by clicking the name box list arrow and selecting its name.

# Naming and Moving a Sheet

Each workbook initially contains three worksheets named Sheet1, Sheet2, and Sheet3. When the workbook is opened, the first worksheet is the active sheet. To move from sheet to sheet, click the desired sheet tab located at the bottom of the worksheet window. Sheet tab scrolling buttons, located to the left of the sheet tabs, allow rapid movement among the sheets. To make it easier to identify the sheets in a workbook, you can rename each sheet and then organize them in a logical way. The name appears on the sheet tab. For instance, sheets within a single workbook could be named for individual salespeople to better track performance goals, and the sheets can be moved so they appear in alphabetical order. ◆ Jim wants to be able to easily identify the actual author events and the forecast sheets. He decides to name two sheets in his workbook, then changes their order.

## Steps 1 2 3 4

**1. Click the Sheet1 tab**

Sheet1 becomes active; this is the worksheet that contains the summer information you compiled for the Marketing department. Its tab moves to the front, and the tab for Sheet2 moves to the background.

**2. Click the Sheet2 tab**

Sheet2, containing the spring and fall data, becomes active. Once you have confirmed which sheet is which, you can rename Sheet1 so it has a name that you can easily remember.

**3. Double-click the Sheet1 tab**

The Sheet1 text becomes selected with the default sheet name ("Sheet1") selected. You could also click Format in the menu bar, point to Sheet, then click Rename to select the sheet name.

**4. Type Summer, then press [Enter]**

See Figure B-19. The new name automatically replaces the default name in the tab. Worksheet names can have up to 31 characters, including spaces and punctuation.

**5. Double-click the Sheet2 tab, then rename this sheet Spring-Fall**

Jim decides to rearrange the order of the sheets, so that Summer comes after Spring-Fall.

**6. Click the Summer sheet tab, then drag it to the right of the Spring-Fall sheet tab**

As you drag, the pointer changes to ⬚, the sheet relocation pointer. See Figure B-20. The first sheet in the workbook is now the Spring-Fall sheet. When there are multiple sheets in a workbook, the navigation buttons can be used to scroll through the sheet tabs. Click the leftmost navigation button to display the first sheet tab; click the rightmost navigation button to display the last sheet tab. The left and right buttons move one sheet in their respective directions.

**7. Type your name in cell A12, click File on the menu bar, click Print, click the Entire workbook option button, then click the Preview button**

The Preview screen opens. Each worksheet is displayed on a separate page. You can preview the workbook sheets by clicking the Next and Previous buttons.

**8. Click the Print button on the Preview toolbar**

**9. Save and close the workbook, then exit Excel**

### QuickTip

To delete a worksheet, select the worksheet you want to delete, click Edit on the menu bar, then click Delete sheet. To insert a worksheet, click Insert on the menu bar, then click Worksheet.

FIGURE B-19: Renamed sheet in workbook

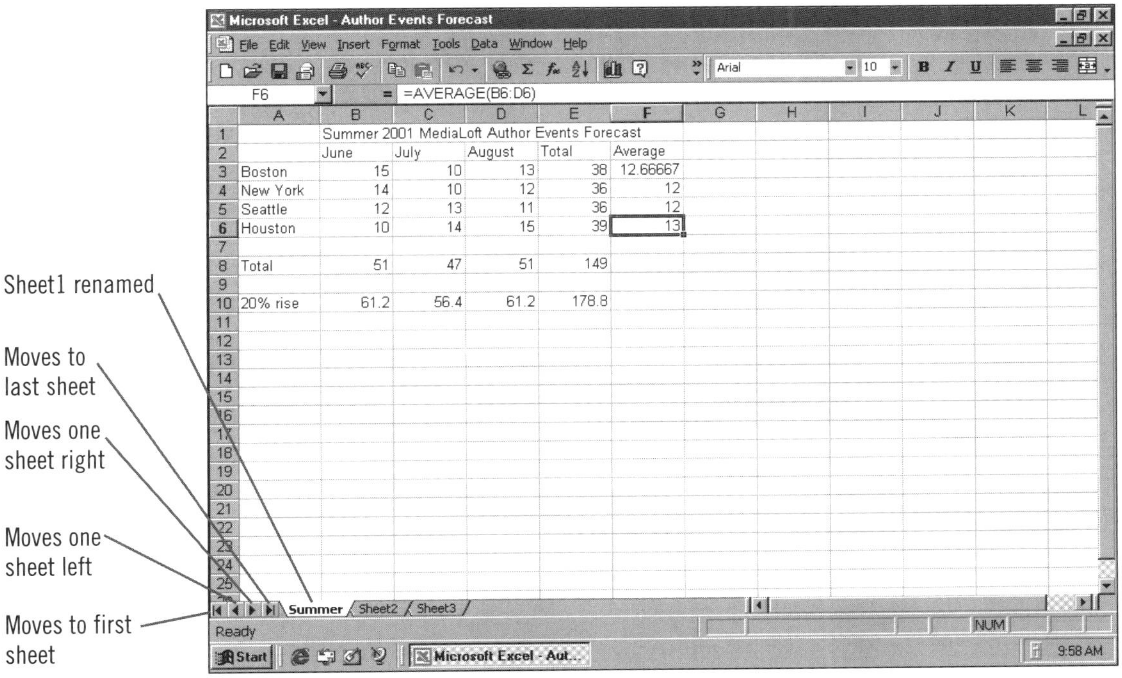

Sheet1 renamed

Moves to last sheet

Moves one sheet right

Moves one sheet left

Moves to first sheet

FIGURE B-20: Moving Summer after Spring-Fall sheet

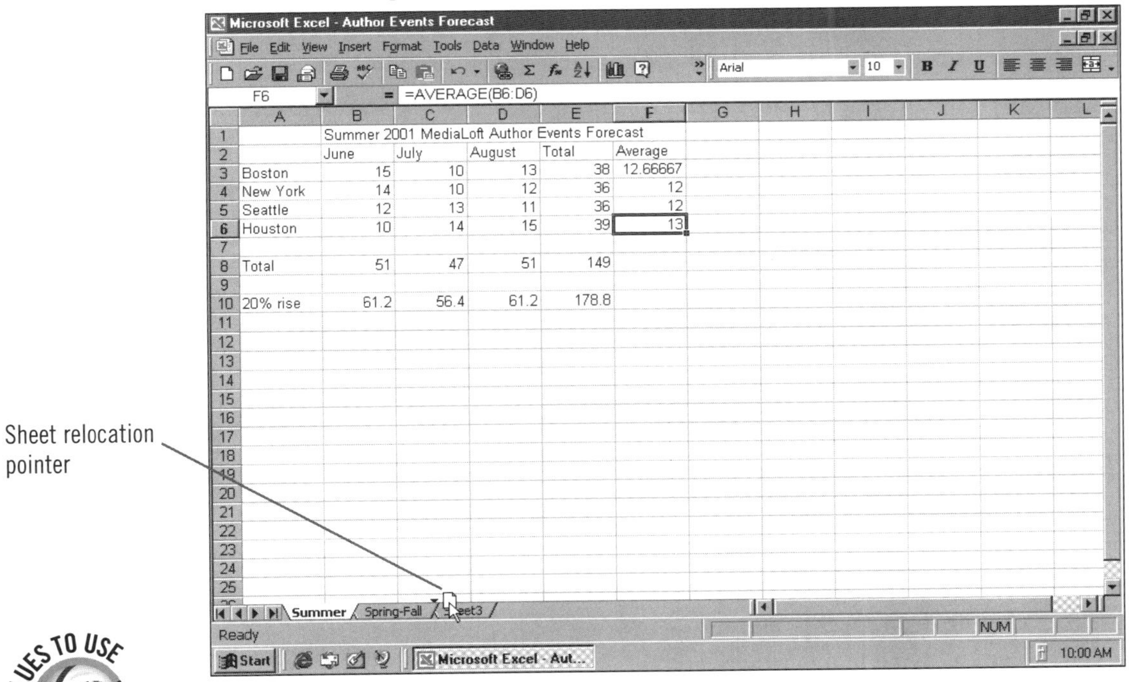

Sheet relocation pointer

## CLUES TO USE

### Moving and copying worksheets

There are times when you may want to move or copy sheets. To move sheets within the current workbook, drag the selected sheet tab along the row of sheet tabs to the new location. To copy, simply press CTRL as you drag the sheet tab and release the mouse button before you release CTRL. Although you have to be careful and carefully check the calculations when doing so, moving and copying worksheets to new workbooks is a relatively simple operation. You must have the workbook that you are copying to, as well as the workbook that you are copying from, open. Select the sheet to copy or move, click File on the menu bar, click Edit, then click Move or Copy sheet. Complete the information in the Move or Copy dialog box. Be sure to click the Create a Copy check box if you are copying rather than moving the worksheet.

# Practice

## ► Concepts Review

Label each element of the Excel worksheet window shown in Figure B-20.

FIGURE B-21

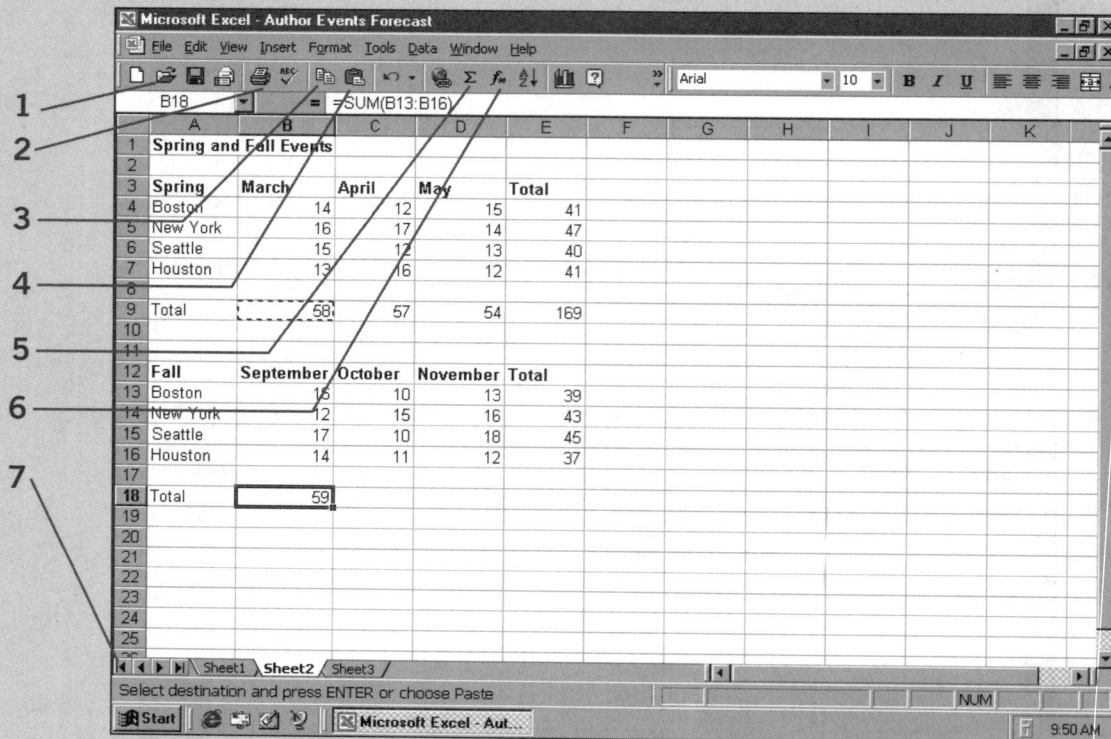

Match the term or button with the statement that describes it.

8. Range
9. Function
10. 🗒
11. 📄
12. Formula

a. A predefined formula that provides a shortcut for commonly used calculations
b. A cell entry that performs a calculation in an Excel worksheet
c. A specified group of cells, which can include the entire worksheet
d. Used to copy cells
e. Used to paste cells

Select the best answer from the list of choices.

13. What type of cell reference changes when it is copied?
   a. Absolute
   b. Circular
   c. Looping
   d. Relative

14. What character is used to make a reference absolute?
   a. &
   b. ^
   c. $
   d. @

**15. Which button is used to enter data in a cell?**

a. [↶]   c. [⧉]

b. [✕]   d. [✓]

## ▶ Skills Review

**1. Edit cell entries and work with ranges.**
  **a.** Start Excel, open the workbook EX B-2 from your Project Disk and save it as "Office Furnishings."
  **b.** Change the quantity of Tables to 25.
  **c.** Change the price of each of the Desks to 250.
  **d.** Change the quantity of Easels to 17.
  **e.** Name the range B2:B5 "Quantity" and name the range C2:C5 "Price."
  **f.** Type your name in cell A20, then save and preview the worksheet.

**2. Enter formulas.**
  **a.** Click cell B6, then enter the formula B2+B3+B4+B5.
  **b.** Save your work, then preview the data in the Office Furnishings worksheet.

**3. Introduce Excel functions.**
  **a.** Type the label "Min Price" in cell A8.
  **b.** Click cell C8; enter the function MIN(C2:C5).
  **c.** Type the label "Max Price" in cell A9.
  **d.** Create a formula in cell C9 that determines the maximum price.
  **e.** Save your work, then preview the data.

**4. Copy and move cell entries.**
  **a.** Select the range A1:C6, then copy the range to cell A12.
  **b.** Use drag and drop to copy the range D1:E1 to cell D12.
  **c.** Save your work, then preview the worksheet.

**5. Copy formulas with relative cell references.**
  **a.** Click cell D2, then create a formula that multiplies B2 and C2.
  **b.** Copy the formula in D2 into cells D3:D5.
  **c.** Copy the formula in D2 into cells D13:D16.
  **d.** Save and preview the worksheet.

**6. Copy formulas with absolute cell references.**
  **a.** Click cell G2 and type the value 1.375.
  **b.** Click cell E2, then create a formula containing an absolute reference that multiplies D2 and G2.
  **c.** Use the Office Clipboard to copy the formula in E2 into cells E3:E5.
  **d.** Use the Office Clipboard to copy the formula in E2 into cells E13:E16.
  **e.** Change the amount in cell G2 to 2.873.
  **f.** Save the worksheet.

**7. Name and move a sheet.**
  **a.** Name the Sheet1 tab "Furniture."
  **b.** Move the Furniture sheet so it comes after Sheet3.
  **c.** Name the Sheet2 tab "Supplies."
  **d.** Move the Supplies sheet after the Furniture sheet.
  **e.** Save, preview, print and close the workbook, then exit Excel.

# ▶ Independent Challenges

**1.** You are the box-office manager for Brazil Nuts, a popular jazz band. Your responsibilities include tracking seasonal ticket sales for the band's concerts and anticipating ticket sales for the next season. Brazil Nuts sells four types of tickets: reserved seating, general admission, senior citizen tickets, and student tickets.

The 2000–2001 season includes five scheduled concerts: Spring Hop, Summer Blast, Fall Leaves, Winter Snuggle, and Early Thaw. You will plan and build a worksheet that tracks the sales of each of the four ticket types for all five concerts.

To complete this independent challenge:

a. Think about the results you want to see, the information you need to build into these worksheets, and what types of calculations must be performed.

b. Sketch sample worksheets on a piece of paper to indicate how the information should be laid out. What information should go in the columns? In the rows?

c. Start Excel, open a new workbook and save it as "Brazil Nuts" on your Project Disk.

d. Plan and build a worksheet that tracks the sales of each of the four ticket types for all five concerts. Build the worksheets by entering a title, row labels, column headings, and formulas.

e. Enter your own sales data, but assume the following: the Brazil Nuts sold 1000 tickets during the season; reserved seating was the most popular ticket type for all of the shows except for Winter Snuggle; no concert sold more than 20 student tickets.

f. Calculate the total ticket sales for each concert, the total sales for each of the four ticket types, and the total sales for all tickets. Name the worksheet "Sales Data."

g. Copy the Sales Data worksheet and name the copied worksheet "5% Increase." Modify this worksheet in the workbook so that it reflects a 5% increase in sales of all ticket types.

h. Use named ranges to make the worksheet easier to use. (*Hint*: If your columns are too narrow, position the cell pointer in the column you want to widen. To widen the column, click Format on the menu bar, click Column, click Width, choose a new column width, and then click OK.)

i. Type your name in a worksheet cell.

j. Save your work, preview and print the worksheets, then close the workbook and exit Excel.

**2.** You have been promoted to computer lab manager at Learn-It-All, a local computer training center. It is your responsibility to make sure there are enough computers for students during scheduled classes. Currently, you have five classrooms: four with IBM PCs and one with Macintoshes. Classes are scheduled Monday, Wednesday, and Friday in two-hour increments from 9 a.m. to 5 p.m. (the lab closes at 7 p.m.), and each room can currently accommodate 35 computers.

You plan and build a worksheet that tracks the number of students who can currently use available computers per two-hour class. You create your enrollment data, but assume that current enrollment averages at 80% of each room's daily capacity. Using an additional worksheet, you show the impact of an enrollment increase of 20%.

To complete this independent challenge:

a. Think about how to construct these worksheets to create the desired output.

b. Sketch sample paper worksheets to indicate how the information should be laid out.

c. Start Excel, open a new workbook and save it as "Learn-it-All" on your Project Disk.

d. Build the worksheets by entering a title, row labels, column headings, and formulas. Use named ranges to make the worksheets easier to use, and rename the sheets to identify their contents easily.

e. Use separate sheets for actual enrollment and projected changes.

f. Name each sheet so you know what's on it.

g. Type your name in a worksheet cell.

h. Save your work, preview and print the worksheets, then close the workbook and exit Excel.

**3.** The Beautiful You Salon is a small but growing beauty salon that has hired you to organize its accounting records using Excel. The store hopes to track its supplies using Excel once its accounting records are under control. Before you were hired, one of the bookkeepers entered expenses in a workbook, but the analysis was never completed.

To complete this independent challenge:

**a.** Start Excel, open the workbook EX B-3 and save it as "Beautiful You Finances" on your Project Disk. The worksheet includes labels for functions such as the Average, Maximum, and Minimum amounts of each of the expenses in the worksheet.

**b.** Think about what information would be important for the bookkeeping staff to know.

**c.** Use the existing worksheet to create a list of the types of functions and formulas you will use, and the cells where they will be located. Indicate where you will have named ranges.

**d.** Create your sketch using the existing worksheet as a foundation. Your worksheet should use range names in its formulas and functions.

**e.** Rename Sheet1 "Expenses."

**f.** Type your name in a worksheet cell.

**g.** Save your work, then preview and print the worksheet.

**h.** Close the workbook and exit Excel.

WEB WORK

**4.** MediaLoft offers eligible employees a variety of mutual fund options in their 401(k) plan. These mutual funds are posted on MediaLoft's intranet site. As a newly eligible MediaLoft employee, you need to determine which mutual funds you want to invest in.

To complete this independent challenge:

**a.** Start Excel, open a new workbook and save it on your Project Disk as "Mutual Fund Data."

**b.** Connect to the Internet and go to the MediaLoft intranet site at http://www.course.com/illustrated/MediaLoft, click the link for the Human Resources page, then click the Employee Benefits link.

**c.** Copy the available mutual fund data from the intranet site to Sheet1 of your workbook.

**d.** Disconnect from the Internet.

**e.** Name Sheet1 "Current Funds."

**f.** On Sheet2, assume this year's annual contribution to your mutual funds will be $10,000. Name this sheet "Investment."

**g.** Choose no more than 4 of the listed mutual funds for your investment, and decide on a percentage for each fund in your contribution.

**h.** Create formulas that multiply those percentages by the total contribution ($10,000). (*Hint:* Use an absolute reference to determine the dollar amount for each mutual fund.)

**i.** Assume that MediaLoft will match your contribution at a rate of 50¢ to your $1. Create formulas that determine how much your total annual investment will be, including the MediaLoft matching funds.

**j.** Type your name in a worksheet cell.

**k.** Preview, then print the Investment worksheet.

**l.** Save and print your work.

**m.** Exit Excel.

# ▶ Visual Workshop

Create a worksheet similar to Figure B-22 using the skills you learned in this unit. Save the workbook as "Annual Budget" on your Project Disk. Type your name in cell A13, then preview and print the worksheet. (Your toolbars may look different from those shown in the figure.)

**FIGURE B-22**

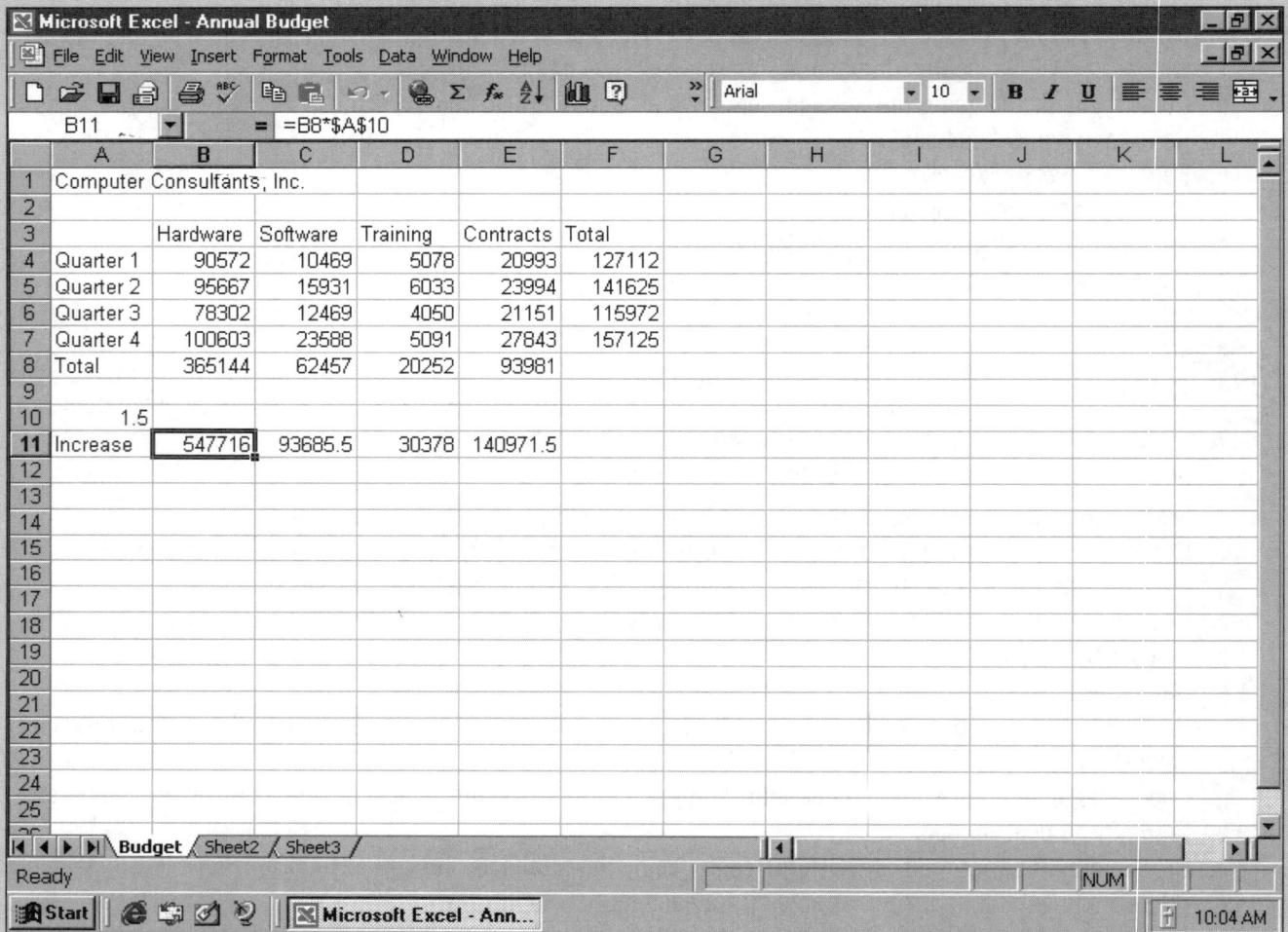

# Formatting

## a Worksheet

- ⌊MOUS⌋ ▶ **Format values**
- ⌊MOUS⌋ ▶ **Use fonts and font sizes**
- ⌊MOUS⌋ ▶ **Change attributes and alignment of labels**
- ⌊MOUS⌋ ▶ **Adjust column widths**
- ⌊MOUS⌋ ▶ **Insert and delete rows and columns**
- ⌊MOUS⌋ ▶ **Apply colors, patterns, and borders**
- ⌊MOUS⌋ ▶ **Use conditional formatting**
- ⌊MOUS⌋ ▶ **Check spelling**

You use Excel's formatting features for a variety of reasons: to make a worksheet more attractive, to make it easier to read, or to emphasize key data. You do this by using colors and different fonts for the cell contents, adjusting column widths, and inserting and deleting columns and rows. The marketing managers at MediaLoft have asked Jim Fernandez to create a workbook that tracks advertising expenses for all MediaLoft stores. Jim has prepared a worksheet for the New York City store containing this information, which can be adapted later for the other stores. Now he uses formatting techniques to make the worksheet easier to read and to call attention to important data.

# Formatting Values

**Excel 2000**

**Formatting** determines how labels and values appear in cells; it does not alter the data in any way. To format a cell, first select it, then apply the formatting. Cells and ranges can be formatted before or after data is entered. If you enter a value in a cell and the cell appears to display the data incorrectly, adjust the cell's format to display the value correctly. The Marketing department has requested that Jim begin by tracking the New York City store's advertising expenses. Jim developed a worksheet that tracks advertising invoices. He entered all the information and now wants to format some of the labels and values. Because some of the changes might also affect column widths, Jim makes all his formatting changes before changing the column widths.

## Steps

1. Start Excel, click **Tools** on the menu bar, click **Customize**, click the **Options tab** in the Customize dialog box, click **Reset my usage data** to restore the default settings, click **Yes**, then click **Close**

2. Open the worksheet **EX C-1** from your Project Disk, then save it as **Ad Expenses**
   The store advertising worksheet appears in Figure C-1. Numeric data can be displayed in a variety of ways, such as having a leading dollar sign. When formatting, you select the range to be formatted up to the last entry in a column or row by selecting the first cell, pressing and holding [Shift], pressing [End], then pressing [→] for the row, or [↓] for the column.

3. Select the range **E4:E32**, then click the **Currency Style button** on the Formatting toolbar
   Excel adds dollar signs and two decimal places to the Cost ea. column data. Excel automatically resizes the column to display all the information supplied by the new formatting. Another option for formatting dollar values is to apply the comma format, which does not include the $ sign.

4. Select the range **G4:I32**, then click the **Comma Style button** on the Formatting toolbar
   The values in columns G, H, and I display the comma format. You can also format percentages using the Formatting toolbar.

5. Select the range **J4:J32**, click the **Percent Style button** on the Formatting toolbar, then click the **Increase Decimal button** on the Formatting toolbar to show one decimal place
   The % of Total column is now formatted with a percent sign (%) and one decimal place. Dates can be reformatted to display ranges in a variety of ways.

6. Select the range **B4:B31**, click **Format** on the menu bar, then click **Cells**
   The Format Cells dialog box opens with the Number tab in front and the Date format already selected. See Figure C-2. There are many types of date formats from which to choose.

7. Select the (first) format **14-Mar-98** in the Type list box, then click **OK**
   You decide you don't need the year to appear in the Inv Due column.

8. Select the range **C4:C31**, click **Format** on the menu bar, click **Cells**, click **14-Mar** in the Type list box, then click **OK**
   Compare your worksheet to Figure C-3.

9. Save your work

FIGURE C-1: Advertising expense worksheet

Your toolbars may not match the toolbars in the figures

FIGURE C-2: Format Cells dialog box

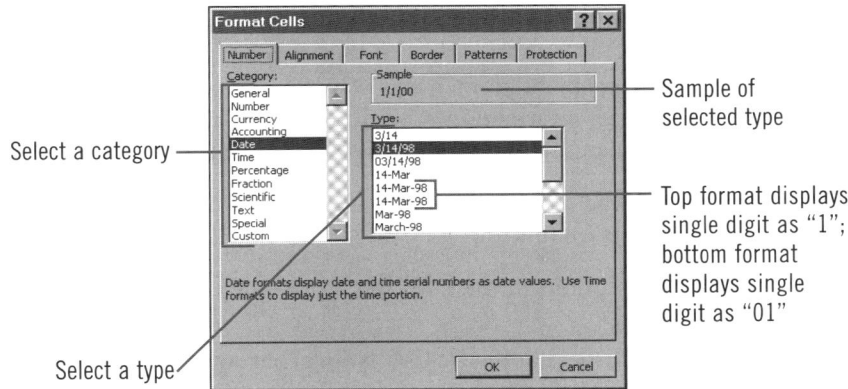

Select a category

Sample of selected type

Top format displays single digit as "1"; bottom format displays single digit as "01"

Select a type

FIGURE C-3: Worksheet with formatted values

Currency Style button

Increase Decimal button

Comma Style button

Percent Style button

Modified date formats

## CLUES TO USE

### Using the Format Painter

A cell's format can be "painted" into other cells using the Format Painter button on the Standard toolbar. This is similar to using drag and drop to copy information, but instead of copying cell contents, you copy only the cell format. Select the cell containing the desired format, then click. The pointer changes to. Use this pointer to select the cell or range you want to contain the painted format.

# Using Fonts and Font Sizes

A **font** is the name given to a collection of characters (letters, numerals, symbols, and punctuation marks) with a specific design. The **font size** is the physical size of the text, measured in units called **points**. The default font in Excel is 10 point Arial. You can change the font, the size, or both of any entry or section in a worksheet by using the Format command on the menu bar or by using the Formatting toolbar. Table C-1 shows several fonts in different sizes. ✎ Now that the data is formatted, Jim wants to change the font and size of the labels and the worksheet title so that they are better distinguished from the data.

## Steps

1. Press **[Ctrl][Home]** to select cell A1

2. Click **Format** on the menu bar, click **Cells**, then click the **Font tab** in the Format Cells dialog box
   See Figure C-5.

3. Scroll down the **Font list** to see an alphabetical listing of the many fonts available on your computer, click **Times New Roman** in the Font list box, click **24** in the Size list box, then click **OK**
   The title font appears in 24 point Times New Roman, and the Formatting toolbar displays the new font and size information. Column headings can be enlarged to make them stand out. You can also change a font and increase the font size using the Formatting toolbar.

4. Select the range **A3:J3**, then click the **Font list arrow** on the Formatting toolbar
   Notice that the fonts on this font list actually look like the font they represent.

5. Click **Times New Roman** in the Font list, click the **Font Size list arrow**, then click **14** in the Font Size list
   Compare your worksheet to Figure C-6. Notice that some of the column headings are now too wide to display fully in the column. Excel does not automatically adjust column widths to accommodate formatting, you have to adjust column widths manually. You'll learn to do this in a later lesson.

6. Save your work

### CLUES TO USE

## Using the Formatting toolbar to change fonts and font sizes

The font and font size of the active cell appear on the Formatting toolbar. Click the Font list arrow, as shown in Figure C-4, to see a list of available fonts. Notice that each font name is displayed in the selected font. If you want to change the font, first select the cell, click the Font list arrow, then click the font you want. You can change the size of selected text in the same way, by clicking the Font Size list arrow to display a list of available point sizes.

**FIGURE C-4: Available fonts on the Formatting toolbar**

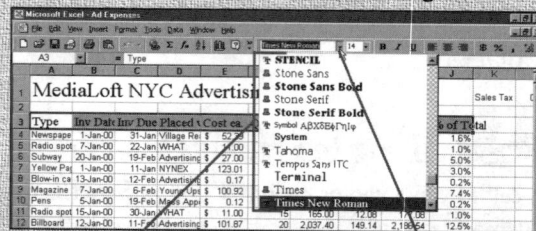

Available fonts installed on your computer (yours may differ)

Font list arrow

FIGURE C-5: **Font tab in the Format Cells dialog box**

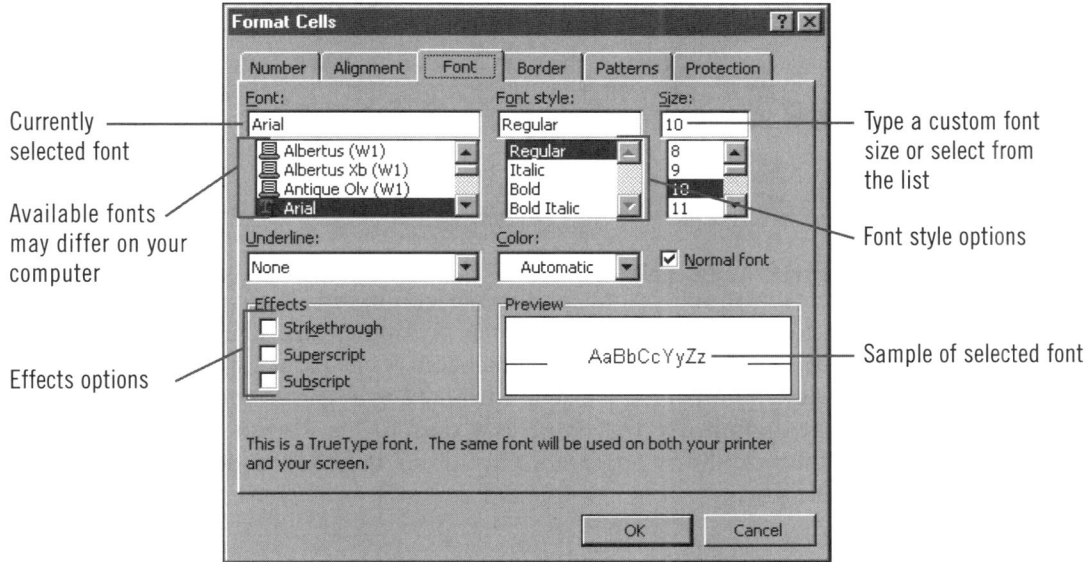

Currently selected font

Available fonts may differ on your computer

Effects options

Type a custom font size or select from the list

Font style options

Sample of selected font

FIGURE C-6: **Worksheet with formatted title and labels**

| | A | B | C | D | E | F | G | H | I | J | K | |
|---|---|---|---|---|---|---|---|---|---|---|---|---|
| 1 | MediaLoft NYC Advertising Expenses | | | | | | | | | | Sales Tax | |
| 2 | | | | | | | | | | | | |
| 3 | Type | Inv Date | Inv Due | Placed | Cost ea. | Quantity | Ext. Cost | Sales T | Total | % of Total | | |
| 4 | Newspape | 1-Jan-00 | 31-Jan | Village Re | $ 52.39 | 5 | 261.95 | 19.17 | 281.12 | 1.6% | | |
| 5 | Radio spot | 7-Jan-00 | 22-Jan | WHAT | $ 11.00 | 15 | 165.00 | 12.08 | 177.08 | 1.0% | | |
| 6 | Subway | 20-Jan-00 | 19-Feb | Advertisinc | $ 27.00 | 30 | 810.00 | 59.29 | 869.29 | 5.0% | | |
| 7 | Yellow Pag | 1-Jan-00 | 11-Jan | NYNEX | $ 123.01 | 4 | 492.04 | 36.02 | 528.06 | 3.0% | | |
| 8 | Blow-in ca | 13-Jan-00 | 12-Feb | Advertisinc | $ 0.17 | 230 | 39.56 | 2.90 | 42.46 | 0.2% | | |

Column headings now 14 point Times New Roman

Title after changing to 24 point Times New Roman

Font and font size of active cell or range

TABLE C-1: **Types of fonts**

| font | 12 point | 24 point | font | 12 point | 24 point |
|---|---|---|---|---|---|
| Arial | Excel | Excel | Palatino | Excel | Excel |
| Comic Sans MS | Excel | Excel | Times | Excel | Excel |

# Changing Attributes and Alignment of Labels

**Attributes** are styling features such as bold, italics, and underlining that you can apply to affect the way text and numbers look in a worksheet. You can also change the **alignment** of labels and values in cells to be left, right, or center. Attributes and alignment can be applied from the Formatting toolbar, or from the Alignment tab of the Format Cells dialog box. See Table C-2 for a list and description of the available attribute and alignment buttons. ◄━━ Now that he has applied the appropriate fonts and font sizes to his worksheet labels, Jim wants to further enhance the worksheet's appearance by adding bold and underline formatting and centering some of the labels.

## Steps

1. Press **[Ctrl][Home]** to move to cell A1, then click the **Bold button** ⊞ on the Formatting toolbar
   The title Advertising Expenses appears in bold.

2. Select the range **A3:J3**, then click the **Underline button** ⊞ on the Formatting toolbar
   Excel underlines the text in the column headings in the selected range.

3. Click cell **A3**, click the **Italics button** ⊞ on the Formatting toolbar, then click ⊞
   The word "Type" appears in boldface italic type. Notice that the Bold, Italics, and Underline buttons are indented. You can apply one or more attributes to text simultaneously.

4. Click ⊞
   Excel removes italics from cell A3 but the bold and underline formatting attributes remain.

5. Select the range **B3:J3**, then click ⊞
   Bold formatting is added to the rest of the labels in the column headings. You want to center the title over the data columns A through J.

6. Select the range **A1:J1**, then click the **Merge and Center button** ⊞ on the Formatting toolbar
   Merge creates one cell out of the 10 cells across the row, then Center centers the text in that newly created large cell. The title "MediaLoft NYC Advertising Expenses" is centered across ten columns. The alignment within individual cells can be changed using toolbar buttons.

7. Select the range **A3:J3**, then click the **Center button** ⊞ on the Formatting toolbar
   Compare your screen to Figure C-7. Although they may be difficult to read, notice that all the headings are centered within their cells.

8. Save your work

### QuickTip
Overuse of any attribute can be distracting and make a workbook less readable. Be consistent, adding emphasis the same way throughout.

### QuickTip
Use formatting shortcuts on any selected range: [Ctrl][B] to bold, [Ctrl][I] to italicize, and [Ctrl][U] to underline.

### QuickTip
To clear all formatting, click Edit on the menu bar, point to Clear, then click Formats.

**TABLE C-2: Attribute and Alignment buttons on the Formatting toolbar**

| button | description | button | description |
|--------|-------------|--------|-------------|
| **B** | Bolds text | ≡ | Aligns text on the left side of the cell |
| *I* | Italicizes text | ≡ | Centers text horizontally within the cell |
| U | Underlines text | ≡ | Aligns text on the right side of the cell |
| ⊞ | Adds lines or borders | ⊞ | Centers text across columns, and combines two or more selected adjacent cells into one cell |

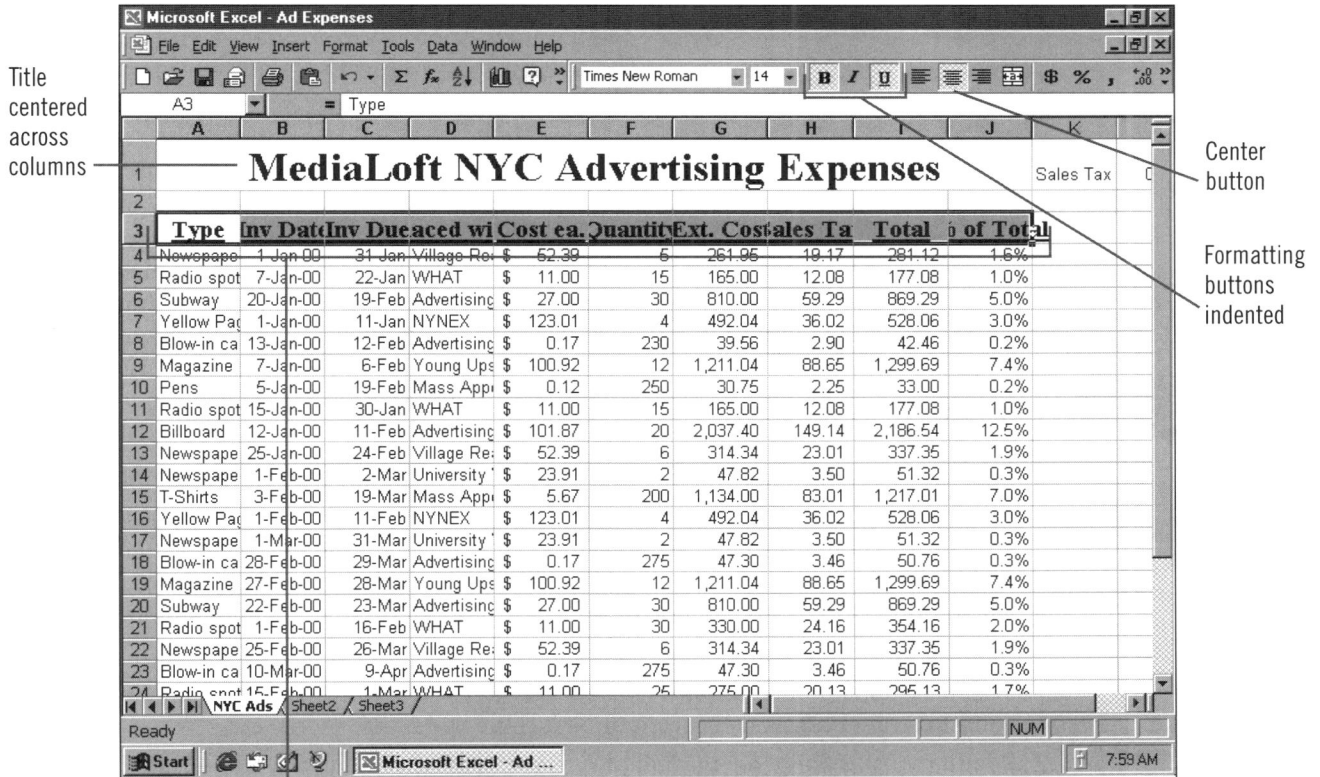

FIGURE C-7: Worksheet with formatting attributes applied

Title centered across columns

Center button

Formatting buttons indented

Column headings centered, bold, and underlined

## Using AutoFormat

Excel also has 17 predefined worksheet formats to make formatting easier and to give you the option of consistently styling your worksheets. AutoFormats are designed for worksheets with labels in the left column and top rows, and totals in the bottom row or right column. To use AutoFormatting, select the data to be formatted instantly—or place your mouse pointer anywhere within the range to be selected—click Format on the menu bar, click AutoFormat, then select a format from the sample boxes, as shown in Figure C-8.

FIGURE C-8: AutoFormat dialog box

Selected AutoFormat

Samples of available formats

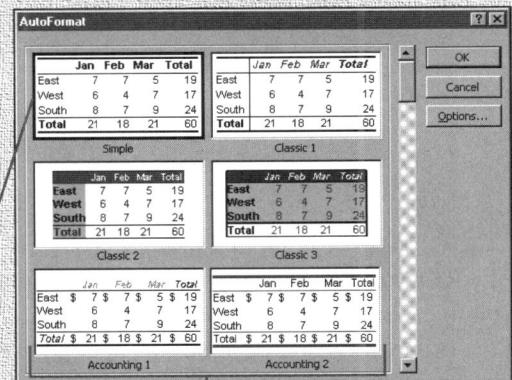

# Adjusting Column Widths

As your worksheet formatting continues, you might need to adjust the width of the columns to make your worksheet more usable. The default column width is 8.43 characters wide, a little less than one inch. With Excel, you can adjust the column width for one or more columns using the mouse or the Column command on the Format menu. Table C-3 describes the commands available on the Format Column menu. You can also adjust the height of rows to accommodate larger font sizes. ✐ Jim notices that some of the labels in column A have been truncated and don't fit in the cells. He decides to adjust the widths of the columns so that the labels display fully.

## Steps 1234

**1.** Position the pointer on the column line between columns A and B selector buttons

The pointer changes to ✛, as shown in Figure C-9. You position the pointer on the right edge of the column that you are adjusting. Then you can drag the column edge, resizing it using the mouse.

**2.** Click and drag the ✛ pointer to the right until column A is wide enough to accommodate all of the text entries in column A

Yellow Pages is the widest entry. The **AutoFit** feature lets you use the mouse to resize a column so it automatically accommodates the widest entry in a cell.

### QuickTip

To reset columns to the default width, select the columns, then use the Column Standard Width command on the Format menu. Click OK in the dialog box to accept the default width.

**3.** Position the pointer on the column line between columns B and C in the column selector until it changes to ✛, then double-click

The width of column B is automatically resized to fit the widest entry, in this case, the column label.

**4.** Use **AutoFit** to resize columns C, D, and J

You can also use the Column Width command on the Format menu to adjust several columns to the same width. Columns can be adjusted by selecting any cell in the column.

**5.** Select the range F5:I5

**6.** Click **Format** on the menu bar, point to **Column**, then click **Width**

The Column Width dialog box appears. Move the dialog box, if necessary, by dragging it by its title bar so you can see the contents of the worksheet. The column width measurement is based on the number of characters in the Normal font (in this case, Arial).

**7.** Type **11** in the Column Width text box, then click **OK**

The column widths change to reflect the new settings. See Figure C-10. If "######" displays after you adjust a column of values, the column is too narrow to display the contents. You need to increase column width until it is wide enough to display the values.

**8.** Save your work

### CLUES TO USE

## Specifying row height

The Row Height command on the Format menu allows you to customize row height to improve readability. Row height is calculated in points, units of measure also used for fonts—one inch equals 72 points. The row height must exceed the size of the font you are using. Normally, you don't need to adjust row heights manually. If you format something in a row to be a larger point size, Excel will adjust the row to fit the largest point size in the row. You can also adjust row height by placing the ✛ pointer under the row selector button and dragging to the desired height.

FIGURE C-9: Preparing to change the column width

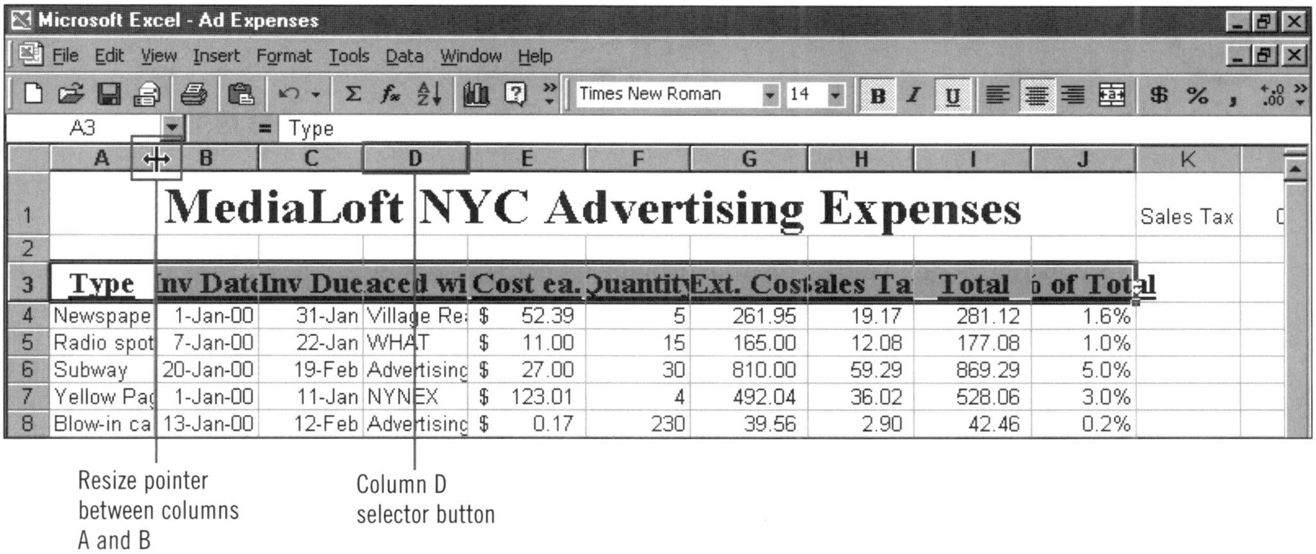

Resize pointer between columns A and B

Column D selector button

FIGURE C-10: Worksheet with column widths adjusted

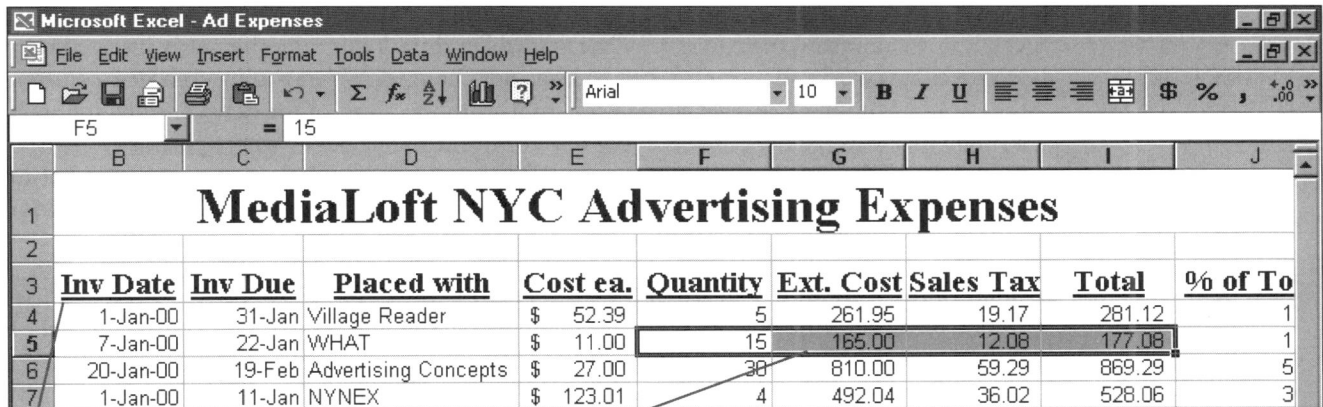

Columns widened to display text

Columns widened to same width

TABLE C-3: Format Column commands

| command | description |
| --- | --- |
| Width | Sets the width to a specific number of characters |
| AutoFit Selection | Fits the widest entry |
| Hide | Hide(s) column(s) |
| Unhide | Unhide(s) column(s) |
| Standard Width | Resets to default widths |

# Inserting and Deleting Rows and Columns

As you modify a worksheet, you might find it necessary to insert or delete rows and columns to keep your worksheet current. For example, you might need to insert rows to accommodate new inventory products or remove a column of yearly totals that are no longer current.  ✏️  Jim has already improved the appearance of his worksheet by formatting the labels and values in the worksheet. Now he decides to improve the overall appearance of the worksheet by inserting a row between the last row of data and the totals. Jim has located a row of inaccurate data that should be deleted, as well as a column that is not necessary.

## Steps 1234

**1. Right-click cell A32, then click Insert**

The Insert dialog box opens. See Figure C-11. You can choose to insert a column or a row, or you can shift the data in the cells in the active column right or in the active row down. An additional row between the last row of data and totals will visually separate the totals.

**2. Click the Entire Row option button, then click OK**

A blank row is inserted between the totals and the Billboard data for March 2000. Excel inserts rows above the cell pointer and inserts columns to the left of the cell pointer. When you insert a new row, the contents of the worksheet shift down from the newly inserted row. Notice that the formula result in cell E33 has not changed. When you insert a new column, the contents of the worksheet shift to the right from the point of the new column. To insert a single row, you can also click the row selector immediately below where you want the new row, right-click, and then click Insert. To insert multiple rows, select the same number of rows as you want to insert. A row can easily be selected for deletion using its **row selector button**, the gray box containing the row number to the left of the worksheet.

**3. Click the row 27 selector button**

Hats from Mass Appeal Inc. will no longer be part of the advertising campaign. All of row 27 is selected, as shown in Figure C-12.

**4. Click Edit in the menu bar, then click Delete**

Excel deletes row 27, and all rows below this shift up one row.

**5. Click the column J selector button**

The percentage information is calculated elsewhere and is no longer needed in this worksheet.

**6. Click Edit in the menu bar, then click Delete**

Excel deletes column J. The remaining columns to the right shift left one column. You are satisfied with the appearance of the worksheet and decide to save the changes.

**7. Save your work**

FIGURE C-11: Insert dialog box

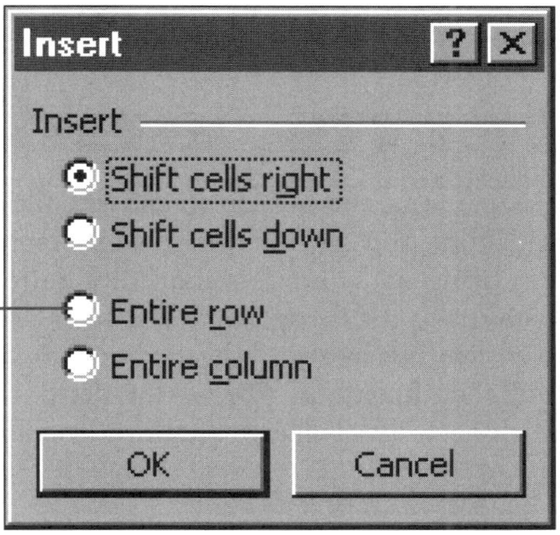

Click here to insert row

FIGURE C-12: **Worksheet with row 27 selected**

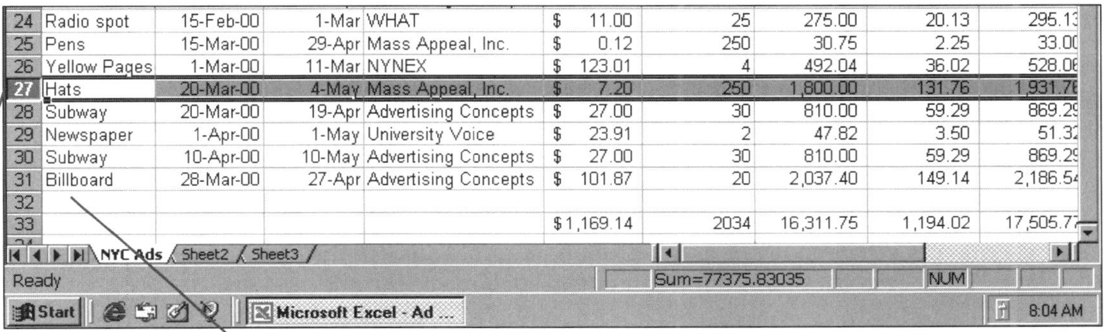

| | A | B | C | D | | E | F | G | H | I |
|---|---|---|---|---|---|---|---|---|---|---|
| 24 | Radio spot | 15-Feb-00 | 1-Mar | WHAT | $ | 11.00 | 25 | 275.00 | 20.13 | 295.13 |
| 25 | Pens | 15-Mar-00 | 29-Apr | Mass Appeal, Inc. | $ | 0.12 | 250 | 30.75 | 2.25 | 33.00 |
| 26 | Yellow Pages | 1-Mar-00 | 11-Mar | NYNEX | $ | 123.01 | 4 | 492.04 | 36.02 | 528.06 |
| 27 | Hats | 20-Mar-00 | 4-May | Mass Appeal, Inc. | $ | 7.20 | 250 | 1,800.00 | 131.76 | 1,931.76 |
| 28 | Subway | 20-Mar-00 | 19-Apr | Advertising Concepts | $ | 27.00 | 30 | 810.00 | 59.29 | 869.29 |
| 29 | Newspaper | 1-Apr-00 | 1-May | University Voice | $ | 23.91 | 2 | 47.82 | 3.50 | 51.32 |
| 30 | Subway | 10-Apr-00 | 10-May | Advertising Concepts | $ | 27.00 | 30 | 810.00 | 59.29 | 869.29 |
| 31 | Billboard | 28-Mar-00 | 27-Apr | Advertising Concepts | $ | 101.87 | 20 | 2,037.40 | 149.14 | 2,186.54 |
| 32 | | | | | | | | | | |
| 33 | | | | | | $1,169.14 | 2034 | 16,311.75 | 1,194.02 | 17,505.77 |

Row 27 selector button

Inserted row

Ready   Sum=77375.83035   NUM

Start   Microsoft Excel - Ad ...   8:04 AM

## CLUES TO USE

## Using dummy columns and rows

When you add or delete a column or row within a range used in a formula, Excel automatically adjusts the formula to reflect the change. However, when you add a column or row at the end of a range used in a formula, you must modify the formula to reflect the additional column or row. To eliminate having to edit the formula, you can include a dummy column and dummy row which is a blank column or row included at the bottom of—but within—the range you use for that formula, as shown in Figure C-13. Then if you add another column or row to the end of the range, the formula will automatically be modified to include the new data.

FIGURE C-13: **Formula with dummy row**

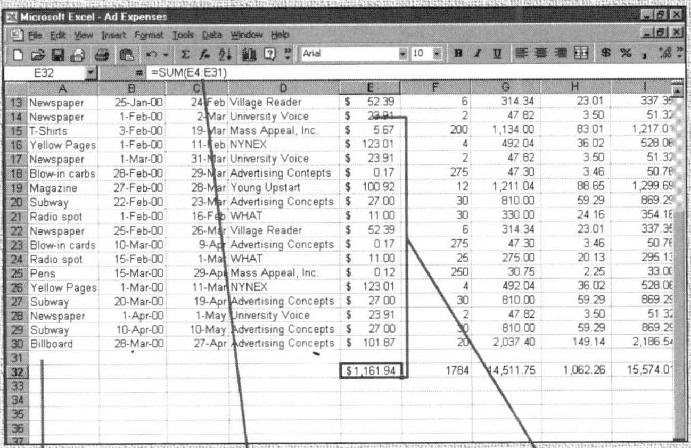

Dummy row

Formula with dummy row

Rows included in formula

Excel 2000

# Applying Colors, Patterns, and Borders

You can use colors, patterns, and borders to enhance the overall appearance of a worksheet and to improve its readability. You can add these enhancements using the Patterns tab in the Format Cells dialog box or by using the Borders and Color buttons on the Formatting toolbar. You can apply color or patterns to the background of a cell or range or to cell contents. And, you can apply borders to all the cells in a worksheet or only to selected cells. See Table C-4 for a list of border buttons and their functions. ✎ Jim decides to add a pattern, a border, and color to the title of the worksheet. This will give the worksheet a more professional appearance.

## Steps 1 2 3 4

1. Press **[Ctrl][Home]** to select cell **A1**, then click the **Fill Color list arrow** 🎨 on the Formatting toolbar
   The color palette appears.

2. Click **Turquoise** (fourth row, fourth color from the right)
   Cell A1 has a turquoise background, as shown in Figure C-14. Notice that Cell A1 spans columns A-I because of the Merge and Center command used for the title.

3. Click **Format** on the menu bar, then click **Cells**
   The Format Cells dialog box opens.

4. Click the **Patterns tab**, as shown in Figure C-15, if it is not already displayed
   When choosing a background pattern, consider that a high contrast between foreground and background increases the readability of the cell contents.

5. Click the **Pattern list arrow**, click the **Thin Diagonal Crosshatch Pattern** (third row, last pattern on the right), then click **OK**
   A border also enhances a cell's appearance. Unlike underlining, which is a text formatting tool, borders extend the width of the cell.

6. Click the **Borders list arrow** ▦ on the Formatting toolbar, then click the **Thick Bottom Border** (second row, second border from the left) on the Borders palette
   It can be difficult to view a border while the cell or range formatted with a border is selected.

7. Click cell **A3**
   The border is a nice enhancement. Font color can distinguish labels in a worksheet.

8. Select the range **A3:I3**, click the **Font Color list arrow** 🅰 on the Formatting toolbar, then click **Blue** (second row from the top, third color from the right) on the palette
   The text changes color, as shown in Figure C-16.

9. Click the **Print Preview button** 🔍 on the Standard toolbar, preview the first page, click **Next** to preview the second page, click **Close** on the Print Preview toolbar, then save your work

### CLUES TO USE

### Using color to organize a worksheet

You can use color to give a distinctive look to each part of a worksheet. For example, you might want to apply a light blue to all the rows containing one category of data and a light green to all the rows containing another category of data. Be consistent throughout a group of worksheets, and try to avoid colors that are too bright and distracting.

FIGURE C-14: Background color added to cell

Cell A1 is affected by
fill color

FIGURE C-15: Patterns tab in the Format Cells dialog box

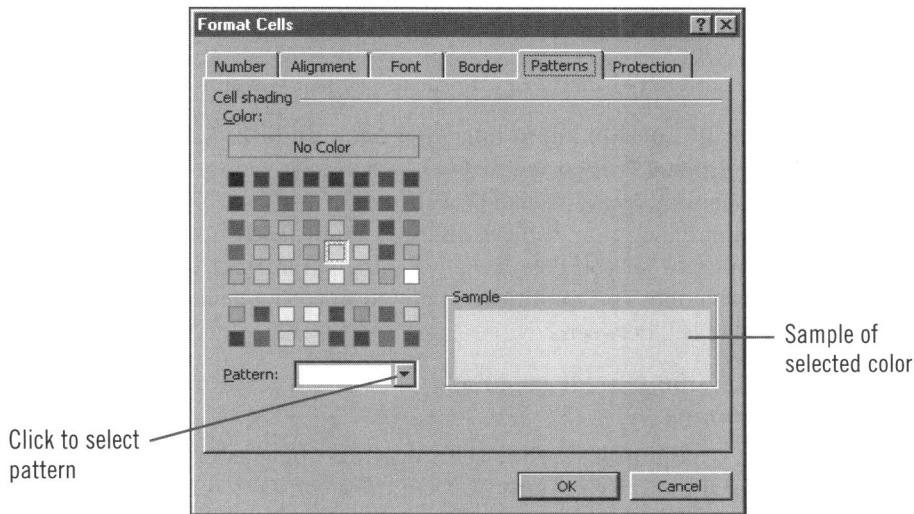

Click to select
pattern

Sample of
selected color

FIGURE C-16: Worksheet with colors, patterns, and border

TABLE C-4: Border buttons

| button | function | button | function | button | function |
|---|---|---|---|---|---|
| | Top Border | | Inside Horizontal Border | | Thick Bottom Border |
| | Bottom Border | | Inside Vertical Border | | Top and Bottom Border |
| | Left Border | | Outside Border | | Top and Double Bottom Border |
| | Right Border | | No Border | | Top and Thick Bottom Border |
| | Inside Border | | Bottom Double Border | | Thick Border |

# Using Conditional Formatting

Formatting attributes make worksheets look professional and help distinguish different data. These same attributes can be applied depending on specific outcomes in cells. Automatically applying formatting attributes based on cell values is called **conditional formatting**. If the data meets your criteria, Excel applies the formats you specify. You might, for example, want advertising costs above a certain number to display in red boldface and lower values to display in blue. Jim wants the worksheet to include conditional formatting so that extended advertising costs greater than $175 display in red boldface. He creates the conditional format in the first cell in the extended cost column.

## Steps

1. **Click cell G4**
   Use the scroll bars if necessary, to make column G visible.

2. **Click Format on the menu bar, then click Conditional Formatting**
   The Conditional Formatting dialog box opens, as shown in Figure C-17. Depending on the logical operator you've selected (such as "greater than" or "not equal to"), the Conditional Formatting dialog box displays different input fields. You can define up to three different conditions that let you determine outcome parameters, and then assign formatting attributes to each one. The condition is defined first. The default setting for the first condition is "Cell Value Is" "between."

### Trouble?
If the Office Assistant appears, close it by clicking the No, don't provide help now button.

3. **To change the current condition, click the Operator list arrow, then click greater than or equal to**
   The first condition is that the cell value must be greater than or equal to some value. See Table C-5 for a list of options. You can use a constant, formula, cell reference, or date. That value is set in the third box.

4. **Click the Value text box, then type 175**
   Once the value is assigned, the condition's formatting attributes are defined in the Format Cells dialog box.

5. **Click Format, click the Color list arrow, click Red (third row, first column on the left), click Bold in the Font style list box, click OK, then click OK to close the Conditional Formatting dialog box**
   The value, 261.95, in cell G4 is formatted in bold red numbers because it is greater than 175, meeting the condition to apply the format. The conditional format, like any other formatting, can be copied to other cells in a column.

6. **With cell G4 selected, click the Format Painter button 🖌 on the Standard toolbar, then drag the ➕🖌 Formatting pointer to select the range G5:G30**
   Once the formatting is copied, you reposition the cell pointer to review the results.

7. **Click cell G4**
   Compare your results to Figure C-18. All cells with values greater than or equal to 175 in column G are displayed in bold red text.

8. **Press [Ctrl][Home] to move to cell A1**

9. **Save your work**

FIGURE C-17: Conditional Formatting dialog box

Click to select operator

Click to delete existing condition(s)

Click to add additional condition(s)

Enter value in the value text box

Click to define format of cells that meet the condition

FIGURE C-18: Worksheet with conditional formatting

Format Painter button

Results of conditional formatting

TABLE C-5: Conditional Formatting Options

| option | mathematical equivalent | option | mathematical equivalent |
|---|---|---|---|
| Between | X>Y<Z | Greater than | Z>Y |
| Not between | B≯C≮A | Less than | Y<Z |
| Equal to | A=B | Greater than or equal to | A>=B |
| Not equal to | A≠B | Less than or equal to | Z<=Y |

CLUES TO USE

## Deleting conditional formatting

Because it's likely that the conditions you define will change, any of the conditional formats defined can be deleted. Select the cell(s) containing conditional formatting, click Format on the menu bar, click Conditional Formatting, then click the Delete button. The Delete Conditional Format dialog box opens, as shown in Figure C-19. Click the checkboxes for any of the conditions you want to delete, then click OK. The previously assigned formatting is deleted—leaving the cell's contents intact.

FIGURE C-19: Delete Conditional Format dialog box

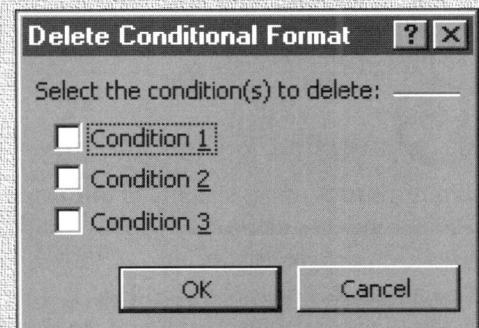

# Checking Spelling

You may think your worksheet is complete, but if you haven't checked for spelling errors, you risk undermining the professional value of your work. A single misspelled word can cast doubt on the validity of your numbers. The spell checker in Excel is also shared by Word, PowerPoint, and Access, so any words you've added to the dictionary using those programs are available in Excel. Jim has completed the formatting for his worksheet and is ready to check its spelling.

## Steps

1. **Click the Spelling button** on the Standard toolbar

   The Spelling dialog box opens, as shown in Figure C-20, with MediaLoft selected as the first misspelled word in the worksheet. The spell checker starts from the active cell and compares words in the worksheet to those in its dictionary. Any word not found in the dictionary causes the spell checker to stop. At that point, you can decide to Ignore, Change, or Add the word to the active dictionary. For any word, (such as MediaLoft or "Inv", the abbreviation of invoice) you have the option to Ignore or Ignore All cases the spell checker cites as incorrect.

2. **Click Ignore All for MediaLoft**

   The spell checker found the word "cards" misspelled and offers "crabs" as one possible alternative. As words are found, you can choose to ignore them, fix the error, or select from a list of alternatives.

3. **Scroll through the Suggestions list, click cards, then click Change**

   The word "Concepts" is also misspelled and the spell checker suggests the correct spelling.

4. **Click Change**

   When no more incorrect words are found, Excel displays the message box shown in Figure C-21.

5. **Click OK**

6. **Press [Ctrl][Home]**

7. **Type your name in cell A2**

8. **Save your work, then preview and print the worksheet**

9. **Click File on the menu bar, then click Exit to close the workbook and exit Excel**

### CLUES TO USE

#### Modifying the spell checker

Each of us uses words specific to our profession or task. Because the dictionary supplied with Microsoft Office cannot possibly include all the words that each of us needs, it is possible to add words to the dictionary shared by all the components in the suite. To customize the Microsoft Office dictionary used by the spell checker, click Add when a word that you know to be correct (but was not in the dictionary) is found. From then on, that word will no longer be considered misspelled by the spell checker.

FIGURE C-20: Spelling dialog box

Misspelled word —

Type replacement
word here or click a
suggestion

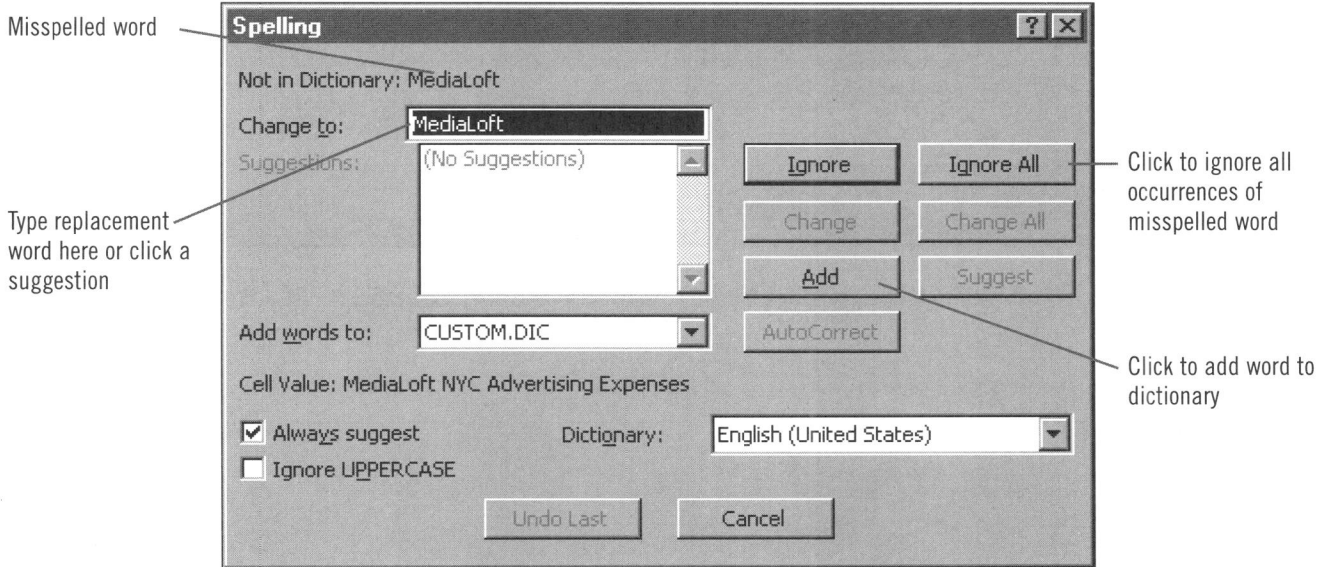

Click to ignore all
occurrences of
misspelled word

Click to add word to
dictionary

FIGURE C-21: Spelling completed alert box

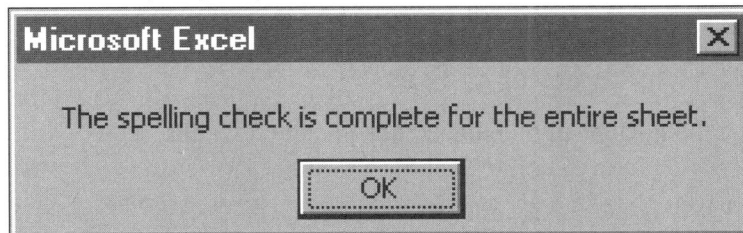

# Practice

## ▶ Concepts Review

Label each element of the Excel worksheet window shown in Figure C-22.

FIGURE C-22

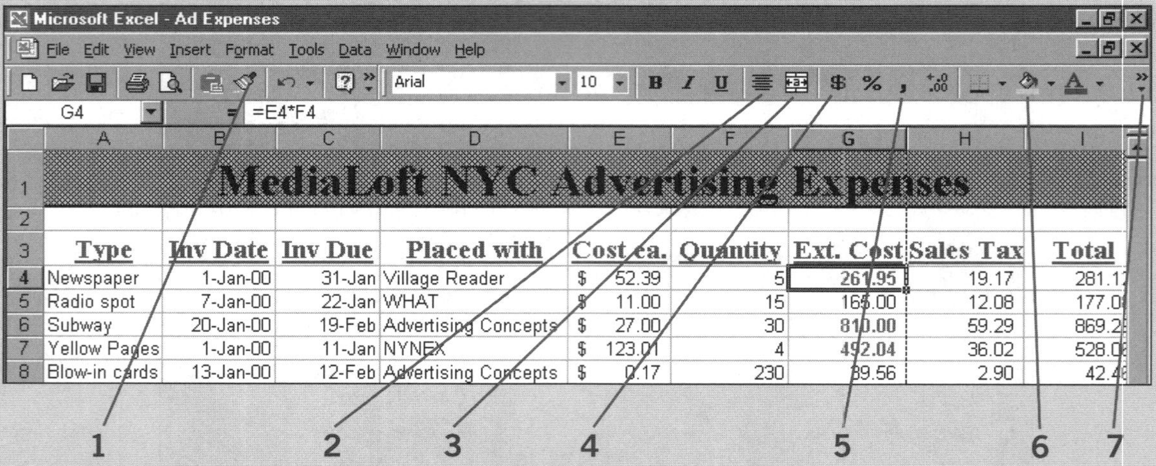

Match command or button with the statement that describes it.

8. Format Cells
9. Edit Delete
10. Format Conditional Formatting
11. ▣
12. $
13. ✓

a. Changes appearance of cell depending on result
b. Erases the contents of a cell
c. Checks the spelling in a worksheet
d. Changes the appearance of selected cells
e. Pastes the contents of the Clipboard in the current cell
f. Changes the format to Currency

Select the best answer from the list of choices.

14. Which button increases the number of decimal places in selected cells?
   a. ,
   b. .00→
   c. ✐
   d. →.0

15. Each of the following operators can be used in conditional formatting, *except*
   a. Equal to.
   b. Greater than.
   c. Similar to.
   d. Not between.

16. How many conditional formats can be created in any cell?
   a. 1
   b. 2
   c. 3
   d. 4

**17. Which button center-aligns the contents of a single cell?**

   **a.** ▦               **c.** ≣

   **b.** ≣               **d.** ≣

**18. Which of the following is an example of the comma format?**

   **a.** $5,555.55           **c.** 55.55%

   **b.** 5555.55             **d.** 5,555.55

# ▶ Skills Review

**1. Format values.**

   **a.** Start Excel and open a new workbook.

   **b.** Enter the information from Table C-6 in your worksheet. Begin in cell A1, and do not leave any blank rows or columns.

   **c.** Add the bold attribute to the equipment descriptions, as well as the Description and Totals labels.

   **d.** Add the italics attribute to the Price and Sold labels.

   **e.** Apply the Comma format to the Price and Sold data.

   **f.** Insert formulas in the Totals column (multiply the price by the number sold).

   **g.** Apply the Currency format to the Totals data.

   **h.** Save this workbook as "Sports Equipment" on your Project Disk.

**TABLE C-6**

| Best Sports Supreme, Inc. | | | |
|---|---|---|---|
| Quarterly Sales Sheet | | | |
| Description | Price | Sold | Totals |
| Ski boots | 250 | 1104 | |
| Rollerblades | 175 | 1805 | |
| Baseball bats | 95 | 1098 | |
| Footballs | 35 | 1254 | |

**2. Use fonts and font sizes.**

   **a.** Select the range of cells containing the column titles.

   **b.** Change the font of the column titles to Times New Roman.

   **c.** Increase the font size of the column titles to 14 point.

   **d.** Resize the columns as necessary.

   **e.** Select the range of values in the Price column.

   **f.** Format the range using the Currency Style button.

   **g.** Resize the columns, if necessary.

   **h.** Save your changes.

**3. Change attributes and alignment of labels.**

   **a.** Select the worksheet title Best Sports Supreme, Inc., then click the Bold button to apply boldface to the title.

   **b.** Use the Merge and Center button to center the title over columns A through D.

   **c.** Select the label Quarterly Sales Sheet, then click the Underline button to apply underlining to the label.

   **d.** Select the range of cells containing the column titles, then click the Center button to center the column titles.

   **e.** Save your changes, then preview and print the workbook.

**4. Adjust column widths.**

   **a.** Use the AutoFit feature to resize the Price column.

   **b.** Use the Format menu to resize the Description column to 16 and the Sold column to 9.

   **c.** Save your changes.

## 5. Insert and delete rows and columns.
**a.** Insert a new row between rows 4 and 5.

**b.** Add Best Sports Supreme's newest product—a baseball jersey—in the newly inserted row. Enter "45" for the price and "360" for the number sold.

**c.** Use the fill handle to copy the formula in cell D4 to cell D5.

**d.** Add a new column between the Description and Price columns with the title "Location."

**e.** Delete the "Location" column.

**f.** Save your changes, then preview the workbook.

## 6. Apply colors, patterns, and borders.
**a.** Add a border around the value data.

**b.** Apply a lime background color to the Description column.

**c.** Apply a green background to the column labels in cells B3:D3.

**d.** Change the color of the font in the first row of the data to green.

**e.** Add a pattern fill to the title in Row 1.

**f.** Type your name in an empty cell, then save your work.

**g.** Print the worksheet, then close the workbook.

## 7. Use conditional formatting.
**a.** Open the file EX C-2 from your Project Disk and save it as "Quarterly Report."

**b.** Create conditional formatting that changes values to blue if they are greater than 2500, and changes them to green if less than 700.

**c.** Use the Bold button and Center button to format the column headings and row titles.

**d.** Column A should be wide enough to accommodate the contents of cells A3:A9.

**e.** AutoFit the remaining columns.

**f.** Use Merge and Center in Row 1 to center the title over columns A:E.

**g.** Format the title Reading Room, Inc. using 14 point Times New Roman text. Fill the cell with a color and pattern of your choice.

**h.** Type your name in an empty cell, then apply a green background and make the text color yellow.

**i.** Use the Edit menu to clear the cell formats of the cell with your name, then save your changes.

## 8. Check spelling.
**a.** Check the spelling in the worksheet using the spell checker.

**b.** Correct any spelling errors.

**c.** Save your changes, then preview and print the workbook.

**d.** Save, close the workbook, then exit Excel.

# ▶ Independent Challenges

**1.** Now that the Beautiful You Salon's accounting records are on Excel, they would like you to work on the inventory. Although more items will be added later, enough have been entered in a worksheet for you to begin your modifications.
To complete this independent challenge:

**a.** Start Excel, open the workbook EX C-3 on your Project Disk, and save it as "BY Inventory."
**b.** Create a formula that calculates the value of the inventory on hand for each item.
**c.** Use an absolute reference to calculate the sale price of each item.
**d.** Use enhancements to make the title, column headings, and row headings more attractive.
**e.** Make sure all columns are wide enough to see the data.
**f.** Add a row under #2 Curlers for "Nail Files," price paid $0.25, sold individually (each), with 59 on hand.
**g.** Before printing, preview the file so you know what the worksheet will look like. Adjust any items as needed, check spelling, and print a copy.
**h.** Use conditional formatting to display which items have 25 or less on hand. Choose colors and formatting.
**i.** Use cell formatting to add borders around the data in the Item column.
**j.** Delete the row with #3 Curlers.
**k.** Type your name in an empty cell, then preview and print the worksheet.
**l.** Save, close the workbook, then exit Excel.

**2.** Continuing your efforts with the Community Action Center, you need to examine the membership in comparison to the community more closely. To make the existing data look more professional and easier to read, you've decided to use attributes and your formatting abilities.
To complete this independent challenge:

**a.** Start Excel, open the workbook EX C-4 on your Project Disk, and save it as "Community Action."
**b.** Remove any blank columns.
**c.** Format the Annual Revenue column using the Currency format.
**d.** Make all columns wide enough to fit their data.
**e.** Use formatting enhancements, such as fonts, font sizes, and text attributes to make the worksheet more attractive.
**f.** Center-align the contents of cells containing column labels.
**g.** Design conditional formatting so that Number of Employee data greater than 50 employees displays in blue.
**h.** Before printing, preview the file so you know what the worksheet will look like. Adjust any items as needed, check spelling, type your name in an empty cell, save your work, and then print a copy.
**i.** Close the workbook and exit Excel.

**3.** Classic Instruments is a Miami-based company that manufactures high-quality pens and markers. As the finance manager, one of your responsibilities is to analyze the monthly reports from your five district sales offices. Your boss, Joanne Bennington, has just asked you to prepare a quarterly sales report for an upcoming meeting. Since several top executives will be attending this meeting, Joanne reminds you that the report must look professional. In particular, she asks you to emphasize the company's surge in profits during the last month and to highlight the fact that the Northeastern district continues to outpace the other districts.

To complete this independent challenge:

**a.** Plan and build a worksheet that shows the company's sales during the last three months. Make sure you include:

- The number of pens sold (units sold) and the associated revenues (total sales) for each of the five district sales offices. The five Classic Instruments sales districts include: Northeastern, Midwestern, Southeastern, Southern, and Western.
- Calculations that show month-by-month totals and a three-month cumulative total.
- Calculations that show each district's share of sales (percent of units sold).
- Formatting enhancements to emphasize the recent month's sales surge and the Northeastern district's sales leadership.

**b.** Prepare a worksheet plan that states your goal, lists the worksheet data you'll need, and identifies the formulas for the different calculations.

**c.** Sketch a sample worksheet on a piece of paper, indicating how the information should be organized and formatted. How will you calculate the totals? What formulas can you copy to save time and keystrokes? Do any of these formulas need to use an absolute reference? How will you show dollar amounts? What information should be shown in bold? Do you need to use more than one font? More than one point size?

**d.** Start Excel, then build the worksheet with your own sales data. Enter the titles and labels first, then enter the numbers and formulas. Save the workbook as "Classic Instruments" on your Project Disk.

**e.** Make enhancements to the worksheet. Adjust the column widths as necessary. Change the row height of row 1 to 30 points. Format labels and values, and change attributes and alignment.

**f.** Add a column that calculates a 15% increase in sales. Use an absolute cell reference in this calculation.

**g.** Type your name in an empty cell.

**h.** Before printing, preview the file so you know what the worksheet will look like. Adjust any items as needed, check spelling, and then print a copy.

**i.** Save your work before closing the file and exiting Excel.

WEB WORK

**4.** As the MediaLoft office manager, you've been asked to assemble data on currently available office suites for use in a business environment. You use the World Wide Web to retrieve information about current software and then post the information on the MediaLoft intranet site. You also create an attractive worksheet for distribution to department managers.
To complete this independent challenge:

**a.** Start Excel, then open a new workbook and save it as "Software Comparison" on your Project Disk.

**b.** Connect to the Internet, go to the MediaLoft intranet site at http://www.course.com/illustrated/MediaLoft, then click the link for the Accounting page.

**c.** Print the Office Suite Analysis, disconnect from the Internet, then enter the data in the Software Comparison workbook.

**d.** Create a title for the worksheet in cell A1. Use the Merge and Center command to center the title over the worksheet columns.

**e.** Make sure each column is resized to accommodate its widest contents.

**f.** Format the labels for each suite manufacturer in bold, 12 point, Times New Roman font.

**g.** Format the labels for the type of program (for example, spreadsheets) in italics, 12 point, Times New Roman font.

**h.** Create a background color and a border for the title. Use a pattern to enhance the text.

**i.** Right-align the label for the suite price.

**j.** Use conditional formatting so that suites costing more than $375 display in red.

**k.** Type your name in a visible worksheet cell.

**l.** Save and print your work, then exit Excel.

Excel 2000

# ▶ Visual Workshop

Create the worksheet shown in Figure C-23, using skills you learned in this unit. Open the file EX C-5 on your Project Disk and save it as "Projected March Advertising Invoices." Create a conditional format in the Cost ea. column so that entries greater than 60 are displayed in red. (*Hint:* The only additional font used in this exercise is Times New Roman. It is 22 points in row 1, and 16 points in row 3.)

**FIGURE C-23**

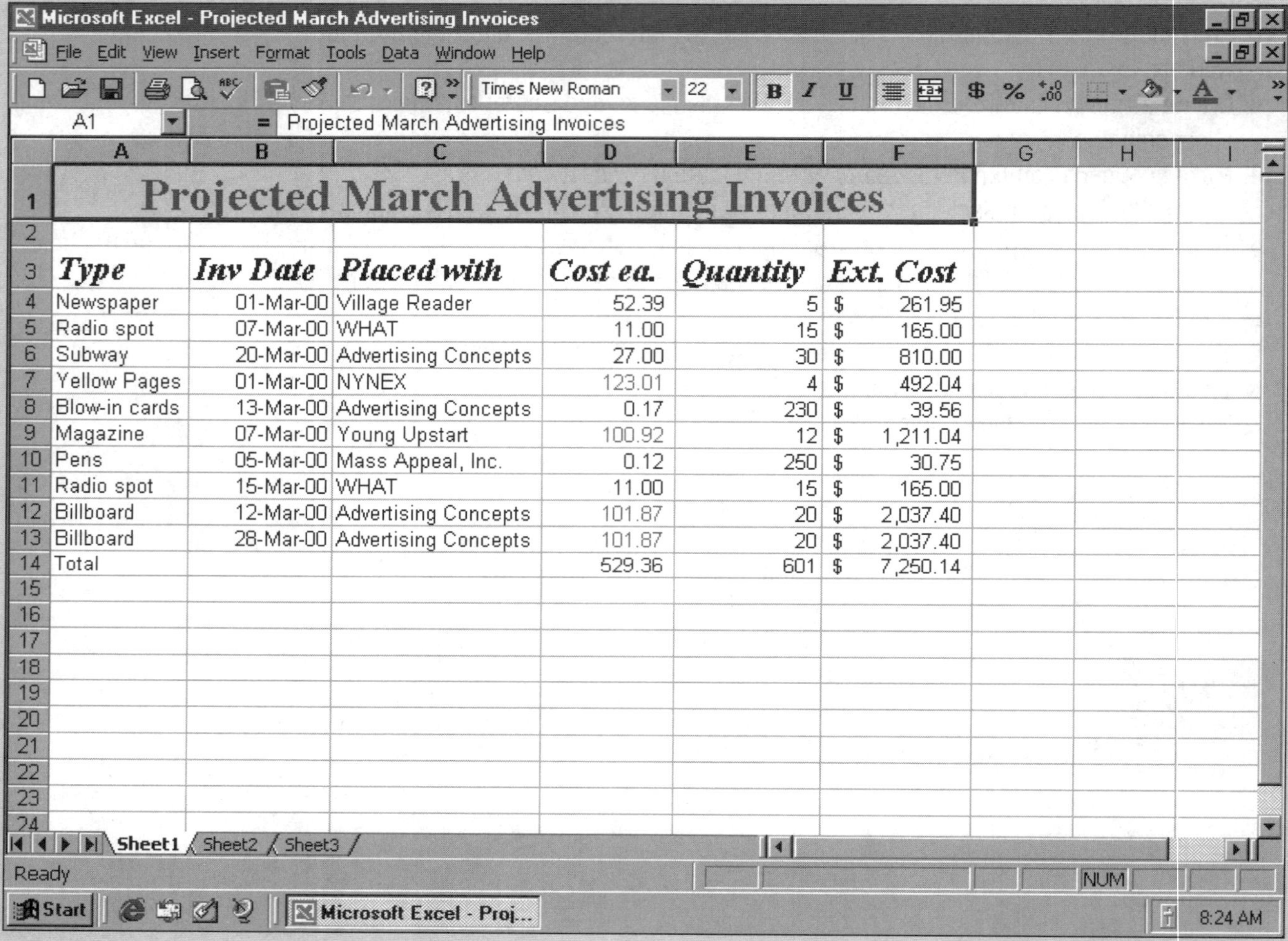

| | Type | Inv Date | Placed with | Cost ea. | Quantity | Ext. Cost |
|---|------|----------|-------------|----------|----------|-----------|
| 1 | Projected March Advertising Invoices | | | | | |
| 2 | | | | | | |
| 3 | Type | Inv Date | Placed with | Cost ea. | Quantity | Ext. Cost |
| 4 | Newspaper | 01-Mar-00 | Village Reader | 52.39 | 5 | $ 261.95 |
| 5 | Radio spot | 07-Mar-00 | WHAT | 11.00 | 15 | $ 165.00 |
| 6 | Subway | 20-Mar-00 | Advertising Concepts | 27.00 | 30 | $ 810.00 |
| 7 | Yellow Pages | 01-Mar-00 | NYNEX | 123.01 | 4 | $ 492.04 |
| 8 | Blow-in cards | 13-Mar-00 | Advertising Concepts | 0.17 | 230 | $ 39.56 |
| 9 | Magazine | 07-Mar-00 | Young Upstart | 100.92 | 12 | $ 1,211.04 |
| 10 | Pens | 05-Mar-00 | Mass Appeal, Inc. | 0.12 | 250 | $ 30.75 |
| 11 | Radio spot | 15-Mar-00 | WHAT | 11.00 | 15 | $ 165.00 |
| 12 | Billboard | 12-Mar-00 | Advertising Concepts | 101.87 | 20 | $ 2,037.40 |
| 13 | Billboard | 28-Mar-00 | Advertising Concepts | 101.87 | 20 | $ 2,037.40 |
| 14 | Total | | | 529.36 | 601 | $ 7,250.14 |

# Working

## with Charts

► **Plan and design a chart**

MOUS ► **Create a chart**

MOUS ► **Move and resize a chart**

MOUS ► **Edit a chart**

MOUS ► **Format a chart**

MOUS ► **Enhance a chart**

MOUS ► **Annotate and draw on a chart**

MOUS ► **Preview and print a chart**

Worksheets provide an effective way to organize information, but they are not always the best format for presenting data to others. Information in a selected range or worksheet can easily be converted to the visual format of a chart. Charts graphically communicate the relationships of data in a worksheet. In this unit, you will learn how to create a chart, how to edit a chart and change the chart type, how to add text annotations and arrows to a chart, and how to preview and print a chart. ➤ For the annual meeting Jim Fernandez needs to create a chart showing the six-month sales history at MediaLoft for the stores in the eastern division. He wants to illustrate the trend of growth in this division.

# Planning and Designing a Chart

Before creating a chart, you need to plan the information you want your chart to show and how you want it to look. ✏️  In early June, the Marketing department launched a regional advertising campaign for the eastern division. The results of the campaign were increased sales during the fall months. Jim wants his chart for the annual meeting to illustrate the growth trend of sales in MediaLoft's eastern division stores and to highlight this dramatic sales increase.

## Details

Jim uses the worksheet shown in Figure D-1 and the following guidelines to plan the chart:

### 🔑 Determine the purpose of the chart, and identify the data relationships you want to communicate visually

You want to create a chart that shows sales throughout MediaLoft's eastern division from July through December. In particular, you want to highlight the increase in sales that occurred as a result of the advertising campaign.

### 🔑 Determine the results you want to see, and decide which chart type is most appropriate to use

Different charts have different strengths and display data in various ways. How you want your data displayed—and how you want that data interpreted—can help you determine the best chart type to use. Table D-1 describes several different types of charts and when each one is best used. Because you want to compare data (sales in multiple locations) over a time period (the months July through December), you decide to use a column chart.

### 🔑 Identify the worksheet data you want the chart to illustrate

You are using data from the worksheet titled "MediaLoft Eastern Division Stores" as shown in Figure D-1. This worksheet contains the sales data for the four stores in the eastern division from July through December.

### 🔑 Sketch the chart, then use your sketch to decide where the chart elements should be placed

You sketch your chart as shown in Figure D-2. You put the months on the horizontal axis (the **x-axis**) and the monthly sales figures on the vertical axis (the **y-axis**). The **tick marks** on the y-axis create a scale of measure for each value. Each value in a cell you select for your chart is a **data point**. In any chart, a **data marker** visually represents each data point, which in this case is a column. A collection of related data points is a **data series**. In this chart, there are four data series (Boston, Chicago, Kansas City, and New York), so you include a **legend** to make it easy to identify them.

FIGURE D-1: Worksheet containing sales data

| | A | B | C | D | E | F | G | H | I | J | K |
|---|---|---|---|---|---|---|---|---|---|---|---|
| 1 | | | | MediaLoft Eastern Division Stores | | | | | | | |
| 2 | | | | FY 2000 Sales Following Advertising Campaign | | | | | | | |
| 3 | | | | | | | | | | | |
| 4 | | | | | | | | | | | |
| 5 | | July | August | September | October | November | December | Total | | | |
| 6 | Boston | 12,000 | 12,000 | 15,500 | 20,000 | 21,000 | 20,500 | $103,500 | | | |
| 7 | Chicago | 14,500 | 16,000 | 17,500 | 18,000 | 18,500 | 19,000 | $101,000 | | | |
| 8 | Kansas City | 9,500 | 10,000 | 15,000 | 16,000 | 17,000 | 15,500 | $103,500 | | | |
| 9 | New York | 15,000 | 13,000 | 16,500 | 19,000 | 20,000 | 21,000 | $83,000 | | | |
| 10 | Total | $51,000 | $51,000 | $64,500 | $73,000 | $76,500 | $76,000 | $391,000 | | | |
| 11 | | | | | | | | | | | |
| 12 | | | | | | | | | | | |

FIGURE D-2: Sketch of the column chart

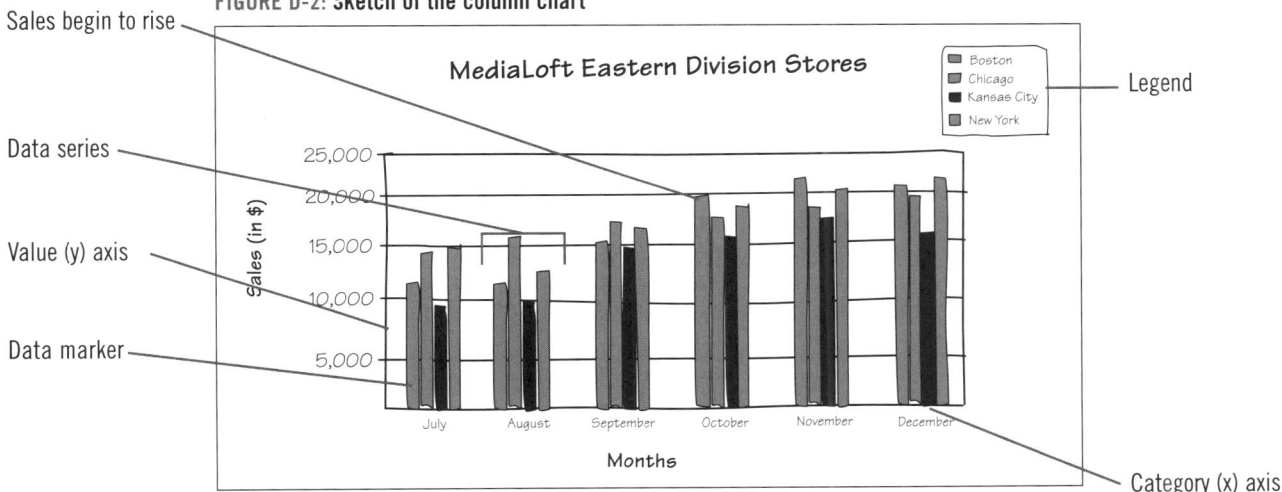

TABLE D-1: Commonly used chart types

| type | button | description |
|---|---|---|
| Area | | Shows how volume changes over time |
| Bar | | Compares distinct objects over time using a horizontal format; sometimes referred to as a horizontal bar chart in other spreadsheet programs |
| Column | | Compares distinct objects over time using a vertical format; the Excel default; sometimes referred to as a bar chart in other spreadsheet programs |
| Line | | Compares trends over even time intervals; similar to an area chart |
| Pie | | Compares sizes of pieces as part of a whole; can have slices pulled away from the pie, or "exploded" |
| XY (scatter) | | Compares trends over uneven time or measurement intervals; used in scientific and engineering disciplines for trend spotting and extrapolation |
| Combination | none | Combines a column and line chart to compare data requiring different scales of measure |

# Creating a Chart

To create a chart in Excel, you first select the range containing the data you want to chart. Once you've selected a range, you can use the Excel Chart Wizard to lead you through the process of creating the chart. ◄━━━ Using the worksheet containing the sales data for the eastern division, Jim creates a chart that shows the growth trend that occurred as a result of the advertising campaign.

**Steps 1 2 3 4**

**QuickTip**

To reset toolbars, click Tools on the menu bar, click Customize, click Reset my usage data, click Yes, then click Close.

**Trouble?**

Click the More Buttons button 〉〉 to locate buttons that are not visible on your toolbars.

**1.** Start Excel, reset your toolbars to their default settings, open the workbook **EX D-1** from your Project Disk, then save it as **MediaLoft Sales-Eastern Division**

You want the chart to include the monthly sales figures for each of the eastern division stores, as well as month and store labels. You don't include the Total columns because the monthly figures make up the totals and these figures would skew the chart.

**2.** Select the range **A5:G9**, then click the **Chart Wizard button** 📊 on the Standard toolbar

This range includes the cells that will be charted. The Chart Wizard opens. The Chart Wizard - Step 1 of 4 - Chart Type dialog box lets you choose the type of chart you want to create. See Figure D-3. You can see a preview of the chart by clicking and holding the Press and Hold to View Sample button.

**3.** Click **Next** to accept Column, the default chart type

The Chart Wizard - Step 2 of 4 - Chart Source Data dialog box lets you choose the data being charted and whether the series are in rows or columns. You want to chart the effect of sales for each store over the time period. Currently, the rows are accurately selected as the data series, as specified by the Series in option button located under the Data range. Since you selected the data before clicking the Chart Wizard button, Excel converted the range to absolute values and the correct range =Sheet1!$A$5:$G$9 displays in the Data range text box.

**4.** Click **Next**

The Chart Wizard - Step 3 of 4 - Chart Options dialog box shows a sample chart using the data you selected. Notice that the store locations (the rows in the selected range) are plotted according to the months (the columns in the selected range), and that the months were added as labels for each data series. Notice also that there is a legend showing each location and its corresponding color on the chart. Here, you can choose to keep the legend, add a chart title, gridlines, data labels, data table, and add axis titles.

**5.** Click the **Chart title text box**, then type **MediaLoft Sales - Eastern Division**

After a moment, the title appears in the Sample Chart box. See Figure D-4.

**6.** Click **Next**

In the Chart Wizard - Step 4 of 4 - Chart Location dialog box, you determine the placement of the chart in the workbook. You can display a chart as an object on the current sheet, on any other existing sheet, or on a newly created chart sheet. A **chart sheet** in a workbook contains only a chart that is linked to the worksheet data. Displaying the chart as an object in the sheet containing the data will help Jim emphasize his point at the annual meeting.

**Trouble?**

If you are using a small monitor, your chart may appear distorted. If so, you'll need to move it to a blank area of the worksheet and then enlarge it before continuing with the lessons in this unit. See your instructor or technical support person for assistance.

**7.** Click **Finish**

The column chart appears and the Chart toolbar opens, either docked, as shown in Figure D-5, or floating. Your chart might be in a different location and look slightly different. You will adjust the chart's location and size in the next lesson. The **selection handles**, the small squares at the corners and sides of the chart's border, indicate that the chart is selected. Anytime a chart is selected, as it is now, a blue border surrounds the data range, a green border surrounds the row labels, and a purple border surrounds the column labels. If you want to delete a chart, select it, then press [Delete].

**8.** Save your work

**FIGURE D-3: First Chart Wizard dialog box**

Selected chart ——

Chart types ——

Chart sub-types for selected chart ——

**Chart Wizard - Step 1 of 4 - Chart Type**

Standard Types | Custom Types

Chart type:
- Column
- Bar
- Line
- Pie
- XY (Scatter)
- Area
- Doughnut
- Radar
- Surface
- Bubble
- Stock

Chart sub-type:

Clustered Column. Compares values across categories.

Press and Hold to View Sample

Cancel | < Back | Next > | Finish

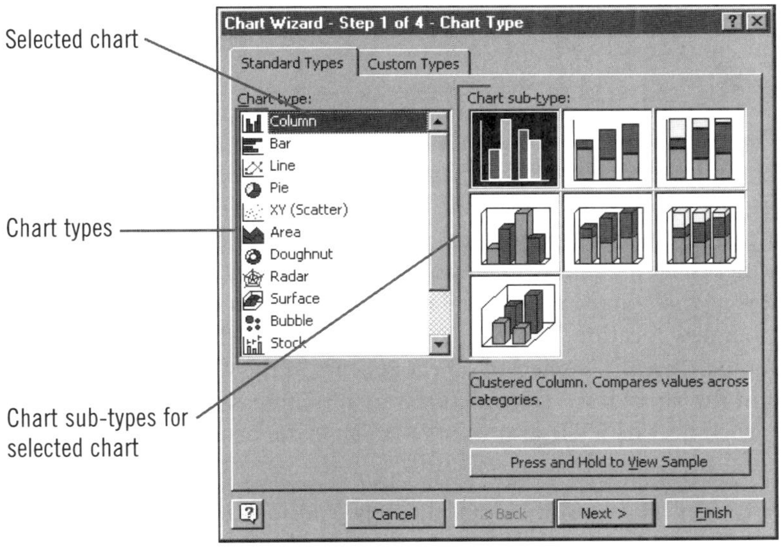

**FIGURE D-4: Third Chart Wizard dialog box**

Type the chart title here ——

Sample chart ——

—— Title added

—— Legend

**Chart Wizard - Step 3 of 4 - Chart Options**

Titles | Axes | Gridlines | Legend | Data Labels | Data Table

Chart title:
ift Sales - Eastern Division

Category (X) axis:

Value (Y) axis:

Second category (X) axis:

Second value (Y) axis:

**MediaLoft Sales - Eastern Division**

Legend: Boston, Chicago, Kansas City, New York

Cancel | < Back | Next > | Finish

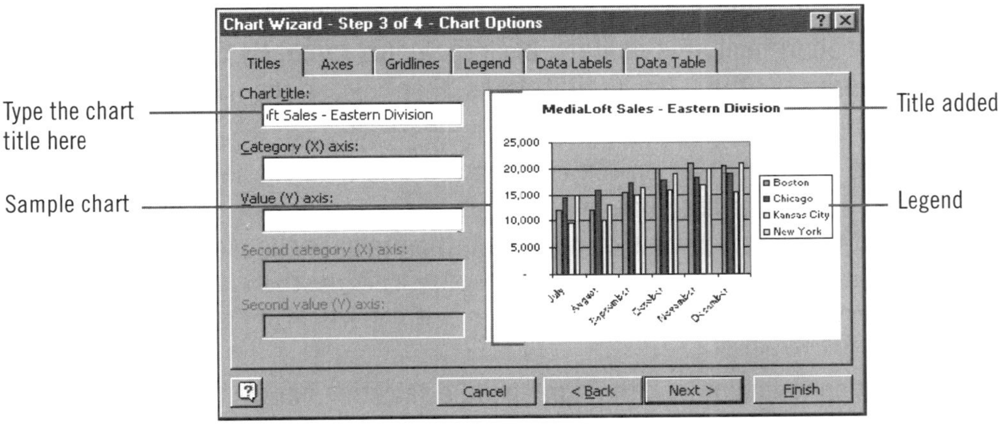

**FIGURE D-5: Worksheet with column chart**

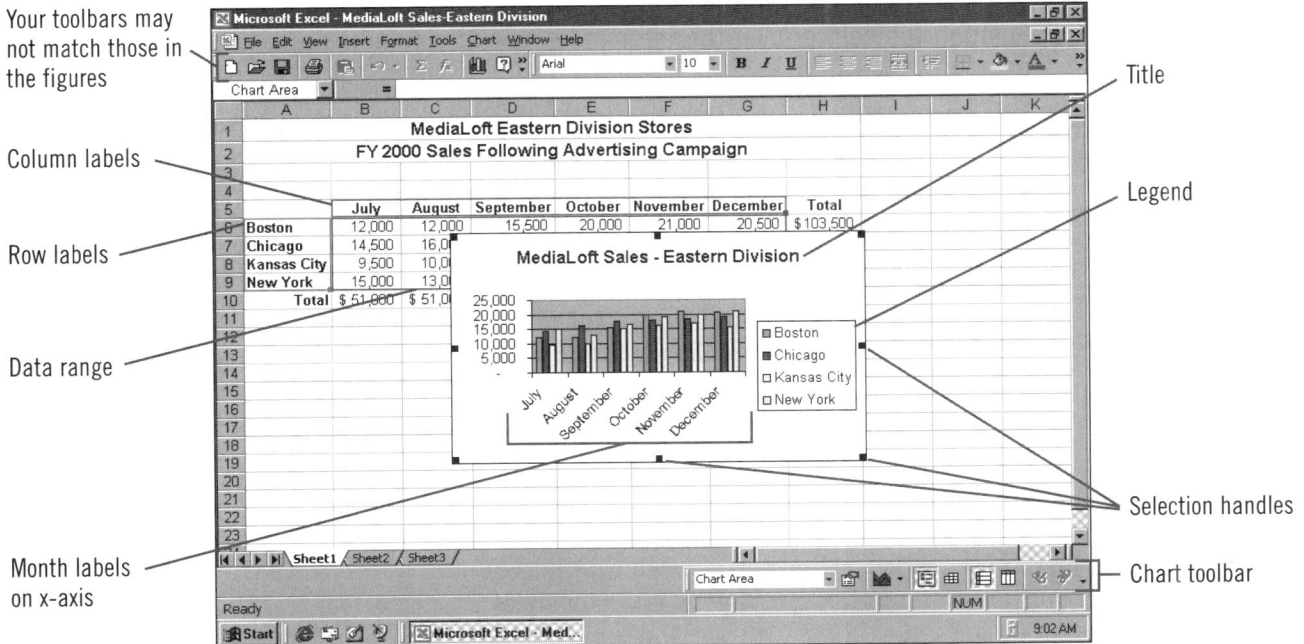

Your toolbars may not match those in the figures ——

Column labels ——

Row labels ——

Data range ——

Month labels on x-axis ——

—— Title

—— Legend

—— Selection handles

—— Chart toolbar

Microsoft Excel - MediaLoft Sales-Eastern Division

File Edit View Insert Format Tools Chart Window Help

Chart Area

|  | A | B | C | D | E | F | G | H |
|---|---|---|---|---|---|---|---|---|
| 1 | | | MediaLoft Eastern Division Stores | | | | | |
| 2 | | | FY 2000 Sales Following Advertising Campaign | | | | | |
| 3 | | | | | | | | |
| 4 | | | | | | | | |
| 5 | | July | August | September | October | November | December | Total |
| 6 | Boston | 12,000 | 12,000 | 15,500 | 20,000 | 21,000 | 20,500 | $103,500 |
| 7 | Chicago | 14,500 | 16,0 | | | | | |
| 8 | Kansas City | 9,500 | 10,0 | | | | | |
| 9 | New York | 15,000 | 13,0 | | | | | |
| 10 | Total | $ 51,000 | $ 51,0 | | | | | |

**MediaLoft Sales - Eastern Division**

Legend: Boston, Chicago, Kansas City, New York

Sheet1 / Sheet2 / Sheet3

Chart Area

Ready

NUM

Start | Microsoft Excel - Med... | 9:02 AM

**WORKING WITH CHARTS** EXCEL D-5

# Moving and Resizing a Chart

**Unit D**
**Excel 2000**

Charts are graphics, or drawn **objects**, and are not in a specific cell or range address. You can move a chart anywhere on a worksheet without affecting formulas or data in the worksheet. Resize a chart to improve its appearance by dragging the selection handles. You can even put a chart on another sheet without worrying about cell formulas. Drawn objects such as charts contain other objects that you can move and resize. To move an object, select it, then drag it or cut and copy it to a new location. To resize an object, use the selection handles. When you select a chart object, the name of the selected object appears in the Chart Objects list box on the Chart toolbar, and in the name box. ⟵⟵⟵ Jim wants to increase the size of the chart and position it below the worksheet data. He also wants to change the position of the legend.

**Steps** 1 2 3 4

**QuickTip**

When a chart is selected, the Chart menu appears on the menu bar.

1. Make sure the chart is still selected, then position the pointer over the chart
   The pointer shape ⬉ indicates that you can move the chart or use a selection handle to resize it. For a table of commonly used pointers, refer to Table D-2. On occasion, the Chart toolbar obscures your view. You can dock the toolbar to make it easier to see your work.

2. If the chart toolbar is floating, click the **Chart toolbar's title bar**, drag it to the **right edge of the status bar** until it docks, then release the mouse button
   The toolbar is docked on the bottom of the screen.

3. Place the ⬉ pointer on the chart, press and hold the left mouse button, using ✛ drag the upper left edge of the chart to the **top of row 13** and the left edge of the chart to the **left border of column A**, then release the mouse button
   A dotted outline of the chart perimeter appears as the chart is being moved. The chart is in the new location. Resizing a chart doesn't affect the data in the chart, only the way the chart looks on the sheet.

4. Position the pointer on the right-middle selection handle until it changes to ↔, then drag the right edge of the chart to the **right edge of column H**
   The chart is widened. See Figure D-6.

5. Position the pointer over the top middle selection handle until it changes to ↕, then drag it to the **top of row 12**

6. If the labels for the months do not fully display, position the pointer over the bottom middle selection handle until it changes to ↕, then drag down to display the months
   You can move the legend to improve the chart's appearance. You want to align the top of the legend with the top of the plot area.

7. Click the **legend** to select it, then drag the **legend** using the ⬉ to the **upper-right corner of the chart** until it is aligned with the plot area
   Selection handles appear around the legend when you click it; "Legend" appears in the Chart Objects list box on the Chart toolbar as well as in the name box, and a dotted outline of the legend perimeter appears as you drag. Changing the original Excel data modifies the legend text.

8. Click cell **A9**, type **NYC**, then click ☑
   See Figure D-7. The legend is repositioned and the legend entry for the New York City store is changed.

9. Save your work

FIGURE D-6: Worksheet with resized and repositioned chart

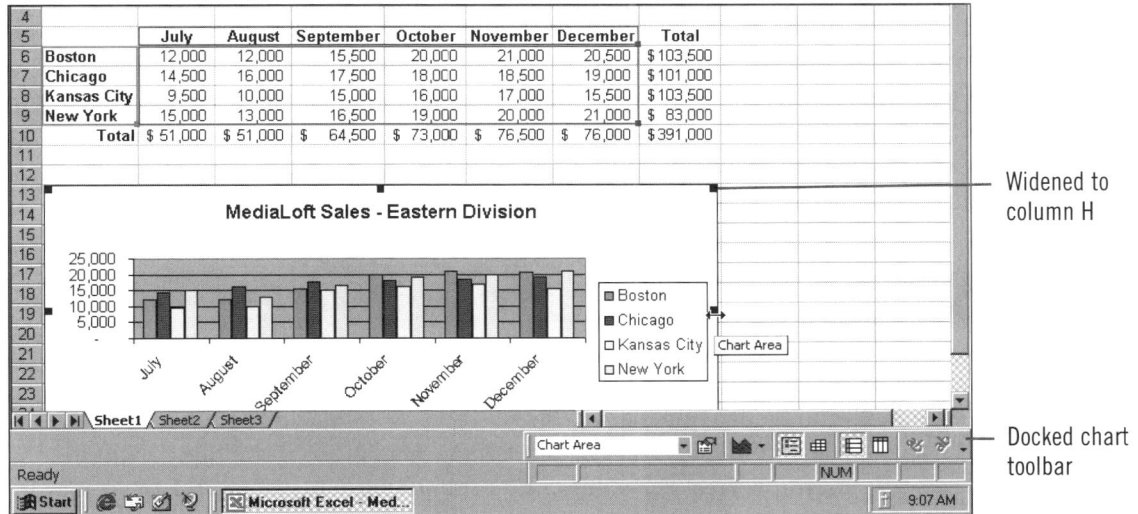

Widened to column H

Docked chart toolbar

FIGURE D-7: Worksheet with repositioned legend

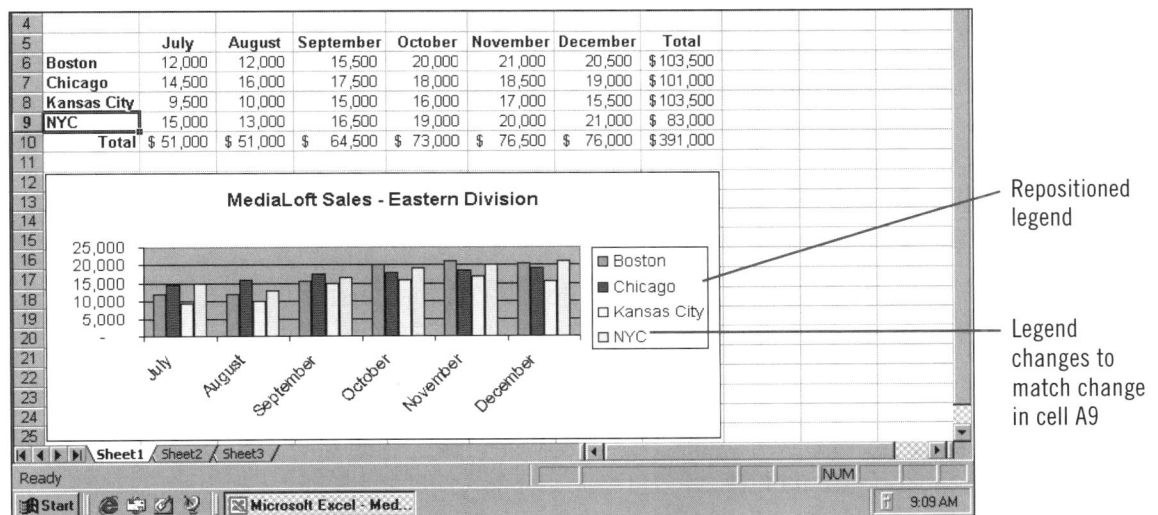

Repositioned legend

Legend changes to match change in cell A9

TABLE D-2: Commonly used pointers

| name | pointer | use | name | pointer | use |
|---|---|---|---|---|---|
| Diagonal resizing | ↗ or ↘ | Change chart shape from corners | I-beam | I | Edit chart text |
| Draw | + | Create shapes | Move chart | ↔↕ | Change chart location |
| Horizontal resizing | ↔ | Change chart shape from left to right | Vertical resizing | ↕ | Changes chart shape from top to bottom |

CLUES TO USE

## Identifying chart objects

There are many objects within a chart and Excel makes it easy to identify each of them. Placing your mouse pointer over a chart object causes a ScreenTip for that object to appear, whether the chart is selected or not. If a chart—or any object in it—is selected, the ScreenTips still appear. In addition, the name of the selected chart object appears in the name box and the Chart Object list box on the Chart toolbar.

# Editing a Chart

Once you've created a chart, it's easy to modify it. You can change data values in the worksheet, and the chart will automatically be updated to reflect the new data. You can also easily change chart types using the buttons on the Chart toolbar.  Jim looks over his worksheet and realizes he entered the wrong data for the Kansas City store in November and December. After he corrects this data, he wants to see how the same data looks using different chart types.

## Steps

**Trouble?**

If you cannot see the chart and data together on your monitor, click View on the menu bar, click Zoom, then click 75%.

**1.** If necessary, scroll the worksheet so that you can see both the chart and row 8, containing the Kansas City sales figures, then place your mouse pointer over the data point to display **Series "Kansas City" Point "December" Value "15,500"**

As you correct the values, the columns for November and December in the chart automatically change.

**2.** Click cell **F8**, type **18000** to correct the November sales figure, press [→], type **19500** in cell **G8**, then click ☑

The Kansas City columns for November and December reflect the increased sales figures. See Figure D-9. The totals are also updated in column H and row 10.

**3.** Select the chart by clicking anywhere within the chart border, then click the **Chart Type list arrow** ⬛▾ on the Chart toolbar

The chart type buttons appear on the Chart Type palette. Table D-3 describes the chart types available.

**4.** Click the **Bar Chart button** ⬛ on the palette

The column chart changes to a bar chart. See Figure D-10. You look at the bar chart, take some notes, and then decide to convert it back to a column chart. You now want to see if the large increase in sales would be better presented with a three-dimensional column chart.

**QuickTip**

Experiment with different formats for your charts until you get just the right look.

**5.** Click the **Chart Type list arrow** ⬛▾, then click the **3-D Column Chart button** ⬛ on the palette

A three-dimensional column chart appears. You notice that the three-dimensional column format is more crowded than the two-dimensional format but gives you a sense of volume.

**6.** Click the **Chart Type list arrow** ⬛▾, then click the **Column Chart button** ⬛ on the palette

**7.** Save your work

### CLUES TO USE

#### Rotating a chart

In a three-dimensional chart, columns or bars can sometimes be obscured by other data series within the same chart. You can rotate the chart until a better view is obtained. Double-click the chart, click the tip of one of its axes (select the Corners object), then drag the handles until a more pleasing view of the data series appears. See Figure D-8.

**FIGURE D-8: 3-D chart rotated with improved view of data series**

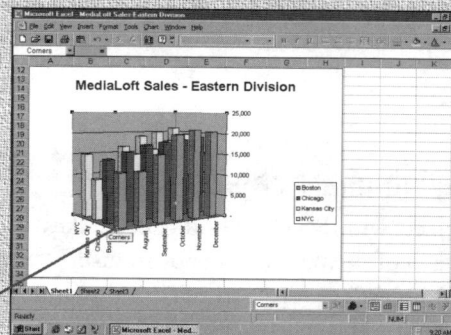

Click to rotate chart

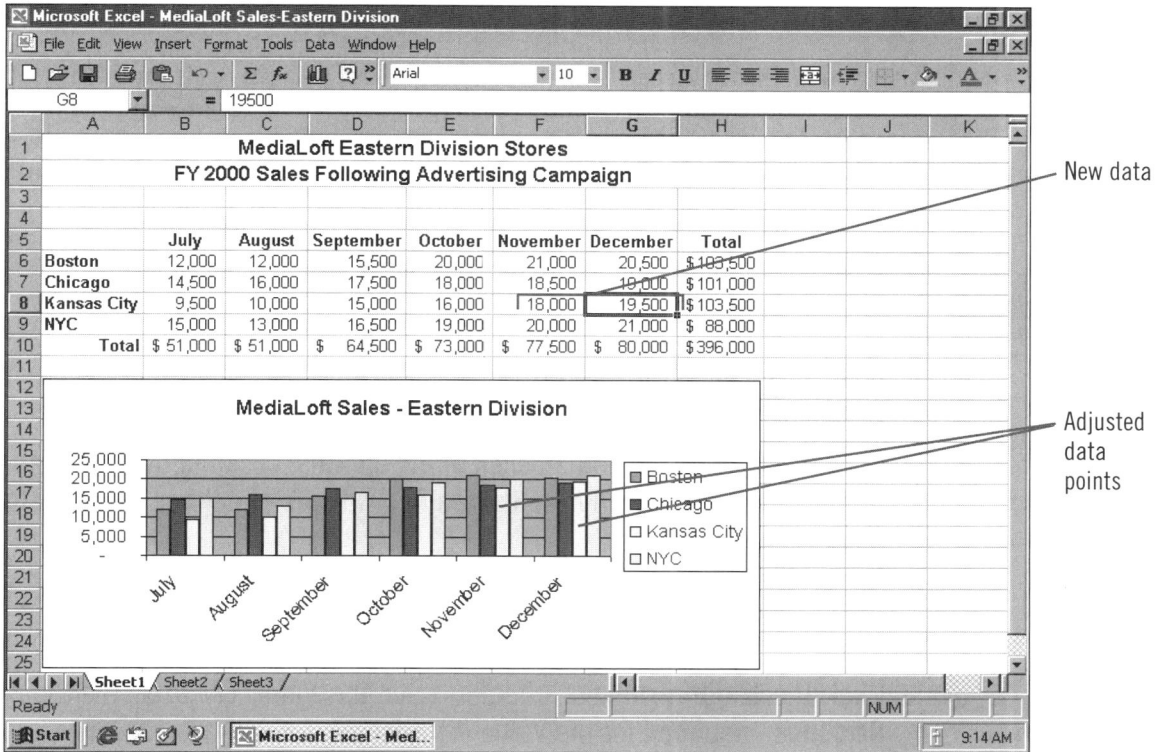

FIGURE D-9: Worksheet with new data entered for Kansas City

New data

Adjusted data points

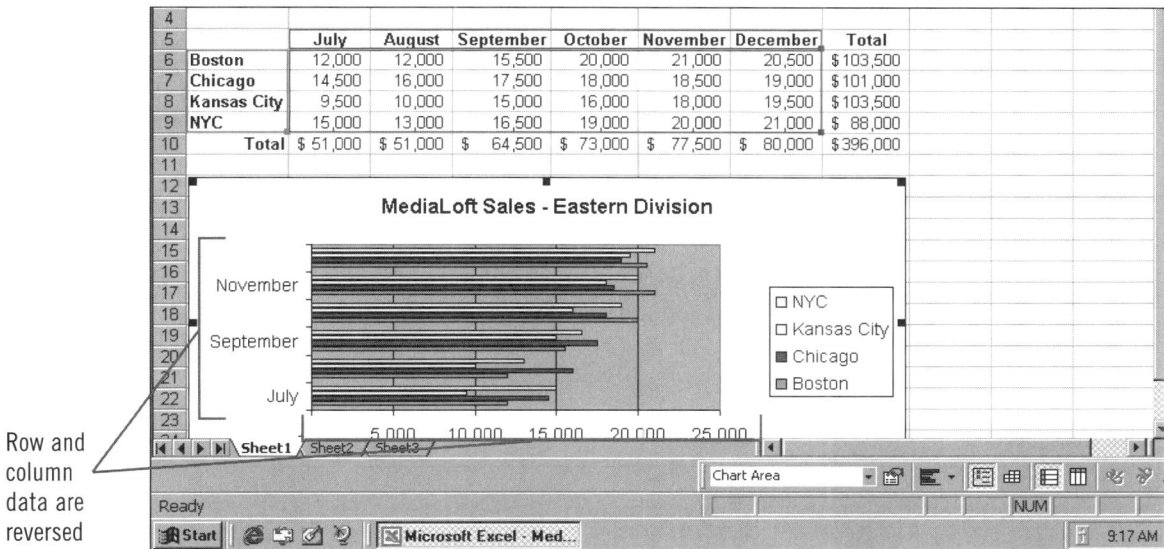

FIGURE D-10: Bar chart

Row and column data are reversed

TABLE D-3: Commonly used chart type buttons

| click | to display a | click | to display a | click | to display a | click | to display a |
|---|---|---|---|---|---|---|---|
| | area chart | | pie chart | | 3-D area chart | | 3-D pie chart |
| | bar chart | | (xy) scatter chart | | 3-D bar chart | | 3-D surface chart |
| | column chart | | doughnut chart | | 3-D column chart | | 3-D cylinder chart |
| | line chart | | radar chart | | 3-D line chart | | 3-D cone chart |

Excel 2000

# Formatting a Chart

After you've created a chart using the Chart Wizard, you can easily modify its appearance. Use the Chart toolbar and Chart menu to change the colors of data series and add or eliminate a legend and gridlines. **Gridlines** are the horizontal and vertical lines in the chart that enable the eye to follow the value on an axis. The button that selects the chart type changes to the last chart type selected. The corresponding Chart toolbar buttons are listed in Table D-4. ▟▔ Jim wants to make some changes in the appearance of his chart. He wants to see if the chart looks better without gridlines, and he wants to change the color of a data series.

## Steps 1 2 3 4

1. **Make sure the chart is still selected**
   Horizontal gridlines currently appear in the chart.

2. **Click Chart on the menu bar, click Chart Options, click the Gridlines tab in the Chart Options dialog box, then click the Major Gridlines checkbox for the Value (Y) axis to remove the check**
   The gridlines disappear from the sample chart in the dialog box, as shown in Figure D-11. Even though gridlines extend from the tick marks on an axis across the plot area, they are not always necessary to the chart's readability.

   > **QuickTip**
   > Minor gridlines show the values between the tick marks.

3. **Click the Major Gridlines checkbox for the Value (Y) axis, then click the Minor Gridlines checkbox for the Value (Y) axis**
   Both major and minor gridlines appear in the sample.

4. **Click the Minor Gridlines checkbox for the Value (Y) axis, then click OK**
   The minor gridlines disappear, leaving only the major gridlines on the Value axis. You can change the color of the columns to better distinguish the data series.

5. **With the chart selected, double-click any light blue column in the NYC data series**
   Handles appear on all the columns in the NYC data series, and the Format Data Series dialog box opens, as shown in Figure D-12.

   > **QuickTip**
   > Add values, labels, and percentages to your chart using the Data Labels tab in the Chart Options dialog box.

6. **Click the Patterns tab, if necessary, click the fuschia box (in the fourth row, first on the left), then click OK**
   All the columns for the series are fuschia, and the legend changes to match the new color. Compare your finished chart to Figure D-13.

7. **Save your work**

**TABLE D-4: Chart enhancement buttons**

| button | use |
|---|---|
| ☷ | Displays formatting dialog box for the selected object on the chart |
| ☷ | Selects chart type (chart type on button changes to last chart type selected) |
| ☷ | Adds/Deletes legend |
| ☷ | Creates a data table within the chart |
| ☷ | Charts data by row |
| ☷ | Charts data by column |
| ☷ | Angles selected text downward |
| ☷ | Angles selected text upward |

FIGURE D-11: **Chart Options dialog box**

Sample chart without gridlines

FIGURE D-12: **Format Data Series dialog box**

Sample of selected color

FIGURE D-13: **Chart with formatted data series**

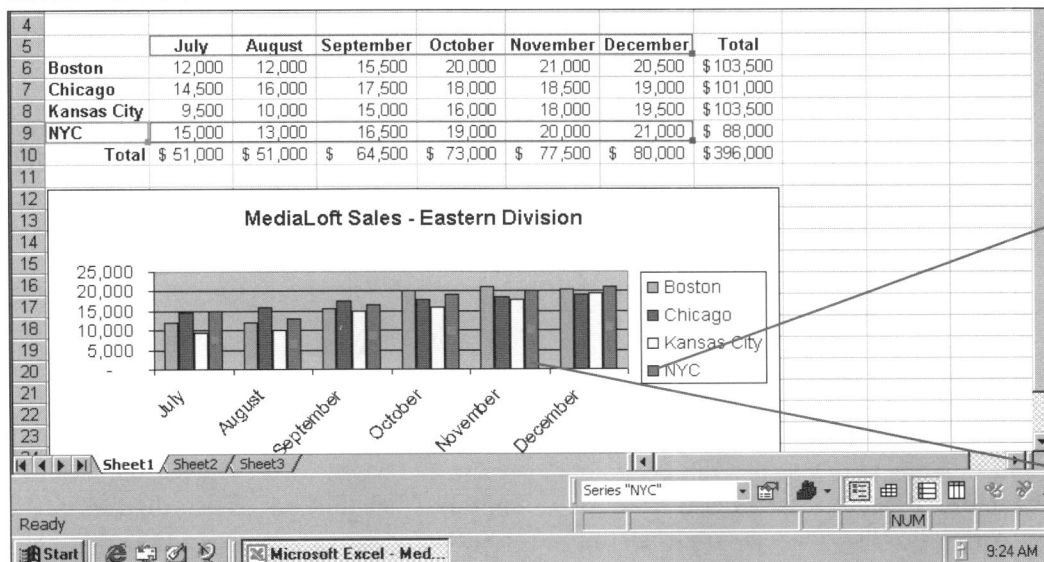

| | July | August | September | October | November | December | Total |
|---|---|---|---|---|---|---|---|
| Boston | 12,000 | 12,000 | 15,500 | 20,000 | 21,000 | 20,500 | $103,500 |
| Chicago | 14,500 | 16,000 | 17,500 | 18,000 | 18,500 | 19,000 | $101,000 |
| Kansas City | 9,500 | 10,000 | 15,000 | 16,000 | 18,000 | 19,500 | $103,500 |
| NYC | 15,000 | 13,000 | 16,500 | 19,000 | 20,000 | 21,000 | $ 88,000 |
| Total | $ 51,000 | $ 51,000 | $ 64,500 | $ 73,000 | $ 77,500 | $ 80,000 | $396,000 |

New color in legend

New color in data series

WORKING WITH CHARTS EXCEL D-11

# Enhancing a Chart

There are many ways to enhance a chart to make it easier to read and understand. You can create titles for the x-axis and y-axis, add graphics, or add background color. You can even format the text you use in a chart. ▬▬▬ Jim wants to improve the appearance of his chart by creating titles for the x-axis and y-axis. He also decides to add a drop shadow to the title.

## Steps 1 2 3 4

**1.** Make sure the chart is selected, click **Chart** on the menu bar, click **Chart Options**, click the **Titles tab** in the Chart Options dialog box, then type **Months** in the Category (X) axis text box

Descriptive text on the x-axis helps a user understand the chart. The word "Months" appears below the month labels in the sample chart, as shown in Figure D-14.

**QuickTip**

To edit the text, position the pointer over the selected text box until it changes to ⊥, click, then edit the text.

**2.** Click the **Value (Y) axis text box**, type **Sales (in $)**, then click **OK**

A selected text box containing "Sales (in $)" appears rotated 90 degrees to the left of the y-axis. Once the Chart Options dialog box is closed, you can move the Value or Category axis titles to new positions by clicking on an edge of the object and dragging it.

**3.** Press **[Esc]** to deselect the Value-axis title

Next you decide that a border with a drop shadow will enhance the chart title.

**4.** Click the **chart title MediaLoft Sales – Eastern Division** to select it

You can create a drop shadow using the Format button on the Chart toolbar.

**QuickTip**

The Format button 📄 opens a dialog box with the appropriate formatting options for the selected chart element. The ScreenTip for the button changes depending on the selected object.

**5.** Click the **Format Chart Title button** 📄 on the Chart toolbar to open the Format Chart Title dialog box, make sure the **Patterns tab** is selected, then click the **Shadow checkbox**

A border with a drop shadow surrounds the title. You can continue to format the title.

**6.** Click the **Font tab** in the Format Chart Title dialog box, click **Times New Roman** in the Font list, click **Bold Italic** in the Font style list, click **OK,** then press **[Esc]** to deselect the chart title

A border with a drop shadow appears around the chart title, and the chart title text is reformatted.

**7.** Click the **Category Axis Title**, click 📄, click the **Font tab**, select **Times New Roman** in the Font list, then click **OK**

The Category Axis Title appears in the Times New Roman font.

**8.** Click the **Value Axis Title**, click 📄, click the **Font tab**, click **Times New Roman** in the Font list, click **OK**, then press **[Esc]** to deselect the title

The Value Axis Title appears in the Times New Roman font. Compare your chart to Figure D-15.

**9.** Save your work

### CLUES TO USE

## Changing text font and alignment in charts

The font and the alignment of axis text can be modified to make it more readable or to better fit within the plot area. With a chart selected, double-click the axis text to be modified. The Format Axis dialog box appears. Click the Font or the Alignment tab, make the desired changes, then click OK.

FIGURE D-14: Sample chart with Category (X) axis text

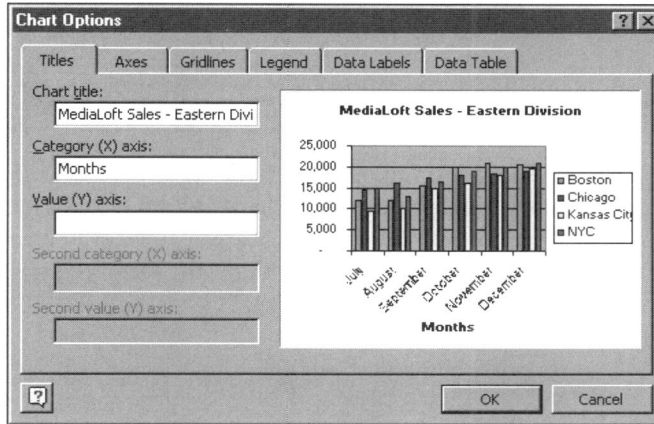

FIGURE D-15: Enhanced chart

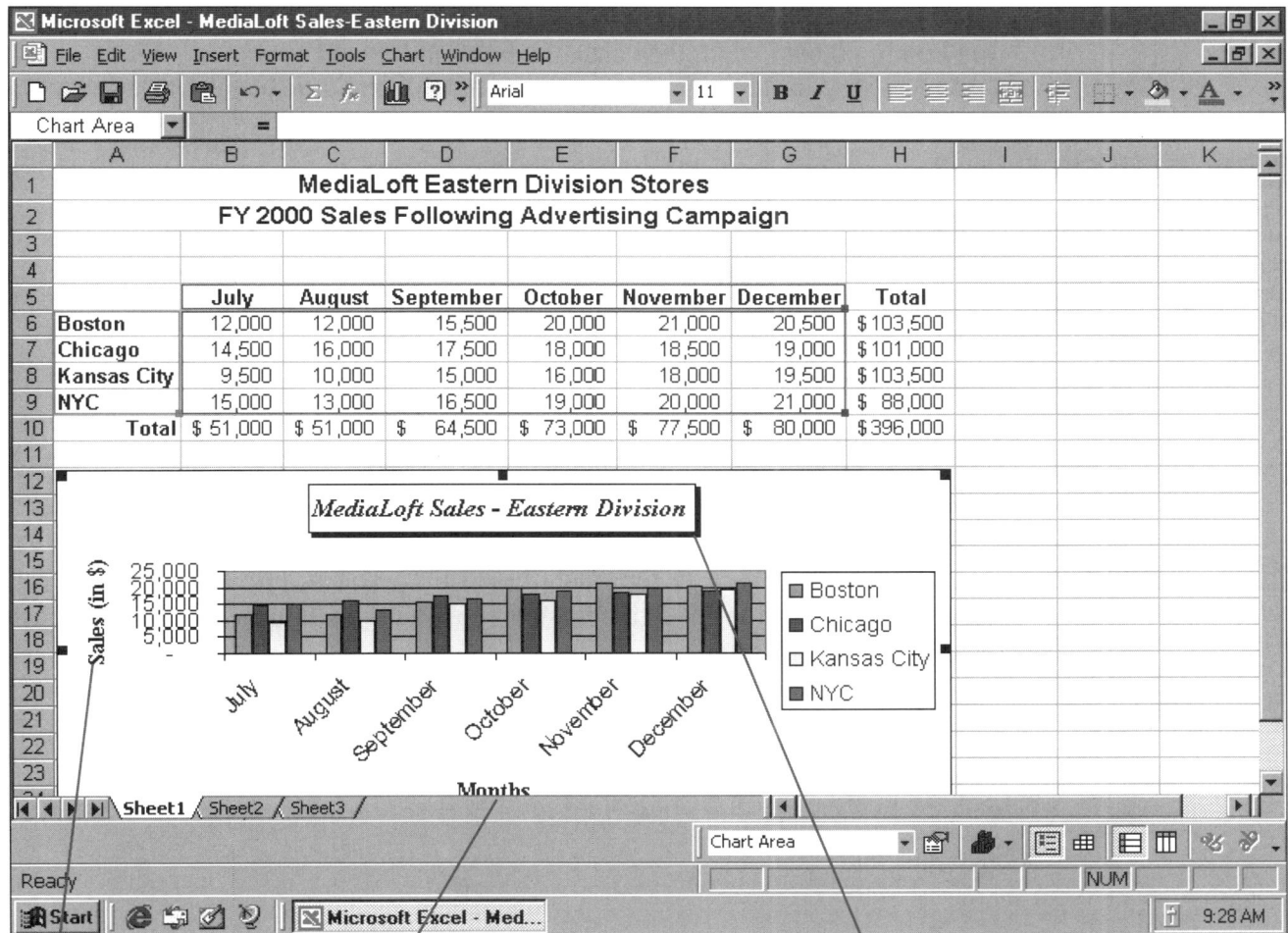

Value axis title          Category axis title          Drop shadow added

# Annotating and Drawing on a Chart

You can add arrows and text annotations to point out critical information in your charts. Text annotations are labels that you add to a chart to further describe the data in it. You can draw lines and arrows that point to the exact locations you want to emphasize. ⬛️ Jim wants to add a text annotation and an arrow to highlight the October sales increase.

## Steps 1234

**1.** Make sure the chart is selected

To call attention to the Boston October sales increase, you can draw an arrow that points to the top of the Boston October data series with the annotation, "Due to ad campaign." With the chart selected, simply typing text in the formula bar creates annotation text.

**2.** Type **Due to ad campaign**, then click the **Enter button** ✓

As you type, the text appears in the formula bar. After you confirm the entry, the text appears in a selected text box within the chart window.

**3.** Point to an edge of the text box so the pointer changes to ⬚

**4.** Drag the text box **above the chart**, as shown in Figure D-16, then release the mouse button

You can add an arrow to point to a specific area or item in a chart using the Drawing toolbar.

**5.** Click the **Drawing button** 🗔 on the Standard toolbar

The Drawing toolbar appears.

**6.** Click the **Arrow button** ⬉ on the Drawing toolbar

The pointer changes to + and the status bar displays "Click and drag to insert an AutoShape." When you draw an arrow, the point farthest from where you start will have the arrowhead.

**7.** Position + under the 't' in the word "to" in the text box, press and hold the **left mouse button**, drag the line to the **Boston column in the October sales series**, then release the mouse button

An arrowhead appears, pointing to Boston October sales. The arrowhead is a selected object in the chart and can be resized, formatted, or deleted just like any other object. Compare your finished chart to Figure D-17.

**8.** Click 🗔 to close the Drawing toolbar

**9.** Save your work

FIGURE D-16: Repositioning text annotation

Outline of
repositioned
annotation

Selected floating
text box

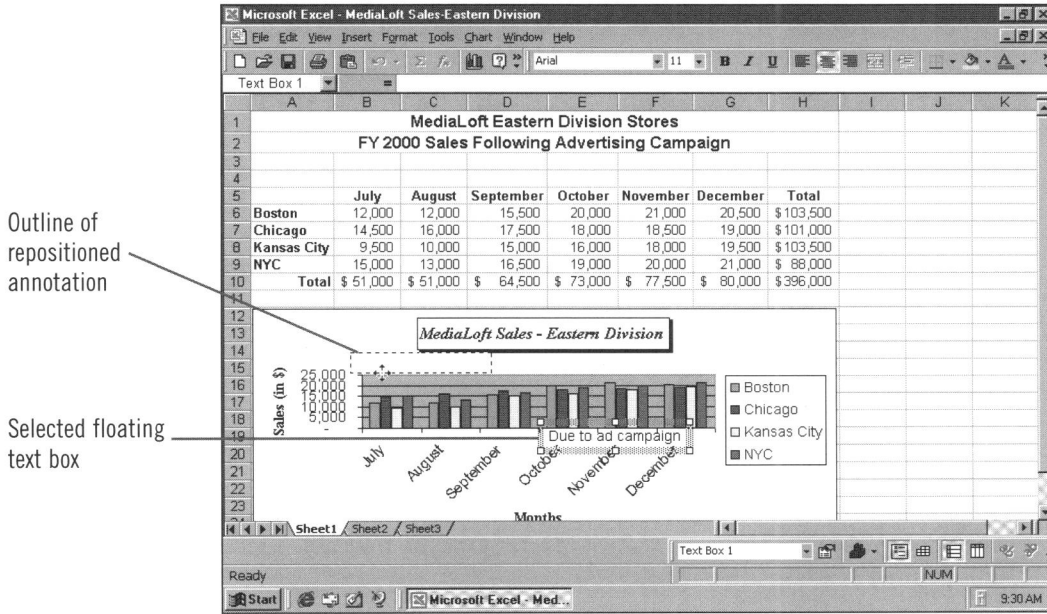

FIGURE D-17: Completed chart with text annotation and arrow

Repositioned text
annotation

Arrow

Boston October
sales

Drawing toolbar

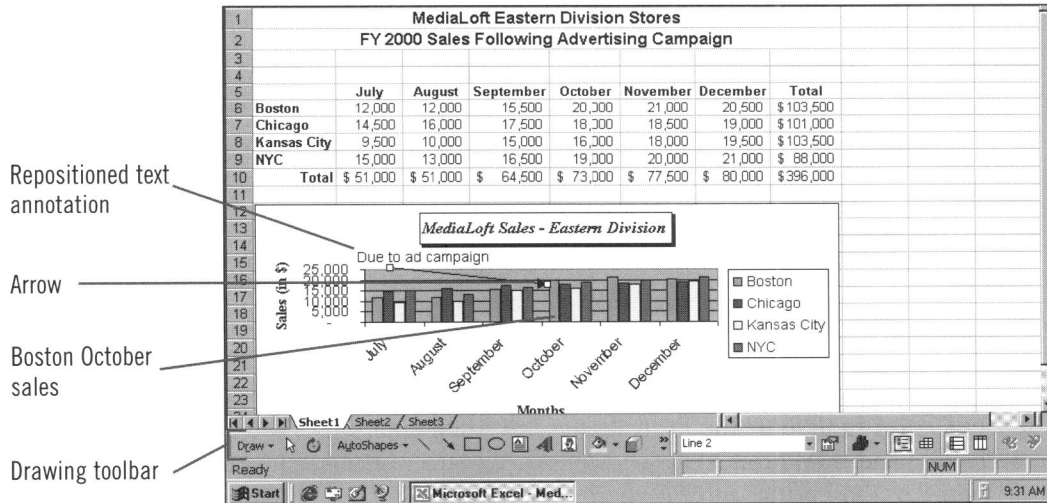

## Exploding a pie slice

Just as an arrow can call attention to a data
series, you can emphasize a pie slice by exploding it, or pulling it away from, the pie chart.
Once the pie chart is selected, click the pie to
select it, click the desired slice to select only the
slice, then drag the slice away from the pie, as
shown in Figure D-18. After you change the
chart type, you may need to adjust arrows
within the chart.

FIGURE D-18: Exploded pie slice

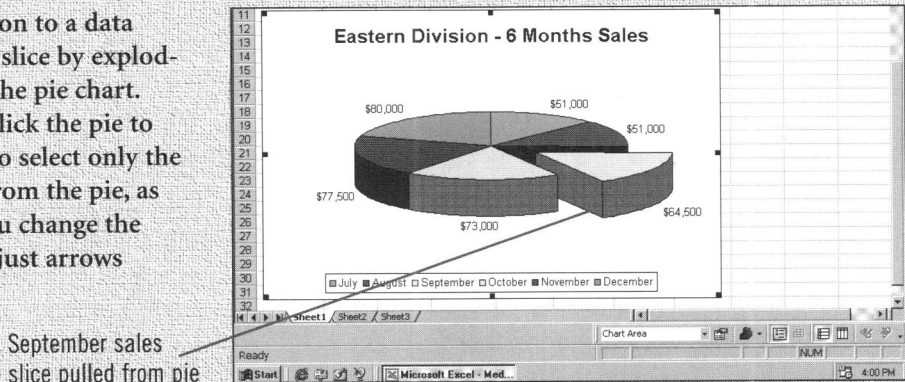

September sales
slice pulled from pie

# Previewing and Printing a Chart

After you complete a chart to your satisfaction, you will need to print it. Previewing a chart gives you a chance to see what your chart looks like before you print it. You can print a chart by itself, or as part of the worksheet. ✏️ Jim wants to print the chart for the annual meeting. He will print the worksheet and the chart together, so that the shareholders can see the actual sales numbers for the eastern division stores.

## Steps 1234

1. **Press [Esc] twice to deselect the arrow and the chart, click cell A35, type your name, press [Enter], then press [Ctrl][Home]**
   If you wanted to print only the chart without the data, you would leave the chart selected. Including your name on a worksheet insures that you'll be able to identify your work when it is printed.

**Trouble?**
Click Margins on the Print Preview toolbar to display Margin lines in the Print Preview window.

2. **Click the Print Preview button 🔍 on the Standard toolbar**
   The Print Preview window opens. You decide that the chart and data would make better use of the page if they were printed in **landscape** orientation—that is, with the text running the long way on the page. Altering the page setup changes the orientation of the page.

3. **Click Setup on the Print Preview toolbar to open the Page Setup dialog box, then click the Page tab**

4. **Click the Landscape option button in the Orientation section as shown in Figure D-19, then click OK**
   Because each page has a left default margin of 0.75", the chart and data will print too far over to the left of the page. You can change this setting using the Margins tab.

5. **Click Setup, click the Margins tab, click the Center on page Horizontally checkbox, then click OK**
   The data and chart are positioned horizontally on the page. See Figure D-20.

6. **Click Print to display the Print dialog box, then click OK**
   The data and chart print and you are returned to the worksheet. If you want, you can choose to preview (and print) only the chart.

7. **Select the chart, then click the Print Preview button 🔍**
   The chart appears in the Print Preview window. If you wanted to, you could print the chart by clicking the Print button on the Print Preview toolbar.

8. **Click Close on the Print Preview toolbar**

9. **Save your work, then close the workbook and exit Excel**

### CLUES TO USE

#### Using the Page Setup dialog box for a chart

When a chart is selected, a different Page Setup dialog box opens than when neither the chart nor data is selected. The Center on Page options are not always available. To accurately position a chart on the page, you could click the Margins button on the Print Preview toolbar. Margin lines appear on the screen and show you exactly how the margins display on the page. The exact placement appears in the status bar when you press and hold the mouse button on the margin line. You can drag the lines to the exact setting you want.

FIGURE D-19: **Page tab of the Page Setup dialog box**

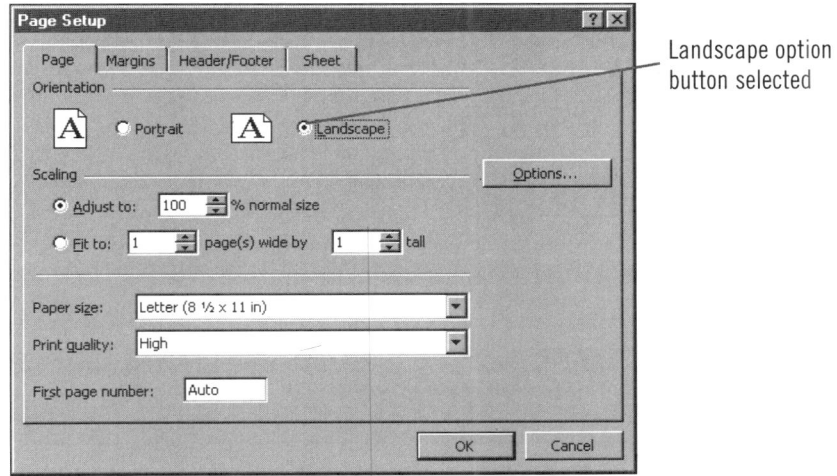

Landscape option
button selected

FIGURE D-20: **Chart and data ready to print**

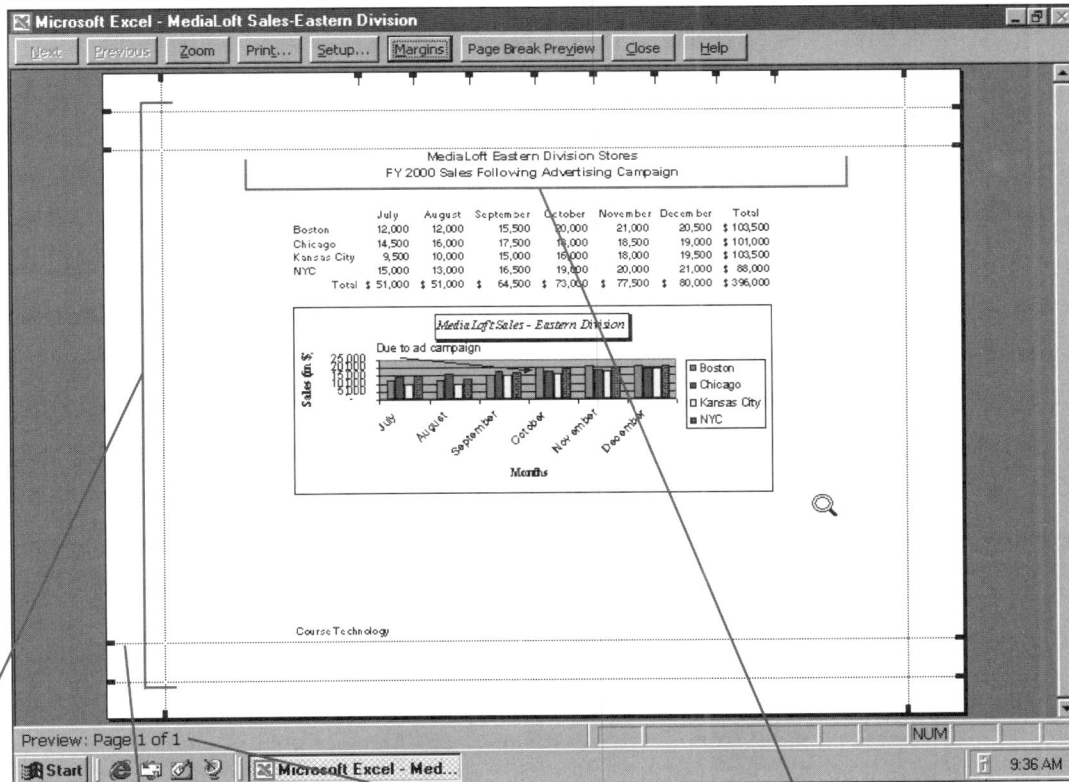

Orientation changed    Margin                    Chart and data will          Centered on page
to landscape                                     print on one page

# Practice

## ► Concepts Review

Label each element of the Excel chart shown in Figure D-21.

FIGURE D-21

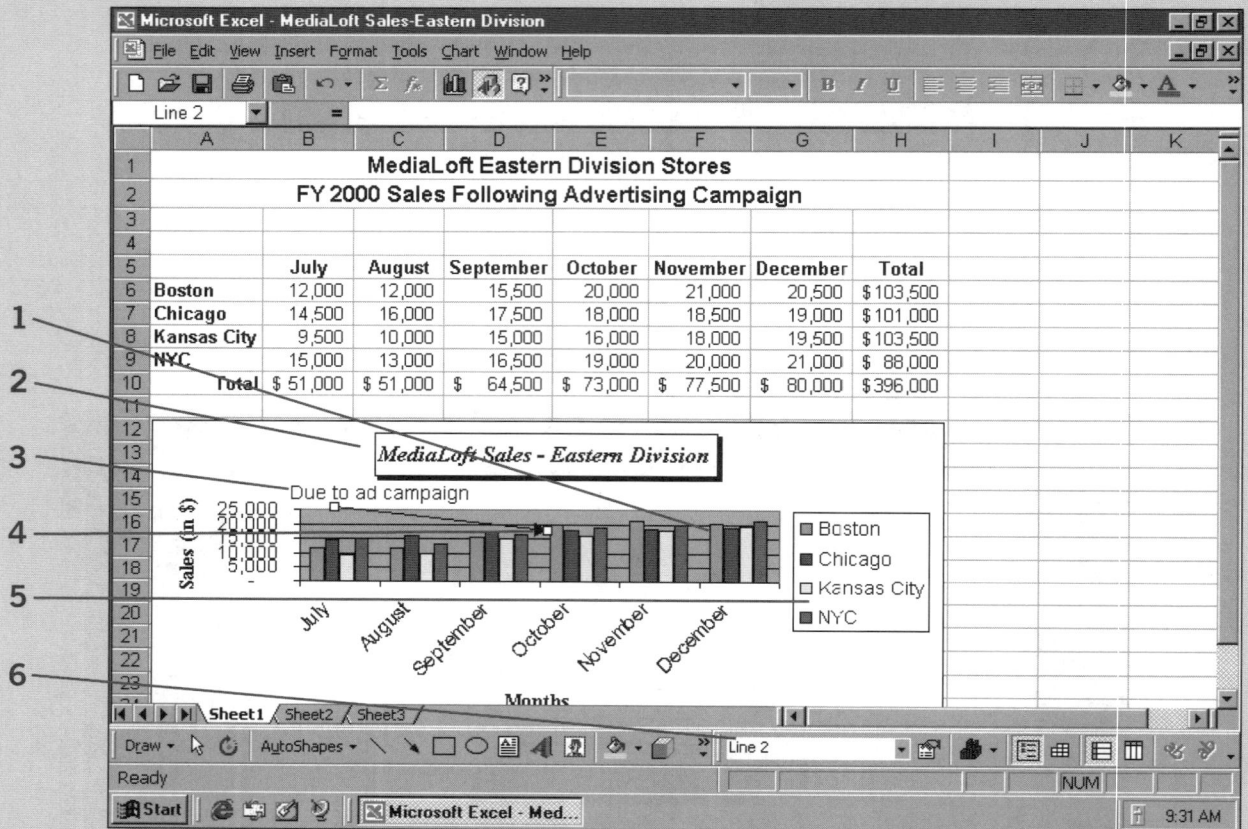

Match each chart type with the statement that describes it.

7. Column
8. Area
9. Pie
10. Combination
11. Line

a. Shows how volume changes over time
b. Compares data as parts of a whole
c. Displays a column and line chart using different scales of measurement
d. Compares trends over even time intervals
e. Compares data over time—the Excel default

Select the best answer from the list of choices.

12. **The object in a chart that identifies patterns used for each data series is a**
    a. Data point.
    b. Plot.
    c. Legend.
    d. Range.

13. **What is the term for a row or column on a chart?**
    a. Range address
    b. Axis title
    c. Chart orientation
    d. Data series

14. **The orientation of a page whose dimensions are 11" by 8½" is**
    a. Sideways.
    b. Longways.
    c. Portrait.
    d. Landscape.

15. **The Value axis is the**
    a. X-axis.
    b. Z-axis.
    c. D-axis.
    d. Y-axis.

16. **The Category axis is the**
    a. X-axis.
    b. Z-axis.
    c. D-axis.
    d. Y-axis.

17. **Which pointer is used to resize a chart object?**
    a. I
    b. ↗
    c. ✛
    d. +

## ► Skills Review

### 1. Create a chart.

a. Start Excel, open a new workbook, then save it as "Software Usage" to your Project Disk.

b. Enter the information from Table D-5 in your worksheet in range A1:F6. Resize columns and rows.

c. Save your work.

d. Select the range you want to chart.

e. Click the Chart Wizard button.

f. Complete the Chart Wizard dialog boxes and build a column chart on the same sheet as the data, having a different color bar for each department. Title the chart "Software Usage by Department."

g. Save your work.

TABLE D-5

|  | Excel | Word | PowerPoint | Access | Publisher |
|---|---|---|---|---|---|
| Accounting | 22 | 15 | 2 | 2 | 1 |
| Marketing | 13 | 35 | 35 | 5 | 32 |
| Engineering | 23 | 5 | 3 | 1 | 0 |
| Personnel | 10 | 25 | 10 | 2 | 25 |
| Production | 6 | 5 | 22 | 0 | 22 |

### 2. Move and resize a chart.

a. Make sure the chart is still selected.

b. Move the chart beneath the data.

c. Drag the chart's selection handles so it is as wide as the screen.

d. Move the legend below the charted data. (*Hint:* Change the legend's position using the Legend button on the Chart toolbar.)

e. Save your work.

### 3. Edit a chart.

a. Change the value in cell B3 to "6." Notice the change in the chart.

b. Select the chart by clicking it.

c. Click the Chart Type list arrow on the Chart toolbar.

d. Click the 3-D Column Chart button.

e. Rotate the chart to move the data.

f. Change the chart back to a column chart.

g. Save your work.

### 4. Format a chart.

a. Make sure the chart is still selected.

b. Use the Chart Options dialog box to turn off the displayed gridlines.

c. Change the font used in the Category and Value labels to Times New Roman.

d. Turn the major gridlines back on.

e. Change the title's font to Times New Roman.

f. Save your work.

5. **Enhance a chart.**
   a. Make sure the chart is still selected, click Chart on the menu bar, click Chart Options, then click the Titles tab.
   b. Click the Category (X) axis text box, then type "Software" in the selected text box below the x-axis.
   c. Click the Value (Y) axis text box, type "Users" in the selected text box to the left of the y-axis, then click OK.
   d. Change the legend entry for "Production" to "Art."
   e. Add a drop shadow to the title.
   f. Save your work.

6. **Annotate and draw on a chart.**
   a. Select the chart.
   b. Create the text annotation "Need More Users."
   c. Drag the text annotation under the title.
   d. Click the Arrow button on the Drawing toolbar.
   e. Click below the text annotation, drag the arrow so it points to the area containing the Access columns, then release the mouse button.
   f. Save your work.

7. **Preview and print a chart.**
   a. Deselect the chart and type your name in cell A30.
   b. Preview the chart and data to see how it will look when printed.
   c. Change the paper orientation to landscape.
   d. Center the data and chart horizontally and vertically on the page.
   e. Click Print in the Print Preview window.
   f. Select the chart.
   g. Preview, then print only the chart.
   h. Save your work, close the workbook, then exit Excel.

Excel 2000

# ► Independent Challenges

**1.** You are the operations manager for the Springfield Theater Group. Each year the city of Springfield applies to various state and federal agencies for matching funds. The city's marketing department wants you to create charts for a report that will be used to document the number of productions in previous years. You need to create charts that show the number of previously produced plays.

To complete this independent challenge:

a. Sketch a sample worksheet on a piece of paper describing how you will create the charts. Which type of chart is best suited for the information you need to display? What kind of chart enhancements will be necessary? Will a 3-D effect make your chart easier to understand?

b. Start Excel, open the workbook EX D-2 from your Project Disk, then save it as "Theater Group."

c. Create a column chart for the data.

d. Change at least one of the colors used in a data series.

e. Create at least two additional charts for the same data to show how different chart types display the same data.

f. After creating the charts, make the appropriate enhancements. Include chart titles, legends, and value and category titles.

g. Add data labels.

h. Type your name in a cell in the worksheet.

i. Before printing, preview the file so you know what the charts will look like. Adjust any items as needed.

j. Save your work. Print the worksheet (charts and data).

k. Close the workbook and exit Excel.

**2.** One of your responsibilities at the Beautiful You Salon is to re-create the company's records using Excel. Another is to convince the current staff that Excel can make daily operations easier and more efficient. You've decided to create charts using the previous year's operating expenses. These charts will be used at the next monthly meeting.

To complete this independent challenge:

a. Decide which data in the worksheet should be charted. Sketch two sample charts. What type of charts are best suited for the information you need to display? What kind of chart enhancements will be necessary?

b. Start Excel, open the workbook EX D-3 from your Project Disk, and save it as "BY Expense Charts."

c. Create a column chart containing the expense data for all four quarters.

d. Using the same data, create two additional charts using different chart types.

e. Add annotated text and arrows (to the initial chart) highlighting any important data or trends that you can see from the charts.

f. In one chart, change the colors of data series, and in another chart, use black-and-white patterns only.

g. Type your name in a cell in the worksheet.

h. Before printing, preview the file so you know what the charts will look like. Adjust any items as needed.

i. Print the charts. Save your work.

j. Close the workbook and exit Excel.

**3.** The Step Lightly Ad Agency is delighted with the way you've organized their membership roster using Excel. The Board of Directors wants to assess certain advertising expenses and has asked you to prepare charts that can be used in their presentation.

To complete this independent challenge:

**a.** Start Excel, open the workbook EX D-4 from your Project Disk, and save it as "Step Lightly."

**b.** Use the raw data for the sample shown in the range A16:B24 to create charts.

**c.** Decide what types of charts would be best suited for this type of data. Sketch two sample charts. What kind of chart enhancements will be necessary?

**d.** Create at least three different chart types that show the distribution of advertising expenses.

**e.** Add annotated text and arrows highlighting important data, such as the largest expense.

**f.** Change the color of at least one data series.

**g.** Add Category and Value axis titles; add a chart title. Format the titles with a font of your choice. Place a drop shadow around the chart title.

**h.** Type your name in a cell in the worksheet.

**i.** Before printing, preview the file so you know what the charts will look like. Adjust any items as needed. Be sure the chart is placed appropriately on the page.

**j.** Print the charts, save your work, then close the workbook and exit Excel.

**WEB WORK**

**4.** During the second quarter of the year, the New York City MediaLoft store decided to analyze sales by type of book for a three-month period. Sales have been steadily increasing and the manager of the store is planning to renovate the space. Depending on which books sell best for the store location, the manager will reallocate the selling floor space accordingly. To be able to present this information to see which types of books are the best sellers, you will chart the analysis to get a graphical representation of the distributions. You decide to create two types of charts for the same data.

To complete this independent challenge:

**a.** Start Excel, open a new workbook, and save it on your Project Disk as "New York Analysis."

**b.** Connect to the Internet, go to the MediaLoft intranet site at http://www.course.com/illustrated/MediaLoft, then click the link for the Accounting page.

**c.** Copy the New York Analysis data into your worksheet.

**d.** Create a column chart with the data series in rows on the same worksheet as the data. Include a descriptive title and the following text: "Type of Book" in the Category axis, and "Sales" in the Value axis.

**e.** Place the chart on the same sheet as the data.

**f.** Move the chart so that it is below the data and the left side of the chart is in column A.

**g.** Format the legend so that it is placed along the bottom of the chart.

**h.** Change the color of the Science Fiction data series to fuschia.

**i.** Remove the gridlines.

**j.** Using the same data, create a 3-D bar chart (use the Clustered bar with the 3-D visual effect) with the data series in rows on a new sheet.

**k.** Add appropriate title(s) to the worksheet and axes.

**l.** Format the Value axis so the numbers display no decimal places, and a 1000 separator (comma).

**m.** Type your name in a visible cell in the worksheet containing the data.

**n.** Preview the chart and change margins as needed.

**o.** Print the worksheet data and column chart, making setup modifications as necessary.

**p.** Print the 3-D bar chart making any setup modifications as necessary.

**q.** Save the workbook and exit Excel.

# ► Visual Workshop

Modify a worksheet using the skills you learned in this unit, using Figure D-22 for reference. Open the file EX D-5 from your Project Disk, and save it as "Quarterly Advertising Budget." Create the chart, then change the data to reflect Figure D-22. Type your name in cell A13, save, preview, and then print your results.

FIGURE D-22

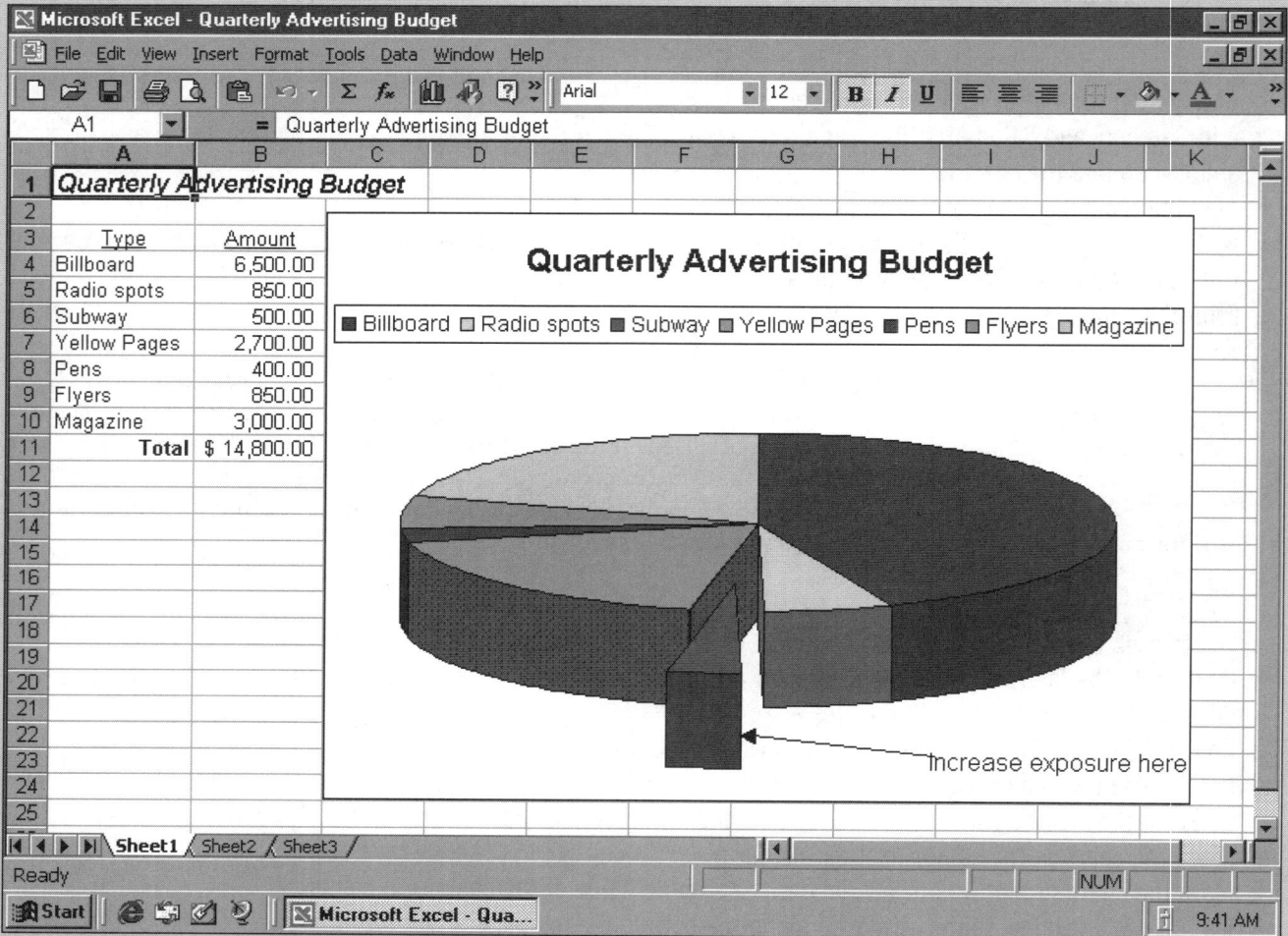

# Excel 2000

Unit **E**

# Working

## with Formulas and Functions

### Objectives

- MOUS ► **Create a formula with several operators**
- MOUS ► **Use names in a formula**
- MOUS ► **Generate multiple totals with AutoSum**
- MOUS ► **Use dates in calculations**
- MOUS ► **Build a conditional formula with the IF function**
- MOUS ► **Use statistical functions**
- MOUS ► **Calculate payments with the PMT function**
- MOUS ► **Display and print formula contents**

Without formulas, Excel would simply be an electronic grid with text and numbers. Used with formulas, Excel becomes a powerful data analysis software tool. As you learn how to analyze data using different types of formulas, including those that call for functions, you will discover more ways to use Excel. In this unit, you will gain a further understanding of Excel formulas and learn how to build several Excel functions. ◄━━ Top management at MediaLoft has asked Jim Fernandez to analyze various company data. To do this, Jim creates several worksheets that require the use of formulas and functions. Because management is considering raising salaries for store managers, Jim's first task is to create a report that compares the payroll deductions and net pay for store managers before and after a proposed raise.

# Creating a Formula with Several Operators

You can create formulas that contain a combination of cell references (for example, Z100 and B2), operators (for example, * [multiplication] and − [subtraction]), and values (for example, 99 or 1.56). You also can create a single formula that performs several calculations. If you enter a formula with more than one operator, Excel performs the calculations in a particular sequence based on algebraic rules called **precedence**; that is, Excel performs the operation(s) within the parentheses first, then performs the other calculations. See Table E-1. ▰▰▰ Jim has been given the gross pay and payroll deductions for the first payroll period and needs to complete his analysis. He also has preformatted, with the Comma style, any cells that are to contain values. Jim begins by entering a formula for net pay that subtracts the payroll deductions from gross pay.

## Steps

**QuickTip**

To return personalized tool-bars and menus to their default state, click Tools on the menu bar, click Customize, click the Options tab in the Customize dialog box, click Reset my usage data to restore the default settings, click Yes, click Close, then close the Drawing toolbar if it is displayed.

1. Start Excel if necessary, open the workbook titled **EX E-1**, then save the workbook as **Pay Info for Store Mgrs**
   The first part of the net pay formula will go in cell B11.

2. Click **Edit** on the menu bar, click **Go To**, then type **B11** in the Reference box and click **OK**
   The Go To command is especially useful when you want to select a cell in a large worksheet.

3. Type **=B6-**
   Remember that you can type cell references in either uppercase or lowercase letters. (Excel automatically converts lowercase cell reference letters to uppercase.) If you make a mistake while building a formula, press [Esc] and begin again. You type the equal sign (=) to tell Excel that a formula follows, B6 to reference the cell containing the gross pay, and the minus sign (−) to indicate that the next entry will be subtracted from cell B6.

**Trouble?**

If you receive a message box indicating "Parentheses do not match," make sure you have included both a left and a right parenthesis.

4. Type **(B7+B8+B9+B10)** then click the **Enter button** ✓ on the formula bar
   The net pay for Payroll Period 1 appears in cell B11, as shown in Figure E-1. (*Note:* Your tool-bars may differ from those in the figure.) Because Excel performs the operations within parentheses first, you can control the order of calculations on the worksheet. (In this case, Excel sums the values in cells B7 through B10 first.) After the operations within the parentheses are completed, Excel performs the operations outside the parentheses. (In this case, Excel subtracts the total of range B7:B10 from cell B6.)

5. Copy the formula in cell **B11** into cells **C11:F11**, then return to cell **A1**
   The formula in cell B11 is copied to the range C11:F11 to complete row 11. See Figure E-2.

6. Save the workbook
   Jim is pleased with the formulas that calculate net pay totals.

TABLE E-1: **Example formulas using parentheses and several operators**

| formula | order of precedence | calculated result |
|---------|--------------------|--------------------|
| =36+(1+3) | Add 1 to 3; then add the result to 36 | 40 |
| =(10−20)/10−5 | Subtract 20 from 10; divide that by 10; then subtract 5 | −6 |
| =(10*2)*(10+2) | Multiply 10 by 2; add 10 to 2; then multiply the results | 240 |

FIGURE E-1: Worksheet showing formula and result

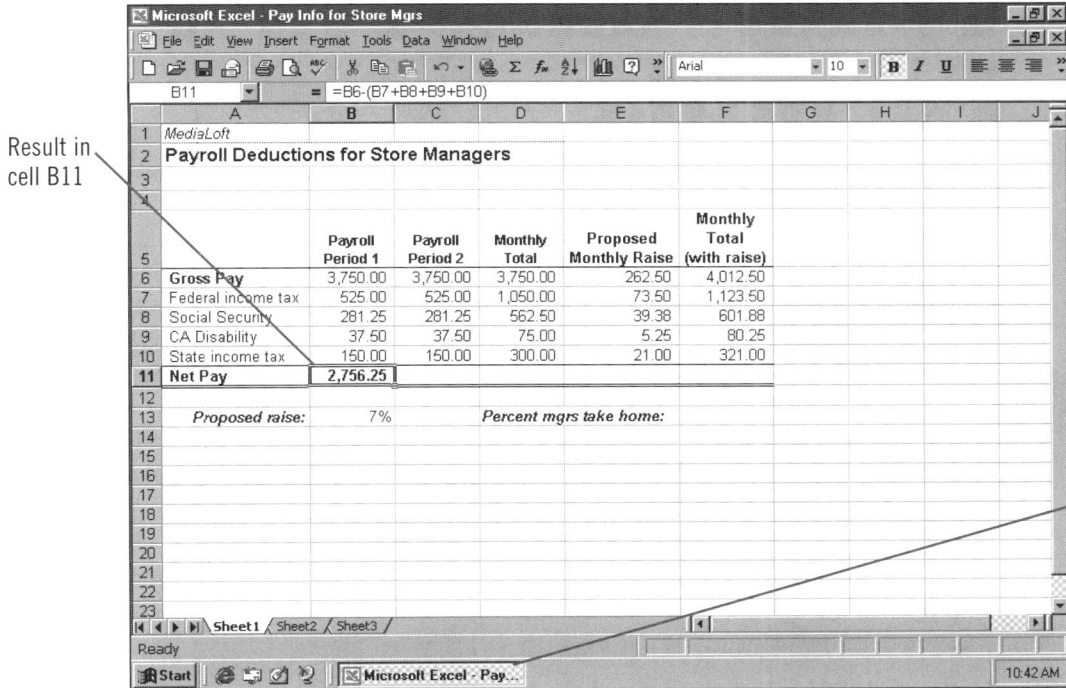

Result in cell B11

Your task bar may show a filename first if you've had other Excel files open

FIGURE E-2: Worksheet with copied formulas

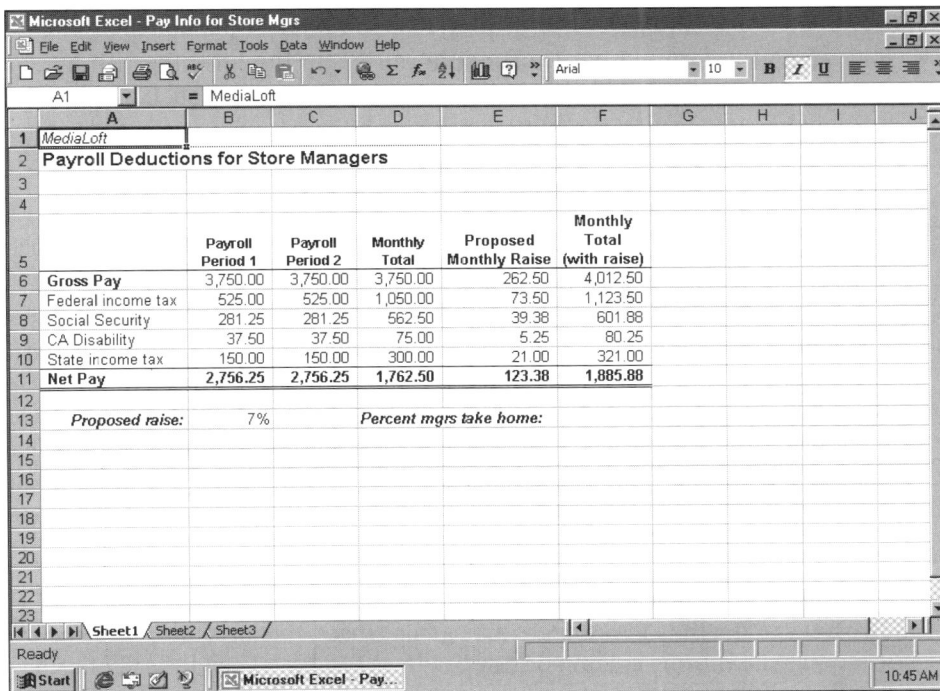

## Using Paste Special to paste formulas and values and to perform calculations

You can use the Paste Special command to quickly enter formulas and values or even to perform quick calculations. Click the cell(s) containing the formula or value you want to copy, click the Copy button on the Standard toolbar, then right-click the cell where you want the result to appear. In the pop-up menu, choose Paste Special, then choose the feature you want to paste and click OK.

# Using Names in a Formula

You can assign names to cells and ranges. Doing so reduces errors and makes a worksheet easier to follow. You also can use names in formulas. Using names in formulas facilitates formula building and provides a frame of reference for formula logic—the names make formulas easy to recognize and maintain. The formula Revenue − Cost, for example, is much easier to comprehend than the formula A2 − D3. You can produce a list of workbook names and their references at any time. ![] Jim wants to include a formula that calculates the percentage of monthly gross pay the managers would actually take home (net pay) if a 7% raise is granted. He starts by naming the cells he'll use in the calculation.

## Steps 1234

1. **Click cell F6, click the name box on the formula bar to select the active cell reference, type Gross_with_Raise, then press [Enter]**
   The name assigned to cell F6, Gross_with_Raise, appears in the name box. Note that you must type underscores instead of spaces between words. Cell F6 is now named Gross_with_Raise to refer to the monthly gross pay amount that includes the 7% raise. The name box displays as much of the name as fits (Gross_with_...). The net pay cell needs a name.

2. **Click cell F11, click the name box, type Net_with_Raise, then press [Enter]**
   The new formula will use names instead of cell references.

3. **Click cell F13, type =Net_with_Raise/Gross_with_Raise, then click the Enter button ![] on the formula bar (make sure you begin the formula with an equal sign)**
   The formula bar now shows the new formula, and the result, 0.47, appears in the cell. If you add names to a worksheet after all the formulas have been entered, you must click Insert on the menu bar, point to Name, click Apply, click the name or names, then click OK. Cell F13 needs to be formatted in Percent style.

4. **Select cell F13, click Format on the menu bar, click Style, click the Style name list arrow, click Percent, then click OK**
   Notice that the result shown in cell F13, 47%, is rounded to the nearest whole percent as shown in Figure E-3. A **style** is a combination of formatting characteristics, such as bold, italic, and underlined. You can use the Style dialog box instead of the Formatting toolbar to apply styles. You can also use it to remove styles: select the cell that has a style and select Normal in the Style name list. To define your own style, select a cell, format it using the formatting toolbar (such as bold, italic, and 14 point), then open the Style dialog box and type a name for your style. Later, you can apply all those formatting characteristics simply by applying your new style from the dialog box.

5. **Enter your name into cell D1, return to cell A1, then save and print the worksheet**
   You can use the Label Ranges dialog box (Insert menu, Name submenu, Label command) to designate existing column or row headings as labels. Then instead of using cell references for the column or row in formulas, you can use the labels instead. (This feature is turned off by default. To turn it on, go to Tools/Options/Calculation tab/Accept labels in formulas.)

6. **Close the workbook**

FIGURE E-3: Worksheet formula that includes cell names

Formula with
cell names

Name box

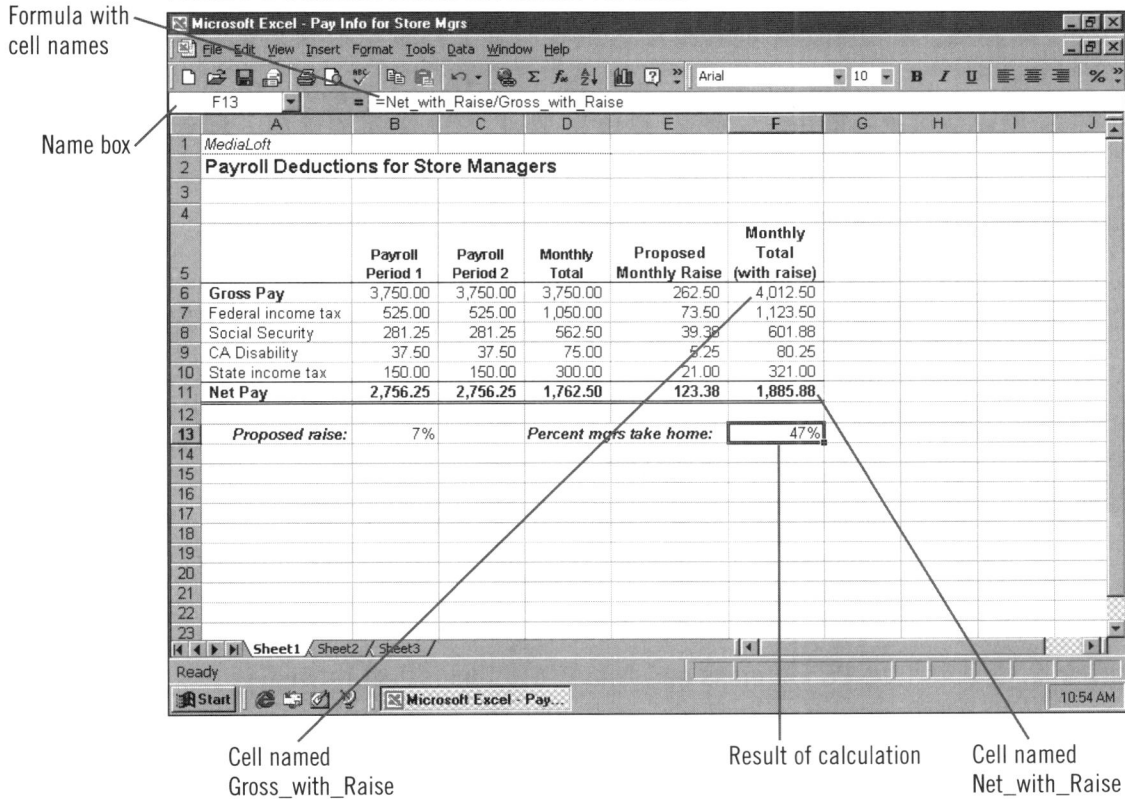

Cell named
Gross_with_Raise

Result of calculation

Cell named
Net_with_Raise

## CLUES TO USE

### Producing a list of names

You might want to verify the names you have in a workbook and the cells they reference. To paste a list of names in a workbook, select a blank cell that has several blank cells beside and beneath it. Click Insert on the menu bar, point to Name, then click Paste. In the Paste Name dialog box, click Paste List. Excel produces a list that includes the sheet name and the cell or range the name identifies. See Figure E-4.

FIGURE E-4: Worksheet with pasted list of names

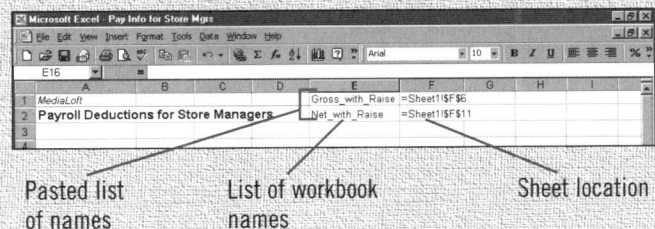

Pasted list
of names

List of workbook
names

Sheet location

# Generating Multiple Totals with AutoSum

In most cases, the result of a function is a value derived from a calculation. Functions can also return results such as text, references, or other information about the worksheet. You enter a function, such as AVERAGE, directly into a cell; you can use the Edit Formula button; or you can insert it with the Paste Function. You can use cell references, ranges, names, and formulas as arguments between the parentheses. (Recall that arguments are the information used in calculating the results of a function.) As with other cell entries, you can cut, copy, and paste functions from one area of the worksheet to another and from one workbook to another. The most widely used Excel function, SUM, calculates worksheet totals and can be entered easily using the AutoSum button on the Standard toolbar. Maria Abbot, MediaLoft's general sales manager, has given Jim a worksheet summarizing store sales. He needs to complete the worksheet totals.

**Steps**

**1.** Open the workbook titled **EX E-2**, type your name into cell D1, then save the workbook as **MediaLoft Sales**

You can use AutoSum to generate two sets of totals at the same time.

**2.** Select range **B5:E9**, press and hold [Ctrl], then select range **B11:E15**

To select nonadjacent cells, you must press and hold [Ctrl] while selecting the additional cells. Compare your selections with Figure E-5. The totals will appear in the last line of each selection.

**3.** Click the **AutoSum button** Σ on the Standard toolbar

When the selected range you want to sum (B5:E9 and B11:E15, in this example) includes a blank cell with data values above it, AutoSum enters the total in the blank cell.

**4.** Select range **B5:F17**, then click Σ

Whenever the selected range you want to sum includes a blank cell in the bottom row or right column, AutoSum enters the total in the blank cell. In this case, Excel ignores the data values and totals only the sums. Although Excel generates totals when you click the AutoSum button, it is a good idea to check the results.

**5.** Click cell **B17**

The formula bar reads =SUM(B15,B9). See Figure E-6. When generating grand totals, Excel automatically references the cells containing SUM functions with a comma separator between cell references. Excel uses commas to separate multiple arguments in all functions, not just in SUM.

**6.** Print the worksheet, then save and close the workbook

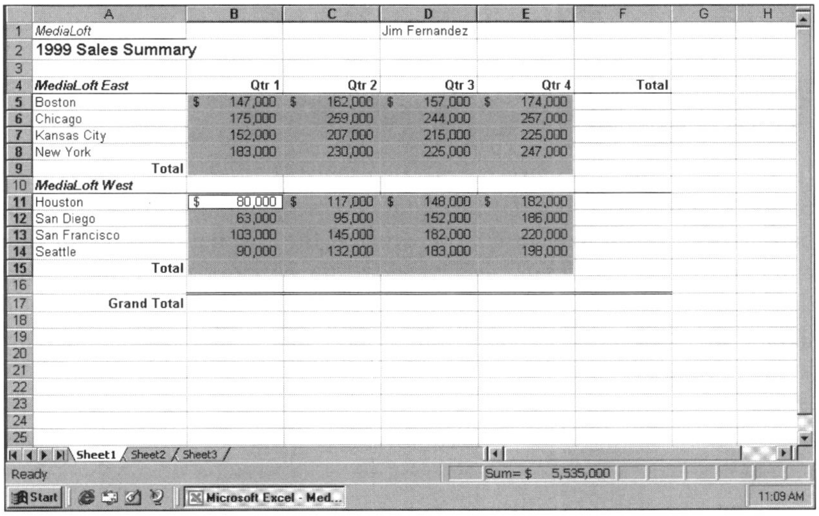

FIGURE E-6: Completed worksheet

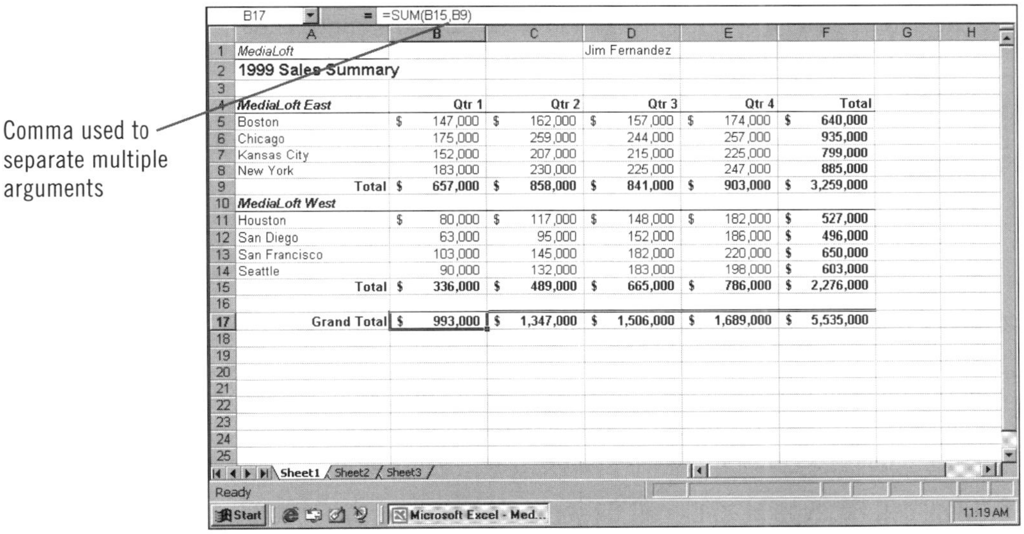

Comma used to separate multiple arguments

## Quick calculations with AutoCalculate

To check a total quickly without entering a formula, just select the range you want to sum, and the answer appears in the status bar next to SUM=. You also can perform other quick calculations, such as averaging or finding the minimum value in a selection. To do this, right-click the AutoCalculate area in the status bar and select from the list of options. The option you select remains in effect and in the status bar until you make another selection. See Figure E-7.

FIGURE E-7: Using AutoCalculate

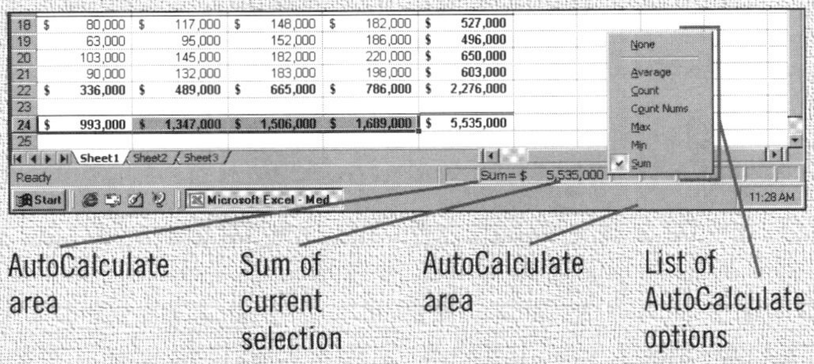

AutoCalculate area

Sum of current selection

AutoCalculate area

List of AutoCalculate options

# Using Dates in Calculations

If you enter dates in a worksheet so that Excel recognizes them as dates, you can sort (arrange) the dates and perform date calculations. For example, you can calculate the number of days between your birth date and today, which is the number of days you have been alive. When you enter an Excel date format, Excel considers the entry a date function, converts the date to a serial date number, and stores that number in the cell. A date's converted serial date is the number of days to that date. Excel automatically assigns the serial date of "1" to January 1, 1900 and counts up from there; the serial date of January 1, 2000, for example, is 36,526. ➤ Jim's next task is to complete the New York Accounts Payable worksheet. He remembers to enter the worksheet dates in a format that Excel recognizes so that he can use date calculation.

## Steps

1. **Open the workbook titled EX E-3, then save the workbook as New York Payables to the appropriate folder on your Project Disk**
   The calculations will be based on the current date, 4/1/00.

2. **Click cell C4, type 4/1/00, then press [Enter]**
   The date appears in cell C4 just as you typed it. You want to enter a formula that calculates the invoice due date, which is 30 days from the invoice date. The formula adds 30 days to the invoice date.

> **QuickTip**
> You also can perform time calculations in Excel. For example, you can enter an employee's starting time and ending time, then calculate how many hours and minutes he or she worked. You must enter time in a format that Excel recognizes; for example, 1:35 PM (h:mm AM/PM).

3. **Click cell E7, type =, click cell B7, type +30, then click the Enter button ✓ on the formula bar**
   Excel calculates the result by converting the 3/1/00 invoice date to a serial date number, adding 30 to it, then automatically formatting the result as a date. See Figure E-8. You can use the same formula to calculate the due dates of the other invoices.

4. **Drag the fill handle to copy the formula in cell E7 into cells E8:E13**
   Cell referencing causes the copied formula to contain the appropriate cell references. Now you are ready to enter the formula that calculates the age of each invoice. You do this by subtracting the invoice date from the current date. Because each invoice age formula must refer to the current date, you must make cell C4, the current date cell, an absolute reference in the formula.

> **QuickTip**
> If you perform date calculations and the intended numeric result displays as a date, format the cell(s) using a number format.

5. **Click cell F7, type =, click cell C4, press [F4] to add the absolute reference symbols ($), type −, click B7, then click ✓**
   The formula bar displays the formula $C$4−B7. The numerical result, 31, appears in cell F7 because there are 31 days between 3/1/00 and 4/1/00. You can use the same formula to calculate the age of the remaining invoices.

6. **Drag the fill handle to copy the formula in F7 to the range F8:F13, then press [Ctrl][Home]**
   The age of each invoice appears in column F, as shown in Figure E-9.

7. **Save the worksheet**

## CLUES TO USE

### Using date functions

When you want Excel to perform a calculation using the current date, you can choose date and time options such as NOW, DATE, and TODAY. DATE inserts any date whose month, day, and year you specify as arguments in the formula palette: =DATE(2000,7,6) will produce July 6, 2000, NOW inserts the current date and time, while TODAY inserts today's date only (you don't have to enter arguments for NOW or TODAY).

FIGURE E-8: Worksheet with formula for invoice due date

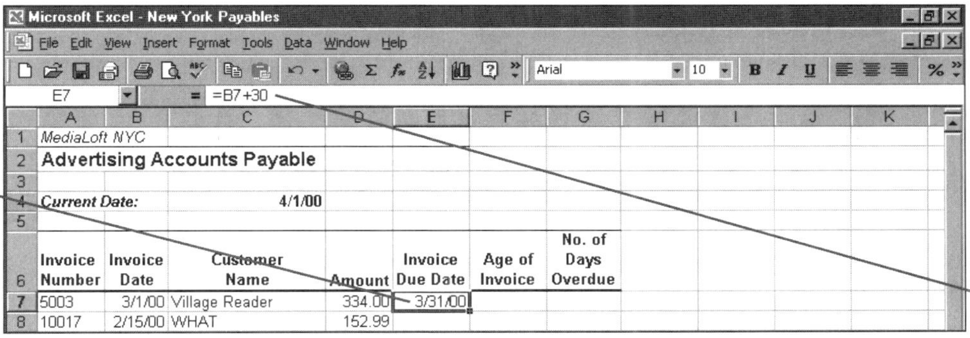

Formula result automatically calculated as date

Formula is invoice date + 30 days

FIGURE E-9: Worksheet with copied formulas

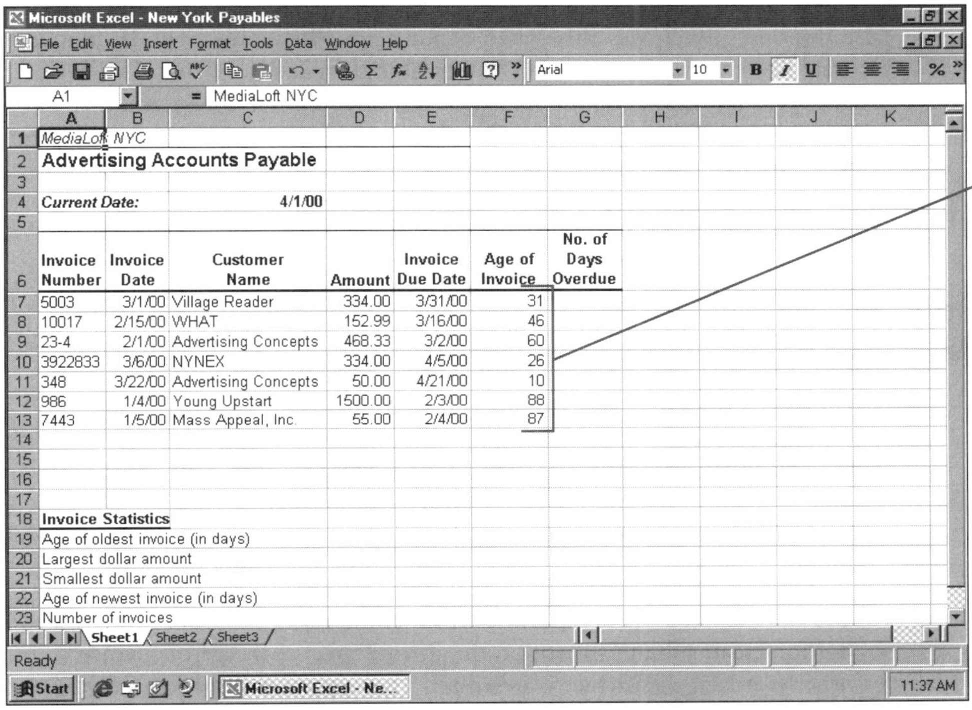

Age of each invoice automatically calculated

## Custom number and date formats

When you use numbers and dates in worksheets or calculations, you can use built-in Excel formats or create your own. The date you entered, 9/1/00, uses the Excel format m/d/yy. You could change it to the format d-mmm, or 1-Sep. The value $3,789 uses the number format $#,### where # represents positive numbers. To apply number formats, click Format on the menu bar, click Cells, then click the Number tab. In the category list, click a category, then specify the exact format in the list or scroll box to the right. To create a custom format, click Custom in the category list, then click a format that resembles the one you want. In the Type box, edit the symbols until they represent the format you want, then click OK. See Figure E-10.

FIGURE E-10: Custom formats on the Number tab in the Format Cells dialog box

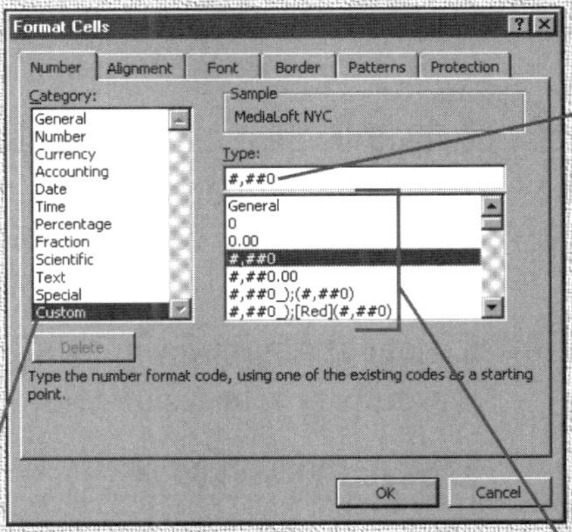

Edit these symbols to customize this format

Custom formats category

Custom formats

# Building a Conditional Formula with the IF Function

You can build a conditional formula using an IF function. A **conditional formula** is one that makes calculations based on stated conditions. For example, you can build a formula to calculate bonuses based on a person's performance rating. If a person is rated a 5 (the stated condition) on a scale of 1 to 5, with 5 being the highest rating, he or she receives 10% of his or her salary as a bonus; otherwise, there is no bonus. When the condition is a question that can be answered with a true or false response, Excel calls this stated condition a **logical test**. The IF function has three parts, separated by commas: a condition or logical test, an action to take if the logical test or condition is true, then an action to take if the logical test or condition is false. Another way of expressing this is: IF(test_cond,do_this,else_this). Translated into an Excel IF function, the formula to calculate bonuses would look something like this: IF(Rating=5,Salary*0.10,0). The translation would be: If the rating equals 5, multiply the salary by 0.10 (the decimal equivalent of 10%), then place the result in the selected cell. If the rating does not equal 5, place a 0 in the cell. When entering the logical test portion of an IF statement, you typically use some combination of the comparison operators listed in Table E-2. ✏ Jim is almost finished with the worksheet. To complete it, he needs to use an IF function that calculates the number of days each invoice is overdue.

## Steps 1234

**1.** Click cell **G7**

The cell pointer is now positioned where the result of the function will appear. You want the formula to calculate the number of days overdue as follows: If the age of the invoice is greater than 30, calculate the days overdue (Age of Invoice − 30), and place the result in cell G7; otherwise, place a 0 (zero) in the cell. The formula will include the IF function and cell references.

**2.** Type **=IF(F7>30,** (be sure to type the comma)

You have entered the first part of the function, the logical test. Notice that you used the symbol for greater than (>). So far, the formula reads: If Age of Invoice is greater than 30 (in other words, if the invoice is overdue). The next part of the formula tells Excel the action to take if the invoice is over 30 days old.

**3.** Type **F7-30,** (be sure to type the comma)

This part of the formula, between the first and second commas, is what you want Excel to do if the logical test is true (that is, if the age of the invoice is over 30). Continuing the translation of the formula, this part means: Take the Age of Invoice value and subtract 30. The last part of the formula tells Excel the action to take if the logical test is false (that is, if the age of the invoice is 30 days or less).

**4.** Type **0**, then click the **Enter button** ✅ on the formula bar (you do not have to type the closing parenthesis) to complete the formula

The formula is complete, and the result, 1 (the number of days overdue), appears in cell G7. See Figure E-11.

**5.** Copy the formula in cell G7 into cells **G8:G13** and return to cell A1

Compare your results with Figure E-12.

**6.** Save the workbook

FIGURE E-11: Worksheet with IF function

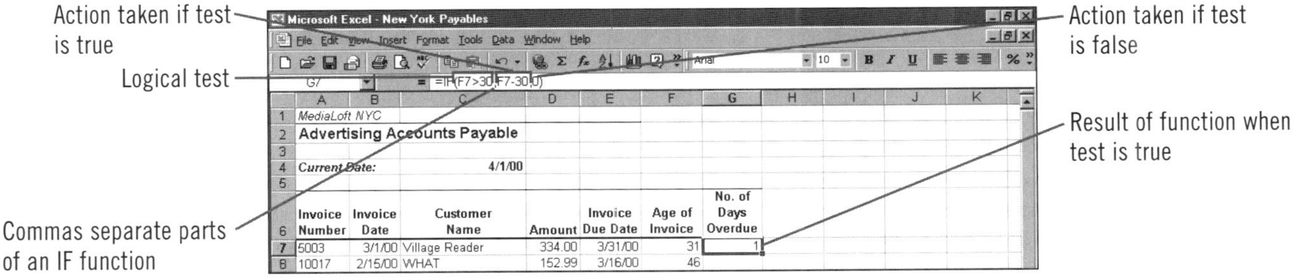

Action taken if test is true
Logical test
Commas separate parts of an IF function
Action taken if test is false
Result of function when test is true

FIGURE E-12: Completed worksheet

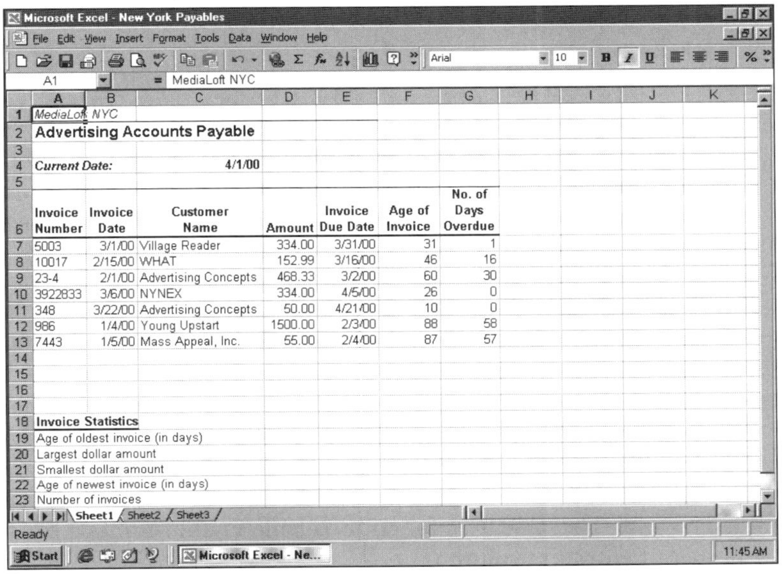

TABLE E-2: Comparison operators

| operator | function |
|---|---|
| < | Less than |
| > | Greater than |
| = | Equal to |
| <= | Less than or equal to |
| >= | Greater than or equal to |
| <> | Not equal to |

### CLUES TO USE

## Inserting and deleting selected cells

As you add formulas to your workbook, you may need to insert or delete cells, not entire rows or columns. When you do this, Excel automatically adjusts cell references to reflect their new locations. To insert cells, click Insert on the menu bar, then click Cells. The Insert dialog box opens, asking if you want to insert a cell and move the selected cell down or to the right of the new one. To delete one or more selected cells, click Edit on the menu bar, click Delete, and, in the Delete dialog box, indicate which way you want to move the adjacent cells. Be careful when using this option that you do not disturb row or column alignment that may be necessary to make sense of the worksheet.

# Using Statistical Functions

Excel offers several hundred worksheet functions. A small group of these functions calculates statistics such as averages, minimum values, and maximum values. See Table E-3 for a brief description of these commonly used functions. ✐ Jim wants to present detailed information about open accounts payable. To do this, he adds some statistical functions to the worksheet. He begins by using the MAX function to calculate the maximum value in a range.

## Steps

1. **Click cell D19, type =MAX(, select range G7:G13, then press [Enter]**
   Excel automatically adds the right parenthesis after you press [Enter]. The age of the oldest invoice (or maximum value in range G7:G13) is 58 days, as shown in cell D19. Next, Jim builds a formula to calculate the largest dollar amount among the outstanding invoices.

2. **In cell D20, type =MAX(, select range D7:D13, then press [Enter]**
   The largest outstanding invoice, for $1500.00, is shown in cell D20. The MIN function finds the smallest dollar amount and the age of the newest invoice.

3. **In cell D21, type =MIN(, select range D7:D13, then press [Enter]; in cell D22, type =MIN(, select range F7:F13, then press [Enter]**
   The smallest dollar amount owed is $50.00, as shown in cell D21, and the newest invoice is 10 days old. The COUNT function calculates the number of invoices by counting the number of entries in column A.

4. **In cell D23, type =, then click the Paste Function button** 🔧 **on the Standard toolbar to open the Paste Function dialog box**

5. **Under Function category, click Statistical, then under Function name, click COUNT**
   After selecting the function name, notice that the description of the COUNT function reads, "Counts the number of cells that contain numbers..." Because the invoice numbers are formatted in General rather than in the Number format, they are considered text entries, not numerical entries, so the COUNT function will not work. There is another function, COUNTA, that counts the number of cells that are not empty and therefore can be used to count the number of invoice number entries.

6. **Under Function name, click COUNTA, then click OK**
   Excel opens the Formula Palette and automatically references the range that is directly above the active cell as the first argument (in this case, range D19:D22, which is not the range you want to count). See Figure E-13. You need to select the correct range of invoice numbers. Because the desired invoice numbers are not visible, you need to collapse the dialog box so that you can select the correct range.

7. **With the Value1 argument selected in the Formula Palette, click the Value1 Collapse Dialog Box button** 📲, **select range A7:A13 in the worksheet, click the Redisplay Dialog Box button** 🖼, **then click OK**
   Cell D23 confirms that there are seven invoices. Compare your worksheet with Figure E-14.

8. **Type your name into cell D1, press [Ctrl][Home], then save, print, and close the workbook**

Edit Formula button

Click to pick a different function

Formula Palette

Collapse Dialog Box button

Result of the COUNTA function

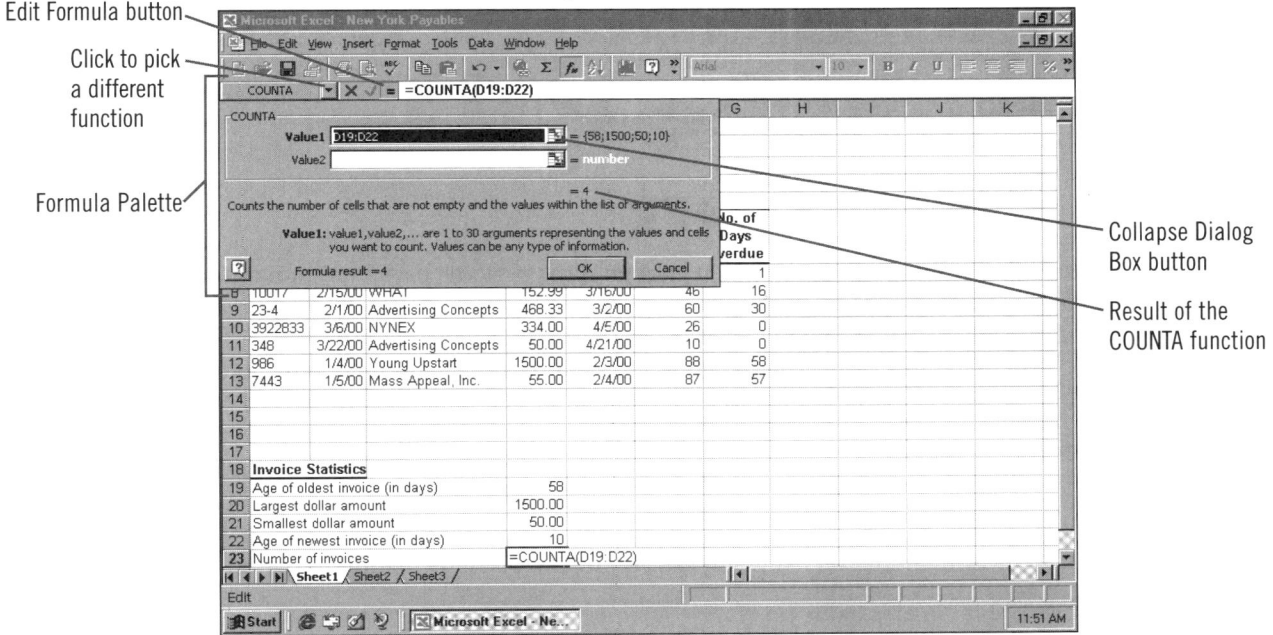

FIGURE E-14: Worksheet with invoice statistics

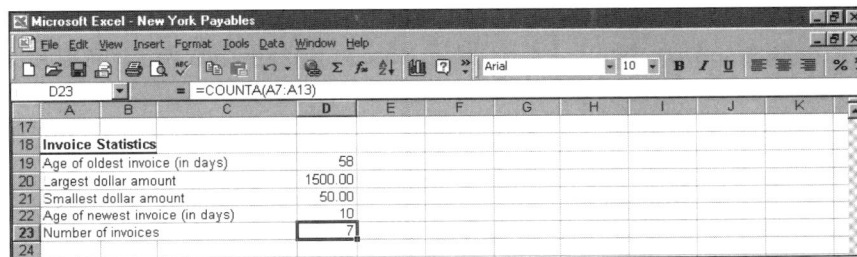

TABLE E-3: Commonly used statistical functions

| function | worksheet action |
|----------|------------------|
| AVERAGE | Calculates an average value |
| COUNT | Counts the number of values |
| COUNTA | Counts the number of nonblank entries |
| MAX | Finds the largest value |
| MIN | Finds the smallest value |
| SUM | Calculates a total |

## CLUES TO USE

### Using the Formula Palette to enter and edit formulas

When you use the Paste Function to build a formula, the Formula Palette displays the name and description for the function and each of its arguments, the current result of the function, and the current result of the entire formula. You also can use the Formula Palette to edit functions in formulas. To open the Formula Palette from either a blank cell or one containing a formula, click the Edit Formula button = on the formula bar.

Excel 2000

# Calculating Payments with the PMT Function

PMT is a financial function that calculates the periodic payment amount for money borrowed. For example, if you want to borrow money to buy a car, the PMT function can calculate your monthly payment on the loan. Let's say you want to borrow $15,000 at 9% interest and pay the loan off in five years. The Excel PMT function can tell you that your monthly payment will be $311.38. The parts of the PMT function are: PMT(rate, nper, pv, fv, type). See Figure E-15 for an illustration of a PMT function that calculates the monthly payment in the car loan example.

For several months, MediaLoft management has been discussing the expansion of the San Diego store. Jim has obtained quotes from three different lenders on borrowing $25,000 to begin the expansion. He obtained loan quotes from a commercial bank, a venture capitalist, and an investment banker. Now Jim can summarize the information using the Excel PMT function.

**Steps** 1 2 3 4

1. **Open the workbook titled EX E-4, then save the workbook as San Diego Financing**
   Jim has already entered all the lender data; you are ready to calculate the commercial loan monthly payment in cell E5.

2. **Click cell E5, type =PMT(C5/12,D5,B5) (make sure you type the commas); then click the Enter button ✓ on the formula bar**
   You must divide the annual interest by 12 because you are calculating monthly, not annual, payments. Note that the payment of ($543.56) in cell E5 is a negative amount. (It appears in red on a color monitor.) Excel displays the result of a PMT function as a negative value to reflect the negative cash flow the loan represents to the borrower. Because you want to show the monthly payment value as a positive number, you can convert the loan amount to a positive number by placing a minus sign in front of the cell reference.

3. **Edit cell E5 so it reads =PMT(C5/12,D5,−B5), then click ✓**
   A positive value of $543.56 now appears in cell E5. See Figure E-16. You can use the same formula to generate the monthly payments for the other loans.

4. **With cell E5 selected, drag the fill handle to select range E5:E7**
   A monthly payment of $818.47 for the venture capitalist loan appears in cell E6. A monthly payment of $1,176.84 for the investment banker loan appears in cell E7. The loans with shorter terms have much higher payments. You will not know the entire financial picture until you calculate the total payments and total interest for each lender.

5. **Click cell F5, type =E5*D5, then press [Tab]; in cell G5, type =F5−B5, then click ✓**

6. **Copy the formulas in cells F5:G5 into the range FG:G7, then return to cell A1**
   You can experiment with different interest rates, loan amounts, or terms for any one of the lenders; the PMT function generates a new set of values automatically. Compare your results with those in Figure E-17.

7. **Enter your name into cell D1, save the workbook, then print the worksheet**

FIGURE E-15: Example of PMT function for car loan

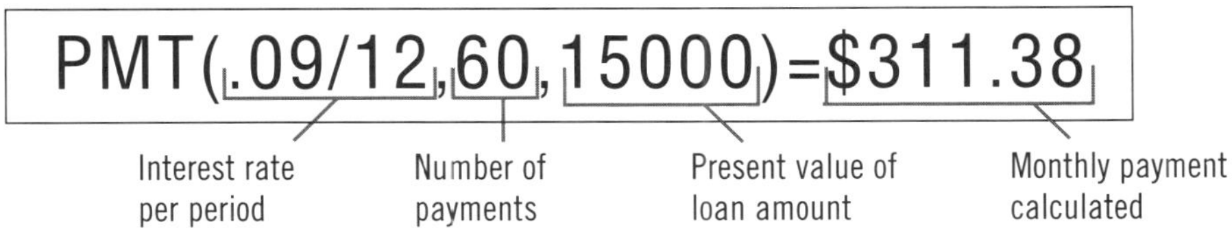

$$\text{PMT}(\underbrace{.09/12}_{\substack{\text{Interest rate} \\ \text{per period}}}, \underbrace{60}_{\substack{\text{Number of} \\ \text{payments}}}, \underbrace{15000}_{\substack{\text{Present value of} \\ \text{loan amount}}}) = \underbrace{\$311.38}_{\substack{\text{Monthly payment} \\ \text{calculated}}}$$

FIGURE E-16: PMT function calculating monthly loan payment

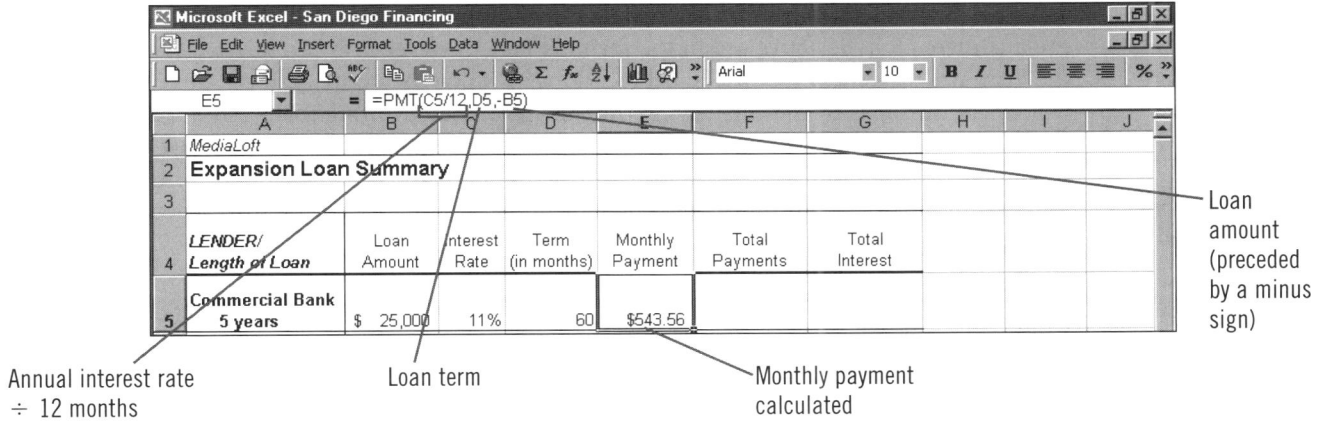

Annual interest rate ÷ 12 months

Loan term

Monthly payment calculated

Loan amount (preceded by a minus sign)

FIGURE E-17: Completed worksheet

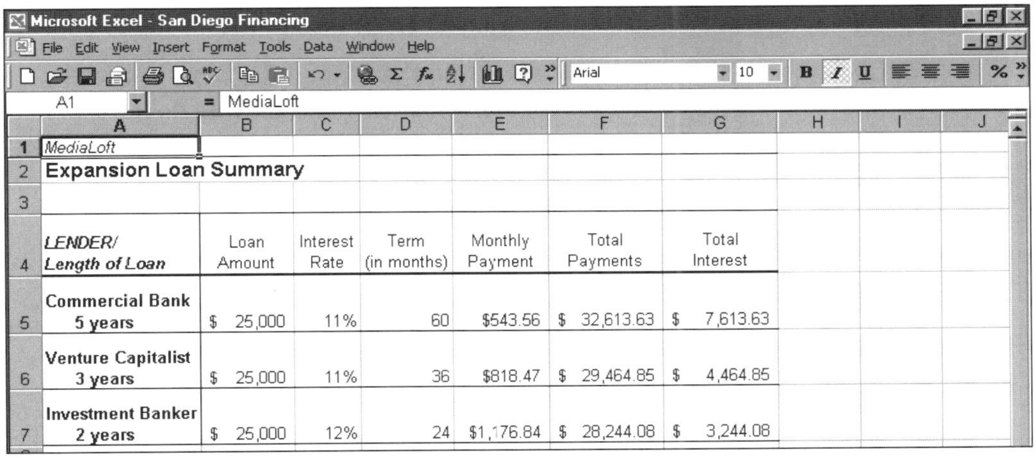

Excel 2000

## Calculating future value with the FV function

You can use the FV (Future Value) function to determine the amount of money a given monthly investment will amount to, at a given interest rate after a given number of payment periods. The syntax is similar to that of the PMT function: FV(rate,nper,pmt,pv,type). For example, suppose you want to invest $1,000 every month for the next 12 months into an account that pays 12% a year, and you want to know how much you will have at the end of 12 months (that is, its future value). You would enter the function FV(.01,12,-1000), and Excel would return the value $12,682.50 as the future value of your investment. As with the PMT function, the units for the rate and nper must be consistent. If you make monthly payments on a three-year loan at 6% annual interest, you would use the rate 6%/12 and 36 periods (12*3). The arguments pv and type are optional; pv is the present value, or the total amount the series of payments is worth now. If you omit it, Excel assumes the pv is 0. The Type argument indicates when the payments are made; 0 is the end of the period and 1 is the beginning of the period.

**WORKING WITH FORMULAS AND FUNCTIONS** EXCEL E-15

# Displaying and Printing Formula Contents

Excel usually displays the result of formula calculations in the worksheet area and displays formula contents for the active cell in the formula bar. However, you can instruct Excel to display the formulas directly in the worksheet locations in which they were entered. You can document worksheet formulas by first displaying the formulas, then printing them. These formula printouts are valuable paper-based worksheet documentation. Because formulas are often longer than their corresponding values, landscape orientation is the best choice for printing formulas. Jim is ready to produce a formula printout to submit with the worksheet.

**1.** Click **Tools** on the menu bar, click **Options**, then click the **View tab**

The View tab of the Options dialog box appears, as shown in Figure E-18.

**2.** Under Window options, click the **Formulas** check box to select it, then click **OK**

The columns widen and retain their original formats.

**3.** Scroll horizontally to bring columns E through G into view

Instead of formula results appearing in the cells, Excel shows the actual formulas. The column widths adjusted automatically to accommodate the formulas.

**4.** Click the **Print Preview button** 🔍 on the Standard toolbar

The status bar reads Preview: Page 1 of 3, indicating that the worksheet will print on three pages. You want to print it on one page and include the row number and column letter headings.

**5.** Click the **Setup button** in the Print Preview window, then click the **Page tab**

**6.** Under Orientation, click the **Landscape option button**; then under Scaling, click the **Fit to option button**

Selecting Landscape instructs Excel to print the worksheet sideways on the page. The Fit to option ensures that the document is printed on a single page.

**7.** Click the **Sheet tab**, under Print click the **Row and column headings check box** to select it, click **OK**, then position the **Zoom pointer** 🔍 over **column A** and click

The worksheet formulas now appear on a single page, in landscape orientation, with row (number) and column (letter) headings. See Figure E-19.

**8.** Click **Print** in the Print Preview window, then click **OK**

After you retrieve the printout, you want to return the worksheet to display formula results. You can do this easily by using a key combination.

**9.** Press **[Ctrl][`]** to redisplay formula results, save and close the workbook, then exit Excel

[Ctrl][`] (grave accent mark) toggles between displaying formula results and displaying formula contents.

FIGURE E-18: **View tab of the Options dialog box**

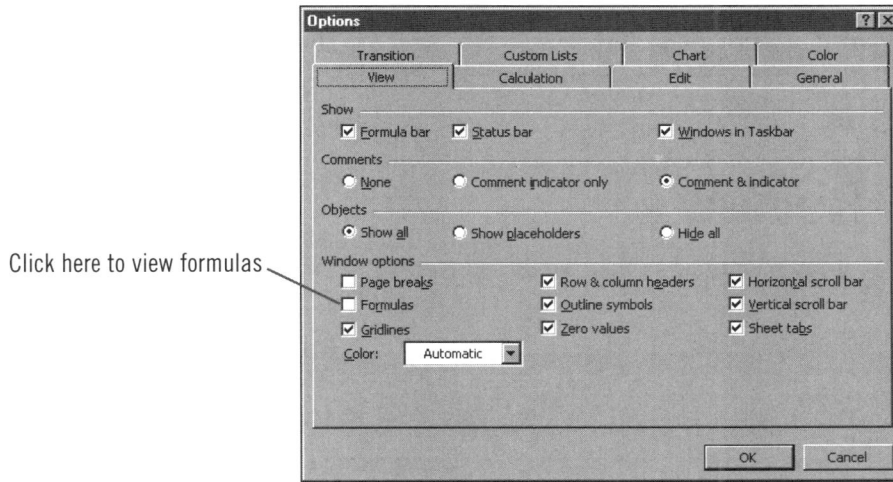

Click here to view formulas

FIGURE E-19: **Print Preview window**

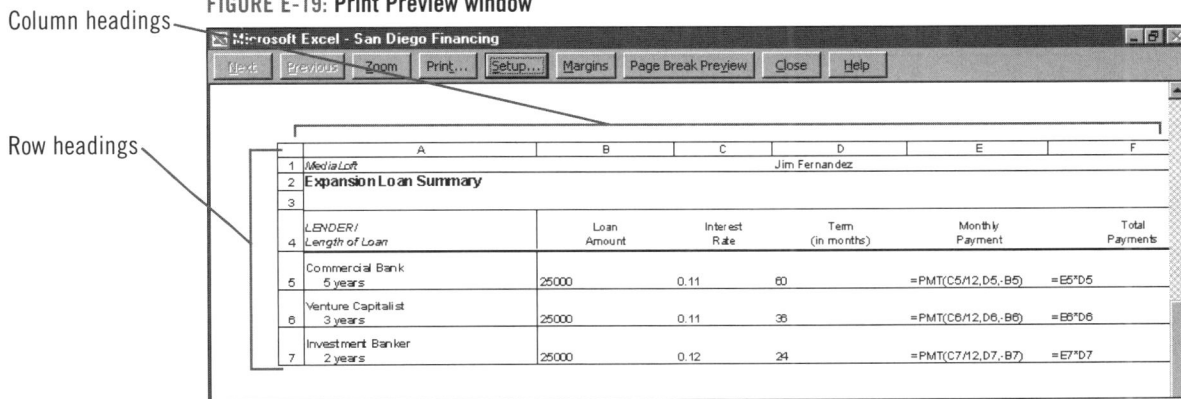

Column headings

Row headings

**Excel 2000**

CLUES TO USE

## Setting margins and alignment when printing part of a worksheet

Sometimes you want to print one part of a worksheet. While you may have set margins for printing the whole worksheet, you can set custom margins to print the smaller section. Select the range you want to print, click File on the menu bar, click Print, under Print what click Selection, then click Preview. In the Print Preview window, click Setup, then click the Margins tab. See Figure E-20. Double-click the margin numbers and type new ones. Use the Center on page check boxes to center the range horizontally or vertically. If you plan to print the range again in the future, save the view after you print: Click View on the menu bar, click Custom Views, click Add, then type a view name and click OK.

FIGURE E-20: **Margins tab in the Page Setup dialog box**

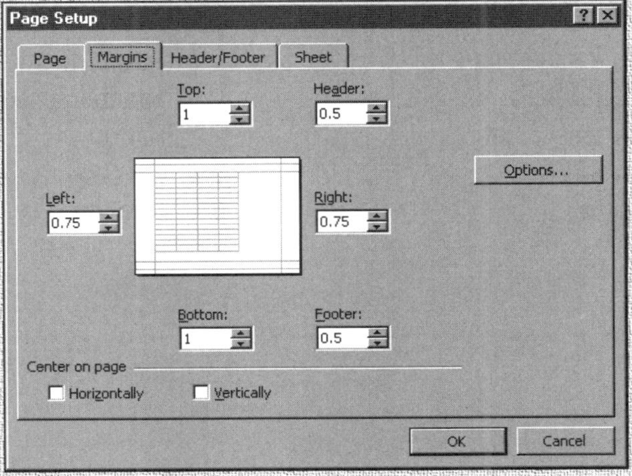

# ► Concepts Review

Label each element of the Excel screen shown in Figure E-21.

FIGURE E-21

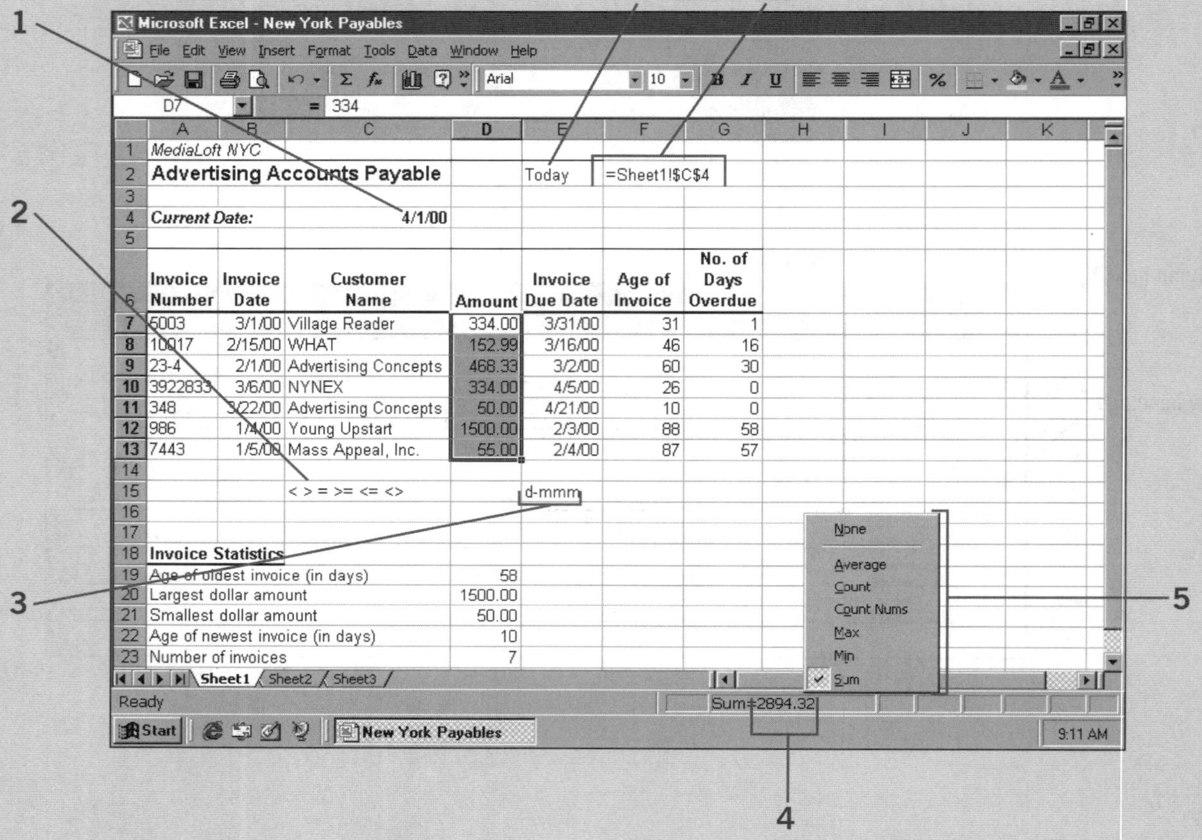

**Match each term with the statement that best describes its function.**

8. Parentheses
9. COUNTA
10. test_cond
11. COUNT
12. pv

a. Part of the IF function in which the conditions are stated
b. Function used to count the number of numerical entries
c. Part of the PMT function that represents the loan amount
d. Function used to count the number of nonblank entries
e. Symbols used in formulas to control formula calculation order

Select the best answer from the list of choices.

**13. To generate a positive payment value when using the PMT function, you must**
   **a.** Enter the function arguments as positive values.
   **b.** Enter the function arguments as negative values.
   **c.** Enter the amount being borrowed as a negative value.
   **d.** Enter the interest rate divisor as a negative value.

**14. When you enter the rate and nper arguments in a PMT function,**
   **a.** Multiply both units by 12.
   **b.** Be consistent in the units used.
   **c.** Divide both values by 12.
   **d.** Use monthly units instead of annual units.

**15. To express conditions such as less than or equal to, you can use a(n)**
   **a.** IF function.
   **b.** Comparison operator.
   **c.** AutoCalculate formula.
   **d.** PMT function.

**16. Which of the following statements is false?**
   **a.** $#,### is an Excel number format.
   **b.** You can create custom number and date formats in Excel.
   **c.** You can use only existing number and date formats in Excel.
   **d.** m/d/yy is an Excel date format.

# ▶ Skills Review

**1. Create a formula with several operators.**
   **a.** Open workbook EX E-5, enter your name into cell D1, and save the workbook as "Manager Bonuses".
   **b.** Select cell C15 using the Go To command.
   **c.** Enter the formula C13+(C14*7).
   **d.** Use the Paste Special command to paste the values in B4:B10 to G4:G10.

**2. Use names in a formula.**
   **a.** Name cell C13 "Dept_Bonus".
   **b.** Name cell C14 "Project_Bonus".
   **c.** In cell E4, enter the formula Dept_Bonus*D4+Project_Bonus.
   **d.** Copy the formula in cell E4 into the range E5:E10.
   **e.** Format range E4:E10 with the Comma Style button.
   **f.** In cell F4, enter a formula that sums C4 and E4.
   **g.** Copy the formula in cell F4 into the range F5:F10.
   **h.** Return to cell A1, then save your work.

**3. Generate multiple totals with AutoSum.**
   **a.** Select range E4:F11.
   **b.** Enter the totals using AutoSum.
   **c.** Format range E11:F11 using the Currency Style button.
   **d.** Return to cell A1, save your work, then preview and print this worksheet.

### 4. Use dates in calculations.

a. Make the Merit Pay sheet active.

b. In cell D6, enter the formula B6+183.

c. Copy the formula in cell D6 into the range D7:D14.

d. Use the NOW function to insert the date and time in cell A3, widening the column as necessary.

e. In cell E18, enter the text "Next Pay Date", and, in cell G18, use the Date function to enter the date 10/1/00.

f. Save your work.

### 5. Build a conditional formula with the IF function.

a. In cell F6, enter the formula IF(C6=5,E6*0.05,0).

b. Copy the formula in cell F6 into the range F7:F14.

c. Apply the comma format with no decimal places to F6:F14.

d. Select the range A4:G4 and delete the cells using the Delete command on the Edit menu. Shift the remaining cells up.

e. Repeat the procedure to delete the cells A15:G15.

f. Use the Cells command on the Insert menu to insert a cell between Department Statistics and Average Salary, moving the remaining cells down.

g. Check your formulas to make sure the cell references have been updated.

h. Save your work.

### 6. Use statistical functions.

a. In cell C18, enter a function to calculate the average salary in the range E5:E13 with no decimal places.

b. In cell C19, enter a function to calculate the largest bonus in the range F5:F13.

c. In cell C20, enter a function to calculate the lowest performance rating in the range C5:C13.

d. In cell C21, enter a function to calculate the number of entries in range A5:A13.

e. Enter your name in cell F3, then save, preview, and print this worksheet.

### 7. Calculate payments with the PMT function.

a. Make the Loan sheet active.

b. In cell B9, enter the formula PMT(B5/12,B6,−B4).

c. In cell B10, enter the formula B9*B6.

d. AutoFit column B, if necessary.

e. In cell B11, enter the formula B10−B4.

f. Enter your name in cell C1, then save and print the worksheet.

### 8. Display and print formula contents.

a. Use the View tab in the Options dialog box to turn formulas on.

b. Adjust the column widths as necessary.

c. Save, preview, and print this worksheet in landscape orientation with the row and column headings.

d. Close the workbook.

## ▶ Independent Challenges

**1.** As manager of Mike's Ice Cream Parlor, you have been asked to create a worksheet that totals the monthly sales of all store products. Your monthly report should include the following:

- Sales totals for the current month for each product
- Sales totals for the last month for each product
- The percent change in sales from last month to this month

To document the report further, you decide to include a printout of the worksheet formulas.
  To complete this independent challenge:

a. Open the workbook titled EX E-6, type your name into cell D1, then save the workbook as "Mike's Sales" to the appropriate folder on your Project Disk.

b. Enter today's date in cell A3. Create and apply a custom format.

c. Complete the headings for weeks 2 through 4. Enter totals for each week and current month totals for each product. Calculate the percent change in sales from last month to this month. (*Hint:* The formula in words would be (Current Month-Last Month)/Last Month.)

d. After you enter the percent change formula for regular ice cream, copy the formula down the column and format the column with the percentage style.

e. Apply a comma format with no decimal places to all numbers and totals.

f. Save, preview, then print the worksheet on a single page. If necessary, print in landscape orientation. If you make any page setup changes, save the worksheet again.

g. Display and print the worksheet formulas, then print the formulas on one page with row and column headings.

h. Close the workbook without saving the changes for displaying formulas.

**2.** You are an auditor with a certified public accounting firm. Fly Away, a manufacturer of skating products, including roller skates and skateboards, has contacted you to audit its financial records. The managers at Fly Away have asked you to assist them in preparing their year-end sales summary. Specifically, they want to add expenses and show the percent of annual expenses that each expense category represents. They also want to show what percent of annual sales each expense category represents. You should include a formula calculating the difference between sales and expenses and another formula calculating expenses divided by sales. The expense categories and their respective dollar amounts are as follows: Building Lease $45,000; Equipment $203,000; Office $23,000; Salary $345,000; Taxes $302,000. Use these expense amounts to prepare the year-end sales and expenses summary for Fly Away.
  To complete this independent challenge:

a. Open the workbook titled EX E-7, type your name into cell D1, then save the workbook as "Fly Away Sales".

b. Name the cell containing the formula for total annual expenses "Annual_Expenses". Use the name Annual_Expenses in the first formula calculating percent of annual expenses. Copy this formula as appropriate and apply the percentage style. Make sure to include a formula that sums all the values for percent of annual expenses, which should equal 1 or 100%.

c. Enter a formula calculating what percent of annual sales each expense category represents. Use the name Annual_Sales in the formula and format it appropriately. Enter formulas calculating annual sales minus annual expenses and expenses divided by sales using only the names Annual_Sales and Annual_Expenses. Add formulas for totals as appropriate.

d. Format the cells using the Currency, Percent, or Comma style. Widen the columns as necessary to display cell contents.

e. Save, preview, then print the worksheet on a single page. If necessary, use landscape orientation. Save any page setup changes you make.

f. Display and print worksheet formulas on a single page with row and column headings.

g. Close the workbook without saving the changes for displaying formulas.

**3.** As the owner of Custom Fit, a general contracting firm specializing in home-storage projects, you are facing yet another business challenge at your firm. Because jobs are taking longer than expected, you decide to take out a loan to purchase some new power tools. According to your estimates, you need a $5,000 loan to purchase the tools. You check three loan sources: the Small Business Administration (SBA), your local bank, and a consortium of investors. Each source offers you a loan on its own terms. The local bank offers you the loan at 9.5% interest over four years. The SBA will loan you the money at 9% interest, but you have to pay it off in three years. The consortium offers you an 8% loan, but they require you to pay it back in two years. To analyze all three loan options, you decide to build a tool loan summary worksheet. Using the loan terms provided, build a worksheet summarizing your options.

To complete this independent challenge:

a. Open a new workbook, type your name in cell A1, then save it as "Custom Fit Loan Options".

b. Enter today's date in cell A3.

c. Enter labels and worksheet data. You need headings for the loan source, loan amount, interest rate, term or number of payments, monthly payment, total payments, and total interest. Fill in the data provided for the three loan sources.

d. Enter formulas as appropriate: a PMT formula for the monthly payment; a formula calculating the total payments based on the monthly payment and term values; and a formula for total interest based on the total payments and the loan amount.

e. Format the worksheet as desired.

f. Save, preview, then print the worksheet on a single page using landscape orientation. Create a printout of worksheet formulas showing row and column headings. Do not save the worksheet with these settings.

**WEB WORK**

**4.** The MediaLoft accounting department has asked you to analyze overall MediaLoft CD sales and look at ways to improve them. The figures you will need are on the MediaLoft intranet site. This site gives employees access to companywide information. Accounting is considering taking out a $25,000 loan to buy new CD display cases for some of its stores.

To complete this independent challenge:

a. Start Excel, then open the File EX E-8, save it as CD Analysis on your Project Disk, and make sure the CD Sales tab is active.

b. Connect to the Internet, go to the MediaLoft intranet site at http://www.course.com/Illustrated/MediaLoft. Click the Accounting link, then click the CD Sales Analysis link. Print the CD Sales Analysis, disconnect from the Internet, and then, starting in cell A2, enter this data on the CD Sales sheet in the CD Analysis workbook, except for the Totals row. Enter formulas to calculate the totals in row 11 and label the row. Enter formulas to calculate the category totals in column F and label the column totals.

c. In row 13, enter a label in column A that reads "Goals", and enter the following sales goals for each quarter:

| Q1 | Q2 | Q3 | Q4 |
|---|---|---|---|
| 317,000 | 327,000 | 372,000 | 400,000 |

d. Enter a formula that totals the goals figures in cell F13.

e. In row 15, enter a label called "Real to Goal", and enter formulas for each loan that calculate the difference between goal and actual sales for each quarter and for the year's total.

f. In row 17, enter another label called "Status". For each quarter, use the IF function that displays the text "Over Goal" if the Real to Goal total is a positive number (in other words, >0). Otherwise, have it print "Under Goal". Format the cells, AutoFit the columns as necessary, and save the worksheet.

g. Go to the CD Loan worksheet and use the PMT function to calculate the monthly payment for each loan, making sure it displays as a positive number.

h. Enter a formula in column F that calculates the total interest for each loan. It should multiply the monthly payment by the term of the loan, and then subtract the original loan amount from the result.

i. For each loan, the respective banks have given MediaLoft a certain number of days to respond, after which their loan offers will no longer be valid. In the Inform by column, enter a formula for each loan that adds the number of days in column G to today's date, displaying the date by which MediaLoft must respond. (*Hint:* Use the TODAY function to enter today's date in the formula.)

j. In cells B8:B10, use Excel functions to enter the shortest term, the lowest rate, and the average interest rate, then display and print the formulas for the CD Loan sheet.

k. Print the CD Sales and CD Loan worksheets, then save and close the workbook.

# ► Visual Workshop

Create the worksheet shown in Figure E-22. (Hint: Enter the items in range C9:C11 as labels by typing an apostrophe before each formula.) Type your name in row 1, and save the workbook as "Car Payment Calculator" to the appropriate folder on your Project Disk. Preview, then print, the worksheet.

FIGURE E-22

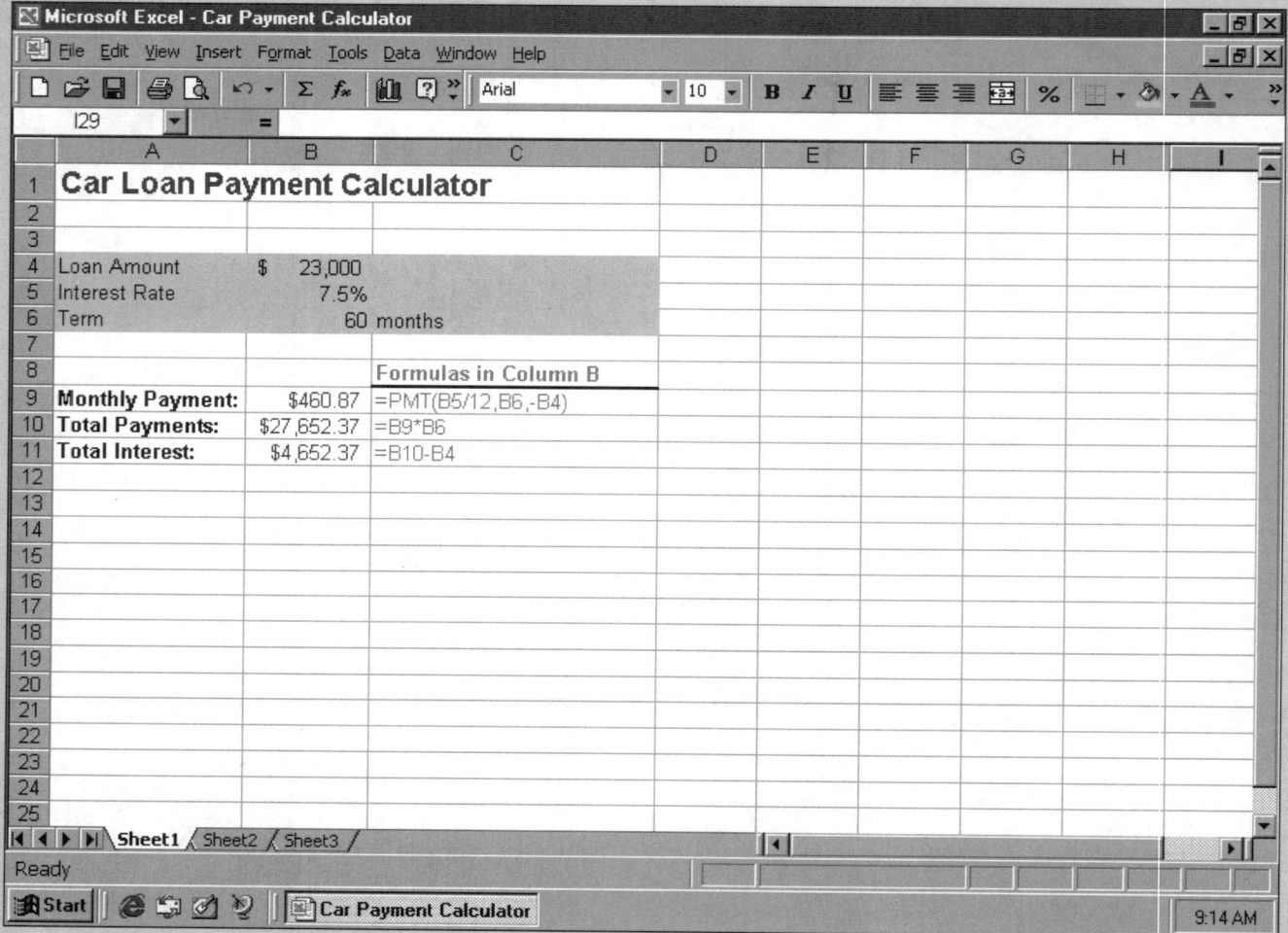

# Managing

## Workbooks and Preparing Them for the Web

### Objectives

- MOUS ▶ **Freeze columns and rows**
- MOUS ▶ **Insert and delete worksheets**
- MOUS ▶ **Consolidate data with 3-D references**
- MOUS ▶ **Hide and protect worksheet areas**
- ▶ **Save custom views of a worksheet**
- MOUS ▶ **Control page breaks and page numbering**
- MOUS ▶ **Create a hyperlink between Excel files**
- MOUS ▶ **Save an Excel file as an HTML document**

In this unit you will learn several Excel features to help you manage and print workbook data. You will also learn how to prepare workbooks for publication on the World Wide Web. ✎━━ MediaLoft's accounting department asks Jim Fernandez to design a timecard summary worksheet to track salary costs for hourly workers. He designs a worksheet using some employees from the MediaLoft Houston store. When the worksheet is complete, the accounting department will add the rest of the employees and place it on the MediaLoft intranet site for review by store managers. Jim will save the worksheet in HTML format for viewing on the site.

# Freezing Columns and Rows

**Excel 2000**

As rows and columns fill up with data, you might need to scroll through the worksheet to add, delete, modify, and view information. Looking at information without row or column labels can be confusing. In Excel, you can temporarily freeze columns and rows, which enables you to view separate areas of your worksheets at the same time. **Panes** are the columns and rows that **freeze**, or remain in place, while you scroll through your worksheet. The freeze feature is especially useful when you're dealing with large worksheets. Sometimes, though, even freezing is not sufficient. In those cases, you can create as many as four areas, or panes, on the screen at one time and move freely within each of them. ▰▰▰ Jim needs to verify the total hours worked, hourly pay rate, and total pay for salespeople Paul Cristifano and Virginia Young. Because the worksheet is becoming more difficult to read as its size increases, Jim needs to freeze the column and row labels.

**Steps**

### QuickTip

To return personalized toolbars and menus to their default state, click Tools on the menu bar, click Customize, click Reset my usage data on the Options tab, click Yes, then click Close.

1. **Start Excel if necessary, open the workbook titled EX F-1, save it as Timecard Summary, scroll through the Monday worksheet to view the data and click cell D6**
   You move to cell D6 because you want to freeze columns A, B, and C. By doing so, you will be able to see each employee's last name, first name, and timecard number on the screen when you scroll to the right. Because you want to scroll down the worksheet and still be able to read the column headings, you also freeze the labels in rows 1 through 5. Excel freezes the columns to the left and the rows above the cell pointer.

2. **Click Window on the menu bar, then click Freeze Panes**
   A thin line appears along the column border to the left of the active cell, and another line appears along the row above the active cell indicating that columns A through C and rows 1 through 5 are frozen.

### QuickTip

To easily change worksheet data without manual scrolling, click Edit on the menu bar, click Replace, then enter text you want to find and text you want to replace it with. Use the Find Next, Replace, and Replace All buttons to find and replace occurrences of the found text with the replacement text.

3. **Scroll to the right until columns A through C and L through O are visible**
   Because columns A, B, and C are frozen, they remain on the screen; columns D through K are temporarily hidden from view. Notice that the information you are looking for in row 13 (last name, total hours, hourly pay rate, and total pay for Paul Cristifano) is readily available. You jot down Paul's data but still need to verify Virginia Young's information.

4. **Scroll down until row 26 is visible**
   Notice that in addition to columns A through C, rows 1 through 5 remain on the screen as well. See Figure F-1. Jim jots down the information for Virginia Young. Even though a pane is frozen, you can click in the frozen area of the worksheet and edit the contents of the cells there, if necessary.

### QuickTip

When you open an existing workbook, the cell pointer is in the cell it was in when you last saved the workbook. Press [Ctrl][Home] to return to cell A1 prior to saving and closing a workbook.

5. **Press [Ctrl][Home]**
   Because the panes are frozen, the cell pointer moves to cell D6, not A1.

6. **Click Window on the menu bar, then click Unfreeze Panes**
   The panes are unfrozen.

7. **Return to cell A1, then save the workbook**

**FIGURE F-1: Scrolled worksheet with frozen rows and columns**

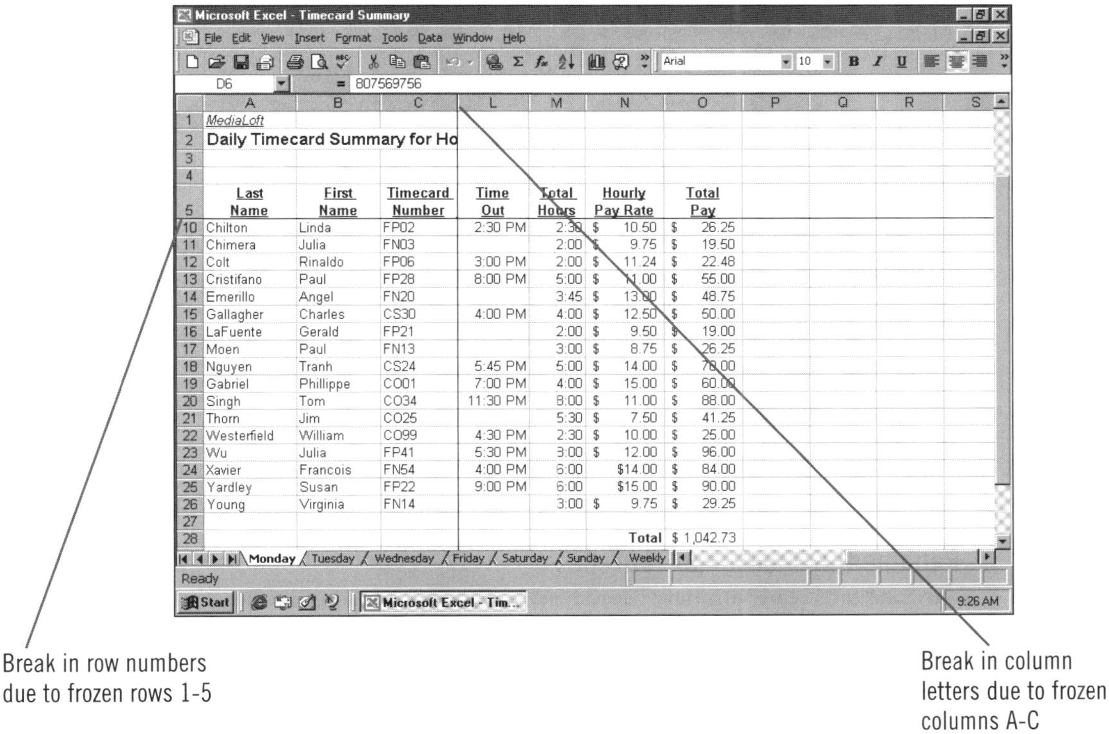

Break in row numbers due to frozen rows 1-5

Break in column letters due to frozen columns A-C

---

**CLUES TO USE**

## Splitting the worksheet into multiple panes

Excel provides a way to split the worksheet area into vertical and/or horizontal panes, so that you can click inside any one pane and scroll to locate desired information in that pane while the other panes remain in place. See Figure F-2. To split a worksheet area into multiple panes, drag the split box (the small box at the top of the vertical scroll bar or at the right end of the horizontal scroll bar) in the direction you want the split to appear. To remove the split, move the mouse over the split until the pointer changes to a double pointed arrow, then double-click.

**FIGURE F-2: Worksheet split into two horizontal panes**

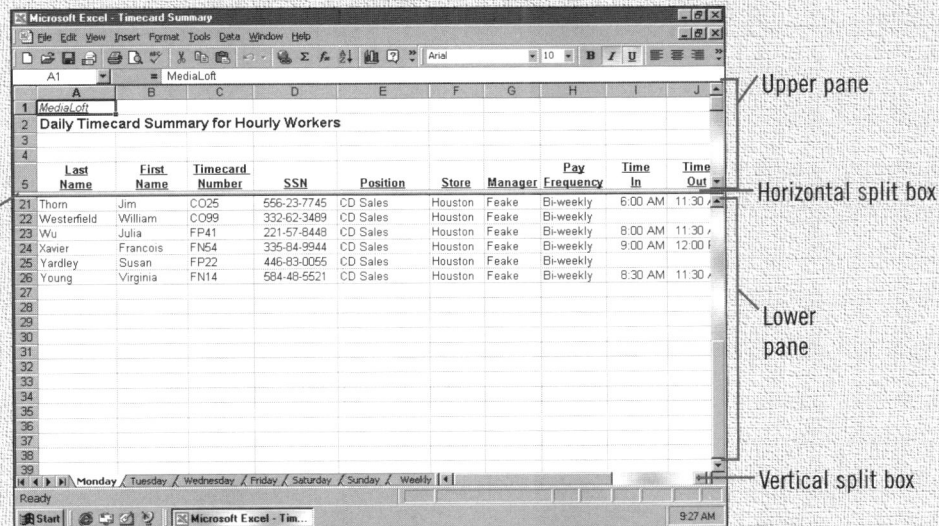

Upper pane

Horizontal split box

Break in row numbers due to split window

Lower pane

Vertical split box

# Inserting and Deleting Worksheets

You can insert and delete worksheets in a workbook as needed. For example, because new workbooks open with only three sheets available (Sheet1, Sheet2, and Sheet3), you need to insert at least one more sheet if you want to have four quarterly worksheets in an annual financial budget workbook. You can do this by using commands on the menu bar or pop-up menu. ✐ Jim was in a hurry when he added the sheet tabs to the Timecard Summary workbook. He needs to insert a sheet for Thursday and delete the sheet for Sunday because these Houston workers do not work on Sundays.

## Steps

1. **Click the Friday sheet tab, click Insert on the menu bar, then click Worksheet**
   Excel automatically inserts a new sheet tab labeled Sheet1 to the left of the Friday sheet.

2. **Rename the Sheet1 tab Thursday**
   Now the tabs read Monday, Tuesday, Wednesday, Thursday, Friday, and Saturday. The tab for the Weekly Summary is not visible, but you still need to delete the Sunday worksheet.

3. **Click the Sunday sheet tab, move the pointer over the Sunday tab, then click the right mouse button**
   A pop-up menu appears. See Figure F-3. The pop-up menu allows you to insert, delete, rename, move, or copy sheets, select all the sheets, or view any Visual Basic programming code in a workbook.

4. **Click Delete on the pop-up menu**
   A message box warns that the selected sheet will be deleted permanently. You must acknowledge the message before proceeding.

5. **Click OK**
   The Sunday sheet is deleted. Next, to check your work, you view a menu of worksheets in the workbook.

6. **Move the mouse pointer over any tab scrolling button, then right-click**
   When you right-click a tab scrolling button, Excel automatically opens a menu of the worksheets in the active workbook. Compare your list with Figure F-4.

7. **Click Monday, return to cell A1, then save the workbook**

Click to delete
selected sheet

Insert...
Delete
Rename
Move or Copy...
Select All Sheets
View Code

Active worksheet

Right-click any
tab scrolling
button to
display menu
of worksheets

Menu of
worksheets

Excel 2000

## Specifying headers and footers

As you prepare a workbook for others to view, it is helpful to give them as much data as possible about the worksheet—how many pages, who created it on what date, and the like. You can do this easily in a **header** or **footer**, information that prints at the top or bottom of each printed page. Headers and footers are visible on screen only in Print Preview. To add a header, for example, click View on the menu bar, click Header and Footer, click Custom Header, and you see a dialog box similar to that in Figure F-5. Both the header and the footer are divided into three sections, and you can enter information in any or all of them. Type information such as your name and click the icons to enter the page number ⊞, total pages ⊟, date 📅, time ⊙, filename 📄, or sheet name ⊡ to enter codes that represent these items. Click OK, view the preview on the Header and Footer tab, then click OK again.

FIGURE F-5: Header dialog box

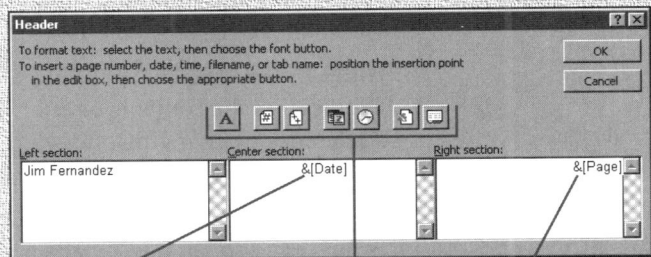

Symbol for date

Click these icons to
insert information
into header sections

Symbol for page
number

# Consolidating Data with 3-D References

When you want to summarize similar data that exists in different sheets or workbooks, you can combine and display it in one sheet. For example, you might have departmental sales figures on four different store sheets that you want to add together, or **consolidate**, on one summary sheet that shows total departmental sales for all stores. The best way to consolidate data is to use cell references to the various sheets on a consolidation, or summary, sheet. Because they reference other sheets that are usually behind the summary sheet, such references effectively create another dimension in the workbook and are called **3-D references**. You can reference data in other sheets and in other workbooks. Referencing cells is a better method than retyping calculated results because the data values on which calculated totals depend might change. If you reference the values instead, any changes to the original values are automatically reflected in the consolidation sheet. ✎ Although Jim does not have timecard data for the remaining days of the week, he wants to test the Weekly Summary sheet that will consolidate the timesheet data. He does this by creating a reference from the total pay data in the Monday sheet to the Weekly Summary sheet. First, he freezes panes to improve the view of the worksheets prior to initiating the reference between them.

## Steps 1 2 3 4

1. On the Monday sheet, click cell **D6**, click **Window** on the menu bar, click **Freeze Panes**, then scroll horizontally to bring columns L through O into view

2. Right-click a **tab scrolling button**, then click **Weekly Summary**
   Because the Weekly Summary sheet (which is the consolidation sheet) will contain the reference, the cell pointer must reside there when you initiate the reference. To make a simple **reference** within the same sheet or between sheets, position the cell pointer in the cell to contain the reference, type = (equal sign), position the cell pointer in the cell to be referenced, and then enter the information.

   **Trouble?**
   If you have difficulty referencing cells between sheets, press [Esc] and begin again.

3. While in the Weekly Summary sheet, click cell **C6**, type **=**, activate the Monday sheet, click cell **O6**, then click the **Enter button** ☑ on the formula bar
   The formula bar reads =Monday!O6. See Figure F-6. *Monday* references the Monday sheet. The ! (exclamation point) is an **external reference indicator** meaning that the cell referenced is outside the active sheet; O6 is the actual cell reference in the external sheet. The result, $33.00, appears in cell C6 of the Weekly Summary sheet, showing the reference to the value displayed in cell O6 of the Monday sheet.

4. While in the Weekly Summary sheet, copy cell **C6** into cells **C7:C26**
   Excel copies the contents of cell C6 with its relative reference down the column. You can test a reference by changing one cell that it is based on and seeing if the reference changes.

5. Activate the Monday sheet, edit cell L6 to read **6:30 PM**, then activate the Weekly Summary sheet
   Cell C6 now shows $41.25. Changing Beryl Arenson's "time out" from 5:30 to 6:30 increased her pay from $33.00 to $41.25. This makes sense because Beryl's hours went from four to five, and her hourly salary is $8.25. The reference to Monday's total pay was automatically updated in the Weekly Summary sheet. See Figure F-7.

6. Preview, then print the Weekly Summary sheet
   To preview and print an entire workbook, click File on the menu bar, click Print, click to select the Entire Workbook option button, then click Preview. In the Preview window, you can page through the entire workbook. When you click Print, the entire workbook will print.

7. Activate the Monday sheet, then unfreeze the panes

8. Save the workbook

FIGURE F-6: Worksheet showing referenced cell

Sheet referenced

Cell referenced

Formula referencing cell

External reference indicator

Referenced value

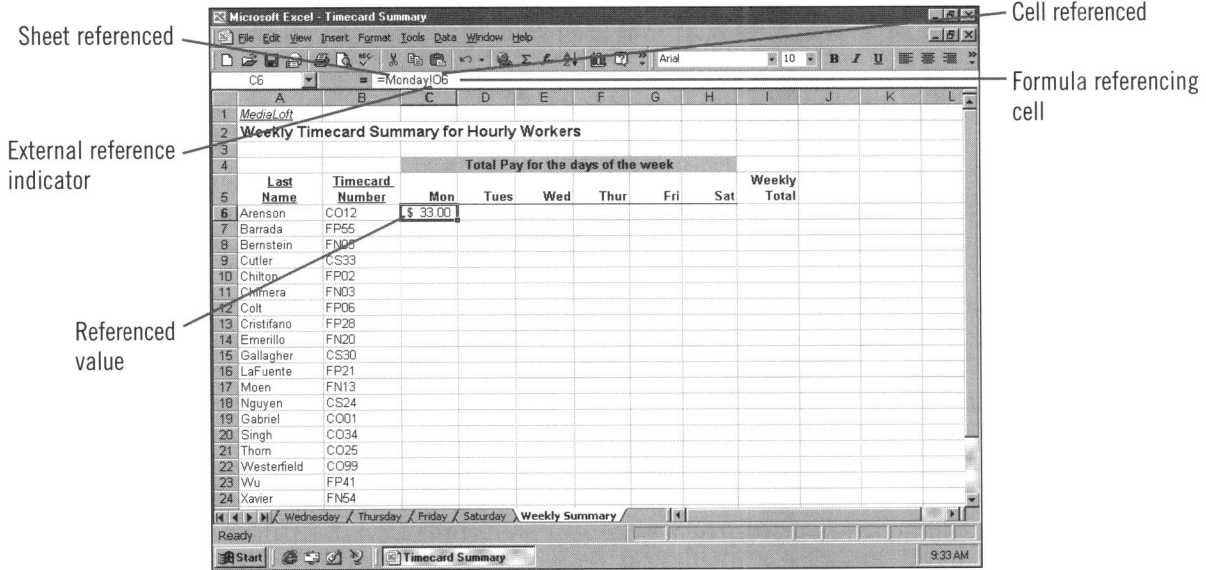

FIGURE F-7: Weekly Summary worksheet with updated reference

Updated value

Copied values also reference the Monday sheet

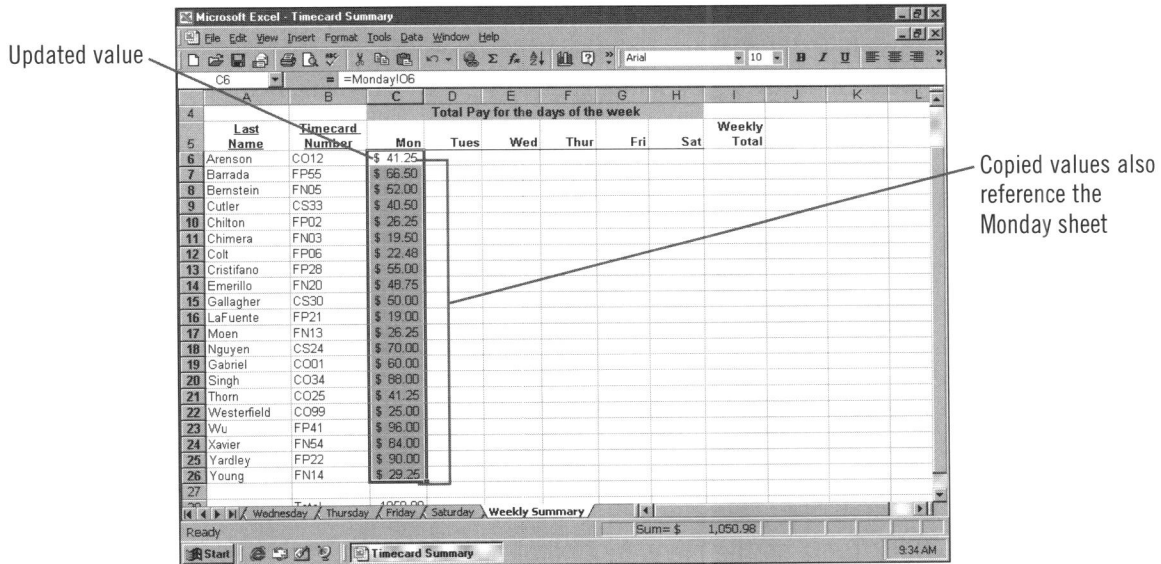

## Consolidating data from different workbooks using linking

Just as you can reference data between cells in a worksheet and between sheets, you can reference data between workbooks dynamically so that changes made in referenced cells in one workbook are reflected in the consolidation sheet in the other workbook. This dynamic referencing is called linking. To link a single cell between workbooks, open both workbooks, select the cell to receive the linked data, press = (equal sign), select the cell in the other workbook containing the data to be linked, then press

[Enter]. Excel automatically inserts the name of the referenced workbook in the cell reference. To perform calculations, enter formulas on the consolidation sheet using cells in the supporting sheets. If you are linking more than one cell, you can copy the linked data to the Clipboard, select in the other workbook the upper-left cell to receive the link, click Edit on the menu bar, click Paste Special, then click Paste Link.

# Hiding and Protecting Worksheet Areas

Worksheets can contain sensitive information that you don't want others to view or alter. To protect such information, Excel gives you two basic options. You can **hide** the formulas in selected cells (or rows, columns, or entire sheets), and you can **lock** selected cells, in which case other people will be able to view the data (values, numbers, labels, formulas, etc.) in those cells but not to alter it in any way. See Table F-1 for a list of options you can use to protect a worksheet. You set the lock and hide options in the Format Cells dialog box. You lock and unlock cells by clicking the Locked check box in the Format Cells dialog box Protection tab, and hide and "unhide" cell formulas by clicking the Hidden check box. The lock and hide options will not function unless an Excel protection feature, which you access via the Tools menu, is also activated. A common worksheet protection strategy is to unlock cells in which data will be changed, sometimes referred to as the **data entry area**, and to lock cells in which the data should not be changed. Then, when you protect the worksheet, the unlocked areas can still be changed. ![arrow] Because Jim will assign someone to enter the sensitive timecard information into the worksheet, he plans to hide and lock selected areas of the worksheet.

**Steps** 1 2 3 4

1. **Make sure the Monday sheet is active, select range I6:L27, click Format on the menu bar, click Cells, then click the Protection tab**

   You include row 27, even though it does not contain data, in the event that new data is added to the row later. Notice that the Locked box in the Protection tab is already checked, as shown in Figure F-8. The Locked check box is selected by default, meaning that all the cells in a new workbook start out locked. (Note, however, that cell locking is not applied unless the protection feature is also activated. The protection feature is inactive by default.)

2. **Click the Locked check box to deselect it, then click OK**

   Excel stores time as a fraction of a 24-hour day. In the formula for total pay, hours must be multiplied by 24. This concept might be confusing to the data entry person, so you hide the formulas.

3. **Select range O6:O26, click Format on the menu bar, click Cells, click the Protection tab, click the Hidden check box to select it, then click OK**

   The screen data remains the same (unhidden and unlocked) until you set the protection in the next step.

**QuickTip**

To turn off worksheet protection, click Tools on the menu bar, point to Protection, then click Unprotect Sheet. If prompted for a password, type the password, then click OK. To remove passwords, open the workbook or worksheet using the password, then go to the window where you entered the password, highlight the password, and press [Delete]. Remember that passwords are case sensitive.

4. **Click Tools on the menu bar, point to Protection, then click Protect Sheet**

   The Protect Sheet dialog box opens. You choose not to use a password.

5. **Click OK**

   You are ready to test the new worksheet protection.

6. **Click cell O6**

   Notice that the formula bar is empty because of the hidden formula setting.

7. **In cell O6, type T to confirm that locked cells cannot be changed, then click OK**

   When you attempt to change a locked cell, a message box reminds you of the protected cell's read-only status. See Figure F-9.

8. **Click cell I6, type 9, and notice that Excel allows you to begin the entry, press [Esc] to cancel the entry, then save the workbook**

   Because you unlocked the cells in columns I through L before you protected the worksheet, you can make changes to these cells. Jim is satisfied that the Time In and Time Out data can be changed as necessary.

FIGURE F-8: Protection tab in Format Cells dialog box

Click to remove
checkmark

FIGURE F-9: Reminder of protected cell's read-only status

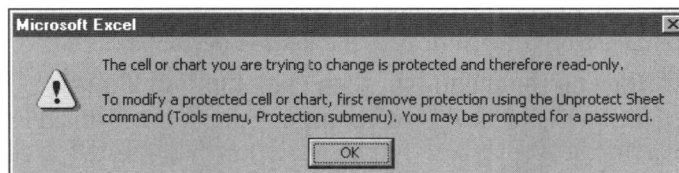

TABLE F-1: Options for hiding and protecting worksheet elements

| task | menu commands |
|------|---------------|
| Hide/Unhide a column | Format, Column, Hide or Unhide |
| Hide/Unhide a formula | Format, Cells, Protection tab, select/deselect Hidden check box |
| Hide/Unhide a row | Format, Row, Hide or Unhide |
| Hide/Unhide a sheet | Format, Sheet, Hide or Unhide |
| Protect workbook | Tools, Protection, Protect Workbook, assign optional password |
| Protect worksheet | Tools, Protection, Protect Sheet, assign optional password |
| Unlock/Relock cells | Format, Cells, Protection tab, deselect/select Locked check box |

*Note: Some of the hide and protect options do not take effect until protection is enabled.*

## CLUES TO USE

### Changing workbook properties

You can also password-protect an entire workbook from being opened or modified by changing its file properties. Click File, click Save As, click Tools, then click General Options. Specify the password(s) for opening or modifying the workbook. You can also use this dialog box to offer users an option to open the workbook in read-only format. To make an entire workbook read-only so that users can open but not change it, click Start on the Taskbar, point to Programs, then click Windows Explorer. Locate and click the filename, click File on the menu bar, click Properties, click the General tab, then, under Attributes, select the Read-only check box.

# Saving Custom Views of a Worksheet

A **view** is a set of display and/or print settings that you can name and save, then access at a later time. By using the Excel Custom Views feature, you can create several different views of a worksheet without having to create separate sheets. For example, if you often switch between portrait and landscape orientations when printing different parts of a worksheet, you can create two views with the appropriate print settings for each view. You set the display and/or print settings first, then name the view. ◢▬▬ Because Jim will generate several reports from his data, he saves the current print and display settings as a custom view. To better view the data to be printed, he decides to use the Zoom box to display the entire worksheet on one screen. The Zoom box has a default setting of 100% magnification and appears on the Standard toolbar.

**Steps**

1. **With the Monday sheet active, select range A1:O28, click the Zoom box list arrow on the Standard toolbar, click Selection, then press [Ctrl][Home] to return to cell A1**
Excel automatically adjusts the display magnification so that the data selected fits on one screen. See Figure F-10. After selecting the **Zoom box**, you also can pick a magnification percentage from the list or type the desired percentage.

2. **Click View on the menu bar, then click Custom Views**
The Custom Views dialog box opens. Any previously defined views for the active worksheet appear in the Views box. In this case, Jim had created a custom view named Generic containing default print and display settings. See Figure F-11.

3. **Click Add**
The Add View dialog box opens, as shown in Figure F-12. Here, you enter a name for the view and decide whether to include print settings and hidden rows, columns, and filter settings. You want to include the selected options.

4. **In the Name box, type Complete Daily Worksheet, then click OK**
After creating a custom view of the worksheet, you return to the worksheet area. You are ready to test the two custom views. In case the views require a change to the worksheet, it's a good idea to turn off worksheet protection.

5. **Click Tools on the menu bar, point to Protection, then click Unprotect Sheet**

6. **Click View on the menu bar, then click Custom Views**
The Custom Views dialog box opens, listing both the Complete Daily Worksheet and Generic views.

7. **Click Generic in the Views list box, click Show, preview the worksheet, then close the Preview**
The Generic custom view returns the worksheet to the Excel default print and display settings. Now you are ready to test the new custom view.

8. **Click View on the menu bar, click Custom Views, click Complete Daily Worksheet in the Views list box, click Show**
The entire worksheet fits on the screen.

9. **Return to the Generic view, then save your work**
Jim is satisfied with the custom view of the worksheet he created.

FIGURE F-10: Selected data fit to one screen

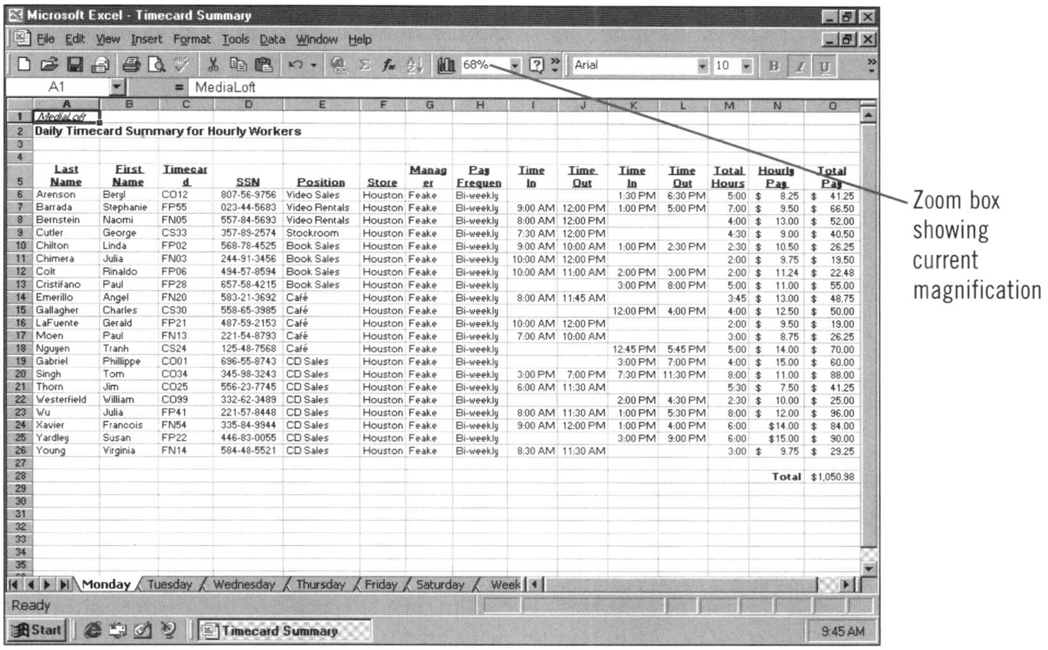

Zoom box showing current magnification

FIGURE F-11: Custom Views dialog box

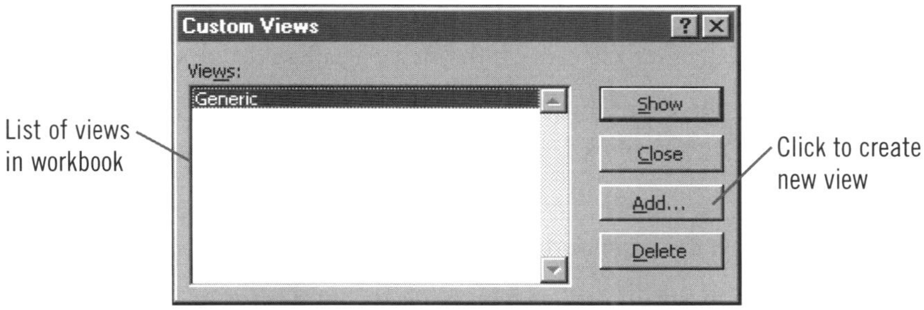

List of views in workbook

Click to create new view

FIGURE F-12: Add View dialog box

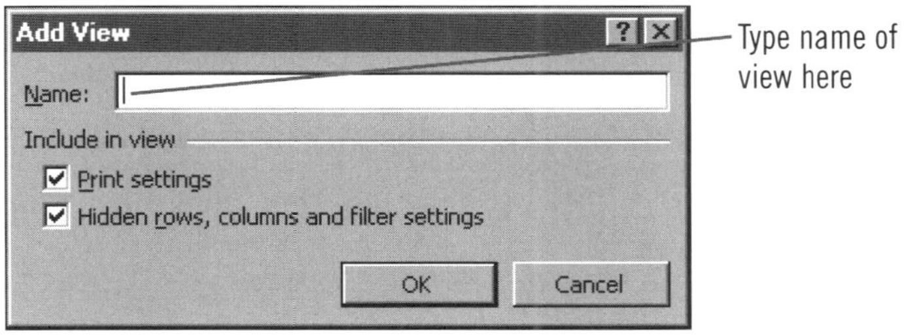

Type name of view here

### CLUES TO USE

## Using a workspace

If you work with several workbooks at a time in a particular arrangement, you can create a **workspace** containing information about their location and window sizes. Then, instead of opening each workbook individually, you can just open the workspace, which will automatically display the workbooks in the sizes and locations saved in the workspace. To create a workspace, open the workbooks and locate and size them as you would like them to appear. Click File on the menu bar, click Save Workspace, then type a name for the workspace file. Then open the workspace file and open the workbooks in their saved locations and sizes. Remember, however, that the workspace file does not contain the workbooks themselves, so you still have to back up the original workbook files. To start the workspace automatically when you turn on your computer, place the workspace file only in your XLStart folder.

# Controlling Page Breaks and Page Numbering

The vertical and horizontal dashed lines in worksheets indicate page breaks. Excel automatically inserts a page break when your worksheet data doesn't fit on one page. These page breaks are **dynamic**, which means they adjust automatically when you insert or delete rows and columns and when you change column widths or row heights. Everything to the left of the first vertical dashed line and above the first horizontal dashed line is printed on the first page. You can override the automatic breaks by choosing the Page Break command on the Insert menu. Table F-2 describes the different types of page breaks you can use. Jim wants another report displaying no more than half the hourly workers on each page. To accomplish this, he must insert a manual page break.

## Steps

**1.** Click cell **A16**, click **Insert** on the menu bar, then click **Page Break**

A dashed line appears between rows 15 and 16, indicating a horizontal page break. See Figure F-13. After you set page breaks, it's a good idea to preview each page.

**2.** Preview the worksheet, then click **Zoom**

Notice that the status bar reads "Page 1 of 4" and that the data for the employees up through Charles Gallagher appears on the first page. Jim decides to place the date in the footer.

**QuickTip**

To insert the page number in a header or footer section yourself, click ☐ in the Header or Footer dialog box.

**3.** While in the Print Preview window, click **Setup**, click the **Header/Footer tab**, click **Custom Footer**, click the **Right section box**, click the **Date button** 📅

**4.** Click the **Left section box**, type your name, then click **OK**

Your name, the page number, and the date appear in the Footer preview area.

**QuickTip**

To remove a manual page break, select any cell directly below or to the right of the page break, click Insert on the menu bar, then click Remove Page Break.

**5.** In the Page Setup dialog box, click **OK**, and, still in Print Preview, check to make sure all the pages show your name and the page numbers, click **Print**, then click **OK**

**6.** Click **View** on the menu bar, click **Custom Views**, click **Add**, type **Half N Half**, then click **OK**

Your new custom view has the page breaks and all current print settings.

**7.** Make sure cell H16 is selected, then click **Insert** on the menu bar and click **Remove Page Break**

**8.** Save the workbook

**TABLE F-2: Page break options**

| type of page break | where to position cell pointer |
| --- | --- |
| **Both horizontal and vertical page breaks** | Select the cell below and to the right of the gridline where you want the breaks to occur |
| **Only a horizontal page break** | Select the cell in column A that is directly below the gridline where you want the page to break |
| **Only a vertical page break** | Select a cell in row 1 that is to the right of the gridline where you want the page to break |

FIGURE F-13: Worksheet with horizontal page break

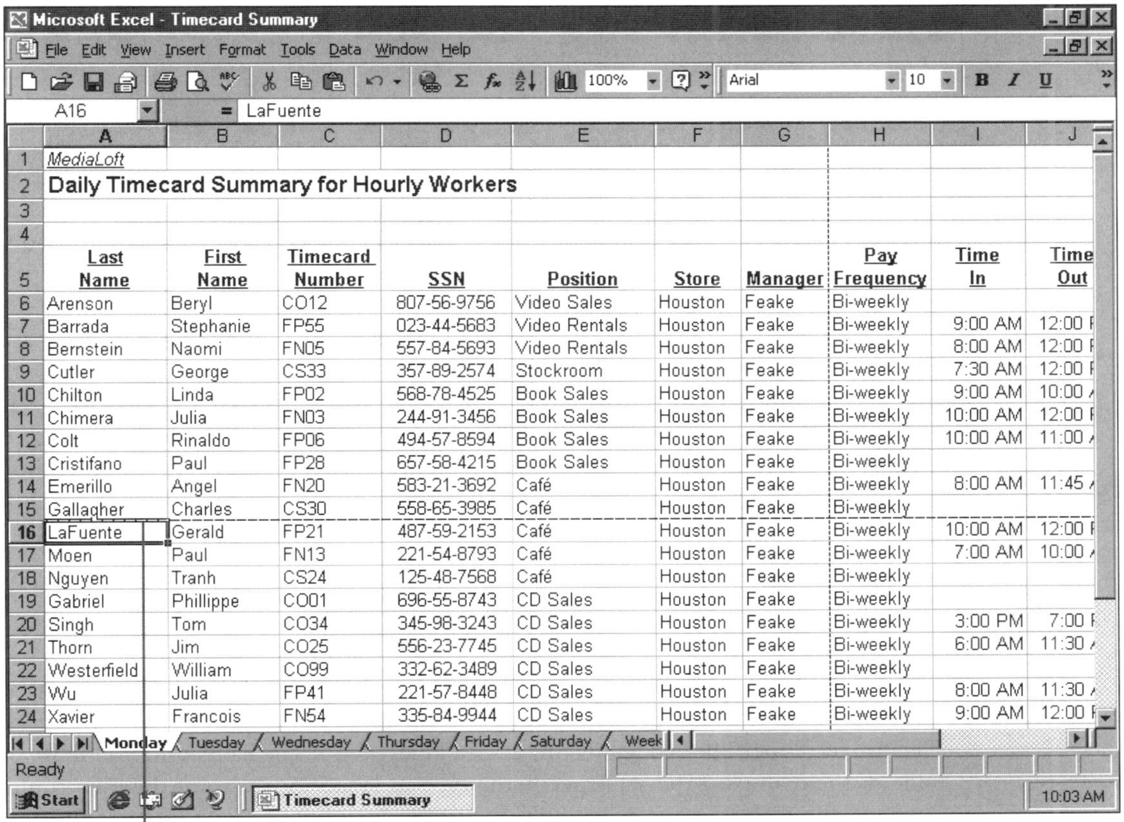

Dashed line indicates horizontal
break after row 15

## Using Page Break Preview

By clicking View on the menu bar, then clicking Page Break Preview, or clicking Page Break Preview in the Print Preview window, you can view and change page breaks manually. (If you see a dialog box asking if you want help, just click OK to close it.) Simply drag the page break lines to the desired location. See Figure F-14. To exit Page Break Preview, click View on the menu bar, then click Normal.

FIGURE F-14: Page Break Preview window

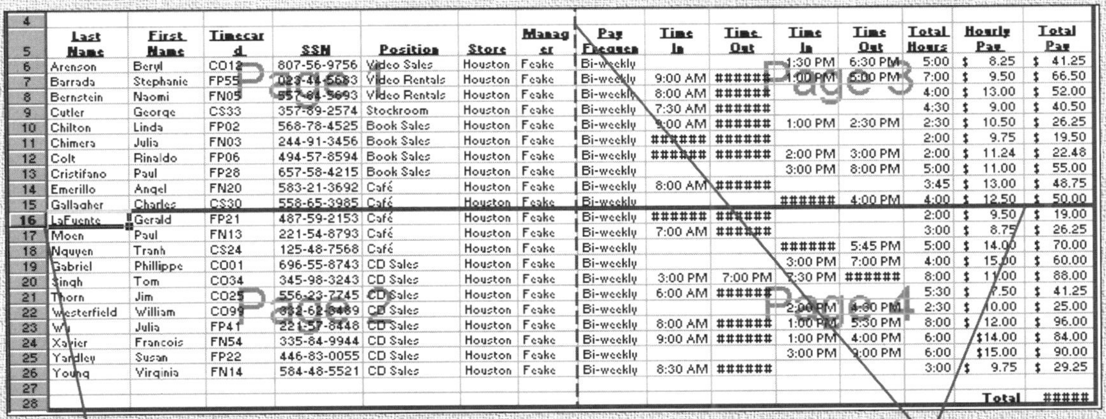

Cell pointer in cell A16

Drag page break lines
to change page breaks

# Creating a Hyperlink between Excel Files

As you manage the content and appearance of your workbooks, you may want the workbook user to have access to information in another workbook. It might be nonessential information or data that is too detailed to place in the workbook itself. In these cases, you can create a **hyperlink**, an object (a filename, a word, a phrase, or a graphic) in a worksheet that, when you click it, will jump to another worksheet, called the **target**. The target can be a document created in another software program or a site on the World Wide Web. For example, in a worksheet that lists customer invoices, at each customer's name, you might create a hyperlink to an Excel file containing payment terms for each customer. You can also use hyperlinks to navigate to other locations in a large worksheet. Jim wants managers who view the Timecard Summary worksheet to be able to view the pay categories for MediaLoft store employees. He creates a hyperlink at the Hourly Pay Rate column heading. Users will click the hyperlink to view the Pay Rate worksheet.

## Steps

1. Display the Monday worksheet

2. Click **Edit**, click **Go To**, type **N5** (the cell containing **the text Hourly Pay Rate**), then click **OK**

3. Click the **Insert Hyperlink button** 🖳 on the Standard toolbar, then click **Existing File or Web Page**, if necessary

   The Insert Hyperlink dialog box opens. See Figure F-15. The icons under Link to: on the left side of the dialog box let you specify the type of location you want the link to jump to: an existing file or Web page, a place in the same document, a new document, or an e-mail address. Since Jim wants users to display a document he has created, the first icon, Existing File or Web Page, is correct and is already selected.

4. Click **File** under Browse for, then in the Link to File dialog box, navigate to your Project Disk and double-click **Pay Rate Classifications**

   The Insert Hyperlink dialog box reappears with the filename you selected in the Type the file or Web page name text box. This document appears when users click this hyperlink. You can also specify the ScreenTip that users will see when they hold the pointer over the hyperlink.

5. Click **ScreenTip**, type **Click here to see MediaLoft pay rate classifications**, click **OK**, then click **OK** again

   Cell N5 now contains underlined blue text, indicating that it is a hyperlink. After you create a hyperlink, you should check it to make sure it jumps to the correct destination.

6. Move the pointer over the **Hourly Pay Rate text**, view the ScreenTip, then click once

   Notice that when you move the pointer over the text, the pointer changes to 🖑, indicating that it is a hyperlink, and the ScreenTip appears. After you click, the Pay Rate Classifications worksheet appears. See Figure F-16. The Web toolbar appears beneath the Standard and Formatting toolbars.

7. Click the **Back button** ⇦ on the Web toolbar, then save the workbook

### CLUES TO USE

#### Using hyperlinks to navigate large worksheets

Hyperlinks are useful in navigating large worksheets or workbooks. You can create a hyperlink from any cell to another cell in the same worksheet, a cell in another worksheet, or a defined name anywhere in the workbook. Under Link to in the Insert Hyperlink dialog box, click Place in This Document. Then type the cell reference and indicate the sheet, or select the named location in the scroll box.

FIGURE F-15: **Insert Hyperlink dialog box**

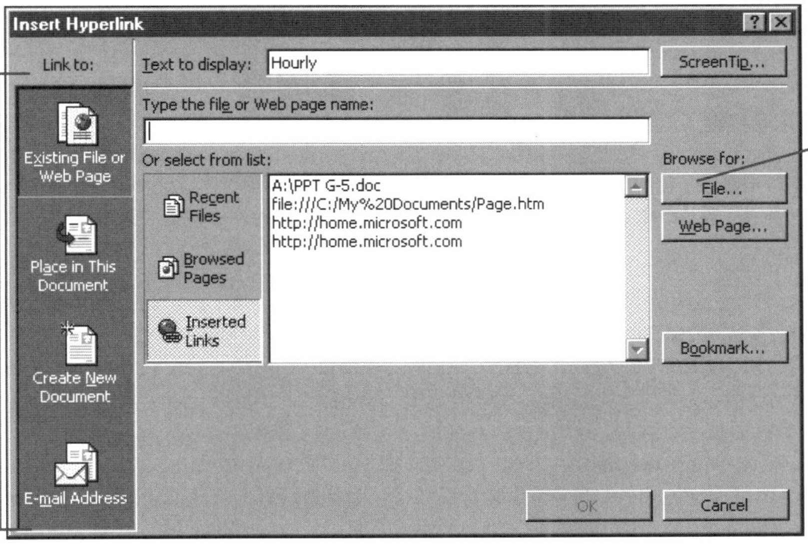

Locations a hyperlink can jump to

Click here to specify hyperlink target file

FIGURE F-16: **Target document**

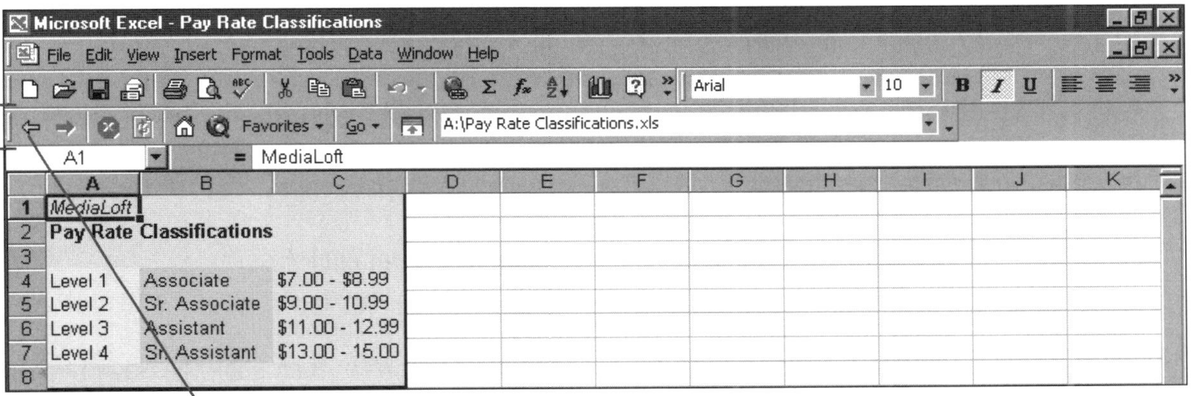

Web toolbar

Click here to return to the Timecard Summary workbook

CLUES TO USE

## Inserting a picture

As you prepare your workbooks for viewing by others on an intranet or on the Internet, you may want to enhance their appearance by adding pictures. You can easily add your own picture, such as a company logo or a scanned picture, or a picture from the Microsoft Clip Gallery. To insert a Clip Gallery picture on a worksheet, click Insert on the menu bar, point to

Picture, then click Clip Art. Click a category, click the image you want to insert, then click the Insert Clip icon. Close the Insert Clip Art window. The picture is an **object** that you can move, resize, or delete. To move a picture, click and then drag it. To resize it, click it once to select it, then drag one of its corners. To delete it, click to select it, then press [Delete].

MANAGING WORKBOOKS AND PREPARING THEM FOR THE WEB EXCEL F-15

# Saving an Excel file as an HTML Document

One way to share Excel data is to publish, or **post**, it online over a network so that others can access it using their Web browsers. The network can be an **intranet**, which is an internal network site used by a particular group of people who work together, or the World Wide Web. The **World Wide Web** is a structure of documents, or pages, connected electronically over a large computer network called the **Internet**, which is made up of smaller networks and computers. If you save and post an entire workbook, users can click worksheet tabs to view each sheet. If you save a single worksheet, you can make the Web page interactive, meaning that users can enter, format, and calculate worksheet data. To post an Excel document to an intranet or the World Wide Web, you must first save it in **HTML (Hypertext Markup Language)**, which is the format that a Web browser can read. ▰▰▰ Jim saves the entire Timecard Summary workbook in HTML format so it can be posted on the MediaLoft intranet for managers' use.

## Steps 1 2 3 4

1. **Click File on the menu bar, then click Save as Web Page**
   The Save As dialog box opens. See Figure F-17. By default, the Entire Workbook option button is selected, which is what Jim wants. However, he wants the title bar of the Web page to be more descriptive than the filename.

2. **Click Change Title**
   The Set Page Title dialog box opens.

3. **Type MediaLoft Houston Timecard Summary, then click OK**
   The Page title area displays the new title. The Save as type list box indicates that the workbook will be saved as a Web page, which is in HTML format.

4. **Change the filename to Timecard Summary - Web, then click the Save in list arrow and locate your Project Disk**

5. **Click Save**
   A dialog box appears, indicating that the custom views you saved earlier will not be part of the HTML file.

6. **Click Yes**
   Excel saves the Web page version as an HTML file in the folder location you specified in the Save As dialog box, and in the same place creates a folder in which it places associated files, such as a file for each worksheet. To make the workbook available to others, you would post all these files on a network server. When the save process is complete, the original XLS file closes and the HTML file opens on your screen.

7. **Click File on the menu bar, click Web Page Preview, then maximize the browser window**
   The workbook opens in your default Web browser, which could be Internet Explorer or Netscape, showing you what it would look like if you opened it on an intranet or on the Internet. See Figure F-18. The Monday worksheet appears as it would if it were on a Web site or intranet, with tabs at the bottom of the screen for each daily sheet. If you wanted to use this document online, you would also need to save the target document (Pay Rate Classifications) in HTML format and post it to the Web site.

8. **Click the Weekly Summary tab**
   The Weekly Summary worksheet appears just as it would in Excel.

9. **Close the Web browser window, then close the Timecard Summary - Web workbook and the Pay Rate Classifications workbook, then exit Excel**

FIGURE F-17: **Save As dialog box**

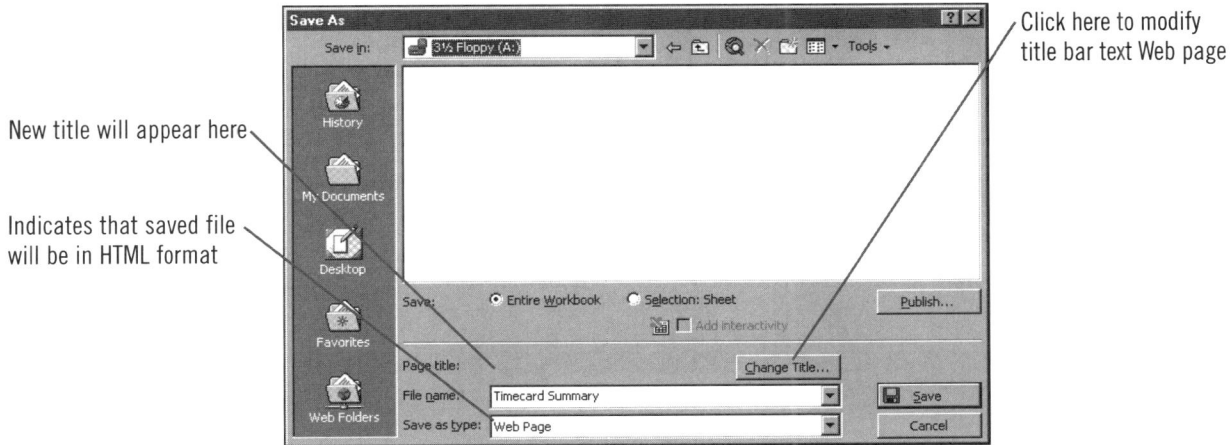

Click here to modify title bar text Web page

New title will appear here

Indicates that saved file will be in HTML format

FIGURE F-18: **Workbook in Web page preview**

Your browser may be Internet Explorer

New title displays in title bar

Browser window

Worksheet tabs allow users to view other sheets in browser

**CLUES TO USE**

## Send a workbook via e-mail

You can send an entire workbook or a worksheet to any e-mail recipient from within Excel. To send a workbook as an attachment to an e-mail message, click File, point to Send to, then click Mail Recipient (as attachment). Fill in the To and Cc information and click Send. See Figure F-19. (If Internet Explorer is not your default Web browser, you may need to respond to additional dialog boxes.) You can also route a workbook to one or more recipients on a routing list that you create. Click File, point to Send to, then click Routing Recipient. Click Create New Contact and enter contact information, then fill in the Routing slip. Depending on your e-mail program, you may have to follow a different procedure. See your instructor or lab resource person for help.

FIGURE F-19: **E-mailing an Excel file as an attachment**

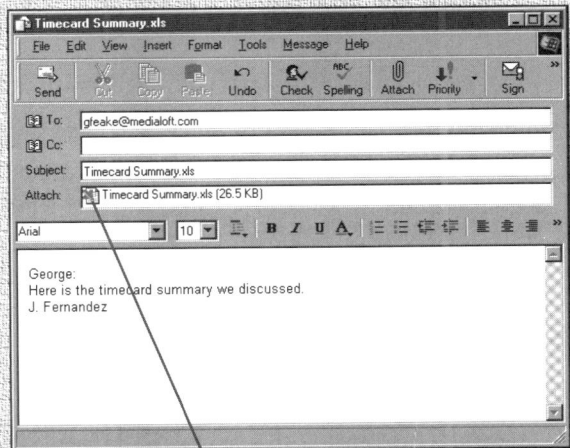

Worksheet is automatically attached to e-mail message

# Practice

## ► Concepts Review

Label each element of the Excel screen shown in Figure F-20.

FIGURE F-20

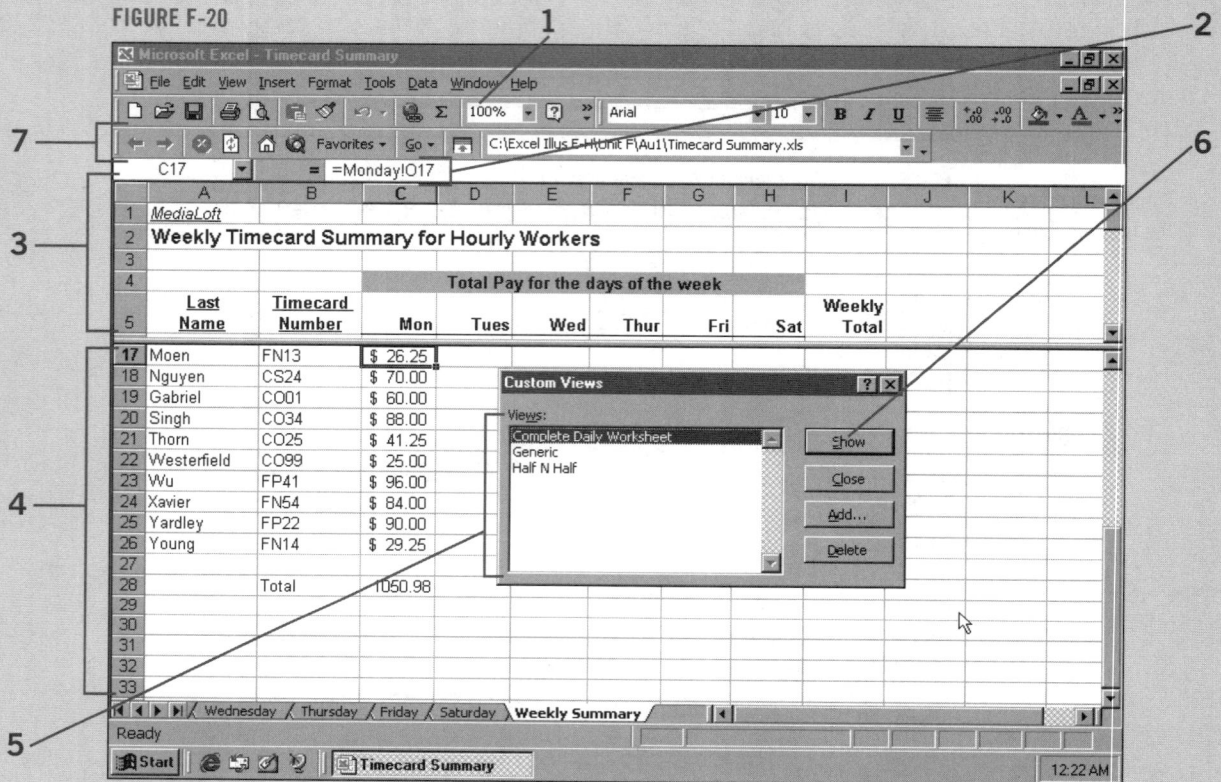

Match each of the terms with the statement that describes its function.

a. **Dashed line**
b. **Hyperlink**
c. **3-D reference**
d. 🖳
e. 🔲

8. Inserts a code to print the total number of pages
9. Uses values from different workbooks
10. Indicates a page break
11. Inserts a code to print the sheet name in a header or footer
12. An object you click to display a target

Select the best answer from the list of choices.

13. You can save frequently used display and print settings by using the _____ feature.
    a. HTML
    b. View menu
    c. Custom Views
    d. Save command

14. You freeze areas of the worksheet to
    a. Freeze data and unlock formulas.
    b. Lock column and row headings in place while you scroll through the worksheet.
    c. Freeze all data in place so that you can see it.
    d. Lock open windows in place.

15. To protect a worksheet, you must first unlock those cells that _____, and then issue the Protect Sheet command.
    a. never change
    b. the user will be allowed to change
    c. have hidden formulas
    d. are locked

# ► Skills Review

1. **Freeze columns and rows.**
   a. Open the workbook titled EX F-2, then save it as "Quarterly Household Budget".
   b. Freeze columns A and B and rows 1 through 3 for improved viewing. (*Hint:* Click cell C4 prior to issuing the Freeze Panes command.)
   c. Scroll until columns A and B and F through H are visible.
   d. Press [Ctrl][Home] to return to cell C4.
   e. Unfreeze the panes.

2. **Insert and delete worksheets.**
   a. With the 2001 sheet active, use the sheet pop-up menu to insert a new Sheet1 to its left.
   b. Delete Sheet1.
   c. Add a custom footer to the 2001 sheet with your name on the left side and the page number on the right side.
   d. Add a custom header with the worksheet name on the left side.
   e. Preview and print the worksheet.

3. **Consolidate data with 3-D references.**
   a. In cell C22, enter a reference to cell G7.
   b. In cell C23, enter a reference to cell G18.
   c. Activate the 2002 worksheet.
   d. In cell C4, enter a reference to cell C4 on the 2001 worksheet.
   e. In the 2002 worksheet, copy the contents of cell C4 into cells C5:C6.
   f. Preview the 2002 worksheet, view the Page Break Preview, and drag the page break so all the data fits on one page.
   g. Print the 2002 worksheet and save your work.

**4. Hide and protect worksheet areas.**

   **a.** On the 2001 sheet, unlock the expense data in the range C10:F17.

   **b.** Protect the sheet without using a password.

   **c.** To make sure the other cells are locked, attempt to make an entry in cell D4.

   **d.** Confirm the message box warning.

   **e.** Change the first-quarter mortgage expense to $3,400.

   **f.** Unprotect the worksheet.

   **g.** Save the workbook.

**5. Save custom views of a worksheet.**

   **a.** Set the zoom on the 2001 worksheet so all the data fits on your screen.

   **b.** Make this a new view called "Entire 2001 Budget".

   **c.** Use the Custom Views dialog box to return to Generic view.

   **d.** Save the workbook.

**6. Control page breaks and page numbering.**

   **a.** Insert a page break above cell A9.

   **b.** Save the view as "Halves".

   **c.** Preview and print the worksheet, then preview and print the entire workbook.

   **d.** Save the workbook.

**7. Create a hyperlink between Excel files.**

   **a.** On the 2001 worksheet, make cell A9 a hyperlink to the file Expense Details, with a ScreenTip that reads "Click here to see expense assumptions".

   **b.** Test the link, then print the Expense Details worksheet.

   **c.** Return to the Household Budget worksheet using the Web toolbar.

   **d.** On the 2002 worksheet, enter the text "Based on 2001 budget" in cell A2.

   **e.** Make the text in cell A2 a hyperlink to cell A1 in the 2001 worksheet. (*Hint:* Use the Place in this document button.)

   **f.** Test the hyperlink.

   **g.** Add any clip art picture to your worksheet, then move and resize it so it doesn't obscure any worksheet information.

**8. Save an Excel file as an HTML document.**

   **a.** Save the entire budget workbook as a Web page with a title bar that reads "Our Budget" and the file named Quarterly Household Budget - Web.

   **b.** Preview the Web page in your browser.

   **c.** Test the worksheet tabs in the browser to make sure they work.

   **d.** Return to Excel, then close the HTML document.

   **e.** Close the Expense Details worksheet, then exit Excel.

# ► Independent Challenges

**1.** You own PC Assist, a software training company. You have added several new entries to the August check register and are ready to enter September's check activity. Because the sheet for August will include much of the same information you need for September, you decide to copy it. Then you will edit the new sheet to fit your needs for September check activity. You will use sheet referencing to enter the beginning balance and beginning check number. Using your own data, you will complete five checks for the September register.

   To complete this independent challenge:

   **a.** Open the workbook entitled EX F-3, then save it as "Update to Check Register".

   **b.** Delete Sheet 2 and Sheet 3, then create a worksheet for September by copying the August sheet.

   **c.** With the September sheet active, delete the data in range A6:E24.

**d.** To update the balance at the beginning of the month, use sheet referencing from the last balance entry in the August sheet.

**e.** Generate the first check number. (*Hint:* Use a formula that references the last check number in August and adds one.)

**f.** Enter data for five checks.

**g.** Add a footer to the September sheet that includes your name left-aligned on the printout and the system date right-aligned on the printout. Add a header that displays the sheet name centered on the printout.

**h.** Save the workbook.

**i.** Preview the entire workbook, then close the Preview window.

**j.** Preview the September worksheet, then print it in landscape orientation on a single page.

**k.** Save and close the workbook, then exit Excel.

**2.** You are a new employee for a computer software manufacturer. You are responsible for tracking the sales of different product lines and determining which computer operating system generates the most software sales each month. Although sales figures vary from month to month, the format in which data is entered does not. Use Table F-3 as a guide to create a worksheet tracking sales across personal computer (PC) platforms by month. Use a separate sheet for each month and create data for three months. Use your own data for the number of software packages sold in the Windows and Macintosh columns for each product. Create a summary sheet with all the sales summary information.

To complete this independent challenge:

**a.** Create a new workbook, then save it as "Software Sales Summary".

**b.** Enter row and column labels, your own data, and formulas for the totals.

**c.** Create a summary sheet that totals the information in all three sheets. Customize the header to include your name and the date. Set the footer to (none). In Page Setup, center the page both horizontally and vertically.

**d.** Save the workbook, then preview and print the four worksheets.

TABLE F-3

| | Windows | Macintosh | Total |
|---|---|---|---|
| **Games Software** | | | |
| Space Wars 99 | | | |
| Safari | | | |
| Flight School | | | |
| Total | | | |
| **Business Software** | | | |
| Word Processing | | | |
| Spreadsheet | | | |
| Presentation | | | |
| Graphics | | | |
| Page Layout | | | |
| Total | | | |
| **Utilities Products** | | | |
| Antivirus | | | |
| File recovery | | | |
| Total | | | |

**3.** You are a college student with two roommates. Each month you receive your long-distance telephone bill. Because no one wants to figure out who owes what, you split the bill three ways. You are sure that one of your roommates makes two-thirds of the long-distance calls. To make the situation more equitable, you decide to create a spreadsheet to track the long-distance phone calls each month. Create a workbook with a separate sheet for each roommate. Track the following information for each month's long-distance calls: date of call, time of call (AM or PM), call minutes, location called, state called, area code, phone number, and call charge. Total the charges for each roommate. Create a summary sheet of all three roommates' charges for the month.

To complete this independent challenge:

**a.** Create a new workbook, then save it as "Monthly Long Distance" to the appropriate folder on your Project Disk.

**b.** Enter column headings and row labels to track each call.

**c.** Use your own data, entering at least three long-distance calls for each roommate.

**d.** Create totals for minutes and charges on each roommate's sheet.

**e.** Create a summary sheet that shows each name and uses cell references to display the total minutes and total charges for each person.

**f.** On the summary sheet, create a hyperlink from each person's name to cell A1 of their respective worksheet.

**g.** Create a workbook with the same type of information for the two people in the apartment next door. Save it as "Next Door".

**h.** Use linking to create a 3-D reference that displays that information on your summary sheet so your roommates can compare their expenses with the neighbors'.

**i.** Change the workbook properties to Read only.

**j.** Save the Monthly Long Distance workbook in HTML format and preview it in your Web browser.

**WEB WORK**

**4.** Maria Abbott, general sales manager at MediaLoft, has asked you to create a projection of MediaLoft advertising expenditures for 1999–2002 that she can put on the company intranet. She wants managers to review this information for an advertising discussion at the next managers meeting. The categories and 1999 figures are already on the site.

**a.** Connect to the Internet, go to the MediaLoft intranet site at http://www.course.com/illustrated/MediaLoft, click the Marketing link, then locate and print the Ad Campaign Summary. Close your browser and disconnect from the Internet.

**b.** Start Excel and create a workbook titled "Ad Campaign Projection". Name Sheet1 "1999", enter the categories and numbers from your printout, and use a formula to calculate the total.

**c.** Add an appropriate worksheet name in cell A1.

**d.** Create figures for the years 2000–2002 and put them in the columns to the right of the 1999 figures, then use font and fill colors to make the worksheet attractive.

**e.** Format all numbers in an appropriate format.

**f.** Use formulas to create totals for each year and for each ad type. Format the totals so they stand out from the other figures and use cell borders as appropriate.

**g.** Create a custom view of the worksheet and save the view using a descriptive name.

**h.** Delete the unused sheets.

**i.** Add your name to the footer, then save and print the worksheet.

**j.** Save your workbook as a Web page, using the filename Ad Campaign Projection - Web, adding descriptive text to the title bar.

**k.** Preview the resulting file in your Web Browser, and test the chart tab.

**l.** Close your browser and Excel.

**Excel 2000**

# ▶ Visual Workshop

Create the worksheet shown in Figure F-21. Save the workbook as "Martinez Agency". Preview, then print, the worksheet. (*Hint:* Notice the hyperlink target on the sheet name at the bottom of the figure.)

**FIGURE F-21**

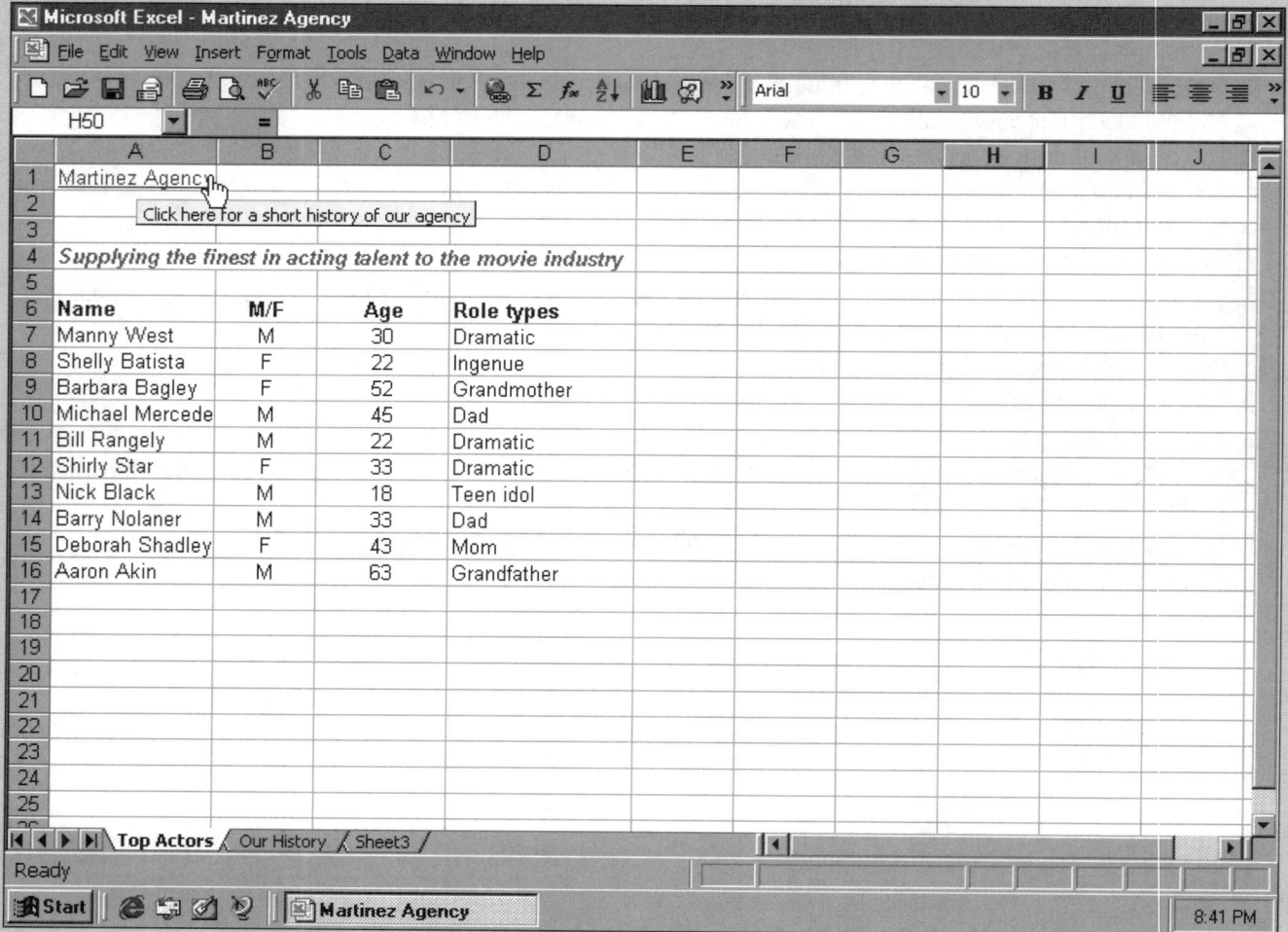

# Automating
## Worksheet Tasks

### Objectives

- ► **Plan a macro**
- [MOUS] ► **Record a macro**
- [MOUS] ► **Run a macro**
- [MOUS] ► **Edit a macro**
- ► **Use shortcut keys with macros**
- ► **Use the Personal Macro Workbook**
- ► **Add a macro as a menu item**
- ► **Create a toolbar for macros**

A **macro** is a set of instructions that performs tasks in the order you specify. You create macros to automate frequently performed Excel tasks that require a series of steps. For example, if you usually type your name and date in a worksheet footer, Excel can record the keystrokes in a macro that types the text and inserts the current date automatically. In this unit, you will plan and design a simple macro, then record and run it. Then you will edit the macro. You will also create a macro to run when you use shortcut keys, store a macro in the Personal Macro Workbook, add a macro option to the Tools menu, and create a new toolbar for macros. ━━ Jim is creating a macro for the accounting department. The macro will automatically insert text that will identify the worksheet as originating in the accounting department.

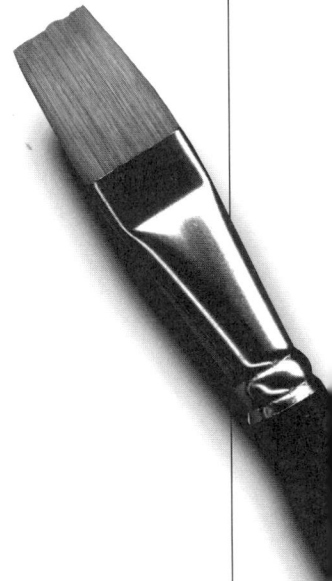

# Planning a Macro

You create macros for tasks that you perform on a regular basis. For example, you can create a macro to enter and format text or to save and print a worksheet. To create a macro, you record the series of actions or write the instructions in a special format. Because the sequence of actions is important, you need to plan the macro carefully before you record it. You use commands on the Tools menu to record, run, and modify macros. ◤◤◤ Jim creates a macro for the accounting department that inserts the text "Accounting Department" in the upper-left corner of any worksheet. He plans the macro using the following guidelines:

## Steps 1 2 3 4

1. **Assign the macro a descriptive name, and write out the steps the macro will perform**
   This planning helps eliminate careless errors. Jim decides to name the macro "DeptStamp". He writes a description of the macro, as shown in Figure G-1. See Table G-1 for a list of macros Jim might create to automate other tasks.

2. **Decide how you will perform the actions you want to record**
   You can use the mouse, the keyboard, or a combination of the two. Jim decides to use both the mouse and keyboard.

3. **Practice the steps you want Excel to record and write them down**
   Jim wrote down the sequence of actions as he performed them, and he is now ready to record and test the macro.

4. **Decide where to locate the description of the macro and the macro itself**
   Macros can be stored in an unused area of the active workbook, in a new workbook, or in the Personal Macro Workbook. Jim stores the macro in a new workbook.

## Macro to create stamp with the department name

Name: DeptStamp

Description: Adds a stamp to the top left of worksheet identifying it as an accounting department worksheet

Steps:
1. Position the cell pointer in cell A1
2. Type Accounting Department, then click the Enter button
3. Click Format on the menu bar, click Cells
4. Click Font tab, under Font style click Bold, under Underline click Single, and under Color click Red, then click OK

Excel 2000

TABLE G-1: Possible macros and their descriptive names

| description of macro | descriptive name |
|---|---|
| Enter a frequently used proper name, such as Jim Fernandez | JimFernandez |
| Enter a frequently used company name, such as MediaLoft | CompanyName |
| Print the active worksheet on a single page, in landscape orientation | FitToLand |
| Turn off the header and footer in the active worksheet | HeadFootOff |
| Show a frequently used custom view, such as a generic view of the worksheet, setting the print and display settings back to the Excel defaults | GenericView |

CLUES TO USE

### Macros and viruses

When you open an Excel Workbook that has macros, you will see a message asking you if you want to enable or disable macros. This is because macros can contain viruses, destructive software programs that can damage your computer files. If you know your workbook came from a trusted source, click Enable macros. If you are not sure of the workbook's source, click Disable macros. If you disable the macros in a workbook, you will not be able to use them in the workbook. For more information, see the Excel Help topic About Viruses and workbook macros.

# Recording a Macro

The easiest way to create a macro is to record it using the Excel Macro Recorder. You simply turn the Macro Recorder on, enter the keystrokes, select the commands you want the macro to perform, then stop the recorder. As you record the macro, each action is translated into programming code that you can later view and modify. ⬤⬤⬤⬤ Jim wants to create a macro that enters a department stamp in cell A1 of the active worksheet. He creates this macro by recording his actions.

## Steps 1234

1. **Start Excel if necessary, click the New button ▫ on the Standard toolbar, then save the blank workbook as My Excel Macros**
   Now you are ready to start recording the macro.

2. **Click Tools on the menu bar, point to Macro, then click Record New Macro**
   The Record Macro dialog box opens. See Figure G-2. Notice the default name Macro1 is selected. You can either assign this name or type a new name. The first character of a macro name must be a letter; the remaining characters can be letters, numbers, or underscores; (spaces are not allowed in macro names; use underscores in place of spaces). This dialog box also allows you to assign a shortcut key for running the macro and to instruct Excel where to store the macro.

3. **Type DeptStamp in the Macro name box**

4. **If the Store macro in list arrow box does not read "This Workbook", click the list arrow and select This Workbook**

5. **If the Description text box does not contain your name, select the existing name, type your own name, then click OK**
   The dialog box closes. Excel displays the small Stop Recording toolbar containing the Stop Recording button ■, and the word "Recording" appears on the status bar. Take your time performing the steps below. Excel records every keystroke, menu option, and mouse action that you make.

6. **Press [Ctrl][Home]**
   The cell pointer moves to cell A1. When you begin an Excel session, macros record absolute cell references. By beginning the recording in cell A1, you ensure that the macro includes the instruction to select cell A1 as the first step.

7. **Type Accounting Department in cell A1, then click the Enter button ✓ on the formula bar**

8. **Click Format on the menu bar, then click Cells**

9. **Click the Font tab, in the Font style list box click Bold, click the Underline list arrow and click Single, then click the Color list arrow and click red (third row, first color on left)**
   See Figure G-3.

10. **Click OK, click the Stop Recording button ■ on the Stop Recording toolbar, click cell D1 to deselect cell A1, then save the workbook**
    Compare your results with Figure G-4.

FIGURE G-2: Record Macro dialog box

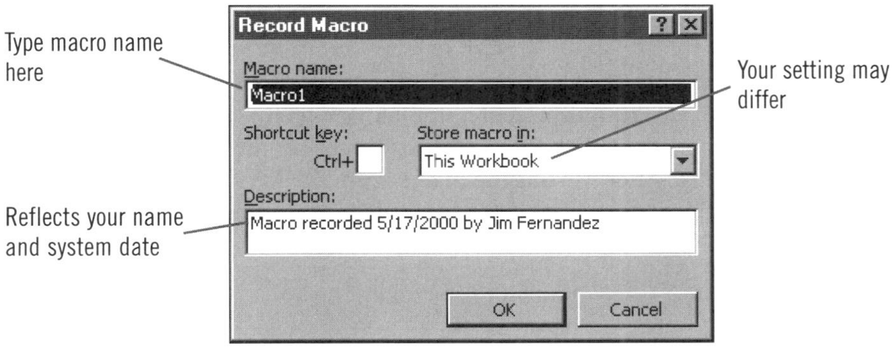

Type macro name here

Record Macro

Macro name:
Macro1

Shortcut key:
Ctrl+

Store macro in:
This Workbook

Your setting may differ

Description:
Macro recorded 5/17/2000 by Jim Fernandez

Reflects your name and system date

OK     Cancel

FIGURE G-3: Font tab of the Format Cells dialog box

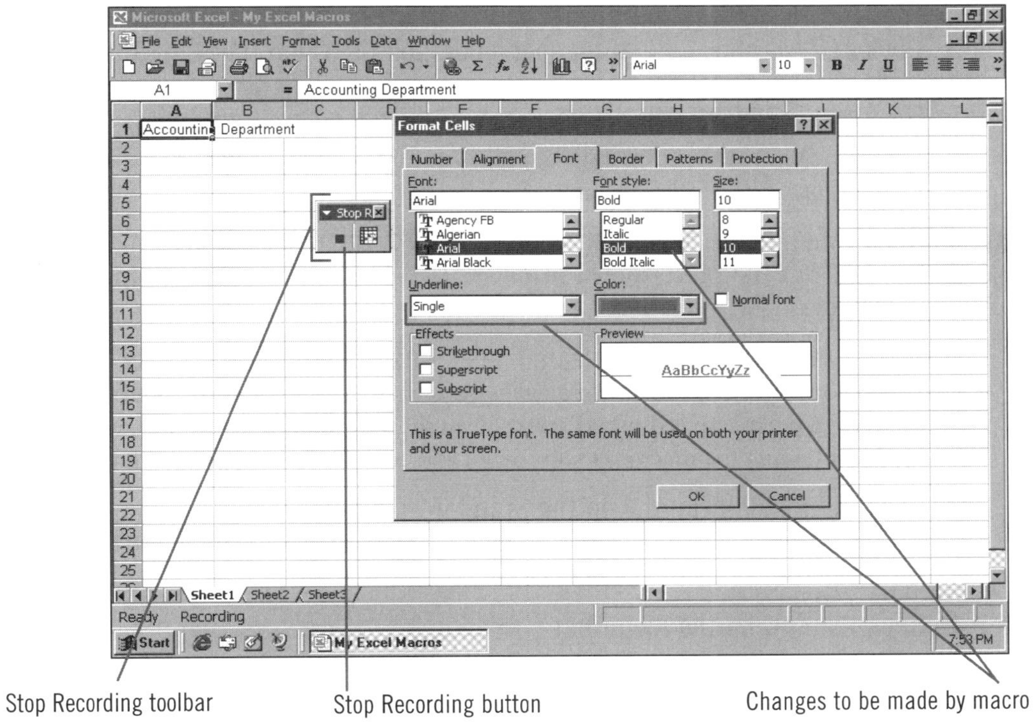

Microsoft Excel - My Excel Macros

File Edit View Insert Format Tools Data Window Help

A1     =  Accounting Department

1  Accounting Department

Stop R

Format Cells

Number | Alignment | Font | Border | Patterns | Protection

Font:
Arial

Agency FB
Algerian
Arial
Arial Black

Font style:
Bold

Regular
Italic
Bold
Bold Italic

Size:
10

8
9
10
11

Underline:
Single

Color:

Normal font

Effects
Strikethrough
Superscript
Subscript

Preview

AaBbCcYyZz

This is a TrueType font. The same font will be used on both your printer and your screen.

OK     Cancel

Sheet1 / Sheet2 / Sheet3

Ready     Recording

Start          My Excel Macros          7:53 PM

Stop Recording toolbar          Stop Recording button          Changes to be made by macro

FIGURE G-4: Personalized department stamp

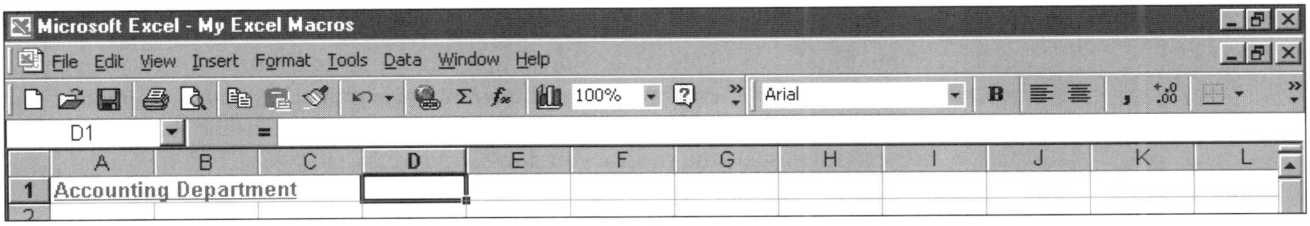

Microsoft Excel - My Excel Macros

File Edit View Insert Format Tools Data Window Help

100%     Arial     B

D1     =

1  Accounting Department

CLUES TO USE

## Using templates to create a workbook

You can create a workbook using an Excel **template**, a special-purpose workbook with formatting and formulas, such as an invoice or income statement. Click File on the menu bar, click New, click the Spreadsheet Solutions or Business planner templates tab, then double-click any template. Excel opens a workbook using that template design.

# Running a Macro

**Excel 2000**

Once you record a macro, you should test it to make sure that the actions performed are correct. To test a macro, you **run**, or execute, it. One way to run a macro is to select the macro in the Macros dialog box, then click Run. ◀▬▬ Jim clears the contents of cell A1 and then tests the DeptStamp macro. After he runs the macro from the My Excel Macros workbook, he decides to test the macro once more from a newly opened workbook.

## Steps

1. **Click cell A1, click Edit on the menu bar, point to Clear, click All, then click any other cell to deselect cell A1**
   When you delete only the contents of a cell, any formatting still remains in the cell. By using the Clear All option on the Edit menu, you can be sure that the cell is free of contents and formatting.

> **QuickTip**
> To delete a macro, select the macro name in the Macro dialog box, click Delete, then click Yes to confirm.

2. **Click Tools on the menu bar, point to Macro, then click Macros**
   The Macro dialog box, shown in Figure G-5, lists all the macros contained in the open workbooks.

3. **Make sure DeptStamp is selected, click Run, then deselect cell A1**
   Watch your screen as the macro quickly plays back the steps you recorded in the previous lesson. When the macro is finished, your screen should look like Figure G-6. As long as the workbook containing the macro remains open, you can run the macro from any open workbook.

4. **Click the New button [icon] on the Standard toolbar**
   Because the new workbook automatically fills the screen, it is difficult to be sure that the My Excel Macros workbook is still open.

5. **Click Window on the menu bar**
   A list of open workbooks appears underneath the menu options. The active workbook name (in this case, Book2) appears with a check mark to its left. The My Excel Macros workbook appears on the menu, so you know it's open. See Figure G-7.

> **QuickTip**
> To stop a macro while it is running, press [Esc].

6. **Deselect cell A1 if necessary, click Tools on the menu bar, point to Macro, click Macros, make sure 'My Excel Macros.xls'!DeptStamp is selected, click Run, then deselect cell A1**
   Cell A1 should look like Figure G-6. Notice that when multiple workbooks are open, the macro name includes the workbook name between single quotation marks, followed by an exclamation point, indicating that the macro is outside the active workbook. Since you use this workbook only to test the macro, you don't need to save it.

7. **Close Book2 without saving changes**
   The My Excel Macros workbook reappears.

---

EXCEL G-6  **AUTOMATING WORKSHEET TASKS**

FIGURE G-5: Macro dialog box

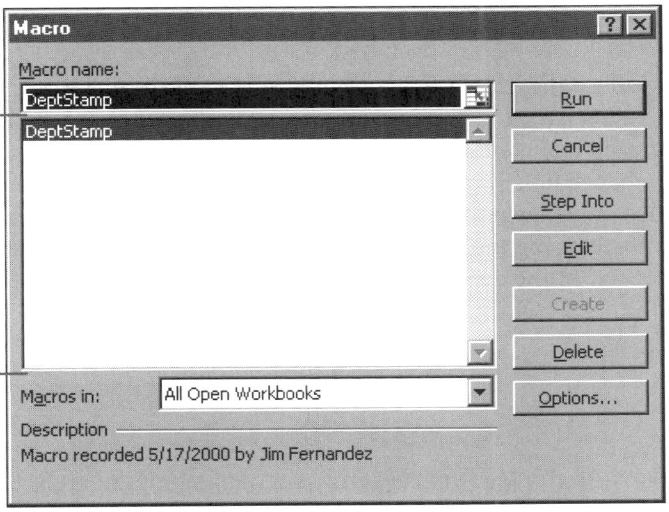

Lists macros stored
in open workbooks

FIGURE G-6: Result of running DeptStamp macro

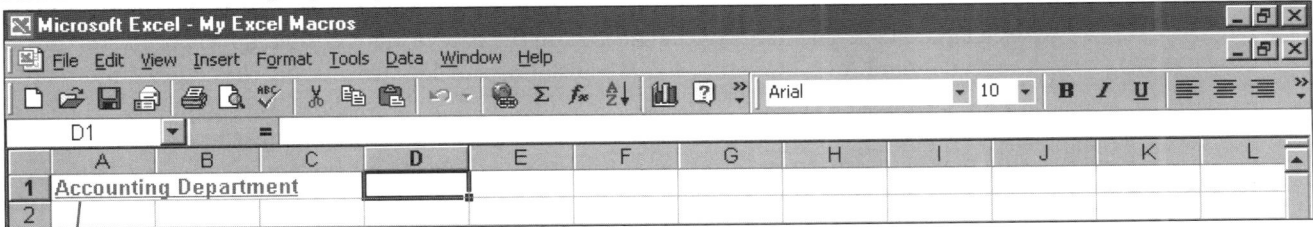

DeptStamp macro
inserts formatted
text in cell A1

FIGURE G-7: Window menu showing list of open workbooks

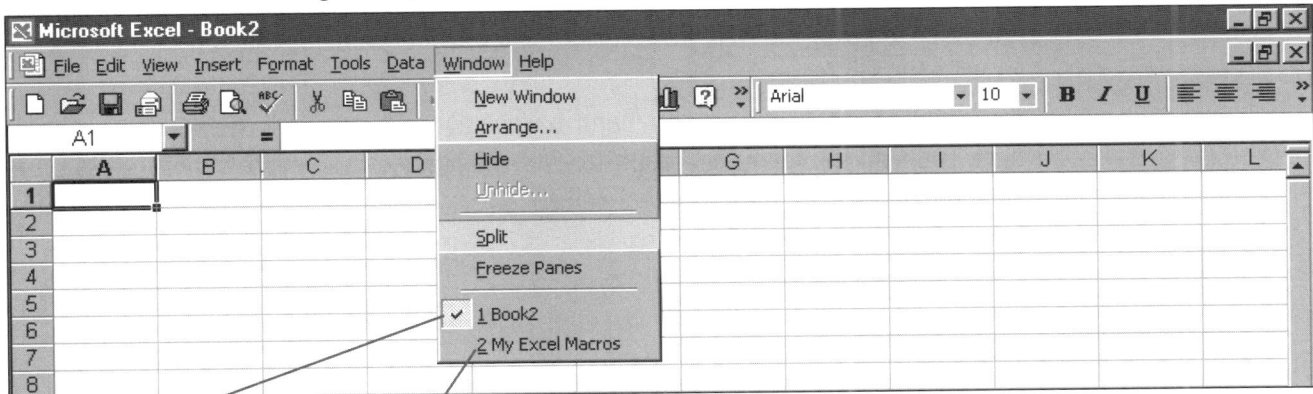

Check mark indicates
active workbook

Indicates this
workbook is still open

# Editing a Macro

When you use the Macro Recorder to create a macro, the instructions are recorded automatically in Visual Basic for Applications programming language. Each macro is stored as a **module**, or program code container, attached to the workbook. Once you record a macro, you might need to change it. If you have a lot of changes to make, it might be best to re-record the macro. If you need to make only minor adjustments, you can edit the macro code, or program instructions, directly using the Visual Basic Editor. ◄══════ Jim wants to modify his macro to change the point size of the department stamp to 12.

## Steps 1 2 3 4

**QuickTip**

Another way to start the Visual Basic Editor is to click Tools on the menu bar, point to Macro, then click Visual Basic Editor, or press [Alt][F11].

1. **Make sure the My Excel Macros workbook is open, click Tools on the menu bar, point to Macro, click Macros, make sure DeptStamp is selected, then click Edit**
   The Visual Basic Editor starts showing the DeptStamp macro steps in a numbered module window (in this case, Module1).

2. **Maximize the window titled My Excel Macros.xls – [Module1 (Code)], then examine the steps in the macro**
   See Figure G-8. The name of the macro and the date it was recorded appear at the top of the module window. Notice that Excel translates your keystrokes and commands into words, known as macro code. For example, the line .FontStyle = "Bold" was generated when you clicked Bold in the Format Cells dialog box. When you make changes in a dialog box during macro recording, Excel automatically stores all the dialog box settings in the macro code. You also see lines of code that you didn't generate directly while recording the DeptStamp macro; for example, .Name = "Arial".

3. **In the line .Size = 10, double-click 10 to select it, then type 12**
   Because Module1 is attached to the workbook and not stored as a separate file, any changes to the module are saved automatically when the workbook is saved.

4. **In the Visual Basic Editor, click File on the menu bar, click Print, then click OK to print the module**
   Review the printout of Module1.

5. **Click File on the menu bar, then click Close and Return to Microsoft Excel**
   You want to rerun the DeptStamp macro to view the point size edit you made using the Visual Basic Editor.

6. **Click cell A1, click Edit on the menu bar, point to Clear, click All, deselect cell A1, click Tools on the menu bar, point to Macro, click Macros, make sure DeptStamp is selected, click Run, then deselect cell A1**
   Compare your results with Figure G-9.

7. **Save the workbook**

FIGURE G-8: Visual Basic Editor showing Module1

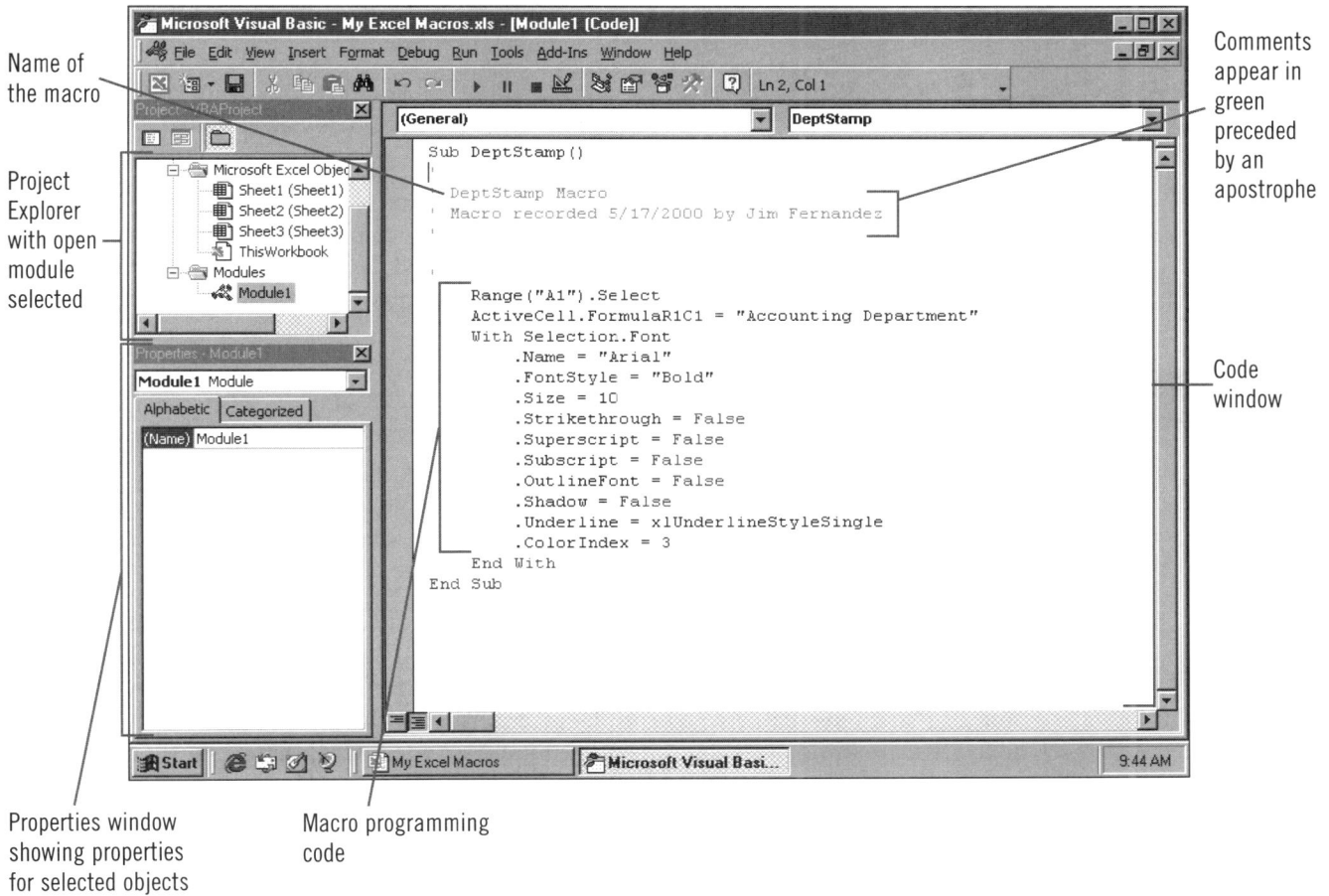

Name of
the macro

Project
Explorer
with open
module
selected

Comments
appear in
green
preceded
by an
apostrophe

```
Sub DeptStamp()

' DeptStamp Macro
' Macro recorded 5/17/2000 by Jim Fernandez
'

'
    Range("A1").Select
    ActiveCell.FormulaR1C1 = "Accounting Department"
    With Selection.Font
        .Name = "Arial"
        .FontStyle = "Bold"
        .Size = 10
        .Strikethrough = False
        .Superscript = False
        .Subscript = False
        .OutlineFont = False
        .Shadow = False
        .Underline = xlUnderlineStyleSingle
        .ColorIndex = 3
    End With
End Sub
```

Code
window

Properties window
showing properties
for selected objects

Macro programming
code

FIGURE G-9: Result of running edited DeptStamp macro

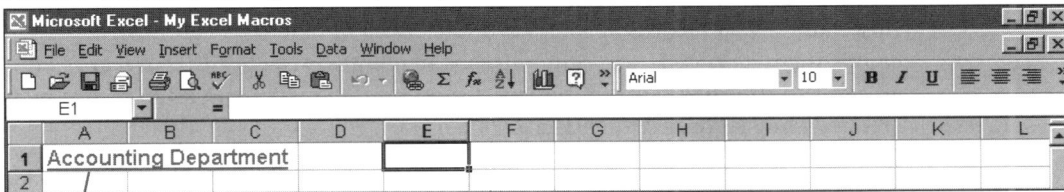

| | A | B | C | D | E | F | G | H | I | J | K | L |
|---|---|---|---|---|---|---|---|---|---|---|---|---|
| 1 | Accounting Department | | | | | | | | | | | |
| 2 | | | | | | | | | | | | |

Font size enlarged
to 12 pt.

## CLUES TO USE

### Adding comments to code

With practice, you will be able to interpret the lines of code within your macro. Others who use your macro, however, might want to know the function of a particular line. You can explain the code by adding comments to the macro. Comments are explanatory text added to the lines of code. When you enter a comment, you must type an apostrophe (') before the comment text. Otherwise, Excel thinks you have entered a command. On a color monitor, comments appear in green after you press [Enter]. See Figure G-8. You also can insert blank lines in the macro code to make the code more readable. To do this, type an apostrophe, then press [Enter].

# Using Shortcut Keys with Macros

In addition to running a macro from the Macro dialog box, you can run a macro by assigning a shortcut key combination. Using shortcut keys to run macros reduces the number of keystrokes required to begin macro playback. You assign shortcut key combinations in the Record Macro dialog box. ➤ Jim also wants to create a macro called CompanyName to enter the company name into a worksheet. He assigns a shortcut key combination to run the macro.

## Steps

**1. Click cell B2**

You will record the macro in cell B2. You want to be able to enter the company name anywhere in a worksheet. Therefore, you will not begin the macro with an instruction to position the cell pointer, as you did in the DeptStamp macro.

**2. Click Tools on the menu bar, point to Macro, then click Record New Macro**

The Record Macro dialog box opens. Notice the option Shortcut key: Ctrl+ followed by a blank box. You can type a letter (A-Z) in the Shortcut key box to assign the key combination of [Ctrl] plus that letter to run the macro. You use the key combination [Ctrl][Shift] plus a letter to avoid overriding any of the Excel's assigned [Ctrl] [letter] shortcut keys, such as [Ctrl][C] for Copy.

**3. With the default macro name selected, type CompanyName, click the Shortcut key text box, press and hold [Shift], type C, then, if necessary, replace the name in the Description box with your name**

Compare your screen with Figure G-10. You are ready to record the CompanyName macro.

**4. Click OK to close the dialog box**

By default, Excel records absolute cell references in macros. Beginning the macro in cell B2 causes the macro code to begin with a statement to select cell B2. Because you want to be able to run this macro in any active cell, you need to instruct Excel to record relative cell references while recording the macro.

### QuickTip

When you begin an Excel session, the Relative Reference button is toggled off, indicating that Excel is recording absolute cell references in macros. Once selected, and until it is toggled off again, the Relative Reference setting remains in effect during the current Excel session.

**5. Click the Relative Reference button 🔲 on the Stop Recording toolbar**

The Relative Reference button is now indented to indicate that it is selected. See Figure G-11. This button is a toggle and retains the relative reference setting until you click it again to turn it off.

**6. Type MediaLoft in cell B2, click the Enter button ☑ on the formula bar, press [Ctrl][I] to italicize the text, click the Stop Recording button ■ on the Stop Recording toolbar, then deselect cell B2**

MediaLoft appears in italics in cell B2. You are ready to run the macro in cell A5 using the shortcut key combination.

**7. Click cell A5, press and hold [Ctrl][Shift], type C, then deselect the cell**

The result appears in cell A5. See Figure G-12. Because the macro played back in the selected cell (A5) instead of the cell where it was recorded (B2), Jim is convinced that the macro recorded relative cell references.

**8. Save the workbook**

FIGURE G-10: **Record Macro dialog box with shortcut key assigned**

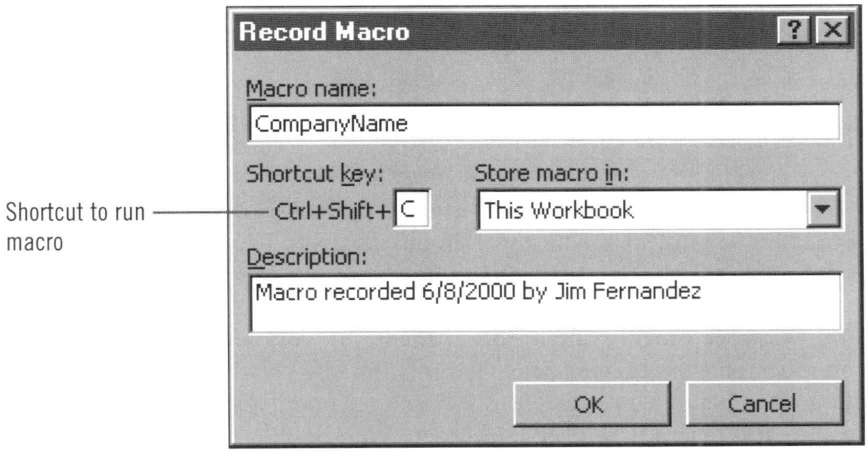

Shortcut to run ──────
macro

**Record Macro** [?][X]

Macro name:
CompanyName

Shortcut key:     Store macro in:
Ctrl+Shift+ C     This Workbook [▼]

Description:
Macro recorded 6/8/2000 by Jim Fernandez

OK     Cancel

FIGURE G-11: **Stop Recording toolbar with Relative Reference
button selected**

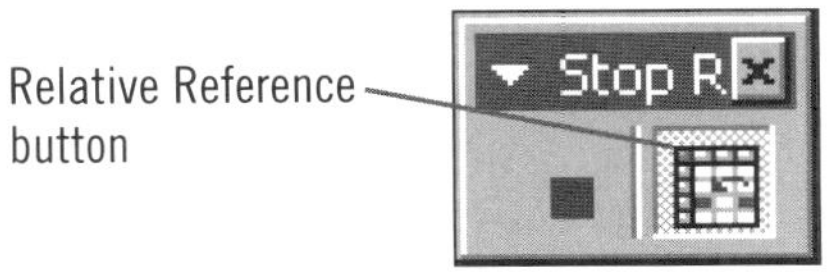

Relative Reference ──────
button

▼ Stop R [X]

FIGURE G-12: **Result of running the CompanyName macro**

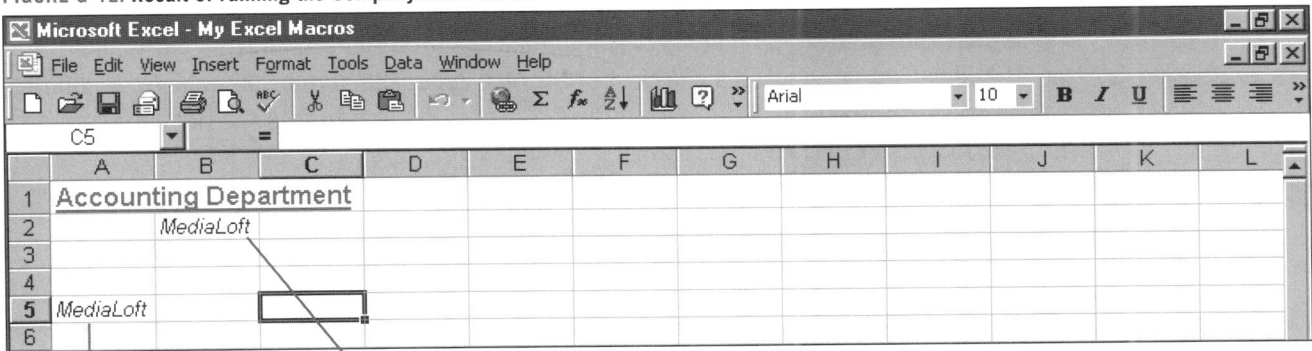

Microsoft Excel - My Excel Macros [_][8][X]

File  Edit  View  Insert  Format  Tools  Data  Window  Help     [_][8][X]

| | A | B | C | D | E | F | G | H | I | J | K | L |
|---|---|---|---|---|---|---|---|---|---|---|---|---|
| 1 | Accounting Department | | | | | | | | | | | |
| 2 | | MediaLoft | | | | | | | | | | |
| 3 | | | | | | | | | | | | |
| 4 | | | | | | | | | | | | |
| 5 | MediaLoft | | | | | | | | | | | |
| 6 | | | | | | | | | | | | |

C5 [▼]  =

Result of running
CompanyName
macro in cell A5

Result of recording
CompanyName
macro in cell B2

# Using the Personal Macro Workbook

You can store commonly used macros in a **Personal Macro Workbook**. The Personal Macro Workbook is always available, unless you specify otherwise, and gives you access to all the macros it contains, regardless of which workbooks are open. The Personal Macro Workbook file is created automatically the first time you choose to store a macro in it. Additional macros are added to the Personal Macro Workbook when you store them there. ◄──── Jim often adds a footer to his worksheets identifying his department, the workbook name, the worksheet name, the page number, and the current date. He saves time by creating a macro that automatically inserts this footer. Because he wants this macro to be available whenever he uses Excel, Jim decides to store this macro in the Personal Macro Workbook.

**Steps** 1234

1. From any cell in the active worksheet, click **Tools** on the menu bar, point to **Macro**, then click **Record New Macro**
   The Record Macro dialog box opens.

**Trouble?**

If you are prompted to replace an existing macro named FooterStamp, click Yes.

2. Type **FooterStamp** in the Macro name box, click the **Shortcut key box**, press and hold **[Shift]**, type **F**, then click the **Store macro in list arrow**
   You have named the macro FooterStamp and assigned it the shortcut combination [Ctrl][Shift][F]. Notice that This Workbook is selected by default, indicating that Excel automatically stores macros in the active workbook. See Figure G-13. You also can choose to store the macro in a new workbook or in the Personal Macro Workbook.

**QuickTip**

If you see a message saying that the Personal Macro Workbook needs to be opened, open it, and then begin again from step 1. Once created, the Personal Macro Workbook file is usually stored in the Windows/Application Data/ Microsoft/Excel/XLSTART folder under the name "Personal".

3. Click **Personal Macro Workbook**, replace the existing name in the Description text box with your own name, if necessary, then click **OK**
   The recorder is on, and you are ready to record the macro keystrokes. (If there is already a macro assigned to this shortcut, display the Personal Macro workbook and delete the FooterStamp macro. Then return to the My Excel Macro workbook and begin again from step 1.)

4. Click **File** on the menu bar, click **Page Setup**, click the **Header/Footer tab** (make sure to do this even if it is already active), click **Custom Footer**, in the Left section box, type **Accounting**, click the **Center section box**, click the **File Name button** 🗐, press **[Spacebar]**, type **/**, press **[Spacebar]**, click the **Tab Name button** 🗐 to insert the sheet name, click the **Right section box**, type your name followed by a comma, press **[Spacebar]**, click the **Date button** 🗐, click **OK** to return to the Header/Footer tab
   The footer stamp is set up, as shown in Figure G-14.

**QuickTip**

You can copy or move macros stored in other work-books to the Personal Macro Workbook using the Visual Basic Editor.

5. Click **OK** to return to the worksheet, then click the **Stop Recording button** 🔳 on the Stop Recording toolbar
   You want to ensure that the macro will set the footer stamp in any active worksheet.

6. Activate Sheet2, in cell A1 type **Testing the FooterStamp macro**, press **[Enter]**, press and hold **[Ctrl][Shift]**, then type **F**
   The FooterStamp macro plays back the sequence of commands.

7. Preview the worksheet to verify that the new footer was inserted

8. Print, then save the worksheet
   Jim is satisfied that the FooterStamp macro works in any active worksheet. Next, Jim adds the macro as a menu item on the Tools menu.

Click to store in new blank workbook

Click to store in active workbook

Click to store in Personal Macro Workbook

**Record Macro**

Macro name:
FooterStamp

Shortcut key:
Ctrl+Shift+ F

Store macro in:
This Workbook

Personal Macro Workbook
New Workbook
This Workbook

Description:
Macro recorded 5/17/

OK        Cancel

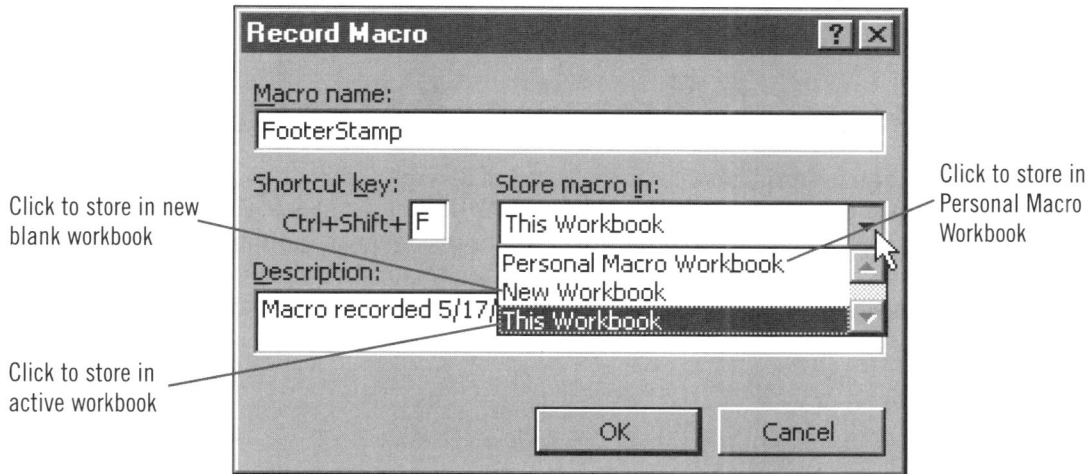

FIGURE G-14: Header/Footer tab showing custom footer settings

**Page Setup**

Page    Margins    Header/Footer    Sheet

Print...

Print Preview

Options...

Header:
(none)

Custom Header...        Custom Footer...

Footer:
Accounting, My Excel Macros / Sheet1, [Student Name], 7/18/

Accounting        My Excel Macros / Sheet1 [Student Name], 7/18/99

Workbook name

Sheet name

Date will reflect your system date

OK        Cancel

## Working with the Personal Macro Workbook

Once created, the Personal Macro Workbook automatically opens each time you start Excel. By default, the Personal Macro Workbook is hidden as a precautionary measure so you don't accidentally add anything to it. When the Personal Macro Workbook is hidden, you can add macros to it but you cannot delete macros from it.

# Adding a Macro as a Menu Item

In addition to storing macros in the Personal Macro Workbook so that they are always available, you can add macros as items on the Excel Worksheet menu bar. The **Worksheet menu bar** is a special toolbar at the top of the Excel screen that you can customize. ◄━━━ To increase the availability of the FooterStamp macro, Jim decides to add it as an item on the Tools menu. First, he adds a custom menu item to the Tools menu, then he assigns the macro to that menu item.

## Steps

1. **Click Tools on the menu bar, click Customize, click the Commands tab, then under Categories, click Macros**
   See Figure G-15.

2. **Click Custom Menu Item under Commands, drag the selection to Tools on the menu bar (the menu opens), then point just under the last menu option, but do not release the mouse button**
   Compare your screen to Figure G-16.

3. **Release the mouse button**
   Now, Custom Menu item is the last item on the Tools menu.

4. **With the Tools menu still open, right-click Custom Menu Item, select the text in the Name box (&Custom Menu Item), type Footer Stamp, then click Assign Macro**
   Unlike a macro name, the name of a custom menu item can have spaces between words, as do all standard menu items. The Assign Macro dialog box opens.

5. **Click PERSONAL.XLS!FooterStamp under Macro name, click OK, then click Close**

6. **Click the Sheet3 tab, in cell A1 type Testing macro menu item, press [Enter], then click Tools on the menu bar**
   The Tools menu appears with the new menu option at the bottom. See Figure G-17.

7. **Click Footer Stamp, preview the worksheet to verify that the footer was inserted, then close the Print Preview window**
   The Print Preview window appears with the footer stamp. Since others using your machine might be confused by the macro on the menu, it's a good idea to remove it.

8. **Click Tools on the menu bar, click Customize, click the Toolbars tab, click Worksheet Menu Bar to select it, click Reset, click OK to confirm, click Close, then click Tools on the menu bar to make sure that the custom item has been deleted**
   Because you did not make any changes to your workbook, you don't need to save it. Next, Jim creates a toolbar for macros and adds macros to it.

FIGURE G-15: Commands tab of the Customize dialog box

Drag to menu location

FIGURE G-16: Tools menu showing placement of Custom Menu Item

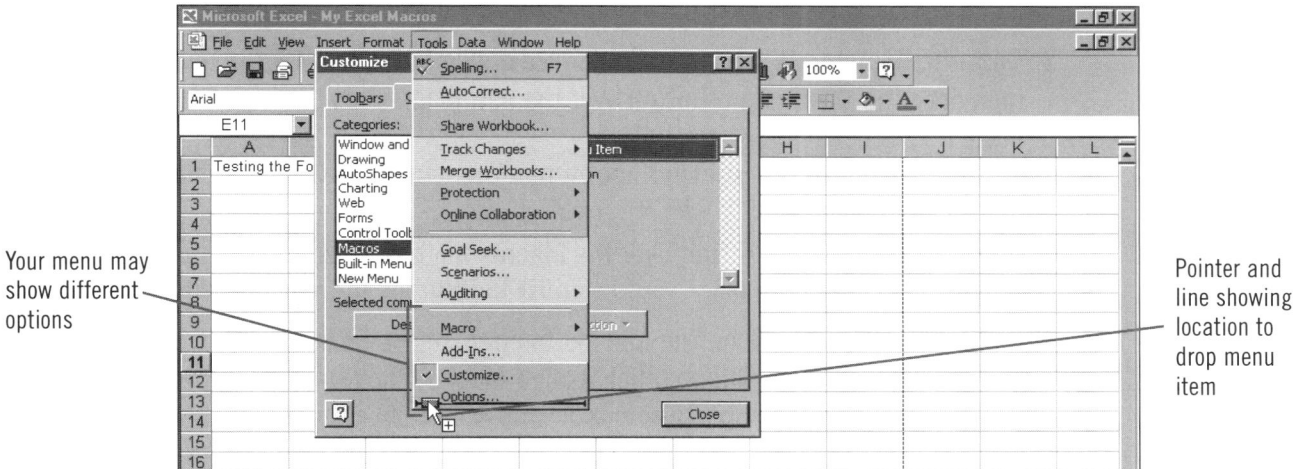

Your menu may show different options

Pointer and line showing location to drop menu item

FIGURE G-17: Tools menu with new Footer Stamp item

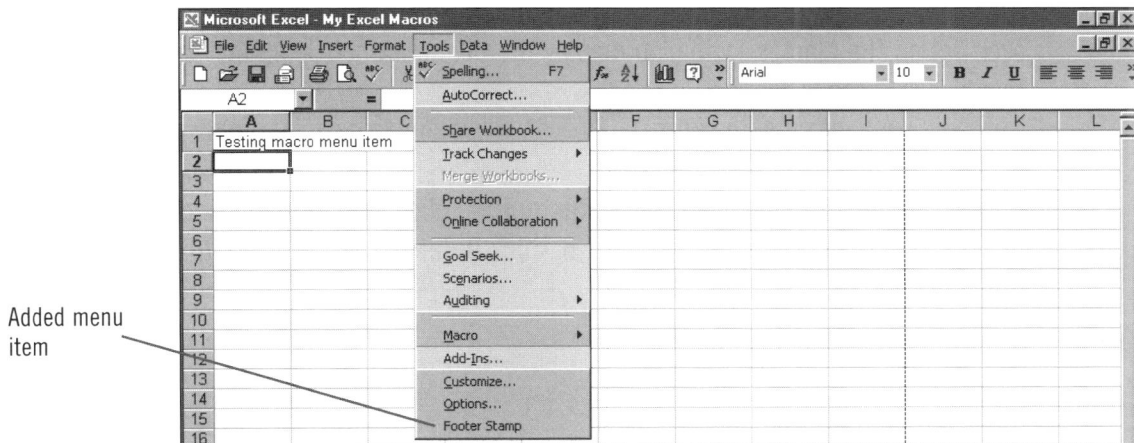

Added menu item

# Creating a Toolbar for Macros

Toolbars contain buttons that allow you to access commonly used commands. You can create your own custom toolbars to organize commands so that you can find and use them quickly. Once you create a toolbar, you then add buttons to access Excel commands such as macros. Jim has decided to create a custom toolbar called Macros that will contain buttons to run two of his macros.

## Steps

1. **With Sheet3 active, click Tools on the menu bar, click Customize, click the Toolbars tab, if necessary, then click New**
   The New Toolbar dialog box opens, as shown in Figure G-18. Under Toolbar name, a default name of Custom1 is selected.

2. **Type Macros, then click OK**
   Excel adds the new toolbar named Macros to the bottom of the list and a small, empty toolbar named Macros opens. See Figure G-19. Notice that you cannot see the entire toolbar name. A toolbar starts small and automatically expands to fit the buttons you assign to it.

3. **Click the Commands tab in the Customize dialog box, click Macros under Categories, then drag the ☺ Custom Button over the new Macros toolbar and release the mouse button**
   The Macros toolbar now contains one button. You want the toolbar to contain two macros, so you need to add one more button.

4. **Drag the ☺ Custom Button over the Macros toolbar again**
   With the two buttons in place, you customize the buttons and assign macros to them.

5. **Right-click the left ☺ on the Macros toolbar, select &Custom Button in the Name box, type Department Stamp, click Assign Macro, click DeptStamp, then click OK**
   With the first toolbar button customized, you are ready to customize the second button.

6. **With the Customize dialog box open, right-click the right ☺ on the Macros toolbar, edit the name to read Company Name, click Change Button Image, click 🏃 (bottom row, third from the left), right-click 🏃, click Assign Macro, click CompanyName to select it, click OK, then close the Customize dialog box**
   The Macros toolbar appears with the two customized macro buttons.

7. **Move the mouse pointer over ☺ on the Macros toolbar to display the macro name (Department Stamp), then click to run the macro; click cell B2, move the mouse pointer over 🏃 on the Macros toolbar to display the macro name (Company Name), click 🏃, then deselect the cell**
   Compare your screen with Figure G-20. The DeptStamp macro automatically replaces the contents of cell A1.

8. **Click Tools on the menu bar, click Customize, click the Toolbars tab, if necessary, under Toolbars click Macros to select it, click Delete, click OK to confirm the deletion, then click Close**

9. **Save, then close the workbooks**

FIGURE G-18: **New Toolbar dialog box**

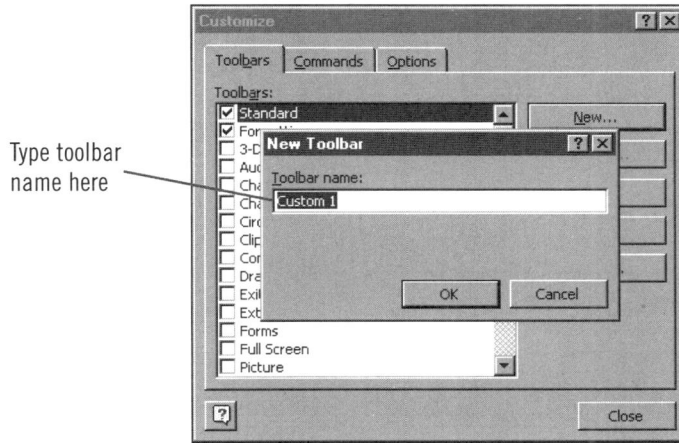

Type toolbar name here

FIGURE G-19: **Customize dialog box with new Macros toolbar**

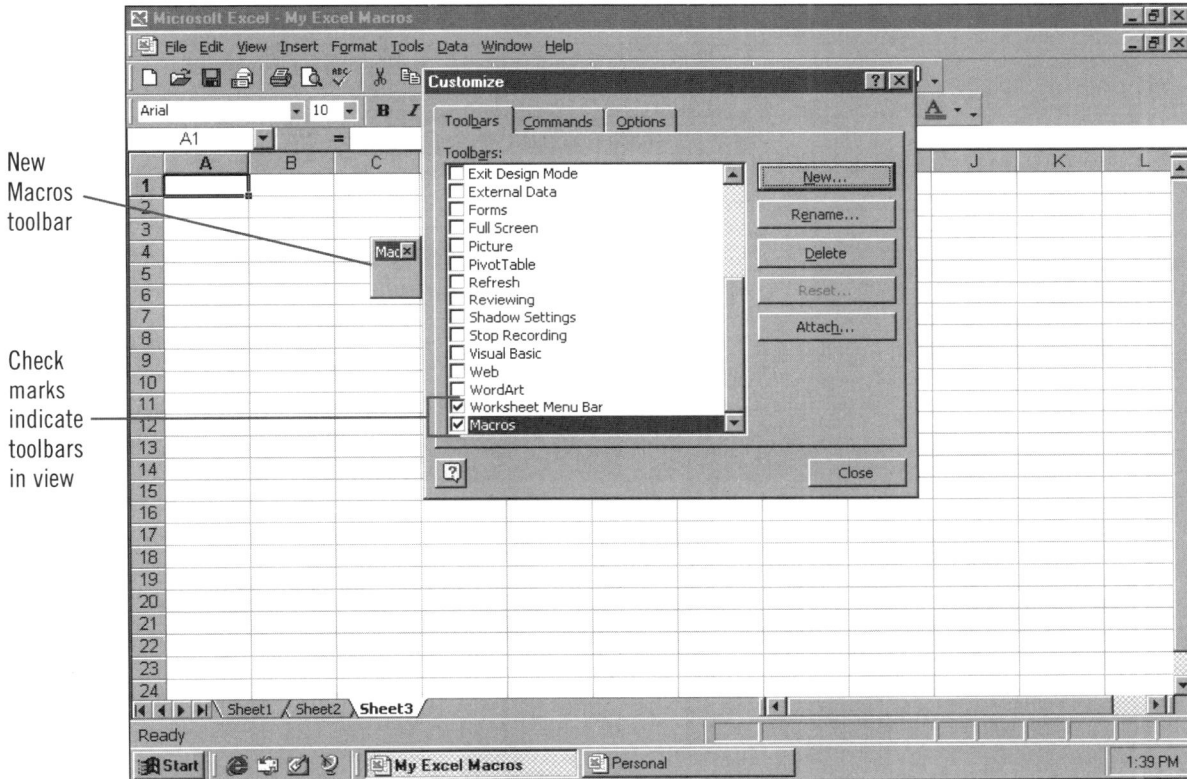

New Macros toolbar

Check marks indicate toolbars in view

FIGURE G-20: **Worksheet showing Macros toolbar with two customized buttons**

Click to run DeptStamp macro

Click to run CompanyName macro

# Practice

## ► Concepts Review

Label each element of the Excel screen shown in Figure G-21.

FIGURE G-21

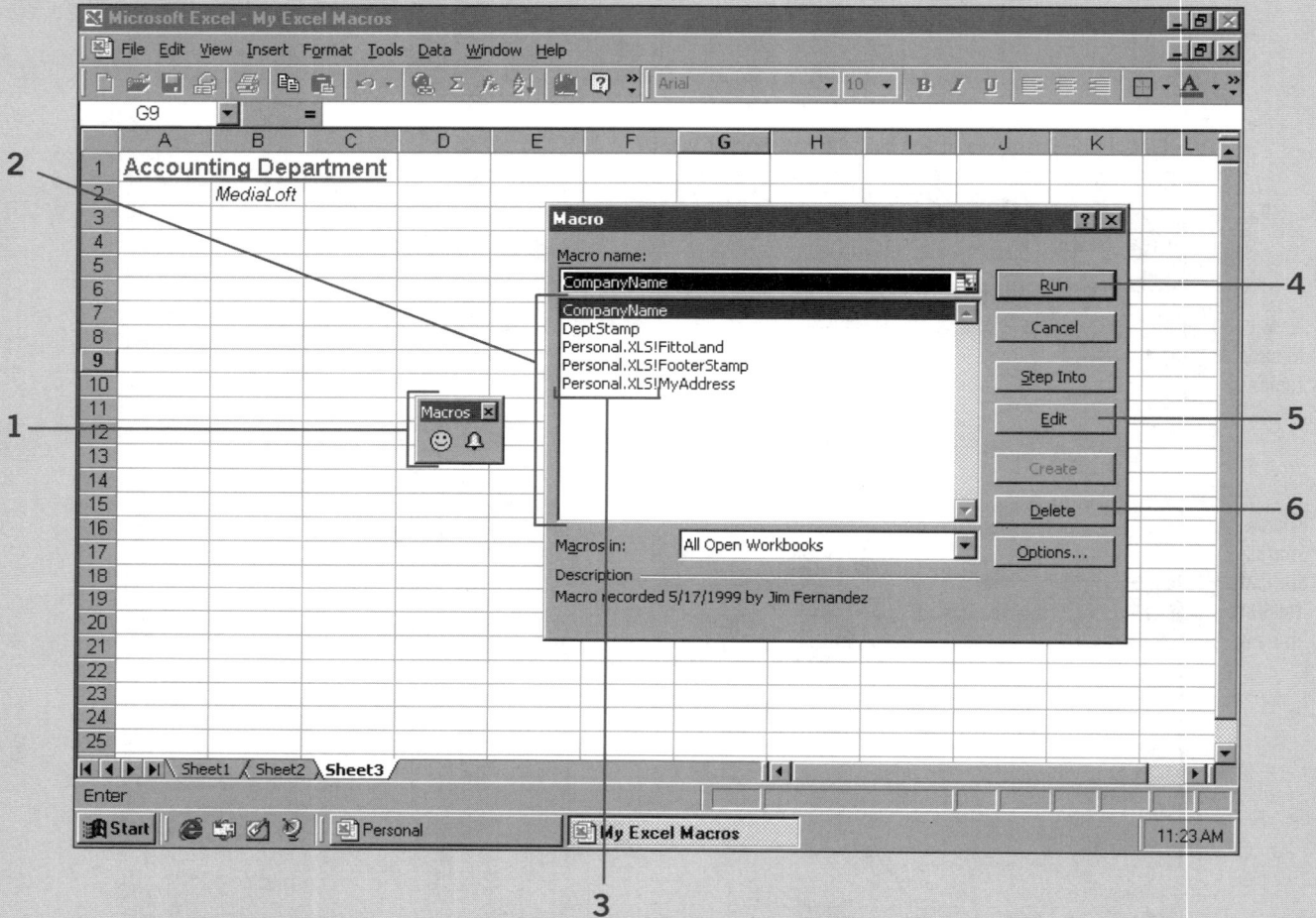

## Select the best answer from the list of choices.

**7. Which of the following is the best candidate for a macro?**
   a. One-button or one-keystroke commands
   b. Often-used sequences of commands or actions
   c. Seldom-used commands or tasks
   d. Nonsequential tasks

**8. When you are recording a macro, you can execute commands by using**
   a. Only the keyboard.
   b. Only the mouse.
   c. Any combination of the keyboard and the mouse.
   d. Only menu commands.

**9. A macro is stored in**
   a. The body of a worksheet used for data.
   b. An unused area to the far right or well below the worksheet contents.
   c. A module attached to a workbook.
   d. A Custom Menu Item.

**10. Which of the following is *not* true about editing a macro?**
   a. You edit macros using the Visual Basic Editor.
   b. A macro cannot be edited and must be recorded again.
   c. You can type changes directly in the existing macro code.
   d. You can make more than one editing change in a macro.

**11. Why is it important to plan a macro?**
   a. Macros won't be stored if they contain errors.
   b. Planning helps prevent careless errors from being introduced into the macro.
   c. It is very difficult to correct errors you make in a macro.
   d. Planning ensures that your macro will not contain errors.

**12. Macros are recorded with relative references**
   a. Only if the Relative Reference button is selected.
   b. In all cases.
   c. Only if relative references are chosen while recording the macro.
   d. Only if the Absolute Reference button is not selected.

**13. You can run macros**
   a. From the Macro dialog box.
   b. From shortcut key combinations.
   c. As items on menus.
   d. Using all of the above.

## ► Skills Review

1. **Record a macro.**
   a. Create a new workbook, then save it as "Macros". You will record a macro titled "MyAddress" that enters and formats your name, address, and telephone number in a worksheet.
   b. Store the macro in the current workbook.
   c. Record the macro, entering your name in cell A1, your street address in cell A2, your city, state, and ZIP code in cell A3, and your telephone number in cell A4.
   d. Format the information as 14-point Arial bold.
   e. Add a border and make the text the color of your choice.
   f. Save the workbook.

2. **Run a macro.**
   a. Clear cell entries in the range affected by the macro.
   b. Run the MyAddress macro in cell A1.
   c. Clear the cell entries generated by running the MyAddress macro.
   d. Save the workbook.

3. **Edit a macro.**
   a. Open the MyAddress macro in the Visual Basic Editor.
   b. Locate the line of code that defines the font size, then change the size to 18 point.
   c. Edit the selected range to A1:E4, which increases it by three columns to accommodate the changed label size. (*Hint*: It is the second Range line in the macro.)
   d. Add a comment line that describes this macro.
   e. Save and print the module, then return to Excel.
   f. Test the macro in Sheet1.
   g. Save the workbook.

4. **Use shortcut keys with macros.**
   a. You will record a macro in the current workbook called "MyName" that records your full name in cell G1.
   b. Assign your macro the shortcut key combination [Ctrl][Shift][N] and store it in the current workbook.
   c. After you record the macro, clear cell G1.
   d. Use the shortcut key combination to run the MyName macro.
   e. Save the workbook.

5. **Use the Personal Macro Workbook.**
   a. You will record a new macro called "FitToLand" that sets print orientation to landscape, scaled to fit on a page.
   b. Store the macro in the Personal Macro Workbook. If you are prompted to replace the existing FitToLand macro, click Yes.
   c. After you record the macro, activate Sheet2, and enter some test data in row 1 that exceeds one page width.
   d. In the Page Setup dialog box, return the orientation to portrait and adjust the capital A to 100 percent of normal size.
   e. Run the macro.
   f. Preview Sheet2 and verify that it's in landscape view and fits on one page.

## 6. Add a macro as a menu item.
**a.** On the Commands tab in the Customize dialog box, specify that you want to create a Custom Menu Item.
**b.** Place the Custom Menu Item at the bottom of the Tools menu.
**c.** Rename the Custom Menu Item "Fit to Landscape".
**d.** Assign the macro PERSONAL.XLS!FitToLand to the command.
**e.** Go to Sheet3 and change the orientation to portrait, then enter some test data in column A.
**f.** Run the Fit to Landscape macro from the Tools menu.
**g.** Preview the worksheet and verify that it is in landscape view.
**h.** Using the Tools, Customize menu options, select the Worksheet Menu bar, and reset.
**i.** Verify that the command has been removed from the Tools menu.
**j.** Save the workbook.

## 7. Create a toolbar for macros.
**a.** With the Macros workbook still open, you will create a new custom toolbar titled "My Info".
**b.** If necessary, drag the new toolbar onto the worksheet.
**c.** Display the Macros command category, then drag the Custom Button to the My Info toolbar.
**d.** Again, drag the Custom Button to the My Info toolbar.
**e.** Rename the first button "My Address", and assign the MyAddress macro to it.
**f.** Rename the second button "My Name", and assign the MyName macro to it.
**g.** Change the second button image to one of your choice.
**h.** On Sheet3, clear the existing cell data, then test both macro buttons on the My Info toolbar.
**i.** Use the Toolbars tab of the Customize dialog box to delete the toolbar named My Info.
**j.** Save and close the workbook, then exit Excel.

▶ # Independent Challenges

**1.** As a computer-support employee of an accounting firm, you need to develop ways to help your fellow employees work more efficiently. Employees have asked for Excel macros that will do the following:

- Delete the current row and insert a blank row
- Delete the current column and insert a blank column
- Format a selected group of cells with a red pattern, in 12-point Times bold italic

To complete this independent challenge:

**a.** Plan and write the steps necessary for each macro.
**b.** Create a new workbook, then save it as "Excel Utility Macros".
**c.** Create a new toolbar called "Helpers".
**d.** Create a macro for each employee request described above.
**e.** Add descriptive comment lines to each module.
**f.** Add each macro to the Tools menu.
**g.** On the Helpers toolbar, install buttons to run the macros.
**h.** Test each macro by using the Run command, the menu command, and the new buttons.
**i.** Save and then print the module for each macro.
**j.** Delete the new toolbar, and reset the Worksheet menu bar.

**2.** You are an analyst in the finance department of a large bank. Every quarter, you produce a number of single-page quarterly budget worksheets. Your manager has informed you that certain worksheets need to contain a footer stamp indicating that the worksheet was produced in the finance department. The footer also should show the date, the current page number of the total pages, and the worksheet filename. You decide that the stamp should not include a header. It's tedious to add the footer stamp and to clear the existing header and footer for the numerous worksheets you produce. You will record a macro to do this.

To complete this independent challenge:

**a.** Plan and write the steps to create the macro.

**b.** Create a new workbook, then save it as "Header and Footer Stamp".

**c.** Create the macro described above. Make sure it adds the footer with the department name and other information, and also clears the existing header.

**d.** Add descriptive comment lines to the macro code.

**e.** Add the macro to the Tools menu.

**f.** Create a toolbar titled "Stamp", then install a button on the toolbar to run the macro.

**g.** Test the macro to make sure it works from the Run command, menu command, and new button.

**h.** Save and print the module for the macro.

**i.** Delete the new toolbar, then reset the Worksheet menu bar.

**3.** You are an administrative assistant to the marketing vice president at Computers, Inc. A major part of your job is to create spreadsheets that project sales results in different markets. It seems that you are constantly changing the print settings so that workbooks print in landscape orientation and are scaled to fit on one page. You have decided that it is time to create a macro to streamline this process.

To complete this independent challenge:

**a.** Plan and write the steps necessary for the macro.

**b.** Create a new workbook, then save it as "Computers Inc Macro".

**c.** Create a macro that changes the page orientation to landscape and scales the worksheet to fit on a page.

**d.** Test the macro.

**e.** Save and print the module sheet.

**f.** Delete any toolbars you created, and reset the Worksheet menu bar.

**WEB WORK**

**4.** The MediaLoft New York store has recently instituted a budgeting process for its café operation. At the end of every monthly sales report created in Excel, the staff lists the four largest budget items and then fills in what it expects the figures to be for the next month.

Jim Fernandez at MediaLoft corporate headquarters has asked you to use Excel macros and the MediaLoft intranet site to help automate this task. The New York store staff will then distribute the macro to all stores so they can easily add the budget figures to their monthly reports.

**a.** Connect to the Internet, go to the MediaLoft intranet site at http://www.course.com/illustrated/MediaLoft, click the Accounting link, then click the Cafe Budget link. Examine the information in the NYC Cafe Expenses chart and note the four largest expense categories. Close your browser and disconnect from the Internet.

**b.** To complete this independent challenge, start Excel, create a new workbook, then save it as "Cafe Budget Macro". Create a macro named "CafeBudget" in the current workbook (activated by the [Shift][Ctrl][B] key combination) that does the following:

- Inserts the names of the four largest expense categories in contiguous cells in a column, starting with the current cell.
- Inserts the word "Total" in the cell below the last category.
- Inserts the words "Next Month's Budget" in the cell just above and to the right of the categories. The managers will insert their budget figures in the four cells below this heading, to the right of each category name.
- Totals the four figures the managers will insert and places the sum to the right of the Total label, just below the four figures.
- Inserts a bottom border on the Next Month's Budget cell and on the cell containing the last of the four figures.
- Boldfaces the Total text and the cell to its right that will contain the total.
- Places a thick box border around all the information, fills the area with a light green color, and autofits the column information where necessary.
- Makes the cell to the right of the first category the active cell.

**c.** Clear the worksheet of all contents and formats and test the macro. Edit or rerecord the macro as necessary.

**d.** Make a custom menu item on the Tools menu called "Cafe Budget" that will run the macro you created.

**e.** Create a custom toolbar named "Budgets" with a button containing the image of a calculator on it, and assign the button to your CafeBudget macro.

**f.** Test the custom menu item and the custom toolbar button, clearing the worksheet before running each one.

**g.** Save your workbook, print the results of the macro, then open the macro in the Visual Basic Editor and print the macro code.

**h.** Return to Excel, save and close the workbook, then exit Excel.

**Excel 2000**

# ▶ Visual Workshop

Create the macro shown in Figure G-22. (*Hint:* Save a blank workbook as "File Utility Macros", then create a macro called SaveClose that saves a previously named workbook. Finally, include the line ActiveWorkbook. Close in the module, as shown in the figure.) Print the module. Test the macro. The line "Macro recorded...by..." will reflect your system date and name.

FIGURE G-22

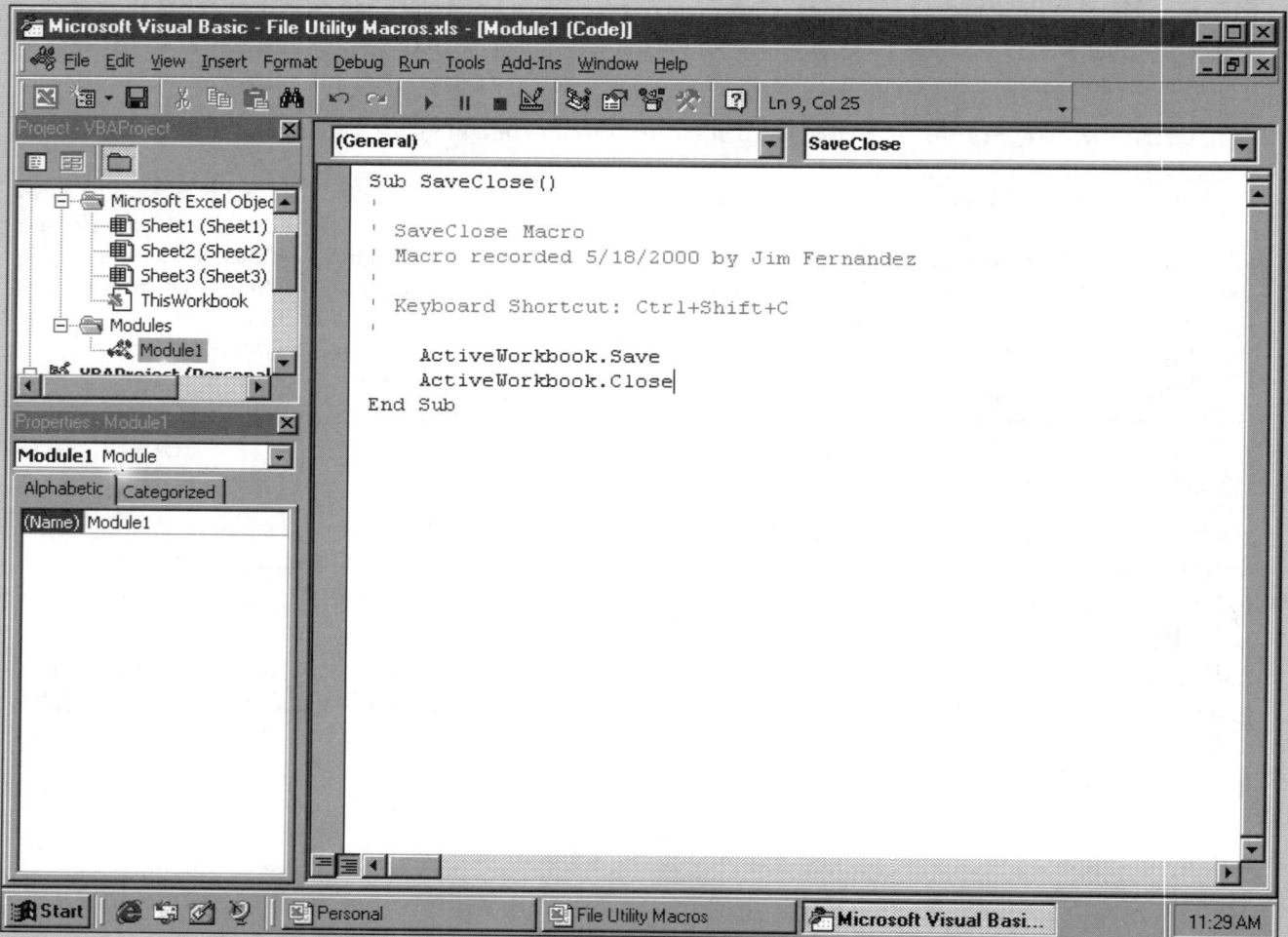

# Using

## Lists

### Objectives

- ► **Plan a list**
- ► **Create a list**
- MOUS ► **Add records with the data form**
- MOUS ► **Find records**
- MOUS ► **Delete records**
- MOUS ► **Sort a list by one field**
- MOUS ► **Sort a list by multiple fields**
- MOUS ► **Print a list**

A **database** is an organized collection of related information. Examples of databases include a telephone book, a card catalog, and a roster of company employees. Excel refers to a database as a **list**. Using an Excel list, you can organize and manage worksheet information so that you can quickly find needed data for projects, reports, and charts. In this unit, you'll learn how to plan and create a list; add, change, find, and delete information in a list; and then sort and print a list.

MediaLoft uses lists to analyze new customer information. Jim Fernandez needs to build and manage a list of new customers as part of the ongoing strategy to focus the company's advertising dollars.

# Unit H

# Planning a List

When planning a list, consider what information the list will contain and how you will work with the data now and in the future. Lists are organized into records. A **record** contains data about an object or person. Records, in turn, are divided into fields. **Fields** are columns in the list; each field describes a characteristic about the record, such as a customer's last name or street address. Each field has a **field name**, a column label that describes the field. See Table H-1 for additional planning guidelines. ◆━━━ Jim will compile a list of new customers. Before entering the data into an Excel worksheet, he plans his list using the following guidelines:

## Details

### Identify the purpose of the list

Determine the kind of information the list should contain. Jim will use the list to identify areas of the country in which new customers live.

### Plan the structure of the list

Determine the fields that make up a record. Jim has customer cards that contain information about each new customer. Figure H-1 shows a typical card. Each customer in the list will have a record. The fields in the record correspond to the information on the cards.

### Write down the names of the fields

Field names can be up to 255 characters in length (the maximum column width), although shorter names are easier to see in the cells. Field names appear in the first row of a list. Jim writes down field names that describe each piece of information shown in Figure H-1.

### Determine any special number formatting required in the list

Most lists contain both text and numbers. When planning a list, consider whether any fields require specific number formatting or prefixes. Jim notes that some Zip codes begin with zero. Because Excel automatically drops a leading zero, Jim must type an apostrophe (') when he enters a Zip code that begins with 0 (zero). The apostrophe tells Excel that the cell contains a label rather than a value. If a column contains both numbers and numbers that contain a text character, such as an apostrophe ('), you should format all the numbers as text. Otherwise, the numbers are sorted first, and the numbers that contain text characters are sorted after that; for example, 11542, 60614, 87105, '01810, '02115. To instruct Excel to sort the Zip codes properly, Jim enters all Zip codes with a leading apostrophe.

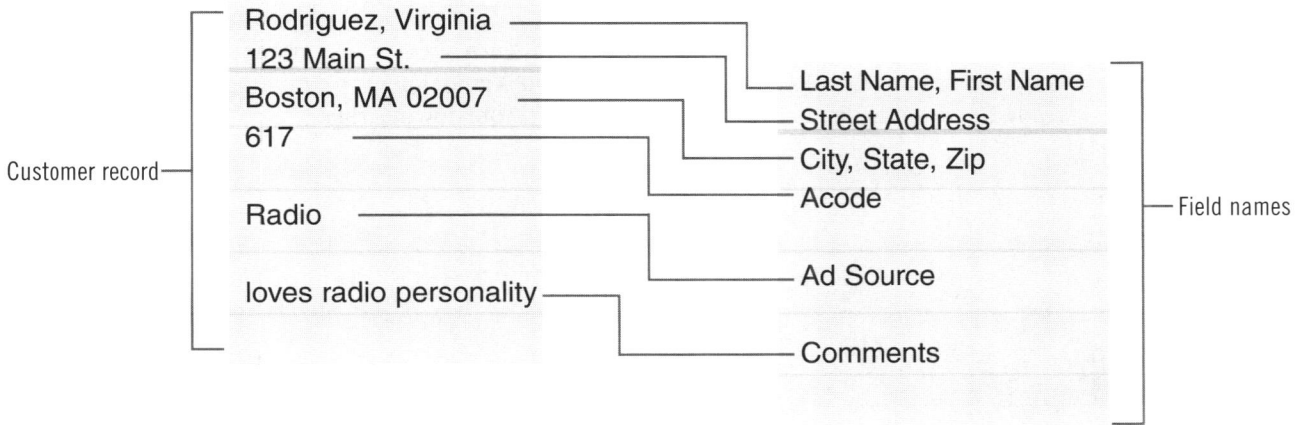

FIGURE H-1: Customer record and corresponding field names

TABLE H-1: Guidelines for planning a list

| size and location guidelines | row and column content guidelines |
|---|---|
| Devote an entire worksheet to your list and list summary information because some list management features can be used on only one list at a time | Plan and design your list so that all rows have similar items in the same column |
| Leave at least one blank column and one blank row between your list and list summary data. Doing this helps Excel select your list when it performs list management tasks such as sorting | Do not insert extra spaces at the beginning of a cell because that can affect sorting and searching |
| Avoid placing critical data to the left or right of the list | Use the same format for all cells in a column |

## CLUES TO USE

### Lists versus databases

If your list contains more records than can fit on one worksheet (that is, more than 65,536), you should consider using database software rather than spreadsheet software.

# Creating a List

Once you have planned the list structure, the sequence of fields, and any appropriate formatting, you need to create field names. Table H-2 provides guidelines for naming fields. ▄▄▄▄▄ Jim is ready to create the list using the field names he wrote down earlier.

## Steps 1 2 3 4

**QuickTip**

To return personalized toolbars and menus to their default state, click Tools on the menu bar, click Customize, click the Options tab in the Customize dialog box, click Reset my usage data to restore the default settings, click Yes, click Close, then close the Drawing toolbar if it is displayed.

**1.** Start Excel if necessary, open the workbook titled **EX H-1**, save it as **New Customer List**, rename Sheet1 as **Practice**, then if necessary maximize the Excel window
It is a good idea to devote an entire worksheet to your list.

**2.** Beginning in cell A1 and moving horizontally, type each field name in a separate cell, as shown in Figure H-2
Always put field names in the first row of the list. Don't worry if your field names are wider than the cells; you will fix this later.

**Trouble?**

If the Bold button or Borders button does not appear on your Formatting toolbar, click the More Buttons button ▸ to view it.

**3.** Select the field headings in range **A1:I1**, then click the **Bold button** 🅱 on the Formatting toolbar; with range A1:I1 still selected, click the **Borders list arrow**, then click the **thick bottom border** (second item from left in the second row)

**4.** Enter the information from Figure H-3 in the rows immediately below the field names, using a leading apostrophe (') for all Zip codes; do not leave any blank rows
If you don't type an apostrophe, Excel deletes the leading zero (0) in the Zip code. The data appears in columns organized by field name.

**QuickTip**

If the field name you plan to use is wider than the data in the column, you can turn on Wrap Text to stack the heading in the cell. Doing this allows you to use descriptive field names and still keep the columns from being unnecessarily wide. If you prefer a keyboard shortcut, you can press [Alt][Enter] to force a line break while entering field names.

**5.** Select the range **A1:I4**, click **Format** on the menu bar, point to **Column**, click **AutoFit Selection**, click anywhere in the worksheet to deselect the range, then save the workbook
Automatically resizing the column widths this way is faster than double-clicking the column divider lines between each pair of columns. Compare your screen with Figure H-4.

**TABLE H-2: Guidelines for naming fields**

| guideline | explanation |
|---|---|
| Use labels to name fields | Numbers can be interpreted as parts of formulas |
| Do not use duplicate field names | Duplicate field names can cause information to be incorrectly entered and sorted |
| Format the field names to stand out from the list data | Use a font, alignment, format, pattern, border, or capitalization style for the column labels that are different from the format of your list data |
| Use descriptive names | Avoid names that might be confused with cell addresses, such as Q4 |

FIGURE H-2: Field names entered and formatted in row 1

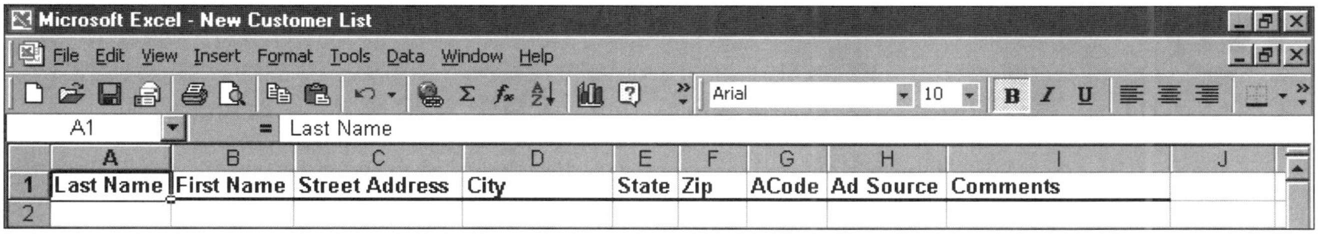

FIGURE H-3: Cards with customer information

| Rodriguez, Virginia | Wong, Sam | Smith, Carol |
|---|---|---|
| 123 Main St. | 2120 Central NE. | 123 Elm St. |
| Boston, MA 02007 | San Francisco, CA 93772 | Watertown, MA 02472 |
| 617 | 415 | 617 |
| | | |
| Radio | Newspaper | Newspaper |
| | | |
| loves radio personality | graphics caught eye | no comments |

FIGURE H-4: List with three records

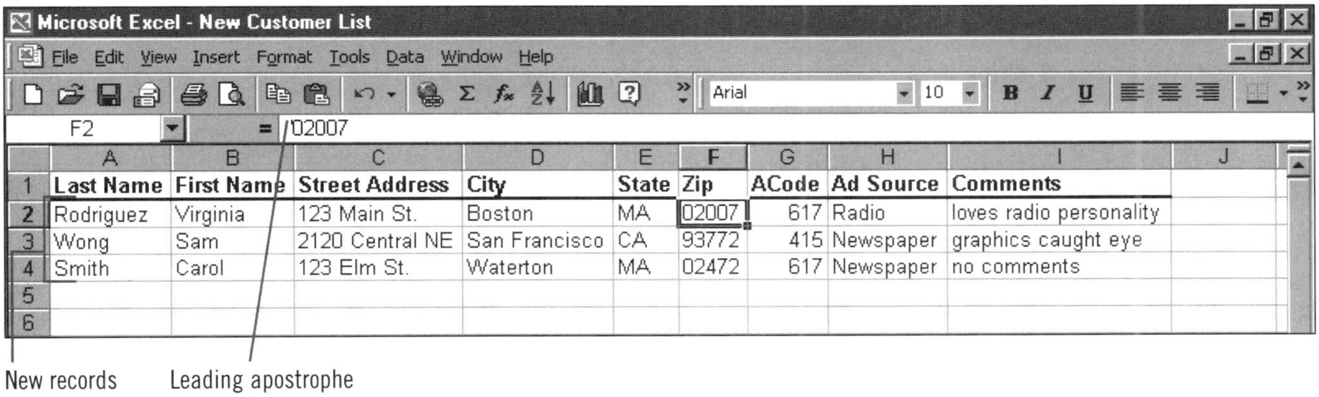

New records    Leading apostrophe

## Maintaining the quality of information in a list

To protect the list information, make sure the data is entered in the correct field. Stress care and consistency to all those who enter the list data. Haphazardly entered data can yield invalid results later when it is manipulated.

Excel 2000

# Adding Records with the Data Form

You can add records to a list by typing data directly into the cells within the list range. Once the field names are created, you also can use the data form as a quick, easy method of data entry. A **data form** is a dialog box that displays one record at a time. By naming a list range in the name box, you can select the list at any time, and all new records you add to the list will be included in the list range. ▰▰▰ Jim has entered all the customer records he had on his cards, but he receives the names of two more customers. He decides to use the Excel data form to add the new customer information.

## Steps 1 2 3 4

**1.** Make sure the New Customer List file is open, then rename Sheet2 **Working List**
Working List contains the nearly complete customer list. Before using the data form to enter the new data, you must define the list range.

**2.** Select the range **A1:I45**, click the **name box** to select the reference to cell **A1** there, type **Database**, then press **[Enter]**
The Database list range name appears in the name box. When you assign the name Database to the list, the commands on the Excel Data menu apply to the list named "Database".

**3.** While the list is still selected, click **Data** on the menu bar, then click **Form**
A data form containing the first record appears, as shown in Figure H-5.

**4.** Click **New**
A blank data form appears with the insertion point in the first field.

**Trouble?**

If you accidentally press [↑] or [↓] while in a data form and find yourself positioned in the wrong record, press [↑] or [↓] until you return to the desired record.

**5.** Type **Chavez** in the Last Name box, then press **[Tab]** to move the insertion point to the next field

**6.** Enter the rest of the information for Jeffrey Chavez, as shown in Figure H-6
Press [Tab] to move the insertion point to the next field, or click in the next field's box to move the insertion point there.

**QuickTip**

Excel 2000 automatically extends formatting and formulas in lists.

**7.** Click **New** to add Jeffrey Chavez's record and open another blank data form, enter the record for Cathy Relman as shown in Figure H-6, then click **Close**
The list records that you add with the data form are placed at the end of the list and are formatted in the same way as the previous records.

**8.** Scroll down the worksheet to bring rows 46 and 47 into view, check both new records, return to cell A1, then save the workbook

FIGURE H-5: Data form showing first record in the list

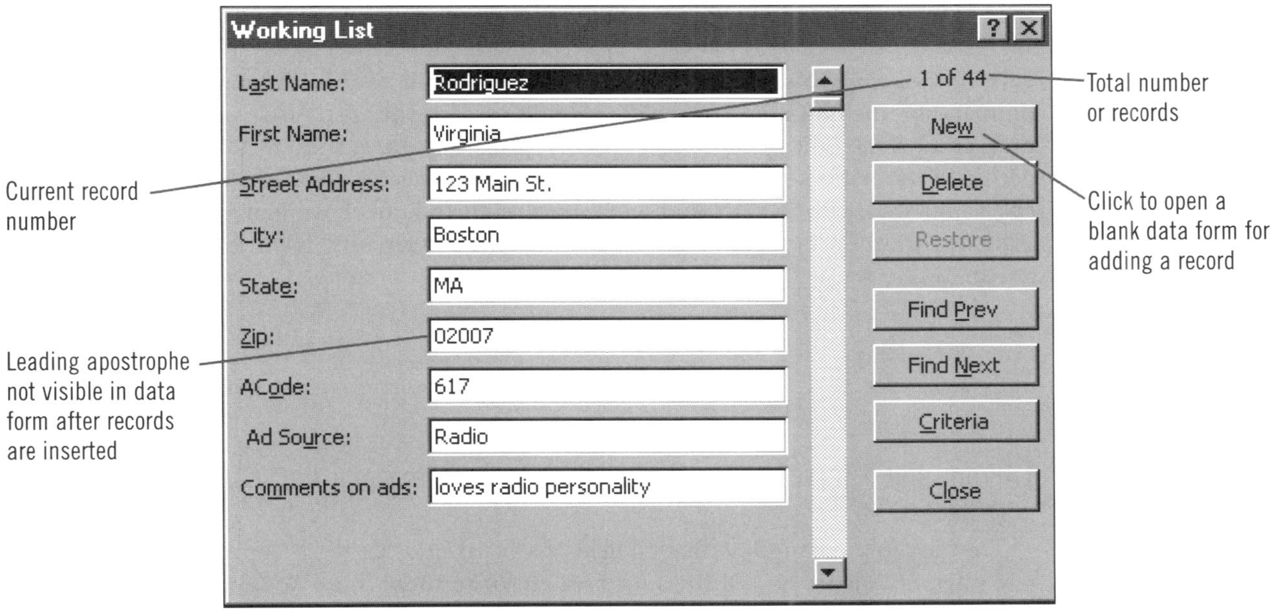

Current record number

Leading apostrophe not visible in data form after records are inserted

Total number or records

Click to open a blank data form for adding a record

FIGURE H-6: Two data forms with information for two new records

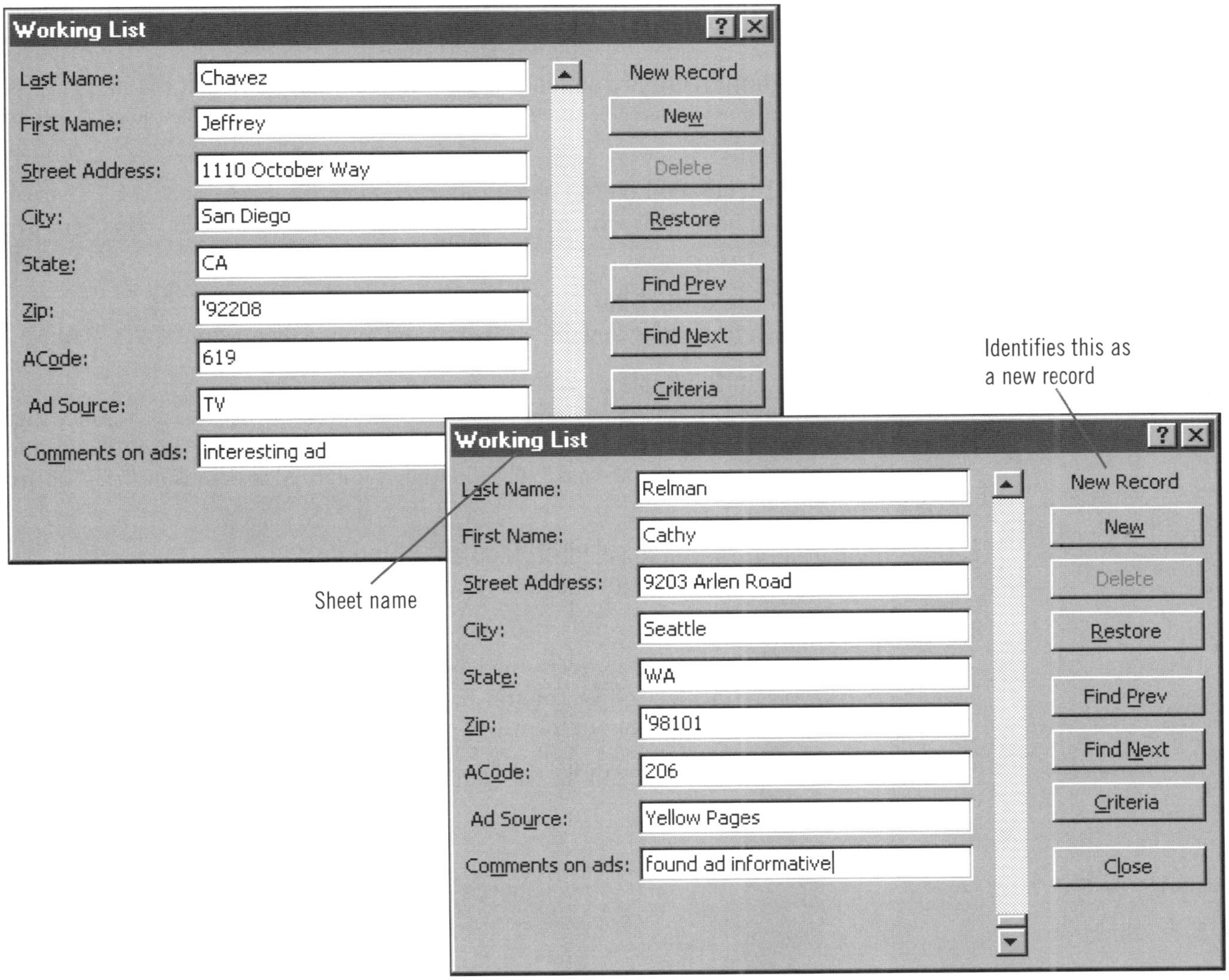

Sheet name

Identifies this as a new record

# Finding Records

From time to time, you need to locate specific records in your list. You can use the Excel Find command on the Edit menu or the data form to search your list. Also, you can use the Replace command on the Edit menu to locate and replace existing entries or portions of entries with specified information. ➤ Jim wants to be more specific about the radio ad source, so he replaces "Radio" with "KWIN Radio." He also wants to know how many of the new customers originated from the company's TV ads. Jim begins by searching for those records with the ad source "TV".

## Steps

**Trouble?**

If you receive the message "No list found", select any cell within the list, then repeat Step 1

1. **From any cell within the list, click Data on the menu bar, click Form, then click Criteria**
   The data form changes so that all fields are blank and "Criteria" appears in the upper-right corner. See Figure H-7. You want to search for records whose Ad Source field contains the label "TV".

2. **Press [Alt][U] to move to the Ad Source box, type TV, then click Find Next**
   Excel displays the first record for a customer who learned about the company through its TV ads. See Figure H-8.

**QuickTip**

You can also use comparison operators when performing a search using the data form. For example, you could specify >50,000 in a Salary field box to return those records in the Salary field with a value greater than $50,000.

3. **Click Find Next until there are no more matching records, then click Close**
   There are six customers whose ad source is TV. Next, Jim wants to make the radio ad source more specific.

4. **Return to cell A1, click Edit on the menu bar, then click Replace**
   The Replace dialog box opens with the insertion point located in the Find what box. See Figure H-9.

5. **Type Radio in the Find what box, then click the Replace with box**
   Jim wants to search for entries containing "Radio" and replace them with "KWIN Radio".

6. **Type KWIN Radio in the Replace with box**
   You are about to perform the search and replace option specified. Because you notice that there are other list entries containing the word "radio" with a lowercase "r" (in the Comments column), you need to make sure that only capitalized instances of the word are replaced.

7. **Click the Match case box to select it, then click Find Next**
   Excel moves the cell pointer to the first occurrence of "Radio".

8. **Click Replace All**
   The dialog box closes, and you complete the replacement and check to make sure all references to "Radio" in the Ad Source column now read "KWIN Radio". Note that in the Comments column, each instance of the word "radio" remains unchanged.

9. **Make sure there are no entries in the Ad Source column that read "Radio", then save the workbook**

FIGURE H-7: Criteria data form

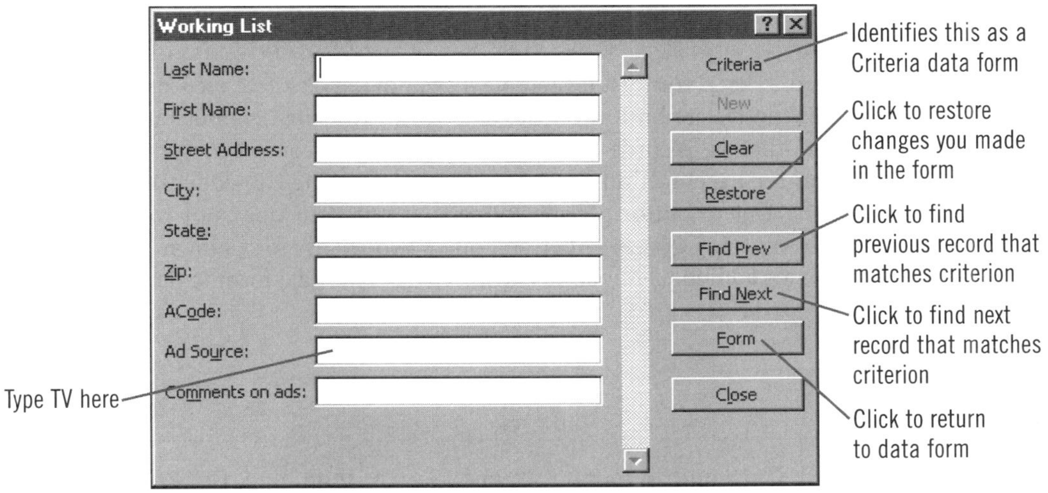
Working List
Last Name:
First Name:
Street Address:
City:
State:
Zip:
ACode:
Ad Source:
Comments on ads:
Criteria
New
Clear
Restore
Find Prev
Find Next
Form
Close
Identifies this as a Criteria data form
Click to restore changes you made in the form
Click to find previous record that matches criterion
Click to find next record that matches criterion
Click to return to data form
Type TV here

FIGURE H-8: Finding a record using the data form

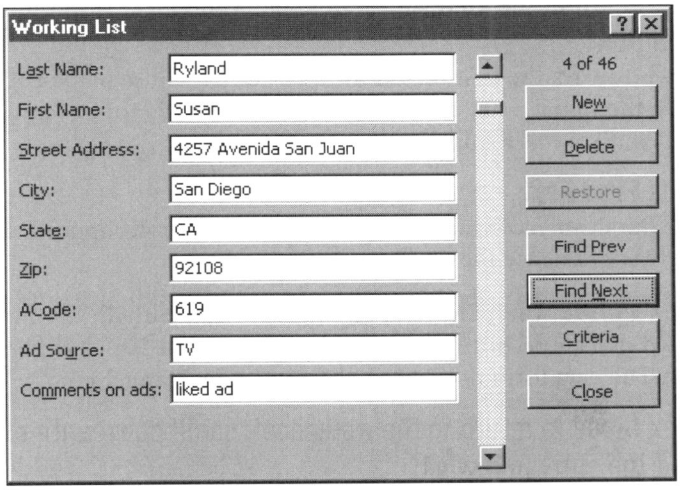
Working List
Last Name: Ryland
First Name: Susan
Street Address: 4257 Avenida San Juan
City: San Diego
State: CA
Zip: 92108
ACode: 619
Ad Source: TV
Comments on ads: liked ad
4 of 46
New
Delete
Restore
Find Prev
Find Next
Criteria
Close

FIGURE H-9: Replace dialog box

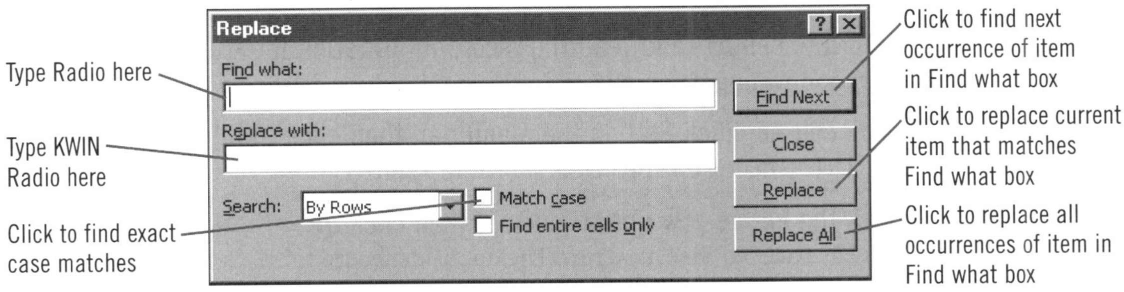
Replace
Find what:
Replace with:
Search: By Rows
Match case
Find entire cells only
Find Next
Close
Replace
Replace All
Type Radio here
Type KWIN Radio here
Click to find exact case matches
Click to find next occurrence of item in Find what box
Click to replace current item that matches Find what box
Click to replace all occurrences of item in Find what box

Excel 2000

CLUES TO USE

## Using wildcards to fine-tune your search

You can use special symbols called **wildcards** when defining search criteria in the data form or Replace dialog box. The question mark (?) wildcard stands for any single character. For example, if you do not know whether a customer's last name is Paulsen or Paulson, you can specify Pauls?n as the search criteria to locate both options. The asterisk (*) wildcard stands for any group of characters. For example, if you specify Jan* as the search criteria in the First Name field, Excel locates all records with first names beginning with Jan (for instance, Jan, Janet, Janice, and so forth).

# Deleting Records

You need to keep your list up to date by removing obsolete records. One way to remove records is to use the Delete button on the data form. You can also delete all records that meet certain criteria—that is, records that have something in common. For example, you can specify a criterion for Excel to find the next record containing Zip code 01879, then remove the record using the Delete button. If specifying one criterion does not meet your needs, you can set multiple criteria. ➤ After he notices two entries for Carolyn Smith, Jim wants to check the database for additional duplicate entries. He uses the data form to delete the duplicate record.

## Steps 1234

**1.** Click **Data** on the menu bar, click **Form**, then click **Criteria**
The Criteria data form appears.

**QuickTip**

You can use the data form to edit records as well as to add, search for, and delete them. Just find the desired record and edit the data directly in the appropriate box.

**2.** Type **Smith** in the **Last Name box**, click the **First Name box**, type **Carolyn**, then click **Find Next**
Excel displays the first record for a customer whose name is Carolyn Smith. You decide to leave the initial entry for Carolyn Smith (record 5 of 46) and delete the second one, once you confirm it is a duplicate.

**3.** Click **Find Next**
The duplicate record for Carolyn Smith, number 40, appears as shown in Figure H-10. You are ready to delete the duplicate entry.

**QuickTip**

Clicking Restore on the data form will not restore deleted record(s).

**4.** Click **Delete**, then click **OK** to confirm the deletion
The duplicate record for Carolyn Smith is deleted, and all the other records move up one row. The data form now shows the record for Manuel Julio.

**5.** Click **Close** to return to the worksheet, scroll down until rows 41-46 are visible, then read the entry in row 41
Notice that the duplicate entry for Carolyn Smith is gone and that Manuel Julio moved up a row and is now in row 41. You also notice a record for K. C. Splint in row 43, which is a duplicate entry.

**6.** Return to cell A1, and read the record information for K. C. Splint in row 8
After confirming the duplicate entry, you decide to delete the row.

**7.** Click cell **A8**, click **Edit** on the menu bar, then click **Delete**
The Delete dialog box opens, as shown in Figure H-11.

**QuickTip**

You can also delete selected cells in a row. Highlight the cells to delete, choose Delete from the Edit menu, and, in the dialog box, indicate if the remaining cells should move up or to the left to replace the selection. Use this command with caution in lists, since with lists you usually delete an entire row.

**8.** Click the **Entire row option button**, then click **OK**
You have deleted the entire row. The duplicate record for K. C. Splint is deleted and the other records move up to fill in the gap.

**9.** Save the workbook
Recall that you can delete a range name by following these steps: click Insert on the menu bar, point to Name, click Define, highlight the range name, and click delete.

FIGURE H-10: Data form showing duplicate record for Carolyn Smith

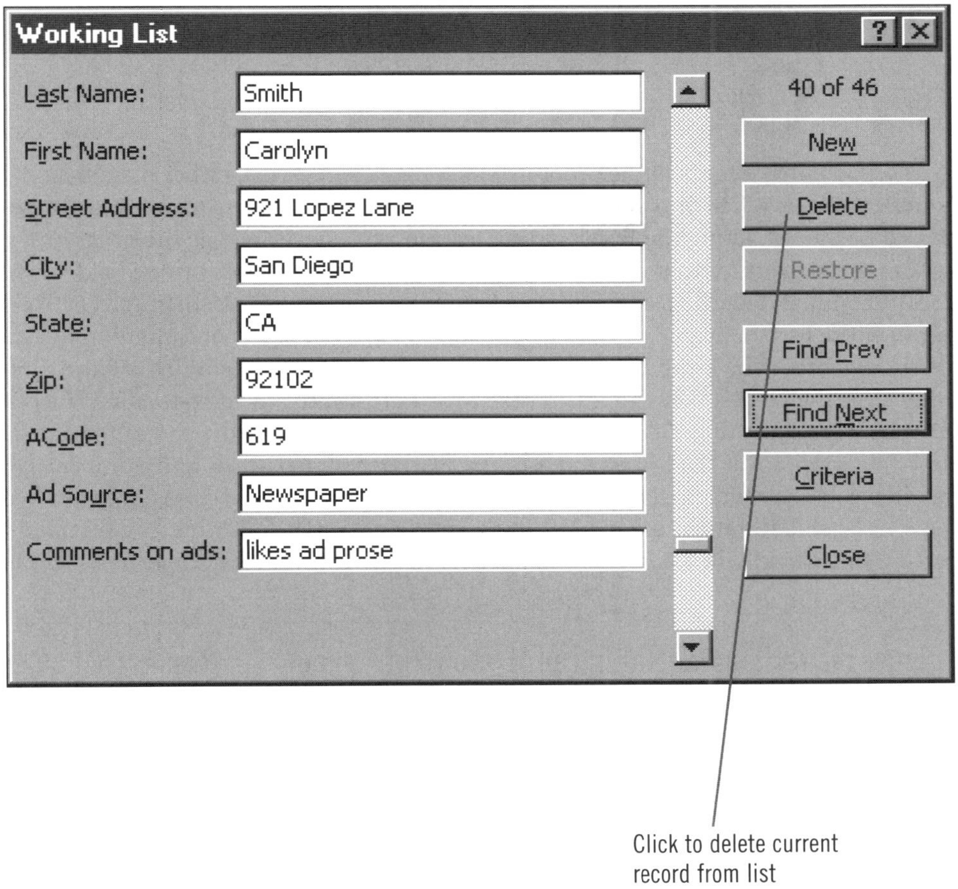

Click to delete current
record from list

FIGURE H-11: Delete dialog box

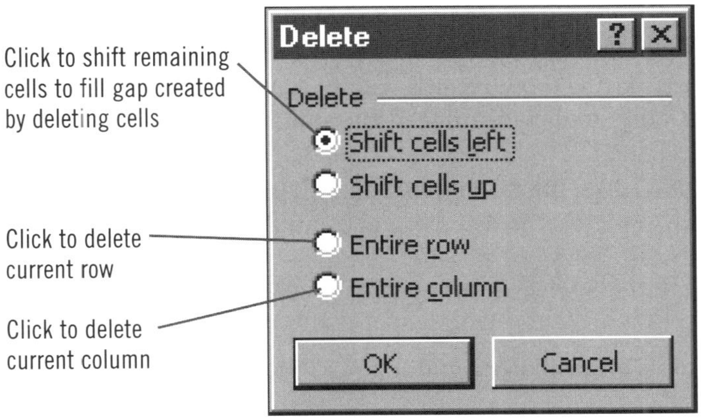

Click to shift remaining
cells to fill gap created
by deleting cells

Click to delete
current row

Click to delete
current column

XXXXXXXXXXXXXXXXXXXXXXXXXXX

## Advantage of deleting records from the worksheet

When you delete a record using the data form, you cannot undo your deletion. When you delete a record by deleting the row in which it resides inside the worksheet area, however, you can immediately restore the record by using the Undo command on the Edit menu, using the Undo button, or pressing [Ctrl][Z].

# Sorting a List by One Field

Usually, you enter records in the order in which they are received, rather than in alphabetical or numerical order. When you add records to a list using the data form, the records are added to the end of the list. Using the Excel sorting feature, you can rearrange the order of the records. You can use the sort buttons on the Standard toolbar to sort records by one field, or you can use the Sort command on the Data menu to perform more complicated sorts. Alternatively, you can sort an entire list or any portion of a list, or you can arrange sorted information in ascending or descending order. In ascending order, the lowest value (the beginning of the alphabet, for instance, or the earliest date) appears at the top of the list. In a field containing labels and numbers, numbers come first. In descending order, the highest value (the end of the alphabet or the latest date) appears at the top of the list. In a field containing labels and numbers, labels come first. Table H-3 provides examples of ascending and descending sorts. ✏️ Because Jim wants to be able to return the records to their original order following any sorts, he begins by creating a new field called Entry Order. Then he will perform several single field sorts on the list.

## Steps 1234

**QuickTip**

Before you sort records, it is a good idea to make a backup copy of your list or create a field that numbers the records so you can return them to their original order, if necessary.

1. Enter the text and format in cell J1 shown in Figure H-12, then AutoFit column J

2. Type **1** in cell J2, press **[Enter]**, type **2** in cell J3, press **[Enter]**, select cells **J2:J3**, drag the fill handle to cell **J45**
   With the Entry Order column complete, as shown in Figure H-12, you are ready to sort the list in ascending order by last name. You must position the cell pointer within the column you want to sort prior to issuing the sort command.

**Trouble?**

If your sort does not perform as intended, press [Ctrl][Z] immediately to undo the sort and repeat the step.

3. Return to cell A1, then click the **Sort Ascending button** ⬇️ on the Standard toolbar
   Excel instantly rearranges the records in ascending order by last name, as shown in Figure H-13. You can easily sort the list in descending order by any field.

4. Click cell **G1**, then click the **Sort Descending button** ⬇️ on the Standard toolbar
   Excel sorts the list, placing those records with higher-digit area codes at the top. Jim wants to update the list range to include original entry order.

5. Select the range **A1:J45**, click the **name box**, type **Database**, then press **[Enter]**
   You are now ready to return the list to original entry order.

6. Click cell **J1**, click the **Sort Ascending button** ⬇️ on the Standard toolbar, then save the workbook
   The list is back to its original order, and the workbook is saved.

**TABLE H-3: Sort order options and examples**

| option | alphabetic | numeric | date | alphanumeric | |
|--------|-----------|---------|------|--------------|--|
| Ascending | A, B, C | 7, 8, 9 | 1/1, 2/1, 3/1 | 12A, 99B, DX8, QT7 | |
| Descending | C, B, A | 9, 8, 7 | 3/1, 2/1, 1/1 | QT7, DX8, 99B, 12A | |

FIGURE H-12: **List with Entry Order field added**

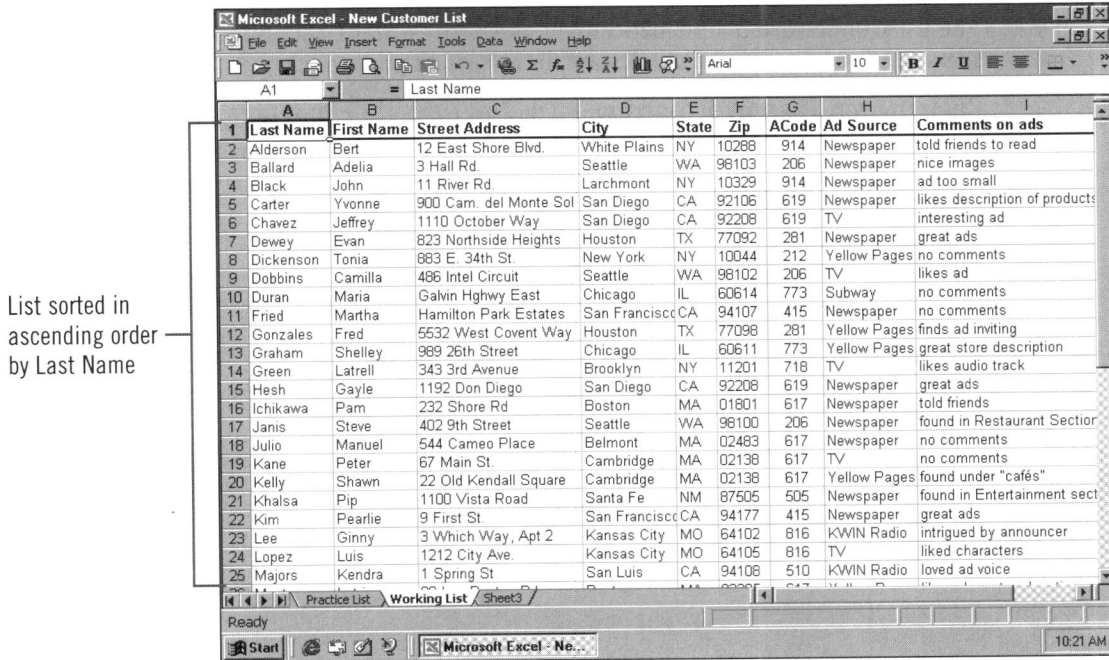

New field

Drag to fill
in values

FIGURE H-13: **List sorted alphabetically by Last Name**

List sorted in
ascending order
by Last Name

## Rotating and indenting to improve label appearance

The column label you added in cell J1 is considerably wider than the data in the column. In cases like this, you can adjust the format of any label or value: Select the cell, click Format on the menu bar, click Cells, and on the Alignment tab drag the red diamond under

Orientation to 90 degrees. You can also add space to the left of any label or value by selecting the cells(s) and clicking the Increase Indent button on the Formatting toolbar.

# Sorting a List by Multiple Fields

You can sort lists by as many as three fields by specifying **sort keys**, the criteria on which the sort is based. To perform sorts on multiple fields, you must use the Sort dialog box, which you access through the Sort command on the Data menu. ━━ Jim wants to sort the records alphabetically by state first, then within the state by Zip code.

## Steps

**1.** Click the **name box list arrow**, then click **Database**
The list is selected. To sort the list by more than one field, you will need to use the Sort command on the Data menu.

**QuickTip**

You can specify a capitalization sort by clicking Options in the Sort dialog box, then clicking the Case sensitive box. When you choose this option, lowercase entries precede uppercase entries.

**2.** Click **Data** on the menu bar, then click **Sort**
The Sort dialog box opens, as shown in Figure H-14. You want to sort the list by state and then by Zip code.

**3.** Click the **Sort by** list arrow, click **State**, then click the **Ascending option button** to select it, if necessary
The list will be sorted alphabetically in ascending order (A-Z) by the State field. A second sort criterion will sort the entries within each state grouping.

**4.** Click the top **Then by list arrow**, click **Zip**, then click the **Descending option button**
You also could sort by a third key by selecting a field in the bottom Then by list box.

**5.** Click **OK** to execute the sort, press **[Ctrl][Home]**, then scroll through the list to see the result of the sort
The list is sorted alphabetically by state in ascending order, then within each state by Zip code in descending order. Compare your results with Figure H-15.

**6.** Return to cell A1, then save the workbook

FIGURE H-14: Sort dialog box

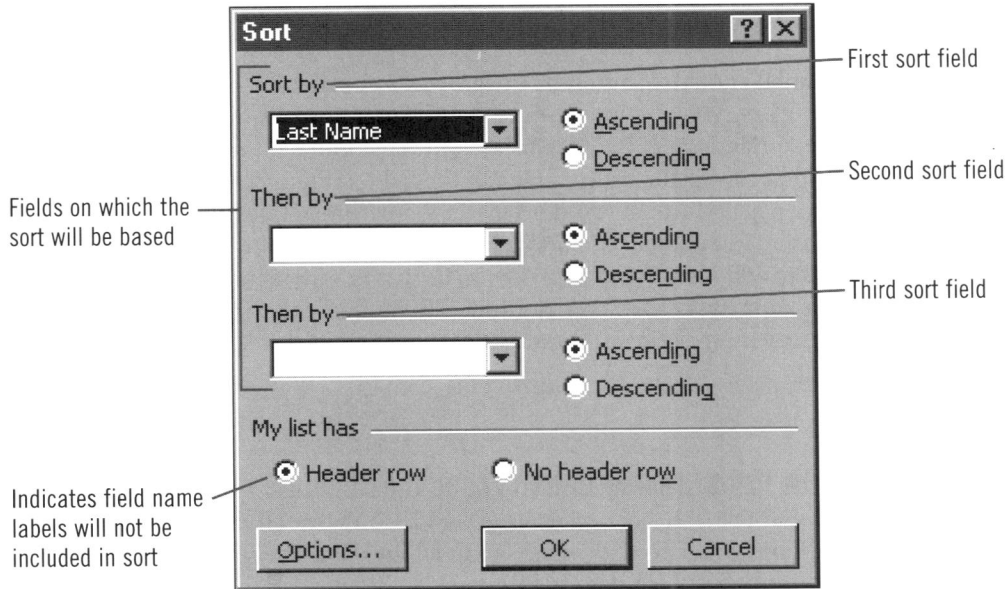

First sort field

Fields on which the sort will be based

Second sort field

Third sort field

Indicates field name labels will not be included in sort

FIGURE H-15: List sorted by multiple fields

First sort by state

Second sort by Zip code within state

## Specifying a custom sort order

You can identify a custom sort order for the field selected in the Sort by box. To do this, click Options in the Sort dialog box, click the First key sort order list arrow, then click the desired custom order.

Commonly used custom sort orders are days of the week (Mon, Tues, Wed, etc.) and months (Jan, Feb, Mar, etc.); alphabetic sorts do not sort these items properly.

# Printing a List

If a list is small enough to fit on one page, you can print it as you would any other Excel worksheet. If you have more columns than can fit on a portrait-oriented page, try setting the page orientation to landscape. Because lists often have more rows than can fit on a page, you can define the first row of the list (containing the field names) as the **print title**, which prints at the top of every page. Most lists do not have any descriptive information above the field names on the worksheet. To augment the information contained in the field names, you can use headers and footers to add identifying text, such as the list title or report date. If you want to exclude any fields from your list report, you can hide the desired columns from view so that they do not print. ➤ Jim has finished updating his list and is ready to print it. He begins by previewing the list.

## Steps 1 2 3 4

1. **Click the Print Preview button 🔍 on the Standard toolbar**
   Notice that the status bar reads Page 1 of 2. You want all the fields in the list to fit on a single page, but you'll need two pages to fit all the data. The landscape page orientation and the Fit to options will help you do this.

**QuickTip**

You can print multiple ranges at the same time by clicking the Print area box in the Sheet tab. Then drag to the select areas you wish to print.

2. **From the Print Preview window, click Setup, click the Page tab, click the Landscape option button under Orientation, click the Fit to option button under Scaling, double-click the tall box and type 2, click OK, then click Next**
   The list still does not fit on a single page. Because the records on page 2 appear without column headings, you want to set up the first row of the list, containing the field names, as a repeating print title.

**QuickTip**

You can also use the sheet tab to specify whether you want gridlines, high or low print quality, and row and column headings.

3. **Click Close to exit the Print Preview window, click File on the menu bar, click Page Setup, click the Sheet tab, click the Rows to repeat at top box under Print titles, click any cell in row 1, then click OK**
   When you select row 1 as a print title, Excel automatically inserts an absolute reference to a beginning row to repeat at the top of each page—in this case, the print title to repeat beginning and ending with row 1. See Figure H-16.

4. **Click Print Preview, click Next to view the second page, then click Zoom**
   Setting up a print title to repeat row 1 causes the field names to appear at the top of each printed page. You can use the worksheet header to provide information about the list.

5. **Click Setup, click the Header/Footer tab, click Custom Header, click the Left section box and type your name, then click the Center section box and type MediaLoft–New Customer List**

6. **Select the header text in the Center section box, click the Font button 🅰, change the font size to 14 and the style to Bold, click OK, click OK again to return to the Header/Footer tab, then click OK to preview the list**
   Page 2 of the report appears as shown in Figure H-17.

**QuickTip**

To print a selected area instead of the entire worksheet, select the area, click File, click Print, and, under Print what, click Selection.

7. **Click Print to print the worksheet, then save and close the workbook**
   To print more than one worksheet, select each sheet tab while holding down the [Shift ] or [Ctrl] keys, then click the print button on the standard toolbar.

FIGURE H-16: **Sheet tab of the Page Setup dialog box**

Indicates row 1 will appear at top of each printed page

Indicates which columns will appear at left of each printed page

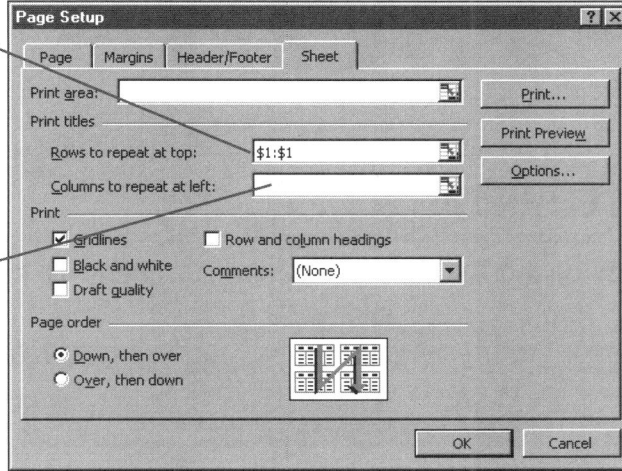

FIGURE H-17: **Print Preview window showing page 2 of completed report**

List header

Row 1 of list repeated as a print title

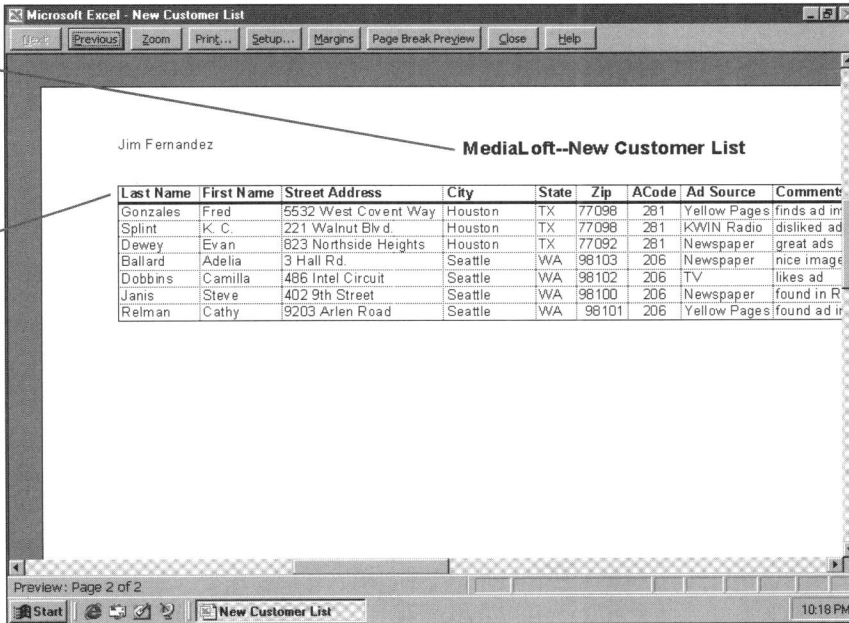

## Setting a print area

There are times when you want to print only part of a worksheet. You can do this in the Print dialog box by choosing Selection under Print what. But if you want to print a selected area repeatedly, it's best to define a **print area**, which will print when you click the Print button on the Standard toolbar. To set a print area, click View on the menu bar, then click Page Break Preview. In the preview window, select the area you want to print. Right-click the area, then select Set Print Area. The print area becomes outlined in a blue border. You can

drag the border to extend the print area (see Figure H-18) or add nonadjacent cells to it by selecting them, right-clicking them, then selecting Add to Print Area. To clear a print area, click File on the menu bar, point to Print Area, then click Clear Print Area.

FIGURE H-18: **Defined print area**

# Practice

## ► Concepts Review

Label each of the elements of the Excel screen shown in Figure H-19.

FIGURE H-19

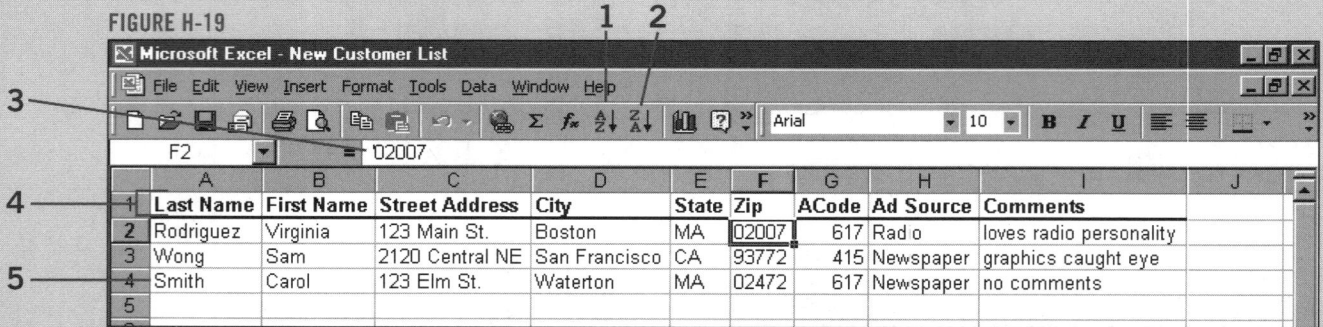

**Match each term with the statement that best describes it.**

6. **List**
7. **Record**
8. **Database**
9. **Sort**
10. **Field name**

a. Arrange records in a particular sequence
b. Organized collection of related information in Excel
c. Row in an Excel list
d. Type of software used for lists containing more than 65,536 records
e. Label positioned at the top of the column identifying data for that field

Select the best answer from the list of choices.

11. Which of the following Excel sorting options do you use to sort a list of employee names in A-to-Z order?
    a. Ascending
    b. Absolute
    c. Alphabetic
    d. Descending

12. Which of the following series is in descending order?
    a. 4, 5, 6, A, B, C
    b. C, B, A, 6, 5, 4
    c. 8, 7, 6, 5, 6, 7
    d. 8, 6, 4, C, B, A

13. Once the _____ is defined, any new records added to the list using the data form are included in the _____.
    a. database, database
    b. data form, data form
    c. worksheet, worksheet
    d. list range, list range

14. When printing a list on multiple pages, you can define a print title containing repeating row(s) to
    a. Include appropriate fields in the printout.
    b. Include field names at the top of each printed page.
    c. Include the header in list reports.
    d. Exclude from the printout all rows under the first row.

## ▶ Skills Review

1. **Create a list.**
    a. Create a new workbook, then save it as "MediaLoft New York Employee List".
    b. In cell A1, type the title "MediaLoft New York Employees".
    c. Enter the field names and records using the information in Table H-4.
    d. Apply bold formatting to the field names.
    e. Center the entries in the Years, Full/Part Time, and Training? fields.
    f. Adjust the column widths to make the data readable.
    g. Save, then print the list.

TABLE H-4

| Last Name | First Name | Years | Position | Full/Part Time | Training? |
|---|---|---|---|---|---|
| Lustig | Sarah | 3 | Book Sales | F | Y |
| Marino | Donato | 2 | CD Sales | P | N |
| Khederian | Jay | 4 | Video Sales | F | Y |
| Finney | Carol | 1 | Stock | F | N |
| Rabinowicz | Miriam | 2 | Café Sales | P | Y |

**2. Add records with the data form.**

   **a.** Select all the records in the list, including the field names, then define the range as "Database".

   **b.** Open the data form and add a new record for David Gitano, a one-year employee in Book Sales. David is full time and has not completed the training.

   **c.** Add a new record for George Worley, the café manager. George is full time, has worked there two years, and he has completed the training.

   **d.** Save the list.

**3. Find and delete records.**

   **a.** Find the record for Carol Finney.

   **b.** Delete the record.

   **c.** Save the list.

**4. Sort a list by one field.**

   **a.** Select the Database list range.

   **b.** Sort the list alphabetically in ascending order by last name.

   **c.** Save the list.

**5. Sort a list by multiple fields.**

   **a.** Select the Database list range.

   **b.** Sort the list alphabetically in ascending order, first by whether or not the employees have completed training and then by last name.

   **c.** Save the list.

**6. Print a list.**

   **a.** Add a header that reads "Employee Information" in the center and that includes your name on the right; format both header items in bold.

   **b.** Set the print area to include the range A1:F9.

   **c.** Delete the database range.

   **d.** Print the list, then save and close the workbook.

   **e.** Exit Excel.

# ► Independent Challenges

**1.** Your advertising firm, Personalize IT, sells specialty items imprinted with the customer's name and/or logo such as hats, pens, and T-shirts. Plan and build a list of information with a minimum of 10 records using the three items sold. Your list should contain at least five different customers. (Some customers will place more than one order.) Each record should contain the customer's name, item(s) sold, and the individual and extended cost of the item(s). Enter your own data and make sure you include at least the following list fields:

- Item—Describe the item.
- Cost-Ea.—What is the item's individual cost?
- Quantity—How many items did the customer purchase?
- Ext. Cost—What is the total purchase price?
- Customer—Who purchased the item?

To complete this independent challenge:

a. Prepare a list plan that states your goal, outlines the data you'll need, and identifies the list elements.

b. Sketch a sample list on a piece of paper, indicating how the list should be built. What information should go in the columns? In the rows? Which of the data fields will be formatted as labels? As values?

c. Build the list first by entering the field names, then by entering the records. Remember, you will invent your own data. Save the workbook as "Personalize IT".

d. Reformat the list, as needed. For example, you might need to adjust the column widths to make the data more readable. Also, remember to check your spelling.

e. Sort the list in ascending order by item, then by Customer, then by Quantity.

f. Select only the cells with data in the last row. Use the Delete command on the Edit menu to delete those cells, moving the existing cells up to fill the space.

g. Type your name in a blank cell and review the worksheet; adjust any items as needed; then print a copy.

h. Save your work before closing.

**2.** You are taking a class titled "Television Shows: Past and Present" at a local community college. The instructor has provided you with an Excel list of television programs from the '60s and '70s. She has included fields tracking the following information: the number of years the show was a favorite, favorite character, least favorite character, the show's length in minutes, the show's biggest star, and comments about the show. The instructor has included data for each show in the list. She has asked you to add a field (column label) and two records (shows of your choosing) to the list. Because the list should cover only 30-minute shows, you need to delete any records for shows longer than 30 minutes. Also, your instructor wants you to sort the list by show name and format the list as needed prior to printing. Feel free to change any of the list data to suit your tastes and opinions.

To complete this independent challenge:

a. Open the workbook titled EX H-2, then save it as "Television Shows of the Past".

b. Using your own data, add a field, then use the data form to add two records to the list. Make sure to enter information in every field.

c. Delete any records having show lengths other than 30. (*Hint*: Use the Criteria data form to set the criteria, then find and delete any matching records.)

d. Make any formatting changes to the list as needed and save the list.

e. Sort the list in ascending order by show name.

f. Preview, then print the list. Adjust any items as needed so that the list can be printed on a single page.

g. Sort the list again, this time in descending order by number of years the show was a favorite.

h. Change the header to read "Television Shows of the Past: '60s and '70s".

i. Type your name in a blank cell, then preview and print the list.

j. Save the workbook.

**3.** You work as a sales clerk at Nite Owl Video. Your roommate and co-worker, Albert Lee, has put together a list of his favorite movie actors and actresses. He has asked you to add several names to the list so he can determine which artists and what kinds of films you enjoy most. He has recorded information in the following fields: artist's first and last name, life span, birthplace, the genre or type of role the artist plays most (for example, dramatic or comedic), the name of a film for which the artist has received or been nominated for an Academy Award, and, finally, two additional films featuring the artist. Using your own data, add at least two artists known for dramatic roles and two artists known for comedic roles.

To complete this independent challenge:

**a.** Open the workbook titled EX H-3, then add at least four records using the criteria mentioned above. Remember, you are creating and entering your own movie data for all relevant fields.

**b.** Save the workbook as "Film Star Favorites". Make formatting changes to the list as needed. Remember to check your spelling.

**c.** Sort the list alphabetically by Genre. Perform a second sort by Last Name.

**d.** Preview the list, adjust any items as needed, then print a copy of the list sorted by Genre and Last Name.

**e.** Sort the list again, this time in descending order by the Life Span field, then by Last Name.

**f.** Enter your name in a blank cell, then print a copy of the list sorted by Life Span and Last Name.

**g.** Save your work.

**WEB WORK**

**4.** You work at MediaLoft corporate headquarters, and the Products Department has asked you to create a database to keep track of all CD products that win the People's Choice poll. The poll is new and will be conducted monthly.

To complete this independent challenge:

a. Start Excel, and create a new file with the following list headings: Artist LN, Artist FN, Title, Category, and In Stock, and save the file as "People's Choice". Format the title row with formats of your choice.

b. Connect to the Internet, and go to the MediaLoft intranet site at http://www.course.com/Illustrated/MediaLoft. Click the Products link, and print the page, which contains a table entitled "Results of People's Choice Poll". Disconnect from the Internet.

c. Use the information from the table to create the first six records of your list. For the In Stock column, show the first three products as in stock (Y) and the second three as not in stock (N). AutoFit the columns and save the file.

d. Open the file EX H-4, copy the records, and paste them into your database.

e. Find the CD by Jim Brickman.

f. Find the CD with the title "Mellow".

g. Use the Replace command to find all the records in the Rock category and change the category name to Rock N Roll. Adjust the column widths as necessary.

h. Sort the list by category.

i. Add a new field for Month, indicating the month each recording won the award. Assign a month (January, February, or March) to each winner so that each category has one winner per month.

j. Sort the list by month.

k. Sort the list by category and the artist's last name.

l. Sort by stock status, category, and the artist's last name.

m. Print the list, then save and close the file.

# ▶ Visual Workshop

Create the worksheet shown in Figure H-20. Save the workbook as "Famous Jazz Performers". Once you've entered the field names and records, sort the list by Contribution to Jazz and then by Last Name. Change the page setup so that the list is centered on the page horizontally and the header reads "Famous Jazz Performers". Preview and print the list, then save the workbook.

**FIGURE H-20**

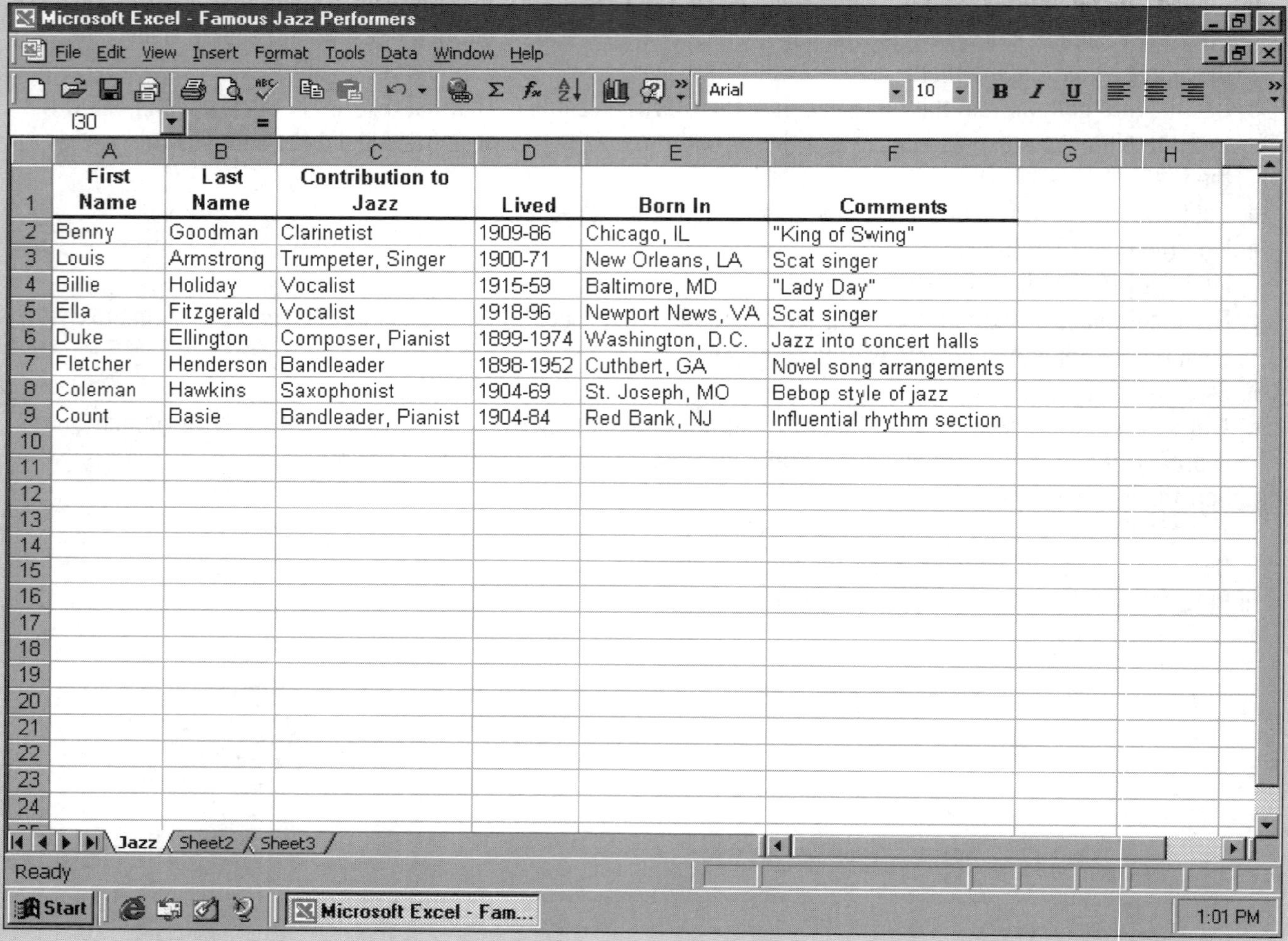

| | First Name | Last Name | Contribution to Jazz | Lived | Born In | Comments |
|---|---|---|---|---|---|---|
| 2 | Benny | Goodman | Clarinetist | 1909-86 | Chicago, IL | "King of Swing" |
| 3 | Louis | Armstrong | Trumpeter, Singer | 1900-71 | New Orleans, LA | Scat singer |
| 4 | Billie | Holiday | Vocalist | 1915-59 | Baltimore, MD | "Lady Day" |
| 5 | Ella | Fitzgerald | Vocalist | 1918-96 | Newport News, VA | Scat singer |
| 6 | Duke | Ellington | Composer, Pianist | 1899-1974 | Washington, D.C. | Jazz into concert halls |
| 7 | Fletcher | Henderson | Bandleader | 1898-1952 | Cuthbert, GA | Novel song arrangements |
| 8 | Coleman | Hawkins | Saxophonist | 1904-69 | St. Joseph, MO | Bebop style of jazz |
| 9 | Count | Basie | Bandleader, Pianist | 1904-84 | Red Bank, NJ | Influential rhythm section |

# Excel 2000 MOUS Certification Objectives

Below is a list of the Microsoft™ Office User Specialist program objectives for Core Excel 2000 skills showing where each MOUS objective is covered in the Lessons and Practice. This table lists the Core MOUS certification skills covered in the units in this book (Units A-H). For more information on which Illustrated titles meet MOUS certification, please see the inside cover of this book.

| MOUS standardized coding number | Activity | Lesson page where skill is covered | Location in lesson where skill is covered | Practice |
|---|---|---|---|---|
| **XL2000.1** | **Working with cells** | | | |
| XL2000.1.1 | Use Undo and Redo | Excel B-4 | Steps 7–8, QuickTip | |
| XL2000.1.2 | Clear cell content | Excel A-10 | Trouble, Step 2 | Skills Review |
| XL2000.1.3 | Enter text, dates, and numbers | Excel A-10 | Steps 2–7 | Skills Review, Independent Challenges 2–4 |
| | | Excel B-4 | Step 7 | Skills Review |
| XL2000.1.4 | Edit cell content | Excel B-4 | Steps 3–10 | Skills Review, Independent Challenges 2–3 |
| XL2000.1.5 | Go to a specific cell | Excel E-2 | Step 3 | Skills Review |
| XL2000.1.6 | Insert and delete selected cells | Excel E-11 | Clues to Use | Skills Review |
| XL2000.1.7 | Cut, copy, paste, paste special and move selected cells, use the Office Clipboard | Excel B-10 Excel B-11 Excel B-14 | Steps 2–4 Clues to Use QuickTip | Skills Review, Independent Challenges 1–4 |
| | Paste Special | Excel B-11 Excel E-3 | Clues to Use Clues to Use | Skills Review Skills Review |
| XL2000.1.8 | Use Find and Replace | Excel F-2 | QuickTip | |
| XL2000.1.9 | Clear cell formats | Excel C-6 | QuickTip | Skills Review |

| MOUS standardized coding number | Activity | Lesson page where skill is covered | Location in lesson where skill is covered | Practice | |
|---|---|---|---|---|---|
| XL2000.1.10 | Work with series (AutoFill) | Excel B-14<br>Excel B-15 | Step 3<br>Clues to Use | Skills Review | |
| XL2000.1.11 | Create hyperlinks | Excel F-14 | Steps 1–7 | | |
| **XL2000.2** | **Working with files** | | | | |
| XL2000.2.1 | Use Save | Excel A-10 | Step 8 | Skills Review | |
| XL2000.2.2 | Use Save As (different name, location, format) | Excel A-8<br>Excel F-16 | Steps 5–6<br>Steps 1–8 | Skills Review<br>Skills Review | |
| XL2000.2.3 | Locate and open an existing workbook | Excel A-8 | Steps 1–4 | Skills Review | |
| XL2000.2.4 | Create a folder | Excel F-16 | QuickTip | | |
| XL2000.2.5 | Use templates to create a new workbook | Excel G-5 | Clues to Use | | |
| XL2000.2.6 | Save a worksheet/workbook as a Web page | Excel F-16 | Steps 1–7 | Skills Review | |
| XL2000.2.7 | Send a workbook via e-mail | Excel F-17 | Clues to Use | | |
| XL2000.2.8 | Use the Office Assistant | Excel A-14 | Steps 1–6,<br>Clues to Use | Independent Challenge 1 | |
| **XL2000.3** | **Formatting worksheets** | | | | |
| XL2000.3.1 | Apply font styles (typeface, size, color and styles) | Excel C-4<br><br>Excel C-6 | Steps 2–5,<br>Clues to Use<br>Steps 2–7 | Skills Review<br>Independent Challenges 1–4,<br>Visual Workshop | |
| XL2000.3.2 | Apply number formats (currency, percent, dates, comma) | Excel C-2 | Steps 3–5 | Skills Review,<br>Independent Challenges 1–4,<br>Visual Workshop | |

| MOUS standardized coding number | Activity | Lesson page where skill is covered | Location in lesson where skill is covered | Practice |
|---|---|---|---|---|
| XL2000.3.3 | Modify size of rows and columns | Excel C-8<br>Excel C-9 | Steps 1–7<br>Clues to Use | Skills Review,<br>Independent Challenges 1–4 |
| XL2000.3.4 | Modify alignment of cell content | Excel C-6 | Step 7 | Skills Review,<br>Independent Challenges 1–4 |
| XL2000.3.5 | Adjust the decimal place | Excel C-1 | Step 5 | Skills Review |
| XL2000.3.6 | Use the Format Painter | Excel C-3<br>Excel C-14 | Clues to Use<br>Step 6 | Skills Review,<br>Independent Challenges 1–4 |
| XL2000.3.7 | Apply autoformat | Excel C-7 | Clues to Use | |
| XL2000.3.8 | Apply cell borders and shading | Excel C-12 | Steps 2–8 | Skills Review,<br>Independent Challenges 1–4 |
| XL2000.3.9 | Merging cells | Excel C-6 | Step 6 | Skills Review,<br>Independent Challenge 2 |
| XL2000.3.10 | Rotate text and change indents | Excel H-13 | Clues to Use | |
| XL2000.3.11 | Define, apply, and remove a style | Excel E-4 | Step 4 | |
| **XL2000.4** | **Page setup and printing** | | | |
| XL2000.4.1 | Preview and print worksheets & workbooks | Excel A-12<br><br>Excel B-18<br><br>Excel F-6 | Steps 1–5<br><br>Step 7<br><br>Step 6 | Skills Review,<br>Independent Challenges 2–4<br>Skills Review,<br>Visual Workshop<br>Skills Review,<br>Independent Challenge 1 |
| XL2000.4.2 | Use Web Page Preview | Excel F-16 | Step 7 | |
| XL2000.4.3 | Print a selection | Excel H-16 | QuickTip | |
| XL2000.4.4 | Change page orientation and scaling | Excel D-16<br>Excel E-16 | Steps 2–5<br>Step 6 | Skills Review |

| MOUS standardized coding number | Activity | Lesson page where skill is covered | Location in lesson where skill is covered | Practice |
|---|---|---|---|---|
| XL2000.4.5 | Set page margins and centering | Excel E-17 | Clues to Use | Skills Review |
| XL2000.4.6 | Insert and remove a page break | Excel F-12 | Steps 1–6 Clues to Use | |
| XL2000.4.7 | Set print, and clear a print area | Excel H-17 | Clues to Use | Skills Review |
| XL2000.4.8 | Set up headers and footers | Excel F-5 | Clues to Use | Skills Review |
| XL2000.4.9 | Set print titles and options (gridlines, print quality, row & column headings) | Excel H-16 | QuickTip | |
| **XL2000.5** | **Working with worksheets & workbooks** | | | |
| XL2000.5.1 | Insert and delete rows and columns | Excel C-10 | Steps 1–6 | Skills Review |
| XL2000.5.2 | Hide and unhide rows and columns | Excel F-8 Excel F-8 | Step 3 Table F-1 | |
| XL2000.5.3 | Freeze and unfreeze rows and columns | Excel F-2 | Steps 2–7 | Skills Review |
| XL2000.5.4 | Change the zoom setting | Excel F-10 | Step 1 | Skills Review |
| XL2000.5.5 | Move between worksheets in a workbook | Excel B-18 | Steps 1–2 | Skills Review, Independent Challenges 1–4 |
| XL2000.5.6 | Check spelling | Excel C-16 | Steps 1–5 | |
| XL2000.5.7 | Rename a worksheet | Excel B-18 | Steps 3–4 | Skills Review, Independent Challenges 1–4 |
| XL2000.5.8 | Insert and delete worksheets | Excel B-18 | QuickTip | Skills Review |
| XL2000.5.9 | Move and copy worksheets | Excel B-18 Excel B-19 | Step 6 Clues to Use | |

| MOUS standardized coding number | Activity | Lesson page where skill is covered | Location in lesson where skill is covered | Practice |
|---|---|---|---|---|
| XL2000.5.10 | Link worksheets & consolidate data using 3D References | Excel F-6 | Steps 1–8 Clues to Use | Skills Review |
| **XL2000.6** | **Working with formulas & functions** | | | |
| XL2000.6.1 | Enter a range within a formula by dragging | Excel B-8 | Steps 4–6 | |
| XL2000.6.2 | Enter formulas in a cell and using the formula bar | Excel B-6 | Steps 1–4 | Skills Review, Independent Challenges 1–4 |
| XL2000.6.3 | Revise formulas | Excel B-16 | Steps 6–7 | Skills Review, Independent Challenges 1–4 |
| XL2000.6.4 | Use references (absolute and relative) | Excel B-12 Excel B-14 Excel B-16 | Details Steps 1–8 Steps 1–8 | Skills Review, Independent Challenges 1, 4 |
| XL2000.6.5 | Use AutoSum | Excel B-8 | Steps 2–4 | Skills Review |
| XL2000.6.6 | Use Paste Function to insert a function | Excel B-8 | Steps 7–9 | |
| XL2000.6.7 | Use basic functions (AVERAGE, SUM, COUNT, MIN, MAX) | Excel B-8 Excel B-9 | Steps 8–9 Clues to Use | Skills Review |
| XL2000.6.8 | Enter functions using the formula palette | Excel E-12 | Steps 6–7 | Skills Review |
| XL2000.6.9 | Use date functions (NOW and DATE) | Excel E-8 | Clues to Use | Skills Review |
| XL2000.6.10 | Use financial functions (FV and PMT) | PMT Excel E-14 FV Excel E-15 | Steps 2–5 Clues to Use | Skills Review Skills Review |
| XL2000.6.11 | Use logical functions (IF) | E-10 | Steps 1–5 | Skills Review |

| MOUS standardized coding number | Activity | Lesson page where skill is covered | Location in lesson where skill is covered | Practice |
|---|---|---|---|---|
| **XL2000.7** | **Using charts and objects** | | | |
| XL2000.7.1 | Preview and print charts | Excel D-16 | Steps 2–8 | Skills Review, Independent Challenges 1–4, Visual Workshop |
| XL2000.7.2 | Use chart wizard to create a chart | Excel D-4 | Steps 2–7 | Skills Review, Independent Challenges 1–4, Visual Workshop |
| XL2000.7.3 | Modify charts | Excel D-6 Excel D-8 Excel D-10 | Steps 2–8 Steps 2–6 Steps 2–6 | Skills Review, Independent Challenges 1–4, Visual Workshop |
| XL2000.7.4 | Insert, move, and delete an object (picture) | Excel F-15 | Clues to Use | Skills Review |
| XL2000.7.5 | Create and modify lines and objects | Excel D-12 Excel D-14 | Steps 4–8 Steps 2–8 | |

# Project Files List

To complete many of the lessons and practice exercises in this book, students need to use a Project File that is supplied by Course Technology and stored on a Project Disk. Below is a list of the files that are supplied, and the unit or practice exercise to which the files correspond. For information on how to obtain Project Files, please see the inside cover of this book. The following list only includes Project Files that are supplied; it does not include the files students create from scratch or the files students create by revising the supplied files.

| Unit | File supplied on Project Disk | Location file is used in unit |
|------|-------------------------------|-------------------------------|
| Excel Unit A | EX A-1.xls | Lessons |
| | EX A-2.xls | Skills Review |
| Excel Unit B | EX B-1.xls | Lessons |
| | EX B-2.xls | Skills Review |
| | EX B-3.xls | Independent Challenge 3 |
| Excel Unit C | EX C-1.xls | Lessons |
| | EX C-2.xls | Skills Review |
| | EX C-3.xls | Independent Challenge 1 |
| | EX C-4.xls | Independent Challenge 2 |
| | EX C-5.xls | Visual Workshop |
| Excel Unit D | EX D-1.xls | Lessons |
| | EX D-2.xls | Independent Challenge 1 |
| | EX D-3.xls | Independent Challenge 2 |
| | EX D-4.xls | Independent Challenge 3 |
| | EX D-5.xls | Visual Workshop |
| Excel Unit E | EX E-1.xls | Lessons |
| | EX E-2.xls | |
| | EX E-3.xls | |
| | EX E-4.xls | |
| | EX E-5.xls | Skills Review |
| | EX E-6.xls | Independent Challenge 1 |
| | EX E-7.xls | Independent Challenge 2 |
| | EX E-8.xls | Independent Challenge 4 |
| Excel Unit F | EX F-1.xls | Lessons |
| | Pay Rate Classifications | |
| | EX F-2.xls | Skills Review |
| | Expense Details | |
| | EX F-3.xls | Independent Challenge 1 |

| Unit | File supplied on Project Disk | Location file is used in unit | |
|------|-------------------------------|-------------------------------|---|
| **Excel Unit G** | No files supplied | | |
| **Excel Unit H** | EX H-1.xls | Lessons | |
| | EX H-2.xls | Independent Challenge 2 | |
| | EX H-3.xls | Independent Challenge 3 | |
| | EX H-4.xls | Independent Challenge 4 | |

# Glossary

**3-D references** A reference that uses values on other sheets or workbooks, effectively creating another dimension to a workbook.

**Absolute reference** A cell reference that contains a dollar sign before the column letter and/or row number to indicate the absolute, or fixed, contents of specific cells. For example, the formula $A$1+$B$1 calculates only the sum of these specific cells no matter where the formula is copied in the workbook.

**Active cell** The current location of the cell pointer.

**Address** The location of a specific cell or range expressed by the coordinates of column and row; for example, A1.

**Alignment** The horizontal placement of cell contents; for example, left, center, or right.

**Anchors** Cells listed in a range address. For example, in the formula =SUM(A1:A15), A1 and A15 are anchors.

**Area chart** A line chart in which each area is given a solid color or pattern to emphasize the relationship between the pieces of charted information.

**Arguments** Information a function needs to create the answer. In an expression, multiple arguments are separated by commas. All of the arguments are enclosed in parentheses; for example, =SUM(A1:B1).

**Arithmetic operator** A symbol used in a formula, such as + or -, / or *, to perform mathematical operations.

**Attribute** The styling features such as bold, italics, and underlining that can be applied to cell contents.

**AutoComplete** A feature that automatically completes labels entered in adjoining cells in a column.

**AutoFill** A feature that creates a series of text or numbers when a range is selected using the fill handle.

**AutoFit** A feature that automatically adjusts the width of a column to accommodate its widest entry when the boundary to the right of the column selector is double-clicked.

**AutoFormat** Preset schemes that can be applied to format a range instantly. Excel comes with 16 AutoFormats that include colors, fonts, and numeric formatting.

**AutoSum** A feature that automatically creates totals using the AutoSum button.

**Background color** The color applied to the background of a cell.

**Bar chart** A chart that shows information as a series of (horizontal) bars.

**Border** The edge of a selected area of a worksheet. Lines and color can be applied to borders.

**Cancel button** The X in the formula bar; it removes information from the formula bar and restores the previous cell entry.

**Cell** The intersection of a column and row in a worksheet.

**Cell address** The unique location identified by intersecting column and row coordinates.

**Cell pointer** A highlighted rectangle around a cell that indicates the active cell.

**Cell reference** The address or name that identifies a cell's position in a worksheet; it consists of a letter that identifies the cell's column and a number that identifies its row; for example, cell B3. Cell references in worksheets can be used in formulas and are relative or absolute.

**Chart** A graphic representation of information from a worksheet. Types include 2-D and 3-D column, bar, pie, area, and line charts.

**Chart sheet** A separate sheet that contains a chart linked to worksheet data.

**Chart title** The name assigned to a chart.

**Chart Wizard** A series of dialog boxes that helps create or modify a chart.

**Check box** A square box in a dialog box that can be clicked to turn an option on or off.

**Clear** A command on the Edit menu used to erase a cell's contents, formatting, or both.

**Clipboard** A temporary storage area for cut or copied items that are available for pasting. See *Office Clipboard*.

**Clipboard toolbar** A toolbar that shows the contents of the Office Clipboard; contains buttons for copying and pasting items to and from the Office Clipboard.

**Close** A command that closes the file so you can no longer work with it, but keeps Excel open so that you can continue to work on other workbooks.

**Column chart** The default chart type in Excel that displays information as a series of (vertical) columns.

**Column selector button** The gray box containing the letter above the column.

**Conditional format** The format of a cell based on its value or the outcome of a formula.

**Conditional formula** A formula that makes calculations based on stated conditions, such as calculating a rebate based on a purchase amount.

**Consolidate** To add together values on multiple worksheets and display the result on another worksheet.

**Control menu box** A box in the upper-left corner of a window used to resize or close a window.

**Copy** A command that copies the content of selected cells and places it on the Clipboard.

**Cut**  A command that removes the cell contents from the selected area of a worksheet and places them on the Clipboard.

**Data entry area**  The unlocked portion of a worksheet where users are able to enter and change data.

**Data form**  In an Excel list (or database), a dialog box that displays one record at a time.

**Data marker**  A graphical representation of a data point, such as a bar or column.

**Data point**  Individual piece of data plotted in a chart.

**Data series**  The selected range in a worksheet that Excel converts into a graphic and displays as a chart.

**Database**  An organized collection of related information. In Excel, a database is called a list.

**Delete**  A command that removes cell contents from a worksheet.

**Dialog box**  A window that opens when more information is needed to carry out a command.

**Dummy column/row**  Blank column or row included at the end of a range that enables a formula to adjust when columns or rows are added or deleted.

**Dynamic page breaks**  In a larger workbook, horizontal or vertical dashed lines that represent the place where pages print separately. They also adjust automatically when you insert or delete rows or columns, or change column widths or row heights.

**Edit**  A change made to the contents of a cell or worksheet.

**Electronic spreadsheet**  A computer program that performs calculations on data and organizes information into worksheets. A worksheet is divided into columns and rows, which form individual cells.

**Enter button**  The check mark in the formula bar used to confirm an entry.

**Exploding pie slice**  A slice of a pie chart that has been pulled away from the whole pie to add emphasis.

**External reference indicator**  The exclamation point (!) used in a formula to indicate that a referenced cell is outside the active sheet.

**Field**  In a list (an Excel database), a column that describes a characteristic about records, such as first name or city.

**Field name**  A column label that describes a field.

**Fill color**  Cell background color.

**Fill Down**  A command that duplicates the contents of the selected cells in the range selected below the cell pointer.

**Fill handle**  A small square in the lower-right corner of the active cell used to copy cell contents.

**Fill Right**  A command that duplicates the contents of the selected cells in the range selected to the right of the cell pointer.

**Find**  A command used to locate information the user specifies.

**Floating toolbar**  A toolbar within its own window that is not anchored along an edge of the worksheet.

**Font**  The typeface or design of a set of characters (letters, numbers, symbols, and punctuation marks).

**Footer**  Information that prints at the bottom of each printed page; on screen, a footer is visible only in Print Preview. To add a footer, use the Header and Footer command on the View menu.

**Format**  The appearance of text and numbers, including color, font, attributes, borders, and shading. See also *Number format*.

**Format Painter**  A feature used to copy the formatting applied to one set of text or in one cell to another.

**Formula**  A set of instructions used to perform numeric calculations (adding, multiplying, averaging, etc.).

**Formula bar**  The area below the menu bar and above the Excel workspace where you enter and edit data in a worksheet cell. The formula bar becomes active when you start typing or editing cell data. It includes the Enter button and the Cancel button.

**Freeze**  To hold in place selected columns or rows when scrolling in a worksheet that is divided in panes. See also *panes*.

**Function**  A special, predefined formula that provides a shortcut for a commonly used calculation; for example, AVERAGE.

**Gridlines**  Horizontal and/or vertical lines within a chart that make the chart easier to read.

**Header**  Information that prints at the top of each printed page; on screen, a header is visible only in Print Preview. To add a header, use the Header and Footer command on the View menu.

**Hide**  To make rows, columns, formulas, or sheets invisible to workbook users.

**HTML**  Hypertext Markup Language, the format of pages that a Web browser such as Internet Explorer or Netscape Navigator can read.

**Hyperlink**  An object (a filename, a word, a phrase, or a graphic) in a worksheet that, when you click it, will display another worksheet, called the target.

**Input**  Information that produces desired results in a worksheet.

**Insertion point**  Blinking I-beam that appears in the formula bar during entry and editing.

**Internet**  A large computer network made up of smaller networks and computers.

**Intranet**  An internal network site used by a particular group of people who work together.

**Label**  Descriptive text or other information that identifies the rows and columns of a worksheet. Labels are not included in calculations.

**Label prefix** A character that identifies an entry as a label and controls the way it appears in the cell.

**Landscape orientation** A print setting that positions the worksheet on the page so the page is wider than it is tall.

**Legend** A key explaining how information is represented by colors or patterns in a chart.

**Line chart** A graph of data that is mapped by a series of lines. Line charts show changes in data or categories of data over time and can be used to document trends.

**Linking** The dynamic referencing of data in other workbooks, so that when data in the other workbooks is changed, the references in the current workbook are automatically updated.

**List** The Excel term for a database, an organized collection of related information.

**Lock** To secure a row, column, or sheet so that data there cannot be changed.

**Logical test** The first part of an IF function; if the logical test is true, then the second part of the function is applied, and if it is false, then the third part of the function is applied. In the function IF(Balance>1,000,Rate*0.05,0), the 5% rate is applied to balances over $1,000.

**Macro** A set of instructions, or code, that performs tasks in the order you specify.

**Mixed reference** Formula containing both a relative and an absolute reference.

**Mode indicator** A box located at the lower-left corner of the status bar that informs you of the program's status. For example, when Excel is performing a task, the word "Wait" appears.

**More Buttons button** A button you click on a toolbar to view toolbar buttons that are not currently visible.

**Mouse pointer** A symbol that indicates the current location of the mouse on the desktop. The mouse pointer changes its shape at times; for example, when you insert data, select a range, position a chart, change the size of a window, or select a topic in Help.

**Moving border** The dashed line that appears around a cell or range that is copied to the Clipboard.

**Name box** The left-most area in the formula bar that shows the cell reference or name of the active cell. For example, A1 refers to cell A1 of the active worksheet. You can also get a list of names in a workbook using the Name list arrow.

**Named range** A range of cells given a meaningful name; it retains its name when moved and can be referenced in a formula.

**Number format** A format applied to values to express numeric concepts, such as currency, date, and percentage.

**Object** A chart or graphic image that can be moved and resized and contains handles when selected.

**Office Assistant** An animated character that appears to offer tips, answer questions, and provide access to the program's Help system.

**Office Clipboard** A temporary storage area shared by all Office programs that can be used to cut, copy, and paste multiple items within and between Office programs. The Office Clipboard can hold up to 12 items collected from any Office program. See also *Clipboard toolbar*.

**Open** A command that retrieves a workbook from a disk and displays it on the screen.

**Order of precedence** The order in which Excel calculates parts of a formula: (1) exponents, (2) multiplication and division, and (3) addition and subtraction.

**Output** The end result of a worksheet.

**Panes** Sections into which you can divide a worksheet when you want to work on separate parts of the worksheet at the same time; one pane freezes, or remains in place, while you scroll in another pane until you see the desired information.

**Paste** A command that moves information on the Clipboard to a new location. Excel pastes the formula, rather than the result, unless the Paste Special command is used.

**Paste Function** A series of dialog boxes that lists and describes all Excel functions and assists the user in function creation.

**Pie chart** A circular chart that represents data as slices of pie. A pie chart is useful for showing the relationship of parts to a whole; pie slices can be extracted for emphasis. See also *Exploding pie slice*.

**Point** A unit of measure used for fonts and row height. One inch equals 72 points.

**Pointing method** Specifying formula cell references by selecting the desired cell with your mouse instead of typing its cell reference; this eliminates typing errors.

**Portrait orientation** A print setting that positions the worksheet on the page so the page is taller than it is wide.

**Precedence** Algebraic rules that Excel uses to determine the order of calculations in a formula with more than one operator.

**Print Preview** A command you can use to view the worksheet as it will look when printed.

**Print title** In a list that spans more than one page, the field names that print at the top of every printed page.

**Program** Task-oriented software (such as Excel or Word) that enables you to perform a certain type of task, such as data calculation or word processing.

**Programs menu** The Windows 95/98 Start menu that lists all available programs on your computer.

**Range** A selected group of adjacent cells.

**Range format** A format applied to a selected range in a worksheet.

**Record** In a list (an Excel database), data about an object or a person.

**Relative cell reference**  A type of cell reference used to indicate a relative position in the worksheet. It allows you to copy and move formulas from one area to another of the same dimensions. Excel automatically changes the column and row numbers to reflect the new position.

**Replace**  A command used to find one set of criteria and replace it with new information.

**Reset usage data**  An option that returns personalized toolbars and menus to their default settings.

**Row height**  The vertical dimension of a cell.

**Row selector button**  The gray box containing the number to the left of the row.

**Save**  A command used to permanently store your workbook and any changes you make to a file on a disk. The first time you save a workbook you must give it a filename.

**Save As**  A command used to create a duplicate of the current workbook with a new filename. Used the first time you save a workbook.

**Selection handles**  Small boxes appearing along the corners and sides of charts and graphic images that are used for moving and resizing.

**Series of labels**  Pre-programmed series, such as days of the week and months of the year. They are formed by typing the first word of the series, then dragging the fill handle to the desired cell.

**Sheet**  Another term used for a *worksheet*.

**Sheet tab**  A description at the bottom of each worksheet that identifies it in a workbook. In an open workbook, move to a worksheet by clicking its sheet tab. Also known as *Worksheet tab*.

**Sheet tab scrolling buttons**  Buttons that enable you to move among sheets within a workbook.

**Sort keys**  Criteria on which a sort, or a reordering of data, is based.

**Spell check**  A command that attempts to match all text in a worksheet with the words in the dictionary.

**Start**  To open a software program so you can use it.

**Status bar**  The bar at the bottom of the Excel window that provides information about various keys, commands, and processes.

**Target**  The location that a hyperlink displays after you click it.

**Text annotations**  Labels added to a chart to draw attention to a particular area.

**Text color**  The color applied to the text within a cell.

**Tick marks**  Notations of a scale of measure on a chart axis.

**Title bar**  The bar at the top of the window that indicates the program name and the name of the current worksheet.

**Toggle button**  A button that turns a feature on and off.

**Toolbar**  A bar that contains buttons that give you quick access to the most frequently used commands.

**Truncate**  To shorten the display of a cell based on the width of a cell.

**Values**  Numbers, formulas, or functions used in calculations.

**View**  A set of display or print settings that you can name and save for access at another time. You can save multiple views of a worksheet.

**What-if analysis**  A decision-making feature in which data is changed and automatically recalculated.

**Wildcard**  A special symbol you use in defining search criteria in the data form or Replace dialog box. The most common types of wildcards are the question mark (?), which stands for any single character, and the asterisk (*), which represents any group of characters.

**Window**  A rectangular area of a screen where you view and work on a worksheet.

**Workbook**  A collection of related worksheets contained within a single file.

**Worksheet**  An electronic spreadsheet containing 256 columns by 65,536 rows.

**Worksheet tab**  See *Sheet tab*.

**Worksheet window**  The worksheet area in which data is entered.

**World Wide Web**  A structure of documents, called pages, connected electronically over a large computer network called the Internet.

**X-axis**  The horizontal line in a chart.

**X-axis label**  A label describing the x-axis of a chart.

**Y-axis**  The vertical line in a chart.

**Y-axis label**  A label describing the y-axis of a chart.

**Zoom**  A feature that enables you to focus on a larger or smaller part of the worksheet in Print Preview.

# Index

# Index

# BMW M3

# BMW *M3*

## The complete history of these ultimate driving machines

BMW M3

Graham Robson

Haynes Publishing

First published in July 2013

A catalogue record for this book is available from the British Library

ISBN 978 0 85733 292 9

Library of Congress control no. 2013932261

Published by Haynes Publishing,
Sparkford, Yeovil, Somerset BA22 7JJ, UK
Tel: 01963 442030 Fax: 01963 440001
Int. tel: +44 1963 442030 Int. fax: +44 1963 440001
E-mail: sales@haynes.co.uk
Website: www.haynes.co.uk

Haynes North America Inc.
861 Lawrence Drive, Newbury Park,
California 91320, USA

Printed in the USA by Odcombe Press LP,
1299 Bridgestone Parkway, La Vergne, TN 37086

# Contents

# Introduction and Acknowledgements

Thirty years ago, BMW set out to produce a new saloon car to compete in touring car racing, aware that at least 5,000 would need to be built to ensure sporting homologation. The resulting car was the original M3, and it first went on sale in 1986.

Naturally, they hoped it would be a winner, but did BMW ever dream that this charismatic new model would prove to be such a worldwide success? Or that it was establishing a pedigree that not only made the acronym 'M3' legendary, but that would lead to more than a quarter of a million such cars being produced in the ensuing 25 years?

In all that time, several different types and generations of M3 road car have passed through my hands, and on each occasion I have been amazed by the way the company always managed to combine astonishing performance with superb build quality, tenacious roadholding with comfortable road manners, and all manner of equipment (some of us still call these 'toys') fitted to keep abreast of less-exciting opposition.

With all that performance on tap, the amazing thing is that I managed to retain my driving licence intact. There were occasions, however, when I was on a racetrack, or on an unrestricted German autobahn, when I achieved unfamiliarly high speeds. Unfamiliar to me anyway … good morning officer!

Then, of course, there is the M3's everlasting motorsport record. The first time I saw an M3 performing on a racetrack was at Silverstone in the rain, and the first time I saw a 'works'-blessed rally car in full flight was on serpentine tarmac roads in Corsica. On both occasions, I couldn't understand how such a car could possibly keep up with, and sometimes vanquish, rivals with a lot more power – but it could.

All this explains why, when the M3 reached its quarter century in 2011, I set out to chronicle the record, the highlights and most of the changes made to the car's pedigree in all that time. I realised even then that, without producing a book of *Encyclopaedia Britannica* length, I could not possibly cover every detail – but I hope I have got the flavour and the balance about right. However, as the M3 pedigree continues to mature, and new generations appear regularly, I am sure that updates will be needed in the future.

Nor could I have done this without tapping into other, more reliable, M3 knowledge and expertise. In the past, and right up to the present day, I have been privileged to consult BMW AG in Munich (and to visit their immaculately kept archive), the same help being provided by BMW (UK) Ltd at Bracknell. This time too, I also thought it wise to contact the true enthusiasts in the BMW Car Club, especially Richard Baxter (chairman of the M-Power section), who made sure that my ramblings were, at least, scanned for accuracy at an early stage.

It is with very grateful thanks, that I also acknowledge the immeasurable help given to me by both BMW (UK) and BMW AG, in sourcing, locating, and making available the mass of illustrations that appear in these pages.

Will there be scope for me to write more about the M3 in the future? If BMW continues to sell such amazing cars, I am sure there will….

GRAHAM ROBSON

**RIGHT: The most highly tuned of M3 four-cylinder road-car engines was the 238bhp/2,467cc version, as fitted to 600 Evolution III models in 1989/1990.**

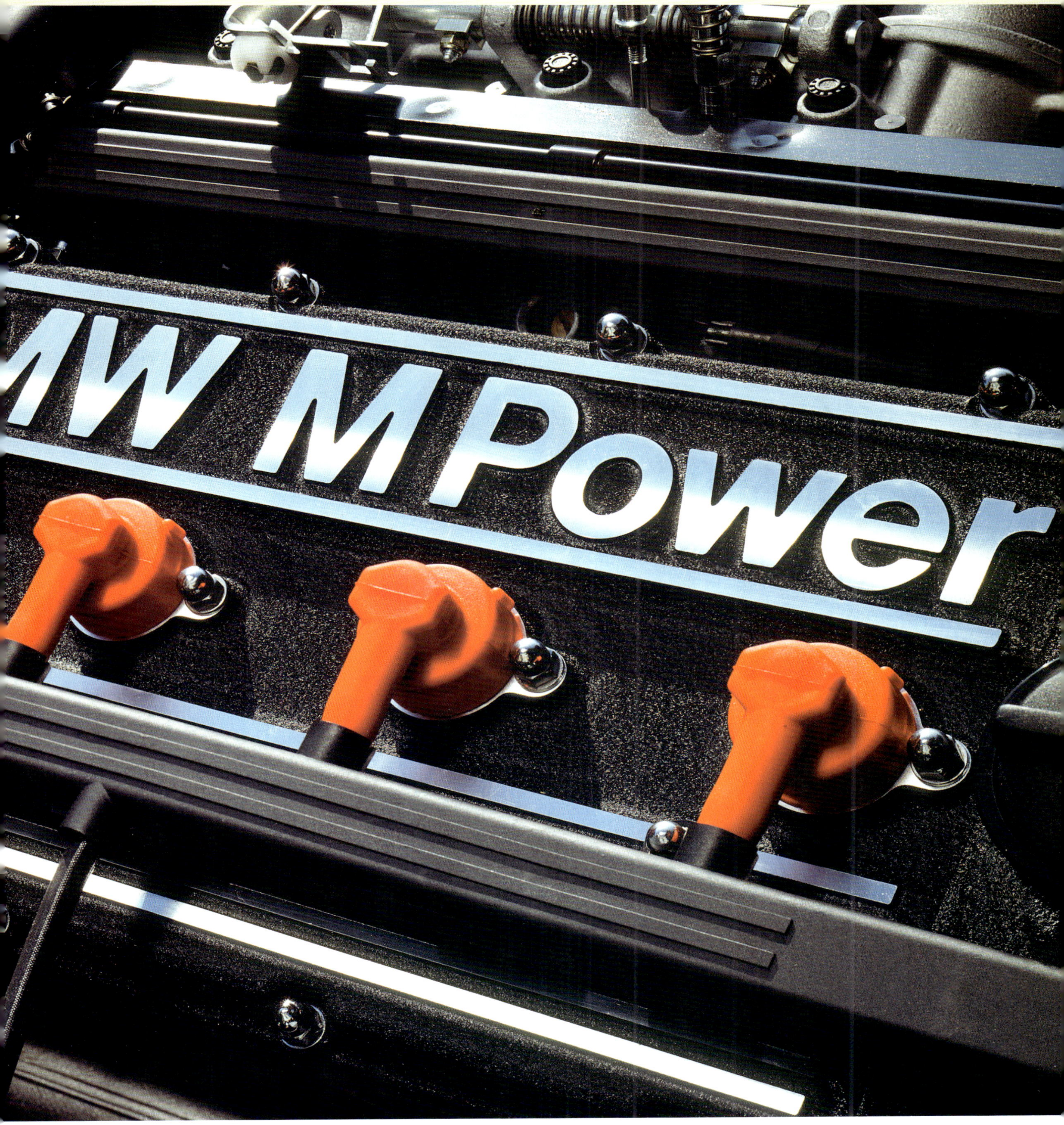
MW M Power

## M3 time line

| | |
|---|---|
| 1978 | Launch of first-ever M-badged BMW, the mid-engined M1 supercar. Only 454 built from 1979 to 1981. |
| 1981 | Project work on a new 'M3' began in Germany. |
| July 1985 | Official preview of new M3 Saloon. Sales to begin in 1986. |
| September 1986 | Sales of M3 began. |
| February 1987 | M3 'Evolution I' (505 produced) put on sale. |
| March 1987 | Sporting homologation achieved, to enable racing and rallying in Group A competition to begin. |
| March 1988 | M3 'Evolution II' (220bhp, etc.) went on sale (501 produced). |
| May 1988 | M3 Cabriolet announced. |
| April 1989 | M3 Cecotto/Ravaglia, with chassis changes, put on limited sale. |
| September 1989 | M3 (215bhp version) put on limited sale. |
| December 1989 | M3 Sport Evolution III, with 238bhp, put on sale (600 produced). |
| December 1990 | End of original E30 Coupé production. |
| June 1991 | End of E30 Cabriolet production. |
| Late 1992 | Launch of second-generation M3, based on new E36 structure, with 3.0-litre six-cylinder engine. |
| January 1994 | Introduction of E36-type Cabriolet. |
| July 1994 | Introduction of E36-type M3 Saloon. |
| December 1994 | Introduction of limited-edition E36 M3 GT 'homologation special' with 295bhp. |
| 1995 | Introduction of E36 M3 Lightweight (LTW), a USA-market-only special edition. |
| July 1995 | Introduction of new E36 Evolution range, with 3.2-litre engine, direct replacement for the original E36. |
| Early 1996 | SMG sequential gear change feature became optional. |
| May 1998 | End of M3 Saloon model production. |
| September 1999 | End of E36/M3 assembly – the Cabriolet being the last of all. |
| October 2000 | Introduction of new E46 M3 Coupé. No SMG option at first. |
| Spring 2001 | Introduction of new E46 M3 Convertible. |
| Summer 2001 | Re-introduction of SMG transmission option. |
| Early 2003 | M3 CSL went on sale. |
| Early 2004 | M3 CSL assembly ended. |
| Summer 2006 | Final E46 types – Coupés and Convertibles – produced. |
| Summer 2007 | Introduction of new-generation V8-engined E92 Coupé. |
| Early 2008 | Introduction of new-generation E90 four-door Saloon, and E93 metal hard-top Convertible. Seven-speed semi-automatic transmission now available. |
| November 2009 | Introduction of limited-production M3 GTS Coupé. 135 cars built. |
| June 2011 | Introduction of limited-edition CRT Saloon. Just 67 cars produced. |
| End 2011 | E90 M3 Saloon discontinued. |
| 2013 | Preview of new-generation M3 model. |

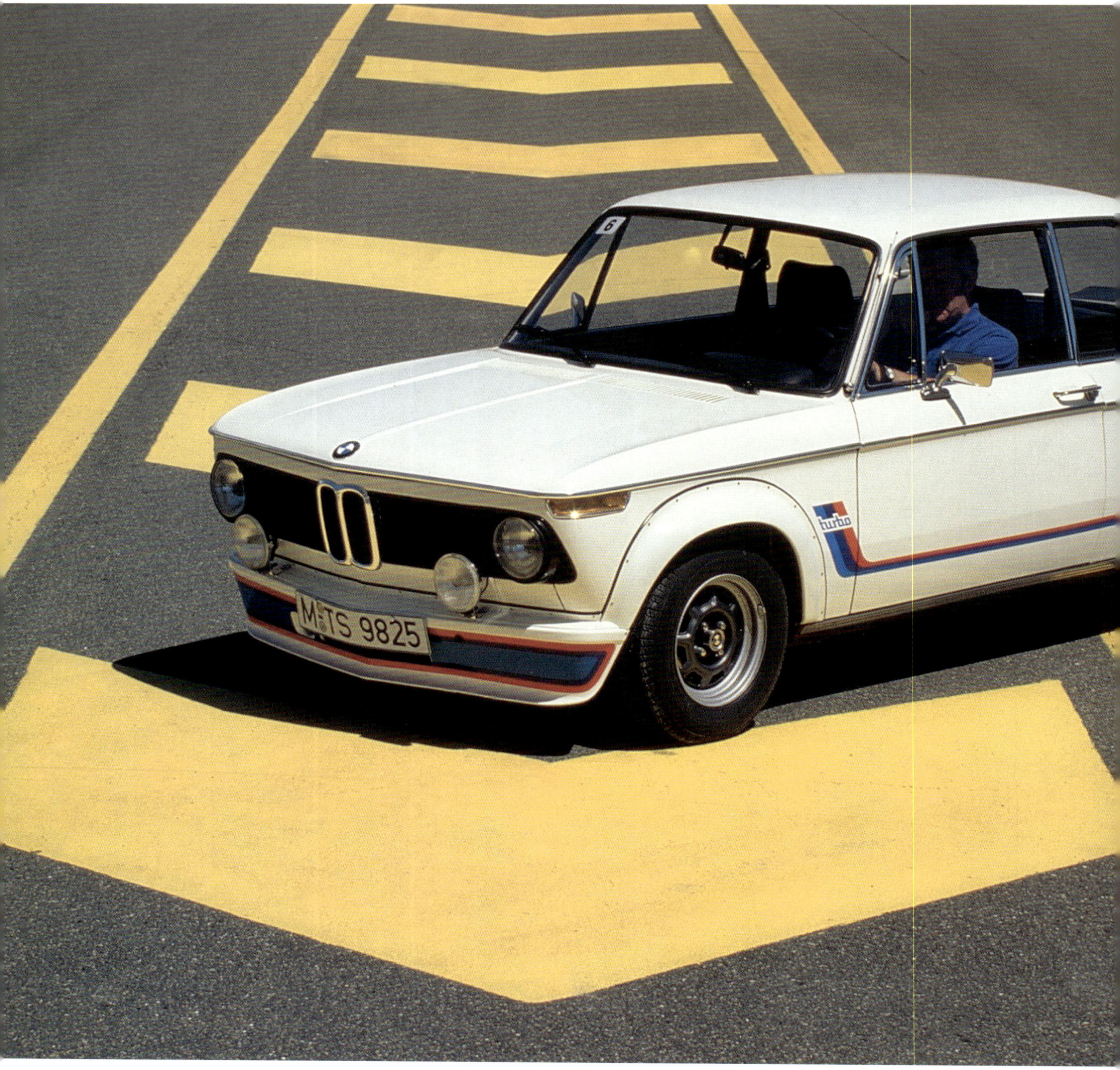
M TS 9825
turbo

# BMW's motorsport tradition – including the M1 Supercar

Although BMWs began winning rallies and production-car races in the 1930s, it was not until the 1960s that they really achieved success at international level. This was when the cars, which began to win touring car races, all used one or other version of a new generation of overhead-camshaft engine design that formed the heart of what became known as the 'Neue Klasse' ('New Class') family of models. This range really rescued BMW from financial disaster in 1961, and the magnificent M3 models that we know so well today stem from the developments, updates, and replacements for that engine.

In the beginning, the company that would eventually take on the BMW acronym had built expensive Wartburg cars at Eisenach in Germany. The first BMW-badged cars of all were modified developments of the cute little British Austin Seven, which were then being manufactured by Dixi (also of Eisenach), and it was only later that BMW came to develop its own chassis, its own body styles and – most important of all – its own engines.

Soon, and throughout the 1930s, BMW's technical advance was swift and remarkable. First of all, in 1932, there was the 3/20 (which featured swing-axle independent rear suspension and an overhead-valve four-cylinder engine), followed by the 303 of 1933, which had BMW's first-ever six-cylinder engine. The 315 of 1934 was the first BMW to use a tubular frame, the 319 of 1935 had a 1,911cc six-cylinder engine – all of which led up to the launch of the 328 two-seater sports car of 1936.

It was the 328 (no question) that laid the foundations of the several sporting BMWs that would follow in the 1940s and beyond, for it featured an 80bhp/1,911cc engine, used a cylinder head with hemispherical combustion chambers, delivered a top speed of up to 95mph, and proved to be remarkably successful on the road, in rallies and on the racetrack. BMW didn't make many of them – only 461 between 1936 and 1940 – but at a stroke they made most of their rivals look old-fashioned and technically obsolete.

The Second World War, which followed between 1939 and 1945, was technically encouraging for BMW, but ultimately resulted in utter devastation of the business. In that time a series of massive, magnificently-engineered, radial aircraft engines was produced – the German fighter and bomber aircraft that used these engines were formidably fast and robust – but Allied bombing eventually reduced the Eisenach and Munich factories to something approaching smoking ruins.

Worst of all was that, with the end of the war and the partitioning of old Germany by the victorious powers, the Eisenach factory, where all

**ABOVE: BMW had only been producing its own-design cars for seven years when it introduced the splendid 328 sports car in 1936. At a stroke, it made all other sports cars look dowdy and old-fashioned.**

**PREVIOUS PAGE: BMW's first truly high-performance Saloon was the turbocharged 2002 Turbo of 1973–1974, with a modified version of the Neue Klasse four-cylinder engine. Even so, the first of the M3s would not employ turbocharging.**

the original-generation cars had been produced, found itself on the eastern side of the Iron Curtain – the impassable border barrier which was set up between the Soviet Union and the other liberating powers. With this it seemed that the BMW pedigree might wither and die.

Or would it? This was the time when BMW's indomitable spirit, visionary planning and sheer bloody-mindedness all kicked in. To rebuild BMW, the business would have to be centred on the Munich factories, where a workforce began to gather once again. This literally had to be tackled from the ground up, and although that was almost impossibly demanding at times, the spirit of the company's managers, engineers and workforce never faltered.

Money was always short and profits hard to come by, but from 1945 to the end of the 1950s,

when BMW so nearly collapsed financially, they kept the faith, kept up their efforts to rejuvenate, rebuild and modernise factories and business equipment and, somehow, just survived. In the beginning BMW repaired military machinery, then produced cooking utensils, building fittings, bicycles, baking equipment and agricultural machines. Then, from 1948, the first post-war motorcycles – the R24 types – were produced.

But no cars, as yet. Although 2,500 people were once again working at the downtown Munich factory by 1949, they were building up production of motorcycles, not cars, and it was not until 1951 that the first new-type BMW car – the big, bulbous, 'Baroque Angel' (as it was nicknamed) – was previewed. Sales began in 1952, and an ultra-sporting version called the 507 followed. But to provide volume to grow the business, and to improve cash flow, BMW also introduced, then produced, tens of thousands of tiny Isetta bubble-cars, the larger 600s which grew out of them, and the smart 700 series (in which Michelotti was much involved as consultant stylist).

Unhappily, by the end of the 1950s, there was still a yawning gap in the range between the 30bhp/697cc 700 and the massive 100bhp/ V8/2,580cc 502 Saloon. Sales drooped, losses mounted, and for a time the business looked as if it might fail, or even fall into the hands of Daimler-Benz, whose Mercedes-Benz range of private cars was already highly profitable, and which was bent on expansion.

It is now a well-known facet of BMW history that a merger was proposed; that a stormy meeting held in Munich to confirm the deal lasted for nine hours; that the merger was rejected by shareholders; and that a new financial godfather, the industrialist Herbert Quandt, then came on to the scene. Since then – more than half a century – Quandt interests have been dominant at BMW.

## BMW – WHAT'S IN A NAME?

Wartburg cars were built in Eisenach, Germany, in 1898, but it was not until 1916 that an original military aero engine was produced, and in 1917 a new enterprise – BMW (Bayerische Motoren Werke) – took shape, and based itself in Munich. Thereafter, the company moved on to producing motorcycles in Munich, and in 1928 it bought a small car-making company called Dixi, which just happened to be in Eisenach, so integration into the existing BMW factories seemed to be straightforward enough. Having spent a year or so producing Dixis, which were licence-built Austin Sevens that had been designed in Britain, the company evolved its own derivative, calling it the BMW 3/15, this being the very first BMW-badged car.

The original company of 1916 had been the Bayerische Flugzeugwerke AG (which translates as Bavarian Aircraft Works). Other small engineering companies were subsequently absorbed, and BMW became the dominant acronym at the Milbertshofen factory in the northern outskirts of Munich. The site, now thoroughly modernised, has been the company's HQ ever since.

LEFT: The 2-litre 328 engine of 1936 used part-spherical combustion chambers, and a novel type of valve gear drive to produce 85bhp, which was extremely powerful at this period in automotive history.

## The 'New Class'

At last, enough capital was made available for BMW to invest in a new medium-sized car, and an all-new model which management dubbed Der Neue Klasse (the New Class) was finalised. Officially badged as the 1500 (but 1600, 1800 and 2000 types would soon follow in rapid succession), and first shown to the public in 1961, this was probably the most important single new car which BMW ever announced, and one which had as big an impact on the company as – say – the Model T had had at Ford, the Beetle at VW, and the Mini at BMC. It was, in other words, a complete game-changer, with features on which BMW would continue to build in the next 50 years.

To summarise, this was the first BMW to use a monocoque body/chassis structure, the first to use MacPherson-strut independent front suspension, and the first to use an all-new four-cylinder overhead-camshaft engine. It was this engine, in which guru Alex von Falkenhausen had played a big part, which would be such a strong link to BMW's long-term future. As explained in Appendix A, this was the classic basic engine that would run and run, and would eventually be redesigned in every respect, but would still be recognisable as the ancestor of the M3 power unit that was to be introduced 25 years later in 1986.

Because of the obvious financial constraints, at first there was only one model in the New Class – a four-door Saloon – but as the 1960s progressed, different, extra, and smaller body-shells, two-door styles, convertibles and a 'Touring' (really an estate car, but BMW never embraced that phrase) were all added. Not only that, but the engine got bigger, more powerful, and soon embraced Bosch fuel injection as one of the fuelling options. One can quite see, I am sure, where and how the pedigree that led to the birth of the M3 became established.

Over the years, the 1500 grew up and was replaced in 1972 by the first of the 5-Series family. In the meantime, 1966 saw the appearance of a smaller-bodied car called the 1600-2, which rapidly grew to include 2002 (2-litre) derivatives, and became the ultra successful 'entry-level' BMW that gave way to the original 3-Series type in 1975.

## Alex von Falkenhausen

Born in 1907, Alex von Falkenhausen was, by the 1930s, working at BMW as a significant young engineer in the development of the 320-Series models (which included the 328 sports car), one of his colleagues being Dr Fritz Fiedler, who designed the unique cylinder head of the 328.

Allied bombing during the Second World War had destroyed much of BMW's infrastructure, and subsequent geopolitical upheavals saw the factory behind the 'Iron Curtain' in East Germany. So von Falkenhausen opened a garage in Munich to restore and tune up 328s, and from 1949 he started building AFM single-seater 2-litre F2 race cars. This venture, however, could not hope to compete successfully against the might of Ferrari and

LEFT: Alex von Falkenhausen was closely involved with BMW from the 1930s all the way until the mid-1970s, and was ultimately responsible for the high-performance engines that evolved from the original Neue Klasse engine of 1961.

Maserati and, lacking funds to match their efforts, von Falkenhausen was obliged to close down the operation.

From 1954, therefore, he rejoined the engineering staff of BMW in Munich, soon took on management of the Rennsportabteilung (racing) operation there, inspired the birth of the new generation of overhead-camshaft Neue Klasse engines (four-cylinder and, later, six-cylinder), finally retiring in 1975, though remaining as a much-respected 'elder statesman' until he died in 1989.

ABOVE: After struggling to stay afloat in the 1950s, BMW's rebirth finally came in 1961, with the launch of the original, all-new, Neue Klasse Saloon.

LEFT: 2002 Turbo of 1973–1974, with a modified version of the Neue Klasse four-cylinder engine.

## 1, 3 AND 5 – THE NUMBERS GAME

Many years ago, BMW concluded that it needed to evolve a new system of model naming that would make their cars quite unmistakable from any other. Up to then, for instance, there had been BMW 700s, 1600s, 2002s and 2800s, but in future the use of many more engines and specifications was going to make this confusing.

Starting with the medium-sized 520 of 1972, BMW decided on a logical way of defining anything in the range, which has persisted to this day. The physically smallest range of cars in the range had always been the 1-Series, the medium range the 3-Series, the medium-large range the 5-Series, and the large type the 7-Series. Two other 'sub-types' have also been added – 6-Series and 8-Series, which were specialised Coupé derivatives of the 5-Series and 7-Series respectively, but even up to the time of writing there has never been a 2-Series or 4-Series type, though the adoption of both of those was suggested from time to time.

Where appropriate, the M-for-Motorsport prefix has been added – and surely nothing could be simpler.

Here, at least, was the '3' badging that would be carried over to the M3 of 1986, but there was still much to evolve at BMW before that exciting model came along. In the meantime, the 2002 eventually became 2002tii (with fuel injection), the short-lived 2002 Turbo (complete with a 170bhp/2.0-litre turbocharged four-cylinder engine), and there was an ever-growing series of smart two-door Coupés with bodies built by Karmann.

## A new 'six' and the first 'M' cars

In and around all this, production soared to match an ongoing growth in sales, and the range continued to expand. Sometimes officially, and at other times by giving rather less obvious financial support, BMW got involved in motorsport, and soon became known for producing formidably strong and successful circuit race cars, though rallying rarely figured.

By the time the original 3-Series was launched in 1975, BMW was making more than 200,000 cars a year, they had taken over the ailing Glas

RIGHT: BMW started its four-valves per cylinder development programme with the lofty and complex Apfelbeck engine of 1966 – here seen in a Brabham BT7 F1 car.

LEFT: Old friends reunited in 1973 – Alex von Falkenhausen (right) and race driver Hans Stuck, the elder. Both Stuck and his son (who became known as 'Hanschen') drove and raced BMWs many times between the 1930s and the 1980s.

BELOW: To follow the unsuccessful Apfelbeck engine, BMW developed this conventional four-valve/twin-cam F2 power unit, which was the true ancestor of all subsequent four-valve engines developed in the next forty years.

**ABOVE:** In 1979 and 1980, the Procar series of M1-only races were held at F1 weekends, using race-prepared Group 4-specification cars that produced 470bhp. They looked magnificent, and were very effective.

**RIGHT:** The M1's 3.5-litre twin-cam, four-valves-per cylinder engine not only produced a lot of power but was also beautifully detailed.

**OPPOSITE:** Massed ranks of race-prepared M1s made quite a sensation in the Procar series (which ran at F1 events) in 1979 and 1980 – this was Monaco.

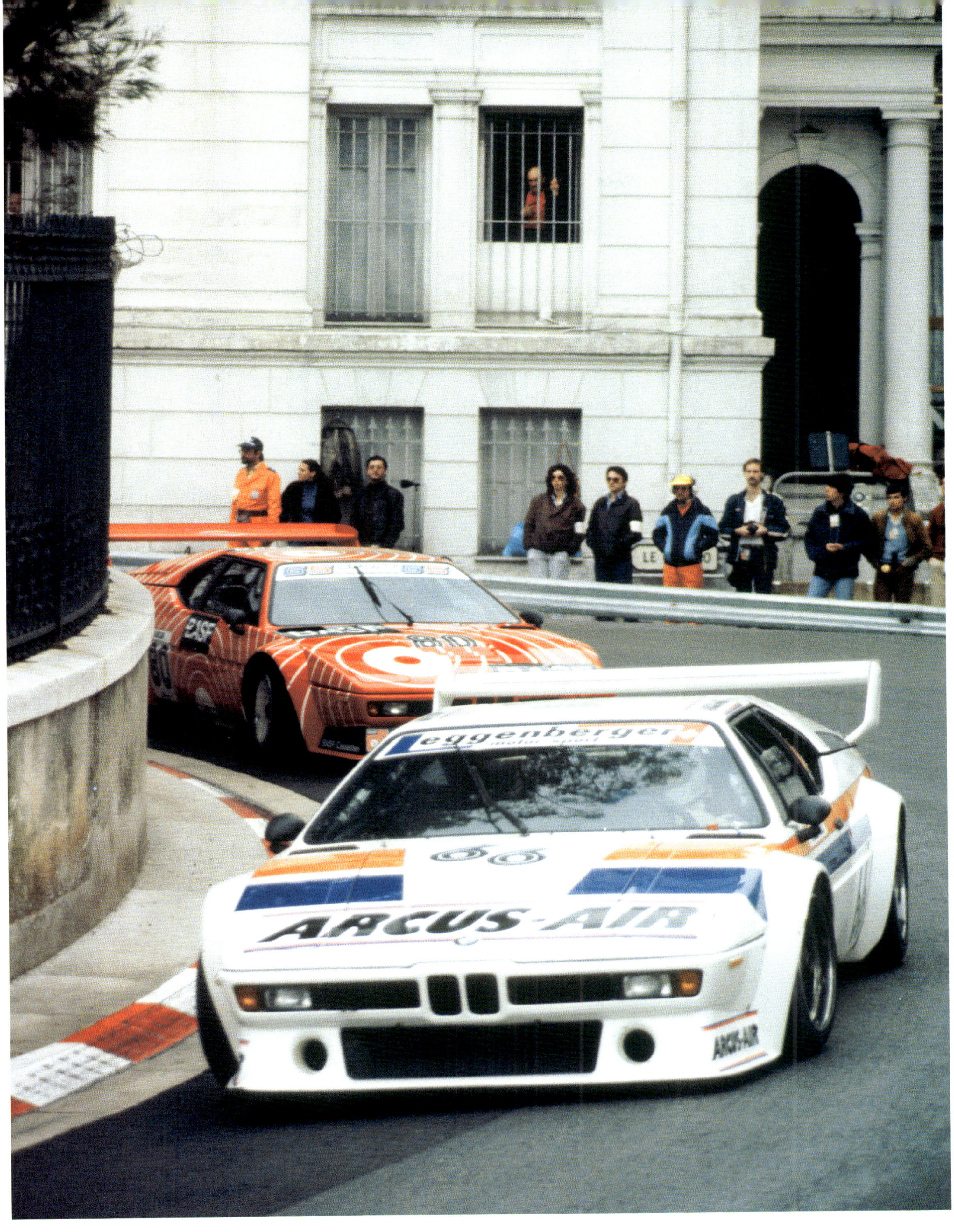
eggenberger
ARCUS-AIR

concern (allowing BMW to build a new and more modern factory at Dingolfing) and the first of the illustrious six-cylinder models – the 2500/2800 3-litre machines – had been launched. Those new big 'six' types, need I add, used engines that were direct descendants of the already respected 'four', and shared any number of components, such as valve gear, pistons, connecting rods and other details.

The BMW Motorsport GmbH operation gradually built up during the 1970s (it was established in 1972), and it was this successful division, headed by Jochen Neerpasch (who had joined BMW from Ford-Germany, where he had been running a successful Capri race programme), which laid firm foundations. Having turned the 3-litre-engined Coupé into the more specialised and extrovert 3.0CSL type, which featured a magnificent 3.5-litre engine and several flamboyant aerodynamic add-ons, making it a dominant touring car racer, he then turned his attention to the very first of the M (for Motorsport) badged BMWs – the M1 supercar.

Although the M1 looked gorgeous, had astonishing performance, and was at least the equal of any of the mid-engined cars that were coming out of Italy at the time, for BMW it was neither a financial nor a marketing success.

**ABOVE:** For the early 1980s, BMW developed an astonishing 1.5-litre turbocharged version of the original Neue Klasse engine, complete with M1-type valve gear, while still retaining the road-car's cylinder block.

**LEFT:** The amazingly powerful turbocharged 1.5-litre BMW F1 engine powered Nelson Piquet's Brabham to World Championship success in 1983. This was the car racing in Brazil.

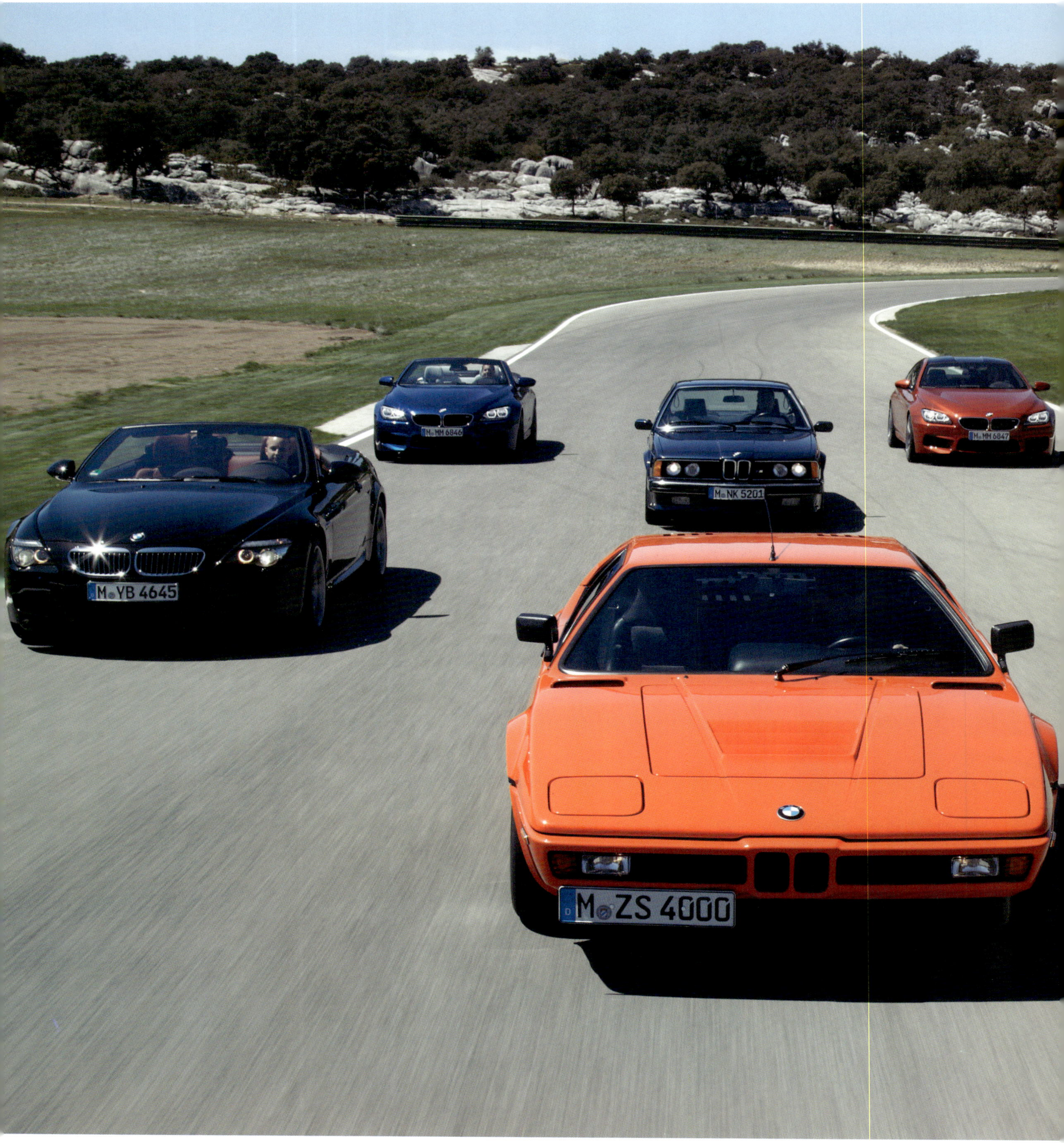
M YB 4645
M MM 6846
M NK 5201
M MM 6847
M ZS 4000

For one thing, the FIA Group 4 sports car racing series, for which it was originally designed, died before birth (leaving the M1 with nowhere to go and no stage on which to perform), and for another, the original manufacturing plan – which was that Lamborghini should have been responsible for building all the cars – fell to pieces when Lamborghini's finances collapsed.

In the end, just 454 such cars were made – a few of them featuring in one-model races at support events held during the 1979 and 1980 F1 seasons – and it was all over by 1981. All of them, however, had one very important innovation that would influence the layout of every subsequent M-Series model – their engines featured twin overhead camshafts, four valves per cylinder, and Kugelfischer fuel injection. These 277bhp/3,453cc engines had been developed on the basis of the company's existing 'larger' six-cylinder power units, and proved right away that Paul Rosche's engineers knew all about high-performance engines.

## FOUR VALVES PER CYLINDER

Each and every M-Series model in BMW's range has always had what all enthusiasts call a 'four-valve' engine. More accurately, every engine has had twin-overhead-camshaft cylinder heads, with gas flow managed by two inlet valves and two exhaust valves.

As with many rival concerns, BMW took time to evolve, and refine the basic layout that has now been adopted by almost every major high-performance engine builder in the world. BMW's first high-performance engine was the 1,911cc six-cylinder unit used in the 1936 328 (which featured hemispherical combustion chambers and a positive forest of pushrods and rocker arms to make all the valves work, but only had two valves per cylinder), and the original single overhead camshaft engine was the 1,499cc unit designed for the original 'New Class' 1500 of 1961.

Developments of the 'New Class' four, and of the six-cylinder unit which evolved from it, were right for every BMW built until 1978, when the magnificent mid-engined M1 appeared, complete with twin-cam cylinder heads and four valves per cylinder. It was that engine, and its evolution, which inspired so many other four-valve BMW engines in the future.

The first-ever four-valve BMW engine was, of course, the 1.6-litre Apfelbeck F2 racing engine, and the more conventional 1.6-litre and 2.0-litre versions that followed it, but it was the four-valve, twin-cam engine of the M1 that sparked off so much more.

## Chapter 1

# E30 – the original M3
## 1986–1991

If motorsport's governing body, the Federation Internationale de l'Automobile (FIA) had not decided to revise all the Groups under which motor sporting events were to be held in the 1980s, BMW's now legendary M3 might never have been developed. Until then, motor races and rallies had been organised according to Groups 1 to 6 inclusive, and sporting homologation (the procedure for gaining approval to enter) had become increasingly complex: the length, detail and scope of the new official documentation confirms this.

To face up to this set of rules, manufacturers tended to develop a series of what became known as 'homologation special' cars (some two-seaters, but mainly four-seaters) whereby a particular sub-model of a particular range was built to be suitable for a particular motorsport formula, often with a rather exotic 'standard' specification, sold in tiny numbers to meet the rules, and then campaigned by those who could afford them. Unsurprisingly, the 'road car' version of these cars was often rather unpleasant to drive, and undeveloped in several details. Even to meet Group 2 rules, only 1,000 such cars had to be built, and in Group 4 only 400 were needed: added to this was the fact that several makers played fast and loose with their 'counting' to gain early homologation.

Car makers such as Ford (with the Escort RS1800), Fiat (with the 131 Abarth) and Lancia (with the mid-engined Stratos) all played this homologation game to perfection – making no more cars than they needed to, and certainly not worrying too much about making an overall profit – but on the other hand some sizeable concerns, such as BMW and Mercedes-Benz, were not prepared to do that. Once BMW's old 3.0CSL had been retired, and both the contemporary 5-Series and 6-Series models had proved to be a little too heavy and cumbersome for touring car racing, the Munich concern really had no car with which to compete at the top level.

Then, as the 1980s opened, the tide turned, for after sustaining a great deal of pressure from manufacturers all around the world, the FIA made a momentous announcement. Starting in 1982 the old groupings were to be swept away, to be replaced with a new system of lettered (rather than numbered) categories – these being Group N (which required 5,000 'showroom' specification cars to be built), Group A (the same 5,000-off cars, but with a number of performance-raising technical freedoms allowed: and this was where motorsport expertise really kicked in) and Group B (200 very special cars of what I might call the M1 type). At the time of the announcement in 1980, Group B looked likely to become the most popular category for international rallying (especially as four-wheel drive was to be allowed for the very first time), but Group A was expected to take over as the formula under which many international motor racing events and most important championships would take place.

**PREVIOUS PAGES:**
**This front view of the original M3 of 1986/1987 shows that many detail changes had been made to the basic body-shell, including the provision of flared wheel arches, and a different front spoiler…**

**ABOVE: …with the same attention to detail being given to the rear end, also including flared arches, a raised boot lid, a functional rear spoiler and a different rear bumper.**

Although they were already committed to a high-profile and very-expensive programme of developing 1.5-litre turbocharged engines for F1 racing (see the image on page 28), BMW concluded that not only did they have enough technical expertise, but there were promising new-model road-car developments in the pipeline that might allow them once again to become competitive in touring car racing. But it was going to require new thinking, bold product planning, and decisive action into the bargain: it went without saying that this could not be slipped through the corporate mesh without gaining board approval, for the investment would be considerable.

The reasons were obvious. To qualify for Group A homologation, the new regulations insisted that a company would have to build a minimum of 5,000 cars within a 12-month period. This, by definition, meant that an average of at least one hundred cars would have to be completed every week — more if possible, to get the cars approved and homologated in good time — and such cars would have to be based on a more mundane series production machine, and should ideally share the same final assembly facilities.

This was never going to be easy, even for a company as profitable and ambitious as BMW. To quote a contemporary motor industry pundit who had a great deal of experience in such matters: 'Anyone can build one car – that's easy – and even building 20 cars is possible, given available finance. But building 200 Group B cars, or 5,000 Group A cars means that big money has to be spent on tooling for special pieces….' Not that BMW needed reminding of this, for they had just gone through that self-same process with the beautiful mid-engined M1 Coupé.

Nevertheless, the company decided to develop a new Group A Saloon model based on the still secret new-generation 3-Series (the E30 range, which was due to be announced in 1982). It was a big decision, and one that would require considerable investment. The plan was to produce the necessary 5,000 cars within a year of assembly beginning, even if this figure was at the top end of what its planners saw as a natural sales ceiling for cars of this sort.

BMW, to their great credit, boldly faced up to this from the beginning, deciding that they could meet the challenge. Like all German motor companies, they would develop every aspect of the machine to their own demanding standards and would only put a model on sale once the company was happy that (a) it was of the high quality expected of any modern BMW, and that (b) it would be competitive in motorsport.

For all the obvious publicity reasons, it was to be called the M3 (there was never an M2, by the way). At the stroke of a pen, therefore, one of the most charismatic of all new-model titles was born.

Even before work began – and the records show that it was engine work that started the ball rolling in 1981 – BMW had to sit down and work out just how specialised a car they could afford to build. They decided that ideally a new M3 should be based on the up-and-coming second-generation 3-Series, not only because at the time this car would be very publicity-worthy, but because it would be relatively light, and a choice of available engines meant that it could surely be made competitive as a competition car.

## 3-Series – an ideal 'base' car

By the early 1980s the 3-Series and the larger 5-Series were behind the company's success, and sales of these cars were producing the bulk of its profits. The heritage of the 3-Series could be traced back to the original Neue Klasse cars of 1961, and it still had all the features that had made that car so popular.

As already mentioned in the Prologue, the Neue Klasse was eventually joined by the first '02' cars in 1966, and it was these machines, complete with their 98.4in/2,500mm wheelbase platforms, allied to two-door bodywork and a choice of overhead-camshaft four-cylinder engines, which had established a familiar DNA. All in all, more than 850,000 of all types would be produced in 11 years, before an even more significant car – the original E21 3-Series range – took over in 1975.

This was the BMW that was breaking all previous production records when thoughts turned towards making an M3, for in nine years no fewer than 1,364,039 examples would be built. Even so, many more of the second-generation (E30) 3-Series, on which the original M3 would be based, would eventually be built.

All the best Group A competition cars have been designed from the first day to be competitive

in motorsport, not merely as fast road cars that later called for modification to make them competitive. To do this it was necessary to understand the provisions, the tightly-written regulations and – most important of all – the multifarious technical 'freedoms' and optional equipment that were built into the rules.

In Group A the changing of body panel materials for motorsport use, for instance, was absolutely forbidden (no aluminium or GRP substitutes), whereas the provision of an entirely different optional gearbox (if listed on the homologation form) was approved. For motor racing and rallying, different wheels, brakes and suspension items could always be used (though in most cases they had to be mentioned and illustrated in the homologation forms), but a change

ABOVE: **For the early 1980s, BMW developed an astonishing 1.5-litre turbocharged version of the original Neue Klasse engine, complete with M1-type valve gear, while still retaining the road car's cylinder block...and this was a complete strip down of that famous power unit. The original M3 engine, which followed, would learn much from this design.**

of basic specification (of fuelling, or of suspension layout) was forbidden. For use in motorsport, changes to the aerodynamic shape of the basic road car were not allowed.

I mention this because all such provisos were totally central to the way that the M3 took shape. For pragmatic and financial reasons, the new car was to be based on the body-shell/structure of the two-door E30 BMW, so most changes that would make the car competitive on the racetrack would have to be developed, and specified at the design stage. This, for instance, meant that any new-type spoilers and wheel-arch extensions would have to be fitted to every one of the first 5,000 road cars built – and by definition this meant that BMW's influential design/styling department would have to be consulted at every stage.

In this case, though, the entire project started with the need to choose in which class in the Group A category the car was to compete. With the decision made to retain a normally-aspirated engine (and one that would comfortably fit into the confines of the E30 series engine bay) the choice, it seemed, was between a four-cylinder engine of perhaps 2.0 litres and a six-cylinder engine of up to 2.5 litres, though the question of taking advantage

of a lower minimum weight limit in the 2.0-litre class was also a factor.

Decisions, decisions – but in the end the company's growing mass of experience with its rugged four-cylinder engine, against its still very limited knowledge of power-tuning the 'small' six-cylinder engine, proved crucial. The choice, then, of a twin overhead camshaft, four valves per cylinder head 'four' was almost a 'no-brainer', for by that time BMW had a great deal of experience – and motor racing success – with that layout.

Not only that, but because it had high ambitions, the company opted for the largest possible version of the four-cylinder engine which could be made reliable for long-distance 'endurance' racing – for, by definition, if such an engine could satisfy that requirement, de-tuned versions would surely be suitable for use in the road cars.

Such an engine was to be a 2.3-litre (coded S14 at first), and in many ways it would bear a distinct resemblance to earlier BMW 'twin-cams', whether four-cylinder or six-cylinder – notably those used in the M1 of the late 1970s, and in the M535i and original M5 types which preceded the M3 in the development cycle.

The close family link between the Neue Klasse four-cylinder engine and the larger six-cylinder engine, which formed the basis of the M1/M5 models, has already been mentioned, but the following brief survey of engine dimensions may be instructive:

| Engine | Bore x Stroke (mm) | Capacity (cc) |
| --- | --- | --- |
| 4-cylinder F1 | 89 x 60 | 1,499 |
| 4-cylinder 2-litre | 89 x 80 | 1,990 |
| 6-cylinder M1/M5 | 93.4 x 84 | 3,453 |
| As chosen for the 4-cylinder M3 | 93.4 x 84 | 2,302 |

The four-cylinder M3 engine, therefore, would use the same bore, stroke, valves and valve gear, and the same general internal porting arrangements as the six-cylinder M1/M535i had employed since the late 1970s.

[As was to happen so often in the future, BMW then muddied the waters a little in 1984 by announcing the original M5 model, whose six-cylinder engine had shrunk to 3,430cc, with a bore and stroke of 92 x 86mm!]

To get the show on the road, the story goes that in 1981 the very first M3 test engine was constructed by traditional motor industry 'knife-and-fork' methods of the sort that any Coventry-based engineer would have been proud. According to BMW engine guru Paul Rosche (and I quote this with grateful thanks to my fellow author Jeremy Walton): 'You know how we make the first M3 engine in 1981? I tell you. We slice the end from an M635 24-valve head; two cylinders are removed, and water passages closed off. Yes, now we have a cylinder head to put on the iron block "four". That's what we needed to show us the M3 could work!'

It was as logical – but by no means as simple – as that. The mocked-up engine worked, it worked well, and produced what BMW was sure would be competitive power. But mountains more work remained before the engine, and the car itself,

## Paul Rosche

Born and bred in Munich, Paul Rosche started working for BMW in 1957, and did not retire until 42 years later in 1999. Throughout that time, he concentrated on the design and development of automotive engines – almost always high-performance engines – and was recognised as one of the leading exponents at this art (and I use the word advisedly) throughout the world.

Having been involved, from the start, with the M10 (Neue Klasse) engine, he soon moved on to F2 race engine development, including the difficult-to-tame Apfelbeck design, but then with what some call the 'Cosworth-clone' that became the dominant 2-litre F2 engine of the 1970s.

What followed? First of all the 3.5-litre 'Batmobile' (3.0 CSL) engines, then the original four-valve M1 six-cylinder engine, followed by the amazingly powerful 1.5-litre F1 engine – which of course retained the standard cast-iron cylinder block.

LEFT: BMW's long-serving engine design chief, Paul Rosche, had already led the team which developed successful turbocharged F1 engines in the early 1980s, before he turned his attention to developing the original M3 power unit.

As is made clear in Chapter 1, the original M3 engine was directly developed from the M1 power unit – it was, in effect, two-thirds of that engine. The six-cylinder M3 engines of the 1990s also came under Rosche's scrutiny, and his crowning glories were the unique 6.1-litre/627bhp V12 engine which was supplied to McLaren for the F1 road car, the first of the 3.5-litre V10 F1 engines, which began to win races in the early 2000s, and the V8/V10 duo of engines developed especially for the M3 and M5 ranges of that same decade.

By then Rosche had retired, leaving behind him a heritage that would take a considerable amount of effort to match in future years.

ABOVE: Although the original M3 engine was bulky (wide, in particular) it fitted comfortably into the engine bay of the E30-type 3-Series body-shell, where it was canted over to the right at an angle of 30°.

Tens of thousands of hours on the test bed, on the road and – yes – on race circuits like the 'old' Nürburgring, would have to go in to final development of the road car version of this engine, which, like other four-cylinder types in the 3-Series body-shells, would be leant over at an angle of 30° in the engine bay. The decision was then taken to make the road car available in all markets, no matter what exhaust emission regulations were to apply, and this meant that the engine settings – particularly of the latest Bosch ML Motronic engine management system – would have to be refined to make the engine available in catalytic and non-catalytic convertor form. This all took time, and millions of Deutschmarks, and the fact that it also had to meet every known drive-by noise test was also a factor, as was the decision to put the M3 on the US market in due course. It was a great credit to all in Munich that the derivative with what was thought to be a power-sapping catalyst in the exhaust system, and other system and settings changes, produced 195bhp, whereas the uncluttered version produced 200bhp.

The biggest and most costly investment decisions centred around the specification of the M3's body-shell, for although BMW's engineers (particularly the motorsport engineers) had a long wish list of how they would like to improve the basic specification of the 3-Series shell, there were financial, practical and regulatory reasons why some could not be included.

First and foremost, it was decided that each and every original-generation M3 should have a two-door saloon structure – not only to reduce the weight of the complete car (two-door cars tend to be a bit lighter than four-door cars), but to ensure that the structure of the competition derivatives could be made as rigid as possible.

Not only that, but it was also concluded that this new model should only be built with left-hand steering. Although right-hand steering (particularly a right-mounted steering column) could probably have been inserted into the engine bay without too much hassle, the company reasoned that (a) left-hand-drive was best for use on many motor racing circuits, and that (b) the vast majority of all M3 road cars would be sold in left-hand-drive territory.

Although the development team was obliged to retain much of the standard E30/two-door

would be ready for sale. It is worth recalling that the M3 road car was not revealed for a further four years – the summer of 1985, in fact – and deliveries of road cars did not start until September 1986.

[There were, and are, no easy short cuts for this process, and all schedules are partly governed by the amount of investment ready to be ploughed in, and by the number of engineers, planners and vehicle builders allocated to the task. Purely for interest, the author notes that BMW's big sporting rival of the period – Ford with its Sierra RS Cosworth – was not even to conceive that car until late 1983, and it was officially launched in March 1985, with customer deliveries beginning in the summer of 1986.]

body-shell, they made as many changes as were allowed by a cost-conscious board of directors. The fact is that the internal shell structure was basically an E30, but other authorities on BMW history have claimed that almost every external panel except the bonnet was changed. The front grille, complete with four circular headlamps, was easily recognisable, but every other exterior panel was noticeably special. As was the case with other successful 'homologation specials' of the period, the transformation from normal 3-Series to M3 was done neatly, without breaking the investment bank, but with the maximum possible boost to the car's overall potential.

The most obvious visual changes were to the wings and the boot lid/spoiler arrangement, and it is significant to note that these were made without altering the basic internal body-shell. New front and rear steel wings were employed, with gracefully flared wheel arches, these features being engineered so that ultra-wide racing wheels and tyres (BMW had plans to use 10in rims) could be fitted without infringing the Group A regulations. Like the standard pressings that they displaced, these were in pressed steel. Although it would have been easy for the road cars to look under-tyred, this was obviated by making 7in x 15in cast alloy BBS wheels standard, along with 205/55VR15 tyres.

Changes made at the rear of the car were at once visually obvious, but suitably subtle. Naturally,

**ABOVE: Not only was the fully-prepared E30 M3 a potential race winner, but also the standard road car was one of the fastest A-to-B machines in the business at the time.**

BMW wanted to add downforce at the rear, which explained the use of a transverse spoiler, but extensive wind-tunnel testing provided benefits in two other quarters. One was a more steeply raked (by 3°) rear window glass and the other an entirely new plastic boot lid, which sat 1.57in (40mm) higher off the ground than the standard pressing. The rear and side windows were bonded into place.

SMC plastic was also employed for the under-door sills, for the big rear bumper/valance and for the three-piece front bumper/spoiler. The sum total of all these changes, which had been finalised with the cooperation of the design/styling department in Munich, was that the new car's overall drag coefficient came down significantly from Cd = 0.38 to Cd = 0.33. Maybe that doesn't sound much – but it translates into more than 13% less drag at all speeds, which was going to make a big difference at high (racing) and lower (road car touring) speeds.

In the fullness of time – BMW was well known for its typically German attitude to diligent testing, to careful development, and to the elimination of faults wherever possible – the road car was ready to meet its public. Although the company was aiming the new M3 at saloon car racing, it was not about to rush the car into the showrooms until it was convinced that the necessary 5,000 cars (necessary, that is, to gain Group A sporting

**RIGHT: This neat four-valve installation was for the original E30 M3, and was very closely related to that already used in the six-cylinder M1 of the late 1970s. Cosworth had laid down the template for cylinder head design in the mid-1960s, and every rival (BMW included) studied their findings very carefully in the years that followed.**

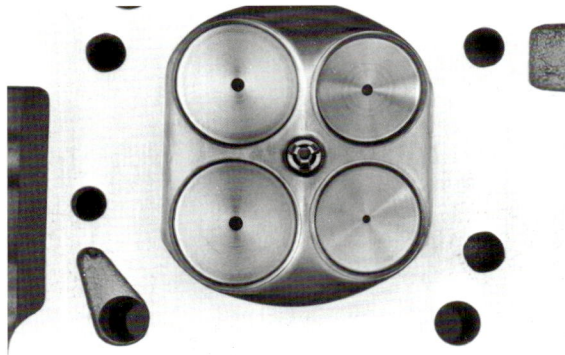

**RIGHT: After five years of development work, this was the finalised version of the original M3's 200bhp/2.3-litre engine – ultra-powerful and carefully detailed, just as one would expect.**

homologation) could be produced. It was no surprise that the original M3 road car did not break cover until the summer and autumn of 1985 – and even then it was not ready for deliveries to begin at once.

Sneak pictures had already been taken of M3 development cars being tested at the famous old Nürburgring circuit before BMW revealed the first official pictures and details of the new machine in July 1985. At the same time, it became increasingly clear that the new car would only be available with left-hand steering. When hearing this news, some cynics and know-alls suggested that this policy would change when the demand for right-hand steering became known – but they were wrong, as no right-hand-drive E30-type M3 was ever officially made.

Because BMW elected to launch a whole range of new 3-Series types at the Frankfurt Show, the M3's public debut almost went by default, and

**ABOVE: Instrument panel displays have advanced considerably in recent years. In 1986, this was the layout of instruments, controls and the steering wheel of the original M3, as they faced the driver. Each and every E30 was a left-hand-drive machine.**

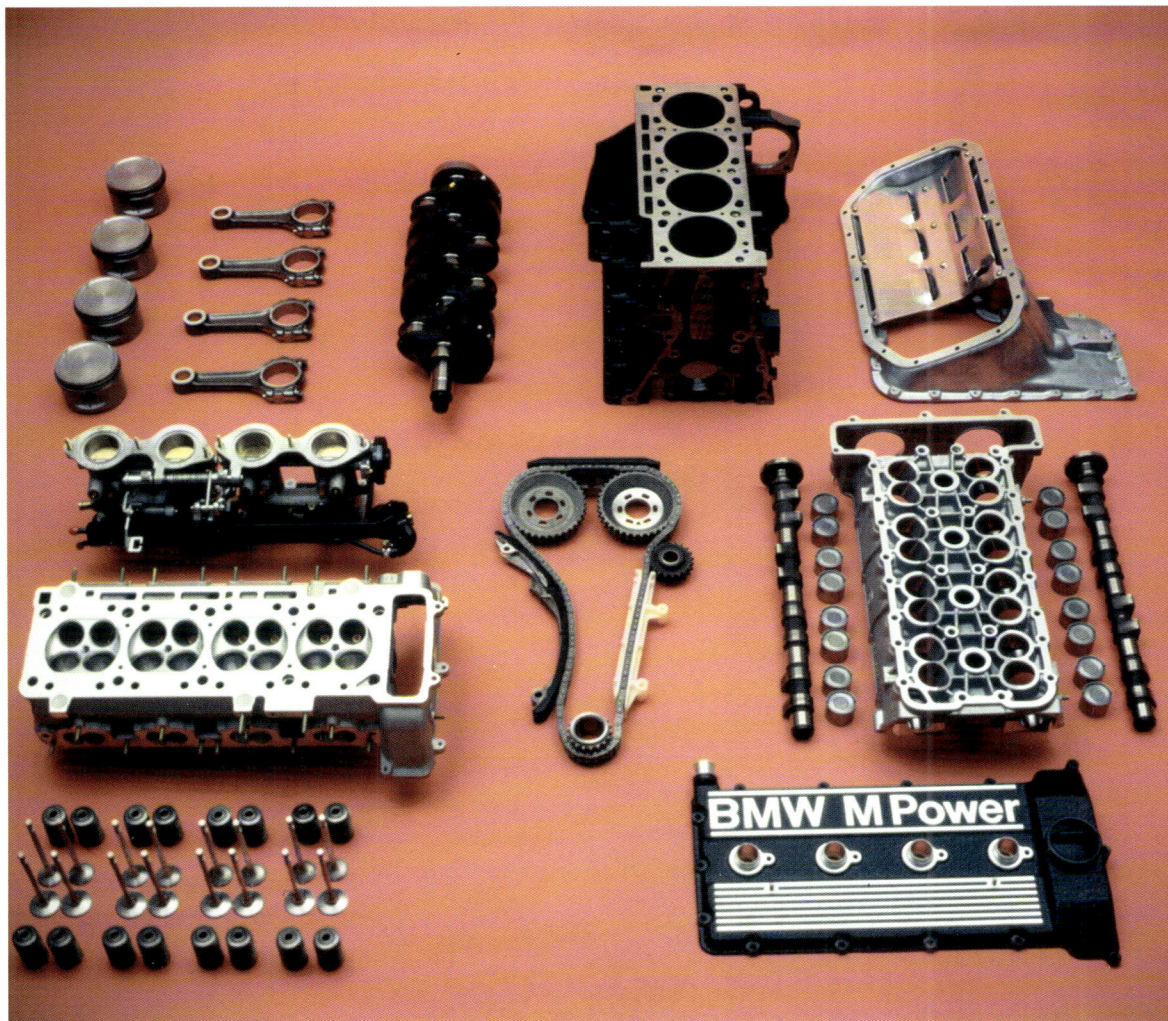

**LEFT: BMW had no secrets to hide away from the public in the 1980s, so when the M3 went on sale, this carefully laid out display of all the engine parts was made available. Much of what appeared here would reappear, in modified detail, in later engines.**

RIGHT: Specially posed
to show just how alike
the Group A E30 M3 race
car was to its road-going
relative, these two cars
make their own point.

little was made of it at the time. Of course, the new six-cylinder/2.5-litre 325i, the four-wheel-drive version of the 325i, a BMW-built (as opposed to Baur-built) 325i Cabriolet and a 324d (diesel) were all commercially, and therefore financially, more important, so BMW made no secret of the fact that the M3 would now go back into the shadows, to finish off its development. Later, it also became clear that they had probably been forced into a premature launch because of the way that Ford had already previewed the Sierra RS Cosworth well over a year before deliveries of that car would commence.

And so it was that, although they knew that a 200bhp/145mph M3 model was soon to be put on sale, every BMW enthusiast had to resort to rumour, counter-rumour, and a bid to get to the head of dealer waiting lists. Full series production eventually got under way immediately after BMW's midsummer 'shut-down' in 1986, though at least 30 'pilot-build' cars were completed in time for the ambitious press launch, which was held at the Italian motor racing circuit of Mugello in May 1986.

Once things got going, BMW was anxious to get 5,000 cars built by the spring of 1987 so cost £24,670), it was an appealing, capable and clearly attractive package, so it was no surprise when the world's media handed out great buckets of praise. There was no question, however, that by UK standards the original M3 was an expensive car (and the compulsory left-hand-drive cannot have helped), which explains why only 55 such cars were sold in 1987, 58 in 1988, and 62 in 1989.

With my very grateful thanks to *Autocar* (at the time that most conservative of motoring magazines) for allowing me to publish so much, the following is a substantial portion of their full road test, which was published in April 1987, and which reflects the opinions of most of the motoring media of the day: 'For an homologation special, BMW's M3 offers a remarkable combination of performance, refinement and practicality. Its price tag may seem high but, as our test team discovered, it is certainly a lot of car for the money....

'Under the steel shell, and composite body add-ons, BMW has paid particular attention to directional stability. Wheel castor is increased three-fold, the anti-roll bars are a larger diameter, and the steering modified to give increased feel.

'Apart from the tuned shock absorbers and rear springs, the rear axle assembly is the same as other 3-Series BMWs. The brake system, however, is not. Both front and rear discs are bigger and thicker with reinforced calipers. Larger 5-Series size wheel bearings are incorporated on special front stub axles for increased durability.... Standard safety items include ABS anti-lock brakes and a limited-slip differential, designed to operate with 25 per cent locking action. BMW does not offer any extras with the M3, although metallic paint is a no-cost action....

'With 200bhp to play with in a car weighing under 25cwt [under 2,800lb/1,270kg], performance is naturally one of the M3's strong suits. Our mean maximum speed of 139mph was achieved in driving rain on a very wet track, and there would certainly be another couple of mph to come in ideal conditions – BMW in fact claims 146mph. At the best one-way speed of 140mph the engine is spinning at 6,600rpm, just 150rpm below the power peak, which demonstrates near-ideal gearing.... We took 7,000rpm as the limit for our in-gear figures, and this equates in maximum speeds in the gears of 40, 62, 84 and 118mph.

that the race cars could take part in early-season events, and in fact no fewer than 2,396 examples were completed by the end of calendar year 1986. Even though it was quite an expensive car, sales were always buoyant. Purely as an example, when the M3 (still in left-hand-drive, of course) finally went on sale in the UK in April 1987, it cost £22,750, whereas the current 2.5-litre six-cylinder-engined 325i Sport two-door Saloon cost a mere £16,685, though in that case power-assisted steering cost an extra £495.

In spite of the high price (although, at the time, the 185bhp-engined Mercedes-Benz 190E 2.3-16

'Standing starts were conducted on a still-damp track and yielded a mean 0–60mph time of 7.1sec. 0–30mph still came up in 2.8sec though, with perhaps another 0.3sec to come off that on a perfectly dry surface. This compares well with BMW's quoted 6.7sec to 62mph, and shows the superior traction of rear-wheel drive in the wet – a powerful front-wheel-drive car would have been lucky to get within a second of its potential in such conditions.

'The close-ratio Getrag five-speed gearbox has a dog-leg first, and the gear-change is sprung to the centre 2nd/3rd gear plane. The gate is rather vague and it was all too easy to find fourth instead of second when going for a quick ratio swap. Obviously, the box was designed with competition use in mind, where first is only used on the starting grid, but for normal road use it does require some care.

'The M3's 200bhp from a normally aspirated engine might seem like the recipe for a very peaky power delivery, but this is far from the case. The 16-valve unit is in fact extremely flexible, and will pull without hesitation from well below 1,000rpm. Its mid-range punch is very impressive indeed, as a glance at the in-gear acceleration figures will confirm, and the power is, of course, delivered without any troublesome turbo-lag.

'For a car offering this sort of performance, an overall fuel consumption figure of over 20mpg is very good indeed. Our figure of 20.3mpg includes the speed-testing sessions, and is a tribute to the efficiency of the 16-valve engine and its Bosch management system. The average owner could certainly expect over 22mpg, giving a range of 300 miles from the 15.4-gallon tank.

'The engine, although it can't match the smoothness of BMW's six-cylinder units, is still remarkably civilised. There is the characteristic rasp that many sporting 16-valve power plants produce, but the noise levels in the cabin are very well controlled – when accelerating hard there is just enough noise to get the adrenalin pumping.

'On the motorway both wind and tyre noise are very subdued, so that the dominant noise is from the engine. The motor is turning over at almost 4,000rpm at 80mph, but that is the price for the sporting nature of the overall gearing. In fact, because fifth gear is where fourth would

normally be, there is a great temptation to change up another gear to a non-existent sixth.

'Although tyre noise is well suppressed, the suspension is definitely on the sporting side of firm. At high speeds the ride is very good, even on very badly surfaced corners, but at lower speeds most surface irregularities are transmitted to the interior. The very comfortable seats and driving position more than make up for this, though, and the M3 is a surprisingly relaxed high-speed cruiser.

'Handling is very predictable in both wet and dry conditions, with mild understeer generated at moderate cruising speeds with a very gradual transition to mild oversteer on a suddenly closed throttle. The overall feel is of a very well-balanced car, one that can be turned through corners deceptively quickly, and one that also feels very safe at the limit of adhesion.

'The uprated steering and revised front suspension geometry allows a driver to feel precisely what the wheels are doing and though the rack is still a little low-geared for a true competition machine (with 3.6 turns lock-to-lock) it received universal praise for both response and feel. The power-assisted steering is well weighted especially at speed and not excessively round town.

'High-speed cornering is accompanied by minimal body roll, and in the dry the M3 hugs the road surface, generating very high forces in the process. Also worthy of note is the M3's ability to run arrow-straight, even in very windy weather. This particular aspect was experienced when circulating the high-speed banked track at maximum speed in the wet, where the M3 tracked perfectly straight and was unfussed by the less than perfect road surface and side winds. BMW's attention to aerodynamic refinements has obviously paid off.

'Of the homologation specials which have passed through our hands recently, and that list includes the Mercedes-Benz 190 2.3-16 and Ford Sierra Cosworth, the BMW M3 is without doubt the most well-mannered from a handling point of view. There are no quirks to take into consideration, nor is there any tendency for the car to move about on uneven road surfaces, or tramline in the ruts often found on well-used motorway sections.

'You might expect something of a compromise in terms of ride quality and though the suspension is up-rated all round, and the M3 rolls on low-

**LEFT:** Already on its way to becoming one of the most charismatic model names of all time, the 'M3' badge figured strongly on the tail of the original E30-type car.

profile 55-series rubber with their low shoulders, the sacrifice in ride comfort is marginal. At speed the car feels well composed and is able to soak up even quite severe irregularities without complaint. It is only when negotiating road imperfections at low speeds that a driver begins to notice the increased stiffness, though to be fair, the ride quality is no less competent than that of most current sports cars.

'The much improved, servo-assisted, four-wheel disc braking system (ventilated up front), provides a reassuring degree of stopping power with a progressive and well-weighted pedal action. The M3 came through the fade tests unscathed – there was a slight and predictable rise in pedal pressures through the ten high-speed stops. The standard equipment ABS system came into operation with a 50lb effort during retardation tests, thereby limiting the deceleration figures to a maximum of 0.80g. This figure is not outstanding for a car of this type, but when you consider the figures were taken in the wet, it doesn't look bad at all....'

Finally, in summary: 'The M3 is perhaps the most successful homologation-inspired road/racer offered by a manufacturer to date. The car is as docile in town traffic as any driver could wish and easy to manoeuvre due to its compact proportions. Then when you hit the open road and pour on the power the chassis handles all the demands a driver makes upon it, whatever the road surface.... The fact of the matter is that the M3 makes a very sensible road car: it looks the part with its decidedly sporty styling, is not over the top, but very purposeful.

'In road trim the M3 may not have the legs of the Sierra Cosworth, but what it lacks in performance it more than compensates for with its easier road manners and better directional stability at speed. The Mercedes-Benz 190E 2.3-16 can match the BMW in this respect, but its engine of similar specification is less responsive, thanks to the larger and heavier body-shell. Nor is the Mercedes as nimble as the BMW....'

Following this sort of report – and those published in more excitable publications, of which there were many – demand for M3s rose considerably. BMW, it is known, would have been happy to sell a few more than the initially-required 5,000 cars, but then let the demand settle down (as, indeed, it did with other such special-purpose production cars throughout Europe) but in this case there was no slump.

BMW, in fact, made no attempt to get its car homologated without producing the necessary number of cars, nor claiming to have built enough examples before actually achieving the target. Those were the days when FISA (the sporting arm of the FIA) mounted an inspection of the production process, always inviting along an expert from a rival company as part of that visit, and Ford UK's homologation specialist, John Griffiths, remembers making several such visits to such companies in that time.

The fact is that in the early months of 1987 BMW was producing more than 200 M3s every week to reach their initial target of 5,000 cars by the end of February, and such was the continued demand for cars that they would complete no fewer than 6,396 before the end of the calendar year.

## M3 Evolution I

In the meantime, the inexorable drive to keep on improving the car for motorsport purposes had begun. One of the provisions of the FIA Group A homologation process was that, once the initial quantities had been completed (the authorities were adamant about this – extra cars could only be built to follow the original 'homologation' run), then once a year, manufacturers could produce a more specialised derivative of the base car, called an 'Evolution' model, which might, for example, have an enhanced engine specification, altered aerodynamic properties, or modified suspension. However, the same basic body-shell had to be retained, and a minimum of 500 such cars had to be produced, inspected, and counted, before homologation could be granted.

With this in mind, and immediately after the first 5,000 cars had been manufactured, BMW set about producing its first evolution type which has come to be titled rather unimaginatively as 'Evolution I', and concentrated on building these between February and May 1987. The figures later released show that just 505 such cars were produced, of which only seven were sold in the UK.

Compared with the original, there were no aerodynamic changes/improvements, but there had been time to finalise a few engine improvements, all of these being aimed at making the M3 a better competition car. There were modifications to the cylinder head, the throttle butterfly manifolds and the butterfly flanges, while there was a two-piece exhaust manifold, modified exhaust funnel and additional throttle nozzles.

These engines, incidentally, were marked with a white painted dot on the butterfly flange, as well as by a letter 'E' stamped beneath the butterfly manifold on the cylinder block – but one needed a mirror to be able to observe this! To repeat, it had been worth producing this package for motorsport purposes, but no change/enhancement in the peak power and torque figures was claimed by the factory.

By comparison with what was to follow – and with what BMW's rivals were planning – this was

LEFT: The first M3 Evolution of 1987 (505 were produced) was intended to make the race cars even more competitive, and featured an extended front spoiler and a lighter-material boot lid.

minor stuff, but it was effective, and ensured that the still-novel competition cars were as competitive as possible in their first season.

## M3 Evolution II

Almost exactly a year after Evolution I had been unveiled – just as soon as the FIA regulations would allow it – it was time for 'Evolution II' to follow. This time just 501 such cars were produced between March 1988 and May 1988 (500 being the magic minimum required to gain sporting homologation), and this time there were substantial updates to the body-shell/equipment, the suspension and to the engine.

For the enthusiast who wanted to have the very latest in M3s, this was a very desirable machine. We now know that 51 such cars came to the UK – selling at the rather eye-wateringly high price of £26,960, they were bound to be rather exclusive purchases – and in this case the changes were made to make the race car more competitive.

Visually, Evo II differed significantly from Evo I by having an extended front lower spoiler, a

ABOVE The 'Evolution' version of the M3 engine was more powerful than the original (220bhp instead of 200bhp) but there were no obvious external differences to flag up this improvement.

ABOVE: **The E30 M3 Evolution II came along in 1988 (501 were produced) with bigger, fatter (16in) wheels/tyres, and the 220bhp engine.**

double-blade rear spoiler across the boot lid, and the boot lid itself was made from lighter material. Carbon fibre was never used on the road cars (the sporting homologation papers mentioned 'plastic', 'glass-fibre polyester' and 'polyurethane'), but featured, in places, on the fully-modified competition cars.

The special front and rear spoilers were now made of slimmer, more lightweight, materials, while the plastic boot lid, the bumper supports, the rear window and the rear side windows had also been put on a diet. The weight saving was only 10kg/22lb, but for motorsport teams this effort was thought worth it.

The engine itself, though still of 2,302cc, had received a significant make-over, giving a package that included an 11.0:1 compression ratio, new camshaft profiles, pistons and a lightened flywheel allied to a different Bosch Motronic chip. The result was that peak power rose to 220bhp at 6,750rpm, and peak torque to 180lb ft. Allied to this, the overall gearing of the road car had been raised, not only by the fitment of a 3.15:1 final drive ratio, but by the use of new 7.5 x 16in BBS road wheels and 225/45-16 tyres. Even though independent tests showed that this car was certainly no lighter than before, it was capable of 148mph, and felt even more responsive and well balanced than the original.

## The first drop-top M3

While all this 'evolution' activity was going ahead, sales and production of the mainstream M3 settled down to 50 and 70 cars every week, for once the 'first 5,000' homologation target had been achieved BMW was not anxious to see stocks of unsold M3s building up. In some ways, the more important development work in 1987 (and the initial launch in 1988) was the work going into adapting the M3 chassis and drive line into BMW's later 3-Series Cabriolet body style.

[At this moment I should recall that drop-top 3-Series cars, all with two passenger doors, had been available from 1977. At first these were created for BMW by the same specialist coachbuilders (Baur of Stuttgart) who had been providing such a service since the 1930s, but BMW then elected to manufacture their own Cabriolet, previewing it in 1985, and delivering the first production cars for sale, from the Regensburg factory, in 1986.]

The M3 Cabriolet, which was previewed in 1987, was only a styling mock-up of the finalised package, but the production package of 1988 (deliveries began in mid-year) was an intriguing amalgam of conventional and M3-type styles, all hiding 100% M3 engineering. From the nose to the windscreen, the M3 Cabriolet was exactly like the two-door Saloon, while the under-door sills, the flared rear wheel arches and the special rear bumper were also the same. Because of the construction of a cabriolet body-shell, however, a standard 3-Series opening boot lid was retained, and there was no rear spoiler.

The fold-back Convertible roof and the main structure of the shell was shared with the mainstream 3-Series Cabriolets, the roof being raised and lowered electrically, and there was no roll cage or any such safety device over the cockpit. Because this was such a specialised M3, it was not even considered practical for it to be assembled at the Regensburg plant, so the job was allocated to the M3 Motorsport centre at Garching, a suburb in the north of Munich, situated approximately halfway between the main downtown complex and the new international airport.

Almost by definition, this sort of batch production – only 786 Cabriolets would be produced in four years, with a maximum of 300 being built in the 'run-out' year of 1991 – resulted in a high price tag. This explains, for sure, why the UK price was no less than £37,250 – which compares, for instance, with British hatchback runabout prices of £6,000 or so – and may explain, partly, why only 33 such machines were delivered to British customers!

Because of the special circumstances in which the Cabriolet was being built, assembly of this derivative would carry on even after the building of the more numerous E30 two-door Saloon types had ended. Whereas the last Saloon was assembled in December 1990 (like all E30 Saloons, this was done at or around a factory 'shut-down' period – Christmas in this case – to allow the main assembly plant to be re-equipped,

BELOW: By the end of the 1980s, the M3's Evolution models offered these magnificently contoured seats.

**ABOVE: To many people's surprise, BMW launched a Convertible version of the E30 M3 model in 1988, eventually producing 786 such cars. It was an intriguing and carefully developed amalgam of M3 chassis engineering and the existing well-liked 3-Series Cabriolet style.**

so that manufacture of the totally different E36 family could begin in 1991), production of Cabriolets continued at Garching (actually more were being produced than at any time in the previous three years) until June 1991.

There would then be almost a three-year gap before the next Cabriolet type – the E36 – was put on sale in 1994.

## More and yet more variety

In the meantime, detail development of the well-established E30 two-door Saloon continued steadily and, just to confuse future historians,

this was also the period when there were special editions of special editions. First of all, at the end of 1988, there was what was rather grandiloquently named the 'Europa Meister 88 Celebration' model, which was a 150-off car intended to commemorate the M3's success in the European Touring Car Championship (see Chapter 2). Although these cars had full trim and equipment, allied to the then-normal 195bhp engine with an exhaust catalyst, each and every one was signed by the successful race driver Roberto Ravaglia, who had won the World Touring Car Championship in an M3 in 1987.

Next up, and previewed in April 1989, was

the motorsport homologation (approval) papers, for no fewer than 600 such cars (the minimum FIA requirement was, of course, 500) would be produced in the mainstream factories in the early months of the year.

Developed because BMW wanted the M3 to continue to be competitive against Mercedes-Benz in the German Touring Car Championship (the DTM), where a 2.5-litre engine size limit applied, the Evolution III featured changes to the engine, the suspension and also to the aerodynamics of the car – and, no question, it was the ultimate of the E30 series. It was faster, tougher and more suitable for conversion into a motor racing machine, and none of the clientele seemed to mind that, at the same time, it was neither as smooth nor as docile as the original had been.

By pushing all previously accepted BMW standards to the limit, the motorsport engineers had managed to increase the capacity of the now venerable, but still rugged, four-cylinder engine to 2,467cc – this being done by adopting bore and stroke dimensions of 95 x 87mm, which compared with the 2,302cc/93.4 x 84mm dimensions of the earlier type. In both cases the increases seemed tiny (and so they were), but as there was now so little room left for expansion inside the original block, these changes were all that could be squeezed out of the existing casting while maintaining reliability.

Although the compression ratio in the cylinder head was slightly reduced from the original – from 10.5:1 to 10.2:1 (probably a result of increasing the cylinder bore/piston area without making any changes to the cylinder head's combustion chamber itself) – the top end featured larger inlet valves, sodium-cooled exhaust valves, a more ambitious camshaft grind, and attention to the internal cooling of the engine, pistons and bores themselves.

The result was a significant increase in power on the road car, and a similar improvement in the car's competitiveness. On the road cars, peak power went up from 215bhp to 238bhp at 7,000rpm and, equally important, peak torque was up from 170lb ft at 4,600rpm to 177lb ft at 4,750rpm. On the road, however, the performance boost was not noticed so much

a version known familiarly as the 'Cecotto', or 'Ravaglia' special – the names being the two most prominent M3 race drivers of the day – and once again, mechanically, these were in standard M3 condition, though in fact they were the first M3s to use the up-rated 215bhp three-way-catalysed version of the engine, which was about to become standard on all cars.

For 1990, however, there was to be one important and final twist in the anything-to-improve-the-M3-for-motorsport theme, with the launch of the Evolution III Sport model. Like Evolution I and Evolution II models, this was always intended as a genuine 'once-a-year' addition to

## First-generation M3 (E30 type) production figures

The number of M3s built between 1985 and 1991, according to BMW's own meticulously preserved statistics, were as follows:

|  | 2-door Coupé | Cabriolet |
|---|---|---|
| 1985 | 1 | – |
| 1986 | 2,396 | – |
| 1987 | 6,396 | – |
| 1988 | 3,426 | 130 |
| 1989 | 2,541 | 180 |
| 1990 | 2,424 | 176 |
| 1991 | – | 300 |
| | | |
| Totals | **17,184** | **786** |

*The single car produced in 1985 was presumably what motor industry experts call a 'pilot-build' production car – although numerous (uncounted) prototypes had already been built and tested before that time.*

from the increased power output, but from the very significant hold on the car's unladen weight and its various aerodynamic advantages.

[As will be made clear in Chapter 2, the power of full race-car E30 M3s, prepared to Group A regulations, increased steadily in the 1987–1992 period. Starting at about 295bhp in 1987, by 1989 this had been nudged up to 315bhp/320bhp, but the final increase in engine size led to 330bhp (at 9,200rpm) becoming available, and before the end a few engines were encouraged to produce up to 365bhp. This was quite enough to make the final M3s competitive against their deadly rivals from Mercedes-Benz, and the cars were still winning when attention finally turned to the newer, sleeker E36 variety in the mid-1990s.]

The M3 Evolution III, in fact, was one of the cars which was so subtly changed, and improved, compared with its predecessor, that one really needed to stand the two side-by-side to spot the differences. Each and every style change on the Evo III was made for motorsport purposes, though for two compelling reasons (the cost of investment, and the limits imposed by international motorsport regulations) these all took the form of 'add-ons' rather than fundamental changes to the shell itself.

For aerodynamic reasons, both front and rear spoilers were provided with additional flaps – these being on the underside of the spoiler at the front, and in the form of what the motorsport fraternity calls a 'Gurney flap' across the top of the boot-lid spoiler at the rear. Both extensions had a choice of three positions, which were set, or could be altered, by Allen screw fixings. At the front, like the Evo II, there were no extra driving lights fitted, their apertures being usefully employed to direct cooling air to the front brakes.

More detail was applied to 'managing' the air flow at the front of the car, for instance by changing the shape of the vanes in the familiar BMW 'kidney' grille, and by placing rubber inserts around the headlamp mountings, the front grille supports and the bonnet surround. These, however, were minor by comparison with the use of new bolt-on front wings, with larger openings for the wheels, which not only covered the Evo III road car's 225/45R16 tyres, but which allowed the serious racers to use 18in wheels with 9in rim widths.

Much detail, and typically thorough, work had gone into putting the rest of the car on a diet, which included fitting a smaller fuel tank (62 litres instead of 70 litres), along with more attention to the already special bumpers, spoilers and the boot lid. It was a battle that was neither won nor lost – one is reminded of another (non-BMW) noted engineer who once said: 'You fight, and you fight, and you fight – and you still lose 50lb!'

Although the so-called stripped-out Evo III was developed with motorsport in mind, and weighed 1,200kg, it was very expensive – those cars which reached the UK, still in LHD form, were priced at £34,500 (and available only in Jet Black or Brilliant Red) – yet if such features were pre-ordered, it was also possible to have cost (and weight!) increasing features such as an electric sun roof, electric door window lifts, leather seats, electronic damper control, opening rear quarter windows…and more, and more; so it was possible to spend more than £40,000 on a 'fully-loaded' example.

Perhaps a peak output of 238bhp does not sound much by modern standards, but for a normally-aspirated engine of the late 1980s/1990 period it was quite outstanding. In the road versions, the power unit was still amazingly flexible, but there was a distinct lack of torque at low speeds. Everything suddenly seemed to chime in, in glorious and raucous harmony, at about 4,000rpm, after which this sturdy engine barked its way up to 7,000rpm, making the Evo III one of the fastest of all road cars for this period.

The reputation of the E30 was now at its height and, amazingly for what was a self-proclaimed 'homologation special' (where cars tend to go in and out of fashion amazingly quickly), it was still in sturdy demand. Even in 1990, when the entire world of enthusiast motoring seemed to know that a totally new generation of 3-Series was about to go on sale, up to 50 cars a week were regularly being manufactured.

Even so, this is the right time to summarise what the E30 M3 had already achieved for BMW. Not only was it a car that had fulfilled every promise in motorsport – where race organisers ran events in which the regulations were demonstrably fair,

an M3 would still be competitive – but it outsold every previous M-badged BMW. Its character was what the customer seemed to enjoy, for thousands had now fallen in love with a car that was variously summarised as 'gruff', 'purposeful', 'hairy-chested' and 'manly'. To their amazement, BMW had also discovered that many people also wanted to combine open-air motoring with M-badging – hence the launch of the Cabriolet – and that others were anxious to see such levels of performance and all-round capability combined with a truly up-market equipment and appointments 'package'.

BMW listened, learned, and acted accordingly. After a total of 17,184 two-door Saloons had been built, and although the M3 badge would disappear from the showrooms for much of 1991 and 1992, much new engineering work was already being done behind the scenes. A new generation of 3-Series – the E36 – was on the way.

**BELOW: Except that it did not incorporate the raised boot lid and transverse rear spoiler of the Saloon, the Cabriolet version of the original M3 was an equally effective ultra-fast road car.**

WÜRTH
Cecotto
WARSTEINER
SCHNITZER
Wintershall ViVA 1
Wintershall
Das Motorenöl
BBS
EINE KÖNIGIN UNTER DEN BIEREN
Warsteiner
DEKRA
3
WARSTEINER
WARSTEINER
YOKOHAMA
Eibach
BILSTEIN
NGK
RECARO
BBS

## Chapter 2

# E30 in motorsport –
## World Champions, European Champions, and so much more

Sometimes, in motorsport, it helps to be patient. It took more than five years to move the original M3 project from 'good idea' to 'told you so' race winner – but it was all worth it. Once the M3 went on sale towards the end of 1986, progress on the tracks was rapid, and the very first international race victory followed in April 1987. After that, there seemed to be no end to the M3's successes, for the original E30 model went on to become one of the dominant saloon car racers all over the world.

However, although BMW, and the teams which supported them, were always ready and willing to go motor racing in M3s, they had to wait for sporting homologation to be achieved, and this did not happen until 1 March 1987. As expected, by that time the company had not only developed many effective competition tune-up pieces, but was ready to supply them to any M3 customer who could wave the appropriate (high!) number of Deutschmarks in front of the motorsport division.

Although the records show that competitive BMWs raced at any and all levels during that first 1987 season, as far as the company was concerned the emphasis was always on the much-hyped World Touring Car Championship (which was new for that year), and in international series in Germany and other European nations.

Much hype? Perhaps. This masterly summary, written in 1988 (about the 1987 series) by the distinguished motoring writer Joe Saward in *Autosport*, perfectly encapsulates everything that had gone before: 'For the previous four seasons Group A touring car racing had grown steadily, its influence spread gradually around the world. A World Championship was suggested a couple of years ago and all those involved were enthusiastic that it would be successful. Television was interested in a championship where overtaking actually happened. Decisions were made and major investment began in a worldwide future. This was to be a new era. There would be a new generation of cars, of budgets, and of drivers. There would be races all over the world. Suddenly increasing numbers of manufacturers were interested....'

The problem was that the sport's governing body, the FIA, then trampled on the hope of the promoters with its heavy bureaucratic feet, insisting that teams could only compete if they paid a large sum of money up front ($60,000 per car, which in total for all the teams was rumoured to reach $900,000 by the end of 1987), and guaranteed to appear at every race. Interest from potentially serious competitors (such as Holden/Tom Walkinshaw, for instance) suddenly evaporated, and in the end there would only be two truly competitive cars – BMW and Ford. Alfa Romeo, with its 75 Turbo, tried hard to keep up with BMW but would withdraw before the end of the year.

Money was not a problem for BMW (the

company was highly profitable at this time, and ambitious too), and the biggest of their worries was that Ford had elected to use the new Sierra RS Cosworth, whose 2-litre engine was turbocharged, and who were threatening to homologate an even more powerful version of that car, the RS500, in the middle of the season. BMW, however, were confident of being able to produce well over 300bhp from their 2.3-litre engine, and hired Schnitzer, Bigazzi and CiBiEmme to deliver the goods on their behalf. Schnitzer was heavily backed by Warsteiner (the drinks concern) and Wintershall.

Everything that you might expect to be done to turn an M3 into a competitive Group A race car was done in 1987, and the cost does not

bear thinking about. By putting the cars strictly on to a weight-saving diet, and by using as many exotic materials as the regulations allowed, they were brought in at an homologated weight of 2,116lb/960kg (the 'showroom' weight was 2,640lb/1,200kg): one reason for this was that the already special shell of the M3 road car was made even more special for race cars by being constructed with lightweight (still steel, where appropriate) panels, and with the ruthless ripping out of all unnecessary trim and fittings.

The shells were given sturdy roll cages, racing (foam-filled bag) fuel tanks and, of course, the lightest of all possible racing seats. The power steering was eliminated (race drivers can cope easily at high speeds) and the rack ratio was changed to give quicker response.

Among the many suspension changes (which naturally included much valuable input from the German specialists Bilstein) were aluminium front sprint struts with adjustable plates (for height, that is), adjustable anti-roll bars at front and rear, and special reinforced semi-trailing rear suspension arms. Special close-ratio gearboxes, up-rated front and rear disc brakes, and one-nut fixing for special 9in x 17in road wheels all added to a well-thought-out suspension package.

Along with this there was an engine which had been marginally increased by a slight overbore (to 2,332cc), with different camshaft profiles and a modified Bosch Motronic engine management system, and even at the start of the season more than 300bhp was available. Over the years, more and more development would produce more and more power, but unlike the M3's rivals, which had turbochargers, nothing dramatic was ever to be expected.

Although the start of the season was farcical for all concerned, it rapidly settled down into a straightforward battle between BMW and the Swiss-prepared Fords. Once the Ford RS500 had been homologated, BMW found it difficult to keep up with its 500bhp engine, but wherever reliability, handling, and sheer professionalism counted for more, then the M3 was always the pacesetter.

At Monza in March, for the original 500km race, the Fords were thrown out before the start because the Italian scrutineers did not like their modified engine management systems. BMW's M3s, on the

## FORD SIERRA RS COSWORTH – the elephant in the room

If Ford had not read the same set of rules as BMW in the early 1980s, and had not set about to build an even more extreme type of Group A contender, the M3's motorsport career might have been even more successful than it actually was.

Ford set out at about the same time (1983) as BMW to develop their new car and based it on the newly-launched Sierra, but made one crucial extra decision: although they retained a 2-litre four-cylinder engine, they decided to ask Cosworth to produce a new four-valve/twin-cam engine for them, and to turbocharge it. Both cars went into production in the summer of 1986, and both achieved Group A homologation in early 1987.

Even though the turbo boost effectively gave Ford access to a larger-capacity engine, and therefore a theoretical advantage over BMW in race-prepared form, in standard form and on the open road, the two rival road cars had very similar peak power outputs. Even so, and as detailed in Chapter 2, on the race track (and certainly in terms of reliability) the M3 often had the beating of the original Ford, and would go on to provide race-winning transport for many distinguished drivers in the next few years.

It was only when Ford pushed the interpretation of sporting Group A regulations to their limit, and built an evolution run of 500 Sierra RS500 Cosworths in the summer of 1987, that their turbocharged race cars were able to run with more than 500bhp. In outright pace, therefore, after this the M3s – even 'works'-backed cars like the Schnitzer machines – found it difficult to lead every race, though their normally-aspirated reliability ensured that they continued to win events and championships all around the world for years to come.

other hand, finished 1-2-3-4-5-6-8, and there was great joy both in the paddock and back in Munich. Until after the race, that is, when the scrutineers threw out all the BMWs.

The scrutineers said: 'Seven BMWs were disqualified because the material of the rear bonnet was not in conformity with the homologation form….' They were referring to the boot lids, which on the race cars were of carbon fibre, rather than the 'plastic' lids that were homologated. The Italians, it seemed, were being punctilious about the correct use of language – but of course this was not Italian, and no Italian car was involved.

Only weeks later, at the Jarama circuit in Spain, some essence of common sense had been restored, both teams having made enough changes to keep the scrutineers happy. All the top drivers made it to the end, with the Pirro/Ravaglia Schnitzer M3 taking its first win of the year. BMW won again at Dijon in May, where the race was stopped when a thunderstorm of biblical proportions descended on the French circuit.

The Schnitzer cars could then only finish second and third at the Nürburgring 500km race

ABOVE: This specially posed study shows that the fully-prepared E30-type M3 race car engine bay (right) looked very similar to that of the road car, showing just how much thought had been given to the design of the car before production began.

**ABOVE: In 1987, the combination of Schnitzer-prepared M3s with Roberto Ravaglia behind the wheel was almost unbeatable – and Ravaglia became World Touring Car Champion in that season.**

in July. In fact, M3s finished 2-3-4-5-6-7, which, considering that this was something of a 'home circuit' race for the Germans, went down very well in Munich. They made up for this with outright victory in the Spa 24 Hours race in August.

This was set to be a battle of the titans by any standards, for at Spa there were no fewer than 13 M3s lining up against eight Ford Sierra RS500 Cosworths and eight Alfa Romeo 75 Turbos. It was no wonder that all the forecasts of lap records being smashed were confirmed. Although the monstrously-powerful turbocharged Fords led for many hours, the works-backed M3s plugged on, and on, and on – and after 24 hours, which included every potential weather condition from sunshine to heavy rain (and even some early-morning mist), it was the cars from Munich that took first, second, third and fifth. There were six M3s in the top ten.

In terms of outright victories, however, the M3's World Championship season was now almost past its peak, for no other car could thereafter keep up with the Fords. Even so, at Brno, in Czechoslovakia, M3s took 3-4-5-7-8, and quite

dominated the Class 2 (up to 2.5-litre) category, with Roberto Ravaglia looking more and more likely to be the BMW driver who would eventually take the drivers' crown at the end of the season.

The scene was set, however, for a concentrated nine-week period between mid-September to mid-November 1987 when there would be five races in four countries and three continents – at Silverstone in the UK, Bathurst and Calder in Australia, Wellington in New Zealand and Fuji in Japan. Controversy about the acceptable limits of interpretation of homologation regulations boiled over, and disqualifications followed, yet BMW M3 drivers managed to score maximum points in three races. When the dust had settled (and it took until the spring of 1988 for every ruffled feather to be patted down) BMW driver Roberto Ravaglia (who always ran in Schnitzer-prepared cars) emerged as champion, while the two Schnitzer-prepared M3s took second and third in the team standings.

It was not controversy over the performance and suitability of the cars that caused so much trouble at this time (for by then there was no question that the M3 had become the world's most successful normally-aspirated saloon race car) but rather the way that the cars were being built. To quote a contemporary authority on the subject: 'For several years Group A racing has been run by an unofficial cartel. The cars might not have been entirely "legal", but agreements could be reached among the leading runners to ensure stability.... The cartel – and it isn't hard to work out which teams might be involved, though they would probably deny such a thing – solves a problem by compromises. We'll do this if you do that: it is a system that has had tacit agreement from FISA.

'The series would have remained untainted by controversy this year but for the Australians, who reckoned the play was better, and consequently screwed everything up. They figured that Australia had the best Group A in the world and everyone else could go to hell....'

All this, however, stayed hidden at Silverstone, for in Europe there was still a cosy agreement between BMW and the Eggenberger Ford team about interpreting the regulations. Not only that, but BMW, with its M3 race car power output limited to 300–330bhp at the time, realised that they could not match the monstrous 500bhp which Ford's latest Sierra RS500 Cosworths were developing.

Although the M3 race cars were incredibly fleet and nimble, they could not dominate the front of the starting grids, or the races themselves. On the other hand, they were probably more accomplished in race craft, in the choice of drivers, in the clever

LEFT: The immaculately prepared and detailed E30 race car engine of 1987, when it was already producing 300bhp from 2.3 litres. More was to come in the years that followed.

**ABOVE:** Roberto Ravaglia on the downhill 'snake' section of the fabulous circuit at Bathurst, Australia, on his way to consolidate his lead in the 1987 World Touring Car Drivers' Championship.

use of race tactics, and in every peripheral aspect of top-level touring car racing. Then, if by chance it rained, where adhesion and handling balance became more important than brute performance....

And at Silverstone it rained, and rained, and rained. Even though the Sierras had qualified a full five seconds a lap faster than the best of the M3s, this mattered not one jot during the race itself. Wet for the entire three hours that this 500km/311-mile race took to unfold, it was led by the Sierras until each and every one of them struck mechanical trouble. The BMWs, on the other hand, slipped, slithered, wriggled and danced their way around the Northamptonshire circuit, and ended up fighting among themselves for outright victory.

At the end of an afternoon that saw the CiBiEmme-prepared M3 (driven by Calderari/ Mancini) beating the Schnitzer-built Ravaglia/Pirro car to the chequered flag by just four seconds, Roberto Ravaglia found himself taking maximum points, and beginning to edge towards the drivers' title. Back at Munich, however, BMW didn't mind which of their sponsored teams was winning, just so long as one of them did.

Then came the high-profile James Hardie 1000 race at Bathurst in Australia, a 1,000km/625-mile marathon around Mount Panorama in hot weather, which took seven hours to complete, where Europe's best faced up to Australia's best – this meaning that they had to fight against locally-prepared M3s, Sierras, Nissan Skyline Turbos, and fearsome 4.9-litre Holden Commodores.

This was not, to be honest, the M3's finest hour (the best of the European cars finished ninth, no fewer than seven 2min 30sec laps off the pace), but it was the events that followed which caused such controversy, and distress, among the WTCC 'circus' – and indirectly led to it being cancelled at the end of its one and only season.

Six seconds off pole position after qualifying (and finding that the M3s built locally by Frank Gardner's team were their equal in pace) both the CiBiEmme and Schnitzer teams settled down to complete a gruelling day's racing – and gruelling it was, for two of the Schnitzer cars retired, one with transmission failure and the other with engine problems. Not only that, but all were soundly beaten by the locally-built Gardner M3 of Jim

Richards/Tony Longhurst.

For the M3s that made it to the finish, this would have been bad enough – but the entire event (and, as it happened, the standing of the entire World Championship) was then thrown into turmoil by the post-event disqualification of the winning Ford Sierra RS500 Cosworths. This, it transpired, was because of the way the Australian scrutineers interpreted Group A regulations about car body modifications, the end result being that they objected to certain aspects of the Sierras' rear wheel arch/panel modifications, which the cars had been using all season, and which had never before been protested by the BMW teams.

Weeks afterwards, the Sierra disqualifications were confirmed, the BMW M3s moved up to fourth, sixth and seventh, with outright victory going to a 4.9-litre Holden, which just happened to be a locally-built car, driven by Australians. How do you spell 'chauvinism' in Strine?

Just one week later, at Calder, a partly banked oval track north of Melbourne in Australia hosted a 500km race, where things returned to something like European normality. BMW fought Ford in what

had become a familiar manner, while the local 4.9-litre Holdens could not keep up. Even though the Fords flaunted their usual 200bhp power bonus, the Schnitzer M3s showed their usual pace and reliability. At the end of a gruelling event, the BMWs took second, third and fourth places overall, the Nissan Skylines and the Holdens were humbled, and Roberto Ravaglia took another step towards the drivers' title.

In the next two weeks the European BMWs had to lick their long-distance wounds, re-prepare their cars, make minor modifications to keep the scrutineers happy, and fly their outfits over the Tasman Sea to Wellington in New Zealand. At this end of the season, there was no time to make the cars faster, or to handle better – all that could be done was that they should be refreshed as much as possible.

In spite of the blustery weather, and the way that the Clerk of the Course had aborted the original rolling start because he thought the leading (European, need I say?) cars were holding up the field too much before unleashing themselves over the line, this turned out to be a thoroughly

**BELOW:** Roberto Ravaglia was also a winner in M3s at German (DTM) level. This Evo III derivative is seen in 1989 leading a massive traffic jam of other M3s, Mercedes-Benz and Ford Sierra RS500 Cosworth rivals.

predictable 500km WTCC race. Once again, three of the world's fastest M3s – two from Schnitzer and one from CiBiEmme – finished in the top seven places, Emanuele Pirro and Roberto Ravaglia took a fine second place overall in a Schnitzer-prepared car, just 22 seconds behind the best of the 500bhp Sierras, and it became increasingly likely that both BMW and Roberto Ravaglia would become world champions.

One event, however, in this busy calendar, remained. Three weeks after Wellington, and eight gruelling months after the season had begun at Monza, the cars finally gathered at the Fuji circuit in Japan. Now that it was certain that the Sierras would not be reinstated from their disqualification at Bathurst (that news came through on Friday the 13th!), it seemed that BMW could, indeed, become world champions.

Even though this was another 500km race, and held in dry conditions, in the end the awards would be shared almost equally, and in spite of spirited opposition from the latest Japanese touring cars, it was dominated by the usual two European brands – BMW and Ford. After more than three hours of flat-out saloon car racing, five BMWs and three Ford Sierras took the top eight places.

On this super-fast circuit the 500bhp Sierras could not be matched, but M3s took third, fourth, sixth, seventh and eighth places. Not only that, but Roberto Ravaglia had been driving the third-placed M3, this being enough to make him the World Touring Car Champion – by a single point! As far as the entrants were concerned, the two 'official' Schnitzer M3s took second and third overall in their first full season of motor racing.

BMW's euphoria was short-lived, for before planning to go ahead to compete even more successfully in 1988 could begin, the WTCC series was brutally killed off! Once again to quote Joe Saward: 'Within a few short months, despite signs that the Championship had not only survived such absurd early treatment, but was actually growing, it was shot down by the guardians of the sport, as efficiently as if a German student had tried to land a Cessna in Red Square [this had recently happened in Moscow].... The whole affair was a disgrace. Still, one must suppose that this is what happens when a pyromaniac takes control of a fire station....'

## European and other campaigns

Although the assassination of the World Touring Car Championship was a cruel blow to BMW, all around the world there had been, and still was, much touring car racing in which a properly-prepared E30 M3 could not only be competitive, but always likely to win. The secret was not in the outright performance of these cars – I have already made it clear that, wherever they were eligible, rival cars with vastly larger engines, or with turbocharged power units, could be faster – but the question lay in their reliability. Year-long experience at world level had shown just what stamina an M3 race car could have, and this was proved, time and time again, around the world.

In 1987, a measure of this was laid down in the European Championship (which effectively was overshadowed by the World series). Seven events were held – the season starting at Britain's Donington Park and ending at Nogaro in France – all but one of them being won outright by an M3 (Eggenberger, with its turbocharged Ford Sierra RS Cosworths, won at Zolder in Belgium).

The Entrants' category was won by the Linder Motorsport M3 team, who concentrated on 'Europe' and did not appear at 'World' level, while both the leading World teams, Schnitzer and CiBiEmme, made token appearances, and it was that team's star drivers, Winni Vogt and Altfrid

OPPOSITE TOP: The Schnitzer-prepared E30 M3 in its original 1987 form with Roberto Ravaglia at the wheel at the Nürburgring...

OPPOSITE BELOW: ...and Eric van der Poele in a sister car at the same circuit at a DTM event.

BELOW: Johnny Cecotto (left) and Roberto Ravaglia (right) were two of the most successful drivers in the M3 race car programme in the late 1980s – both of them race winners, and both eventually having M3 special-edition road cars named after them!

Heger, who dominated the drivers' standings. BMW M3 drivers finished first, second, fifth, sixth, seventh and eighth in that table. Dominant? You could say so.

Because of the killing off of the World series, it was the European Championship which got most of the 'works' cars' attention in 1988, but right away it became apparent that high costs, controversy over vehicle homologation, and motorsport 'political' infighting were going to spoil the pure motor racing aspect. For the spectators, however, the good news was that the fight between the world's best BMW M3s – now in the latest Evolution form – and the world's best rivals, would continue.

At the end of the season there was some good news for BMW, and some disappointing news. Although Roberto Ravaglia, driving Schnitzer-prepared M3s, once again won the Drivers' Championship, BMW's normally-aspirated 2.3-litre cars were outpaced by the hugely-powerful turbocharged Ford Sierras. Despite BMW ending the season with some outright victories to celebrate – particularly in the prestigious 24-hour marathon at the Spa Circuit in Belgium – it became clear that the Championship would not be run again because of the high and ever-rising costs.

This time around it was Schnitzer (aided by the Bigazzi team, who were not as close to the factory as Schnitzer) who got most of the support from Munich, always entering two immaculately prepared cars, though high-level machinations led to them starting the season using German-made Pirelli race tyres instead of the Japanese Yokohamas, which had been suitable in 1987: that decision would be reversed later in the year!

Starting at Monza in March, and ending at Nogaro in September, there were 11 events in the series, in which two of the M3 drivers – Ravaglia and Eric van de Poele – usually rivalled each other, and managed to finish on every occasion. This was a credit both to them and to the rock-solid reliability of the race-prepared M3s, which handled well and put down every one of their 320 to 350bhp (claims varied from source to source) at all times.

Ford's Texaco-sponsored Sierras, let us be honest, took eight outright victories in the 1988 series, while the Schnitzer M3s won three times, and were always as competitive as possible everywhere else. BMW's first big win of the year

came at Donington Park in April, when both Fords failed, and the M3s (led by Ravaglia) took a processional victory. Then, in July, came the monumentally difficult 24 Hours race at Spa in Belgium, where reliability always seemed to matter more than outright performance.

Sierras led from the start, but soon began to wilt, for (as touring car specialist Graham Smith later commented in *Autosport*): 'Pursued by a howling pack of M3s, the Schnitzer, Prodrive and Bigazzi cars were packed tightly behind and closed in relentlessly, before taking the lead in the early hours of Sunday morning. Both Eggenberger [Ford's entrant] and Schnitzer held their lead drivers back until the very last moment, trying to guess which of their cars would be the one to finish most strongly.

'One by one, Schnitzer's M3 challengers dropped by the wayside, leaving the Heger/Quester/Ravaglia car to score a memorable victory that gave the Italian a valuable double helping of points....'

There was more good fortune to follow in Belgium, at Zolder, three weeks later, for sunny weather at the start of the race turned into a torrential downpour later, which suited the M3s perfectly, the result being a third outright victory of the season, with Ravaglia and van de Poele sharing the driving honours.

And yet, and yet – no amount of short-term celebration could hide the fact that by this time top-level touring car racing was becoming too costly for all but a few well-backed teams, and although there would always, it seemed, be an M3 outfit among them, there would not be a sufficiently large field to make events worth promoting. Thus it was that although the M3 was demonstrably the most versatile racing saloon car in the world, there would be no further European-wide, or worldwide, series for it to prove that point.

## Racing – at home in Germany, and elsewhere

BMW made sure that properly-specified, and properly-developed E30 M3s were ready to go motor racing as soon as Group A homologation was achieved in March 1987, the result being that there were victories as far away as in Australia, and

as close to home as Germany.

In Germany, in the DTM (Deutsche Tourenwagen Meisterschaft – though this name would be changed in the 2000s), which had originally been founded in 1984 to run under Group A regulations, BMW was already present; its old but still game M635 Coupés being competitive to the end. From 1987, however, it was time for a premeditated assault by the new-generation M3s.

Through a weight handicapping system imposed by the organisers the competition was kept as close as the organisers could 'fix' it (and I use that word in the most appropriate sense). Cars that won too often, or were thought to have too much power – like the turbocharged Ford Sierras – had to carry extra lead weights bolted to their floor pans.

The reformed BMW Junior team was run on the factory's behalf by Zakspeed from workshops based at the Nürburgring, and the drivers were Eric van de Poele of Belgium, and Marc Hessel. At the end of an eventful season, where the BMW/Ford battle was complicated by rivals using old-type Ford Sierra XR4Tis to stay on

terms, M3s won seven races outright, and were always competitive. Van de Poele's M3 won the Championship, though the gallant Belgian did not actually win a single race!

Elsewhere, Fabien Giroix's M3 won the French Championship, Jim Richards won the Australian Championship and there were other M3 series victories in Portugal, Holland, Italy and Finland. The German car was clearly setting all the standards for future years.

All over Europe, in 1988 it was a similar story, with championship after championship being contested by the fleet M3s and the grossly powerful Sierra RS500 Cosworths, and in many cases the constant repeat of familiar names and circuits would become positively routine. The M3, of course, proved itself to be such a dominant 'class car' – there is no question that it was the best and most versatile touring car in the world at this time – and unless series regulations were deliberately skewed to render it uncompetitive, it was always likely to win. In the 1988 British Championship, for instance, a 500bhp Ford might have won all the races, but BMW dealer Frank

ABOVE: **Marc Hessel campaigned this works-backed E30 M3 in the German Championship (DTM) in 1987, taking third overall in the series, which was won by Eric van de Poele in a sister M3.**

RIGHT: This M3 race car (from the DTM of 1987) not only sports on its windscreen strip a sponsor label from Zakspeed (who had previously leaned towards Ford cars but was now running the BMW Junior race team), but also displays a considerable amount of damage to the right-side door panel. Motor racing is meant to be a no-contact sport!

BELOW: Eric van de Poele of Belgium won the German (DTM) Championship in 1987, driving E30 M3s – here seen at the race near Berlin earlier in that season.

Sytner's M3 won its 3-litre class so often that it ensured a championship victory.

In the fast-improving German DTM series, for instance, BMW's deadly rivals Mercedes-Benz also put in a big effort with their Cosworth-powered 190E 2.3-16s. Although a Sierra won the series

outright, little could match the reliability of the M3s, the result being that there were no fewer than five M3s in the top ten standings. In a desperately close end to the season, Markus Oestreich's M3 took fourth place overall.

In 1989, M3s took national championship titles almost wherever they competed, and just one double-page seasonal survey in *Autosport* makes that point. Covering the German, French and Italian series, it showed that M3s won all of them. In Italy, Alfa Romeo were truly annoyed that they could not triumph on home soil, and in France there was only one French car (a Renault) able to finish in the top eight.

That was the year in the DTM when the German authorities always moved swiftly to apply 'weight penalties' if one type of car became too dominant – which explains why the Fords won many races, but could not win the Championship. Fresh from his World (1987) and European (1988) crownings, Roberto Ravaglia's Schnitzer-prepared M3s won three races and finished in the top six almost every time he started one of the 11 races, eventually winning this series too, with other M3s driven by

Fabien Giroix (third), Steve Soper (fifth) and Johnny Cecotto (seventh). However, because Mercedes-Benz had upgraded their contender from 2.3-litres to 2.5 litres, BMW realised that they would certainly have to push the E30 M3 to its limits in future, and set about finalising the changes which would lead to the homologation of Evolution III for 1990.

For BMW, however, 1989 proved to be a frustrating year in the British Touring Car Championship, for although cars prepared by Prodrive, and sponsored by BMW Finance and Mobil, were faster and more reliable than ever, they were handicapped by an absurd class system. Absurd? Try this, from *Autosport*'s Nick Phillips starting his annual survey: 'The overall champion was John Cleland in his Vauxhall Astra GTE, highlighting the anomalies of a system which allows a car finishing races around 15th overall to win the Championship.'

Accordingly, the fact that BMW's James Weaver won his (3.0-litre) class 11 times in 13 races, but failed to set up fastest race lap on one occasion, meant that according to the BTCC system he had to settle for second place in the end!

The prospect of success in the BTCC in 1990 looked even less promising when the authorities imposed a 2-litre class, and threatened to make that the 'standard' for the rest of the 1990s (which it was, for this is where, and how, the Super Touring category took root), but at least Prodrive were allowed to develop hybrid engines using short-stroke (320i) dimension crankshafts, as a single-season concession. [This, of course, was the year in which almost every other M3 raced with the latest Evolution capacity of engines – 2,493cc, as a slight over-bore of the road car's 2,467cc. Illogical? You might say so.]

As ever in this period of history, it was the enormously powerful Sierra RS500 Cosworths that won the races, but it was the M3s that won the 2-litre class so regularly, and Frank Sytner took second overall in the series. An end-of-season road test for the media showed that this car's handling was as acrobatic and peerless as ever, while the engine produced 265bhp at 8,500rpm. It was interesting to note that Matter of Germany had provided the fully-Group-A-prepared shells to Prodrive, and that although a Getrag gearbox casing was retained, it used internals that had been engineered and manufactured by Prodrive.

All over Europe, it seemed, the very latest 2.5-litre Evolution M3s were as competitive as ever, even though production of road cars was about to end, for they beat Alfa Romeo on their home ground in Italy (Roberto Ravaglia was the star driver), and beat all other brands in France (Jean-Pierre Malcher doing the honours), while in the German series there was a season-long battle against 'works' Audi V8 Quattros and the latest Mercedes-Benz 190E 2.5-16 models, which resulted in second place for Johnny Cecotto's Schnitzer-built M3: even so, Cecotto would have won outright if he had not been eliminated in a first-corner accident on the final race at Hockenheim. This was when his M3 was hit by an AMG Mercedes-Benz driven by…Michael Schumacher!

BMW's star showing in 1990, however, came in the Spa 24 Hours race, which was now open to many other types of car, including a positive fleet of Group N Porsche 911 Carreras, which started alongside more familiar rivals such as the Eggenberger Sierra RS500 Cosworths. Even though the M3s were outpaced on lap times, they proved to be more reliable, were not obliged to make as many refuelling stops, and were always fighting for the lead. In the end, only one Sierra survived the 24 hours, whereas M3s took first, second, fourth and fifth places – the leading places being taken by the two Schnitzer cars whose star drivers included Johnny Cecotto, Dieter Quester and Marc Duez. The use of Yokohama tyres, it seemed, was an important factor in this endurance victory.

Now, however, it was definitely 'Indian Summer' time for the E30 model, whether on the road or on the racetracks of the world. As already noted in Chapter 1, the last of the road cars was built at the end of 1990 (although Cabriolet assembly would continue for a time in 1991), and new models plus new racing regulations would soon render the cars obsolete in racing too.

So, was the E30 M3's success in saloon car racing now beyond its peak? It was, after all, beginning to look like a machine with 'old engineering', and with the next-generation (E36) M3 not yet available, and with new four-wheel-drive competition from Nissan becoming available, the future looked bleak.

Even so, in the 1991 24 Hours Nürburgring race, a Schnitzer-prepared (and, therefore, factory backed) final-evolution M3 driven by Joachim Winkelhock, Kris Nissen and Armin Hahne won that gruelling race in fine style, while a year later the Team Bigazzi organisation, using an Evolution M3, employed the stellar driving line-up of Johnny Cecotto, Christian Danner, Jean-Michel Martin and Marc Duez to repeat the feat, even though this was a race which had to be stopped for several hours during the night because of the thick fog which settles on the Eiffel mountains!

It was a similar, but not quite so successful, story over the border, relatively close by, at the Spa 24 Hours race. In 1991, for instance, a unique set of race regulations obliged the ultimate-specification E30 cars to run against 580bhp Nissan GT-Rs and 3.2-litre Porsche Carrera 2s. If the opposition could maintain its reliability, was there ever any doubt that the M3s would be overwhelmed?

Amazingly, though, victory in a whole variety of national championships was still to come in the early 1990s, so the news that BMW had sold no fewer than 330 competition-prepared E30 M3s (whether as complete cars, or as kits to make road cars competitive in far-flung territories) came as no surprise. No rival other than perhaps Ford with its large array of 16-valve RS1600s and RS1800s could match that achievement.

In the UK, the 'Indian summer' came in the 1991 British Championship, which was the first British series to be run under the new-fangled Super Touring rules. This was a formula that applied a 2-litre engine limit, an 8,500rpm rev limit and a minimum car weight limit, while leaving much of the chassis and technical regulations open. One concession was to allow engine sizes to be changed, which meant that the M3s could therefore have short-stroke cranks, and be instantly competitive: they were claimed to be running with 270bhp. Clearly the motor racing fraternity thought this was a great deal, for in a season when 25 different cars appeared (some of them starting every one of the 13 rounds), no fewer than 16 of them were M3s!

That season, in fact, became one of the high-points in Team Securicor's existence (the low point would follow when team principal Vic Lee spent some time incarcerated 'at Her Majesty's pleasure' for committing contraband offences and using team cars and the race-car transporter to carry illegal substances), when Lee built two brand new M3 race cars to be driven by Will Hoy and Ray Bellm. Lee later admitted that during the winter of 1990 he had spent many hours not only studying the new UK Super Touring rules, but had combed through a detailed list of everything that BMW had ever put on sale for the original M3 race cars, and came up with a unique detail specification – one such being to place the fuel tank very low, under the floor, and forward of the rear axle line. Engines came from Eurotech, transmissions came from Hollinger in Australia, Listerine provided major sponsorship, and with preparation in workshops on Silverstone's trading estate, that team was set to match, and hopefully beat, the Mobil-backed 'works' cars from Prodrive.

The result was a resounding triumph. Will Hoy won three races outright, and also reached the podium on seven other occasions, ending up as Drivers' Champion ahead of every other M3, and the fast-developing Vauxhall Cavaliers. Steve Soper's Prodrive car also won three races, but Steve had commitments elsewhere in Europe too, which meant that he could not start on six occasions.

Although the three works-backed teams were by no means as dominant in their domestic (German) series, their cars and their drivers were still good enough to win six races outright. Here, though, was a championship that allowed large-engined cars (like Audi's V8, which also had four-wheel drive), though discrepancies in performance were balanced by a weight-penalty-for-success formula that often frustrated the entrants and the drivers too. Steve Soper, Johnny Cecotto, and Joachim Winkelhock all won races, but at the end of the season Cecotto and Soper had to settle for fourth and fifth in the Drivers' Championship standings.

By 1992 the E30 M3 was still competitive in national race series in several countries, but as the new-shape E36 cars had now been announced, it was thought that they should be used wherever possible. This new range's race car fortunes, sometimes as genuine M3s and (increasingly) as much-modified 318Ss, are recounted in Chapter 7.

There was, however, one astonishing high-profile success to celebrate in 1992, which came at the season's most high-profile endurance race – the Spa 24 Hours. As in recent seasons, the organisers imposed their own special set of regulations, which allowed cars as various as the old-type E30 M3s to compete against full-house 3.6-litre turbocharged Nissan GT-Rs, and Porsche Carrera 2s. No fewer than five German Championship M3s therefore turned up, all of them with the latest 2.5-litre Evolution engines (which, for use in Germany, apparently produced 370bhp), all of them in BMW Fina Bastos livery, these cars being run by the Schnitzer, Bigazzi and CiBiEmme teams who normally campaigned them in Germany.

In spite of the engine size and power of the rival cars, the M3s set the fastest times in qualifying, for the Nissan seemed to be off-colour, and none of the Porsche 911s could match up. Early in the race the Nissan took the lead, but looked likely to have to make several more pit stops for refuelling and for tyre changes. Less than five hours after the start, one of these pit stops was bungled, there was a major fire because of spilt fuel, and the car was eliminated.

The M3s then set about scrapping among themselves – because there were three different operating teams, there were no team orders – and by half distance just two of the cars were fighting it out. Towards the end, the car which had been crewed by a Brit, a Belgian and a German (with Steve Soper as team leader) was still lagging behind, but Soper put in a superhuman effort, caught and passed van de Poele's car on the

ABOVE: **Out of production maybe, but in 1992 a race-prepared M3 was still a winning tool – this was the Steve Soper/Jean-Michel Martin/Christian Danner car on its way to a narrow victory in the Spa 24 Hour race in 1992, which was really the E30 M3's last outright victory at this level.**

penultimate lap of the 24 hour event, and ended up taking the chequered flag by just 0.49 seconds! BMW took first, second and third in the race, with the best of the rest – a Porsche – being no less than 28 laps behind. It was a peerless way to bring the 'works-backed' race career of this amazing machine to a close.

Not that this was the end of BMW victories in long-distance 'Endurance' races (see Chapter 7 for a description of how later-generation M3s fared). Even in 1994, by which time the charismatic E30 M3 had been out of production for nearly four years, the Nürburgring 24 Hour touring car race was won by Karl-Heinz Wlazik, Frank Katthöfer and Fred Rosterg in a privately-prepared example. In the mid-1990s, though, changes in regulations would often mean that what we might call 'pure' M3s were no longer eligible, while much-modified versions of larger-production 3-Series types (318iS and 320i, for example) could be used instead.

## Rallying – right car for tarmac, but no four-wheel drive

Although the agile, lightweight, original M3 looked ideal for use in international rallying, in the 1980s that sport was rapidly moving away from its roots. In what many people still consider as the 'Golden Days', rallies were held on tarmac surfaced special stages, and four-wheel-drive machines were specifically banned. In the early 1980s that all changed, for more and more events used loose-surfaced special stages, and (worse still for BMW) four-wheel-drive cars were allowed to compete on equal terms. Even when the anything-goes days of Group B were brought abruptly to an end in 1986, it rapidly became essential to have four-wheel drive to be competitive in the Group A events, which became compulsory – and the M3 was not, and was not likely to be, that sort of a machine.

Because BMW was totally committed to the development of cars for circuit racing, and had not had any sort of official 'works' rally team for many years, in 1986–1987 they made no effort to produce an M3 that would be suited to tarmac rallying. This was a great pity, for with the single exception of the Ford Sierra RS Cosworth, at that time no other two-wheel-drive Group A car could match the power-weight ratio of the M3, none were

as nimble, and none could put their power down so well and so effectively.

In spite of the pressure that was applied by some well-known and well-financed teams in Europe, BMW therefore refused to be drawn into giving official support to rallying. Instead, they made a deal with David Richards' recently-formed Prodrive organisation (which was, and is, based in the UK, and whose preceding company had recently been preparing Porsche 911 SC RSs), whereby Prodrive would have privileged access to the BMW parts bins, would continue to liaise with the factory, and would provide comprehensive kits of cars – even complete rally-ready cars – to order.

BMW itself would provide complete engines, tuned to power and torque levels that Prodrive deemed appropriate for rallying, for we must not forget that BMW was almost ignorant (and certainly disdainful) of rallying. In the first year or so, the 2.3-litre engines produced about 270bhp, which reputedly rose to 285bhp in 1988, and to 295bhp in 1989. In the next two or three years, a remarkable number of such cars would be built, and would chalk up victories in many different territories.

Within limits – the limits, that is, of the suitability of the events in which BMW M3s might be competitive – this strategy worked well, but Prodrive made it look too easy at first, by noting that the car was homologated on 1 March 1987, and by supplying the car which won a prestigious World rally – the Tour de Corse – just nine weeks later! That particular car (registered in Southern Ireland because of UK Type Approval difficulties) was GXI 9427 – and it would go on to record more major victories in future years.

In the Tour de Corse, it was Grenoble-born Bernard Béguin who won the event outright, his Prodrive-built M3 carrying sponsorship from Rothmans (the tobacco concern) and Motul (the French oil company). Clearly the conditions were ideal for an M3, for on the serpentine stages of Corsica, the BMW set nine fastest stage times, led for all but a few hours, and seemed to have the comfortable beating of the Lancia and Renault works teams. This, though, was the single high point of the world season, though M3s were always competitive at European and international level: Béguin, for instance, also won in Antibes towards the end of the year.

Although the Belgian Patrick Snyers won the Belgian Rally Championship, and put up some fine M3 performances in the European Rally Championship itself (latterly his cars had a six-speed gearbox, which had of course been homologated with the race teams in mind), the only World-level showing of note of the year was in Corsica once again, where François Chatriot took fifth place in a Prodrive-built/Bastos + Motul-sponsored car (FXI 318).

Snyers, in fact, finished second in the European Rally Championship, having recorded outright wins in the Boucles de Spa, Garrigues (France), Madeira, Manx International (Isle of Man) and the Controz (using either GXI 9427 – his 1987 car – or one of the newer cars used in the Tour de Corse earlier in the year). He also took second place in 24 Hours of Ypres, and went on to become Belgian rally champion. Elsewhere, M3s won many events that were held on tarmac-surfaced stages, but it was increasingly obvious that four-wheel-drive rivals, and the events which were increasingly being tailored to suit them, would bring that success to an end in the near future.

Even so, in 1989 Marc Duez took fifth place in Portugal (in EDZ 4346), this being the M3's best-ever result in a loose-surface event, while François Chatriot (in ADZ 9667) took second place overall in the Tour de Corse. Not only that, but there were six outright wins at European Championship level – four of them by François Chatriot (driving ADZ 9667, yet another Prodrive-built car). Duez became Belgian champion, while Chatriot won the French Championship.

Now, though, as far as rallying was concerned, it really was almost all over. BMW had more or less disappeared from the world rally scene, yet there were still three outright wins to come in Europe in 1990, two of them to François Chatriot (who also became French rally champion that year), and J-M Ponce won two European events in Spain in 1991.

With rallying now dominated by four-wheel-drive cars, and the E30 M3 out of production, this was the end of the M3's top-level rallying career. However, with development of an entirely different type of M3 – the E36 – well under way, the future still looked exciting for the brand.

**BELOW: Until rival manufacturers produced ultra-special four-wheel-drive cars, the original type M3 was a formidably competitive tarmac rally car too. In 1987, the first year of its competition career, this car, driven by Bernard Beguin, won the World Championship Tour de Corse event. The British company Prodrive eventually specialised in rally preparation of such cars, and they won all around Europe.**

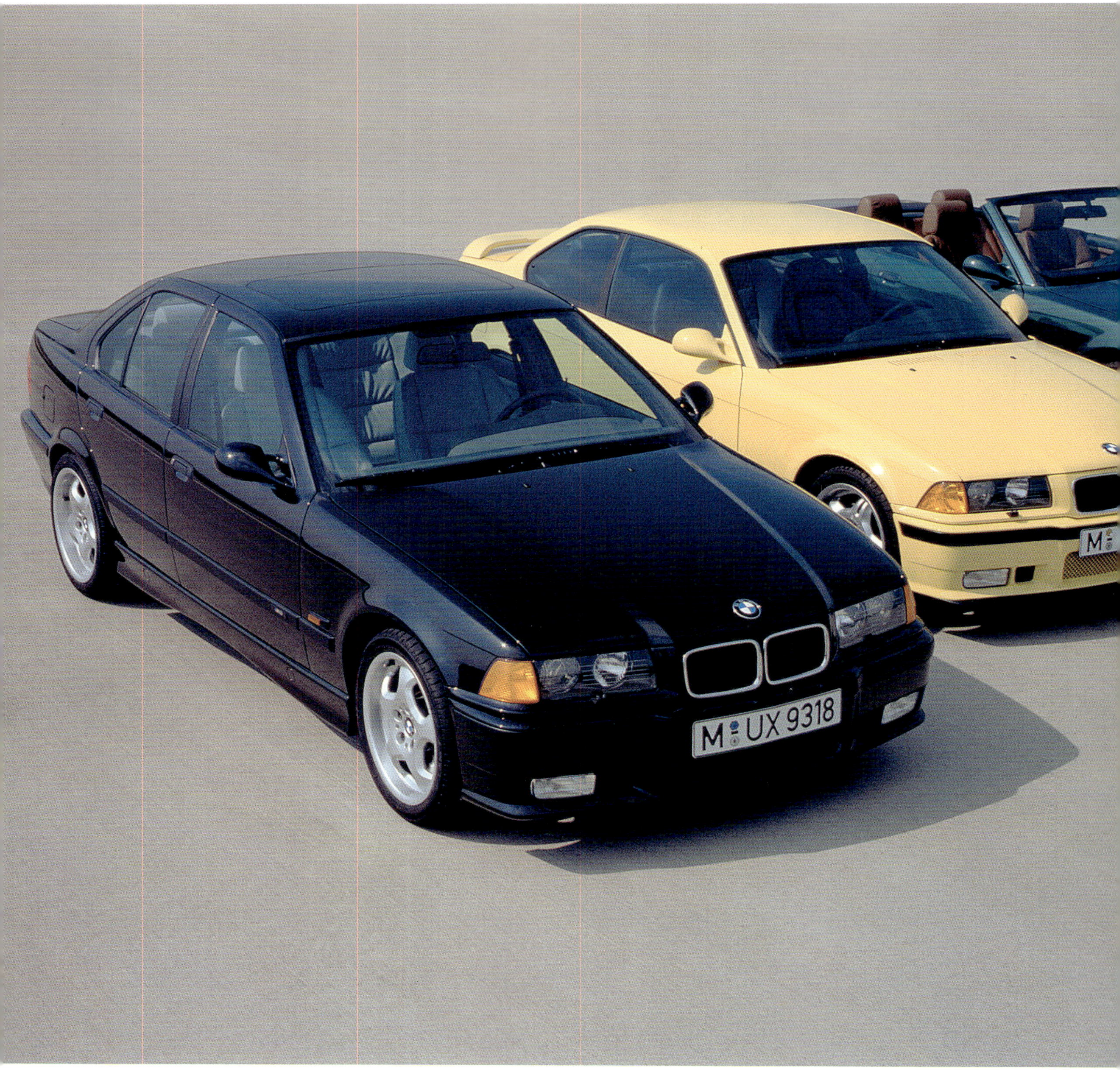
M UX 9318

## Chapter 3

# E36 models –
## the first six-cylinder cars

I t was late in 1992 before the first of a new second-generation M3 (what is now more familiarly known as the E36 variety) became available. By that time the M3 pedigree was six years old, and it was nearly two years since the last of the original (E30) type of M3 two-door Saloons had been available. BMW enthusiasts, it could be said, were salivating.

There was nothing sinister behind the delay, for BMW had gone about its new-model design and launch programme in its usual measured and methodical manner. There would indeed be a new-generation M3, they decided, and it must be a logical development of the new-generation E36 variety. However, since most components in that range were new (as opposed to being modified versions of E30 parts) this was going to take time. In particular, because of the fundamental change in regulations that had recently been enacted, BMW could no longer entertain any world-level motorsport ambitions for its new-type M3 (though they still wanted to shine in German and other European and overseas series), and was set on using a six-cylinder engine in an M3 for the first time.

The new-generation (actually the third-generation) 3-Series on which a future M3 would be based, had officially been launched at the end of 1990, with sales beginning almost immediately. Significantly, at first only a four-door Saloon type was announced (there was never to be a two-door

Saloon), with the forecast of a two-door Coupé type (which was to have a unique style, and therefore unique body-shell, based on the same new platform) to follow. As BMW made it crystal clear at the time, the success of the 3-Series was vital to the company, for every year this range made up half of its total global production.

To keep up with perceived market trends, this new 3-Series was to be at once a larger, more technically complex, and (in marketing terms) a more flexible range than what had gone before. It was indeed to be a larger car in every respect, with a totally new 'chassis' platform. Compared with the E30, therefore, the original E36 Saloon was to have a 5in (127mm) longer wheelbase than before, the entire car was 4in (102mm) longer, and 2in (51mm) wider, and the new platform ran on larger 15in wheels, even for the entry-level types.

Most important, though, were the twin technical facts that the new platform was to use a much more sophisticated independent rear suspension (one which BMW soon came to describe as 'multi-link') and that there was to be a range of engines which included 1.6-litre and 1.8-litre 'fours', along with 2.0-litre and 2.5-litre 'six' varieties.

Because, for the new car, BMW had taken the big step of up-rating its power units (and, by inference, would soon swap several rough-and-rorty four-cylinder engines for a silky-smooth, sweet-singing 'six' in the M3), the engine and the

**PREVIOUS PAGES: By 1995, the E36 M3 range had blossomed to three different sub models – left to right: Saloon, Coupé and Convertible – each of which was a marketing success.**

**BELOW: To assist in the long-term development of M-type cars, BMW opened its new Motorsport centre in 1990.**

rationale behind it need to be explained. After all, this engine and developments of it would be at the heart of all M3s built from 1992 to 2007.

As summarised in the panel on page 200 (although for the E36 this was a 'six', compared with the two older six-cylinder types that BMW had been using through the 1970s and 1980s) it was radically new in many ways, and capable of much further development. BMW had been manufacturing modern sixes since 1968 (and what we might call a 'small' six since 1977), but this was a third-generation six, which the new M3 would thoroughly deserve. When the new power unit was introduced in 1990 for use in the very latest 3-Series and 5-Series ranges, although there were some similarities with the previous 'small' six – the 30° canted-over installation in the cars, the cylinder spacings, the bore and stroke dimensions, the location of many components, and some elements of the cast-iron cylinder block – in almost every aspect there was new thinking on show.

To sum up (compared with the original small six): there were twin-overhead camshafts rather than single-cam heads, four valves per cylinder rather than two valves, and chain drive to those camshafts instead of an internally-cogged belt. In many ways, the cylinder head layout was visually similar to that of the original M3, but not in component detail, and (except for the camshaft drive) was rather like that of the four-cylinder twin-cam that had been inserted in the 318iS just months earlier. In so many ways, therefore, it followed the 'classic' layout that many other manufacturers were then adopting, with a centrally-positioned spark plug, with a narrow angle between the lines of valves, and with pent-roof shaped combustion chambers.

Bosch fuel injection, allied to their latest DME (Digital Motor Electronics) 3.1 engine management system, a plastic inlet manifold, and a catalytic converter in the exhaust system was standard on all types, and even on the original (non-M3) 525i

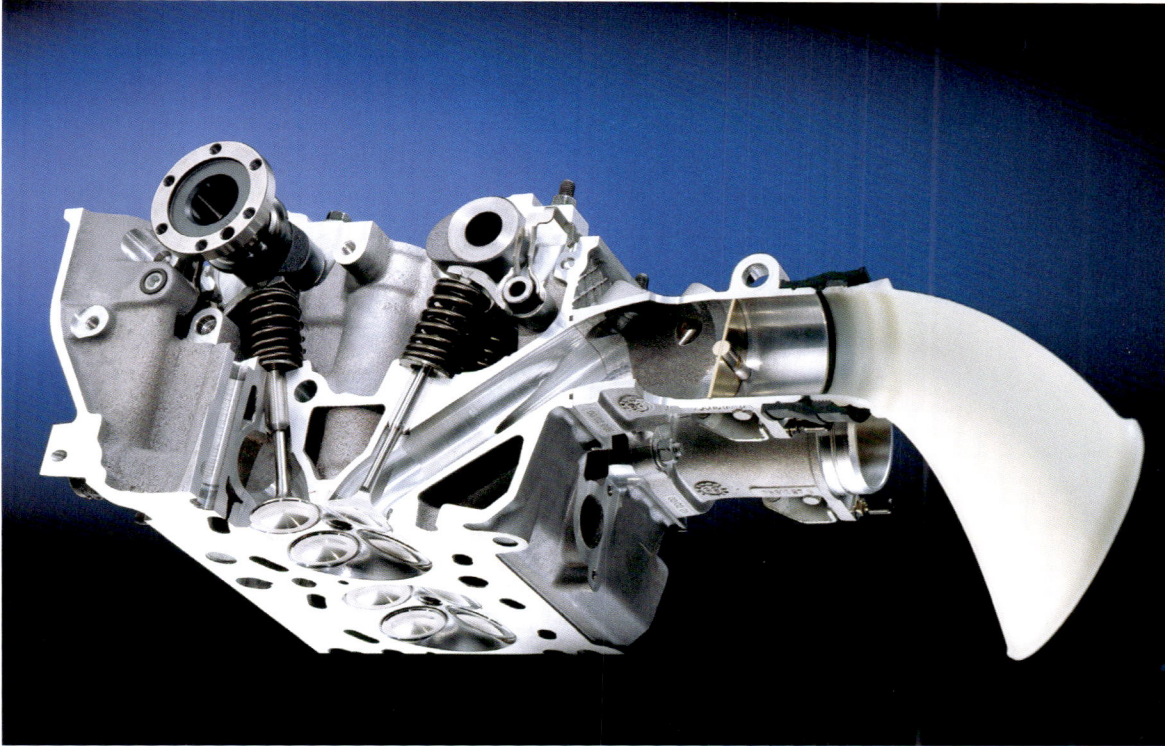

LEFT: This cross-section shows BMW's well-established, and very neatly-detailed, four-valve/twin-cam cylinder-head layout in six-cylinder form.

model the compression ratio was no less than 10.0:1. On that car, for 1991, the 2,494cc 'six' was rated at 189bhp at 5,900rpm.

When this new engine was announced (originally for the latest-generation 5-Series cars, but soon in 3-Series types and eventually for the E36 M3 model), BMW made much of all the new technology, which included what they called a 'stationary ignition distributor system with coils integrated into the cylinder head', along with hydraulic valve tappets. Although it was agreed that there was more machinery in the new engine than before, and that there had been an overall weight increase, the weight of the engine assembly had been kept down to a creditable 428lb/194kg – and this was still with a conventional seven-main-bearing cast-iron cylinder block.

What was fascinating was that BMW revealed that this six-cylinder unit was so compact that although the spacing between adjacent cylinders was just 91mm (this is one of the crucial 'identification marks' that tend to live with an engine through its entire, often long, career), even on the original series-production 2,494cc engine the cylinder bores themselves were of 84mm, which did not leave much scope for them to be enlarged in the future. In due time, we would learn that

the cylinder bore of the E36 M3 engine would be 86mm, and that the ultimate stretch for the engine, made in 2000, was only to be 87mm.

A quick analysis of the cylinder head/combustion chamber layout is instructive – if only that it confirms just how fundamental the launch of what we might call the 'Cosworth/DFV/4-valve' layout had been in 1967. Since that moment, engine designers throughout the world had studied the Cosworth unit, then studied the four-cylinder Ford-based units that followed on, and concluded that this was a logical way to go themselves.

On this six-cylinder BMW engine the line of inlet valves was set at 20° 15min from vertical, while the line of exhausts was set at 19° 15min – these criteria being exactly (not approximately, but exactly) the same as on the larger original M1 (six) and M3 (four) four-valve units. Paul Rosche and his team thought that they understood all the constructional air flow and water (cooling) flow characteristics of such engines, and were not about to make big mistakes by trying something else on the new smaller 'six'.

Equally important was the feature in which BMW was a pioneer, that of providing what BMW initially called VACC (Variable Camshaft Control) but later renamed VANOS. This provided electronic

OPPOSITE: The limited-
production Z1 sports
car was the BMW that
signalled new thinking in
the chassis department,
for it was the first new
model to use what
BMW soon began to
call the 'five-link' rear
suspension.

control over the inlet camshaft timing, where the overall timing could be varied progressively, all the way from giving either maximum breathing capacity at full throttle, or maximum fuel efficiency at lighter loads. This device was housed within the aluminium casting at the front of the cylinder head.

According to BMW: 'VACC also ensures a very even spread of torque throughout the rev range. As a result this engine develops more torque at idle speed (and at any other engine revs) than the old [E30] M3 did, even at its peak....'

The introduction of a new type of independent rear suspension on the E36 family was probably even more significant, for it finally spelled out the end of BMW's long love affair with semi-trailing links and coil springs, which they had first adopted on BMW 600 bubble cars at the end of the 1950s. While such layouts were very space-efficient, and not too costly to manufacture, because of the inherent changes of wheel camber that took place between full bump and full rebound, they had several flaws in terms of roadholding and ultimate grip – something that E30-type M3 owners had already come to recognise very well!

The new 'multi-link' system had first been seen on the limited-production BMW Z1 sports car of the late 1980s and, although we did not know it at this time, it was now set to be adopted on many new-design BMWs (and eventually on the BMW-owned Mini brand) in the future.

It had to work, of course, and indeed it did work. To quote one technical sage when the new car was launched: 'The new 3 [-Series] stomps all over the old in terms of roadholding and on-

the-limit handling. Both aspects have been transformed, thanks to the wider track, equal weight distribution, and most of all, the hugely impressive new rear suspension. Based on the design of the Z1's rear axle, this "central arm" system has, among its aims, the maintaining of constant toe-in whatever the spring load, in order to provide the handling neutrality the old model lacked. Success is absolute.'

However, to describe the location and articulation of the new suspension's locating links in space, is as difficult as trying to describe a beautiful woman's shape without using sweeping hand signals in the air – so let me merely suggest that this was a combination of transverse links allied to trailing links, along with neatly packaged coil springs, separate telescopic dampers and an anti-roll bar, all arranged under and around a steel cross member which also housed the rear differential. This, need I add, had to be carefully packaged so that it interfered as little as possible with the desired shape of the floor-pan, the fuel tank, the exhaust system and the spare wheel, which were all close to it. The plastic fuel tank, in fact, now spread all the way across the underside of the car, ahead of the rear suspension.

The result, once finally developed, was not only a more compact installation than that of the old-type semi-trailing arm had ever been, but one in which there was a more precise control of rear tyre/wheel articulation. BMW expected great things of it, and M3 enthusiasts looked forward to seeing it fitted to the next-generation M3, which must surely follow.

When the new E36 car appeared, it was immediately seen to be smoother, more aerodynamically shaped and more spacious than the E30, and except for elements of the transmissions there appeared to be no carry-over of major components. Not for nothing did BMW management admit that it was probably the most important launch they had made for almost a decade, as 3-Series production and sales were currently making up so much of the company's business worldwide. More than 4.5 million of all 02 and earlier 3-Series cars had already been made – so the new car would have to continue to uphold a remarkable reputation.

The front and rear screens were much more

BELOW: Like other
German manufacturers
of high-performance
cars, BMW spends
much time exercising its
test vehicles at the old
Nürburgring race circuit,
this being the HQ of that
operation. Specialists
in the capture of 'sneak
photos' spend much time
hanging around here.

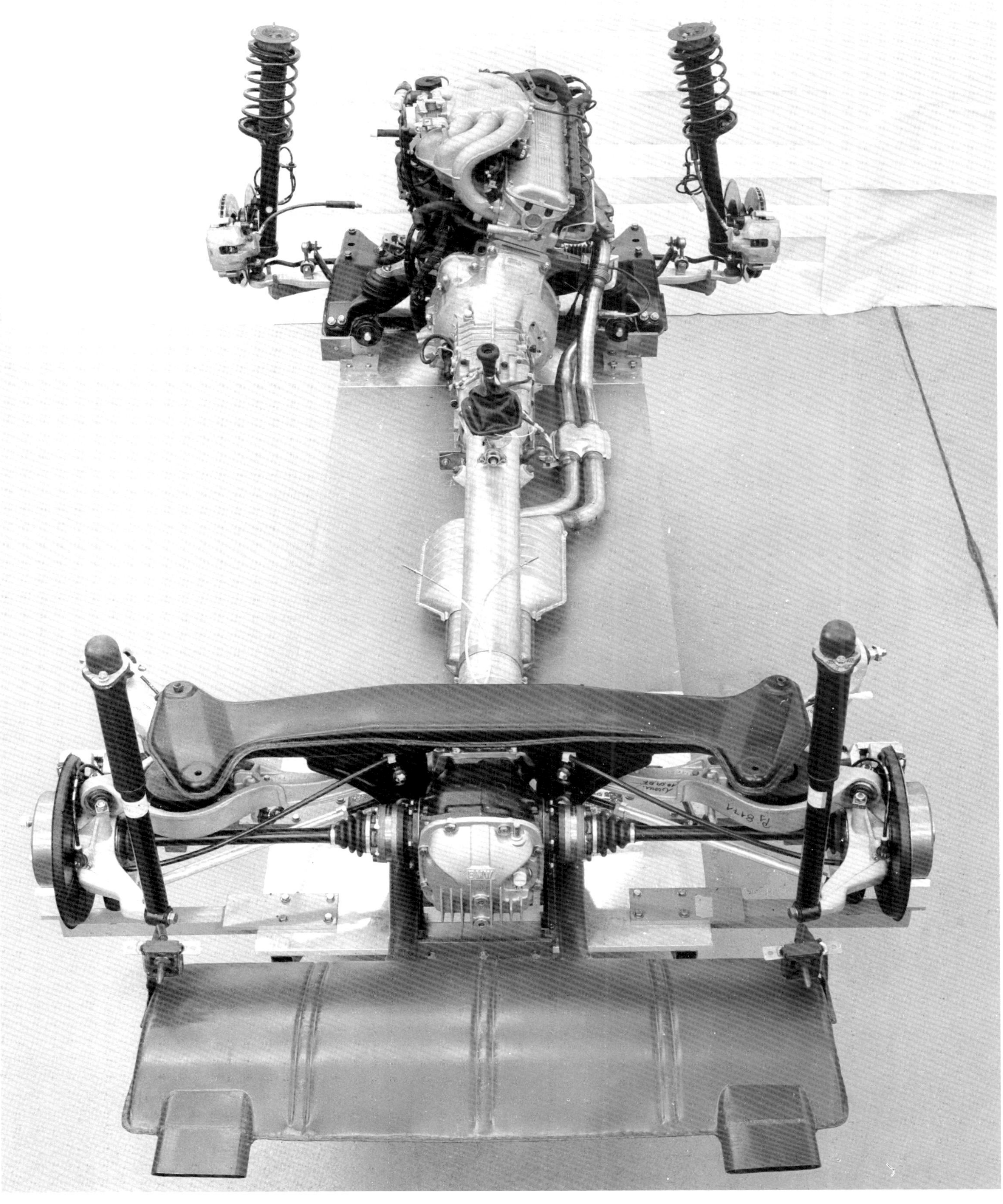

sleekly aligned than before, and the detailing, particularly around the front end and the wheel arches, was more carefully considered – all of which was confirmed by the drag coefficient of the lowest-specification car, which was a startlingly encouraging Cd = 0.29.

On top of that, the overall rigidity of the body-shell was claimed to be much enhanced (by no less than 45% on the four-door Saloon), while more than half of the shell panels were now of rust-resistant galvanised steel. Although it was the ultra-modern 24-valve engines and the complex independent rear suspension that made most of the technology headlines, it is worth recalling that all types had power-assisted steering, and disc brakes on all four wheels were naturally standard on the six-cylinder derivatives.

Deliveries of mainstream four-door E36 Saloons began early in 1991, but it would be some time before BMW fulfilled its promise to produce Touring (estate car, that is), Cabriolet and two-door derivatives, and those longing for an M3 version of the new car would have to wait even longer. In the end a new-type two-door Coupé model (which the

more excitable motoring pundits had said might be called a 4-Series, but this never happened) was introduced in the first days of 1992.

Although still recognisably based on the 3-Series platform (and retaining that car's new 106in/2,692mm wheelbase platform), this time it was definitely more two-door Coupé than two-door Saloon. Apart from the front end, which was shared with the E36 Saloon, virtually every skin panel was new. One well-received styling detail was that on this car, front and rear body mouldings were mainly in body colour, rather than in the rather drab grey of the four-door Saloons.

The roof panel of the new two-door car was 1in (25.4mm) lower, the front and rear screens were more steeply raked, the bonnet was longer and the tail was lower. The boot itself was quite small (the author speaks with long-term experience of these models), but BMW was readily excused on the grounds of how attractive the model looked. Initially there was to be a choice of three engines – the latest 16-valve 318S 'four', along with the 2-litre and 2.5-litre 24-valve 'sixes' – which had already been put on sale in the E36 four-door model.

**BELOW: With a body style much sleeker than that of the original (E30) M3 type, and with a 286bhp/3.0-litre six-cylinder engine under the bonnet, the second-generation M3 Coupé was a formidably fast car.**

ABOVE: The 286bhp
six-cylinder engine was
neatly packaged in the
engine bay of the original
E36 M3.

With two-door sales beginning (all round Europe) early in 1992, the scene was now set for the launch of a new M3, but this would still not occur for some months yet. In the meantime, potential buyers salivated at the rumours that a new-generation car would have an ultra-powerful six-cylinder engine, and that it would be available in left-hand and right-hand drive.

## E36 M3 – the new car arrives, at last

Finally – and it was, after all, almost two years after the last of the much-loved E30-type M3 Saloons had been manufactured – the new-generation E36-type M3 was previewed. As widely forecast, initially it was to be a two-door Coupé, not a two-door Saloon, and also as rumoured, it had a very powerful six-cylinder engine. Except that it now did not fall competitively into any readily-available motorsport category, and by definition was going to

cost quite a bit more than the earlier M3 had ever done, it was greeted by an enthusiastic public.

This, make no mistake, was no longer the type of 'homologation special' that could be driven, but only under sufferance and with compromises, on the public highway, but a genuine, carefully-developed, refined and completely equipped road burner. Not only larger and heavier than its predecessor, it was also a much more sophisticated machine. Although it was at once more powerful and faster than before, it did not need any exotic materials, or aerodynamic aids, to make that possible. Not only that, but with the exception of the new front and rear bumpers, and the special 17in road wheels, it looked almost exactly like the 3-Series Coupé from which it had evolved.

There was more. The engine was not only ultra-powerful but also extremely refined, every possible noise and exhaust emission regulation could

**ABOVE: Compared with the original M3, the second-generation ('E36') model was sleeker and, under the skin, much more powerful, for in 1992 (when the new cars were launched) the 3.0-litre six-cylinder power unit produced 286bhp.**

be met, and the top speed would be an easily-reached and electronically-limited 155mph/250kph. Although this was not spelt out in any gloating detail, one rhetorical question asked at this time was: 'Why buy a Porsche 911 when the new M3 could match it in all respects, and could carry four people in great comfort?'

Now to the visual differences from other 3-Series Coupés. First of all, the entire body-shell had been lowered by 1.2in (30mm), this being achieved simply by making suitable changes to the front and rear suspension. New front bumper/apron, new rear apron, and modified side skirts were allied to what BMW claimed as 'aerodynamic' door mirrors, while the whole car was painted in the same colour (the mainstream Coupé had black front, side and under-skirt detailing).

The front bumper/apron featured three sizeable air intakes, those on the flanks being intended to channel air towards the enlarged front discs, and the centre one to enhance cooling of the radiator/engine bay. All these features, allied to the extrovert 7.5in x 17in alloy wheels (shod with 235/40ZR17 tyres), made their point without appearing over-the-top or unsuitable. This, incidentally, was the first M3 in which optional 8.5in-wide rims could be ordered for the rear wheels to increase traction and to subtly alter the front/rear handling balance.

Compared with the E30 variety, which was already gathering 'classic' status around it, the new car set out to be at once understated, yet a much faster open-road car. The character of the two types was totally different, and intentionally so. On the earlier car, there was the constant reminder that this was really a de-tuned race car, and that many compromises had been made to make it competitive: while on the new E36 there was the sense that a racing career could all still be possible, but that this time it was primarily intended to be the normal, carefully-developed flagship of the entire range.

Maybe the pundit who wrote this got it absolutely right: 'The truth is (and BMW admits it) that this car is no successor to the M3 at all. It would like you to think of it as a car cut from the mould of the M635CSi (hence the 286bhp power output), a swift and efficient express, all wrapped up in a beautiful coupé shell.'

LEFT: To show that the latest M3 was not only a very fast car, but was also one that was practical and roomy, BMW revealed this drawing of the 'package' of the latest E46 model.

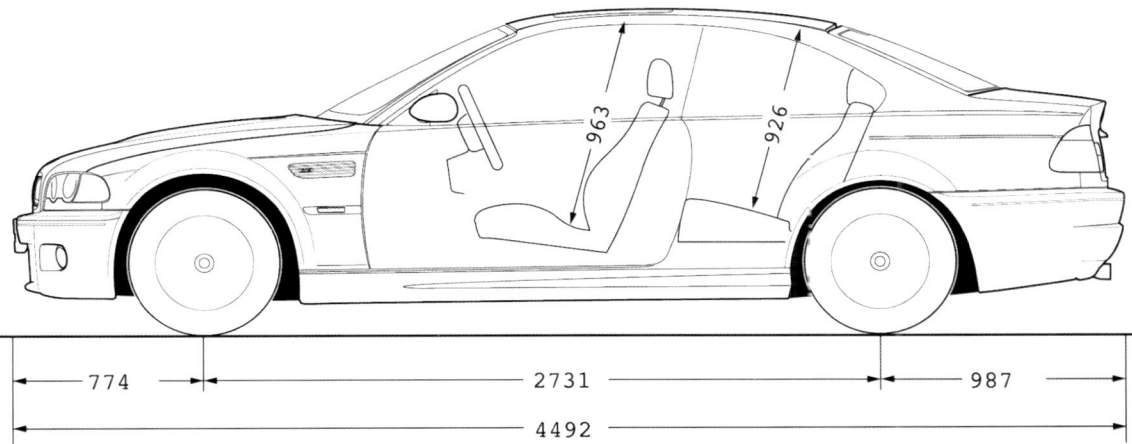

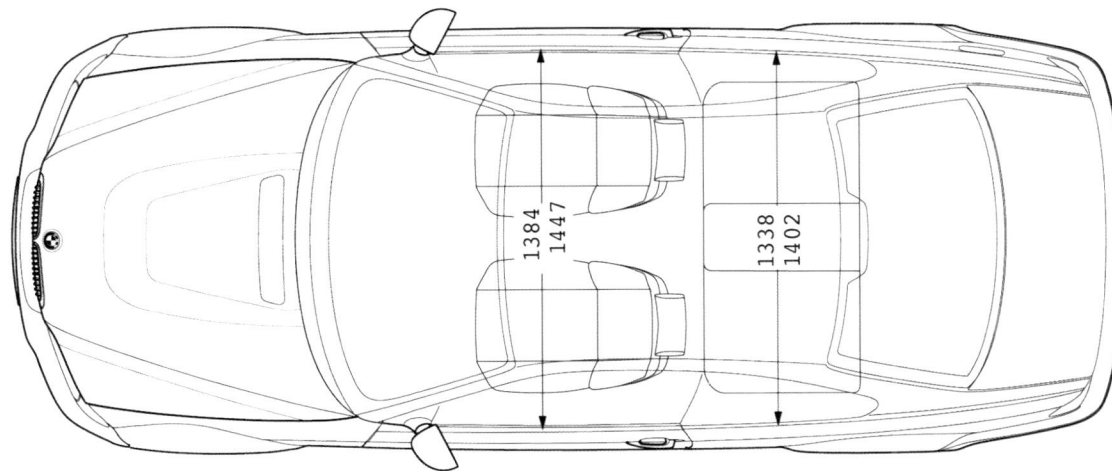

Maße in mm (ohne Gewähr)

W 101 - 1508    W 102 - 1525    L 101 - 2731    W 3 - 1384 Schulterraum vorn
W 103 - 1780    W 104 - 1924    L 104 -   774    W10 - 1447 Ellenbogenbreite vorn
H 100 - 1383                    L 105 -   987    W 4 - 1338 Schulterraum 2.Sitzreihe
                                L 103 - 4492    W11 - 1402 Ellenbogenbreite 2.Sitzreihe
                                H 61 -   963
                                H 63 -   926

It was the running gear – really the engine, transmission and rear-suspension package – that told its own story. The transmission (as usual, a five-speed from Getrag) was as efficient, slick-changing, and seemingly bombproof as usual, though the pattern of the change had been altered to eliminate the 'dog-leg' first ratio position, while the newfangled rear suspension delivered everything promised, which included a claim from BMW that on a reasonably smooth test track its chassis could generate more than 1.0g on corners.

It was the six-cylinder engine, however, which attracted most superlatives, for in spite of what some diehards said about a 'lack of charisma' (which presumably meant that it no longer fizzed, rumbled and snarled under pressure) this was a remarkable piece of engineering. As detailed in Appendix C, BMW's small 'six' had started life in 1977 as a two-valve single-ohc design, but from 1990 had been completely re-engineered in four-valve twin-ohc form. For those hankering after future enlargement, and who wanted more and yet more power, the only major snag was that it had originally been designed to fit into a rather snug 3-Series engine bay – and to do this it was quite short, the result being that the basic, immutable, spacing of the cylinder bores was restricted to 91mm, just the same (BMW engineers pointed out) as that dimension adopted on the company's existing four-cylinder and 12-cylinder engines.

Before work began on producing an M3 tune from this 24-valve engine, it was being produced as a 2,494cc unit, with bore and stroke dimensions of 84mm x 75mm (the earlier two-valve/single-

cam type had also featured a less highly-specified 'economy' version of 2,693cc with a long-stroke of 81mm). After a great deal of development, heart searching and testing, the M-Sport team finally decided that they could enlarge the engine to the full 3 litres (2,990cc in fact) by increasing the cylinder bore to 86mm (those extra two millimetres were the most, they thought, which could even be considered), and using a lengthy 85.8mm stroke.

[It was not until the M3 pedigree progressed even further, especially into the E46 variety of the early 2000s, that we all realised just how close to the practical size limit this engine had already been in 1992.]

All the effort seemed to be worth it, for with the aid of Bosch's very latest engine management system, and yet more attention to camshaft profiles, this engine proved to develop 286bhp at 7,000rpm. Not only that, but it pulled like a lusty horse from low and medium speeds, for peak torque occurred at 3,600rpm, after which the torque curve was almost flat to 6,000rpm. BMW, it seems, was proud to flag up the 95bhp/litre power figure (which was a new record for a normally-aspirated European road-car engine at the time, they said, and rightly so), noting the flat torque curve that went with it, and challenging any rival to match it. For a time no one could.

Under the skin, too, the E36 M3 was like the mass-production E36, but different in almost every detail. As already mentioned, the entire car had been lowered by 30mm (1.2in), but road springs and damper rates had been revised, anti-roll bar rates had been increased, while at the front there were modified track control arms and stub axles to provide different geometry. The power-assisted steering had a variable ratio, the ventilated disc brakes were enlarged to 12.4in (315mm) at the front and 12.3in (313mm) at the rear, and those distinctive cast-alloy 17in wheels filled the wheel-arch cut-outs to perfection.

There was only one disappointment – and this, to be fair, was almost inevitable. It was that the new car was considerably heavier than the old. BMW had always been happy to boast that the E30 3 had weighed only 2,646lb (1,200kg), so they were mildly defensive about the weight of the new car, which turned the scales at no less than 3,212lb (1,460kg).

## Theme and variations

By mid-1993, and even before the new E36 Coupé had been made available on all world markets, the rumours of a widening of the range began to spread. This M3, it was suggested, would shortly be available in Convertible and four-door Saloon form – which, if true, meant that BMW was indeed serious about expanding the appeal of this ultra-high-performance model. With all this in mind, it was no surprise to learn that E36 M3 production was to be centred at Regensburg, a considerable distance north of Munich, where a vast and modern BMW assembly plant had been set up in the 1980s (though a few cars, it seems, would also be assembled, mainly from kits supplied from Germany, in the small BMW plant at Rosslyn, in South Africa, which was concentrating on building up its 3-Series expertise).

In the meantime, independent road tests confirmed just how fast the new Coupé undoubtedly was. When *Autocar & Motor* tested a right-hand-drive car in the summer of 1993, they recorded a top speed of 162mph (7mph above the theoretically limited-to-155mph gait of home market cars), and no less than 132mph in fourth gear, allied to 0–60mph acceleration in 5.4sec, 0–100mph acceleration in 13.1sec, and the sort of overall potential that made almost every other car in this class obsolete.

It was, of course, an expensive car all over the world. In the UK, the 'sticker' price was £32,450, which made it price-comparable with cars like the Jaguar XJS 4.0 coupé and the front-engined Porsche 968. However, it was altogether typical of the way that BMW was aiming at what we might call the hard-driving 'executive' market that there was a long list of available extras, and it was easily possible to push up that price to £36,000 and more.

Air conditioning? Yes, for £1,440 at first. Cruise control? £375. Full leather trim? £1,040. Anti-theft installation? £465. Sports steering wheel with driver air bag? £560. These were the days, too, when no radio installation was even offered by BMW, and customers had to do their own deal with the dealer/supplier before getting that essential piece of kit.

But was it worth it? With the generous approval of *Autocar & Motor*, I would like to reproduce their closing remarks in an otherwise adulatory test:

'Verdict: BMW had two goals to achieve with the new M3. The first was to make it appeal to a wider commercial market, and it has certainly done that. The car is more user friendly now, not merely because it is available for the first time in right-hand-drive form, but because it is quieter, roomier and a sight more economical than was previously the case.

'The second was to do all this without diluting the original car's fabulously raw thoroughbred driver appeal, but here we feel it has been only partially successful. And the trouble, we suspect, was that it was impossible to do both.

'The truth is that, in its darkest confessional moment, BMW knows this just as much as we do. It is, after all, the company that produced the original M3. However, somewhere along the line, a decision was taken to make the new M3 not a real M3 but instead a car more in the mould of the old M635CSi: an easy-going tool that will appeal to more of the people for more of the time, but not one that will pull so passionately on the heart strings of the serious enthusiast.

'Does that mean the M3 has gone soft, then?

No. Any car with an engine this good that is linked to a chassis this well developed deserves praise of the highest order, especially since it unlocks the door to such giant-killing cross-country ability. Even so, we can't help but shed a tear for the demise of the genuine M3. It was a unique car that will, it seems, remain that way forever....'

[But was this a case of the super-enthusiasts not completely understanding developments in the market place? The same breed of road testers had said the same about Ford's recent approach to civilising the original whale-tail Sierra RS Cosworth – when in the real world, sales of the four-door Sapphire Cosworth, and later the Cosworth 4x4, were far higher than those of the original model had ever been.]

No matter, the new-generation M3 was now fast making its mark, and in any case BMW had many other diversification plans for the brand in 1994. For sale in the USA, meeting the latest exhaust emissions regulations meant that the new car had to be delivered with a much-detuned 240bhp engine (and with peak torque of 225lb ft). Even so, that derivative of the new machine could

still sprint up to 60mph in 5.6 seconds, and top out at an electronically-limited 137mph. Notably, for this market there was also a ZF automatic transmission option – this being the very first M3 on which such an option became available.

In 1994, however, the two major launches were of the E36 M3 Cabriolet (which was officially previewed in January) and the E36 M3 four-door Saloon (July). M3 Cabriolets, of course, had been seen before, but the launch of a four-door Saloon, which made no concessions to the fiercely powerful chassis hidden away, was a real departure. This, if nothing else, indicated that BMW was in the M3 business seriously, and aiming to be so, long term.

Although it was ferociously more expensive to buy, the specification of the latest Cabriolet was logical in every way, for technically and mechanically it was almost the same as that of the still-fresh M3 Coupé. The principal style change was the elimination of the 'splitter' from the base of the front spoiler, while there was a new type of five-spoke alloy wheel (that would, in fact, be seen on other M3s in the coming months). There

had been no cynical attempt to save weight (the full electric operation of the folding soft top was retained, for instance), and since the body-shell of this type of M3 was reinforced under the floor to enhance stiffness, it was about 176lb (80kg) heavier than the Coupé.

When the Saloon appeared in mid-summer, there were no surprises either, for the only visible body enhancement was the deeper front spoiler and 8.5in rear wheel rims – and there was no sign of any rear-end spoiler. Under the skin, the whole car was slightly lower compared with the other 3-Series Saloons, and compared with the other E36 M3s it had softer suspension settings. Customers were also delighted when BMW decided to price the four-door at exactly the same level as the Coupé.

## ... and more variations

Although the E36 model range immediately began to sell far faster than the original M3 had ever done (more than 70,000 of all types would be produced), it was also one where the basic

**BELOW: The E36-type M3 Convertible appeared in 1994, and became a very popular open-top cruiser.**

**ABOVE:** With motor sport in mind, the E36 M3 GT Coupé was launched as a limited-edition model, with many weight-saving and aerodynamic features...

**RIGHT:** ...including this two-tier rear spoiler.

specification rarely seemed to settle down for long. Not only did a much-changed 'Evolution' type appear towards the end of 1995 (this type is covered in Chapter 4), but also there seemed to be a constant stream of special editions and product changes to keep one's attention. It is to these cars that we must now turn our attention:

## M3 GT

At the end of 1994, BMW introduced a strictly limited-edition version of the Coupé, calling it the M3 GT. However, although it was allegedly built to comply with race regulations to be applied to the 1995 Le Mans 24 Hour race, it is difficult to see how it could have been competitive against other more specialised machines.

In fact, this was yet another 'homologation special' type such as BMW was totally expert in developing, produced to make the car more suitable for use in the FIA GT Class II, in IMSA GT racing in the USA and in other international long-distance races.

A total of 350 left-hand-drive cars (priced approximately £2,500 above the standard model) were originally constructed in the winter of 1994/1995, along with 50 'Individual' right-hand-drive cars for sale in the UK (other sources suggest that 356 of the original type were actually made) all of them painted in British Racing Green, with what was described as a 'Mexico Green' interior.

Minor changes (mainly electronic) were made to the 2,990cc engine, the claimed peak power going up to 295bhp (the remainder of the drive line and transmission was not changed), while the suspension was lowered and stiffened. Visual changes – not only making the car more attractive, but making it significantly better as a motorsport proposition – included adding a 'splitter' to the front bumper/spoiler, and fitting a two-tier rear spoiler to the back corner of the boot lid.

Many of the interior plastic cockpit mouldings had been replaced by Kevlar parts, but this was really an unnecessary cosmetic change as there was no structural significance in what was done. BMW certainly did not claim any weight-saving for this car.

ABOVE: When the E36 M3 was launched in 1992, any thoughts of preparing a race car version were discounted.

## Not for sale but …

Two BMW innovations that 'went public' in 1994 were of interest to M3 fanatics, but neither came to the market place at the time.

First, as announced in October, BMW admitted that in mid-1995 they would increase the size of their 'mainstream' six-cylinder engine from 2,494cc to 2,793cc. Although this did not affect the M3 line (where the engine was already out to 2,990cc), the announcement that mainstream engines would also get an aluminium block/crankcase was important. That this would reduce the engine weight by 69lb (31.5kg) was initially thought to be significant and exciting for the M3 – but the fact is that BMW had no plans to add such a lightweight component to M3 models. As noted earlier in this chapter, the cylinder bore dimensions of the 2,990cc engine were already perilously large, and close to reliability limits, and it was thought that such dimensions would not be tolerated in an alloy casting.

Similarly, the appearance of sneak pictures (and BMW's later reluctant admission of the car's existence) of the short-wheelbase hatchback

3-Series Compact, which had been given all the appropriate M3 treatment, also generated more speculation than truthful analysis. The fact is that this was, and would remain, just a 'look-see' project.

In November 1994, Friebbert Holz of the Motorsport Department commented: 'We are responding to customer demand for a slightly stronger engine in the Compact, although we have yet to decide whether it will be a four- or six-cylinder unit. For sure we intend the car to be a lot cheaper than the current M3 Saloon and Coupé, and it will definitely have a multi-valve engine, but at this stage we are not prepared to say more.'

It is worth recalling that each and every one of the first-generation Compact cars used an E30-type chassis platform, together with the old-type semi-trailing arm independent rear suspension that had already been abandoned on E36 M3 models, which may explain why BMW was reluctant to use the full-power M3 engines in this model. In the end, little more was ever heard of this car, though a single, full-house 321bhp/3.2-litre-engined car was completed, seen and tested in 1996.

## M3 Lightweight (LTW)

Compared with the M3 GT, the LTW (Lightweight) Coupé model, which became available in the USA in 1995, was an altogether more ambitious and comprehensive update of the E36 Coupé, this being specifically intended to make the car more competitive against the latest Porsche 911 in certain classes of racing in the USA.

Within the limits of regulation changes, and economic practicalities at the Regensburg factory, this was a comprehensively updated machine, which was rare at the time (116 are reputed to have been sold to the public, and a further handful were retained by approved racing teams in the USA) and is even rarer today. Major efforts had been made to reduce the weight of the machine.

All cars were built without what might be called luxury items – no radios, no air-conditioning systems, no leather seats, no toolkits and no sunshine roofs. The doors had aluminium skins instead of steel. Bodies came without what BMW called an under-bonnet 'insulation blanket', and much of the habitual sound-deadening had also been removed. However, a large rear spoiler was standard, and all cars were finished in plain Alpine White. All in all, this allowed BMW to claim a weight reduction of at least 220lb (100kg).

Mechanically, an effort was made to supply these cars with production-built engines 'at the upper end of design tolerance' (make of that what you will), the ECU speed-limiter was removed, so that the cars easily soared over the nominal M3 speed 'barrier' of 155mph, and the rear axle ratio was changed from 3.15:1 to 3.23:1. The suspension also received attention, for stiffened spring and damper settings were all chosen. Although the tyre size of 235/40R17 was retained, these were on 7.5in-rim front wheels and 8.5in-rim rear wheels.

All cars were delivered direct to a company known as the Prototype Technology Group (PTG) Racing in Virginia, USA, where a great deal of extra preparation kit, aimed at making the cars even more suitable for racing or, at least, for 'track-day' work, was made available, this concentrating on improvements to the engine's lubrication performance, and to its on-circuit aerodynamic balance.

## The M3's future

By 1995, the M3 was selling in quite unprecedented numbers, with almost 10,000 cars being completed in every 12-month period. Of those, the Coupé was by far the most popular, and to the surprise of many market analysts sales of the Saloon struggled to get on terms with the other two types.

No matter. With more than 25,000 E36s already built since launch in 1992, BMW was now intent on pushing ahead further – and in October 1995 the public found out what this meant. More power, a new transmission, and even more 'toys' were on the way.

**BELOW: Each and every evolution of the 24-valve, twin-ohc, six-cylinder engine used in M3s from 1992 to 2007 was immaculately turned out.**

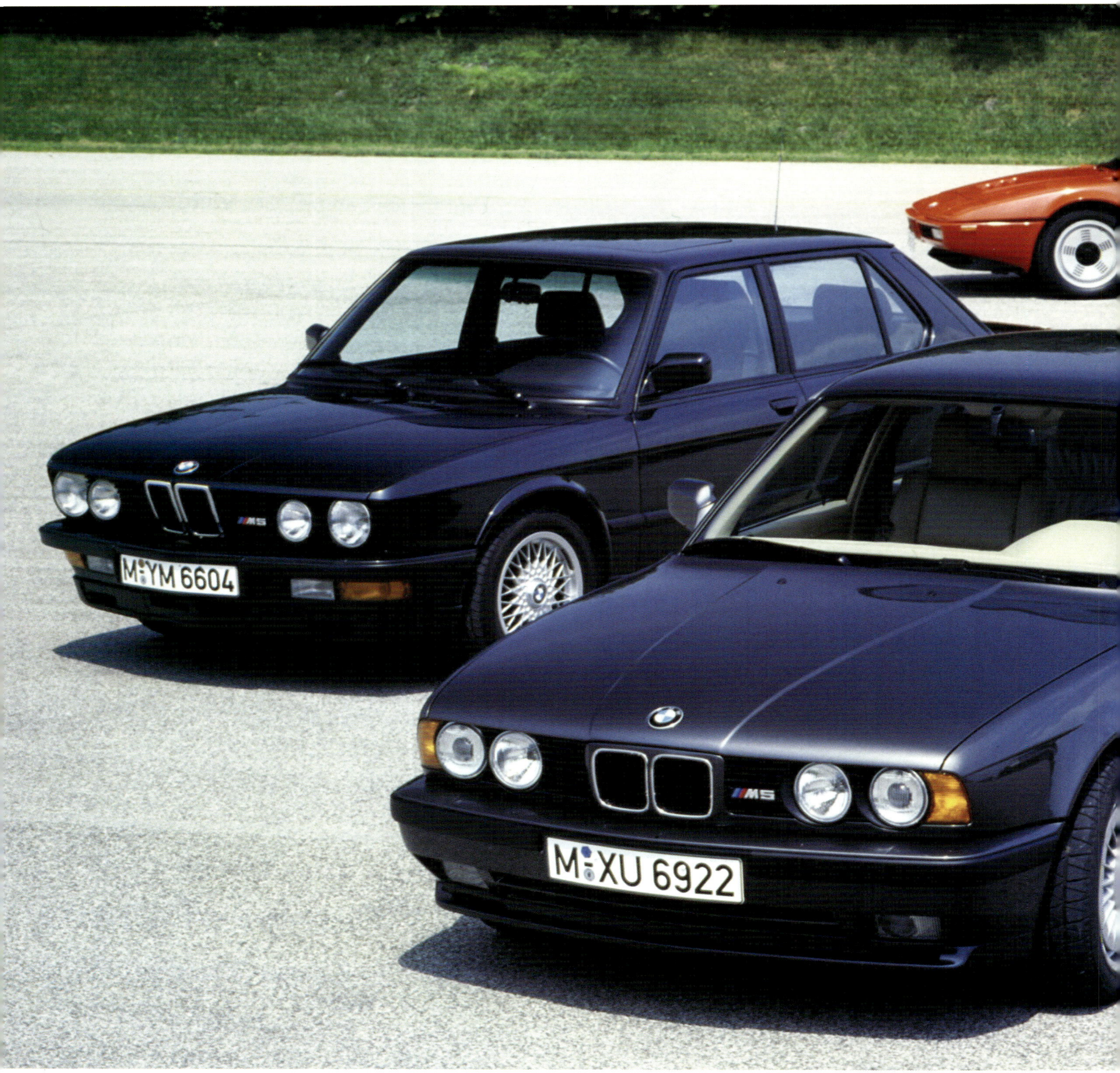
M YM 6604
M XU 6922

# Blood relative –
## The M5 evolves as a 'sister' car

As already mentioned at the beginning of this book, the first BMW to carry the 'M' badge was the mid-engined M1, and the original M3 was also pre-dated by another now-legendary series of BMWs – the M5s. The original M5 preceded the M3 by two years, and as time went on, the two ranges followed each other. Because of the way BMW's new-model programme was structured – and it was, believe me, structured very thoughtfully – a new edition of the M5 would usually appear some time before the equivalent M3 made its bow.

Because the one type often shared technology with the other, I should now spend a short time – an Interlude, if you will excuse that expression – summarising how the M5 pedigree has changed over the years. In each case I have listed BMW's own 'project code' for a particular series, and the years in which such a car was on the market.

**LEFT: The second-generation M5 – the E34-based Saloon – arrived in 1988, and although it retained the 24-valve 'six', it had been enlarged slightly to produce 315bhp from 3,535cc. Because it could reach 155mph before an electronic limiter cut in, it was widely praised as the then ultimate in high-performance sports saloons. Here it is seen posed with the earlier E28 type (left of the group), with the iconic M1 in the background.**

## M535i (E12-based, 1980–1981)

(Basic specification: Front-engined, five-seater, four-door Saloon; 3,453cc, 218bhp, six-cylinder. 1,410 cars built.)

Cashing in on the growing reputation of the 'M' badge, which had appeared on the mid-engined M1 Supercar, BMW introduced a specialised version of the E12-type 5-Series Saloon car of the early 1980s. Only ever built on the basis of the four-door Saloon, this was the 'flagship' derivative of the 5-Series, and except for the level of equipment now fitted, it did not have a specially-tuned engine, and was virtually the same as other six-cylinder 5-Series cars of the day.

It used a single-overhead-camshaft version of the well-known six-cylinder engine (in other words, it did not have the twin-cam head of the M1) complete with Bosch L-Jetronic fuel injection.

Three years later, the following pair proved more worthy successors to the rather 'milk-and-water' E12 M535i.

**BELOW: The M535i of 1980 was the very first of the M-labelled BMW saloons, but because it did not have a specially-developed engine – it was fitted with the conventional 218bhp/3.5-litre single-cam 'six' – it was not a true M-model as many BMW owners care to remember them.**

## M535i (E28-based, 1984–1987)

(Basic specification: Front-engined, five-seater, four-door Saloon; 3,430cc, 218bhp, six-cylinder. 9,483 cars built.)

Although not as fierce or as specialised as the original M5, which was launched at the same time, this E28-based M-model was effectively the successor to the original M535i that had been built three years earlier. Like that car, it retained the existing single-cam six-cylinder engine, and was produced at the same time as the first-generation M5.

## M5 (E28-based, 1984–1988)

(Basic specification: Front-engined, five-seater, four-door Saloon; 3,453cc, 286bhp (256bhp for sale in the USA), six-cylinder. 2,241 cars built.)

Announced before the M3, on sale before the M3, and never intended as a pure competition car, this was the first production-based car on which the engineering team was allowed to work its entire M-for-Motorsport magic on the engine, the transmission, the suspension and the equipment in general. It was the first of the Saloons to use the twin-cam/24-valve engine, which had originally made its name in the mid-engined M1. After first being built in downtown Munich, assembly was rapidly relocated to the specialised Garching plant north of the city centre.

The next-generation M5, which followed in 1988, was a formidable machine.

LEFT: By the standards of the day, the original M5 of 1984 was an exciting piece of kit, for it combined the luxury of a 5-Series four-door body style with a 286bhp, 24-valve, 3.5-litre engine, this being a development of the M1's power unit.

## M5 (E34-based, 1988–1995)

(Basic specification: Front-engined, five-seater, four-door Saloon; 3,535cc, 315bhp (310bhp in USA), six-cylinder. 8,344 cars built.)

Widely praised when new, and still revered as a 'classic' car to this day, the E34 version of the M5 was a magnificent machine, at once sleeker, more powerful, faster and more capable than the E28-based car that it replaced. Careful and judicious development work produced an even more powerful version of the existing 24-valve engine, which used yet another combination of bore and stroke (93.4 x 86mm instead of 93.4 x 84mm), and produced a remarkable 315bhp. The top speed was an electronically-limited 155mph.

The 1991 version of the M5 pedigree was an update of the car that had already been on sale for three years, but it had a larger and more powerful engine.

## M5 (E39-based, 1998–2004)

(Basic specification: Front-engined, five-seater, four-door Saloon; 4,941cc, 400bhp, V8. 20,482 cars built.)

Based on the latest E39 5-Series, the third-generation M5 was the first of the entire M-family to be equipped with a V8 engine, this being the company's latest 4.9-litre/32-valve power unit, and it was allied to a six-speed gearbox. This was used on many other medium-sized and larger BMWs of the period. Larger, faster, heavier and more technically advanced than any previous M-badged car, this M5 regularly got plaudits as the best M-badged car yet made. No fewer than 20,482 such machines would be produced.

The next generation of M5, the E60-based car, was a quite sensational car in that it boasted an entirely special 507bhp, 5-litre V10 engine.

**RIGHT: The third-generation M5, the E39 type based on the latest 5-Series family, was launched in 1998, and was the first M-badged car to be equipped with a V8 engine, a 4.9-litre unit rated at 400bhp.**

## M5 3.8 (E34-based, 1991–1995)

(Basic specification: Front engined, five-seater, four-door Saloon or five-door Estate Car; 3,795cc, 340bhp, six-cylinder. 3,014 Saloons, 891 Estate Cars built.)

From late 1991, the already excellent E34-based M5 was treated to a whole package of improvements that not only included Adaptive M Technic suspension (which automatically reset the Boge gas dampers to suit different driving habits) but also a 340bhp/3,795cc version of the six-cylinder engine. This derivative of the M5 was never marketed in the USA. From mid-1994, a six-speed Getrag transmission became standard, this being the first usage of this box on a BMW saloon car.

After a break in M5 production and marketing, a new-generation model (based on the latest E39 5-Series) appeared in 1998. Production of the new type, incidentally, was carried out at the 'mainstream' 5-Series plant, the ex-Hans-Glas site at Dingolfing, north-east of Munich.

## M5 (E60 based, 2004–2010)

(Basic specification: Front-engined, five-seater, four-door Saloon or five-door Estate Car; 4,999cc, 507bhp, V10. 20,548 cars built.)

This was the M-badged BMW that made almost all previous M-badged cars look and feel obsolete. Not only was it based on the latest generation 5-Series Saloon, which had been launched a year earlier, but it had a phenomenal new 4,999cc/507bhp 90° V10 engine, and this was usually linked to a seven-speed SMG III sequential-change transmission, though a conventional six-speed Getrag manual was also available in the USA. Ultra fast (the limited top speed was 155mph, but it would otherwise have been easily capable of 200mph), it was at the time the ultimate in BMWs.

**RIGHT: By any standards, the fourth-generation M5 of 2004 made almost every other fast saloon in the world look obsolete, for it was equipped with a specially-designed 90° V10 engine, which produced 507bhp. If electronic means had not been employed to limit its top speed, it must have been close to a 200mph machine.**

## AMAZING V10 ENGINE

When the latest M5 was announced in 2004, it appeared to have bucked the usually rigorous BMW cost-controlling system. The power advantage it had over its predecessors came from a brand-new engine for which there was no obvious place in the corporate scheme of things. Not only was it a V10 power unit – never before had BMW produced a V10 road-car engine – it was a 90° V10 at that.

The connection (the inspiration, more like) was Formula 1 racing. V10 engines had been compulsory in that formula since the late 1990s, so when BMW (which had been out of the formula since its turbocharged 1.5-litre units had become obsolete in the 1980s) decided to make a comeback by supplying engines to Williams, it was to be with a brand-new 3-litre V10 engine. This was successful, and immediately gave a boost to BMW's high-performance image.

Then, when BMW started looking around for a new engine to power the E60 M5 of 2004, they chose to develop another all-new V10, which they coded the S85B50 project. Except for the general layout – which included the 90° V-angle and the four-valve/twin-cam cylinder heads – there was absolutely no connection with the race engine of the period, and not a single component was shared.

**LEFT:** By the early 2000s, BMW had returned to F1 racing, which specified the use of V10 engines, so when the time came to launch a new M5 in 2004, the company designed a brand-new 90° V10 engine to pay homage to its motor racing presence, though the F1 and road V10 did not share a single part. This was the cutaway drawing of the M5's new V10, showing how complex a power unit it actually was.

**ABOVE:** The V10 engine of 2004 was specifically designed to fit into the new-generation M5's engine bay...

**RIGHT:** ...and this is the display of all the componentry that helped to produce 507bhp from 5 litres.

The new V10 road-car engine, which was coded S85, featured a cylinder bore of 92mm, a stroke of 75.2mm, and a swept volume of 4,999cc, all being based around an aluminium-silicon die-cast block casting, along with an aluminium bed plate for additional thickness. Naturally it also featured Double VANOS variable valve timing on each cylinder head, a complex four oil-pump lubricating system, ten individually electrically-controlled throttle valves, and an electrically driven water pump. The four camshafts were chain driven, for BMW's one-time love affair with cogged belt drive was well and truly over. Even though it was more complex than the previous M5's series-production V8, it only weighed 1kg (2.2lb) more, and fitted comfortably into the engine bay.

BMW made it clear that although their F1 V10s revved to 19,000rpm and beyond, and had to be stripped for rebuild after only 500 miles of racing, the new S85 would be expected to be

serviceable for 200,000 hard road miles, and more. Even so, the camshaft and breathing details were set so that the maximum torque (385lb ft) occurred at no less than 6,100rpm, and the peak power (a magnificent 507bhp) was developed at 8,250rpm. If electronic limits had not been placed on the car's systems, so that it could not normally exceed 155mph (250kph), BMW agreed that the latest M5 would certainly have been capable of more than 200mph – and the rest of the running gear, including the sturdy new Getrag seven-speed sequential manual gearbox, had been evolved to suit.

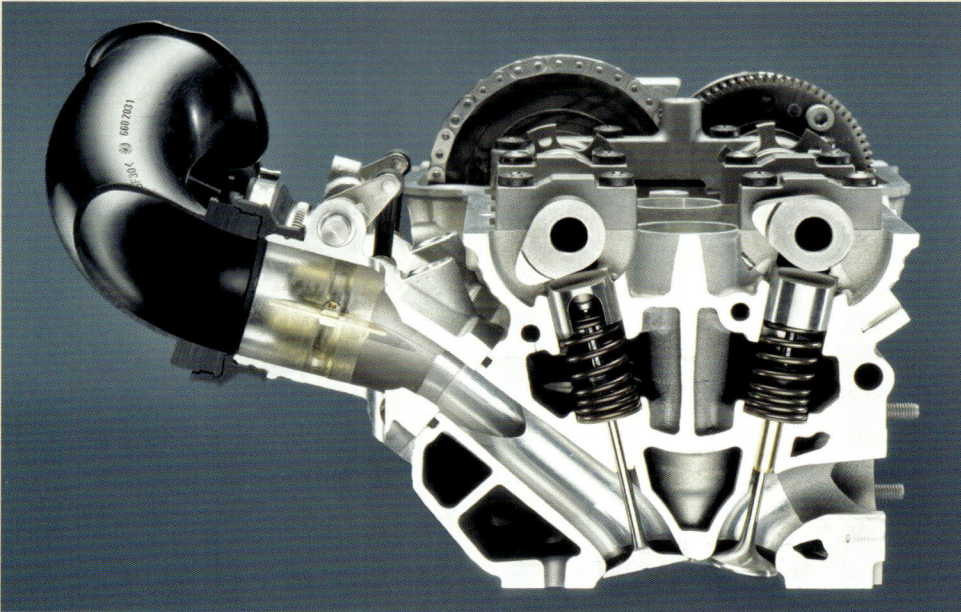

**ABOVE:** This shows just how compact, yet demonstrably efficient, was the top end/valve gear of the M5's V10 power unit. All the details would soon be applied to the V8 engine to be used in the E90-style M3.

**RIGHT:** This was a display example of the early-2000s P83 3-litre BMW F1 V10 engine – shown simply to prove that it had absolutely nothing in common with the 5-litre V10 that powered the M5 from 2004!

## M5 (F10-based, introduced in 2011)

(Basic specification: Front-engined, five-seater, four-door Saloon; 4,395cc, 552bhp, V8 or 2,993cc, 381bhp, diesel six-cylinder.)

Compared with the previous M5 (of 2004–2010), which it replaced in 2011, the new-generation car was at once slightly less special but still amazingly capable. Like other M5s, it had a four-door, five-seater body style based on the other mass-production 5-Series cars of the day. This time, however, the ultra-specialised V10 of the old model had been dropped, and had been replaced by a turbocharged 4.4-litre V8 (developing 552bhp instead of 507bhp) allied to a seven-speed dual-clutch semi-automatic transmission (a six-speed conventional manual transmission was retained for USA-market cars), and for the first time there was to be an ultra-powerful diesel option. Once again, its potential 200mph-plus top speed was throttled back to 155mph by an electronic limiter.

**Launched in 2011, the fifth-generation M5 might have been slightly less specialised than the car it replaced, but with 552bhp from its turbocharged 4.4-litre engine it was still a phenomenally fast machine. For the first time on a BMW M-badged car, there was also a diesel-engined alternative.**

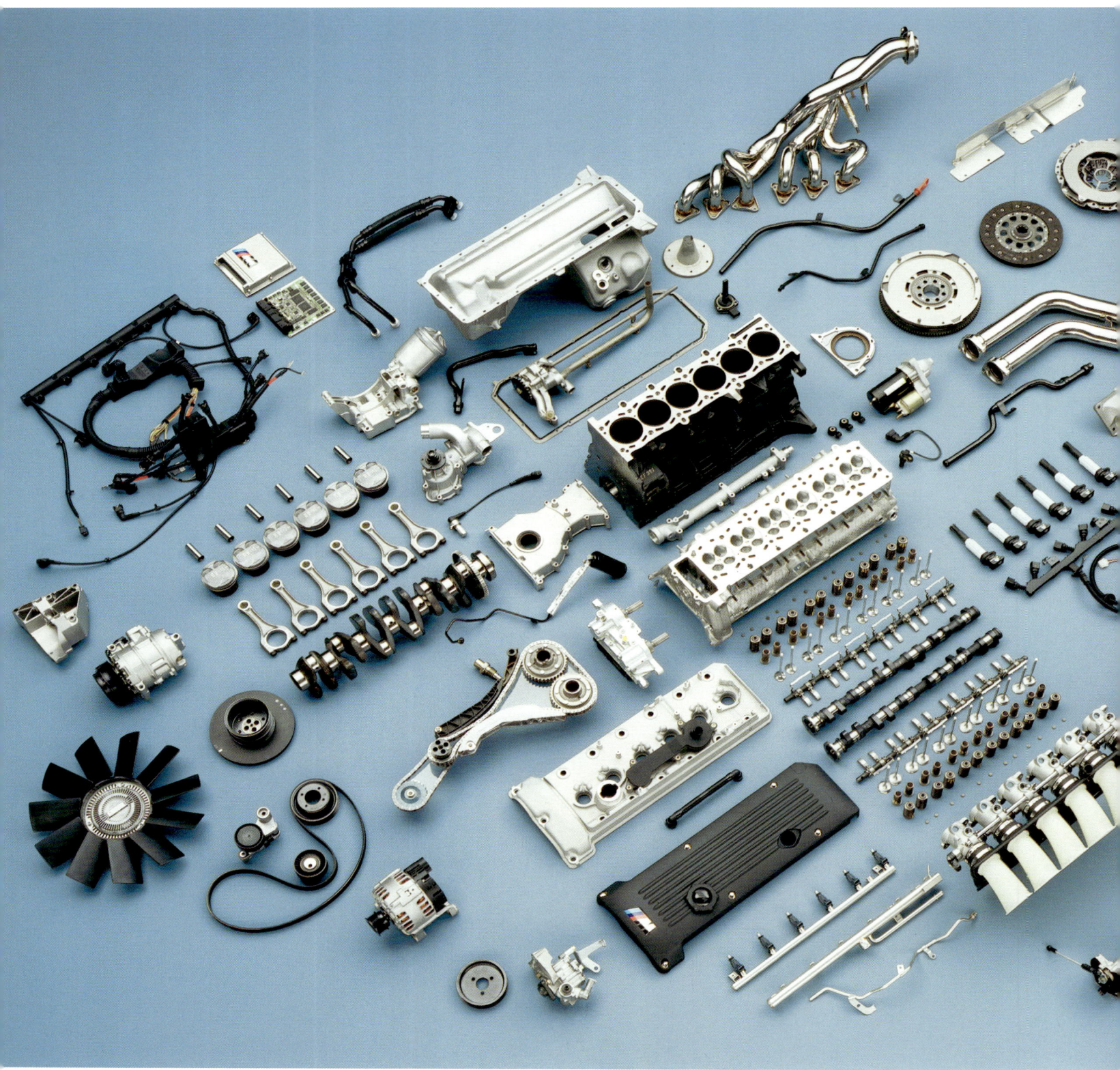

## Chapter 4

# E36 Evolution –
# more power, more performance, more variety

Almost every observer was surprised, to put it politely, when what became known as the 'Evolution' version of the E36-type M3 appeared in July 1995. It was so soon – only three years after the original six-cylinder M3s had gone on the market. So why had it happened so unexpectedly, for with 286bhp the M3 still seemed to be at the pinnacle of whatever performance table of such cars was assembled; and no one was complaining about the styling. Was there a hidden meaning?

On sober reflection there seemed to be two possible main reasons. One was that a number of noisy and influential motoring pundits had written less-than-laudatory reviews of the original E36 M3 along the lines of: 'Well, it's very fast, and very well equipped, but it doesn't have the same character as the original M3.' The other (perhaps more commercially significant) was that BMW had themselves recently introduced the 328i, which took over as the flagship of the mainstream 3-Series line, was more powerful than the 325i had been, and was a significant amount closer to M3 performance than the earlier cars had been.

For these reasons, and after the usual analytical 'why don't we?' conversations at Motorsport, Paul Rosche's department was allowed to take another detailed look at the still-new M3 E36, and to decide what they thought should be done to make an already-excellent

car even better. As ever, they were also allowed to look around the many technical divisions in Munich, and take an early 'pick' of technical innovations with which other BMW departments were already dabbling, which explains why this new car became the first BMW-badged car to use what became known as the 'Double VANOS' adjustable camshaft timing, and the next in line to be allowed to use the six-speed Getrag gearbox recently fitted to the latest M5.

First thoughts about this, the first major evolution to the E36-style M3, actually began soon after that car was launched in 1992, but for purely practical reasons there were other priorities that had to be settled before such development work could become serious. Not only did work have to be completed on the all-new V12 engine, which was to be supplied to McLaren for use in the McLaren F1 road car (technical details of this car were fully revealed in 1992), but also there was ongoing work to be completed on the current E34 M5, which included the new Getrag six-speed gearbox.

Serious detail development work on what I will call the E36 'Mk 2', therefore, did not begin until the winter of 1993/1994 – just as the original range of three E36 M3 cars (Coupé, Saloon and Cabriolet) reached the production stage. Although there were to be strict budgetary limits on the scope of the changes proposed, Rosche's team

ABOVE: By 2000, the 3.2-litre engines fitted to M3s had almost reached their development peak.

PREVIOUS PAGE: By 2000, the classic 24-valve six-cylinder engine had reached its zenith, in 3.2-litre form, but there was still a chance to extract a little more from this set of superbly detailed components.

were given free rein to look at every aspect of the car, to make proposals, and to wait anxiously for top management to approve, or disapprove of what they wanted to do.

In the end, what got through to the customers was significant, encouraging, but not revolutionary. Although modifications to the chassis turned the M3 into a tauter machine than before, the most important changes were concentrated on the engine and the transmission.

Superficially, the engine set for use in the Evolution model was much the same as it had become in the original car – but, as well as a small enlargement, there were in fact major improvements to the VANOS valve timing mechanism, and also to the fuel injection/engine management system. These, of course, were not merely made for the sole benefit of the M3, but

would eventually be adopted for other versions of the six-cylinder engine used in 3-Series, 5-Series and even 7-Series road cars too.

## Engine – major changes

Motorsport, of course, was always on the lookout for more power, more control and (in general terms) more efficiency. In many cases in history, more power could be found by increasing the size of the engine (to use that oft-quoted Americanism: 'There is no substitute for cubic inches'), but as far as the M3's six-cylinder engine was concerned, there was a major problem.

This, which has already been discussed in Chapter 3 and in Appendix C, was that the original engine had been laid out to be very compact along its seven-main-bearing cylinder block, such

## McLAREN F1 ROAD CAR – BMW V12 ENGINE

I make mention of this impressive power unit for it was, effectively, a blood relation of the six-cylinder engines used in the E36 and E46 M3 ranges of the period. Designed to order for McLaren, and specifically for their use in the three-seater F1 road car (it was not related to another V12 in BMW's road-car range), this S70/2 engine was an amazingly powerful V12 in which many details would later be refined and used in E36 Evolution and E46 M3s. Work began in Munich in March 1991, the first prototype engine ran on a test-bed before the end of the year, and the first engine was delivered to McLaren for installation in March 1992.

Based around what looked otherwise like a conventional aluminium alloy cylinder block and cylinder heads, it measured 6,064cc, with a bore and stroke of 86mm and 87mm respectively. Purely for interest (and BMW insist that this was no more than a convenient coincidence), I note that the cylinder bore was exactly the same as the 2,990cc BMW 'six', whereas the stroke was unique. Because of this coincidence, the detailing of the cylinder head, valve gear and gas-flow layouts was, indeed, very similar to that of the existing M3-type 'six'.

Chronologically, the V12 engine was, in fact, the first from BMW to use Double VANOS valve timing control (naturally enough, on each cylinder head) – this feature is described on page 100.

The power output of this engine was a colossal and hyper-impressive 627bhp at 7,400rpm, with an electronically-monitored peak torque of 479lb ft developed all the way from 4,000 to 7,000rpm. The engine itself, incidentally, weighed 586lb (266kg), which was substantial enough – but then it had a very substantial power output.

The performance of the F1 road car was itself quite colossal too. The only authorised road test of an F1 was carried out by *Autocar* in May 1994. The top speed was 'in excess of 230mph' (at which the engine was turning over at approx 7,500rpm). In standing start sprints it passed 60mph in a mere 3.2sec, 100mph in 6.3sec and 200mph in 28.0sec. The standing start quarter mile was dismissed in a mere 11.1sec, which was something quite out of the ordinary for any other road car of the period.

In the end, incidentally, McLaren built a total of 106 ultra-expensive F1 road cars, of which 28 were race-modified cars.

that the distance between cylinder bore centres was a mere 91mm. Because of the colossally expensive tooling installed at BMW to machine the cylinder blocks, there was no economically sensible way that this dimension could ever be changed, and since the cylinder bore of the E36 M3's engine was already 86mm, it was very close to the maximum that could be used without the cylinder walls becoming perilously thin.

Much of the detail work, which eventually found a use in this latest engine, had already been done by the same team when working on the McLaren V12 engine. This engine, incidentally, was a 6.1-litre power unit, in which the cylinder bore was 86mm and in which the general layout of the cylinder head, valve gear and breathing arrangements was very similar (see the panel 'McLaren F1 road car – BMW V12 engine' on page 95).

Not only did Rosche's team want to release more power from the revised engine, but they also wanted to retain full control of its behaviour, which explains why the engine was slightly enlarged,

and why a new engine management system was developed and installed. For the reasons mentioned above, the new bores could only be increased very slightly from 86mm to 86.4mm.

However, at the same time, a new longer-stroke crankshaft was employed (91mm instead of the original 85.8mm), which still allowed the power unit to be revved all the way up to 7,400rpm and beyond. This gave a capacity of 3,201cc; at which point every BMW enthusiast assumed there would simply be no further 'stretch' to come. They were wrong – but only just!

With the compression ratio also raised from 10.8:1 to 11.3:1, there had also been creditable improvements in power and torque, these being summarised as follows:

| Model | Engine size (cc) | Peak power (bhp at rpm) | Peak torque (lb ft at rpm) |
|---|---|---|---|
| M3 E36 | 2,990 | 286/7,000 | 236/3 600 |
| M3 E36 Evolution | 3,201 | 321/7,400 | 258/3,250 |

BELOW: Double VANOS first appeared on BMW's six-cylinder engine in 1995 – being unobtrusively placed at the front of the cylinder head/camshaft junction. This, in fact, is a non-M3 derivative of the power unit, with different manifolding and other details.

**LEFT:** This cutaway drawing shows the neat, yet intricate, detail of the Double VANOS adjustable valve-timing feature on E36 M3 Evolution and later models.

**BELOW:** Equally as fast as the E36 Evolution coupe, the four-door saloon was even more versatile.

BMW was delighted to point out that, apart from the engine they were already supplying to McLaren for the F1 road car, this was the first normally-aspirated road-car engine they had ever put on sale with a specific output of more than 100bhp/litre.

Much other detail work had gone into developing this engine, which included lightweight pistons, a two-mass flywheel, a modified engine vibration damper, low-friction graphite-coated connecting rods, larger diameter inlet valves, a second oil pump to nullify any unwanted oil surge from greater cornering forces, a revised and very complex (as can be seen!) exhaust manifold, and two quick-to-warm-up exhaust catalysts.

As with the new V12 engine currently being supplied to McLaren, the company had also developed and refined its VANOS variable valve timing system, which had previously only worked on the inlet valves. Now it was to work on inlet and exhaust valves, the whole of a complex little system being hidden in a light-alloy cover that was mounted at the front of the cylinder head.

At the time, it was claimed to be the most sophisticated variable valve timing control system that had so far been applied to a European car, and effectively gave this generation of 24-valve twin-cam six-cylinder engine the ability to behave like a highly-tuned power unit when operating in the upper rev range, and yet to have more conventional camshaft behaviour when the car was cruising, or lugging around town at low rpm.

This feature was so important to the ongoing evolution of M3 technology, and to BMW's engine expertise in general, that a more detailed description is appropriate. Tucked away inside that alloy cover was a combination of precision

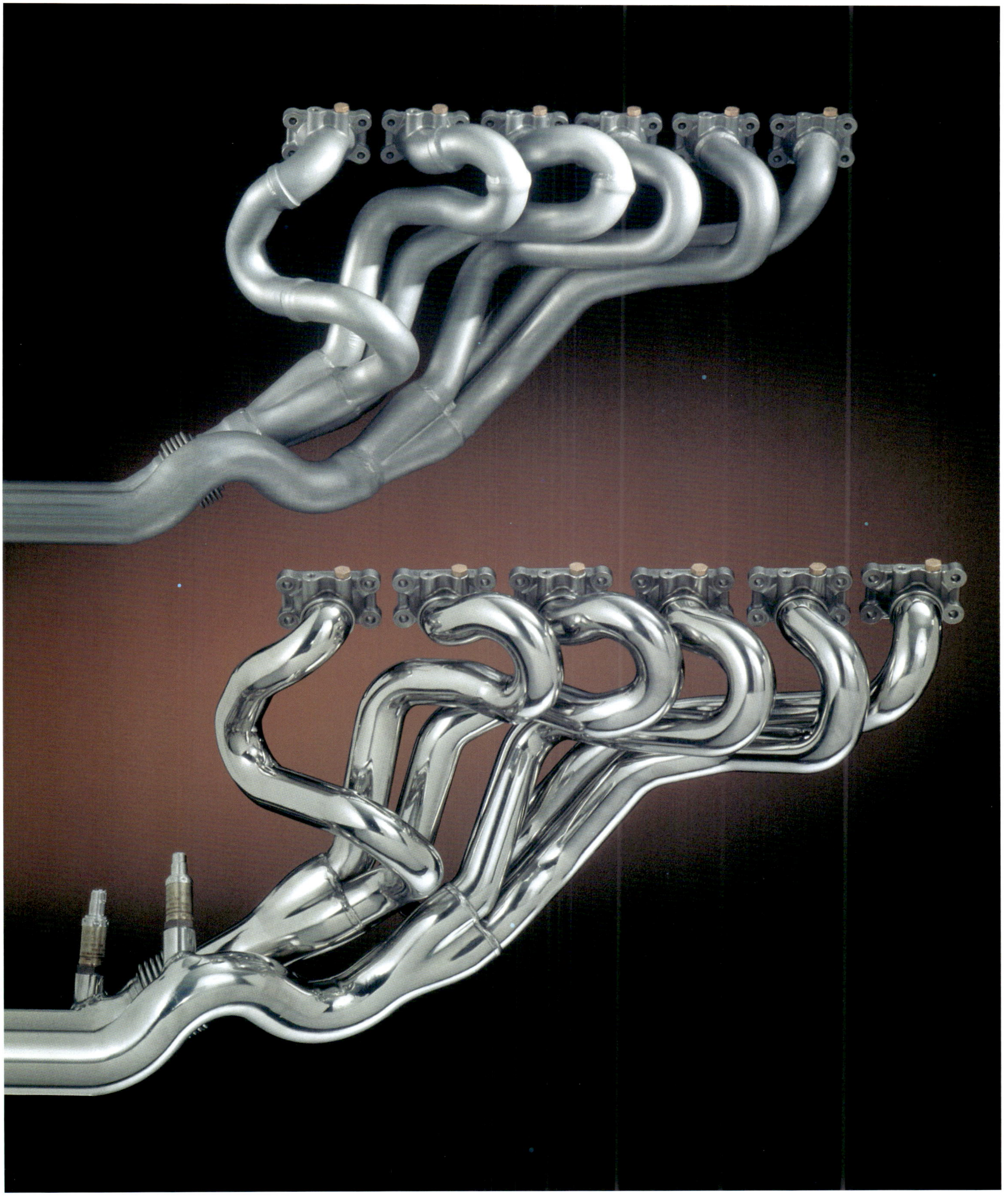

engineering, hydraulic actuators and electronic sensor controls, continually selecting ideal positions for the inlet and exhaust camshafts to take up in their operating cycles at any particular instant. It is worth noting that while the original VANOS installation (that only operated on the inlet camshaft) could vary the timing by up to 40° of rotation, the new Double VANOS installation extended the possible inlet cam adjustment to 62°, while the exhaust camshaft could be rotated by up to 40°.

The main advantage of such an installation, which was entirely automatically operated (for the driver could only affect what was going on by his throttle foot position and use of engine revs at a particular moment), was that it could effectively change the engine from giving a 'supersports' peaky delivery, to one which at once had more lower speed torque, and reduced fuel consumption. BMW claimed that this provided better fuel consumption overall, and reduced exhaust emissions – remarkable for an engine with such a high specific output.

So, how was it done? BMW, for sure, was not about to give away every detail, in case rivals hastened to copy it all, but all the settings of the camshaft timings were decided by the new MSS50 engine management system, the actual rotation of the camshaft into its ideal position being carried out by a mechanism interspersed between the camshaft drive chain, and the camshaft itself. This becomes clearer if one studies the drawing so helpfully provided by BMW (see page 97). A pair of delicately machined pistons, acting under oil pressure of 100 bar (normal atmospheric pressure is 1.0 bar, of course), could rotate each shaft to its desired position in a mere 250 milliseconds.

This leads on logically to the other major innovation on the engine for this car – the new MSS50 engine management system, which BMW claimed was the first-ever 'in-house' system developed by a major car manufacturer. This was not done because BMW was unhappy with its previous major supplier (Bosch): it was all part of a new major product strategy.

In fact, it was not quite as independent a project as might be thought, and could not have been developed by Motorsport alone (for this was a long, technically challenging and complex affair), so Motorsport had cooperated with their own mainstream engineers and with Siemens, whose own electronic expertise was well-proven and well-regarded. To quote from the original claims, this system was said to be capable of issuing up to 20 million instructions per second. Its function was to provide instructions specific to each individual engine cylinder, for there were six individual ignition coils.

All ignition functions, and all anti-knock controls were combined with electronic mapping for the Double VANOS variable camshaft timing (as described above), as well as monitoring engine oil levels, the fuel cut-off for the immobiliser, protection for the well-being of the exhaust catalyst – and it was all said to be self-diagnostic. This, if no other feature, meant that a home-based mechanic could no longer maintain (or, if necessary, repair) a car like the latest E36 M3 model!

## Transmission and suspension changes

All this product action, incidentally, was backed by the introduction of a six-speed all-synchromesh Getrag gearbox, which was an innovation for the M3, although such a six-speed transmission had already been launched in the latest M5 model, and other large-engined 8-Series, 7-Series and 5-Series BMWs. Chronologically, the first six-speed-box BMW had been the V12-engined 850CSi of 1989, but that technology soon spread to other models in the company's range.

Getrag was a specialist company that had been founded at Ludwigsburg (north of Stuttgart), Germany, in 1935. It had grown enormously in the post-war years, and had become BMW's principal supplier of manual gearboxes. In these modern times, of course, six-speed manual transmissions are to be found in scores of different cars, built all round the world, but in the 1990s this type was still considered rare, and exotic. As far as BMW was concerned, the colossal high performance that their modern cars were becoming capable of – and the continued availability of many kilometres of unrestricted autobahns in Germany – meant that they had to find a transmission solution which

**ABOVE: Getrag's sturdy all-synchromesh six-speed gearbox was a feature of the E36 Evolution model – this being a display of the original assembly as already fitted to contemporary M5 types.**

ensured that engines would not overspeed at high road speeds, while at the same time ensuring that the overall gearing was still low enough to allow low-speed transit of traffic-congested towns and cities.

It is fascinating to see how Getrag/BMW had arranged the ratios to be used, and these comparative figures between the original E36 M3 and the E36 Evolution M3 are taken directly from the official specification sheets:

| Model | Gearbox forward internal gear ratios | | | | | | Final drive ratio |
|---|---|---|---|---|---|---|---|
| **E36** | | | | | | | |
| (five-speed) | 4.20 | 2.49 | 1.66 | 1.24 | 1.00 | | 3.15:1 |
| **E36 Evolution** | | | | | | | |
| (six-speed) | 4.23 | 2.51 | 1.67 | 1.23 | 1.00 | 0.83 | 3.23:1 |

Clearly, in going from the five-speed transmission to the six-speeder, the object had been to provide a 'longer' (higher) sixth gear to bring down the engine revs being pulled at normal highway cruising speeds and, please note, there was a small, but definite, difference in the rear axle final drive itself, which had already been seen on the latest M5, and which had a 25% locking factor setting.

While all this mechanical effort was going on, Motorsport had also been allowed to revisit the chassis settings to try to turn this car back, significantly but not dramatically, from what the clientele now saw as the rather 'soft' character of the original E36 M3 towards the character of the E30 model. Naturally (I say 'naturally' as it seemed to be the default go-to solution for all German high-performance car manufacturers of the period) the team had chosen to use the difficult surroundings of the old Nürburgring Nordschleife motor racing circuit where, frankly, improvements in lap times were usually thought to be more significant than improvements in the ride or transient handling abilities of a car.

Changes and refinements were made to both ends of the car – to the MacPherson strut at the front end, and to the multi-link independent rear suspension. These changes were in connection with outright handling improvements, with the characteristics of the latest breed of 17in Michelin Pilot tyres, with other chassis changes (which included a minor reduction of the rear track dimension) and with the adoption of some new-type 8-Series details in the mounting/set-up of the front end. Firmer springs and dampers were adopted, the anti-roll bars were stiffened up and changes were made to the power-assisted steering so that it was 'quicker' in spirited use.

This was not all, for it was also the time to adopt the all-disc brake installation as recently applied to the M5 – the front brakes now using the 'floating disc' principle to help reduce any tendency for the discs to warp prematurely. At the same time, the latest Teves Mk IV anti-lock braking was adopted.

Compared to the extensive work done to the running gear, there were few style updates to the cars, visually or structurally. No changes had been made to the basic shape (the 'sheet metal', as our trans-Atlantic colleagues would say), or to its aerodynamic aids, but the Coupés and Cabriolets were given aluminium door skins, which was claimed to have saved 12kg (26.5lb) from each door assembly. New for 1996, however, were indicator lenses that were not clear, a new high-level third brake light and a grille that was painted matt black instead of being colour-coded as before. Inside the cabin, reflecting BMW's obsession for providing safe machinery, there were now twin air bags.

In a way, the Coupé could still be described as 'hard core', for it had certain features that were not shared with the other types, and was significantly lighter than they were. Cabriolets had the electrically-operated soft-

BELOW: This display model, so typical of the E36, E46 and E90 models, shows how compact was the five-link independent rear suspension fitted to all these cars. Incidentally, normally the fuel tank would be housed ahead of this assembly, wrapped around and over the propeller shaft.

top mechanism provided on other 3-Series Cabriolets of the period, which weighed considerably more, and lacked the specialised M-Sport seats. The Saloon, when it appeared, was seen to retain steel passenger door skins, had electrically-operated rear windows, but did not have the M-tuned suspension.

Although revealed in July 1995, this much-improved M3 did not go on show to the general public until September of the same year, when it was one of the stars of the Frankfurt Motor Show. Production of the original E36 M3 had already ended, and the BMW showrooms were clear, before the first Coupés were produced in October 1995. The four-door Saloon derivative followed almost at once, and the latest Cabriolet completed the line-up in January 1996.

Inevitably, the cars in the new M3 range cost slightly more than those they replaced. On the German home market the increase was about £1,600, while in the UK the line-up in early 1996 was:

| | |
|---|---|
| **M3 Coupé** | £36,550 |
| **M3 Cabriolet** | £41,800 |
| **M3 Saloon** | £36,550 |

Even though the cars had always sold very well (once again I emphasise that they had easily outsold the original E30-generation M3s), BMW – who had seemed to have been slightly puzzled, disappointed and even mildly irritated by the attitude of the motoring media to their original E36 – were anxious to know what would be thought of the new type.

They need not have worried, for it was as if a magic wand had been waved! The sporting character (supposedly hidden from 1992 to 1995) had come rushing back with a vengeance, and the latest M3 was dubbed the quickest BMW road car yet put on sale. With the ability to sprint up to 60mph in little more than 5sec, to 100mph in no more than 13sec, and with a top speed most firmly limited (electronically) to 155mph, it was only the M1, which had been an ultra-special type of BMW 'road car', that could still out-rank it.

ABOVE: In the cabin of the E36 Evolution model, the only indication the driver got of a new Getrag transmission was the marking of six forward speeds on the gear shift knob.

Road testers did not bother to compare the latest car with any other high-performance saloon, but instead chose to discuss rivals like the latest Ferraris. In terms of the quality of construction, and the equipment offered as standard on the M3, they found that Munich's finest was now sitting proudly on top of the heap. To quote just one highly-experienced writer: 'It is devastatingly quick, point to point, certainly, and undoubtedly more enjoyable to drive than the previous iteration. That lofty sixth gear, the greatly improved high-speed stability and towering through-the-gears performance are beyond question....'

This author's own personal experience – not in an M3, but (if you understand me) fighting against it – confirms all this. Over in Germany in the late 1990s, I was sometimes bustling along a derestricted autobahn at speeds that would have seen me thrown into prison in the UK, and had cause, on several occasions, to give battle with the latest M3s. The car I was in? Let's just say that it had a rear-mounted engine, and it could not get away from BMW's best.

RIGHT: This was the
sturdy SMG (Sequential
Manual Gearbox) gear
lever, available as an
option on M3s from 1996
in Europe and from 1998
in the UK. As explained
in the text, there were
three possible modes,
manual, semi-manual
and automatic – this
installation being built
around a six-speed
Getrag manual gearbox,
but with a mass of
electronic controls.

## Change and improvement

Once the latest E36 types were on sale, M-Sport
kept on working at ways of making them even
better. USA deliveries began in 1996 and, as
happened so often in that period of automotive
history, the engine had its own unique specification.
Although the engine size had been increased to 3.2
litres, the peak power was still pegged at no more
than 240bhp (at 6,000rpm), and because the open-
road speed limits were so fiercely policed in that
vast nation, BMW retained the old-type five-speed
transmission: the electronically-limited top speed
remaining at 139mph in this case. Coupés were
available from 1996 onward, with Saloons added in
1997, and Cabriolets in 1998.

The first major upgrade of the European-
specification cars then followed in the summer
of 1996, when an optional Sequential Manual
Gearbox (SMG) was put on sale, originally only
on left-hand-drive cars, at the stirringly ambitious
(Sterling-equivalent) price of £2,500. BMW (and
Getrag, which provided the assembly) made much
of the fact that this was a sophisticated upgrade
of a manual transmission, and retained a normal

single-plate clutch, rather than the quasi-automatic/
torque converter assembly being offered by some
rivals. Accordingly, they insisted, this was far
sportier in feel and delivery, and could give owners
the same feel as the racing drivers who had first
experienced such a change in recent years. Apart
from the extra cost involved, the only apparent
downside of this installation was that it all weighed
18kg (40lb) more than the conventional manual
transmission.

BELOW: This was the
linkage, and hydraulic
circuitry, of the original
SMG transmission,
available as an option on
the M3 from 1996.

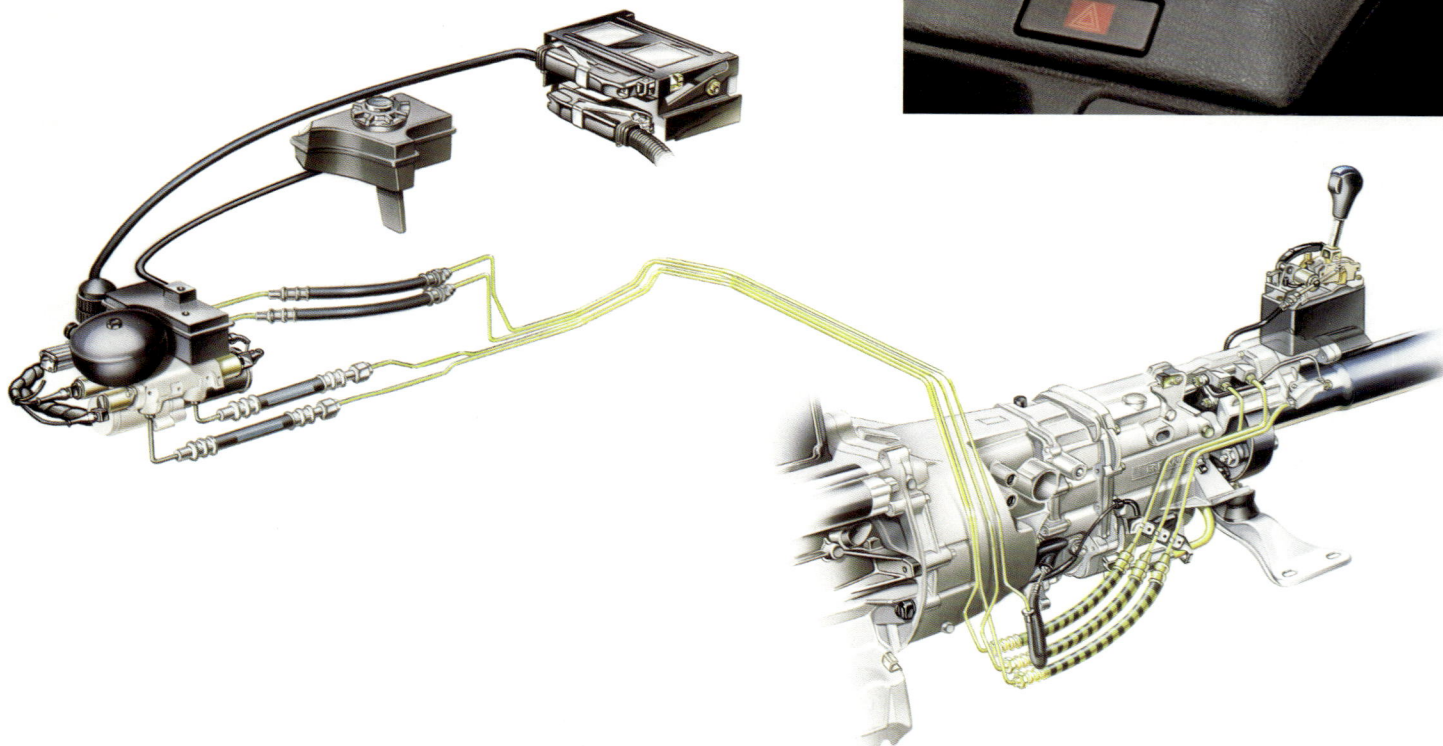

[It was important to make this clear, BMW insisted, because on larger and less sporting BMWs of the day – certain V8-engined versions of 5-Series and 7-Series models, for instance – there was a 'Steptronic' transmission alternative, but that was based on a fully automatic transmission, and was provided by ZF!]

The SMG installation featured computer-controlled changes, which did away with a conventional clutch pedal, and the gearbox interior ratios were those of the normal M3 manual gearbox. The system allowed for two programmes to be employed – one was a fully-automatic E (for Economy) mode, the other being a 'manual' S (for Sport) mode. These could be selected via a control/gear lever that was in the conventional place on the centre console, and the operation of which was in two planes.

By pushing the lever across to the right (i.e. remote from the driver of a left-hand-drive car), the 'E' mode was engaged, and by pulling across to the left, the S mode took over. Simple plus or minus signs indicated upward or downward changes. When 'S' mode was selected, and the driver

pushed (forward for a down-change) or pulled (rearwards for an upward change) a gear-change was instantaneously made, with the computer looking after clutch disengagement, rev-matching and engagement once again, there being no need for the driver to feather the throttle pedal in any way. BMW claimed that 'instantaneous' actually meant 250 milliseconds, and noted that there was a safeguard against over-revving in any case.

In a typically painstaking way, BMW and Getrag had been working on such a piece of kit for some years before it was made available, and all were at pains to emphasise that it was meant to make the car better and more pleasurable to drive, rather than any faster, which it most assuredly was not.

In a way, they had tried to think of everything before unleashing it on the public. Sequential automatically engaged first gear whenever the car came to a standstill, selected the appropriate gear after emergency braking had taken place, and automatically applied engine braking in slippery conditions. There was a 'winter' auto mode which ensured, too, that the standing start was made in second gear, and the electronic brain behind all this

ABOVE: This ghosted cutaway drawing shows just how comprehensive the fitment of the SMG transmission option actually was to the E36 Evolution chassis.

RIGHT: Hidden away
from the driver, of
course, the gear change
lever on the original
SMG (Sequential Manual
Gearbox) was a complex
piece of kit.

would not allow a down-change if it calculated that this would otherwise over-rev the engine as a result.

In other words, this took much of the decision making, and quite a bit of risk, out of the hands of the driver – for the 'leave it all to me' syndrome was well and truly evident at all times. But it was an approach to selling cars (to selling M3s in particular), which clearly worked. In 1993 (the first year the E36 M3 was on sale) 6,712 had been sold, followed by 10,764 in 1994, 11,964 in 1995, and now 11,789 in 1996. The only rival whose sales even approached those levels was another German brand (Porsche), and they sold nothing else. For them, it was their hard-grafted bread-and-butter, while for BMW the M3 was a magnificent gilt-on-the-gingerbread extra. No one, particularly the shareholders of BMW AG, was complaining about that.

By 1998, however, the Evolution derivative of the E36 M3 was what the aviation industry calls a 'mature product' – which meant that although it was still state-of-the-[automotive] art in many ways, BMW no longer had any significant plans to make major changes to the specification. Bearing in mind that the launch of M-for-Motorsport models

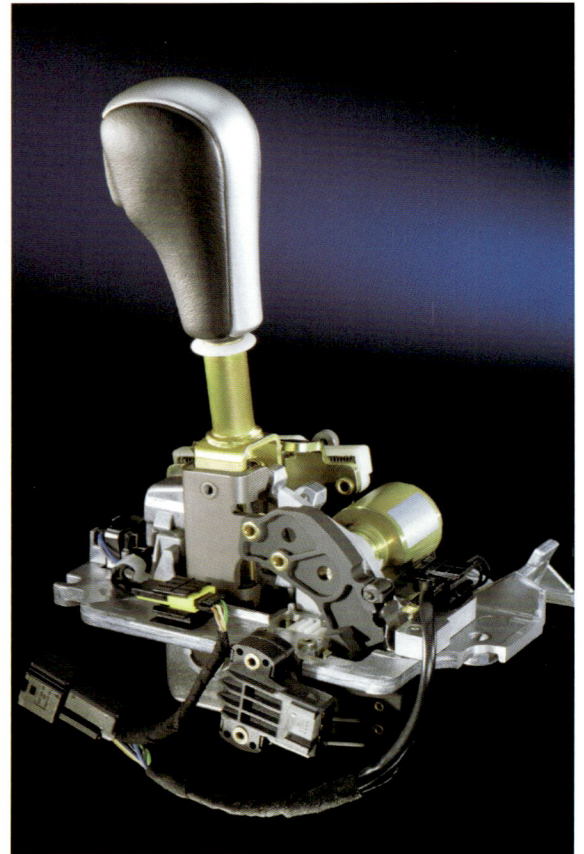

RIGHT: When the SMG
gearbox option was
specified in 1996, this
was the engineering
detail of the main
gearbox and change
linkage.

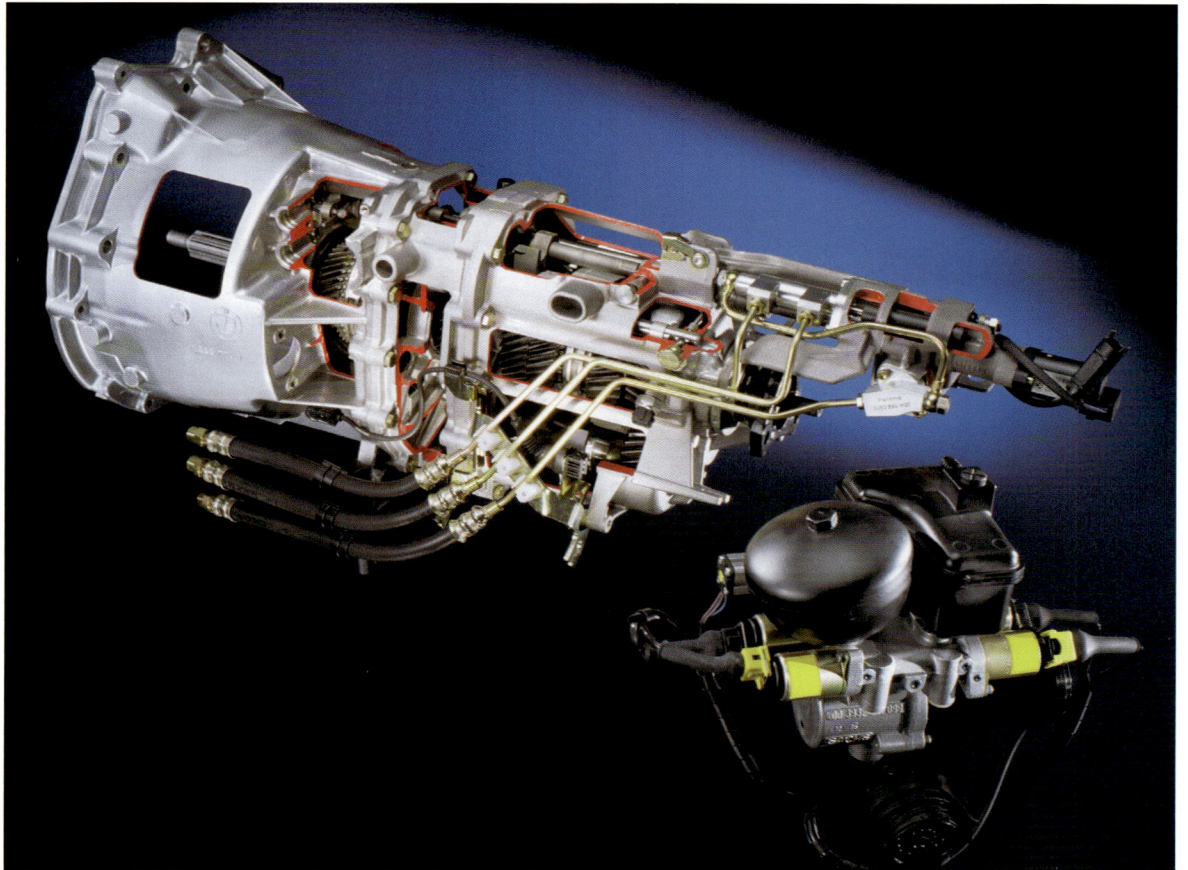

always lagged behind that of the mainstream version, the miracle was that it still sold so well even after the next-generation (E46, that is) 3-Series was previewed.

By the end of 1997, the Saloon version of the E36-type M3 had been discontinued, yet the introduction of the SMG version for the UK market was held back until January 1998, just days before the mainstream E46 type made its appearance. Once this was done, and after BMW GB set an ambitious premium of £1,735 (resulting in a total retail price of £40,155 for the SMG-equipped M3 Coupé), the company could remind everyone that it had technology of a type almost identical to that offered on a Ferrari F355 F1. It was very popular with European buyers (more than half of whom were choosing SMG rather than a 'normal' manual gear change) and there seemed to be no loss of outright performance.

Independent road tests showed that, although the SMG installation still had some rough edges (the change quality was not yet as smooth as some testers – or even BMW if the truth be told – would wish), it did not turn this car's performance into anything less than astonishing. No one, for sure, was going to complain about 0–60mph sprint times of 5.3sec, or 0–100mph in 12.9sec, nor of the (electronically-limited) top speed of 155mph, especially as that was also matched by 155mph in fifth gear, an amazing 138mph in fourth, and no less than 102mph in third.

BMW, however, were slightly disappointed by the media's reaction to the SMG installation, for *Autocar*'s report on the system was so typical of many: 'Worse still is the way the SMG operates in either of its two auto modes. Gear changes occur reasonably smoothly on light throttle openings (although still nowhere near as smoothly as they do in a regular auto), but on half-throttle openings they are irritatingly jerky, and seem to happen at different revs from one minute to the next, again a result of the gearbox trying to learn the habits of its driver....'

In all other respects, though, this iteration of the M3 was as outstanding as any M3 had ever been, in that it offered a seductive combination of superb performance, ride, handling, braking, comfort and equipment, which was not offered by its so-called rivals.

For the E36 series, however, the end was now in sight, as the introductory remarks in the next chapter make clear. A new-generation 3-Series – the E46 type – was officially unveiled in February 1998, with the M3 derivative of that car to follow in due course.

All in all, the second-generation E36 (plus E36 Evolution) M3 had enjoyed a stellar career by that time, as these production totals clearly show:

| | | |
|---|---|---|
| **Coupé** | 46,525 | Last built in April 1999 |
| **Cabriolet** | 12,114 | Last built in September 1999 |
| **Saloon** | 12,435 | Last built in May 1998 |
| Total | 69,194 | |

The effort put in to making all these cars suitable for sale in North America had also paid off, and handsomely. Even though the North American version was by no means as fast as the European-market type, USA buyers had purchased 18,961 Ccupés, 7,760 Saloons and 6,211 Convertibles (32,932 in all), which represented nearly half of the sum total of all E36 Evos produced.

But it was now time to move on, and the next type of M3 (the E46 variety) duly appeared in September 1999.

## Second-generation M3 (E36 type) production figures

Starting in 1992, the following numbers of M3s were built:

| | 2-door Coupés | 4-door Saloons | Cabriolets |
|---|---|---|---|
| 1992 | 470 (+50 CKD) | – | - |
| 1993 | 6,080 (+632 CKD) | – | 3 |
| 1994 | 9,289 (+66 CKD) | 288 | 1,118 |
| 1995 | 9,828 | 1,282 | 860 |
| 1996 | 6,896 | 3,639 | 1,248 |
| 1997 | 5,873 | 4,740 | 1,135 |
| 1998 | 4,422 | 2,486 | 4,682 |
| 1999 | 2,919 | – | 3,068 |
| **Totals** | **46,525** | **12,435** | **12,114** |

*According to the records, the CKD cars were sent out to South Africa, for assembly there, and for sale in that country.*

## Chapter 5

# E46 range –
## refining a great formula, 2000–2006

From 1998, the existing M3 (the E36 Evolution type) began to live on borrowed time, for an all-new 3-Series range, internally known as the E46, had been officially previewed in February of that year, and would go on sale in the autumn of the same year. Styled under the direction of BMW's controversial Chris Bangle and, as ever, intended to make up at least 50 per cent of BMW's expanding production facilities, it was at once very similar to, but different in almost every detail from the E36 that it replaced.

Some years ago, a renowned top man from a rival car-producing concern was heard to say that he never consulted his dealer chain about the features to be fitted to a replacement model 'because all they ask for is more of the same' – in other words they tended to be interested in evolution, rather than revolution. BMW, for sure, did not follow the same philosophy, as each succeeding 3-Series (and accordingly, each M3 model) now seemed to be recognisably developed from the previous type.

But why not, as commercially this seemed to work? Even in 1998, BMW was already selling close to 400,000 3-Series cars (of all types) in every calendar year, and was building them at various sites in Germany (principally at Munich and Regensburg), in South Africa and (to get the new plant up, running and humming) in South Carolina, USA, which was now the home of the Z3 sports

car. Plans were already laid to make and sell even more in the 2000s.

BMW, however, has never made it simple for historians (or enthusiasts) to trace pedigrees and trends, for the original mainstream E46 was first launched only as a four-door Saloon. At the same time, the balance of the 'old' E36 family – Touring, Coupé, Cabriolet and short-wheelbase Compact – continued in full-scale production, and would sell in considerable numbers for the next two years. There was no immediate sign of the arrival of an E46-based M3 – nor would there be for a couple of years.

Except that the E46 as a whole played 'mix-and-match' with the existing, but ever-improving, range of engines – four- and six-cylinder, petrol and diesel, normally-aspirated and turbocharged – the rest of the car was entirely new, and this would have a central effect on the M3 derivative which followed. Based on a totally new steel platform, it was larger than the E36 in every way, and intended to be even more versatile in what it offered. And for why? BMW explained that they had packaging, visual design, engineering and crash safety requirements in mind, and that some versions would have no fewer than eight air bags installed.

As a consequence (and because almost every new car ever made, by whatever company, tends to be slightly larger and more roomy than the range it replaces), it had a 25mm (1.0in) longer

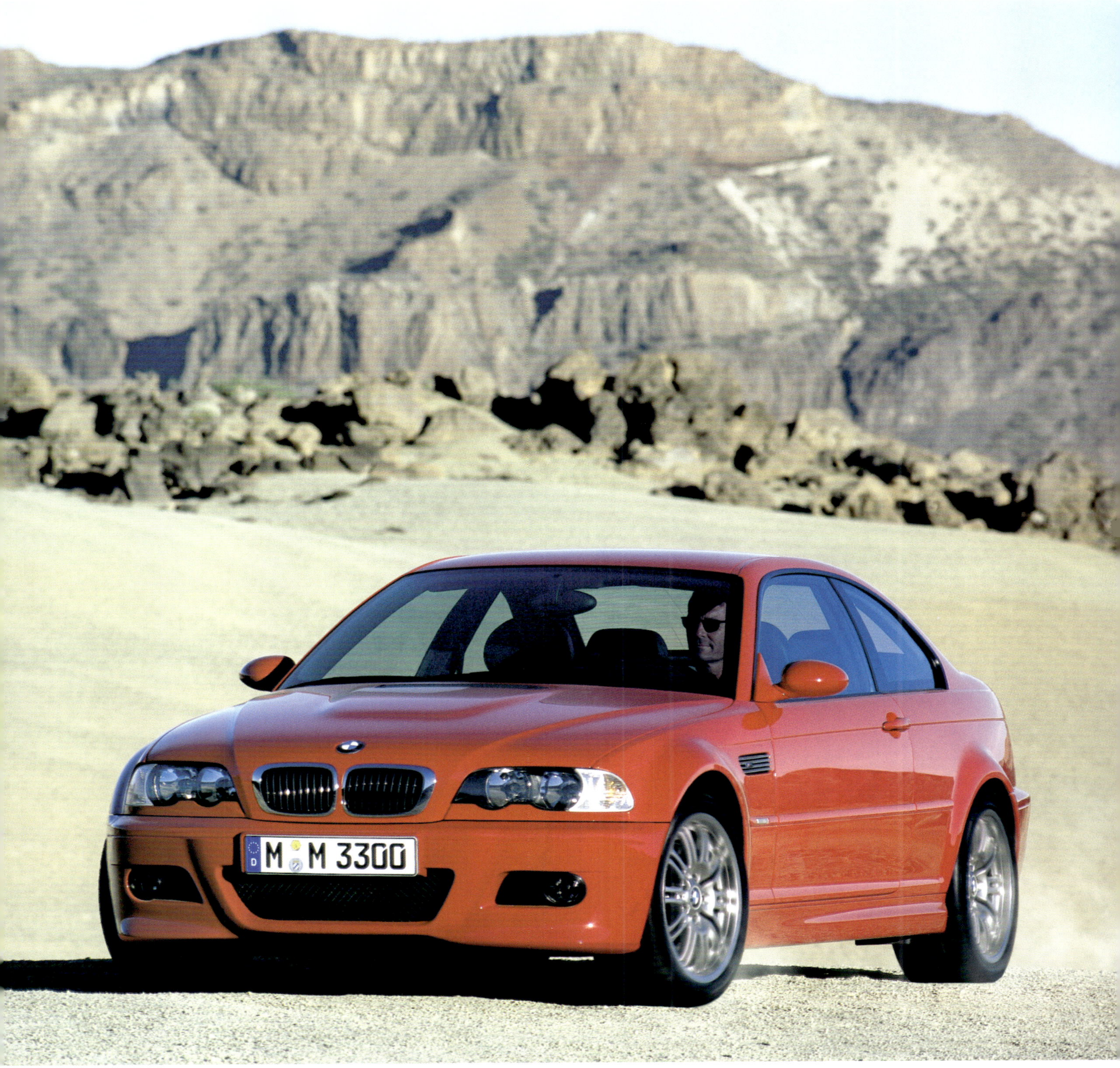
M M 3300

**ABOVE: In 2000, BMW was proud to issue this 'ghosted' cutaway of the E46 M3 in Coupé form, which illustrated why a domed bonnet style was needed to accommodate the vast air cleaner of the mighty engine. Apart from the body-shell itself, the Convertible would have the same basic layout.**

**PREVIOUS PAGES: This was the original type of E46 put on sale in 2000, based around the longer and wider platform of the latest series of 3-Series. Love that registration number!**

wheelbase, wider tracks (by 63mm (2.5in) at the front and 57mm (2.25in) at the rear), was 41mm (1.6in) wider, 38mm (1.5in) longer, and (in Saloon form at least) 23mm (0.9in) taller. BMW also claimed that the new car even had a slighter better drag coefficient than before.

All of this was just a taster of what was to follow, for the Coupé version was not scheduled to go on sale until 1999, and the Cabriolet and Tourer types even later than that. In the meantime, Motorsport got on with the development and completion of new-generation M3 prototypes – and in those days of spy cameras (and BMW's fixation with trying out the new developments at the Nürburgring from their dedicated test centre) it was not long before the first images were seen in the media.

Even in mid-1998, an impressive number of technical details had somehow leaked out, and some of the more excitable rumours had already been quashed. 'They' said that there had been a proposal to use V8 engines (yet the company's

existing V8 was really too bulky, and too heavy, to be used in a 3-Series shell), while some thought that the six-cylinder engine would be increased to 3.4 litres, which was quite impractical because of the limits on cylinder bore which had already been approached.

Pre-launch teaser then followed teaser, not least following the launch of the 3-Series E46 Coupé in February 1999, on which the next-generation M3 seemed certain to be based. Although BMW was still not saying anything, officially at least, about the forthcoming M3, the company made it very clear that although it shared the same platform as the E46 Saloon, the Coupé (whose profiles, if not its detail engineering, would be carried forward for the next-generation M3) had an entirely unique body superstructure, with no important panels being shared. It was 46mm (1.8in) lower than the Saloon, the screen was raked by an extra 2°, and the suspension settings had yet again been reworked. Although 16in road wheels were standard, there was an option of 17in, or even 18in, wheels – which gave a hint as to how the eventual M3 specification would settle down.

With the mainstream E46 Coupé securely launched, it would surely not be long before the appearance of the next generation M3, and this appearance duly came (rather prematurely, as it turned out) at the Frankfurt Show in September 1999. Work had begun in 1996, the main battle having been to keep the weight of the new car down as much as possible (it was a losing battle), one result of which being that it was decided to produce the new M3 with aluminium doors, bonnet panel and boot lid. However, it was not until February 2000 that BMW was ready to show off the car in detail.

Originally available only as a two-door Coupé, in detail it was to be so very different from the mainstream E46 Coupé on which it was based. The two structures might have been the same, but the detail, and the intended function, of the two types were widely different. Visually, and by comparison with the E36 variety that it succeeded, the structure of the new car was at once more specialised and more 'visible' than the mainstream variety. In the words of BMW publicists, the new car looked much more 'aggressive' than before.

The new 'aggression' shone out from every aspect. At the front there was a deep spoiler that included a large central air scoop to channel air to the engine's water radiator, which was shielded by black mesh. The central scoop was flanked on either side by vents (surrounding the driving lamps), which channelled air to the big front disc brakes. Above (and this had been made economically possible by the decision to use light-alloy skin panels) there was a noticeable dome, or bulge, in the bonnet panel, the intent of which was to allow more air to circulate around the inlet side of the highly-tuned six-cylinder engine.

Along the flanks, both the under-door sills and the rear-view door mirrors had received attention from the stylists, but much the most obvious detail features were the uniquely-styled alloy wheels (which had ten 'double' spokes), the inclusion of flared front and rear wheel arches, and the cooling vents in the front wings, which were positioned above and behind the front wheel-arch cut-outs.

**BELOW:** This depiction of the rolling chassis of the E46 M3 of 2000 shows that the entire 'chassis' was packed with running gear, such that the fuel tank had to be located low down and ahead of the rear suspension, and the exhaust silencer draped across the tail with four separate outlets.

All were strictly functional – the flared arches being specified to allow for the massive 18in wheels and tyres to be fitted without hindrance, and the vents to aid the air flow through the crowded engine bay. By comparison, the rear end looked positively restrained, though the rear 'bumper' was a massive composite moulding, and the four exhaust outlets (which emanated from the vast transversely-positioned silencer box) told their own story.

Since this was a car that was going to sell (in the UK, at least) for the equivalent of £40,000 and more, the comprehensive high level of interior trim, fixtures and fittings was only to be expected; this car now being a long way, both in terms of time (14 years) and in aspiration, from the original E30 M3 of 1986. For the new E46 the customer expected, and got, a choice of interior trim levels, electrically-adjustable figure-hugging front seats (which were closely related to those fitted to the latest M5 model), and a full range of instruments. In addition, there was a full complement of air bags ahead and to each side of the passengers, air conditioning, satellite navigation, a trip/economy computer, and cruise control, all in the standard specification.

Technically, the important news – or, as it transpired, the non-news – was in the running gear, for apart from further tune-up work on the famous six-cylinder engine, the installation was still very much unchanged. Before the E46 M3 was introduced, and even at official preview time in September 1999, there had been those wild rumours (already mentioned) that the engine was to be increased in size to 3.4 litres, and even that a new type of V8 engine installation was being considered. The facts were more mundane that that.

In February 2000, Adolf Prommesberger, who was then head of BMW's M Division, admitted: 'We studied the V8 for the M3. In fact, we got as far as constructing prototypes. In the end we decided to stick with the six. It wasn't the cheapest route, but the correct one.'

But where did stories of a 200cc enlargement of the six-cylinder engine come from when, as already described in Chapter 4, this was never going to be practical? Even when the E46 M3 car was rather prematurely revealed in September 1999 (but without technical details being ratified), a company spokesman seems to have confirmed this enlargement and stated: 'We've gone about as far as we can go. The spacing between the cylinders is such that we'd have to alter the architecture if we wanted to go higher.'

Which was at once true, or – shall we say

BELOW: Launched in 2000, the E46 iteration of the M3 used an entirely new body-shell, and was fitted with many light-alloy panels. This side view shows off the identifying details, including the discreet vents to the engine bay, positioned behind the front wheel arches.

– economical with the truth of what had actually been considered, and then actually done. A simple calculation shows that if the already long stroke of the engine was to be retained (and, let us not forget, that making it longer would perhaps have affected the high-revving qualities of the existing power unit), new bore dimensions of 89mm would have been needed to deliver the 200cc increase (actually to 3,397cc). And, since the distance between bore centres was only an absolutely immovable 91mm, which was surely never practical, as the cylinder walls would have been too thin. At this time BMW made it very clear that there could never be any further enlargements, not even for 'homologation special' motorsport requirements, and that reboring was quite out of the question.

What actually happened is that the engineers looked, looked again, tested, and firmly crossed their fingers before deciding to use a bore dimension of 87mm, which was just 0.6mm more

ABOVE: E46 in action and, incidentally, showing off the new-style 18in ten-double-spoke alloy road wheels. To aid traction, the rear rims were one whole inch wider than the fronts.

**ABOVE:** This cutaway of the 3.2-litre engine, dated 2000, shows that the cylinder bores were all 'Siamesed', and that there was no way that any further bore expansion could take place. Even so, for the M3s of the late 1990s and early 2000s, this was a phenomenal power unit.

than it had been on the previous M3. That increase provided an extra 44cc; the resulting swept volume being 3,245cc – the absolute limit that could be entertained.

Much work, on the other hand, had been done on all detail aspects of this remarkable engine, which retained its cast-iron cylinder block, its Double VANOS monitoring of the twin overhead camshafts, and the exquisite production detailing of an engine that could soar up to 8,000rpm. Attention had been given to cylinder block and cylinder head cooling, the Double VANOS installation itself had received roller bearings, and there was the possibility of even more overlap between the inlet and exhaust valve timings. Although the architecture was as before, BMW made claims that very few actual components were carried over from the earlier 3,201cc engine:

it is interesting to learn that BMW even dabbled with the idea of saving yet more weight by using a magnesium-alloy cylinder block, before deciding to play safe and use a cast-iron block as before.

An all-new in-house-developed MSS54 digital engine management system took over, which also incorporated ETBC (Electronic Throttle Butterfly Control), which was a new control system already developed for the M5, this being an electronic layout which could instantly re-map the drive-by-wire throttle linkage. MSS54, incidentally, was claimed to be able to make 20 million (and that is no misprint) decisions every second, and was definitely the most sophisticated of this type in use on a road-car installation.

For comparison, therefore, this is how the latest engine compared with the formidable former engine of the E36 Evolution model:

ABOVE AND LEFT: The E46 M3 might have been a tyre-stripping extrovert, but BMW saw no point in making it uncomfortable to drive. This was the well-equipped and carefully detailed cabin and instrument display.

ABOVE: The six-cylinder used in the E46 was positively the last enlargement possible for this amazing power unit. As released in 2000, it produced a sturdy 343bhp from 3,245cc.

| Model | Engine size (cc) | Peak power (bhp at rpm) | Peak torque (lb ft at rpm) |
|---|---|---|---|
| M3 E36 Evolution | 3,201 | 321/7,400 | 258/3,250 |
| E46 | 3,245 | 343/7,900 | 269/4,900 |

… and if this was indeed to be the final fling, it was a magnificent way for the pedigree of the 'six' to reach its peak.

Although there was no such sequence of innovation in the transmission – the E46 used the same basic six-speed Getrag gearbox that had already featured in the E36 Evolution (fifth ratio being the direct ratio, and sixth being, effectively, the 'overdrive') – the rear differential now incorporated an electronically-controlled lock-up/limited-slip action to optimise traction in all conditions, this having been developed by the British company, GKN.

What was interesting at this stage was that BMW made so little mention of a high-priced SMG (sequential change) option, for customer reaction to the original system offered on E36 Evolution cars had been somewhat mixed. BMW, to their credit, admitted that they were not totally happy with this installation and had taken the system back behind closed doors to carry out more development work. It was due to return, for sure, but not for a while yet.

BMW boasted that during development they had carried out no less than 60,000 miles (100,000km) of fast development driving around the Nürburgring's famous Nordschleife circuit, and had progressively changed, improved, or idealised the basic E46 suspension and steering so that very few standard parts remained. They were determined, it seems, to make this car better than any of its predecessors, and better – they insisted – than any other BMW.

The fact that the E46 'chassis' platform was distinctly larger than that of the E36 gave the team every chance to make this handle even better than any previous M3 had done. Not only were 18in road wheels standardised, but also the rear driven wheels had 9in width rims and 255/40-section Michelin Pilot Sport or Continental Sport Contact tyres (which were considerably larger than the front – 225/45 and 8in rims). Spring, damper and anti-roll bar settings were all specially developed, and not shared with other types, while the whole car had been lowered by 15mm (0.6in).

To match this, the new car had massive floating and ventilated disc brakes at front and rear, which were allied to an ABS anti-lock mechanism. Not only that, but the same delicately engineered wheel sensors were used to actuate the ASR

BELOW: M3 enthusiasts readily identified the E46 from any angle, especially from the three-quarter front end, where the extrovert spoiler and the front wing vents were all visible.

traction control, and the DSC III dynamic stability control. This combination arranged not only for the maximum possible traction and braking, but balance in all road conditions – and could even apply a little selective braking control if it detected any incipient oversteer. Frustrating for the ultra-keen extrovert driver, who might want to take his new M3 on track days? Just in case, BMW had thoughtfully provided a switch that could disable this kit!

Here was a new car which retained the same proportions as the now obsolete E36 type, but one which looked even more purpose-built, and even more menacingly fast than before; this being precisely what the designers and planners had hoped. Even with the massive 18in wheels, and with the flared arches, which added 20mm (0.8in) to the width of the machine, it could still be built on

the same assembly lines at Regensburg as other E46-generation 3-Series models.

Even by BMW standards, however, it took time to get the car finally ready for sale and, for instance, to build up adequate supplies of special items, such as the unique light-alloy body panels, and the unique wide-rim wheels. In fact, final work on the production lines at Regensburg was completed during the summer 'shut-down' (holiday) period, and the new car went on sale in Germany in October 2000 at a price equivalent to a UK level of £32,250.

In the meantime, the Convertible version of the E46 M3 finally broke cover, with all technical details being publicised in November 2000, and with first deliveries promised for the spring of 2001. At the same time it emerged that there would not be a four-door saloon version of this particular M3, so

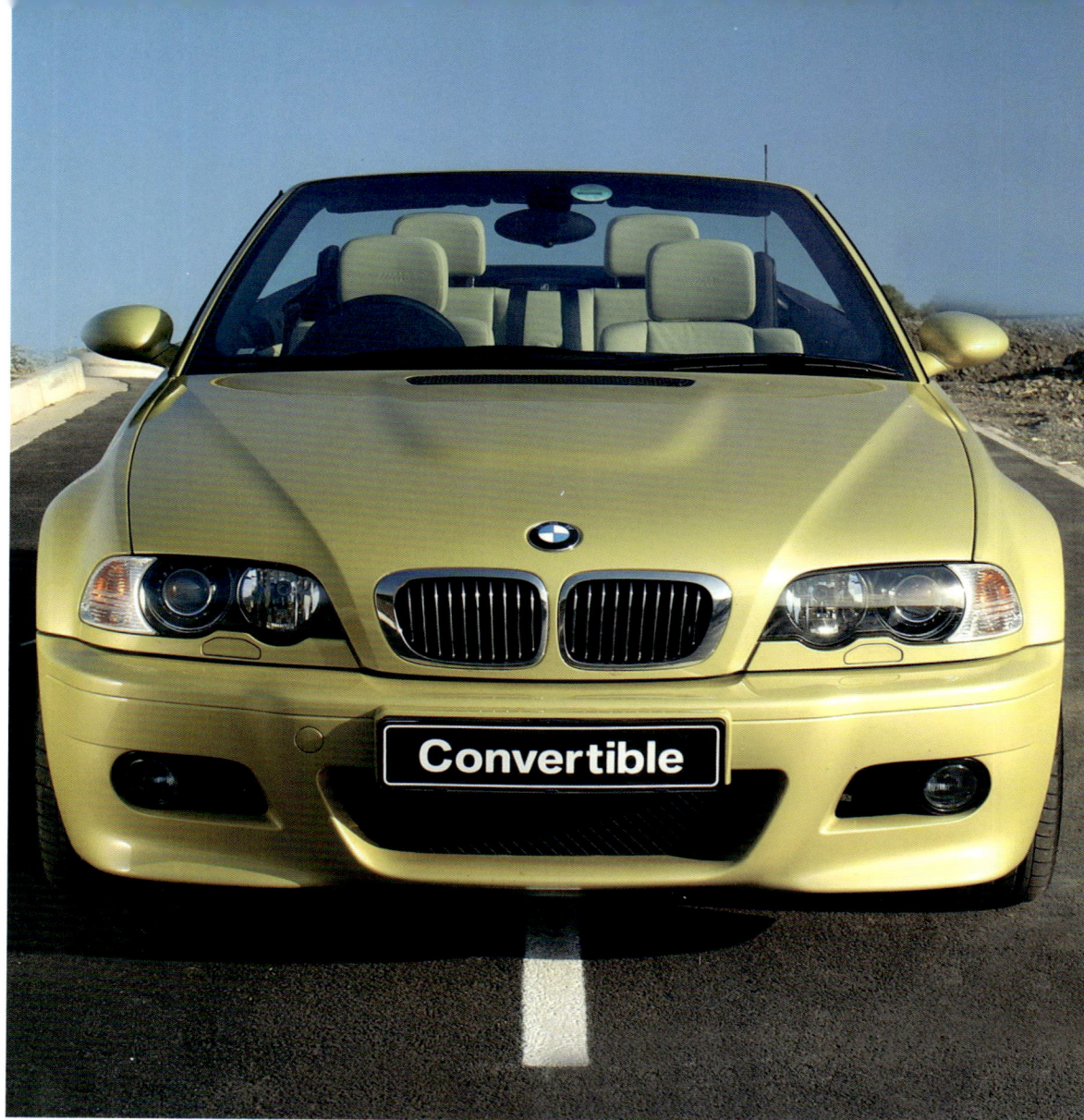

the range was already complete, with just two body styles.

Although the new Convertible was mechanically almost identical to the E46 M3, it was expected to cost quite substantially more. Compared with the mainstream E46 Convertible, which was already in production and on sale, the already stiffened body-shell was made yet more robust in M3 form by having extra beams welded in within the sills, and across the floor-pan. Unavoidably this meant that there would be a weight penalty – the Convertible being estimated to weigh up to 150kg (330lb) more than the Coupé.

Visually, the new Convertible took on all the special features already seen on the Coupé – front and rear spoilers, domed bonnet panel, flared front and rear wheel arches, vents in the front wings, along with the electro-hydraulically operated soft

top, which was moved by pressing just a single button on the fascia.

Compared with the previous E36 generation, the cars intended for sale in the North American market were much more powerful, and therefore much faster, than before. This improvement was achieved as a result of much development work, which included a complete revamping of the exhaust system, and particularly of the placement of close-coupled catalytic converters near to the engine exhaust manifold itself. Whereas the 1998/1999 E36 models had engines with 321bhp (European spec.) and a mere 240bhp (USA spec.) for 2001 the Euro-spec. E46 cars had 343bhp, which this time was followed closely by American-spec. cars with 333bhp. For all markets, therefore, BMW applied electronic controls to limit top speeds to 155mph, though they openly admitted

LEFT: From the rear end, the E46 Convertible showed off the same special rear bumper moulding and, of course, the four exhaust outlets.

that if such devices were not fitted, then the cars could have reached 180mph in complete safety and comfort!

By almost any standard, therefore, the E46 seemed to be a significantly better car than the best of the E36s had ever been. Once the first UK-market cars arrived they sold for £38,500. The queues built up, and when the motoring press got their hands on cars they positively salivated about the performance and character of the new machines.

Once again with grateful thanks to my good friends on *Autocar* magazine, I can confirm that almost every red-blooded journo was bowled over by the new car. In their Twin Test of 2001 (which compared the E46 M3 with a Mercedes-Benz C32 AMG V6 Kompressor), extracts from their fulsome words include: 'We already respect the new BMW M3 as the greatest M car to date…. Although being noted for their engineering excellence, the M3 is a timely reminder of how well the M boys can tweak a car's looks. Deeply dished, gunmetal-finished 18in alloy wheels, aggressive bumpers and sill extensions and – crucially – flared arches distance the M3 from any other 3-Series….'

The performance, too, was quite remarkable. Limiting the top speed to 155mph was, of course, just a nod towards the noisy environmentalists throughout Europe, though there must have been some slight tolerance in electronic settings, as this road test recorded 160mph. Nothing, however, could detract from the 157mph attainable in fifth gear, 139mph in fourth and 102mph in third. The acceleration figures of 0–60mph in 4.8sec, 0–100mph in 11.5sec, and a standing start quarter-mile sprint in 13.4sec, are jaw-dropping examples.

Handling, braking and general fast road behaviour were all deemed impeccable, and the complete package was found to be superior to that of the Mercedes-Benz model that cost at least £7,000 more, while the general build quality was much preferred. And, in summary: 'The M3 is an enormous achievement for BMW, a company that has been berated for moving away from its core sporting brand identity of late…. The M3 is a dynamic masterpiece: its engine is among the best ever made, and its chassis capable and entertaining in equal measures…. The M3 is a landmark sports coupé.'

Was it any wonder that sales continued to surge ahead in every market, from its home territory in Germany to North America, and especially in performance-mad countries like our own?

## Variations

Early in 2001, and to everyone's astonishment, BMW admitted that they were developing a 4-litre V8-engined version of the new E46 M3. But before customers could get too overexcited, they also made it clear that this would be a strictly limited-edition (*very* limited, as it transpired) derivative of the Coupé, and that it was intended to be raced in the American Le Mans Series (ALMS) of 2001, when the cars were entered and campaigned by Schnitzer Motorsport. More details of this programme are included in Chapter 7.

At this point it is only appropriate to relate that this particular car was known as the M3 GTR, and was powered by a 493bhp, 3,997cc V8 engine – a prototype unit which had no connection with the V8s already being used in 5-Series and 7-Series models. Although it was highly successful in sport in 2001, this car's prospects were well and truly damaged when the organising body pointed out that its rules stated that such cars (even in de-tuned form) had to be sold in two continents within 12 months.

To get round this rule, BMW decided to sell ten (ten, not 10,000, you understand) such road cars at the end of the season, all of them with left-hand drive, and the race engine would be de-tuned from 450bhp, but would retain its dry sump lubrication, and would still be backed by a six-speed gearbox. For 'road' use, the engine would be rated at

350bhp at 7,250rpm, with peak torque of 269lb ft at 5,000 rpm (which still sounded very 'racy' indeed).

Not only this, but even the road car was due to have a lightweight carbon-fibre reinforced plastic roof, front and rear spoilers, along with even more use of aluminium in the suspension component links. The roof was to be unpainted, there would be four large additional cooling slots in the bonnet panel, carbon trim on the fascia, and lightweight bucket driving seats. Even so, and in spite of their undoubted exclusivity, at a price of 250,000 Euros each ($218,000) the demand was non-existent. When the ALMS rules for 2002 were then issued, stating that 100 cars and 1,000 engines had to be built for a car to qualify, BMW withdrew from that category of motorsport, and the M3 GTR's one-year career was effectively over.

During 2001 the reappearance of the SMG (Sequential Manual Gearbox), now to be known as SMGII, as an option for the new E46, was commercially much more important, and – as it transpired – much more successful than the original. The first SMG installation, frankly, was not as good as the customers would have hoped, and BMW had certainly not been satisfied, which explains why it had not reappeared when the E46 M3 was launched.

Much development (and much input both from Getrag and from Sachs) had taken place in the intervening period. When it finally became available once again, in upgraded form, SMG featured the familiar electro-hydraulic control of all gear-changes, the feature of the driver never having to operate a (non-existent) clutch pedal, and – this time – for a simple centre-console-mounted gear lever to be accompanied by twin gear-change paddles mounted behind the steering wheel. Although this was all based on the Getrag six-speed manual transmission, drivers could opt for fully automatic or sequential manual modes, and changes were described as lightning fast – significantly faster than those of the original SMG type. There was a minor weight penalty, claimed to be just 8kg (17.6lb), but no one was complaining about that.

New for SMGII was what might be described as a 'launch control system'. After deactivating the dynamic stability control which (electronically) frowned on all such signs of driver exuberance, with the S6 driver programme selected, and the gear lever pushed well forward, the accelerator could be fully depressed, and the maximum possible acceleration was achieved. All this was

**ABOVE:** 'OK, if the rules insist, we'll make you a road-car version of the 4-litre V8-engined M3 GTR of 2001....' Ten such cars were produced at the end of the season, but the programme was then immediately cancelled. Note the extra cooling louvres in the bonnet of the 'road' car.

BELOW: An improved type of SMG sequential transmission option, which had not been a complete success on late-model E36s, was relaunched in 2001 for the E46. On that car, the driver had a choice of either using a conventional gear lever, or a pair of paddles that were positioned behind the steering wheel.

available for substantial money (£2,400 in the UK), but for a system greeted at the time as the very best available, this seemed to be reasonable value.

M3 followers then got even more excited in the autumn of 2001 when BMW previewed a new derivative of the Coupé, which they titled M3 CSL. This was to be a lightened, stripped-out version of the latest E46 M3, and in many ways was meant to emulate an earlier strategy adopted by BMW in the 1970s. At that time, the company's most exciting road car was the 3.0CSi (a four-seater Coupé) that the company was using as a 'works' saloon car racer. Its main problem was that it was too heavy, and lacked certain aerodynamic features. Accordingly, in 1972, the 3.0CSL (Coupé Sports Lightweight) was launched, this not only being considerably lighter than the original, but also having spoilers and (eventually) other aerodynamic features to improve high-speed grip and handling.

The 'CSL' part of the new M3's title harked back to the 3.0CSL Coupé, for although there were to be no obvious aerodynamic changes, there was to be significantly more power, and the whole car was to go on a weight-saving diet, by dint of the use of exotic materials, and by the deletion of what could be called 'luxury' equipment and features.

In an attempt to save up to 150kg (330lb) – this saving would be trimmed back as development proceeded – the new car would be delivered without air conditioning, electric seat adjustment and sun roof, though the full array of six air bags would be retained. Not only that, but there would also be lighter body panels (the use of carbon fibre was forecast, but not detailed at first).

BMW made it clear that they were so serious about this derivative that if the reception given to the machine was favourable at the Frankfurt Show of September 2001, and in the media, they were prepared to build at least 1,000 examples, starting in 2002, even though this type would not be sold in North America. They need not have worried, so preparations began in earnest. By April 2002 the company had decided to put the car into production – not as a replacement for the E46 M3,

RIGHT: In this rather colourful way, BMW showed off the SMGII installation of electro-hydraulic controls that helped to convert the six-speed Getrag gearbox to clutchless operation.

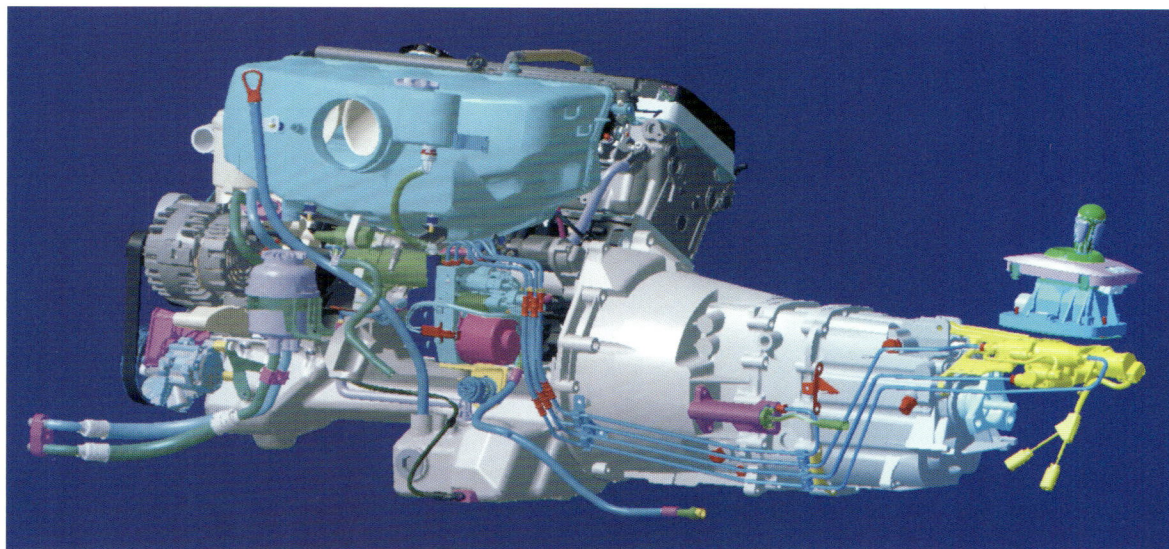

# BMW lebt
# mit dem Motorsport

BMW ist mit dem Rennsport groß geworden. Menschen und Automobile sind mit ihm gewachsen und von ihm geprägt.
Dem sportlichen Elan entspricht das sportliche Konzept, das sich am Menschen orientiert, im Rennen erprobt und in der Konstruktion verwirklicht.

In diesem Sinn treibt BMW Motorsport.

Mit einer neuen Gesellschaft: der BMW Motorsport GmbH.
Unter neuem Zeichen und neuem optischen Akzent.
Mit dem Ziel, das bessere Automobil zu bauen.

The was the 3.0CSL 'Batmobile' of the mid-1970s, which brought so much touring car racing success to the BMW brand. When the lightweight E46 M3 came along, it is easy to see why the charismatic initials 'CSL' were once again chosen.

**ABOVE:** Although the M3 CSL of 2003–2004 carried no badges to shout its presence, M3 fanatics immediately recognised it by way of the massive rear tyres, and by the unique little boot lid spoiler.

**RIGHT:** The E46 CSL model was lightened as far as possible, including these dramatically shaped seats.

but as a derivative of that design.

It was all achieved with typical German thoroughness. Not only was the CSL to be lighter, and more powerful, than before, but it was also to have larger and different-styled BBS wheels, a different ride height, modified suspension settings, sharper steering, different front and rear spoilers, and the use of the latest six-speed SMGII semi-automatic transmission as standard. The braking installation, too, had been upgraded. Surprisingly, there were now only to be two air intakes in the front spoiler (that normally inserted in the right side having been omitted), and the driving lamps had been deleted from their habitual low-mounted position.

By the summer of 2002, BMW was ready to show off the complete package (though they were almost excessively modest in stating that they might, just might, make more changes if the reactions demanded it, especially as they had only produced five hard-working prototypes so far). Already they admitted that they could reduce

**TOP:** This high side view of the CSL gives little away, other than to emphasise the use of uniquely-styled road wheels. There is no external indication of the use of a weight-saving carbon-fibre roof panel.

**ABOVE:** For the M3 CSL of 2003–2004, the front spoiler was unique in that there were only two lower air intakes, one on the left side, which led direct to the intake box for the inlet manifolding, for the extra driving lights had been deleted.

the weight of production cars by as much as the concept vehicle had achieved – but, nevertheless, cars to be delivered to customers would be at least 150kg (330lb) lighter at the kerbside: that figure was reduced to approx. 110kg (242lb) when the new car finally went on sale in the UK.

As forecast, the air conditioning, the radio/ICE equipment and the electric seat adjustment features had been eliminated (though these could be reinstated at no extra cost if ordered before the car was built), but the truly uplifting news was not only that the sun-roof feature had also been eliminated, but that the entire roof panel was moulded from carbon fibre composite – and even though this apparently saved only about 7kg (15lb) in weight, BMW had thought it worth doing. Other weight-saving measures included the use of an aluminium honeycomb floor to the boot

compartment, a composite rear bulkhead (rear seat to boot, that is), and thinner glass to the rear screen. The passenger doors were also moulded from carbon fibre.

Any thought that the M3 GTR's V8 engine (as used in ALMS racing in 2001) could go into limited production had been abandoned, so if this car was to be faster than the standard M3, the only way it could be done was by producing more power from the existing 3,245cc 'six'. This, of course, was already at the limit of its capacity, but diligent work by the engineers allowed it to be power-tuned to 360bhp, still at the same 7,900rpm of the standard M3.

More development work on the chassis of the E46, and the adoption of ultra-low profile 19in tyres, along with wider front and rear tracks, and a slightly lowered ride height, all meant that the CSL was claimed to handle better than any previous M3. Under the bonnet, there was a large carbon fibre air intake feeding the throttle bodies, and elements of F1 engine technology had allowed a new method of sensing to monitor the ideal fuel-air mixture being provided to take account of the throttle positions. And, so what if it didn't deaden as much of the inlet sound as some spoilsports would have wished? In addition, BMW claimed that weight had been saved by using thinner exhaust manifold piping, the exhaust valve shapes had been optimised, and camshaft profile changes had also been made.

With CSL production only beginning in 2003, after a considerable 'will-they-won't-they?' debate

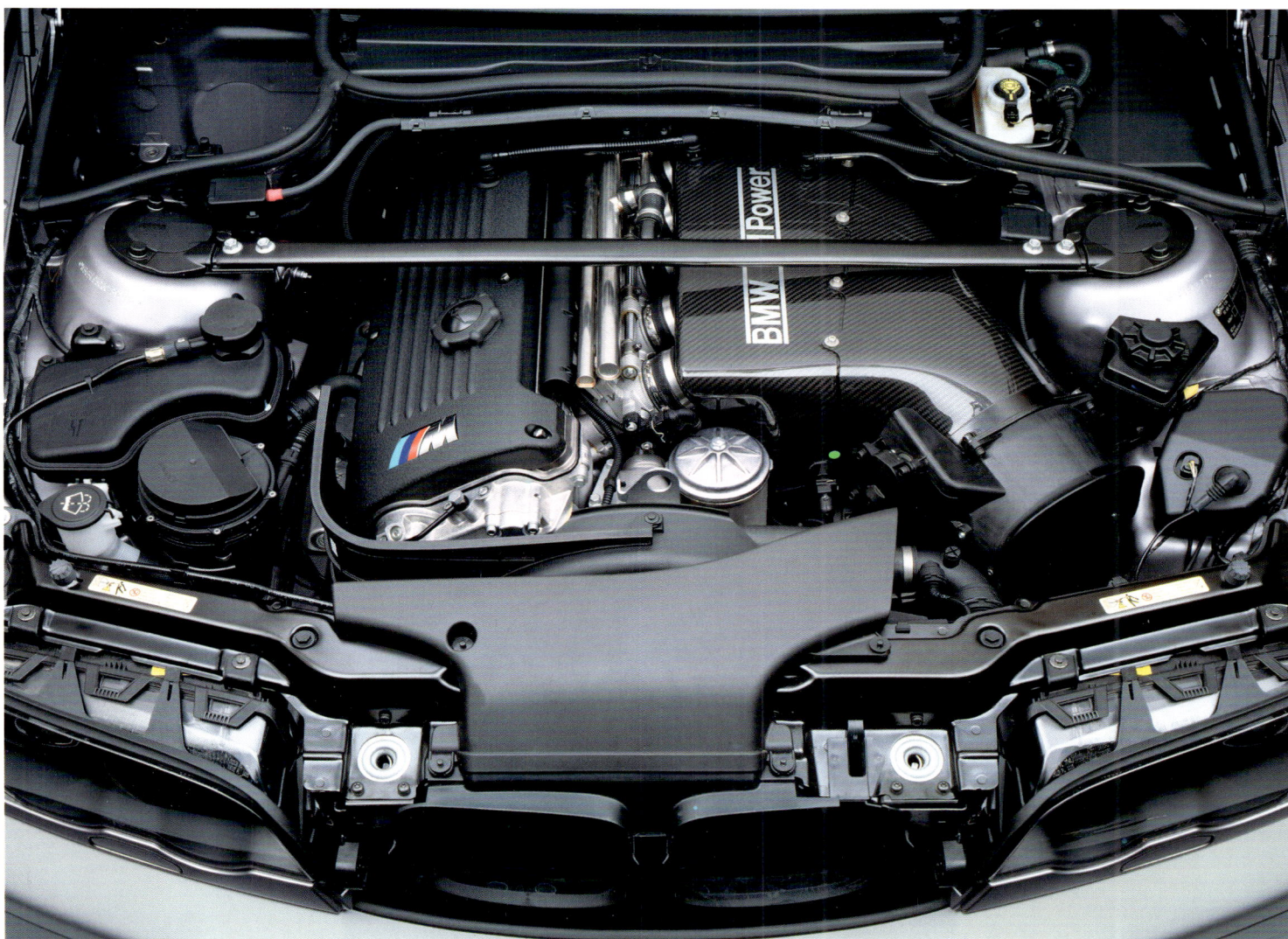

among prospective customers about all the 'toys' that had been included in the project cars, there seemed to be little doubt that the limited production run would soon be sold out. BMW, in fact, had originally promised that a thousand cars would be built, but in the end a total of no fewer than 1,400 were constructed, of which 500 were allocated for UK sale: in the end, just 422 reached these shores. UK sales began in August 2003, at a whopping £58,455 – which was nearly £20,000 higher than that of a 2003-model 'standard' M3. For this market, one optional extra feature was a full day's driver training, for no less than £850.

At such an ambitious price, the M3 CSL simply had to deliver, and to everyone's relief it did just that. The top speed might still be electronically limited to 155mph (UK cars tended to top out at 160mph, but no one in this market complained

about that), but 0–60mph was now achievable in 4.8sec, and 0–100mph in 10.9sec.

Nor was that all, for this M3 CSL was one of only two current production cars (the Ferrari 360 Challenge Stradale being the other) that were optionally fitted with Michelin Pilot Sport Cup tyres (semi-slicks, with soft-compound rubber) though Michelin Pilot Sports were standard. The grip that the latest Michelins could offer was stupendous (BMW claimed up to 1.6g lateral acceleration being possible) and, all in all, this was an amazingly capable road car, of which BMW was justly proud. Its career, however, was short-lived, for production ended in early 2004.

However, although the CSL died young, as it were, its pedigree lived on for some time. Well before the end of 2004, BMW announced that they were ready to start supplying specially-modified

ABOVE: **For the more powerful engine of the M3 CSL, which went on sale in 2003, BMW developed a brand new inlet passage moulded from carbon fibre, which quite dominated the engine bay of this specialised model.**

**ABOVE:** Variation on a theme. The M3 Competition Package/M3 CS of 2005 used some of the CSL's more sporty suspension, wheels and tyres, but retained the standard front spoiler.

**RIGHT:** These were the newly-styled 19in wheels fitted to the M3 CSL. The same wheels were being fitted to the Competition Package/CS model of 2005 above.

M3s to the North American market – and that this derivative would first be shown at the Los Angeles Motor Show in January 2005. To be called the M3 Competition Package, it would include many, but not all, of the M3 CSL's special features. It was typical of BMW's sometimes rather mysterious way of dressing up its intentions. The inference, but not the promise, was that this package, if successful, might be offered on other markets.

ZCP, as it became known, was to be offered in the USA as a $4,000 (£2,620 at the current rate of exchange) option. Because the M3's 3.2-litre engine had now reached the outer limits of its performance/reliability/long-life envelope (rumours of a V8 engine to replace it in the next-generation M3 were already circulating) there were to be no boosts to the power output. The package, therefore, concentrated on improvements to the handling and to the equipment of the existing M3. These were the principal features of ZCP:

- 19in spin-cast BBS wheels, with 8.0in front rim widths, and 9.5in rears.

- Revisions to the suspension spring rates (these, in fact, being due to be fitted to all future USA-specification M3s).

- The compound cross-drilled disc brake rotors of the CSL; the fronts being increased in size to 345mm (13.6in) – these would only fit inside 19in rims.

The steering rack from the CSL, which was 'sharper', with a slightly more direct ratio than before.

The M-Track Mode DSC of the CSL, via a button mounted on the steering wheel.

An Alcantara finish to the steering wheel rim and handbrake grip.

Unique aluminium interior trim details.

The whole to be wrapped in an Interlagos Blue body colour, the only one to be offered on this package.

What was not offered, please note, was the special carbon fibre roof panel, or the front and rear bumper/spoilers that were unique to the M3 CSL.

Early in 2005 BMW did, indeed, put this derivative on European markets, for this car arrived in the UK as the 'M3 CS', where it was priced at £43,555 (a 'normal' M3 cost £41,155 with the conventional six-speed manual gearbox, or £43,250 when the SMGII transmission was specified), and was available with the normal six-speed gearbox.

While it would be true to describe this car as really an up-scale M3, rather than a milk-and-water version of the M3 CSL, the developed handling,

and the 19in wheels and tyres, made it more sporty than the 'base' car.

This generation of M3s had now certainly reached maturity, and BMW made no secret of that. The fabulous six-cylinder engine, they admitted, was at its limits, at least in normally-aspirated guise – the limit of capacity stretch and the limit of reliable road-car power development had both been reached. Work, they admitted, was already going ahead on the development of a new generation M3, and this would have an entirely new type of V8 engine.

Even so, sales stood up well in 2005 and 2006, and production carried on strongly at Regensburg, but with a new-generation 3-Series already announced in the winter of 2004/2005, and already in full flow, time was nearly up for the E46. Once the Coupé and Convertible versions of the new-generation 3-Series cars appeared, in the summer/autumn of 2006, this, by definition, meant that the principal press tooling for body panels, and the assembly jigging, welding and robot facilities for the older E46 type monocoques had already been dismantled.

In the end, the final E46-generation M3 cars were produced in the summer of 2006 – with an amazing total of 85,744 Coupés and Convertibles having been constructed. Now it was time to usher a new M3 derivative into the limelight; and its engine would cause a sensation.

**BELOW: The E46 Convertible was a superfast way to enjoy open-air motoring, and had all the performance and equipment of the Coupé itself. Posed charismatically against the surf of (I guess) the California coast, this gold-painted M3 Convertible showed off the open-type of E46 M3 that sold so well in North America in the mid-2000s.**

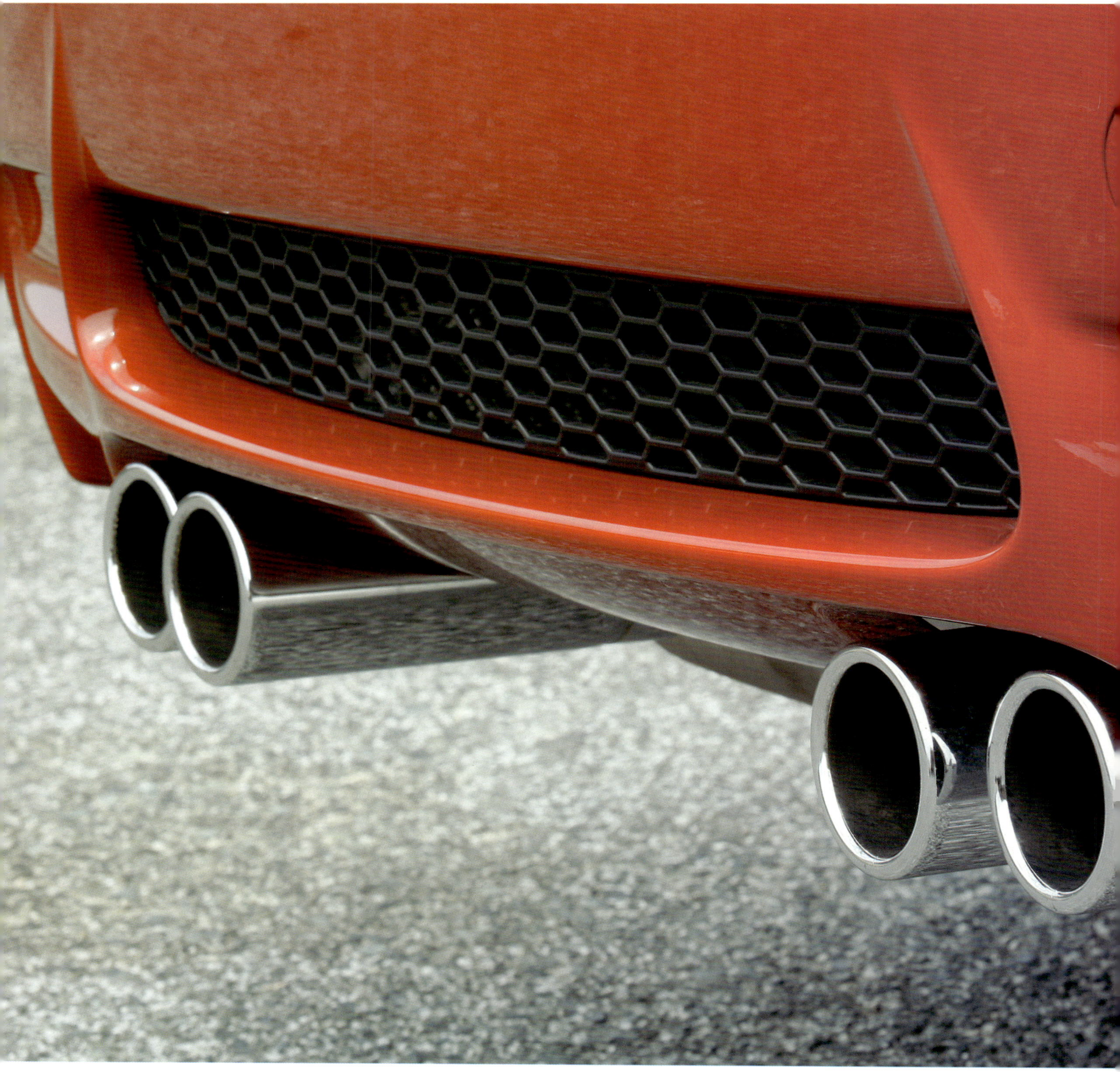

*Chapter 6*

# E90 models –
# with a mighty new V8 engine

**A**lthough the E46 M3 had enjoyed a remarkable career – not just in sales, but also in building a fine image, and in longevity – by the mid-2000s the model was clearly due for replacement. A new-generation 3-Series range (the E90 range) duly made its debut in January 2005, and naturally it was not long before rumours of M3 derivatives of that new model began to circulate. As ever, development of the M3 followed, rather than ran parallel with, the evolution of the mainstream cars. Sneak 'spy' pictures of test cars – always disguised and usually either captured in the city streets of Munich or in high-speed runs on the Nürburgring – began to appear in 2006, but it was not until March 2007, at Geneva Motor Show time, that BMW released the first official details.

By any standards, the E90 3-Series had already been seen and judged as an evolutionary, not revolutionary, development. It was, after all, one of the main cornerstones of the company's business. Not only was it being built in three different German factories, as well as in South Africa, but well over 500,000 such cars were being produced every year, in Saloon, Tourer (estate car), Coupé and Convertible guises.

As expected, compared with the E46 variety, the E90 was slightly larger, heavier, more capacious and more ambitious in all respects than ever before, for the style team led by Chris

Bangle had made sure that the style themes of the new car were evolutionary, and would be readily identifiable to every BMW enthusiast in the world. When the complete original mechanical range was revealed (the most powerful petrol engine of all being the 258bhp magnesium-blocked 3.0-litre 'six'), with every car being fitted with a six-speed manual gearbox as standard, it was clear that an M3 derivative would have to be quite remarkable to sit well on top of this prestigious pile.

With its wheelbase 35mm (1.4in) longer, and being 38mm (1.5in) wider overall, the new car was a little bit bulkier than hitherto, for BMW claimed that the cabin of the body was 49mm (1.9in) longer than before, and that it was no less than 25% stiffer in torsion. BMW, incidentally, insisted that, although the new M3 looked superficially like the other Coupés in the vast 3-Series range, at least 80% of their new car was effectively just that – new. The general mechanical layout was much as before. As expected, there were four-cylinder and six-cylinder petrol and diesel engines in abundance, while the underpinnings (what diehards might have called the 'chassis') had been improved, with much attention given to new detail and (with weight-saving in mind) with more aluminium suspension members replacing the iron and steel of earlier types.

The new-type Coupé appeared in the spring of 2006, and what became known as the E92 (the

M3) duly follcwed it a year later, but BMW was not ready to reveal full details until the summer of 2007, and finally put the car on show later in 2007. Central to the layout of the new car was the all-new 4-litre V8 engine. By the way, originally there had apparently been plans to badge this newcomer as an M4, but in the end the marketing chiefs abandoned the plan, having decided not to waste the heritage that still existed in the prestige of an M3.

Because of BMW's conservative policy to style revisions at this time, the shape of the new car was demonstrably influenced by its now obsolete predecessor. Originally available only as a two-door Coupé, it was later to be joined by four-door Saloon and two-door Convertible types. All the obvious 'signatures' from the E46 type were carried forward, including the massive air intakes

in the front spoiler (with 414bhp available from the new engine, lots of cooling air was certainly needed!), the hot air outlets (from the engine bay) in the front wings behind the front wheel-arch cut-outs, the flared front and rear wheel arches, and (to emphasise the new engine), not two but four exhaust outlets under the rear spoiler. There was also a significant 'power bulge' in the bonnet panel, the need for which became somewhat obvious on lifting the bonnet.

## A new V8 engine for the M3

BMW engineers love designing new engines. If you don't believe that, then beg a tour around BMW's restricted museum collection in Germany – not the glossy museum which stands proudly in central Munich, but a smaller private collection

**FAR LEFT:** BMW called these 'aerodynamic' rear-view mirrors, as fitted to each passenger door on the E92 M3.

**LEFT:** Another recognition point of the E92 M3 was this nicely detailed hot air outlet positioned on the front wings, behind the wheel-arch cut-out.

**LEFT:** Huge front brake discs, not only ventilated, but also cross-drilled, were a feature of the new E90-series M3s.

**LEFT:** Other recognition points of the new E92 M3 Coupé were the weight-saving carbon-fibre roof panel, and the neat little antenna for the GPS-activated sat nav system.

that is held carefully and close to the company's archive. If you are lucky enough to be granted that visit, there you will find all manner of secret BMW engine projects (real engines, not mock-ups) that were designed, built and tested, but never put into production.

Would you, for instance, believe the existence of normally-aspirated V12 F1 engines from the late 1980s (intended to replace the phenomenal turbocharged 1.5-litre units), a series of more modern normally-aspirated V6 engines proposed for road cars, and even one amazingly compact V16 power unit (derived from the existing V12 road-car power unit), which was built, and squeezed (just!) into a 7-Series body-shell? In another part of town, and in other offices, maybe BMW's accountants and their long-term planners sometimes held their heads in their hands and moaned softly when they saw this sort of thing happening, but technically at least there seems to have been nothing which inspired the Motorsport engineers quite so much as designing new power units, even if the investment sums didn't quite add up.

**FAR LEFT:** This front view of the new E92 M3 of 2007 shows that the hugely powerful 414bhp V8 engine (and the big front brakes to keep everything in check) needed a lot of cooling air.

**LEFT:** Well-equipped – plush, even. The front seats/cockpit area of the E92 M3 Coupé made no concessions to the ultra-high performance.

**BELOW:** The new E92 M3 Coupé, in pure side-view, showed a close family relationship to the E46 type which preceded it – yet it was slightly larger all round, and every panel was new.

RIGHT: This was the rear seating area of the E92 M3 Coupe…

BELOW: …which compares closely with that of the M3 Convertible launched shortly afterwards.

LEFT: Lots of 'Big Boys' Toys' in the driving compartment of the E92 M3 Coupé.

The arrival of the brand-new (and, as it appears, short-lived) V8 engine that was fitted to the fourth-generation E90-family M3s of 2007 is a perfect case in point. A few years earlier, and as the new century had opened, the magnificent, but venerable, 3.2-litre straight six, which it was to replace in ultra-high-performance BMWs, was finally approaching its development limits – at least as a normally-aspirated design – and, with more power in mind, a new engine was therefore needed for the next M3 model.

So, since BMW already had a well-proven range of 32-valve V8s in production (and already in use in 5-Series and 7-Series models, as noted in the Interlude section), why should the engineers not use an ultra-sophisticated version of those power units for the M3 too?

No chance. Although it was a fine engine (and in turbocharged form it would eventually go on to produce environmentally clean and stonking amounts of power in cars like the F10-generation M5), the M-pedigree planners concluded that it was a touch too bulky, and too heavy, to suit their mid-2000s M3. They did, however, build

road-going 'mules' to make their point. Instead, an ambitious alternative strategy took shape. Maybe if the M-pedigree had not already been so successful, this would never have taken root, but in the early 2000s, and with the company booming and very profitable, almost anything still seemed to be possible in Munich. The solution, it seemed, was already available, in house.

ABOVE: This was how neatly the new 4.0-litre V8 engine fitted into the E92 M3 engine bay in the late 2000s.

Years earlier, in fact, BMW's top people had decided to give the larger M-badged cars a further image boost by authorising a brand-new 5-litre V10 engine for use in the next-generation (E60-based) M5: this was due to appear in 2004. Oh, by the way, the company was already actively involved in F1 motor racing, where 3-litre V10 engines were still compulsory, and where constructors such as Williams were using BMW engines. Not that there was any likelihood of that particular engine being de-tuned for road use, but why not design another V10, which would nominally be similar, and which would be an ideal strategy for marketing and publicity purposes if properly handled? The design and rationale of that amazing power unit, incidentally, is analysed in the Interlude section.

This, then, is where, when and why BMW set about designing a new type of 90° V10, the S85B50 project, a 5-litre engine that produced 507bhp at 7,750rpm. This was launched in the spring of 2004, and it immediately made almost every other production engine in the world look out-of-date. It was so outstanding, in fact, that it won several international engineering design awards.

That was exciting enough, but at that time BMW also let it be known that this was, effectively, designed to be a 'modular' engine, and that they were already planning to produce an eight-cylinder/4-litre version of it, which would fit neatly into the engine bay of the next-generation M3. And so it was that in 2007 the new-generation M3 was to be powered by a brand-new 90° V8, the S65B40 type – an engine that was to all intents and purposes a new-type V10 with two cylinders chopped off – not actually but figuratively, you understand – and one which had always

RIGHT: V8 engine, front view, completely assembled...

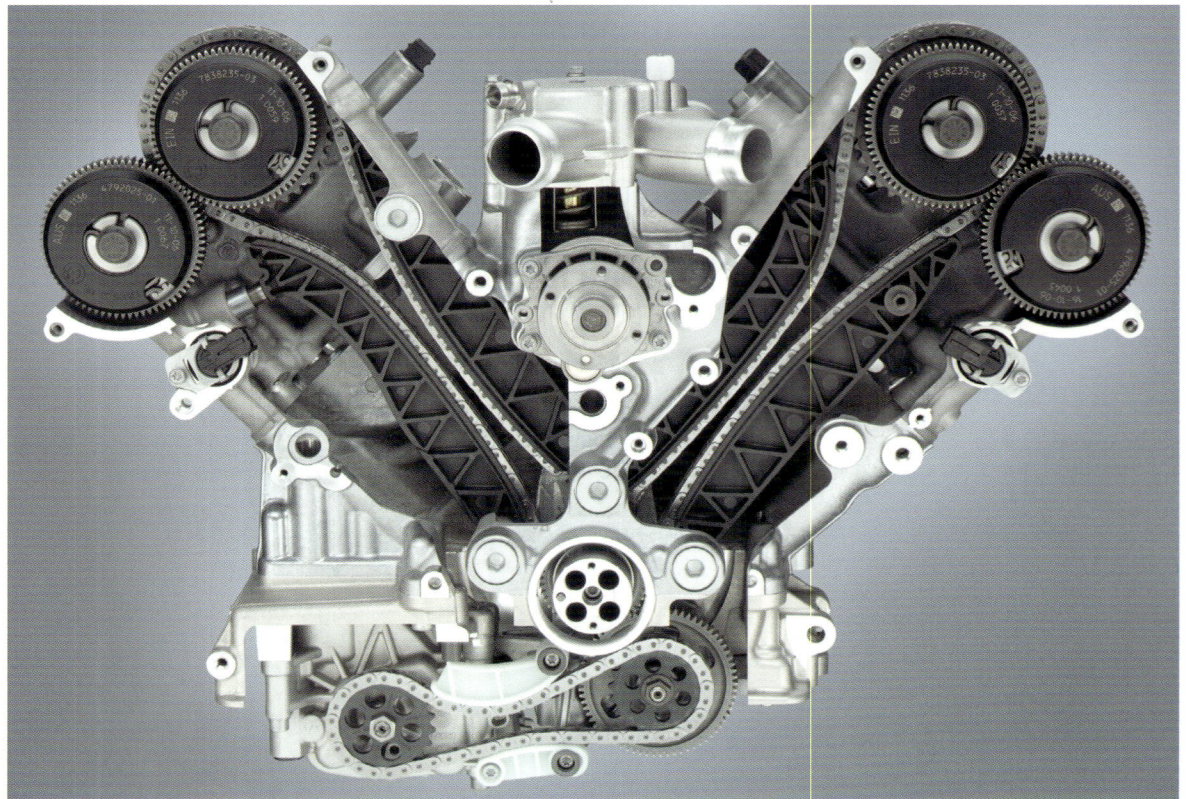

RIGHT: ...and partially stripped, to show the complexities of the chain drive to the four camshafts.

been intended when the first outlines of that V10 had been schemed up in one of the company's computers.

In every respect except that of cost (for this was always going to be a very limited-production machine to be manufactured purely for use in the M3), this was set to be a remarkable power unit, which made every rival gasp, reach for their calculators and wonder if they might ever catch up. With a power output of 414bhp, peaking at 8,300rpm, it was no less than 22% more powerful than the outgoing 3.2-litre 'six', yet it was more compact and (because it used an aluminium cylinder block) weighed 15kg (33lb) less than the old 'six'. Not only that, but it was by no means a 'top-end screamer' – for BMW claimed that 80%

**ABOVE:** The all-new 4-litre V8 engine, destined for the M3 in 2007, under test at the prototype stage.

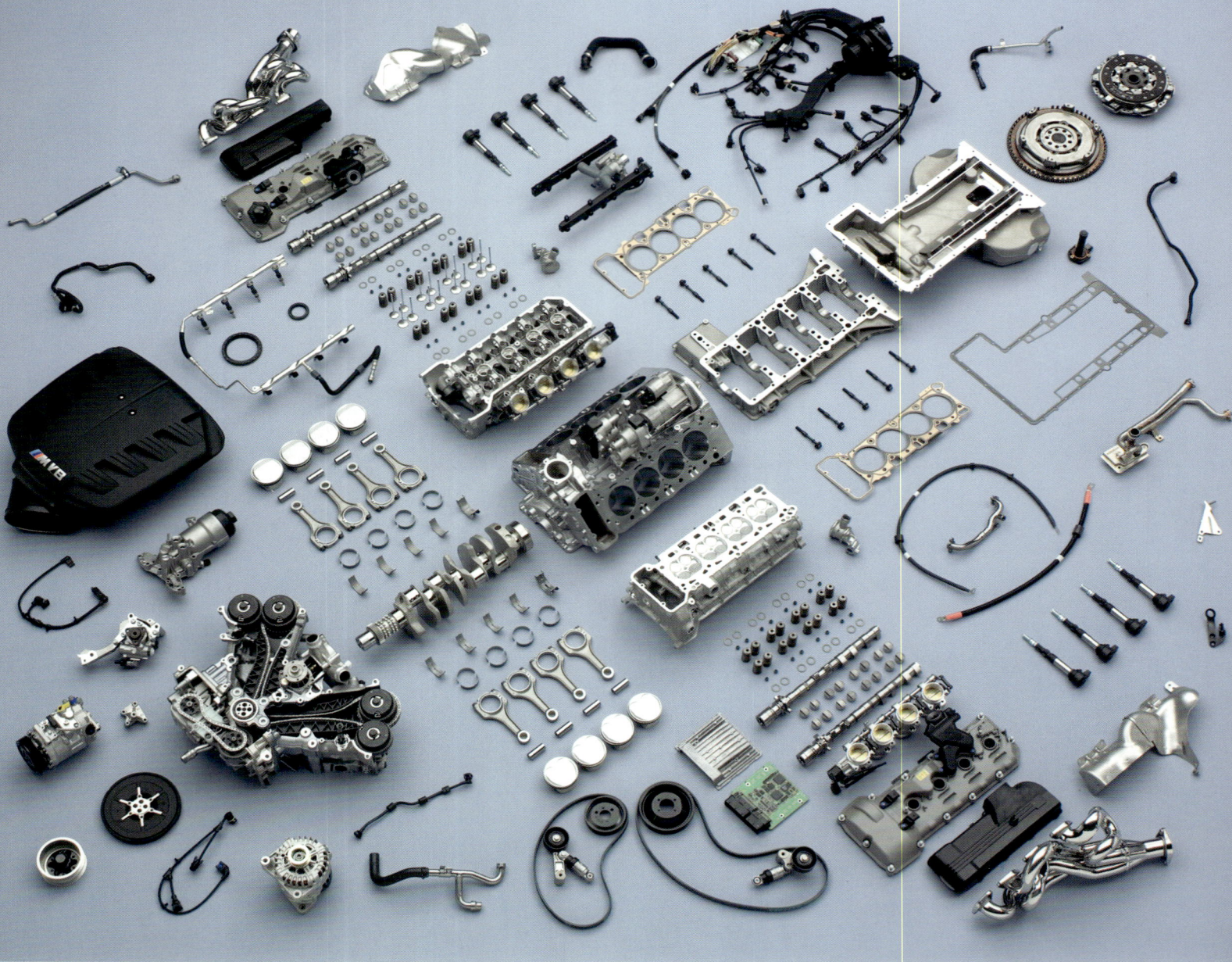

**ABOVE: BMW is always proud to display a completely stripped-out high-performance engine, this being the new-generation 4.0-litre V8 for the M3.**

of peak torque (which occurred at 3,900rpm) was available over a huge 6,500rpm of the rev range.

When it was originally announced, the new E92 model featured the familiar type of six-speed manual Getrag transmission, but there was no longer any sign of the SMG-type of semi-automatic change being available, even as an option. On the other hand, it was made clear that there would, one day, be an optional Getrag transmission system called M-DCT (where DCT stood for Double Clutch Transmission), which would not only have seven forward speeds, but would also be more refined that SMG had ever been.

Before going on to mention this new car's stupendous performance, fabulous roadholding and all-round any-road capability, it is worth noting

that it was yet another M3 that had put on weight compared with its predecessor. As detailed in the panel 'M3 Coupé weights' on page 147, the unladen weight of the latest E92 M3 was no less than 1,655kg (3,649lb), which was 78kg (172lb) more than that of the E46 model that it was replacing, and a colossal 455kg (1,009lb) more than the light, nimble and totally unsurpassable E30 M3 of the late 1980s had been. Time, new safety regulations, middle-aged spread and an inexorable move upmarket had not been kind to the M3.

This, of course, was not entirely BMW's fault, for many weight increases were quite unstoppable because of the need to re-engineer the structure to meet the most stringent of crash test and other safety regulations. But even that 78kg (172lb)

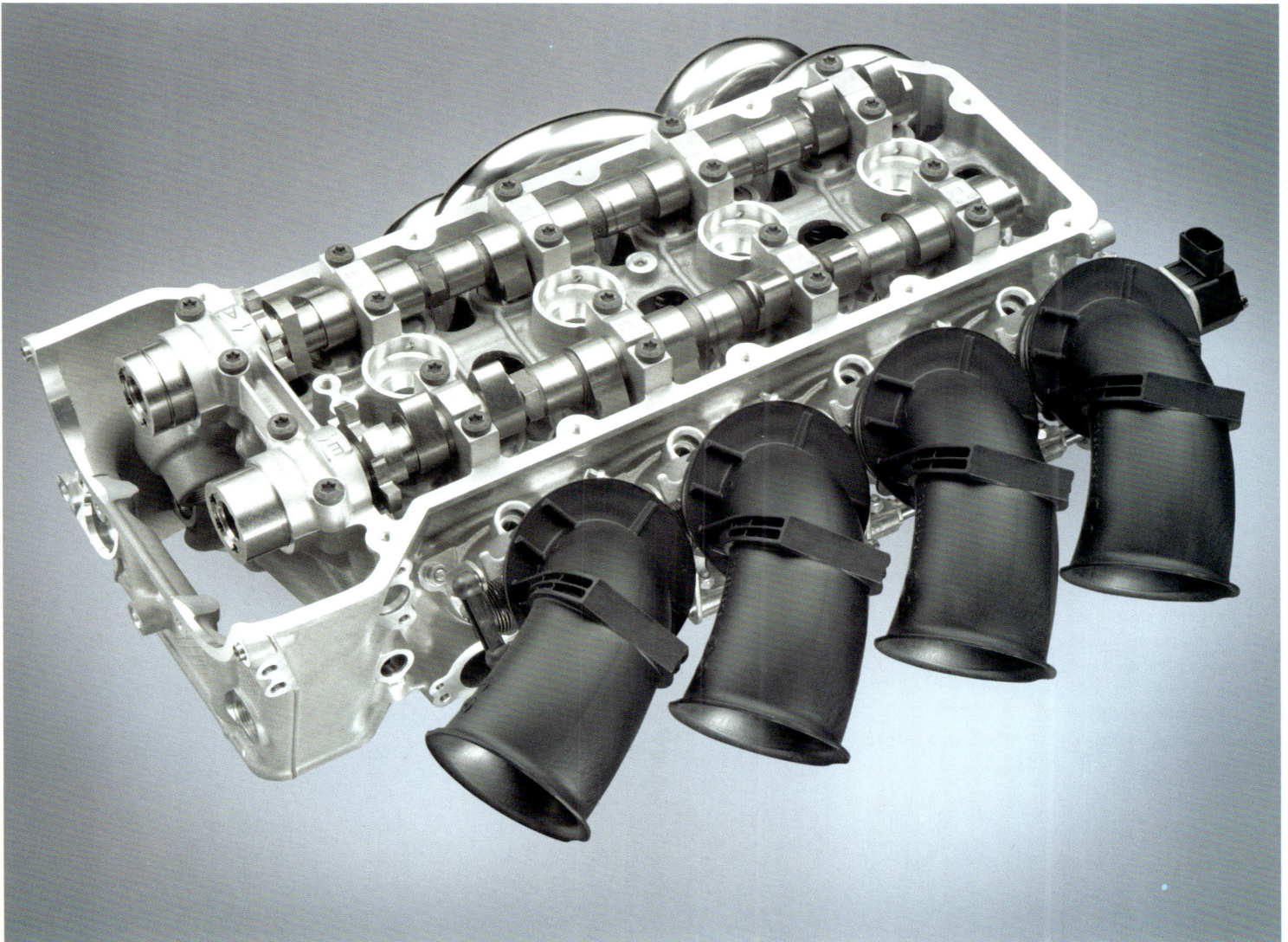

BELOW: One of the V8 cylinder heads already assembled with two camshafts, and the inlet manifold trumpets.

**ABOVE:** A familiar layout? Of course – the classic four-valve arrangement of the engine in the E92 M3 model.

**RIGHT:** The V8 exhaust manifold for the new M3 looks complex enough to have been designed by F1 engineers. And so it was, for the same team had worked on both types of engine.

**OPPOSITE:** It can get mighty hot on the test beds when a 4.0-litre V8 is unleashed at full power!

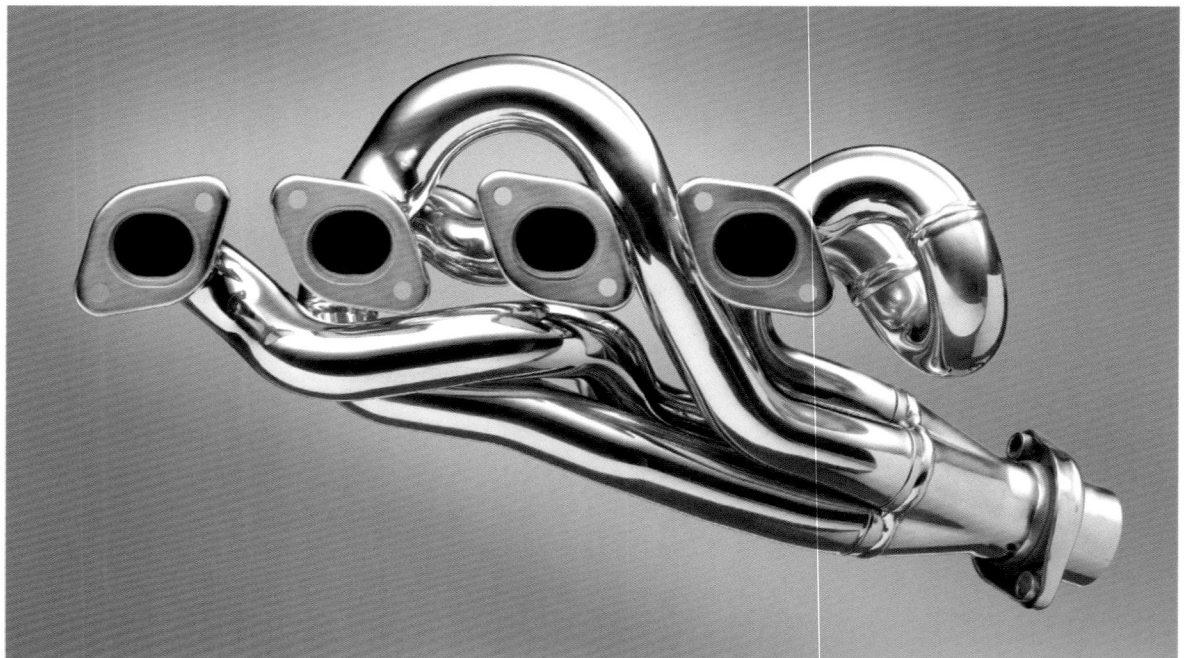

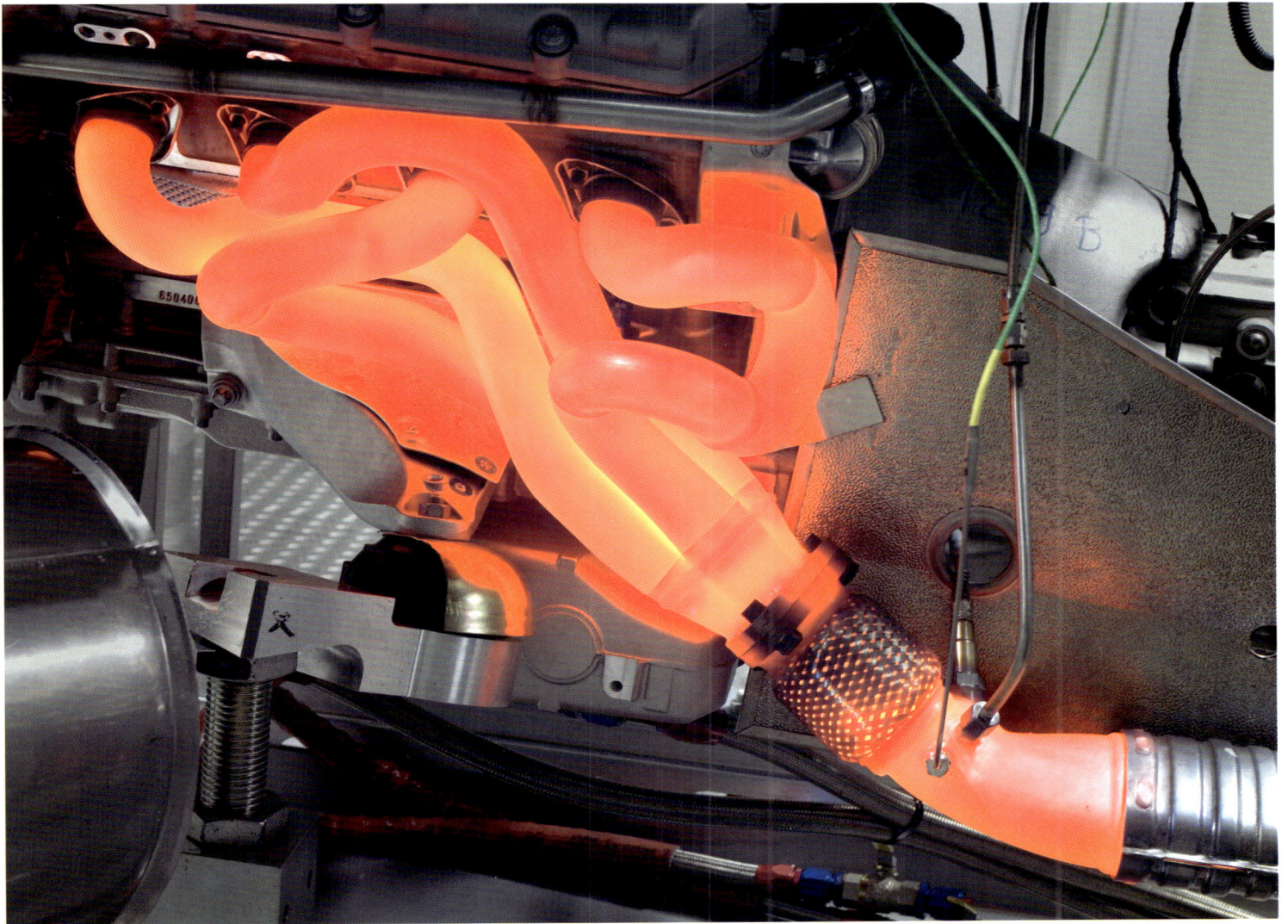

increase compared with the E46 was really the equivalent of carrying one reasonably light fully-grown male passenger alongside the driver all the time. To be fair, BMW had tried their best to minimise the weight penalty, not only by specifying an aluminium bonnet, but also by once again using a carbon fibre roof panel (of the type first used on the E46 M3 CSL a few years earlier).

When production cars finally reached their customers in the summer of 2007, the new M3 Coupé proved to be simply devastatingly fast. The fact that the electronic engine limiter fixed the car's top speed at an internationally agreed 155mph (250kph) was seen to be ludicrous, as the car could also reach the same limited 155mph in fifth gear, along with 145mph in fourth of the six ratios in the Getrag manual transmission.

It was the acceleration of the car, therefore,

## M3 Coupé weights

Cars have put on a lot of weight in the last two decades. The major reason, of course, is that safety regulations have become progressively more difficult to meet. These days, any car expecting to perform well in Euro NCAP crash tests needs a lot more bulk than it once did. Purely to demonstrate, here are unladen weights that BMW provided for each of the major M3 derivatives over the years:

| Derivative | Year launched | Engine (cc) | Peak power (bhp) | Weight (lb/kg) |
|---|---|---|---|---|
| E30 | 1986 | 2,302 | 200 | 2,640/1,200 |
| E36 | 1992 | 2,990 | 286 | 3,219/1,460 |
| E36 Evolution | 1995 | 3,201 | 321 | 3,219/1,460 |
| E46 | 2000 | 3,245 | 343 | 3,477/1,577 |
| E46 CSL | 2003 | 3,245 | 360 | 3,142/1,425 |
| E90 | 2007 | 3,999 | 414 | 3,649/1,655 |

RIGHT: The modern-
generation M3 featured
a twin exhaust system
from front to rear, but
with a single transverse
silencer in the very tail of
the car.

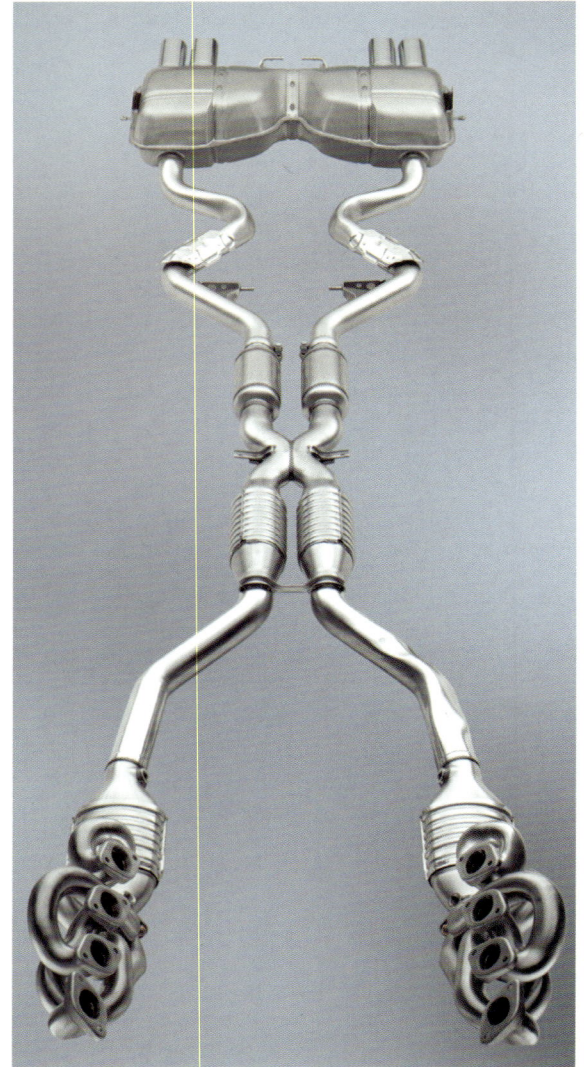

OPPOSITE: Not for the
faint-hearted! BMW's
display model of the
optional Getrag double
clutch gearbox, which
became available on M3s
from 2008.

which caused all the superlatives to roll when road tests were published – 60mph was available from a standing start in just 4.7sec, 0–100mph in 10.2sec, and even 0–150mph in just 26.5sec. Not only that, but what I might describe as the 'snap-action' 50–70mph acceleration when passing another car on the open road took only 3.0sec in third gear, and a quite startling 6.1sec in sixth.

Once one had factored in the reasonable fuel consumption (up to 22–24mpg in everyday use), the excellent roadholding and the high level of standard equipment, then there was little to complain about, though super-sensitive testers made much of the fact that there did not seem to be as much 'feel' in the steering as some of the precious little souls would like.

By the time a car like this particular M3 gets into its new price/marketing bracket, there

always seems to be scope for nit-pickers to complain about some aspect of the equipment, the appearance, the behaviour, or even – if it can ever be quantified – the car's 'character'. BMW knew this, but were supremely confident that they were offering an outstanding package, and began building M3s just as rapidly as the Regensburg factory facilities (and, in particular, the engine facilities in Munich) would allow.

UK price levels in mid-2007, therefore, tell their own story. The new M3 was priced at £50,625, though it was easy to increase that to £53,000 and more if the many options were specified (19in wheels and tyres cost £1,265, for instance) – but to buy similar performance and refinement you would have to pay more for an Audi RS4, £60,810 for a Porsche Carrera (but where were the rear seats?), and where was there anything of similar standing?

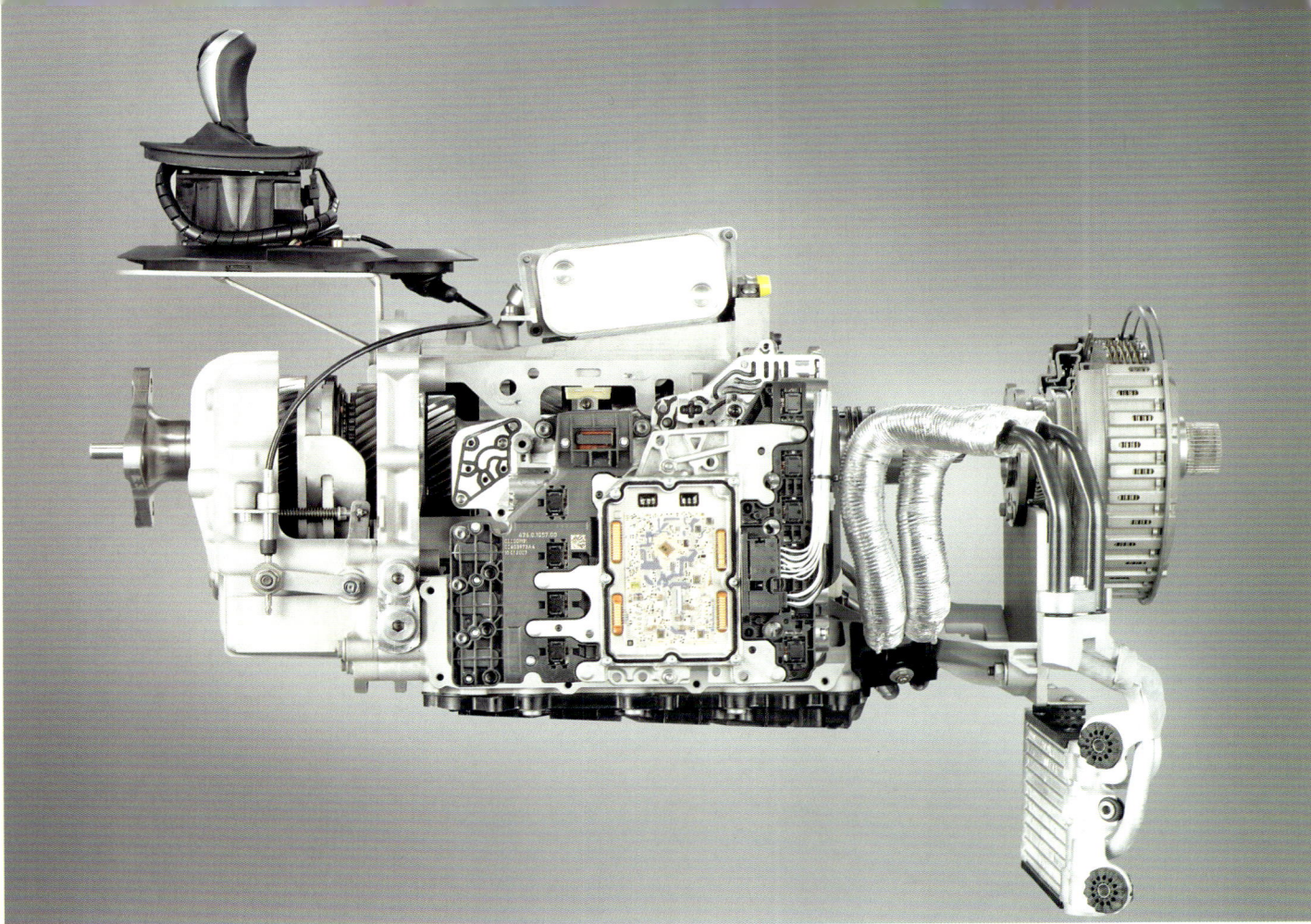

**RIGHT AND BELOW:**
Another two views of the same complex seven-speed Getrag double clutch gearbox.

ABOVE: The E90 M3
four-door Saloon was
launched in 2008, and
was mechanically like
that of the Coupé.

Was it any wonder, therefore, that my esteemed contemporaries on *Autocar* magazine ended their eight-page report with this summary: '… the M3 is not a blunt instrument; there are layers of sophistication, and as something in which to conduct your daily grind it will prove a thrilling companion…for those who love rear-driven M machinery, this is still the best practical performance coupé on sale.'

## More and more variety

In any case, even before the latest M3 went into series production, BMW revealed that they would shortly make an alternative transmission available. Nor was this to be yet another update of the SMG package, which had been available on E36 and E46 types, but a modern double-clutch seven-speeder from Getrag, a type of gearbox which some of BMW's rivals had already adopted.

This new transmission, dubbed M DCT (Double Clutch Transmission), had been on test for some considerable time, and was to be unique to BMW. Not only was it also destined for use in other

3-Series and 5-Series types, but it would also be controlled by a combination of a 'joystick' lever (like that used on M5s and X5s) or by a pair of F1-like paddles located behind the steering wheel rim.

Although DSG (Direct Shift Gearbox) transmissions developed by rivals (particularly for use in VW/Audi group cars) had been available for some little time, they were relatively new to BMW – and to Getrag, which had done the engineering. DSG transmissions evolved to improve on the one, single, basic problem exhibited by the SMG type of 'semi-automatic' transmission, which was that, to change ratios, the engine had to be momentarily disconnected from the transmission, which cut off the transmission of power.

To improve on this, DSGs (or, from this moment, I will use the BMW acronym of DCT) used two friction clutches to eliminate that lag. It is much easier to write what follows, than understand it by looking at models or drawings, and it effectively worked by providing two separate transmissions, still in line, with a pair of clutches between them. One clutch and one transmission look after, say, first, third and fifth gears, while the other clutch

**RIGHT:** This was the front corner of the new M3 four-door Saloon of 2008, technically and visually just the same as that of the Coupé.

**ABOVE:** The new-generation 4.0-litre V8 fitted neatly into the engine bay of the M3, as launched in 2007.

and transmission look after the remainder. When the car starts out from rest, DCT is in first gear in one gearbox, while the other gearbox has already pre-engaged the next ratio above it. When the time comes to change gear, the transmission (and the very clever controls, settings and sensors) simply uses the clutches to switch from the 'odd' gearbox to the 'even' gearbox, ensuring a near-instantaneous change up to the second gear. This done, the 'odd' gearbox immediately pre-selects third gear, ready for the next change … and so the sequence can go on, either up or down.

That, though, would not be available until the spring of 2008, by which time two even more important additions to the range would have arrived – the four-door Saloon and the sleek well-equipped Convertible. For the first time (and this became important to all those who liked to remember such things), each would have its own 'in-house' E-number – E90 for the Saloon, E92 for the Coupé, and E93 for the Convertible.

The four-door (E90) Saloon version went on sale early in 2008, with virtually the same mechanical specification as the established Coupé, which is to say that it retained the 414bhp 4-litre V8 engine and the six-speed transmission. Although the style was unavoidably constrained by that of the series-production cars from which it was based, BMW had managed to use the same type of nose as the Coupé, the same headlamps, grille, bonnet (complete with bulge to accommodate the big V8 engine), the sexy door mirrors and the flared arches incorporating the hot air outlets from the engine bay. Unhappily, although a carbon fibre roof panel had been tried, tested and found satisfactory at the prototype stage, this was not specified on production cars. Cost and the complication of bonding it into place were, apparently, major factors, for the latter caused significant delays at the body manufacturing stage. Except for the discreetly re-profiled rear wings, and the use of a tiny transverse rear spoiler on the boot lid, it was only the four exhaust pipes that really gave the game away.

The bad news was that the bulkier Saloon was unavoidably even heavier than the Coupé – BMW claimed that the extra bulk added 25kg (55lb) – but the good news was that it was still ferociously fast, and of course still absolutely toyed with an electronically-limited top speed of 155mph, which it could reach from rest in no more than 30sec. It was also significantly cheaper than the Coupé – in the UK market, for example, Saloon prices began at

£49,210, compared with £50,625 for the Coupé.

Launched in the same season, however, the new-generation (E93) M3 Convertible was a very specialised machine indeed, for like other versions of the car in this comprehensive new 3-Series range, it featured one of the new breed of fold-away steel hardtops that had suddenly become so popular among European manufacturers at this time. In other times, BMW might have ignored a trend for developing what was a very complicated piece of kit (and one that occupied quite a proportion of the available space in the boot compartment), but the fact that their deadly domestic rivals, Mercedes-Benz, had started building SLKs and larger models with such roofs may just have tipped the balance.

Here was really not just one new model, but two rather different, co-related, models instead.

BELOW: If you could get a friendly technician to disable the limiter on the E90 M3 Saloon (against BMW's advice, of course!) this 2008 Saloon would achieve well over 180mph, and this would be the only lasting view the rivals would get as the car disappeared up the autobahn.

**ABOVE: When launched in 2008, the four-door saloon version of the E90 family was probably the fastest and certainly the most completely developed high-performance five-seater in the world.**

Not only could this car be used as a completely 'top-down' convertible, but it could also be used as a roof-up closed four-seater, ostensibly as sleek as the M3 Coupé, and with almost as much space inside the cabin.

That was the good news. The bad news was that the fold-away roof brought a very significant weight penalty with it of approx 200kg (441lb) compared with the Coupé, and of course the need to sell the car at a much higher price. When launched in the UK, this folding-roof M3 cost £4,610 (9%) more than the Coupé.

Technically, however, this installation was a real tour de force, which not only worked, but also completed the closing/opening action so very elegantly, and which looked so good when the transformation scene was completed. The change from fully open to fully closed could be

carried out from inside the car, or when standing outside it, by pressing the appropriate control on the key fob.

To anyone except the world-weary who watched it; in less than half a minute the changeover would take place like this: Starting from, as an example, the fully open/top down condition, first of all the rear boot lid opened up (it was hinged at the extreme tail, incidentally), followed by the appearance of a three-part stack of roof/rear-quarter panels all tied together with a complex linkage, which was hinged at its forward extremity, close to the rear seat back rest. Electric motors then urged this to extend forward over the passenger compartment, where it gradually opened itself up, and settled down, miraculously, as a coupé roof, with two obvious mating joints in the roof panels, but with no unsightly

**ABOVE AND LEFT:**
Two views of the elegant E93 M3 Convertible, with soft-top stowed, and ready to enjoy another day in a warm, perhaps Mediterranean, climate. The front three-quarter above…
…then the smart three-quarter rear.

**RIGHT:** Although this particular BMW model is not an M3 derivative of the E93, it shows off the way that the intricate folding steel roof unfolded from the boot compartment of the car. Amazingly, there was still spare room for much luggage in the boot! At this point in the sequence, the rear-hinged boot lid is wide open; the three-piece roof has been partly erected...

**RIGHT:** ...while a few seconds later the boot lid has closed down, and the stack of three roof panels is unfurling, ready to dovetail neatly together.

**RIGHT:** In this shot of a (non-M3) E93 Convertible, the three-piece roof is now firmly in place, turning the car into a snug, close-coupled, four-seater Coupé, with as much interior space as the dedicated Coupé itself.

excrescences. Meantime, the boot lid would have closed down too.

All done as if by magic – or, more realistically, by a series of electric motors, sensors, levers and clamps. As already noted, the weight penalty of this mechanism was considerable, which explains why BMW was not anxious to emphasise the performance of the new car. There was, on the other hand, much mention of the special nature of the body-shell – the claim being made that, apart from the chassis platform itself, only the three-piece steel roof and linkage, the boot lid, the windows and the rear lights were the same as those of the mainstream E93 3-Series Convertible. The rest of the shell – the entire front end, the under-door sills, the rear wings and the rear spoiler/bumper – were all shared with the new-type M3 Coupé and, naturally, there were four exhaust pipes at the tail as expected.

ABOVE: When the foldaway steel hardtop of the E93 Convertible was erect, the junction between the three roof panels is clear – one immediately above the shut-line of the doors, the other aligned to the top of the rear window.

LEFT: The rear view, showing off the four exhaust pipes.

## Theme and variations

By the middle of 2008, BMW was proud to announce that they had already built their 300,000th 'M' model, and that they were actively looking to expand the range of such cars. M3 and M5 types, of course, still made up the majority of such sales, but in the next few years M-versions of the 1-Series, the Z4, the X5 and the 6-Series would all come along, and still more derivatives of cars that were still unknown to the public would follow.

Even so, their marketing staff never missed a trick, and made sure that special editions could be made available in different markets. In the UK, in 2009 for instance, there was the 'M3 Coupé Edition' which, though with a familiar mechanical package, combined the standard 414bhp V8 engine with the dual-clutch seven-speed 'automatic' transmission, with the otherwise optional 19in wheels (which were painted black in this application), the whole car being lowered by 10mm (0.4in). At an all-in price of £53,435, it cost £3,010 more than the 'standard' M3 Coupé of the day, yet there was no problem in selling the strictly limited number available.

The M3, however, no longer seemed to be at the forefront of BMW's M-Sport image; not only because other new models (such as those based on 1-Series, 5-Series and even the 6-Series) were continually coming along to gain their share of the limelight, but because it was increasingly becoming treated as what might be called the 'Pet Labrador' of the BMW brand – a creature that everyone liked to have around, to pat on the head whenever encountered, but no longer likely to get any special treatment.

When this happens in today's European motor industry, a company's reflex reaction is often to launch special editions, limited editions, or to announce extra 'packs' to make a well-known machine more salesworthy and newsworthy. In 2009 BMW did just that, but did it properly. Not merely by building M3s in fancy colours with fancy names, but by developing a very different, higher-performance derivative, which was not only an ideal track car (if, that is, one had the funds to keep replacing the soft Pirelli Zero tyres!) but was also totally road legal, and was claimed to be capable of 190mph. Enter, therefore, the M3

**BELOW: Under the orange air-cleaner cover of the M3 GTS inlet manifolds was a 450bhp/4,361cc engine, which was linked to a highly successful double-clutch seven-speed transmission.**

GTS, which was not only more powerful, and more chassis specific, but had a BMW-developed roll cage already installed, and was only sold in one colour – bright orange.

Apart from many details, which will be listed, the GTS was improved in two basic ways – one being that it had more power than ever, the other that quite a lot of weight had been pared off it. The secret of its honed-for-action aerodynamic performance was that it had a body kit based on that used on the latest (non-M3) World Touring Car Championship machines, which is to say that it included a deeper front air dam, and a large freestanding transverse rear aerofoil mounted on pylons on the boot lid.

The engine, itself already a near-unique 90° V8, was made even more powerful by being fitted with a long-stroke crankshaft – the stroke went up, therefore, from the 75.2mm of the 4-litre to 82mm. This produced a capacity of 4,361cc, the peak torque leapt by an appropriate 10%, and peak power rose to a soul-stirring 450bhp, still at 8,300rpm. This time, too, the previously optional seven-speed double-clutch DSG transmission

had been standardised, a lighter-weight exhaust system was developed and no-expense-spared titanium rear silencers ensured optimum flow.

Chassis-wise, the whole car was slightly lowered (by 16mm at the front and by 12mm at the rear), the rear suspension sub-frame was rigidly mounted to the rear body-shell (which unhappily meant that more road noise was transferred to the interior), and there were larger front and rear brake discs, with six-piston calipers at the front, four-piston calipers at the rear. The tyres were fatter than before, but the 19in diameter dimension was retained.

Of equal importance, however, was the considerable weight saving of 276lb (125kg) compared to that of the normal M3 Coupé. This was done not only by dispensing with the rear seats, and using lightweight racing-type front bucket seats, but also by using lightweight components on the centre console and door panels, with polycarbonate rear quarter and rear windows. Owners who wished to pre-order their GTS cars could lose some of these advantages by specifying the full air-conditioning installation,

**ABOVE: Lower, wider, fiercer, yet still road legal, the M3 GTS of 2009/2010 was one of the ultimate statements of M3 engineering.**

From the rear, the very obvious, but totally functional, boot-lid-mounted spoiler made the M3 GTS immediately recognisable.

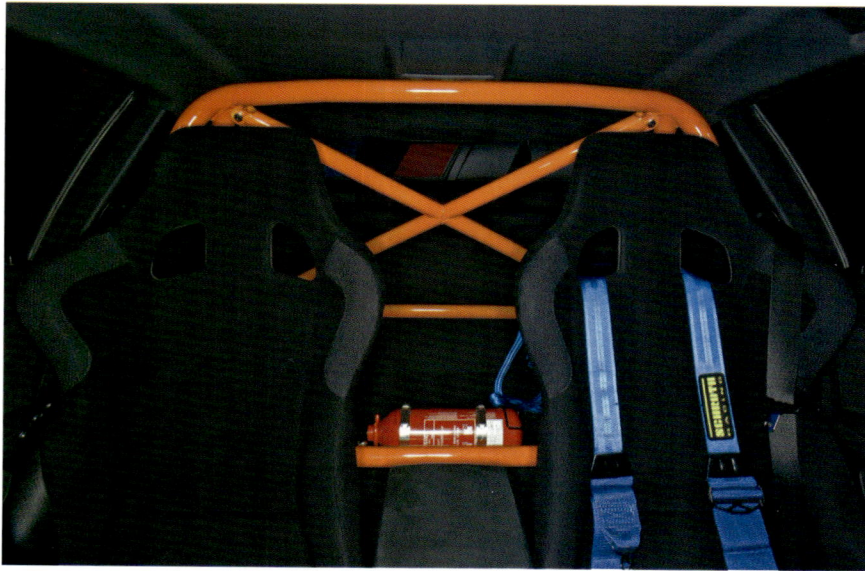

**ABOVE:** Each and every M3 GTS had an orange-painted roll cage fitted to the interior.

**ABOVE RIGHT:**The M3 GTS had 285/30ZR19 Pirelli Zero tyres, those massive aluminium wheels being almost full of equally massive disc brakes.

**RIGHT:** BMW intended the rear spoiler of the M3 GTS to do a job, and it could do this best by being mounted well above the line of the boot lid itself.

and an audio system, neither of which were normally fitted. Six-point safety harnesses and a fire extinguisher were both standard, but roll cage extensions were optional.

This was, it seems, a 'hard core' derivative, but we soon learned not to use that phrase too often in case BMW intended to go even further in the future. Even so, the very limited number of GTSs built – some say that this was just 135 with a very small number coming with right-hand steering at a price north of £115,000 – were soon sold out.

During this period, demand for M3s of all types, which were being produced at Regensburg, continued to be as strong as ever. Waiting lists (especially in the UK) built up from time to time, and several sales territories were 'rationed' as to the number of M3s they could acquire. Incidentally, and as expected, when yet another generation of the mass-production 3-Series made its worldwide debut in the winter of 2011/2012, the wholesale dismantling and replacement of robot settings and assembly jigs meant that it was no longer possible to build M3 versions of the old-type four-door Saloon, so this version quietly disappeared from the price lists, leaving the Coupé and Convertible types to carry on into 2012 and 2013.

In the meantime, the company had not lost its appetite for producing special editions, as yet another 'well, we can if we feel like it' run-out derivative of the four-door Saloon had appeared in June 2011. This was the M3 CRT (the initials standing for Carbon Racing Technology), which in a way was an intriguing amalgam of chassis features from the GTS, innovations of its own, along with a fully-equipped and specified interior.

The clue to the specification was in the 'CRT' model name, for this seemed to be a car which had been showcased to demonstrate just how BMW had harnessed/could harness all the latest developments in carbon fibre, and such related plastics. The CRT used this new material in its bonnet, instead of the normal aluminium pressing, where the weight saving was said to be at least

50%, while there were other carbon details, not least of which were the red/black individual front seats, and two individual rear seats (there was no roll cage in the CRT model). Even though this model had all the usual in-car equipment, including navigation aids and an up-to-date sound system, it was still significantly lighter than the normal M3 Saloon. The overall weight saving was claimed to be 45kg (100lb).

Under the skin – and what an elegant skin it was, because there were neat and individual refreshed air outlets in the carbon bonnet and in the front wing air outlets – the CRT retained the 4.4-litre/450bhp V8 engine originally seen in the GTS of 2010, the result being that the 0–62mph/100kph acceleration sprint was claimed

to be just 4.4sec, which was 0.5sec faster than a normal E90 M3 Saloon.

This, need one emphasise, was an expensive and very specialised car to build, so BMW decided to restrict production to just 67 cars, all of which carried plaques to confirm this exclusivity – and none of these was officially sold in the UK.

## More special editions

By 2012, industry-watchers surely realised that the end was approaching for this generation of M3s when a whole series of 'special editions' began to be marketed worldwide. The M3 ZCP Competition Package had been added to the E92 Coupé for sale in the North American market in 2011, this

BELOW: The M3 CRT (Carbon Racing Technology) was the last of the special edition E90 M3 four-door saloons, and featured a carbon-fibre bonnet.

**ABOVE: The three-quarter rear view of the M3 CRT looked like most other M3 saloons, but used all the chassis equipment of the GTS, and other special carbon-fibre panels and fittings.**

concentrating its changes on the handling of the car, to the electronic controls which governed the damper settings, the Stability Control and the Traction Control settings, at the same time adding the 19in wheels previously seen on the E46 CSL. Then there was the 200-off Lime Rock Park Edition (once again USA only), in which there was more use of carbon-fibre body panels, and the six-speed manual transmission (instead of the seven-speed DCT).

Several special editions were marketed in the UK during 2012. First of all, in March, there was the 'Limited Edition 500' (not a very inspired title, perhaps), which was available in either Coupé or Cabriolet guise, and on 500 specially-allocated cars included the standardisation of £4,000-worth of previously optional extras for a mere

£1,000 premium. Then, in May there was the 'Performance' edition (there were 'Performance' M5s too), which offered no more performance, but would apply special liveries and wheels to a mere 30 cars.

It was, in other words, getting close to the end, though the M3 continued to be a formidable contender in whatever class the pundits intended to force it. As a normal four-seater road car – which the Coupé, indeed, was – its performance put it out of the league of most other European four-seaters, so the pundits tended to compare it with sports coupés such as Porsche 911s and Caymans.

Yet it was, of course, much more than just that. An M3 could cope with heavy and continuous traffic (even though it was a waste of its prodigious talents) with the magnificent V8 engine doing little more than turn over at tick-over speeds while, unleashed, it was one of the world's fastest cars in any A-to-B scramble on surfaced roads. And not only that, for the build quality was up to the expected BMW standards with equipment to match, the air conditioning was as capable as one would expect of a £50,000 car and the cabin was quiet at the most illegal of open-road speeds to which anyone would like to admit.

So what, if the insurance companies tended to load an M3 and its owner with all manner of caveats, and even though the day-to-day consumption of premium-grade fuel could be forced down below the 20mpg mark, and so what if tyre replacement prices were high – this was never meant to be a 'sensible' family car. It was the sort of machine that BMW had evolved over a full generation, and one that was almost an aspirational driver's dream.

Not only that, but over the years the M3 pedigree had developed to combine the colossal capabilities of performance that every road tester concentrated on, along with a high standard of

equipment ('fixtures and fittings', as it were), along with a ride and handling package that made all but the snootiest of testers very happy indeed.

Even so, by mid-2012, it had already been on sale for five seasons without visual changes, and with no more than logical development changes to the engine and transmission. Sneak pictures, and an indiscreet remark or two from BMW personalities, had already indicated what might be in store for 2013 and beyond. Would a new M3 be as outstanding as all the previous types had been?

ABOVE: Neat little fittings for the CRT included red features for the front wing hot air vents, and for the bonnet vents too.

BELOW: The front seat shells of the M3 CRT of 2011 were produced from carbon fibre, not only because this was a very stiff material, but also because it could help reduce vehicle weight.

Chapter 7

# More motor racing –
## DTM, world events, success around the world

Although BMW was as keen as ever to keep up with its motor racing programme, in the early 1990s it became clear that the very latest E36-style M3s would no longer be suitable, eligible, or competitive for the latest type of touring car racing, where regulations ensured that there was either a 2-litre or 2.5-litre engine size limit, or a class structure that rendered the 3.0-litre six-cylinder M3 unsuitable. In fact, there was a time when it looked as if there would no longer be any suitable formulas, in the near future, in which the E36 could compete with any hope of success.

Quite simply, in the late 1980s the success of models like the original E30 M3s, and (in the larger-capacity class) the Ford Sierra RS500 Cosworths, was such that most rival car makers were neither capable, nor financially willing, to keep up. Thus it was that the World series, then the European series, died of neglect (or of high and ever-increasing costs), and a variety of national championships had to take over instead.

Thus it was that by 1992, when the original E36 M3 came on stream, it was the German series (the DTM) and the British series that had become the most high-profile, and therefore the most significant – even though the use of 3-litre-engined cars was not authorised in either series.

Fortunately for BMW enthusiasts, and team entrants, two special-regulations events – the Nürburgring 24 Hours and the Spa [Belgium] 24 Hours – carried on, and in each case it was possible to use modified and sometimes rather specialised versions of the cars that would otherwise be competing in a country's national championships.

Before venturing into Europe (which was, of course, 'home ground' to the Schnitzer teams and the Ravaglias of the touring car race world), a swift analysis of what happened in the UK tells a story which was repeated, in some ways, in other territories.

No British touring car race period has been as exciting, or as close-fought, as that of the 1990s, when events ran to what was known as the 'Super Touring Cars' formula. This was a period during which all eligible cars had to run with normally-aspirated 2-litre engines (which would be rev-limited to 8,500rpm), and there were different weight limits to try to equate traction differences between front-, rear- or even four-wheel-drive cars. Free in some respects, but heavily restricted in others, this package was then progressively adopted by touring car race organisers all over the world. All, however, soon discovered that although these regulations could produce very close racing, this was often followed by technical complication, at very high prices to entrants. Accordingly, by 2000, and because of those high costs, the edifice was in danger of collapse.

**PREVIOUS PAGES:**
**In fully-prepared race condition, the V8-engined E46 GTR of 1993 was a fearsome and successful saloon car racer.**

Originally authorised by the RAC MSA of Britain, to appease other manufacturers who might want to race, but whose cars could not match the BMW E30 M3s and the Sierra RS500 Cosworths, the Super Touring Car formula set out to make all things possible for those willing to spend the money, and to make sure that superficially mechanically mundane cars could be developed to a very high standard. We now know that in the UK it was representatives of Vauxhall and BMW – both of whom could produce competitive 2-litre cars from their existing outclassed machinery – who did most of the lobbying before this was adopted.

In the UK in 1991, this extract from the new rules shows why the new E36 M3 would be at a grave disadvantage:

- Cars had to be saloons, versions of those of which more than 5,000 had been built in the previous 12 months.

- Engines to be 2-litre, normally aspirated, units. Existing power units could be enlarged, or reduced in capacity, to suit this limit (BMW found this acceptable, for the E30 M3 engine could easily be reduced in size).

- Engines to be from that manufacturer's range, but not necessarily those already fitted to the chosen model range. (This rule suited BMW very well, of course, as they had four-cylinder and six-cylinder engines that would fit into a chosen engine bay.)

- Engine speeds to be restricted to 8,500rpm by electronic limiters.

- Two-wheel drive to be the norm, though front-wheel-drive cars could run 221lb (100kg) lighter than rear-drive cars.

Ford, bluntly, said they were not interested at first, though BMW, Renault and Vauxhall were all attracted. For 1991 the RAC MSA then decided to impose these regulations as the new template for British saloon car racing. Everyone expected a straight fight between factory-supported Vauxhalls and a fleet of modified BMW E30 M3s: these used engines with a 93.4mm cylinder bore, like that of

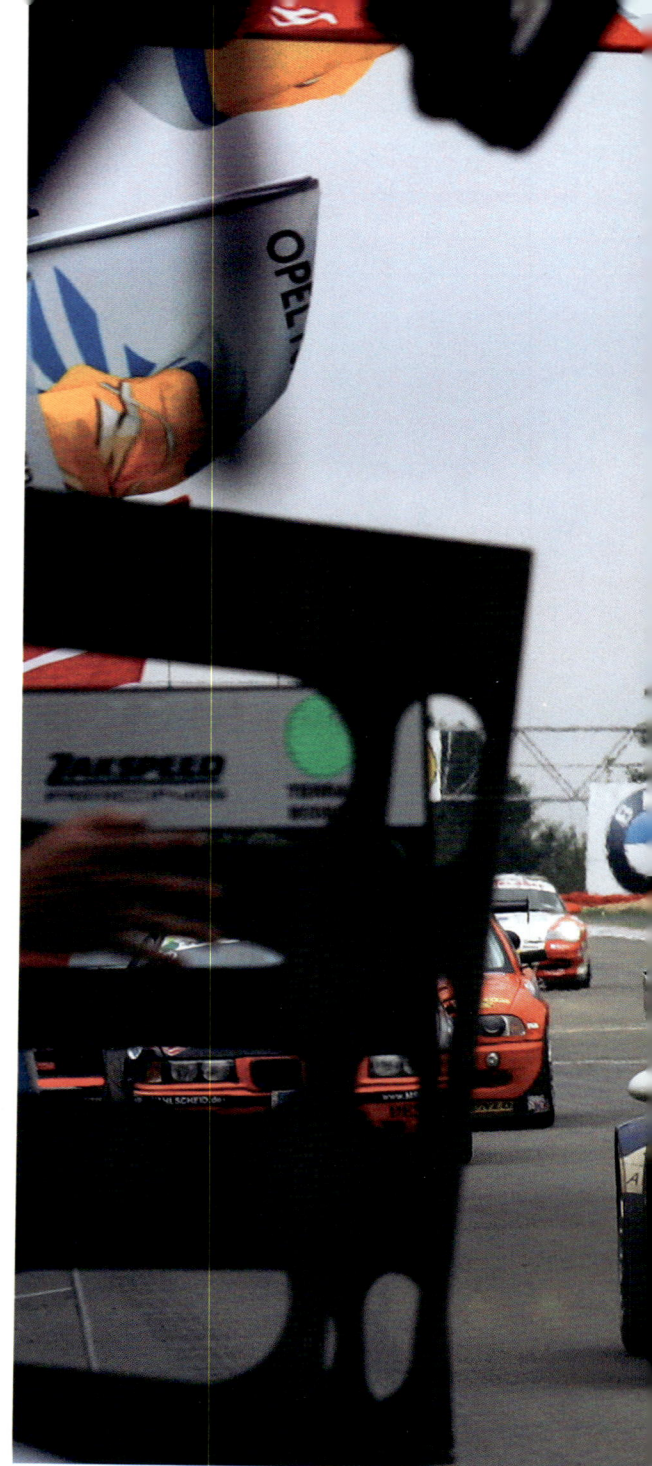

the road-going E30 M3, but with a short stroke (approx 73mm) crankshaft.

Accordingly, at the end of a season in which no fewer than 16 different M3 drivers scored points, Vauxhall's John Cleland won four races, while Andy Rouse's Toyota Carina won three times. The Championship winner, however, was Will Hoy – his M3 being run by the Vic Lee team – who won three races, but stood on the podium a further seven times.

One year on, and once again it was a BMW

ABOVE: **First and second on the grid, first and second to finish the race – beat that if you can. These were the 'works'-assisted E46 GTRs in the Nürburgring 24 Hour race of 1994.**

that won the Championship. Competitive drivers including Championship-winner Tim Harvey used suitably tuned new-shape E36 318i Coupés (which were now allowed to compete) instead of the obsolete M3 (though smaller-capacity four-cylinder E30-type M3 engines, which produced up to 280bhp at 8,500rpm, were still being used). Harvey won six of the 15 races, while all the other plaudits went to Vauxhall Cavaliers (five victories) and Toyota Carinas (four victories).

The next big changes came in 1993, when the regulations were changed once again, obliging all teams to run four-door saloon body-shells. Not only did Ford return, by hiring Andy Rouse to develop the all-new front-wheel-drive Mondeo, but henceforth BMW UK ran a fully-fledged 'works' team using four-door 318iS models. Most pundits agreed that the Mondeo was the real revelation in the 1993 season. Even so, it was BMW's Motorsport Team that won the Championship, with some ease. 'Smoking Jo' Winkelhock (these days, for sure, the 'health police' would baulk at the way that the amiable German would light up a cigarette as soon as his helmet was off, and he was out of the car) won five races, while his teammate Steve Soper won three times.

Then, in 1994, there was another step change – not only in engineering, but also in publicity and marketing interest. Technically, this was a year in which BMW, Ford, Peugeot, Renault, Toyota, Vauxhall – and Volvo – were all prominent, all with approximately 300bhp engines, all running at minimum championship weights, and all making unavoidable physical contact with their rivals from time to time. From mid-season, the regulation defining the minimum weight gap between front-drive and rear-drive cars was reduced by 50kg, to give BMW more of a chance, for by this time every other competitive car in the series had front-wheel drive and was running lighter. Even then that wasn't quite enough, so before the end of the season BMW were allowed to cut another 25kg – yet they were still not winning.

Even so, the stars of the 1995 season were the rejuvenated Vauxhall Cavaliers (John Cleland became Champion, six years on from his Astra success of 1989), and the Renault Lagunas (a team run by the Williams F1 operation) took ten wins, but

the BMW 318s were still off the pace.

Frank Biela, using a four-wheel-drive Audi A4, won eight times in 1996, and this was also the season in which the renowned Schnitzer team brought their BMW experience (plus star drivers Winkelhock and Ravaglia) to the UK for the first time in years. However, not even victories for this, and other rejuvenated teams – four for Menu's Renault Laguna, four for Winkelhock's Schnitzer-prepared BMW 320i, four for Rickard Rydell's Volvo 850, and a creditable three for David Leslie's Honda Accord – could upset that progress. BMW was pleased to finish second in the Manufacturers' Championship, and hoped for more in 1997.

By 1997, racing and technical development in the Super Touring category was at its height, but because of the 2-litre engine size limit there was still no way that the contemporary E36 M3 Evolution could be used. The cars were technically more sophisticated than ever, the racing was ultra-close, and the spectacle made them real crowd-pleasers. Not for nothing did *Autosport*'s annual survey begin: 'Brilliant, unpredictable racing. A host of different winners. A championship whose destiny remained in doubt right up until the closing stages of the season.'

RIGHT: Looking just as purposeful as expected, this was the E36 M3 as prepared for IMSA racing in the USA in 1995, the driver being Hans ('Hanschen') Stuck.

ABOVE: Johnny Cecotto, driving a 1993 M3 E36 GTR (complete with prototype V8 engine) to win the German GT Cup in 1993.

LEFT: Driving the still-new E36 M3, Johnny Cecotto was successful at Zolder in 1993.

However, after 1996, there was no further sign of interest from BMW, and the works-backed Schnitzer team's ambitious plans were never to be realised. Disillusion set in among drivers, teams and (for they had to pay the bills) the manufacturers in 1998, when several, including BMW, made it clear that they would soon withdraw their support because it was all getting too costly for them. Spending a fortune to win, it seemed, was one thing, but spending it to lose was another.

At the end of 2000, with interest down to just three manufacturers (not BMW), an entirely different saloon car race formula was to take over. For the 2000s, it seemed, the eligible cars would have to be slower if not simpler – and BMW was not interested in that approach.

And so it was with several other major racing championships in Europe. Even in the German DTM series, where BMW E30 M3s had provided motive power for the Drivers' Championship winners – Eric van de Poele, Roberto Ravaglia and Hans-Joachim Stuck – three times in the late 1980s, the company steadily lost interest as the regulations changed to allow more and yet more special machinery, as costs rose and (unhappily) as the E30 cars went out of production and in any case became technically obsolete. For 1993, for instance, Group A regulations were abandoned in favour of a more free-and-easy 2.5-litre category, where features like carbon-fibre special chassis, four-wheel drive, ABS brakes and electronic driver aids were all authorised, even though the production car on which some machines were based might not even have them as standard. Costs rose, and continued to rise.

When the DTM was effectively absorbed into the newly-founded International Touring Car Championship in 1996, with some qualifying rounds being held as geographically far apart as Brazil and Japan, cost controls seem to fly out of the window, and the sporting attraction to sensible managements (as opposed to incurable romantics, which BMW most assuredly was not) rapidly evaporated. When every manufacturer except Mercedes-Benz withdrew at the end of 1996, that series abruptly vanished into the ether. The DTM, this time to be renamed Deutsche Tourenwagen Masters, was not revived until 2000.

BELOW: Huge rear wheels, extra wheel arch extensions and a vast rear spoiler – this could only be the E46 of 1993–1994.

ABOVE: **The V8-powered GTR was competitive wherever the regulations allowed it to race – this being at the Nürburgring in 2004.**

In the meantime, the success of the 2-litre 'Super Touring' type of saloon car racing in the UK rapidly saw it being taken up by countries all over the world (including Australia, though in the hearts of that nation's spectators it could never replace the long-standing V8 Championship which was only being contested between domestically-manufactured Ford and Holden cars). Such countries which did adopt Super Touring fell in line with the convention that the cars themselves would have to be current-model four-door saloons which were in regular quantity production, but that engines from another model range could be used, just so long as these were modified to be of 2-litre capacity, and would run only up to 8,500rpm before hitting an electronic rev limiter.

For BMW, therefore, there was still an obvious 'get out of jail' clause, with the concession that alternative engines of the same brand could be used, for there seemed to be no point in trying to reduce the E36-type straight six all the way down to 2.0 litres when the company already

had a robust and still totally competitive 2-litre four-cylinder (the short-stroke version of the E30 M3) which was available in large numbers, and could produce robust, reliable and competitive horsepower.

Paul Rosche's team had evolved an engine which was at once light, and sang its way up to 8,500rpm without complaint, so why should anyone complain if it was put into cars that were not normally sold on the road in such a guise? No one did, of course, and victories continued to pile up. For what can only have been marketing reasons, the cars on which these Super Touring 'specials' were created were often supposedly based on the six-cylinder 320i shell, which was, of course, almost identical in size and bulk to that of the latest M3 Saloons.

Because the cost and complication of DTM was already spiralling out of control, in 1994 the German authorities had set up an alternative series, the Deutsch Tourenwagen Cup, which ran to rules similar to those in Super Touring. In 1995, there

OPPOSITE TOP: Hidden away behind that purposeful nose, complete with functional air intakes, and louvres in the bonnet panel, was the prototype V8 engine of the E46 GTR. This was the final 2005 version of what was a near-unique car.

OPPOSITE BOTTOM: Although not strictly a production car under the rules that existed, the V8-engined E46 GTR was nonetheless eligible to compete in the Nürburgring 24 Hour race. In 2005, there was a fantastic 'double' victory in that famous event.

BELOW: Impressive from any angle, but particularly from above where the extra aerodynamic features used on Schnitzer-prepared V8 GTRs are clear. This shows the car in its final flowering in 2005.

were eight rounds, of which BMW 318is won four races, the Series Champion being Joachim Winkelhock, with his team rival Peter Kox second. A year later, in 1996, Schnitzer-prepared 320is remained competitive in Italy (against the Alfa Romeos), with Johnny Cecotto taking second place.

In 1997, which was surely at the peak of this generation's remarkable powers, modified-M3-engined Super Touring 320is won championships in Australia, Belgium, Germany (the Tourenwagen Cup), Italy, South America, Holland, France and New Zealand. Even as late as 1998, this series (now working purely to Super Touring rules) involved a running battle between BMW and Peugeot, the honours going to Johnny Cecotto and Laurent Aiello, both of them BMW-mounted, in spite of them carrying 25kg of extra weight because of running with rear-wheel drive.

In those years, the new-shape 3-Series cars with old-type M3 engines continued to win races and championships all round the world. Purely as examples: in 1995 Yvan Muller won nine of 18 rounds in the French Super Touring Championship, defeating strong 'works' teams from Opel and Vauxhall Vectra, and in the

same year Steve Soper spent much of his time commuting to and from Japan, where he eventually won the Japanese Championship, defeating a phalanx of Japanese domestic 'works' teams, causing a great deal of 'loss of face'.

In the meantime, and to the delight of the BMW teams who knew just how competitive and reliable an M3-developed car could be, race organisers at the Nürburgring in Germany and at the Spa circuit in Belgium continued to organise 24-hour racing marathons. The fortunes of the E30 M3-based cars prepared for those events has already been told in Chapter 2.

Once again, however, as the years passed by, it was no longer thought suitable for obsolete-shape (E30) M3s to be racing in such events. The cars which entered, and won, so many races in the 1990s and early 2000s might have retained some elements of current and old-style M3 engineering under the skin (most important, too, the teams could still draw on the depths of race-car experience that had been built up at this time), but were invariably entered as 318s and 320s.

At the end of the 2000s, however, from time to time E92-type M3s were once again entered in races that suited their capabilities, and two different

specifications – E92 M3 GT2 and E92 M3 GT4, both with the existing 4-litre V8 engines – were evolved. As examples, Schnitzer prepared GT2 cars for the 1000km of Spa event in 2009, where one of the examples took a praiseworthy fourth overall, and there was even more astonishing success in the 2010 Nürburgring 24 Hour race, where a car driven by Jorg Muller, Augusto Farfus, Pedro Lamy and Uwe Alzen (it was a long and excessively gruelling race!) won outright.

Further afield, GT2 cars entered by Rahal Letterman Racing competed with honour in the 2009 American Le Mans Series. M3 GT2s won the category in the ILMC 1000km race at Zhuhai (a Chinese area, very close indeed to Macau). In 2011, such BMWs finished first and second in the 12 Hours of Sebring race in Florida. Further triumph came for the Rahal Letterman team came in 2011 when, in the ALMS GT Category they won the Manufacturers', Team and Drivers' Championships, the driving team including such world-renowned notables as Andy Priaulx, Oliver Gavin, Dirk Muller and Joey Hand. The same team won two of the ten events outright in 2012.

GT4s started racing in 2009, to an M3 specification which included near-standard (but naturally very carefully-prepared 4-litre V8 engines), but these were intended really as 'customer' race cars for certain types of racing, and there was no involvement, for instance, from fully works-backed teams like Schnitzer.

## M3 GTR – designed for motorsport

In 2001, the M3 GTR (GT Race car?) was a sensational new competition model that made many headlines in the multi-national American Le Mans Series (ALMS), then found itself summarily banned from competition in 2002 by a swingeing change of regulations. Effectively, the 2001 M3 GTR race cars were prototypes, but for 2002 when the company was suddenly faced with the need to meet the hastily revised regulations by making no fewer than 100 de-tuned road cars and (worse, far worse and far more costly) 1,000 engines, they cancelled the entire programme forthwith.

ALMS had been invented in North America, though events were also being held outside

that vast continent, and in the beginning the GT category in which M3s were racing had been dominated by Porsche 911s of one variety or another. When the M3 GTR came along, with one purpose in mind – that of defeating the 911s – it immediately unbalanced the pecking order, the GTR started winning, and furious lobbying to change the regulations began once again.

The original regulations, which cannot possibly have been assembled by anyone with the hidden mental reserves of a motor racing team

manager's mind, effectively tried to impose what we might call 'silhouette' racing, where the race cars would continue to look like road cars that you or I (correction: well-to-do customers, more likely) could buy. The organisers, however, cannot have expected that a company as ambitious and capable as BMW would go ahead and develop a completely new engine to suit!

The rationale behind the stillborn 'production cars' (350bhp, but retaining all the appropriate chassis and running gear features), which BMW promised to make and sell, has already been spelt out in Chapter 5. For the high-profile ALMS series, and to make the M3 competitive once again against the equally-specialised Porsche 911 of the day – the 996 GT3 model – in 2000 (and in great secrecy) the M3 GTR began to take shape. Naturally it took on board all the assembled expertise of earlier BMW 'works' and favoured private teams, but the real secret of this machine was that it was to use a brand new and unique V8 engine: the P60B40 3,997cc V8 power unit.

ABOVE: Specifically designed for the North American ALMS race car series, the V8-engined GTR dominated its category in the 2001 series. Here was one of the victorious cars at Laguna Seca, in California.

It is important to stress that this engine had nothing at all in common with the BMW V8s that were already being used, in big numbers, in existing 5-Series and 7-Series cars, but had been specially designed by the same team of engineers who were already building and developing 850bhp 3-litre V10 F1 engines for the Williams F1 team. Nothing, it seemed to them, was impossible – and they set out to prove it!

A brief look at engine specs, as eventually released by BMW, show that this was a conventional racing V8 by early 2000s standards, in that it was built around a 90° V-formation, of lightweight materials, with steel crank and rods, four valves per cylinder, a 12.0:1 compression ratio, and was originally rated at approximately 450bhp. It does not, incidentally, seem to have had any relationship to the V8 that would eventually be fitted to all E90-generation M3s, starting in 2007.

Amazingly, in race car form it could have been made much more powerful than this, which became clear when one example was shown to the European media at the Vallelunga race circuit towards the end of the 2001 season. Another team driver, Dirk Muller, pointed out the way that intake air for the engine had to be taken through two small inlet trumpets near the front of the car (which included restrictors imposed by regulations) because: 'Without these, the engine would produce between 600–650bhp. But the ALMS rules say we have to run with air restrictors, hence these two plastic trumpets, which is why the car only has about 450bhp in racing trim.'

Visually, the M3 GTR race car had demonstrably been evolved from the E46 M3 Coupé, though it was at once lower, wider and with more obvious aerodynamic add-ons to provide increased downforce. Not only were the front and rear wings fettled to allow ultra-wide 11in rim wheels and 270-section Michelin racing tyres to be fitted, but also the sizes and shapes of the front bumper/lower spoiler, and the rear bumper/diffuser were massively enhanced. There were also extra cooling vents in the bonnet panel, and a big transverse rear spoiler with struts fixed to the Coupé's boot lid panel.

Because the weight had been slashed, right down to 1,120kg (2,469lb), this was an impressively rapid beast, which went on to make mincemeat of its Porsche opposition in 2001, and won the ALMS GT category outright. Fierce and strident lobbying from rivals (notably Porsche) began before the end of that year, which resulted in the authorities deciding that, for it to remain eligible in 2002 the BMW would have to carry an extra 45kg (100lb), and that no fewer than 100 road cars and 1,000 of this unique and magnificent V8 engine would have to be produced.

As already noted in Chapter 5, BMW baulked at this, and withdrew the GTR from motorsport at once. All, however, was not quite lost, and the still-young race cars were preserved. In the mid-2000s, when race regulations continued to be suitable, GTRs prepared by Schnitzer won the Nürburgring 24 Hour race in 2004 and 2005, and other privately-entered cars were also successful. British driver Andy Priaulx was one of the winning drivers in that second year, when he was already on his way to becoming one of the most successful touring car race drivers in the world.

## DTM racing – 2012

As an addendum to this Chapter, I should summarise the remarkably successful return that cars called BMW M3s (but actually including a negligible number of standard parts) made to the German-based DTM (Deutsche Tourenwagen Masters) in 2012. To recapitulate: BMW, having won more than 40 DTM races in the 1980s and 1990s w th E30-generation M3s, had withdrawn from that series as costs got out of hand, and had concentrated more on racing sports car and Formula 1 engine design instead.

Although BMW had not been a part of this series once it was revived in 2000, when the move to impose a standardised chassis and other componentry was proposed, in 2010 a decision was taken to come back in due course. BMW Motorsport then spent the next year or so building up a new design, showed concept cars at the end of 2011, and homologated the new DTM race car design in March 2012. It then made such a successful return from 'retirement' in 2012 that it became the champion manufacturer in that year (beating the long-established and high-profile Audi and Mercedes-Benz teams) but it also provided the cars used by the Drivers' Championship winner, Swiss-born Bruno Spengler.

In the opening paragraph of this section, I rather cautiously used the phrase 'cars called BMW M3s' because, in truth, BMW's DTM cars raced under that name, and looked superficially like an E92 M3 Coupé of the period, but were almost entirely special. Not that this was cheating, because that was the whole object of DTM racing, for all the rival teams' cars were equally as special. Indeed, it was one of the race regulations that only the roof panel of the standard road car should compulsorily be used in the race cars, while the rest of the assembly could be entirely unique. The DTM organisers also pointed out that their rigidly inspected regulations ensured that more than 50 of the components in the design of every DTM car were standardised (or 'spec'), these including the six-speed sequential transmission, the ZF-Sachs four-plate clutch and the rear wing of all the cars.

All the cars in this series (and the 'BMW M3s' were no less so) were intended to be fast and spectacular to watch, and to drive. All had to have rear-wheel drive, and all had to have 4.0-litre V8

**LEFT: After a decade-long absence, BMW returned to the highly prestigious DTM series in 2012 and beat stiff competition from Mercedes-Benz and Audi to win it outright. The regulations allowed BMW to build an entirely special car, though it had visual similarities to the latest E92 M3 road car. Posed next to it, here, is a new-type 335i, complete with a kit of Performance parts.**

engines with a 90° configuration. Much of the bodywork/structure, and the specified safety roll cage, was standardised, the cage being steel and the tub being in carbon fibre. All cars used the same 18in diameter alloy wheels (with 11in front rims and 12in rear rims) shod in Hankook tyres.

On this new BMW, the normally-aspirated 4-litre engine, coded P66, was all-new, though clearly inspired by the 4.0-litre engine of the existing M3 road car, and its peak power output was limited to approximately 480 to 500bhp, because the regulations specified the use of the two 28mm diameter air restrictors in the V8's inlet passages.

With the renowned Schnitzer team running the fastest of the cars – there were six 'M3s' in the permanent 22-car field – and with those cars proving to be remarkably reliable and race-competitive, Bruno Spengler had all the backing he needed. Of the 11 events in the programme (most of them in Germany, but with visits to the UK, Spain and Holland during the year), Spengler won four times, finished second once and finished third once. It was a truly excellent comeback to a series that was far, far different from the one that the company had previously quit in the 1990s.

## Modern BMWs (but not M3s) in saloon car events

In the 21st century, motor racing's authorities have bowed to powerful but sometimes nebulously-defined pressure from 'environmental campaigners' by running major championships for cars with small and yet smaller engines. This, almost by definition, has precluded BMW from entering M3-based cars, although other models have been extremely successful.

Earlier in the 2000s, cars were restricted to 2-litre engines, but the latter-day World Touring Car series was run for turbocharged 1.6-litre cars, and BMW had their share of outright victories (Britain's Andy Priaulx started by being third in the 2003 European Series, then went on to become the winner in 2004, and topped that with a sensational run, when he became World Touring Car Champion in 2005, 2006 and 2007, all of them in BMW cars variously titled 320i or 320Si). By this time, however, the technical connection with the M3 pedigree was increasingly tenuous, and I must bring the story to a (perhaps temporary) halt at this point.

**BELOW: With nearly 500bhp, here is Bruno Spengler's DTM car at Brands Hatch in 2012.**

**ABOVE:** Bruno Spengler's BMW at Zandvoort, in Holland, in the DTM race of 2012. Only the roof panel of this car is from a standard M3, the rest being entirely race-special.

**LEFT:** Racing in the DTM series of 2012 was always very close – this being BMW driver Bruno Spengler's 'M3' leading one of the rival Mercedes-Benz cars to the finish in the last race at Hockenheim.

## Chapter 8

# Fifth-generation M3s and M4s from 2013

In the end, we had to wait until the end of 2012 before any definite news (as opposed to rumours and off-the-record briefings) came of what might be done to replace the existing E92 M3 with a new model. Not that there had been any lack of rumour in the meantime, for the latest-generation 3-Series, on which any new-type M3 would presumably be based, had been launched in the winter of 2011/2012.

The news, when it came, was at once reassuring and confusing. In 2013, it seemed, there would be no launch of a new-generation M3 Coupe (which was rumoured to be the F80 type), but instead there would be an M4 Coupe, and later a convertible. BMW, it seemed, had moved on, was continuing to expand its product range, and was going to separate coupes from other derivatives. Oh, and by the way, there would still be a new M3, one day, but that would be a four-door saloon only and we would have to wait a few more months to get a glimpse of it.

This, it seemed, was all part of BMW's steadily developing long-term strategy, where the '2', and '4' categories, which had been missing from the line-up for several decades, would finally be opened up, and formalised. Over the years, rumours had abounded, but this was the first time that such suggestions were to be turned into fact. In December 2012, when showing a car called a BMW Concept 4 Series Coupe, a BMW

spokesman said that: 'The "4" doesn't just mark the start of a new cycle; it marks the start of a model with its own individual character, and a stand-alone design.'

Because of the time limits imposed when producing this book, the images shown are of that Concept coupe which, although acknowledged to be a faithful representation of the 4-Series production car, may yet have one or two of the more extreme styling details toned down before series production begins. However, what was hidden away – the running gear and the chassis engineering – is what the M3 enthusiast would be most interested in, and for the time being BMW was not about to reveal all that.

Even though the new 4-Series Coupe was to get a new name, it was clear that the basic philosophy of how it had evolved would be the same as before – it would, in other words, be based on the platform and basic chassis engineering of the latest-generation 3-Series; it would have a compact but well-equipped and well-trimmed four-seater cabin; and it would, of course, be the most powerful, the fastest and the most specialised derivative of that range. Although (and designers must excuse a novice here) the 'theme' of the new 4-Series/M4 was very similar to the existing type, the chassis was a logical improvement on what had gone before. Unsurprisingly, the wheelbase of the new 3-Series

**ABOVE: How much of this M4 Concept coupe would make it to production line ? Almost all of it, if the rumours were substantiated.**

**PREVIOUS PAGES: By the mid-2000s, BMW had thoroughly modernised its original downtown HQ and production base in Munich. This aerial view shows the layout in its modern condition. The administrative block – which is affectionately known as the 'four-cylinder building' – and the near-complete Welt (World) marketing and exhibition complex dominate the foreground.**

(which was likely to be shared with the 4-Series) was 5mm/2in longer than before, the overall length having crept up by 93mm/3.7in. Although the new car was no wider than the outgoing model, the front and rear tracks had expanded by some 1.7in, and the styling details lined themselves up like the mass-production 3-Series, first revealed in December 2011.

Although BMW was still reluctant to discuss mechanical details when the 4-Series Concept was first shown (and to make no comment, absolutely no comment, about the running gear which might appear in a new-for-2014 M3 saloon), all the signs were that, once again, there would be a radical change of power train. The reasoning behind this, at corporate level, was that BMW had to meet ever-tightening exhaust pollution and other environmental regulations, and chose to do this by using direct fuel injection and turbocharging.

By 2013, there was already a choice of ten different engines in the latest 3-Series (four of them being diesels, and one being a petrol/hybrid combination). The most powerful of these was the

340bhp Hybrid model, complete with straight-six turbo power.

In the meantime, the fabulous 507bhp 5-litre V10 engine, which had powered the M5 since 2004, had been unceremoniously dropped, for the latest M5, launched as recently as mid-2011, was powered by the latest derivative of BMW's mass-produced V8, a 4.4-litre with twin turbochargers producing 560bhp. The inference, though it was not spelt out in as many words, was that if the specialised V10 had been killed off then the closely related 420bhp V8 that powered the E92 M3 would not have long to live.

For 2014, therefore, it seemed as if the F80 M3 would have a 450bhp straight-six-cylinder engine, which would be complete with direct fuel injection and turbocharging. That engine, it was suggested, would be backed by a choice of manual or automatic transmissions (by Getrag and ZF respectively), and the result would be an explosively fast four-door saloon car which would be faster and more capable than any previous M3.

Was the marketplace impatient? You could say so ...

ABOVE: The first of the new-generation M4 types, the Concept, was clearly aimed at taking over from all previous M3 Coupes.

LEFT: What a dramatic front-end study ! The M4 Concept Coupe was similar, in so many ways, to other BMWs of the early 2010s.

# Not forgetting –
## M Roadsters and Coupés, 1 Series M Coupés, M635CSis, X5Ms and more – an entire M family

It would be quite wrong of me to conclude the story of the M3's development without mentioning some of the other M-badged cars that have been developed and put on sale alongside the M3s throughout their career. The M division, in fact, eventually became a very sizeable part of BMW's automotive business, and continues to expand: the 300,000th M-badged car was built in 2008.

The M treatment has now been applied to BMWs as small as the 1-Series and as bulky as the four-wheel-drive X5 models, and we also know that the company had dabbled with (then rejected) the idea of applying the same magic to even larger machinery. Some of the cars that were put on the market were more specialised than others, and the engineering of some versions was shared with BMW's 'mainstream' engineers, but all of them proudly flaunted the 'M' badge and invariably proved to be a commercial success.

The evolution of the larger M5 models has already been covered in the Interlude (page 82), and what follows are other M-models that have already made it to the showrooms (undoubtedly there will be more in future years), but to avoid this appendix developing into a separate book I have kept the coverage of each 'M family' model to a limited summary.

**RIGHT:** In its day, the 160mph-plus M1 was a match for any contemporary Ferrari, but was very expensive to build. Only 454 such cars were sold in three years, but the M-pedigree was well and truly founded.

## M1 (1979–1981)

(Basic specification: Mid-engined, two-seater Coupé; 3,453cc, 277bhp, six-cylinder. 454 cars built.)

As already made clear in the Prologue, the M1 was the very first M-badged car to be produced by BMW. In many ways this was the most specialised of all M-Type cars, for it had a totally unique chassis, body style and transmission. It was the very first BMW production car to use the four-valve twin-ohc layout that became usual on almost all subsequent BMW M-Types.

**BELOW: The original M-badged BMW was the mid-engined M1, which was revealed in 1978. Not only did it look sensational, but also it was very fast, and was the first BMW to use a four-valves-per-cylinder engine.**

## M635CSi/M6 (1984–1989)

(Basic specification: Front-engined, four-seater, two-door Coupé; 3,453cc, 286bhp, six-cylinder. 5,855 cars built.)

This was a logical combination of the 24-valve twin-ohc engine/transmission drivetrain of the original M5 that was being developed at the same time, with the structure/equipment of the 635CSi, which was a close-coupled four-seater Coupé model based on the platform of the existing 5-Series. One of the ancestors of this car had been the 3.0CSL 'Batmobile' that had done so much for BMW in touring car racing in the 1970s, so its rationale and implied marketing stance was clear. It was also known as the M6 in the USA market.

**ABOVE:** The 6-Series had originally been announced in the mid-1970s. As well as a very successful 2+2-seater sports Coupé, it also proved itself in touring car racing. From 1984, BMW gave this bulky car a 3.5-litre/24-valve M1-type engine transplant, with modified suspension, and some aerodynamic add-ons to suit, calling it the M635CSi.

**LEFT:** To emphasise the new M635CSi's technical links with the M1 (the two cars shared the same 24-valve engine), BMW released this picture. Except for that engine, of course, there were no other items of shared hardware between the two cars.

## M Roadster and Coupé (1997–2002)

(Basic specification: Front-engined, two-seater sports car, or hatchback Coupé; 3,201cc, 321bhp, six-cylinder. 21,693 cars built.)

BMW was expanding vigorously in the mid-1990s, and was building the new-type Z3 range of sports cars and hatchback Coupés in its new production plant in the USA. It elected to combine the chassis of this Z3 model with the power train of the latest E36-generation M3. Although this was not easy, especially as the Z3 was based on the ageing platform of the 3-Series Compact (which had old-type semi-trailing arm rear suspension), it was made possible because a six-cylinder version of the Z3 was already being built. The Coupé version was launched in 1999. Cars sold in the USA used less powerful versions of this engine.

**ABOVE: This was the original Z3M Roadster, which used the E36 Evolution engine and power train, allied to the old-type chassis platform of the Z3.**

**BELOW: Pretty, distinctive, or what? The style of the Z3M of 1999 was, to say the leat, controversial.**

## M6 (V10 version, 2004–2010)

(Basic specification: Front-engined, four-seater, two-door Coupé and Convertible; 4,999cc, 507bhp, V10 – from 2012 4,395cc, 552bhp, V8. 14,143 V10-engined cars built.)

BMW's latest medium/large Coupé (one of a lengthy pedigree of such cars) evolved around the platform of the 5-Series, which had been launched in 2003: it was, itself, put on sale in the same year, and was mechanically a very close relation of the fourth-generation V10-engined M5. Although mechanically similar to the mainstream 5-Series, and using the platform, layout and chassis of that car, 6-Series cars had a four-seater, two-door Coupé style. For a comprehensively revised M6, after a gap in production, the latest turbocharged V8 replaced the limited-production V10 in 2012.

**ABOVE:** The modern generation 6-Series, which relied on the 5-Series and M5 for its chassis/running gear/platform, was an obvious candidate for the 'M-treatment'. The M6, therefore, was launched in 2004, complete with the magnificent 507bhp/5.0-litre V10 engine. Both Coupé and Convertible versions were available.

## Z4M (2005–2008)

(Basic specification: Front-engined, two-seater, two-door sports car; 3,245cc, 340bhp, six-cylinder.)

By the early part of the new century, BMW was virtually playing 'alphabetical spaghetti' with all its models, then engines, and the specialised markets for which new types were intended. The Z4M was a case in point. The original Z3 was a two-seater roadster (a Coupé followed later) announced in 1995 and manufactured at Spartanburg in the USA: the M derivative followed in 1997.

From 2002, the Z4 took over with a much more sophisticated chassis and, predictably, a Z4M type followed suit in 2005. Except for a different front spoiler (to channel more air into the engine bay than for the lower-powered Z4s), a different rear bumper and four exhaust tail pipes, the Z4M looked unchanged.

ABOVE: The M-developed version of the American-built Z4 sports car was announced in 2005, and was powered by a 340bhp, 3.2-litre, six-cylinder engine. There were two different body styles, this being the Roadster...

LEFT: ...and this being the hardtop Coupé.

## X5M (introduced in 2009)

(Basic specification: Front-engined, four-wheel-drive, five-seater SUV (estate car); 4,395cc, 555bhp, V8 – or 2,993cc, 381bhp, diesel, six-cylinder.)

BMW's X5 was its first four-wheel-drive SUV, announced in 1999, and was always manufactured at its newly-built USA factory in South Carolina. After selling hugely, it gave way to the second-generation type in 2006, and was then available with a variety of high-powered petrol and diesel engines, with automatic transmission. The M derivatives followed in 2009, with a choice of ultra-powerful turbocharged petrol and diesel engines.

**RIGHT: Built at its modern assembly plant at Spartanburg, USA, the X5 was BMW's original, very successful, four-wheel-drive SUV. Soon after the second-generation type was launched in 2006, work began on an M-derived version. From 2009 this was put on the market with a choice of 555bhp (petrol) or 381bhp (diesel) engines.**

## X6M (introduced in 2009)

(Basic specification: Front-engined, four-wheel-drive, five-seater, five-door Saloon; 4,395cc, 555bhp, V8 – or 2,993cc, 381bhp, six-cylinder diesel.)

The X6 was what is called a 'cross-over' derivative of the four-wheel-drive X5, retaining the same platform and running gear. On this car, however, there was a sleeker fastback body style, complete with hatchback. Mechanically, therefore, the X6M, which was launched in 2009, mirrored the X5M in every way.

**RIGHT: By the late 2000s there were so many BMWs (some M-badged and some not), that it was easy to get confused. The X6 was a five-door hatchback-styled derivative of the X5, but retained its four-wheel-drive system, while the X6M of 2009 used the same choice of petrol and diesel power as the equivalent X5.**

## 1-Series M Coupé (2011 only)

(Basic specification: Front-engined, rear-wheel-drive, four-seater, two-door Coupé; 2,979cc, 335bhp, six-cylinder. 6,331 cars built.)

Originally launched in 2004, the 1-Series was the 'entry-level' BMW for some years, complete with a conventional driveline, and a controversially ungainly hatchback body style. A two-door Coupé, based on the same platform, was then launched in 2007. For years, BMW had little interest in producing a performance version; then, in 2011, it suddenly announced the 1-Series M Coupé, which featured a 335bhp turbocharged six-cylinder engine. It received rave reviews, but was only ever meant to be a limited-production model, and was effectively replaced by the much-modified M135i in 2012.

## M135i (introduced 2012)

(Basic specification: Front-engined, four-seater, three-door hatch or five-door hatch; 2,979cc, 306bhp, six-cylinder.)

Soon after the revised-generation 1-Series was introduced, BMW announced its first M-type hatchback. This was badged M135i, and had the same three-door hatchback style as the mainstream cars. The 315bhp engine was a turbocharged version of BMW's latest, celebrated, 3.0-litre straight six, and was made available with either a six-speed Getrag manual, or an 8-speed ZF automatic transmission. Sales began in the autumn of 2012.

*This listing, of course, is only complete and correct as at the first printing of this book, and is sure to expand in the future. BMW discovered, years ago, that the 'M' badge was commercially valuable to them, and is sure to exploit it even more in the years to come.*

**LEFT:** Showing how much had changed in a generation, this is the 1-Series M Coupé of 2011 alongside an E30 Sport Evolution of the late 1980s.

**BELOW AND BELOW LEFT:** To follow the success of the limited-production 1-Series M Coupé, BMW launched the more ambitious M135i in 2012, which produced slightly less power (306bhp) but featured a restyled version of the three-door hatchback body-shell that made it into a very desirable and versatile package.

# BMW's four-cylinder engines from 1961

The heart and soul of the original M3, no question, was the high-revving and seemingly ultra-reliable 2.3-litre four-cylinder engine. However, although it might have looked (superficially at least) just like any other four-valve/twin-cam engine of the period, it was a power unit whose elements already had two decades of racing experience behind it before it went on sale in 1986, and it had come a long way in that time.

In the mid-1980s, other series-production 3-Series models were available with a choice of four-cylinder or six-cylinder, petrol or diesel, engines; that four-cylinder engine also finding a home in the larger-bodied 518i models. All such engines had two valves per cylinder, polyspherical-shaped combustion chambers, and single-overhead-camshaft valve gear.

By any standards, the existing four-cylinder engine was quite a venerable unit, for in M10/M12 form it had been in production in Munich for almost 25 years. As originally laid out by a team led by Alex von Falkenhausen, it was a sturdily-detailed unit, complete with cast-iron cylinder block and aluminium cylinder head, the overhead camshaft being driven by chain from the crankshaft. The first engine had an 82mm cylinder bore and a 71mm stroke, giving a swept volume of 1,499cc. It also had a single downdraught Solex carburettor, and was rated at 80bhp at 5,700rpm.

Nevertheless, in the 1960s this had always been intended to be the first, and most humble, of a family that was intended to stay in production for a long time. Within four years there would be 1.6-, 1.8- and 2.0-litre versions. Fuel injection became available on the more upmarket 2-litre types, and the engine was introduced to motorsport. First of all, in 1964/1965, came a model called the 1800TI/SA, which used a 1.8-litre engine with twin-choke Weber carburettors and was rated at 130bhp, and which became a successful (though limited-production) race car.

In the next few years, there was to be a brief racing programme for a turbocharged 2-litre car in touring car races (it was successful, but this was not a production engine), and in 1973 BMW even produced the 2002 Turbo, which was a fierce machine featuring a 170bhp/1,990cc derivation of the engine, in which the power was produced with the aid of Kugelfischer fuel injection allied to a big KKK turbocharger. All this, however, was overshadowed by the continuous development and improvement of engines for single-seater F2 racing, in which BMW eventually became the dominant power unit. It was this engine programme, together with the benefits demonstrated by the almost obscenely powerful turbocharged 1.5-litre F1 engine of the 1980s (see the panel on page 29) that directly led to the M3's power unit.

## F2 power in the 1970s

This all started when motorsport's governing body announced that from 1967 there would be a new Formula 2, in which engines would have to be normally-aspirated and would be limited to 1.6 litres, and in which those engines had to be built up around the basis of a series-production cylinder block. Both Ferrari (with an engine developed from the V6 Dino power unit) and Ford (with the Cosworth FVA that evolved from the Cortina power unit) were immediately seen as favourites – and no one at the time thought of BMW.

BMW, on the other hand, had already thought long and hard about this, and for the first time proposed to design a brand-new engine with twin-overhead camshafts and four valves per cylinder. It was at this point that an Austrian motorcycle engineer, Ludwig Apfelbeck, carried out experiments with what we might call a radial valve engine (in which the valves were arranged around a combustion chamber in the order inlet-exhaust-inlet-exhaust, with a single centrally-positioned spark plug, a complex intermediate link between two camshafts and the head of each valve, and showed up remarkable gas flow results.

BMW inspected this layout, liked what they saw, swallowed a 'brave pill', and applied it to an 89mm x 62.4mm (1,553cc) bottom end. They accepted that to make the installation practical they would need to use eight vertical inlet ports, and to have exhaust ports on both sides of the new cylinder head – four each side. Lucas provided the inlet-port fuel injection installation and, after much test bed work, the engine was rated at a claimed 220bhp at 9,500rpm. An excellently analysed and illustrated description appeared in Britain's *Autocar* magazine in April 1967, in which there was a fine cutaway drawing, yet BMW made sure that details of the Apfelbeck valve gear were not shown.

Although it was a heavy power unit, and none-too-reliable, it seemed to match the Cosworth-Ford's peak FVA power output, but was lacking in mid-range torque. There were some successes, but not enough to convince BMW that this twin-cam solution was better than that of Cosworth's FVA, which was already becoming accepted as the 'classic' for future development.

Accordingly, in 1969 a different type of 16-valver was developed, this still having the diametrically-opposed valve layout, but with no fewer than three spark plugs per cylinder, but even this was not the answer to all their hopes. Although it produced 225bhp at 10,500rpm, and was enough to help Hubert Hahne's BMW-Lola into second place in the European F2 Championship, it was only an interim device.

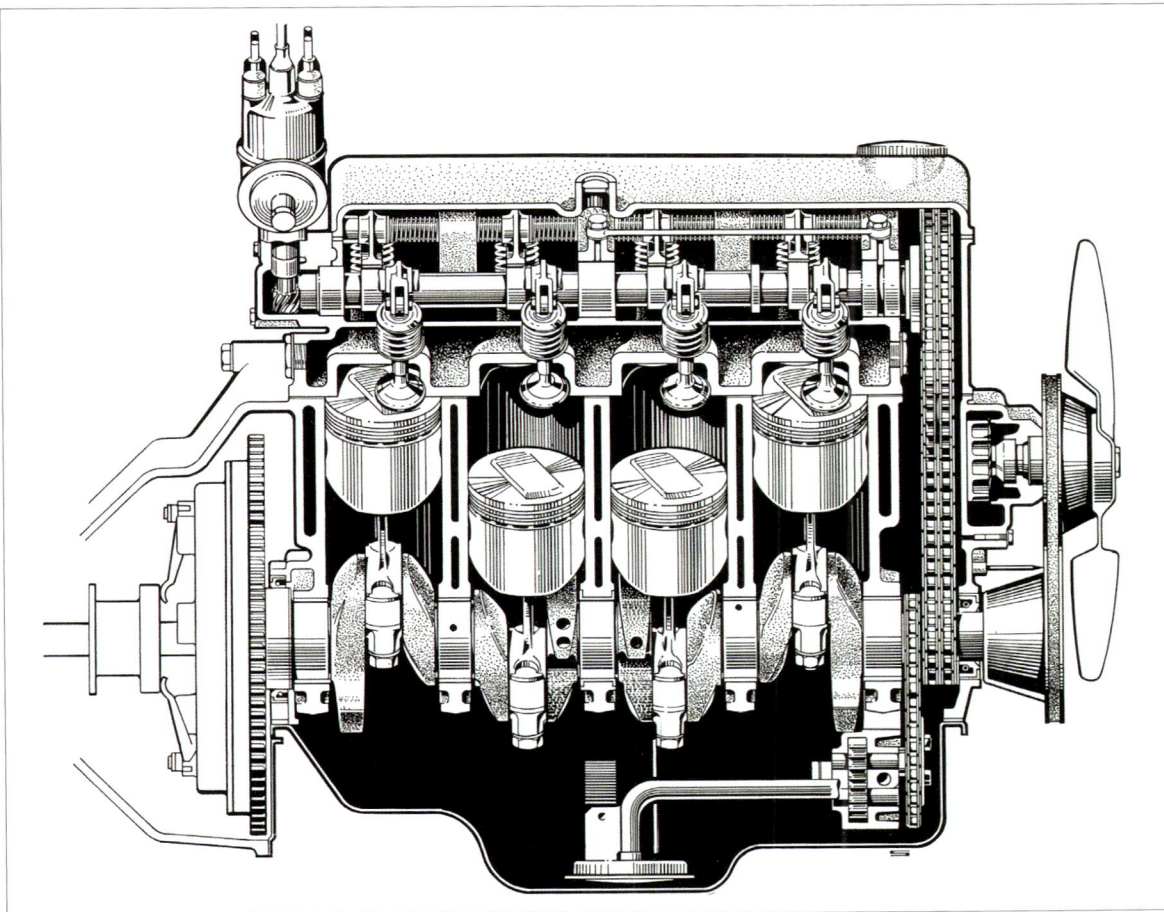

**LEFT:** In 1961, Alex von Falkenhausen finalised the very first of the four-cylinder overhead-camshaft engines that were to power all BMW cars for many years to come.

BELOW: This study shows off all the details of the four-cylinder overhead-camshaft engines.

The race engine that truly led BMW towards dominance (and that would eventually inspire the M3 power unit) was the M12/2, the first of this family to have what we might call a conventional four-valve/twin-cam cylinder head. First seen in 1970, this finally had all the inlet valves on the same side of the engine, in line with the dedicated inlet camshaft, and all the exhaust valves in line, and opposite; though three spark plugs were still specified.

Maturity – and real dominance – then followed in 1972, when Formula 2 regulations were revised so that cars were based on production-based 2.0-litre engines. This situation was ideal for BMW, whose existing M12/M13 engine was already being produced in 2-litre form, whereas the Cosworth FVA and BDA types were both based on 1.5-litre/1.6-litre Ford power units, and needed to be stretched towards that upper limit.

Accordingly, when full race engines were produced, the Fords soon proved difficult to enlarge so far, and began to seem fragile, whereas the BMWs were well placed. The first 2-litre M12 raced at the Salzburgring in May 1972, when Dieter Quester's Chevron B21 won a European 2-litre Sports Car Championship race, but this was only a taster for what would follow.

What we may call the definitive engine – the one that not only led to the development of the M3, but also to the turbocharged F1 power unit – then appeared in 1973, this finally having what I will irreverently call the 'Cosworth lookalike' cylinder head, with merely one single spark plug per cylinder. Engine development guru Paul Rosche once said that in the 1.6-litre engine the three-plug layout was worth perhaps 5–10bhp at more than 10,000rpm, but that there was no difference for 2.0-litre engines.

This engine eventually became quite dominant in 2-litre Formula 2 and racing sports cars, and clearly had great influence on the other engines that BMW was developing at the time.

## Four becomes six...then back to four

This is where the story gets a bit complicated, but becomes logical when the close design relationship between the original Neue Klasse 'four' and the early-type six is recalled. When the time came to develop an engine for the original E30 M3, for the very first prototype 'lash-up', Paul Rosche's team began, literally, by sawing off one end of a 24-valve, six-cylinder cylinder head (see Appendix C) to produce a 16-valve, four-cylinder engine. Although much changed in detail, in the months and years which followed, the E30 M3 engine then evolved as a different power unit from the existing eight-valver, and from the F2/F1 power unit of the day.

It was at about the same time, however, that BMW introduced a radically redesigned range of eight-valve/single-cam/four-cylinder engines, coded M40, which replaced the original M10/M12 types. In 1987 the M40 took over, still with a sturdy cast-iron five-bearing cylinder block, and still with eight valve heads, but fitted with the then-fashionable internally cogged-belt drive for the single overhead camshaft. They were rated at 102bhp for the 1.6-litre and 115bhp for the 1.8-litre.

Less than three years later, however, a 16-valve twin-cam derivative of this modern 1.8-litre M40 engine, the M42, appeared, and was equipped with chain drive, not belt drive, to the two overhead camshafts. Originally this engine was only fitted to the E30 318iS, where it developed 136bhp. Later, it was expanded to cover 1.6-litres all the way to 2.0-litres, and after the 3-Series turned over completely to six-cylinder engineering in later years, it was used gainfully in the smaller, entry-level BMW 1-Series and in the Z3 sports car. After carrying on into the mid-2000s, it was finally ousted by an all-new-generation 1.6-litre unit (the very same engine that had been designed, jointly with Peugeot, for use in many small and small-to-medium-sized Mini, BMW, Peugeot and Citroën models).

# BMW's sweet and silky 'six'

Although BMW's first six-cylinder M3 did not appear until 1992, BMW engines of that general type, family and layout had already been in production since 1977. Like the four-cylinder engine that it replaced from the original M3, however, this silky 'six' was very different in detail from that original power unit. As ever, BMW was proud of its engine design expertise, and never liked to see its power units falling behind the opposition, so there had already been a progressive enlargement of the units, improvements to power ratings, to camshaft layouts, to cylinder head configurations, and to the fuelling and electronic control layouts. This explains why there was so little 'carry-over' from the original 'small' six of 1977 to the massively capable engine that appeared in the E36 M3, in 1992.

When the Type E36 M3 first appeared, it represented a complete step-change in performance, potential and general market specification from the last of the four-cylinder M3s. Not only that, but its engine was a huge leap forward on the original type. Its six-cylinder engine displaced 2,990cc and produced 286bhp at 7,000rpm. Fifteen years earlier, in 1977, the two original M60 six-cylinder power units of this family had capacities of 1,990cc or 2,315cc, and produced a mere 122 or 143bhp. How times had changed.

As already noted in Chapter 3, by the 1970s, BMW already had a six-cylinder engine in its overall range, but this was an older design, large and rather heavy, which had evolved from the original M10 'four', and which was applied to bigger cars in the ever-expanding BMW range. By the 1990s, this had already reached its absolute limit of expansion, at 3.8 litres, and would never be used in M3 types – though for years it was always an important constituent of the M5 family.

The new 'small' M60 engine was specifically designed to be compact, smaller and lighter to enable it to fit into the engine bay of a 3-Series – and to be capable of a lot of careful development and evolution in the years that would follow. It was, in fact, the very first BMW engine to use an internally-cogged belt instead of a chain to drive the overhead camshaft (the original M10 type, of course, had a chain-drive camshaft), and it was also the first truly all-new BMW engine since the arrival of the 'New Class' range in 1961.

The first major redesign of the M60 took place, ready for launch in 1990 ahead of the arrival of the entire family of the E36 3-Series models, this being the occasion when new four-valves-per-cylinder, twin-ohc, versions were introduced. Significantly, these camshafts were to be driven by chain and not by cogged belts, for BMW had now concluded that the life of chains was significantly longer (and more predictable) than that of cogged belts.

Until the arrival of the four-valve/twin-ohc units in 1990, this is how that original engine (a family which would evolve steadily in the future, not least with VANOS valve gear adjustment, and with light-alloy cylinder block features) had already expanded over the years:

| Size (cc) | Bore/stroke (mm) | Peak power | Comments |
|---|---|---|---|
| 1,990 | 80/66 | 122 | Introduced 1977 for 320/6 |
| 2,315 | 80/76.8 | 143 | Introduced 1977 for 323i/6 |
| 2,494 | 84/75 | 171 | Introduced 1984 for 325i |
| 2,693 | 84/81 | 122 | Introduced 1985 for 325e ('e' for 'economy') model |

...after which the twin-cam/24-valve derivatives were launched in February 1990 (they may have looked superficially similar, for they retained similar cast-iron cylinder blocks, but were radically different), and for the latest M3 of October 1992 this naturally led to:

| | | | |
|---|---|---|---|
| 2,990 | 86/85.8 | 286 | Introduced 1992 for the second generation M3 |

...and then, for the E36 Evolution type of 1995, the following was squeezed out:

| | | | |
|---|---|---|---|
| 3,201 | 86.4/91 | 321 | Introduced 1995 |

...with just a tiny further enlargement to follow for the E46 variety:

| | | | |
|---|---|---|---|
| 3,245 | 87/91mm | 343 | Introduced 2000 |

This engine, still with its cast-iron cylinder block and aluminium head, would then carry on in the E46 M3 until that car gave way to the sensational V8-engined E90-family M3 in the first months of 2007. Along the way, of course, it would take on the VANOS (Variable camshaft control) timing feature, first operating on the inlet camshaft only, and later operating as a 'Double VANOS' on both camshafts.

## Afterlife

Although that might have been the end of the story as far as the M3 family was concerned, this was still an engine with a great deal of change, modification, reinvention, and improvement to follow, for even in the early 2010s further innovations were regularly being announced.

An additional 2,793cc derivative was put on sale in the mid-1990s, and from the same period certain versions were treated to an aluminium cylinder block, while a mainstream 2,979cc engine (84 x 89.6mm) type followed. Not only that, but by a long and complex process, six-cylinder turbo-diesel engines became more and more specialised, originally as 2,926cc types, but later as 2,993cc (84 x 90mm) sizes, some with complex and highly efficient bi- and even tri-turbocharging.

That story, it seemed, had a lot more in store for historians as the new century progressed.

# BMW M3 (E30 type) – produced 1986 to 1991

[Initial European specification detailed – other European market types summarised below]

**Layout:** Unit construction steel body/chassis structure. Originally a two-door Saloon, front engine/rear-wheel drive, sold as a four-seater sports Saloon. Only supplied in left-hand drive. Cabriolet version also available from May 1988.

## Engine

| | |
|---|---|
| Type | Four-cylinder, mounted fore-and-aft |
| Block material | Cast iron |
| Head material | Cast aluminium |
| Cylinders | Four in line |
| Cooling | Water |
| Bore and stroke | 93.4 x 84mm |
| Capacity | 2,302cc |
| Main bearings | Five |
| Valves | Four per cylinder, operated by twin overhead camshafts, and bucket-type tappets, with the camshafts driven by chain from the crankshaft |
| Compression ratio | 10.5:1 |
| Fuel supply | Bosch ML Motronic fuel injection |
| Max. power | 200bhp at 6,750rpm |
| Max. torque | 176lb ft at 4,750rpm |

## Transmission

Five-speed manual Getrag gearbox, all synchromesh. Rear axle fitted with limited-slip differential.

| | |
|---|---|
| Clutch | Single plate, diaphragm spring |

## Overall gearbox ratios

| | |
|---|---|
| Top | 3.25 |
| 4th | 4.09 |
| 3rd | 5.75 |
| 2nd | 7.80 |
| 1st | 12.09 |
| Reverse | 13.75 |
| Final drive | 3.25:1 |

## Suspension and steering

| | |
|---|---|
| Front | Independent, by coil springs, MacPherson struts, track control arms and anti-roll bar |
| Rear | Independent, by coil springs, semi-trailing arms and anti-roll bar |
| Steering | Rack-and-pinion, with power assistance |
| Tyres | 205/55VR15 |
| Wheels | Cast-alloy disc, bolt-on fixing |
| Rim width | 7.0in |

## Brakes

| | |
|---|---|
| Type | Disc brakes at front and rear, hydraulically operated, with ABS |
| Size | 11.8in front discs, 9.84in rear discs |

## Dimensions (in/mm)

| | |
|---|---|
| Track | |
|   Front | 56.0/1,412 |
|   Rear | 56.4/1,433 |
| Wheelbase | 100.9/2,562 |
| Overall length | 171.7/4,360 |
| Overall width | 65.9/1,675 |
| Overall height | 53.7/1,365 |
| Unladen weight | 2,640lb/1,200kg |

## UK retail price

| | |
|---|---|
| At launch in 1987 | £22,750 |

Note: When fitted with a catalyst (this was important for the emission-conscious USA market) the engine produced 195bhp at 6,750rpm. For sale only in the Italian market (where there was a special tax regime relating to engine size) the engine was reduced to 1,990cc (93.4 x 72.65mm), the peak power of that unit being 192bhp at 6,900rpm.

USA-market types had a final drive ratio of 4.10:1.

**Evolution 1** models used the same basic technical specification as original types.

**Evolution II** models incorporated the following upgrades:

**Engine**

| | |
|---|---|
| Compression ratio | 11.0:1 |
| Max. power | 220bhp at 6,750rpm |
| Max. torque | 181lb ft at 4,750rpm |

**Transmission**

Final drive ratio 3.15 instead of 3.25:1, with consequent changes to all intermediate overall ratios

**Wheels and tyres**

16in wheels with 7.5in rims, and 225/45ZR16 tyres.

**UK retail price**  £26,960

From 1989 to 1990 (Coupé) and 1990 to 1991 (Cabriolet), the standard cars were equipped with a 215bhp at 6,750rpm (170lb ft at 4,600rpm) version of the catalysed engine.

**Evolution III** (1989/1990) models included the following upgrades, compared with a 'standard' M3 specification:

**Engine**

| | |
|---|---|
| Bore and stroke | 95 x 87mm |
| Capacity | 2,467cc |
| Compression ratio | 10.2:1 |
| Max. power | 238bhp at 7,000rpm |
| Max. torque | 177lb ft at 4,750rpm |

**Transmission**

Final drive ratio 3.15:1 instead of 3.25:1, with consequent changes to all intermediate overall ratios

**Wheels and tyres**

16in wheels with 7.5in rims, and 225/45ZR16 tyres

**UK retail price**  £34,500

Italian-market version, badged as 320iS
To take advantage of certain Italian-market fiscal rules, the M3 was marketed as a '320iS' with the following engine changes:

| | |
|---|---|
| Bore and stroke | 93.4 x 72.65mm |
| Capacity | 1,990cc |
| Max. power | 192bhp at 6,900rpm |
| Max. torque | 161lb ft at 4,900rpm |

## Specifications

# BMW M3 (E36 type) – produced 1992 to 1995

**Layout:** Unit construction steel body/chassis structure. Front engine/rear-wheel drive, sold as a four-door/four-seater sports Saloon, two-door sports Coupé, or two-door Cabriolet.

## Engine

| | |
|---|---|
| Type | Six-cylinder, mounted fore-and-aft |
| Block material | Cast iron |
| Head material | Cast aluminium |
| Cylinders | Six in line |
| Cooling | Water |
| Bore and stroke | 86 x 85.8mm |
| Capacity | 2,990cc |
| Main bearings | Seven |
| Valves | Four per cylinder, operated by twin overhead camshafts, and bucket-type tappets with the camshafts driven by chain from the crankshaft. VANOS control of the inlet camshaft timing |
| Compression ratio | 10.8:1 |
| Fuel supply | Bosch Motronic 3.3 fuel injection |
| Max. power | 286bhp at 7,000rpm |
| Max. torque | 236lb ft at 3,600rpm |

## Transmission

Five-speed manual gearbox, all synchromesh

| | |
|---|---|
| Clutch | Single plate, diaphragm spring |

### Overall gearbox ratios

| | |
|---|---|
| Top | 3.15 |
| 4th | 3.906 |
| 3rd | 5.23 |
| 2nd | 7.84 |
| 1st | 13.23 |
| Reverse | 12.25 |
| Final drive | 3.15:1 |

## Suspension and steering

| | |
|---|---|
| Front | Independent, by coil springs, MacPherson struts, track control arms and anti-roll bar |
| Rear | Independent, by coil springs, multi-link transverse and trailing arms and anti-roll bar |
| Steering | Rack-and-pinion, with power assistance |
| Tyres | 235/40ZR17 (optional 245/40ZR17 at rear) |
| Wheels | Cast-alloy disc, bolt-on fixing |
| Rim width | 7.5in (optional 8.5in at rear with larger tyres) |

## Brakes

| | |
|---|---|
| Type | Disc brakes at front and rear, hydraulically operated, with ABS |
| Size | 12.4in front discs, 12.3in rear discs |

## Dimensions (in/mm)

| | | |
|---|---|---|
| Track | | |
| Front 55.4/1,407 | Rear 55.9/1,421 | |
| Wheelbase | 106.3/2,700 | |
| Overall length | 174.5/4,433 | |
| Overall width | 67.3/1,710 | |
| Overall height | | |
| (Coupé) | 53.8/1,366 | |
| Unladen weight | 3,219lb/1,460kg | |

## UK Retail Price

At launch in 1992(Coupé) £32,450

**M3 GT** (Limited Edition) Note: In 1994 and 1995, BMW also produced a total of 350 M3 GT models, which were based on the two-door Coupé version of the E36 range. Apart from the use of lowered/stiffened suspension, and the addition of a front-end 'splitter' spoiler and a two-tier rear spoiler, the peak engine power output was raised to 295bhp.

**North American market version** Produced in 1995, this derivative had 240bhp and peak torque of 225lb ft.

**M3 LTW** (1995 model) Built as a very limited production 'homologation special', as sold in the USA the LTW (Lightweight) retained the standard 3.0-litre engine, allied to a 3.23:1 final drive ratio, 7.5 x 17in front wheels and 8.5 x 17in rear wheels.

# BMW M3 (E36 Evolution type) – produced 1995 to 1999

**Layout:** Unit construction steel body/chassis structure. Front engine/rear-wheel-drive, sold as a four-door/four-seater sports Saloon, two-door sports Coupé, or two-door Cabriolet.

### Engine

| | |
|---|---|
| Type | Six-cylinder, mounted fore-and-aft |
| Block material | Cast iron |
| Head material | Cast aluminium |
| Cylinders | Six in line |
| Cooling | Water |
| Bore and stroke | 86.4 x 91mm |
| Capacity | 3,201cc |
| Main bearings | Seven |
| Valves | Four per cylinder, operated by twin overhead camshafts, and bucket-type tappets with the camshafts driven by chain from the crankshaft. Double VANOS variable valve timing |
| Compression ratio | 11.3:1 |
| Fuel supply | Bosch Motronic 3.3 fuel injection |
| Max. power | 321bhp at 7,400rpm |
| Max. torque | 258lb ft at 3,250rpm |

### Transmission

Six-speed manual gearbox, all synchromesh

| | |
|---|---|
| Clutch | Single plate, diaphragm spring |

Overall gearbox ratios

| | |
|---|---|
| Top | 2.68 |
| 5th | 3.23 |
| 4th | 5.23 |
| 3rd | 5.39 |
| 2nd | 8.11 |
| 1st | 13.66 |
| Reverse | 12.11 |
| Final drive | 3.23:1 |

An optional SMG (Sequential Manual Gearbox) change was made available on left-hand-drive cars from the autumn of 1996, and on right-hand-drive cars from 1997. The ratios themselves were not changed.

### Suspension and steering

| | |
|---|---|
| Front | Independent, by coil springs, MacPherson struts, track control arms and anti-roll bar |
| Rear | Independent, by coil springs, multi-link transverse and trailing arms and anti-roll bar |
| Steering | Rack-and-pinion, with power assistance |
| Tyres | 225/45ZR17 (front), 245/40ZR17 (rear) |
| Wheels | Cast-alloy disc, bolt-on fixing |
| Rim width | 7.5in (front), 8.5in (rear) |

### Brakes

| | |
|---|---|
| Type | Disc brakes at front and rear, hydraulically operated, with ABS |
| Size | 12.4in front discs, 12.3in rear discs |

### Dimensions (in/mm)

| | |
|---|---|
| Track | |
| Front | 55.4/1,407 |
| Rear | 55.9/1,421 |
| Wheelbase | 106.7/2,710 |
| Overall length | 174.5/4,433 |
| Overall width | 67.3/1,710 |
| Overall height | 53.8/1,366 |
| Unladen weight | 3,219lb/1,460kg |

### UK Retail Price

| | |
|---|---|
| At launch in 1996 | (Coupé) £36,550 |

**Imola Individual** (Limited Edition) Just 200 of these Coupés were built, and were mechanically the same as the GTs produced earlier in the decade. Interior equipment was enhanced, along with special interior and exterior colour combinations. Special front splitters and rear spoilers made the car intrinsically more suitable for race car preparation.

# BMW M3 (E46 type) – produced 2000 to 2006

**Layout:** Unit construction steel body/chassis structure, with aluminium skin panels. Front engine/rear-wheel drive, sold as a two-door sports Coupé or a two-door Cabriolet.

## Engine

| | |
|---|---|
| Type | Six-cylinder, mounted fore-and-aft |
| Block material | Cast iron |
| Head material | Cast aluminium |
| Cylinders | Six in line |
| Cooling | Water |
| Bore and stroke | 87 x 91mm |
| Capacity | 3,245cc |
| Main bearings | Seven |
| Valves | Four per cylinder, operated by twin overhead camshafts, and bucket-type tappets with the camshafts driven by chain from the crankshaft. Double VANOS variable valve timing |
| Compression ratio | 11.5:1 |
| Fuel supply | Bosch Motronic MSSS54 fuel injection/ engine management system |
| Max. power | 343bhp at 7,900rpm |
| Max. torque | 269lb ft at 4,900rpm |

## Transmission

Six-speed manual Getrag gearbox, all synchromesh

| | |
|---|---|
| Clutch | Single plate, diaphragm spring |

Overall gearbox ratios

| | |
|---|---|
| Top | 3.00 |
| 5th | 3.62 |
| 4th | 4.45 |
| 3rd | 6.04 |
| 2nd | 9.16 |
| 1st | 15.31 |
| Reverse | 13.57 |
| Final drive | 3.62:1 |

## Suspension and steering

| | |
|---|---|
| Front | Independent, by coil springs, MacPherson struts, track control arms and anti-roll bar |
| Rear | Independent, multi-link, by coil springs, transverse and trailing arms and anti-roll bar |
| Steering | Rack-and-pinion, with power assistance |
| Tyres | 225/45ZR18 (front), 255/40ZR18 (rear) |
| Wheels | Cast-alloy disc, bolt-on fixing |
| Rim width | 8.0in (front), 9.0in (rear) |

## Brakes

| | |
|---|---|
| Type | Disc brakes at front and rear, hydraulically operated, with ABS |
| Size | 12.8in front discs, 12.8in rear discs |

## Dimensions (in/mm)

| | |
|---|---|
| Track | |
| Front | 59.4/1,508 |
| Rear | 58.2/1,478 |
| Wheelbase | 107.3/2,725 |
| Overall length | 176.8/4,492 |
| Overall width | 70.1/1,780 |
| Overall height | 54.0/1,372 |
| Unladen weight | 3,477lb/1,577kg |

## UK Retail Price

At launch in 2000(Coupé) £38,500

# BMW M3 CSL (E46 type) – produced 2003 to 2004

**Layout:** Unit construction steel body/chassis structure. Front engine/rear-wheel drive, sold as a two-door sports Coupé.

## Engine

| | |
|---|---|
| Type | Six-cylinder, mounted fore-and-aft |
| Block material | Cast iron |
| Head material | Cast aluminium |
| Cylinders | Six in line |
| Cooling | Water |
| Bore and stroke | 87 x 91mm |
| Capacity | 3,245cc |
| Main bearings | Seven |
| Valves | Four per cylinder, operated by twin overhead camshafts, and bucket-type tappets with the camshafts driven by chain from the crankshaft. Double VANOS variable valve timing |
| Compression ratio | 11.5:1 |
| Fuel supply | Bosch Motronic MSSS54 fuel injection/ engine management system |
| Max. power | 360bhp at 7,900rpm |
| Max. torque | 272lb ft at 4,900rpm |

## Transmission

Six-speed SMG (Sequential Manual Gearbox)/manual gearbox, all synchromesh

| | |
|---|---|
| Clutch | Single plate, diaphragm spring |

Overall gearbox ratios

| | |
|---|---|
| Top | 3.00 |
| 5th | 3.62 |
| 4th | 4.45 |
| 3rd | 6.04 |
| 2nd | 9.16 |
| 1st | 15.31 |
| Reverse | 13.57 |
| Final drive | 3.62:1 |

## Suspension and steering

| | |
|---|---|
| Front | Independent, by coil springs, MacPherson struts, track control arms, and anti-roll bar |
| Rear | Independent, by coil springs, multi-link transverse and trailing arms, and anti-roll bar |
| Steering | Rack-and-pinion, with power assistance |
| Tyres | 225/35ZR19 (front), 265/30ZR19 (rear) |
| Wheels | Cast-alloy disc, bolt-on fixing |
| Rim width | 8.5in (front), 9.5in (rear) |

## Brakes

| | |
|---|---|
| Type | Disc brakes at front and rear, hydraulically operated, with ABS |
| Size | 13.4in front discs, 12.8in rear discs |

## Dimensions (in/mm)

| | |
|---|---|
| Track | |
| Front | 59.4/1,508 |
| Rear | 58.2/1,478 |
| Wheelbase | 107.3/2,725 |
| Overall length | 176.8/4,492 |
| Overall width | 70.1/1,780 |
| Overall height | 54.0/1,372 |
| Unladen weight | 3,142lb/1,425kg |

## UK Retail Price

At launch in 2003(Coupé) £58,455

# BMW M3 (E90/E92/E93 types) – produced 2007 to 2012

**Layout:** Unit construction steel body/chassis structure. Front engine/rear-wheel drive, sold as four-door/four-seater sports Saloon (E90), two-door sports Coupé (E92), or two-door Convertible (E93).

## Engine

| | |
|---|---|
| Type | V8, mounted fore-and-aft |
| Block material | Cast aluminium |
| Head material | Cast aluminium |
| Cylinders | Eight in 90° V |
| Cooling | Water |
| Bore and stroke | 92 x 75.2mm |
| Capacity | 3,999cc |
| Main bearings | Five |
| Valves | Four per cylinder, operated by twin overhead camshafts, and bucket-type tappets with the camshafts driven by chain from the crankshaft, and Double VANOS timing control |
| Compression ratio | 12.0:1 |
| Fuel supply | Bosch fuel injection/engine management system |
| Max. power | 414bhp at 8,300rpm |
| Max. torque | 295lb ft at 3,900rpm |

## Transmission

Six-speed manual gearbox, all synchromesh

| | |
|---|---|
| Clutch | Single plate, diaphragm spring |

Overall gearbox ratios

| | |
|---|---|
| Top | 3.35 |
| 5th | 3.85 |
| 4th | 4.58 |
| 3rd | 6.08 |
| 2nd | 9.12 |
| 1st | 15.63 |
| Reverse | 14.17 |
| Final drive | 3.85:1 |

From 2008: Optional seven-speed DSG transmission, all synchromesh.
Overall ratios:

| | |
|---|---|
| Top | 3.15 |
| 6th | 3.78 |
| 5th | 4.38 |
| 4th | 5.29 |
| 3rd | 6.77 |
| 2nd | 9.64 |
| 1st | 15.06 |
| Reverse | 14.02 |
| Final drive | 3.156:1 |

## Suspension and steering

| | |
|---|---|
| Front | Independent, by coil springs, MacPherson struts, track control arms, and anti-roll bar |
| Rear | Independent, by coil springs, multi-link transverse and trailing arms, and anti-roll bar |
| Steering | Rack-and-pinion, with power assistance |
| Tyres | 245/35ZR19 (front), 265/35ZR19 (rear) |
| Wheels | Cast-alloy disc, bolt-on fixing |
| Rim width | 8.5in (front), 9.5in (rear) |

## Brakes

| | |
|---|---|
| Type | Disc brakes at front and rear, hydraulically operated, with ABS |
| Size | 14.2in front discs, 13.8in rear discs |

## Dimensions (in/mm)

| | |
|---|---|
| Track | |
| Front | 60.6/1,538 |
| Rear | 60.6/1,539 |
| Wheelbase | 108.7/2,761 |
| Overall length | 181.7/4,615 |
| Overall width | 71.0/1,804 |
| Overall height | |
| (Coupé) | 55.8in/1,418 |
| Unladen weight | |
| (E92 Coupé) | 3,649lb/1,655kg |

## UK Retail Price

At launch in 2007 (Coupé) £50,625

## M3 GTS Limited Edition – produced in 2010

Specification based on that of the E92 Coupé, except for:

### Engine:

| | |
|---|---|
| Bore and stroke | 92 x 82mm |
| Capacity | 4,361cc |
| Max. power | 450bhp at 8,300rpm |
| Max. torque | 325lb ft at 3,750rpm |

### Transmission

Seven-speed DSG transmission standard, conventional manual gearbox not available

### Suspension

| | |
|---|---|
| Tyres | 255/35ZR19 (front), 285/30ZR19 (rear) |

### Brakes

| | |
|---|---|
| Size | 14.9in front discs, 15.0in rear discs |

### Dimensions

Unladen weight (approx)   3,374lb/1,530kg

# BMW M3 E30 and E36 performance

A summary of the figures achieved by *Autocar* (Britain's most authoritative motoring magazine)
of cars supplied for test by BMW-UK over the years:

| Model | M3 Coupé<br>E30<br>2,302cc<br>200bhp | M3 Coupé<br>E30 Evo II<br>2,302cc<br>220bhp | M3 Coupé<br>E36<br>2,990cc<br>286bhp | M3 Coupé<br>E36 (AMG)<br>3,201cc<br>321bhp |
|---|---|---|---|---|
| Max speed (mph) | 139 | 146 | 162 | 155 |
| Acceleration (sec): | | | | |
| 0–60mph | 7.1 | 6.6 | 5.4 | 5.3 |
| 0–80mph | 11.9 | 11.0 | 8.8 | 8.7 |
| 0–100mph | 19.0 | 17.8 | 13.1 | 12.9 |
| Standing ¼-mile (sec) | 15.7 | 15.2 | 13.9 | 13.9 |
| Consumption (mpg): | | | | |
| Overall | 20.3 | 26.0 | 26.2 | 22.8 |
| Typical | 23.0 | 30.0 | 30.0 | 28.0 |
| Kerb weight (lb/kg) | 2,762/1,252 | 2,809/1,274 | 3,352/1,520 | 3,330/1,510 |
| Year tested | 1987 | 1988 | 1993 | 1998 |
| UK price | £22,750 | £27,381 | £34,915 | £38,525 |

# BMW M3 E46 and E92 performance

A summary of the figures achieved by *Autocar* (Britain's most authoritative motoring magazine) of cars supplied for test by BMW-UK over the years:

| Model | M3 Coupé E46 3,245cc 6-cyl 343bhp | M3 CSL Coupé E46 3,245cc 6-cyl 360bhp | M3 Coupé E92 6-speed 3,999cc V8 414bhp |
|---|---|---|---|
| Max speed (mph)* | 160 | 161 | 155 |
| Acceleration (sec): | | | |
|   0–60mph | 4.8 | 4.8 | 4.7 |
|   0–80mph | 7.7 | 7.6 | 7.2 |
|   0–100mph | 11.5 | 10.9 | 10.2 |
| Standing ¼-mile (sec) | 13.4 | 13.2 | 13.3 |
| Consumption (mpg) | | | |
|   Overall | 21.7 | 21.1 | 19.0 |
|   Typical | 25.0 | 25.0 | 24.0 |
| Kerb weight (lb/kg) | 3,477/1,577 | 3,054/1,385 | 3,649/1,655 |
| Year tested | 2001 | 2003 | 2007 |
| UK price | £38,500 | £58,455 | £50,625 |

* Limited electronically.

# M3 production – 1986 to 2012 inclusive

| | | |
|---|---|---|
| E30 (1986–1991) | All Saloons (including specials/Evolutions) | 17,434 |
| | Cabriolets | 787 |
| E36 (1992–1995) and E36 Evolution (1995–1999) | Coupés | 46,525 |
| | Cabriolets | 12,114 |
| | Saloons | 12,603 |
| E46 (2000–2006) | Coupés and Convertibles | 84,344 |
| E46 CSL (2003–2004) | Coupés | 1,400 |
| E90 (Saloon), E92 (Coupé) and E93 (Convertible) (2007–2013) | All types | In progress |

As the end of E90/92/93 production approaches, total production of all M3 types, therefore, is well over 200,000 units, and that total marches inexorably upwards.

# Index